PENGUIN BOOKS

GLADSTONE

Sir Philip Magnus-Allcroft (1906–88), MA, FRSL, was educated at Westminster School and Wadham College, Oxford. After a period as a Civil Servant, he served during the Second World War as a Major in the Royal Artillery and the Intelligence Corps in Iceland and Italy. In 1943 he married Jewell Allcroft. He was a JP for Shropshire and was also Chairman of the Planning and Records Committee of the Shropshire County Council. His books include *Edmund Burke* (1939), *Sir Walter Raleigh* (1951), *Gladstone: A Biography* (1954), *Kitchener: Portrait of an Imperialist* (1958) and *King Edward the Seventh* (1964). Sir Philip Magnus-Allcroft was awarded the CBE in 1971.

GLADSTONE

A
Biography

BY
PHILIP MAGNUS

PENGUIN BOOKS

PENGUIN BOOKS

Published by the Penguin Group
Penguin Books Ltd, 27 Wrights Lane, London w8 5TZ, England
Penguin Putnam Inc., 375 Hudson Street, New York, New York 10014, USA
Penguin Books Australia Ltd, Ringwood, Victoria, Australia
Penguin Books Canada Ltd, 10 Alcorn Avenue, Toronto, Ontario, Canada M4V 3B2
Penguin Books India (P) Ltd, 11, Community Centre, Panchsheel Park, New Delhi – 110 017, India
Penguin Books (NZ) Ltd, Private Bag 102902, NSMC, Auckland, New Zealand
Penguin Books (South Africa) (Pty) Ltd, 5 Watkins Street, Denver Ext 4, Johannesburg 2094, South Africa

Penguin Books Ltd, Registered Offices: Harmondsworth, Middlesex, England

First published by John Murray 1954
Published as a Classic Penguin 2001

1

Printed and bound in Great Britain by The Bath Press, Bath

TO MY WIFE

CONTENTS

LIST OF ILLUSTRATIONS

LIST OF ILLUSTRATIONS

INTRODUCTION

THE vast majority of mankind have believed, however imperfectly, throughout the ages that the whole of human life is the service of God. That was Gladstone's belief, and he went a great deal further than any statesman in modern times in the attempt to give it practical effect in politics. In the course of that attempt, he courted and, to a large extent, incurred martyrdom for himself as well as for the Liberal Party, which became his instrument, and which, before it broke in his strong grip, owed its unity and enthusiasm almost entirely to him.

Gladstone brought to his task a superabundant vitality of body and mind, and his first need was to find a means of controlling it. Lord Kilbracken, who was once his principal private secretary, said that if a figure of 100 could represent the energy of an ordinary man, and 200 that of an exceptional man, Gladstone's energy would represent a figure of at least 1,000. Mrs. Gladstone told Lord Morley that anyone who wrote her husband's life would have to remember that there were two sides to his nature. One was impetuous, irrestrainable, uncontrollable ; the other was an iron self-mastery which he had achieved at about the age of twenty-three or twenty-four through the natural strength of his character and constant wrestling in prayer.

Gladstone harnessed the energy and passion which he generated to a single, constant, transcendental purpose. He sought to mould himself, his country, and the world to the pattern suggested by his personal religion in which he believed with the pure faith of a child. Political life would have been meaningless to him without that purpose which attained its most outstanding public expression during three successive phases of his long career.

In the first phase, when he was Chancellor of the Exchequer, Gladstone achieved unparalleled success in his policy of setting the individual free from a multitude of obsolete restrictions. He thereby implemented his creed that self-discipline in freedom is the essential condition of the mental health of men and nations, as well as of their material prosperity. The crowning moments were the great Budgets of 1853 and 1860. Gladstone's reputation was made in the field of finance, to which, under Sir Robert Peel's guidance, he graduated directly from that of theology.

During the second phase of his career, Gladstone achieved great success in arousing the moral indignation of the British people against Turkish misrule in the Balkans, and against what he regarded as Disraeli's blindness—typifying that of the great and cautious world—to the transcendental issues which are involved in all tyranny and oppression. The crowning moment was the Midlothian campaign of 1879. Gladstone's efforts in that cause made him the foremost statesman in Great Britain and a moral force in Europe.

During the third and final phase of his career, Gladstone, in his magnificent old age, led a crusade against English misrule in Ireland. The crowning moments were the rejections of his first and second Home Rule Bills in 1886 and 1893. The lamentable results of those two resounding failures belong to history; they were due in part to temperamental defects in Gladstone himself, in part to accident, but mainly to the fact that Gladstone's principal opponents and colleagues were more worldly, and ultimately less far-sighted and high-minded, than he was. Gladstone was undaunted in the face of humiliation and defeat. He towered in moral grandeur over his contemporaries and stood before the world as the inspired prophet of the nineteenth-century liberal experiment.

Gladstone entered public life with such a profound distrust of liberty that he detected what he called ' an element of anti-Christ ' in the great Reform Act of 1832. Experience taught him that the transcendental purpose to which his life was dedicated could only be realized in freedom; and in that gradual discovery lies the key to all his changes. He came to repose his trust in the ability of individual men and women to hear, interpret correctly, and obey the voice of God using their private consciences to inspire and direct mankind. Gladstone fought for the second and third Reform Acts because he had acquired that trust.

In that way Gladstone embarked upon the liberal experiment at a time when the sea of faith was on the ebb, and when, as Matthew Arnold expressed it, there was only to be heard :

> Its melancholy, long, withdrawing roar
> Retreating to the breath
> Of the night wind, down the vast edges drear
> And naked shingles of the world.

Because Gladstone's politics were rooted in dogmatic religion, the decline of faith impaired his strength, weakened his appeal, and made political life, which he had entered with reluctance, increasingly uncongenial to him. There were, however, in his extraordinary combination of gifts such reserves of force that at the time of his death he was still, in his own right, the most venerated and influential statesman in the world.

Gladstone was convinced that God would call him personally to account for his every thought, and word, and act. He prepared·himself accordingly, by keeping records—occasionally copious, but mostly jejune—of all three. He kept back very little ; he had nothing significant to hide ; but he knew from long experience the difficulty of writing accurately and satisfactorily about what he called ' interior matters '. Gladstone was careful, above all, to preserve every letter or document bearing upon his career which seemed in any way important or interesting. About a quarter of a million such documents were preserved, at first in an octagon room which he built as an annexe to his library at Hawarden Castle, and, later, in the muniment room of St. Deiniol's Library, which he founded at Hawarden before he died.

Some 200,000 of those documents were removed to the British Museum in 1930 by direction of the Gladstone trustees. All, with the exception of the correspondence with the Royal Family, which remains in the Museum on loan, were absorbed five years later, on the death of Henry Neville Gladstone (Lord Gladstone of Hawarden), into the archives of the British nation. With a few subsequent additions they have been distributed into 750 volumes (Add. MSS. 44086–44835) which constitute the most important single collection available to students of the later nineteenth century. The Gladstone papers are more voluminous than those of any former prime minister ; Gladstone's nearest competitors in respect of bulk in the British Museum are Thomas Pelham-Holles, Duke of Newcastle, whose papers fill 548 volumes, and Sir Robert Peel whose papers fill 437. Almost all figures of note among Gladstone's contemporaries are represented among his 12,000 correspondents.

Lord Morley's great *Life of Gladstone* was published in 1903. In the introduction to it, the author stated that he stood so near to his subject, that it was difficult to adjust the perspective, the scale, and the relation. A quarter of a century later (1928) the Prime Minister's fourth son, Herbert (Viscount Gladstone), complained that ' luminous and interesting as are Lord Morley's pages, they do not present, for those who did not know Mr. Gladstone, a true and complete view of his personality . . . while the tendency of the modern writers is to seek the truth about great men from the habits and affairs of their private life, Mr. Gladstone seems to be excluded from this process.'

With the approval and co-operation of Gladstone's grandson and present-day representative at Hawarden Castle, Mr. Charles Andrew Gladstone, I have attempted to repair that omission. The years which have lengthened the perspective, and allowed the lava of controversy to cool and harden into history, have suggested a new scale and a new relation, which it has been my purpose to provide.

I am exceedingly grateful to Mr. C. A. Gladstone for making this book possible. There are some 50,000 personal and intimate papers still in the octagon room and library at Hawarden Castle, and I very much appreciate the privilege of having been allowed to carry them all off for long periods to my home. That eased my task. I would like to thank Mr. and Mrs. Gladstone for very great kindness.

I am grateful also to Mr. A. Jefferies Collins, Keeper of Manuscripts and Egerton Librarian at the British Museum. He showed me special kindness which smoothed my way.

To Mr. Arthur Tilney Bassett I find it almost impossible to express my indebtedness. He has been not merely kind but kindness itself. The Gladstone papers were in his charge for many years before they left Hawarden, and his knowledge of them will, in all human probability, never be equalled. The trustees of the British Museum entrusted him with the task of cataloguing the papers in conformity with their methods, and they accorded his work the unique distinction of an independent catalogue. If normal practice had been followed, his work would have been included in one outsize volume listing all manuscripts acquired by the Museum between 1931 and 1935.

I think I may have tried Mr. Bassett's patience at times, but his kindness was unfailing, and I can only record my deep appreciation of the generous help and constant encouragement which he has given me.

Finally I wish to thank Mr. M. R. D. Foot, lecturer in English nineteenth-century history at Keble College, Oxford, and author (with Mrs. Hammond and the late Dr. J. L. Hammond) of *Gladstone and Liberalism* (1952), for his kindness in reading the whole of my typescript, and in making valuable suggestions.

P. M.

Stokesay Court,
Onibury, Shropshire.

CHAPTER 1

A PURE YOUNG MAN
1809–1833

WILLIAM EWART GLADSTONE was born on 29 December, 1809, at 62, Rodney Street, Liverpool. He was named after William Ewart, a close friend of his father. He was the fifth of the six children (four sons and two daughters) of John Gladstone, who was one of Liverpool's foremost citizens. John Gladstone had moved to Liverpool, as a youth, from Leith, the port of Edinburgh. From humble beginnings he made a fortune, which amounted at his death to £600,000, out of commerce with America, India, and the West Indies. He was the eldest in a family of sixteen, and one by one he sent for his six brothers, who were all remarkably vigorous and long-lived, and provided them with careers. He was a man of very strong family affections, and his family worshipped him. William's eyes would sometimes fill with tears when he spoke about his father in later life. " None but his children," he would say, " can know what torrents of tenderness flowed from his heart."

In 1829, John Gladstone purchased for £80,000 the estate of Fasque, near Fettercairn, Kincardineshire. He was created a baronet in 1846 on the recommendation of his friend, Sir Robert Peel. For the sake of euphony he changed his name in 1837 from Gladstones to Gladstone, and from having been a Presbyterian and a Whig he became a zealous member of the Church of England, and a Tory. He and his second wife, Anne Robertson, who was the mother of all his children, were of pure Scottish descent.

In 1809—a year in which Abraham Lincoln, Alfred Tennyson, and Charles Darwin were also born—Britain's vast wealth and sea-power were at the service of the Allies in the long struggle to crush Napoleon. Britain's armies played a notable and often a glorious part in the war, but there was no conscription, and the blood-tax was relatively light. During the twenty-two years between 1793 and 1815 the British death-roll was about 100,000. Protected by their fleets and by the sea the upper class had never been happier or more prosperous. Their rent-rolls mounted with the price of corn, and the property tax at two shillings in the pound did not much trouble them. But the poor suffered greatly from the constant rise in prices, and from war taxes, levied principally on consumer goods, which included the necessities of life.

On society, the great war made no impression. The country-house life of the period is depicted in Jane Austen's novels; no-one thought of asking any of her heroes why they contributed no service of any kind to their country's war effort. The life of the capital is mirrored in the career of George Brummel, who became fashionable in 1799, at the age of twenty-one; no-one thought any the worse of him for having, in the previous year, resigned his commission in the Tenth Hussars, in protest against being ordered to Manchester.

The upper class was able throughout the war to cultivate all the pleasures of the intellect, and of the senses. At its best, the quality of the pattern of life and manners which it enjoyed has rarely been paralleled. Its polished and brilliant surface was unruffled by the hurricane which howled for nearly a quarter of a century about the length and breadth of Europe, and which even crossed the Atlantic to North America before it died.

The Gladstone family was middle class. And to the middle class the long war was a gamble. Many of its members were ruined by the sudden opening and closing of markets, and by violent fluctuations in war prices; but others, like John Gladstone, succeeded in turning to glorious gain the opportunities and necessities which confronted them. To those who were successful, glittering vistas were open. They could buy land and found families; they could mix with the patrician class by taking part in politics; they could send their sons to fashionable schools, and buy them seats in Parliament, or commissions in famous regiments. Class divisions have always been looser in Great Britain than in most continental countries.

John Gladstone himself sat in Parliament from 1818 to 1827, when he was unseated for bribery. His record in the House was undistinguished, and he became involved in a rancid controversy about slavery which was revived soon after his famous son entered Parliament. He had acquired extensive sugar plantations and many slaves in the West Indies, and on one of his properties, in British Guiana, an insurrection was suppressed with cruelty in August, 1823. Some negroes were hanged, or flogged to death, but trouble arose because the planters rashly condemned to death, on hearsay evidence of complicity, a white missionary, John Smith. Before Smith's sentence could be commuted by the authorities at home, he had died of ill-treatment in prison. Henry Brougham raised the matter in

Parliament, but John Gladstone preferred to defend the planters' cause in the Press. He argued that missionaries had acted as revolutionary agents ; that slavery had been sanctioned by providence in certain climates since history began ; that the difficulties in the way of emancipation were insurmountable ; and that the public would be well-advised to concentrate its attention on the condition of the lower classes at home. He was attacked for those views by the abolitionists, but his fellow citizens in Liverpool did not forget how deeply indebted they were to the slave labour for the prosperity of their city. Early in 1824 they subscribed £1,400 to present John Gladstone with a service of plate in token of their sympathy and goodwill.

John Gladstone's negative attitude was characteristic of his age. He was a devout Christian but, until the revolutionary ferment in Europe had subsided, there was a widespread distrust of any form of State interference in the economic or in any other field. The machinery for it was almost non-existent. Men who had built up great enterprises by their unaided efforts were intolerant of an obsolete tradition of Government regulation which had formerly cramped initiative and fostered uninventive techniques. It was difficult to begin to think again about methods of controlling some aspects of the State's economic life, until experience had been gained gradually, by trial and error, about methods of administering the new large-scale industrial and commercial undertakings.

In the meantime, the economists preached *laisser-faire*, and statesmen were afraid of injuring the manufacturers on whom they relied to increase production and lift the burden of taxation. Landowners and moneyed men were well aware that in many respects conditions were bad. In some cases they made attempts to come to grips with problems and to provide remedies. But, lacking the knowledge and the means, the remedies they proposed were mostly futile. A feeling of helplessness was thus engendered, which set up tremendous tensions in many sensitive minds. John Gladstone was himself a sensitive man. For his coat of arms he defiantly adopted[1] 'a savage's head, affronté, distilling drops of blood'. But he sought relief for the acute tensions which troubled him, by building and endowing churches.

The charming circumstances of upper-class life during the previous century had given rise to an optimistic philosophy which discouraged religious enthusiasm. However, the excesses of the French Revolution caused a reaction. Many Whig magnates, it is true, continued

[1] See note on page 17.

light-heartedly to wear infidelity as they wore hair-powder. But in general there was a remarkable and widespread revival in Sunday observance, and in the practice of daily family prayers. By the middle of the nineteenth century Evangelicalism had imposed a common discipline on the whole British nation, including even those sections of it which were deaf to its religious or economic appeals. When William Gladstone entered Parliament, society was beginning to notice the existence of a small number of intense and pure young men, whose views inspired respect, although they often seemed odd and exaggerated.

In the Gladstone household the narrowest form of Evangelical religion prevailed. But two other factors were of importance in conditioning William's mind. In the first place, John Gladstone, like others of his class, owed his success in life to his contempt for economic tradition, and to his practice of carefully weighing every act by rational and empirical standards. He applied similar principles of reason to the management of his growing family. There was no subject which was taken for granted; none which could not be discussed freely between himself and his sons in a spirit of good feeling and good sense. The children were actively encouraged to dispute courteously about every topic, great or small; and in that stimulating atmosphere, William early developed what he called ' a priggish love of argument '. As the youngest boy, his poise, and cautious reserve, were probably encouraged in equal measure.

In the second place, John Gladstone was politically associated with George Canning. And William, even before he went to Eton, sympathized warmly with his father's action in voting with Canning, in 1821, for Roman Catholic emancipation. John Gladstone brought Canning to Liverpool in 1812, and helped the Tory leader to win that seat against the Whig candidates, Henry Brougham and Thomas Creevey, the diarist. On 16 October, 1812, he gave a dinner to Canning at his house in Rodney Street. In the middle of it his youngest boy was carried into the dining-room by his nurse, set on a chair, and told to say, ' Ladies and Gentlemen '. And so, amid laughter and the clink of glasses, William made what in later years he liked to describe as his maiden speech.

George Canning, before he died in 1827, took a fancy to the boy. He enjoyed talking to him, and sent for him when he visited Eton. As late as 1890, Sir Harry Verney, then in his ninetieth year, could remember hearing Canning speak warmly about the bright and

4

attractive son of one of his Liverpool constituents. Some of William's earliest verses, printed in the *Eton Miscellany*, were in praise of Canning, who was pleased when they were shown to him.

Among William's earliest memories were the sound of the guns at Edinburgh Castle saluting the news of Napoleon's abdication in 1814. He remembered also being taken, in London, to a Thanksgiving Service for the victory of Waterloo, at St. Paul's, when he looked down from a gallery on the powdered wig of the Prince Regent. His parents moved in 1815 to a fine new house, which is now pulled down and built over, at the mouth of the Mersey, outside Liverpool. It was named Seaforth House after the head of the family with which Mrs. Gladstone claimed kinship. William attended a preparatory school nearby, in the rectory of a church which his father had built.

William entered Eton in the winter half of 1821, where he fagged for his elder brother, Thomas, who was five years his senior. He used to recall that the reigning adjective in the school at that time had been 'dapper'. George III, old, mad, and blind, had died in the previous year. Turner was painting sunsets at the height of his form ; Byron was making love to Countess Guiccioli at Ravenna ; and Shelley was writing lyrics of matchless beauty at Pisa. John Keate, the headmaster of Eton, believed in flogging boys, but he was in other respects an amiable and popular figure. He was only five feet tall, but his personality towered over the school. Gladstone, who was only once flogged, was extremely happy for the whole of his six years at Eton. He accepted unquestioningly whatever he was taught, and whatever, as he put it, ' insensibly filtered into me from my surroundings'.

The young Gladstone was remarkably good-looking and well-proportioned. He had brown, curly hair and rather pale and delicate features. He was always neat and well-dressed, and in no way outstanding among his contemporaries ; but during his last two years he was a favourite not only of the headmaster, but also of E. C. Hawtrey, the most outstanding of the assistant masters,[1] who was, Gladstone noted, ' always on the lookout for any bud which he could warm with a little sunshine'. The greatest event of Gladstone's school-life was his friendship with Arthur Hallam, the subject of Tennyson's *In Memoriam*, who cast an extraordinary spell over his

[1] Hawtrey succeeded Keate as headmaster in 1834, and became Provost of Eton in 1852.

contemporaries. Hallam, who has a place in the *Dictionary of National Biography* although he died aged twenty-two, was Gladstone's most intimate friend. 'He had', Gladstone wrote, 'in one point a large advantage over me. He had evidently, from the first, a large share of cultivated domestic education. With a father absorbed in diversified business, I had none.' He described that friendship as 'the zenith of my boyhood', and added, characteristically, 'it must have been the nadir of his '. Arthur Hallam, the son of the Whig historian, Henry Hallam, was two years younger than Gladstone, and their friendship began in 1824. They were in different houses, at opposite ends of Eton, but, contrary to the custom of the place, they used to breakfast during alternate weeks in each other's rooms.

Seventy years later, Gladstone wrote of Hallam's life at Eton that 'when looking back, I do not detect in it a single deviation from the ideal, in thought, or word, or act. Tennyson was as happy in having such material ready to his hand, as Hallam was in the opportunity of a friendship so lofty and so fraternal.' But Tennyson was not at Eton, and he did not meet Hallam until they had both arrived at Cambridge. Gladstone, in the meantime, derived immense advantage from a friendship which warmed and kindled his reserved nature. The two boys were strongly contrasted. Hallam matured early, and his personality was clear-cut. Gladstone was slow and vacillating. Hallam was a Foxite, and a Whig. Gladstone was a Pittite, and a Tory. But the friendship was close-knit. Hallam was not strong, and Gladstone used to scull him on the Thames, or walk with him, often to Gray's monument near the churchyard at Stoke Poges, where the famous elegy was said to have been composed. He was fascinated by Hallam's tolerance and sweetness of nature. 'Whatever I may now know of tolerance ', he wrote at the end of his life, in reference to that early friendship, 'has been a lesson drilled into me by the experience of political life.'

Because he took no interest in games, Gladstone was never a popular boy. He became prominent, however, during his last two years, as a debater, and as a schoolboy essayist and poet. During his last year he was co-editor, with George Selwyn, later Bishop of Lichfield, of an ephemeral magazine called *The Eton Miscellany*. After Hallam, his closest friend was Francis Doyle, later a civil servant and an Oxford Professor of Poetry. Gladstone, Hallam, and Doyle were all prominent in the debates of the Eton Society, but they used to meet also in one another's rooms, and out of doors, on long summer afternoons, to discuss questions of the hour, which were not then allowed to be debated in ' Pop '. It is interesting to compare that gifted circle with another, of which Horace Walpole had been the centre, and which had included the poet Gray, nearly a hundred years before. Walpole's ' quadruple alliance ' was sentimental, literary, and rather childish. Although Walpole's father, Sir Robert, was Prime Minister, the boys were not concerned about the outside world. But Gladstone, Hallam, and their friends, were deeply interested in contemporary events, and in practical and moral problems. To the most gifted set at Eton ninety years before, life had seemed a toy. It was regarded by an equivalent set in the 1820s as a supreme responsibility.

Gladstone's habit of sleeping with his windows open summer and winter, which was unusual at that time, could be regarded as symbolic. He was later to fling open many stuffy political windows. He left after the winter half of 1827, and wrote (2 December) in his diary : ' Oh, if anything mortal is sweet, my Eton years, excepting anxieties at home, have been so.' Those anxieties were the illness of his elder sister, Anne, who died in the following year, and the complete breakdown in health of his mother, who remained an invalid until her death in 1835. His mother's illness left Gladstone even more dependent than formerly on the affection of his father, whom he loved with his whole heart and mind.

Gladstone went up to Christ Church, Oxford, on 10 October, 1828. The years of his residence there were increasingly overshadowed by the convulsive struggle for the Reform Bill, which threatened to plunge the country into anarchy and civil war. He spent a ten months' interval before he went up to Oxford in reading and paying visits, and in being privately coached. He saw much of his ailing sister, Anne, whose mind, on religious topics, was less prejudiced than her brother's. She helped to persuade William that the doctrine of baptismal regeneration was not, as he had once supposed, heretical. The way was thus insensibly opened for further changes.

At Eton, Gladstone's religious opinions had been subject to no positive influences. The place was virtually pagan, and sermons in Chapel had been mumbled by toothless Fellows. Even the Confirmation ceremony had been an empty show. There was hardly any preparation, and all Gladstone could remember of the service was the Bishop of Lincoln recommending candidates to cultivate a ' sober ' religion, avoiding the pitfalls of enthusiasm on the one hand and lukewarmness on the other.

7

As he emerged from boyhood, Gladstone became increasingly conscious of the faith which he had formerly taken for granted. He understood the Church after the narrowest fashion of the Evangelical school, whose bigotry he shared, but whose fervour possessed him only by fits and starts. He was convinced that all unbelievers and Unitarians would be damned ; he thought that most Roman Catholics would be ; but that most Nonconformists had a fair chance of salvation.

During Gladstone's first year at Oxford, the mother of his friend James Milnes-Gaskell planted a seed in his mind which germinated. She suggested that salvation might be open to all true Christians, whatever the faults of their opinions. It was as simple as that : ' She supplied me ', he noted, ' with the key to the whole question . . . and it is now my rule to remember her in prayer before the altar.' One side of his nature believed that he had a call to enter the Church. But the other side caused him, before he left Eton, to inscribe and preserve a number of envelopes in copper-plate hand-writing : THE RIGHT HONOURABLE W. E. GLADSTONE, M.P. The conflict, thus begun, lasted until the end of his life.

Gladstone, when he arrived at Oxford, was horrified by its dry Anglican orthodoxy—so hostile to ' vital ' religion. ' The state of religion in Oxford ', he wrote in March, 1829, ' is the most painful spectacle it ever fell to my lot to behold.' He reacted violently against it. The contrast between his own exalted views and the worldly sophistries which he found practised in the society in which he moved, set up a very powerful state of tension in his mind. He sought, instinctively, to discharge that tension by living on the highest moral and intellectual plane of which he was capable. That gave him a great advantage in competition with his fellows, and in December, 1829, he was elected a Student of Christ Church. His election was a significant tribute, for Studentships at that period were in the gift of the Dean and Canons, and they were usually bestowed on relations, or friends, without much regard to merit or suitability.

Gladstone's rooms at Christ Church were on the first floor of the staircase on the north-east side of Canterbury Quad. He told his mother that it was the most fashionable part of the College. He read Classics, but he only started to work really hard—by his own standards—in the summer of 1830, when he began to study mathematics. He founded an Essay Club towards the end of his first year, which was known, by his initials, as *The Weg*.

Gladstone's Oxford friendships were mostly continuations of those begun at Eton, but Hallam was partly lost to him at Cambridge. His most intimate new friend was Joseph Anstice, who became Professor of Classics at King's College, London, at the age of twenty-two, but died prematurely aged thirty. 'I bless and praise God for his presence here', Gladstone noted. Anstice sympathized with Gladstone's religious preoccupations, which often caused him to hear as many as three sermons on a Sunday. He reproached himself constantly for idleness, as well as for uncharitableness, pettiness, illiberality, and obstinacy. He went sometimes, in pursuit of enlightenment, and at the risk of reprimand, to services at the various species of Dissenting chapels.

Gladstone often said in his old age that he had tried unsuccessfully for the Newdigate Prize in 1829, with a poem on Richard Cœur de Lion. This was one of the rare occasions when his memory failed him, for he never competed. His poem was written while he was at Eton, and printed in the *Eton Miscellany*. He tried, however, unsuccessfully, for the Ireland Scholarship in 1830, and again in 1831. His essay, on the second occasion, when he was *proxime accessit* was marked 'desultory, beyond belief'. He was informed that in writing English he needed to guard against 'a vague diffuseness'.

With Hallam, at Cambridge, Gladstone loved to correspond, and he complained that Hallam seemed no longer to cherish their friendship. On 23 June, 1830, Hallam gently rebuked him:

My dear Gladstone,

I read the latter part of your letter with much sorrow . . . I am utterly unworthy of the admiring sentiments you express . . . Circumstance, my dear Gladstone, has separated our paths, but it can never do away with what has been. The stamp of each of our minds is upon the other . . . I am aware that your letter points to something more . . . If you mean that such intercourse as we had at Eton is not likely again to fall to our lot, that is, undoubtedly, a stern truth. But if you intimate that I have ceased, or may cease, to interest myself in your happiness, indeed, Gladstone, you are mistaken.

At that time, Gladstone began to be deeply agitated about his choice of career. On 4 August, he wrote a long and prancing letter to his father about his wish to enter the Church. On that day he entered in his diary, 'God direct me. I am utterly blind.' John Gladstone replied kindly and sensibly, advising the boy to wait until he had completed his education. But he intimated clearly that he thought his son's views somewhat exalted, and that the law would be a suitable profession. On 29 August, 1830, William wrote to his brother John, who was a Lieutenant in the Navy, 'It tortures me to think of an inclination opposed to that of my beloved father.' He added that his temperament was so excitable, that he feared the result of surrendering his mind to worldly 'subjects which have ever proved sufficiently alluring to me, and which I fear would make my life a fever of unsatisfied longing and expectations'. They did.

In that year, 1830, Gladstone served a term as President of the Union, where he was prominent on the Tory side. He liked to believe in later years that he would have joined the Liberal camp much sooner if the accident of the Reform Bill had not thrown his mind into a panic. 'I do not think', he wrote in his old age, 'that the general tendencies of my mind were, in the time of my youth, illiberal,' but 'there was, to my eyes, an element of anti-Christ in the Reform Act.' He considered that Oxford, by planting firmly in his mind a passionate love of truth, had supplied him with the means of extricating himself from that folly. The means had, however, been provided much earlier, in his home, where he had long been encouraged to weigh and discuss freely all subjects.

While his mind was still swathed, as he later described it, in clouds of prejudice, Gladstone, on 16 May, 1831, made a speech in the Union against the Reform Bill which earned him a prodigious reputation. He carried, by 94 votes to 38, a motion that the Bill was unwise and unscrupulous, and that it was calculated to break up the foundations of the social order in Britain and throughout the civilized world. His friend Doyle wrote that when 'Gladstone sat down we all of us felt that an epoch in our lives had occurred'. Gladstone spoke for three-quarters of an hour on the theme that reform spelt revolution. One of his Eton friends, Lord Lincoln, a sensible but rather priggish and solemn youth, was so impressed, that he presently persuaded his father, the Duke of Newcastle, to offer Gladstone one of the seats in Parliament which he controlled.

It would have been helpful to Gladstone if he had had more experience of the world, and if life had not been made quite so easy for him at the start. In that respect he was at a disadvantage by comparison not only with Disraeli, who had to fight his way, but with many of his Eton and Oxford contemporaries whose wholesome and astringent earthiness was the result of being rooted in the soil. Gladstone was too intellectual, academic, and detached. In the month when he delivered his famous speech at the Union, he received a salutary lesson when he tried to convince a working-man that reform had spelt revolution in foreign countries. The man regarded him contemptuously for a moment. Then he spat, and finally exclaimed, "Damn all foreign countries! What has old England to do with foreign countries!"

Gladstone was greatly impressed by that incident, and it is impossible not to regret that he was never afforded an opportunity of widening the basis of his experience. He might have gained much if it had been possible for him to serve for a period in one of his father's enterprises after he left school, and before he entered the University.

In November and December, 1831, Gladstone and his friend Anstice both won Double Firsts in Classics and Mathematics in their Final Examinations. Gladstone had learned to love Oxford with an affection equal to that which he felt for Eton; and crowned with the honours he had earned he took the coach for Cambridge, where he saw Arthur Hallam, and then returned home to decide the question of his career. On 29 December, his twenty-second birthday, he recorded in his diary, 'Politics are fascinating to me; perhaps too fascinating.' On 17 January, 1832, he told his father, in a letter of quite inordinate length and obscurity, that, although he considered it likely that the entire social order would shortly be overturned, he was willing to make the law his profession, and to seek to enter politics. A fortnight later he left England with his brother, Lieutenant John Gladstone, R.N., who was two years his senior, to complete his education by a grand tour of Europe.

Among the places they visited before the tour was unexpectedly interrupted, were Brussels, Paris, Lyons, Turin, Florence, Rome, Naples, Venice, and Milan. In Brussels, on 5 February, they watched five thousand troops march into the Cathedral, and afterwards attended the service. 'The men were small,' Gladstone noted in his diary, 'for both John and I could see over their heads with ease.' On the field of Waterloo they were shown the spot where Lord Anglesey's leg had been buried after it had been carried off by a cannon-ball. The boot in which it had been contained was exhibited.

On 12 February, a Sunday, the two brothers dined in Paris, at the Hotel Meurice, for $4\frac{1}{2}$ francs each, without wine. Gladstone found the city 'a painful sight' because the shops and theatres were not closed on Sunday. 'In England things are bad enough, but by no means so far gone.' A worse shock followed when they reached one of the goals of their pilgrimage—the Vaudois Valley, in north Italy, where lived the descendants of the Protestant martyrs commemorated by Milton in the famous sonnet beginning :

Avenge, O Lord, thy slaughtered saints . . .

Gladstone had formed 'a lofty conception' of those people 'as ideal Christians', and he underwent 'a chill of disappointment at finding them much like other men'. He saw a pastor who was 'without the smallest sign of . . . vital religion'. He gave the man what money he could spare in a packet 'bearing on it what was meant for a pious inscription'. He then went sadly away, consoling himself by composing a set of indifferent verses. He noted that his Protestant temperature was a good deal lowered, and in that mood he reached Rome. Entering St. Peter's for the first time on 31 March, 1832, he experienced a preliminary intimation of the earthquake which was to convulse his mind in Naples six weeks later. He suddenly felt the pain and shame of the schism in the body of Christ's Church ; and he admitted that the Evangelical opinions in which he had been brought up received on that day 'a shock from which they never thoroughly recovered'. They began to dissolve like gossamer threads.

The Italian sun, in fact, was helping to ripen Gladstone's mind in every direction. He saw one day a very lovely girl, a Miss Burke, walking with her sister in St. Peter's. Her beauty seemed to smite him on the forehead, like a physical blow. He was always extremely susceptible. It was, however, in Naples that an event occurred which he considered much the most important and dramatic in his early life. Characteristically, it was a mental and not a physical event.

On 13 May, 1832, Gladstone was idly examining the *Occasional Offices* in the Church of England Prayer-Book. Without warning, his mind was convulsed, as by an earthquake, and, in a flash, Christianity was presented to him in a new guise. Hitherto, like all Evangelicals, he had taken the greatest part of his teaching directly from the Bible. 'But now, the figure of the Church arose before me as a teacher, too.' He recalled that the Church of England was as Catholic as it was Protestant, and that it had been Catholic long before it became Protestant. Thenceforward he felt himself a member of the Universal Church of Christ, with its 'Ministry of

12

symbols, its channels of grace, its unending line of teachers joining from the Head—a sublime conception, based throughout upon historic fact'. He felt no attraction whatever towards the Roman Church, although he continued to attend as many Roman Catholic services as possible. He considered that that Church was much more corrupt and less Catholic than his own, and he was completely satisfied with a High Church Anglican position. Paradoxically, he felt, in consequence, a little more reconciled to the Reform Bill. For he was now able to compare the Reformation in English Church history with the Reform Bill in English political history.

In Naples, Gladstone engaged a singing-master, and throughout the tour he was at great pains to improve his knowledge of Italian and French. Towards the end of June, 1832, in Milan, he received a letter from Lord Lincoln to say that his father, the Duke of New-castle, would be glad to place his influence in the borough of Newark at Gladstone's disposal if he felt ready to enter Parliament.

That proposal was intoxicating, but Gladstone was plunged, by his temperament, into an agony of introspection. The Duke had already written to Gladstone's father, who replied (26 June) that he would advise his son to accept the offer. The Reform Act had finally become law on 7 June, 1832, but the influence possessed in many constituencies by borough-mongers like the Duke of Newcastle was not greatly shaken for many years.[1]

Gladstone's decision had already been made in principle when he abandoned his idea of taking Holy Orders. He accepted the Duke's offer and posted home to join his family at Torquay. But he noted, later, that the remains of his ' devize' for the Church ' operated unfortunately. They made me glorify, in an extreme manner, not only the religious character of the State, which in reality stood low, but the religious mission of the Conservative Party.'

It was arranged between the Duke and John Gladstone that they should each pay half of William's election expenses. Those were expected to amount to a thousand pounds, but in fact, they amounted to two thousand. William, when he reached home, took life easily for some weeks at Torquay, and was troubled to discover how widely he now differed from his eldest brother, Thomas, on the subject of

[1] Mr. Norman Gash in *Politics in the Age of Peel* (1953) estimates that after the Reform Act of 1832, patrons still returned between 59 and 73 members for between 32 and 42 proprietary boroughs in England and Wales. Newark remained, in effect, one of those proprietary boroughs.

religion. Thomas, who had sat in the previous Parliament for a borough which was now disfranchised, was looking for another seat. It had for some time been found necessary to exclude religion altogether from the habitual freedom of their family discussions, but William considered that that exclusion was dangerous and wrong. He now tried, unsuccessfully, to break the ban, which he called 'intolerable'. On 23 September, 1832, he left Torquay for Newark in response to an urgent summons from his prospective constituents. He spent part of the forty-hour journey wondering how he could possibly justify his action in travelling on the Sabbath.

Newark was a two-member constituency which had returned a Tory and a Whig to the previous Parliament. The interest of the fight centred around Gladstone and the Whig member, Thomas Wilde, who was to be Lord Chancellor, eighteen years later, as Lord Truro. Speaking came easily to Gladstone, and he used only the briefest notes. He proved an ideal candidate and enjoyed every minute of the campaign. He wrote to his mother (29 September) : 'Such a stirring succession of outward circumstances as have surrounded me—such a wonderful medley of motives as my canvas has introduced me to—and such a rapid variety of thoughts as these have combined to produce—may be commonplace to experienced politicians, but to me and my habits . . . they bear the aspect of enchantment.' At the same time he firmly resolved that he would dedicate his life to ensuring that the resources of the State were used to further God's immanent purposes. He convinced himself that the career he had adopted contained 'a purpose of the highest utility, namely the endeavour to keep the principles of society right . . . and more especially to oppose the increasing worldliness of modern political principles'. He thought that that might prove a difficult and even visionary object, but that it was well worth the trial.

On 7 September Gladstone wrote to his sister, Helen, his junior by five years : 'The only thing I really *dread* is the fierceness of internal excitement, and that from experience as well as anticipation, I *do* dread. May God pour upon it his tranquillizing influence. It is very painful to feel myself mastered by turbulent emotions which one can condemn, but not control.'

Parliament was dissolved on 3 December, and the Election turned largely on the slavery issue. Gladstone was mocked as a schoolboy and abused as a member of a family which owed all it possessed to slavery. In an Election Address which he issued on 8 December,

14

he said that, while he desired the extinction of slavery, he considered that the ground should first be well prepared ; otherwise emancipation would prove 'more fleeting than a shadow and more empty than a name'. He added : 'I cannot forget that the English factory children are permitted to grow up in almost as great ignorance and deadness of heart as the West Indian negroes.' He reminded the electors that four-fifths of the cotton goods everyone consumed were ' *the produce of slave labour* in Lancashire, and of a system even more injurious than that enforced in the West Indies'. The Duke of Newcastle was startled when he read that statement. Gladstone was always a little liable to stick pins into the sides of anyone who befriended him.

On 9 October, 1832, Gladstone paid his patron a visit at Clumber. He had formed, he noted, 'rather an awful idea of the great borough-mongering Leviathan before I came here, but it was quickly dispelled and his manner set me *too* much at my ease . . . Only *eight* of his children are here at present.' He kept a record of a conversation with the Duke at breakfast on 10 October. A part of it went as follows :

D. of N. : " I confess I have a great notion of the horrors of enthusiasm."

W. E. G. : " Your Grace, I think we must expect to see enthusiasm in the present day, for where, after a long period of prosperity and ease, men's minds are disturbed . . . as at the time of the French Revolution, it naturally happens that opinion starts forth in every variety of form which it can possibly assume."

D. of N. : " Yes, it is so. There can be no doubt that, if we desert God as a nation, he will desert us."

W. E. G. : " Yes, my Lord. And we seem to be approaching a period in which one expects events so awful that the tongue fears to utter them . . . All seems to be in preparation for the grand struggle between the principles of good and evil. The way to this seems to be in preparation by the approaching downfall of the Papacy."

D. of N. : " Yes, Popery is attempting to rally its forces, but I think only preparatory to its utter defeat and destruction."

W. E. G. : " The Roman Catholic religion is so bad, and yet the prospect after its overthrow is so very dreary, that one scarcely knows whether to wish for its continuance, or destruction."

15

D. of N. : " I think there can be little doubt that we ought to wish for its destruction."

W. E. G. : " The question as to what is to succeed is full of interest beyond calculation."

D. of N. : " I fear that infidelity must succeed—for a time at least."

W. E. G. : " It appears to me that those are right who think there are great evils in the state of society—but wrong when they think them so superficial that they can be cured by legislation."

D. of N. : " Yes, all depends upon individuals ; the matter cannot be reached by Act of Parliament."

The Duke was well pleased with his protégé, and Gladstone left Clumber as deeply imbued as Burke had ever been with the virtues of an ' ancient aristocracy, than which the world never saw one more powerful or more pure '. London, he reflected, had a bad effect on them, but ' birth, wealth, station, are, as well as talent and virtue, among the natural elements of power, and we must not war with nature's laws '.

What Gladstone's friends thought about his candidature may be seen in a letter which Hallam wrote to Milnes-Gaskell on 1 October, 1832 : ' In some things he is likely to be obstinate and prejudiced ; but he has a fine fund of high chivalrous Tory sentiment, and a tongue, moreover, to let it loose with. I think he may do a great deal.' It must be remembered that Hallam was a Whig.

Polling took place on 12 December. Gladstone came out top with 887 votes, against 798 for his Tory colleague, W. F. Handley, and 726 for his opponent, Wilde. ' You return me to Parliament,' he told the electors, ' not merely because I am the Duke of Newcastle's man ; but because the man whom the Duke has sent, and the Duke himself, are *your* men.' He had digested the lesson of the Reform Act.

In the first Reformed Parliament, the Tories, who now called themselves Conservatives, were reduced to about 150 out of 658 seats. Their depleted and dispirited ranks were rallied by Sir Robert Peel, who watched eagerly for fresh talent. Before the new House met on 29 January, 1833, Gladstone took rooms at 92, Jermyn Street ; he moved to Albany, off Piccadilly, in March. He had been admitted to Lincoln's Inn on 26 January, and although he was never called to the Bar, he ate his dinners for thirteen terms. He joined the Oxford and Cambridge and the Carlton Clubs. He took little part in the social life of London, but a fine singing voice made him a welcome guest at musical parties. His future rival, Disraeli, had been defeated at High Wycombe, where he had stood as an Independent Radical. He was now launched with his curls and his rings, his extraordinary clothes, and still more extraordinary charm, on a campaign to conquer the London drawing-rooms, while composing a revolutionary epic.

On 1 September, 1833, Disraeli wrote in his diary:

'I have passed the whole of this year in uninterrupted lounging and pleasure.'

On 29 December, 1833, Gladstone wrote in his diary:

'I have now familiarized myself with maxims sanctioning and encouraging a degree of intercourse with society, perhaps attended with much risk.'

(See page 3.) The Arms granted by the College of Heralds in London on 1 July, 1846, were based on those of the Gladstaines of that Ilk in the Lyon Register in Edinburgh during the 1670's, doubtless with the implication that the two lines were of the same stock. The family from which Sir John Gladstone was descended can be shown to have owned land in Lanarkshire and Peebles-shire during the fourteenth century.

CHAPTER 2

PRIVATE LIFE

1833–1839

THE means Gladstone chose to improve his public speaking were probably unique. He read sermons aloud to himself, adding, altering, and omitting passages as he read. His Parliamentary duties had the first claim on his time; but outside those he read more deeply and widely than at any other period of his life. Apart from the Bible and Homer, he always said that he owed most to Dante, Aristotle, St. Augustine, and Bishop Butler. He kept himself physically fit by riding and walking; and one of his first actions in London was to engage a German tutor. He worked hard for some years at that language because he wanted to study the works of the German theologians.

In the first reformed Parliament he sat with the shrunken rump of the Conservative Opposition. He was liable, for a few months, to be confused with his eldest brother, Thomas, who had won Portarlington by a single vote. His principal recollections of the old Houses of Parliament, which were destroyed by fire in 1834, were the discomfort of the lavatories, and the absence of facilities for washing.

On 3 June, 1833, Gladstone made what was, in effect, his maiden speech. The House was in Committee on a Government Bill to emancipate all slaves throughout the Empire. In the course of the long debate, Lord Howick, the son of the Prime Minister, Earl Grey, had, on 14 May, accused Gladstone's father of working his slaves systematically to death. Thomas Gladstone replied three nights later, but William had to wait until 3 June before he found an opportunity to come forward in his father's defence.

Gladstone complained that he and his brother had been given no notice of Lord Howick's intention to attack their father. He would not deny that cases of wanton cruelty had occurred, but he adduced facts and figures to prove that his father was wholly innocent. He would not, he said, defend slavery as an institution. It was a system which 'unquestionably began in crime, in atrocious crime', but 'I do not admit that holding slaves necessarily involves sin, though it does necessarily involve the deepest and heaviest responsibility'.

Gladstone said that while he would welcome a safe and gradual emancipation, he considered that an unconditional emancipation, before the slaves were ripe for freedom, would be 'ruinous to the colonies, to the country, and to the slaves themselves'. He spoke for fifty minutes, and on 7 June the Colonial Secretary, Lord Stanley, in congratulating his youthful opponent, said that he had 'never listened with greater pleasure to any speech than I did to the speech of the Honourable Member for Newark who then addressed the House, I believe, for the first time'. A son defending his father will always evoke sympathy, but the effect of Gladstone's speech was greatly enhanced by his rare good looks, and by his charm of voice and manner. George Keppel, the Whig Member for East Norfolk, noted how completely the ear of the House had been gained by 'a beardless youth with . . . an earnest, intelligent countenance, and large, expressive black eyes'. Sir Robert Peel congratulated Gladstone in the lobby, and King William IV, in a letter to Lord Althorp, the leader of the House of Commons, expressed interest.

The Act abolishing slavery substituted a temporary apprenticeship system in most Colonies. It became law on 1 August, 1834, and John Gladstone received more than £70,000 as his share of the compensation money voted by Parliament. His son was always sensitive to hostile insinuations that he had started his career by maintaining a factious opposition to emancipation. He had, in fact, lost confidence in the slave-owners' agents, and he was discreetly silent during the closing stages of the debate.

The slavery issue was painful for family reasons. But on other questions Gladstone was uninhibited in opposing almost every forward-looking measure which came before Parliament. He supported, it is true, a Bill which his friend, Lord Ashley, later Earl of Shaftesbury, introduced for limiting hours of work in factories. But he opposed the abolition of sinecures, the abolition of flogging for minor offences in the Services, the adoption of a secret ballot at elections, the admission of Dissenters to the Universities, and the admission of Jews to Parliament. He advocated ruthless coercion in Ireland and the maintenance of all the privileges of the Anglican Church Establishment in that country. He argued strongly for the retention of the Corn Laws.

In August, 1833, after the House rose, Gladstone paid his first visit to Fasque, his father's new home in Kincardineshire. He fell in love with it at sight. He was there on 6 October when a letter from Francis Doyle informed him that Arthur Hallam was dead. His brother Thomas had thought Hallam 'affected', but Gladstone told him, 'it has never been my fate to see his equal'. He noted in his diary that, selfish as he was, the news had cut him to the heart.

Gladstone was at Fasque again in the autumn of 1834 when the King took the remarkable step of dismissing his Whig Government. He did so with the whole-hearted goodwill of Lord Melbourne, who had succeeded Lord Grey as Prime Minister, and despite the huge Whig majority in the Commons. The King asked the Duke of Wellington to form an interim Conservative administration until Peel, who was in Italy, could be summoned home.

The Duke cheerfully agreed. Gladstone later considered that Peel ought to have insisted on a General Election before instead of after taking office ; the transaction illustrates with great clarity the difference in constitutional practice between the earlier and later decades of the nineteenth century.

Political ties in 1834 were still regarded, in the main, as personal, and Parliament had not yet taken into its own hands the whole of the executive powers of the Crown. Whig and Tory leaders felt that their first duty was to carry on the Government and to avoid, as far as possible, all conflicts of principle such as that which had arisen during the years of agitation for the Reform Bill. Members of Parliament were not constrained by the terms of Party programmes, or by pledges to constituents. They were so jealous of the executive that the House as a whole exercised that duty of watching and criticizing the Government which has since become for the most part the specialized function of the Opposition.

Another theory of Party had been implicit in many speeches during the Reform Bill debates. It was, however, still in its infancy, and the first serious blow for it was not struck until 1845, when Disraeli attacked Peel for betraying Conservative Election pledges to maintain the Corn Laws. Thereafter the old and the new conceptions existed for many years, side by side. The old theory of Party had been stultified whenever conflicts of principle arose. Such conflicts were, however, the life-blood of the new theory, which required that they should be invented whenever they were not immediately apparent. By the end of the century Parties had become essential organs for the manufacture and sale of policy. The control of the electorate over Parliament was thereby made effective at some cost to the independence of its members.

In 1834 the Whigs were divided and unhappy. Lord Melbourne

considered that by getting himself dismissed he had managed the King and a difficult situation with equal adroitness. The country, although it regarded the King's action as somewhat of an anachronism, was largely indifferent; and the Conservatives, although holding only an insignificant minority of seats in the Commons, were quite content to take over the Government from the Whigs.

At Fasque, on 17 December, 1834, Gladstone received a letter from Sir Robert Peel. It was dated 13 December, and it asked him to call and see the Prime Minister. 'This is a serious call,' he noted. He posted to London, and reached his chambers in Albany at six o'clock on the morning of 20 December. After resting in bed for two and a quarter hours, he waited on Peel at eleven o'clock.

He was offered a Junior Lordship at the Treasury, and he found Peel ' *extremely* kind '. He was told that his friend, Lord Lincoln, would be one of his colleagues, and although he expressed the pleasure which he felt, he recorded characteristically, ' People call Lord Lincoln my friend and he acts as such. But it is well for me to remind myself of the difference of rank between us ... Oh God, that I were better worth having ! '

Three days later, on 23 December, Gladstone dined at the Mansion House. He told Tom that the dinner was a fine sight, but extremely uncomfortable where he sat at the lower end—' scarcely a knife, fork, or plate to be had ! ' However, he had secured a place, and friends assured him that at twenty-five he was the youngest Minister ever appointed solely on his merits.

A General Election was held in the following month, January, 1835. Gladstone was unopposed at Newark. The Conservatives, who made it clear that they were now reconciled to the Reform Act, gained about a hundred seats. They remained in a minority, but Peel continued to carry on the Government.

On 17 January, 1835, at dinner with Lord Lyndhurst, the gay and light-hearted Lord Chancellor, Gladstone and Disraeli met for the first time. Gladstone did not notice Disraeli's presence in his diary, but Disraeli noted that of ' young Gladstone '. He told his sister that ' a swan, very white and tender, and stuffed with truffles ', was ' the best company there '. Having just suffered his third defeat at Wycombe, Disraeli may well have been a little jealous. Years later Gladstone recalled that evening. He said that he had thought Disraeli ' rather dull ', and that he had been astonished by the foppery of his clothes.

On 26 January, Peel sent for Gladstone again, and offered him the

Under-Secretaryship for the Colonies. The previous Under-Secretary had failed to retain his seat. When Gladstone accepted, Peel wrote a charming letter to John Gladstone to say what pleasure it gave him to have an opportunity to promote his son : 'Wherever he may be placed, he is sure to distinguish himself.'

Gladstone had specialized increasingly in colonial subjects, and Peel told him that his family connexion with the West Indies would be an advantage. Lord Aberdeen, the Secretary of State, was in the Upper House, so that Gladstone was left in charge in the Commons. Of Aberdeen, Gladstone formed the highest possible opinion. He was a little dismayed at first by his limp and phlegmatic manner, but he used to say that of all the politicians with whom he had ever been associated, Lord Aberdeen was the only one he felt confident that he had really understood.

Gladstone's first spell of office was very brief, but it stamped his name with a hall-mark. The Government fell on 7 April, 1835, after Lord John Russell had carried an Opposition motion for applying to secular use a portion of the endowments of the Irish Church. It was the sixth time that the Government had been defeated in as many weeks. The House considered that the King's attempt to arrest the tide of liberalism had been accorded a loyal and adequate trial, and that a change of Government was imperative. In his disgust at the turn of events, Gladstone wrote to his mother a few hours before the fatal division was taken :

'If we are beaten to-night, as we are humanly certain to be, Sir Robert Peel will resign to-morrow. And, with him, will depart, not indeed the last hope, for God still reigns, but, in my mind, the last ordinary, available, natural resource against the onset of revolution.' He was not alone in thinking that the deplorable economic condition of the lower classes would combine with the powerful Radical movement to precipitate revolution. But an hour or two after writing that letter, he dined with Lady Salisbury, where he met the King's brother, the Duke of Cumberland. The Duke congratulated him on his speech in defence of the Anglican Church in Ireland, and Gladstone said that he felt he had done all too little to save that Church from harm. The Duke laughed heartily, and swore, as he thumped the young man on the shoulder. He told him that in his opinion the disappearance of bishops' wigs had done the Church more harm than anything else.

Gladstone hurried back to the House to take part in the division.

The Government was once again defeated, and Peel resigned. Two days later the Liberals, led by Melbourne, returned to office.

*   *   *

That year, 1835, was a very unhappy one for Gladstone. He lost office in April, after holding it for barely three months. At about the same time he fell deeply in love with a girl who firmly refused to marry him. And while his mind was most distressed and excited, his mother died rather suddenly at the end of her protracted illness. Finally, he irritated all his family by maintaining a hopeless and unreasonable opposition to a project of marriage which his elder brother Robertson had formed. He objected very strongly because the girl was a Unitarian.

Among Gladstone's contemporaries at Eton had been Walter Farquhar, son of Sir Thomas Farquhar of Polesden Lacy, near Dorking, Surrey. At a ball given by Lady Antrobus in the spring of 1835, Gladstone met Walter's eldest sister, Caroline. She was a great beauty, tall, and very popular, and he resolved to make her his wife if he could. Accordingly, when the House rose for the summer recess, he did not go to Fasque, but stayed in London with the object of pressing his suit. On 29 July, he wrote to Tom :

'Can you recommend me a man of song who could tune my throat a little in the interval before I leave town ? '

Three days later Gladstone wrote to his father :

'Marriage is a subject which, in a general form, has been enough in my mind. But I feel myself beset with some peculiar difficulties, in as much as it would be my duty, if possible, and by seeking help from above it must be possible, to keep a strict guard upon my feelings, until I could have ascertained that the object which might attract them was endowed with those religious convictions which are the only permanent foundation of happiness, and whose necessity for my own case I should ground . . . upon special need in myself.'

On 11 August, Gladstone relieved his feelings in a long poem of no great merit :

. . . .

The lamp of love burned low, but clear,
And brightened like the unfolding year
Beneath the breezes' kiss,
When first at view
My spirit knew
Her presence to be bliss

. . . .

Gladstone had confided to a limited extent in his friend, Owen Blayney Cole. Two years earlier (12 August, 1833) he had told Cole that the new principles which he had adopted in his social life might prove to be of such 'destructive laxity' that already they made his conscience 'start and tremble'. He now wrote to him (5 August, 1835) that he had reached the conclusion that physical beauty was to be considered a real good, so long as the respect paid to it was never allowed to compete with that which is due to 'moral and mental beauty'. Cole's reply (21 August, 1835) may, or may not, have amused Gladstone :

'Who the crippled, crooked, squinting, pock-marked lady, who has taught you to prefer moral to material beauty, may be, I cannot say, but as you have thought proper to conceal her name I will not guess at it. Whoever she is, I am certain that with such well-regulated feelings and pure principles as those avowed in your letter, she cannot fail of being a happy woman when united to you.'

Late on the evening of 22 August, on the day before he was due at Polesden Lacy, Gladstone penned some private 'Reflections' :

'This is an interesting evening of my life. In my solitary chambers, without light, I lay and ruminated on that which lies before me, and about which I have said to myself often during these last weeks, "Shall I grasp at it? Shall I dream of grasping at it?" ... I know that her presence constitutes a tranquil, but a deep delight ... I recognize in her that which one should wish to find in the being whom God should appoint to be as a guardian angel of the soul. I am not wise enough to define this feeling further, or to clothe it with a name.

'And to-morrow, Sunday, on the day of the Lord's rising ... do I venture into her family, in the humble hope and prayer that means may be opened to me of seeing further, of touching more inward chords, of eliciting the holy sounds whose music I must obey. Oh, may that effort be unprofaned : may it be blessed ! Amen !'

The visit to Polesden Lacy was a failure. Gladstone's love-making was so rigorously unprofaned, that no inward chords were touched, and no sounds, holy or otherwise, were elicited. He found no opportunity to speak words of love to Caroline Farquhar. Returning to London, he opened the attack on another front. He wrote a letter (25 August, 1835) from his chambers in Albany to the girl's father, Sir Thomas Farquhar :

'I scarcely dare to conjecture with what feelings you and Lady

Farquhar will receive the request I am about to proffer to you . . .
My father's liberality enables me, his fourth and youngest son, to
contemplate a change of state, I trust, and believe, without impro-
priety, though I would guard myself against appearing to imply that
any great advantages of fortune are ever likely to be within my reach.
Neither would my inclinations, so far as I am acquainted with them,
be such as to render acquisitions of this kind more probable . . .
In my own person I have been blessed by Providence with what,
though anything but great in itself, may nevertheless be deemed so
when viewed in relation to either my expectations or deserts. But
no-one is more conscious than myself that the uncertainty of all things
earthly has perhaps, in the present day, a peculiarly forcible application to one whose destinies have like mine early been committed upon
the perilous contingencies of political life, and who is therefore especially bound to live with reference to those permanent and exalted
objects which belong to our condition as human beings.'

It was natural, no doubt, that in that long letter which hardly did
justice to his feelings, there should have been a great deal more about
Gladstone than about Miss Farquhar : ' It is scarcely necessary to
explain,' he interpolated, ' that what I have said has reference to your
daughter.' On 27 August Lady Farquhar replied on behalf of Sir
Thomas, who was unwell. She regarded Gladstone as a poor
match for her lovely girl who was widely admired, and she wrote
very guardedly. She had, she said, had a long conversation with
Caroline :

' She expressed extreme surprise at the communication, not having
the smallest idea that you entertained any preference for her. She
told me she considered the acquaintance of so short a duration that it
was impossible to form any decision as to the future, or to say whether,
on more intimate acquaintance, a congeniality of tastes and opinions
might lead to any warmer sentiment than at present exists.'

Gladstone immediately consulted Walter Farquhar. On 31 August,
Walter obligingly communicated his sister's views :

' The following are her words. " Are not Mr. G.'s ideas with regard
to religion more strict than I should like to embrace. Many things
which I do not consider wrong, might be viewed in that light by him ;
and, if I married him, it would be with the wish of thinking with him
in everything." '

He warned Gladstone that his sister's fortune amounted to only five
thousand pounds.

Money did not worry Gladstone. His father wrote to him on 6 September :

'When you marry I shall make your income equal to two thousand pounds per annum, and give you a reasonable sum to furnish a house . . . to which the fruits of any fortune the lady may have will be to add.'

Gladstone's efforts, therefore, were concentrated on the task of clearing up the religious difficulty. He wrote to Lady Farquhar (3 September) :

'As to those particular kinds of amusements which most prevail, I do not so much look to the specific opinion which may be entertained as to the lawfulness of this or that one among them, but more— far more—to the temper of mind which limits them to their proper character . . . and which is ready to reject any of them, or all of them, if they should be found at variance with the will of God or hostile to the health of the soul : not as a matter of constraint, but under the influence of a stronger attachment to Him who has redeemed us . . . For that temper I have felt bound to look, and fully believe that I have found it.'

But Lady Farquhar thought otherwise, and was now thoroughly alarmed. Her answer was delivered to Gladstone by hand the next day. She said that she saw no possibility of any 'true union of minds' :

'I have read your letter with great attention, and have reflected upon it deeply, and I am *very* grateful to you for so entire an elucidation of your sentiments. It has given me a much more complete insight into your religious principles than any conversation could have done. Indeed, I must confess to you from what passed between us on Monday, the impression then left on my mind was of a much less "exaggerated" description than that which your letter to-day conveys. After I had read it, my *own* decision was formed. All the apprehensions I expressed to you were revived tenfold . . . But I would not bias her. I left her to decide her own fate. She assured me she felt the responsibility too great. In a union with one whose religious opinions go so far beyond her own, she reads (as I do) the too probable event of family disunion, estrangement and separation from all she most loves. She is bewildered and frightened . . . She begs me to say she sees no other alternative but that of relinquishing a connection which, under other impressions, might have been productive of so much happiness for us all.'

Gladstone was much disturbed by that letter. He turned again to

Walter Farquhar for enlightenment, but he wrote first (4 September) to his mother :

' My hopes are now altogether crushed, and the cord which bound me here is snapped . . . The reason which makes my disappointment bitter and sore to bear in my untamed heart . . . is this. Believing that no purer and less selfish creature moves on earth, and that that purity and unselfish frame of mind are sustained by a love of God glowing in the heart, I find at the same time that the very religion of love itself assumes in my mind so harsh a form as to alienate those who hold its substance . . . I blame myself in a thousand ways, and how much above my practice must my professions have risen, to alarm anyone on the score of religion! '

Walter Farquhar's reply (11 September) to Gladstone's request to know why his letter had produced so unfavourable a reaction is very interesting. It illustrates the manner in which the leaven of seriousness was beginning to penetrate a few sections of society at that time :

My dear Friend,

. . . In my opinion it was this. My mother saw in your statement of principles much what she would have expected me to write. And the absolute necessity of a practice, such as mine, flowing from those principles, being the fixed conviction of her mind, she immediately apprehended that they must lead in your case also to a shunning of those amusements and societies in which she sees no harm, and which it would deeply grieve her to find her daughter shun and disapprove . . . Try to bear up and overcome it, and regain your peace of mind.

On 7 September, Gladstone had to leave London to attend the funeral of one of his uncles ; he went on to Fasque, where his mother's health had taken a sudden turn for the worse. He helped to nurse her devotedly, and he made detailed notes about every incident that occurred. Mrs. Gladstone died on 23 September, 1835, and although her son's attention was necessarily distracted for a time, he experienced a full sense of Christian religious consolation, and in December he resumed his correspondence with Walter Farquhar. He was told plainly (18 December) : ' The barrier you have to overcome is the obtaining my sister's affections.'

Nevertheless, Gladstone fretted about the religious difficulty. On New Year's Day, 1836, he sent Farquhar a paper he had prepared, with a request that it should be laid before Caroline, and Lady Farquhar. He said that he assumed 'the principle of religion . . . to be . . . the surrender of the whole heart and the whole life to God, and the receiving them back from Him to be employed for his purposes.' He considered that marriage should be based upon an identity of views upon that vital matter. A congeniality of tastes and affections would in that way have the best chance of being realized.

Farquhar was not unsympathetic, but after his father's death on 12 January, 1836, when he succeeded to the baronetcy, he pointed out to Gladstone the difficulty and delicacy of his position. On 13 February, Gladstone promised his father that he would try his best to put the affair out of his mind, but that proved impossible. He reported to his father (10 March, 1836) that Farquhar had lately told him that 'someone had declared an old attachment to Miss F., which pecuniary matters alone had prevented him long ago disclosing'. Farquhar believed that his sister was not indifferent to that admirer, and added that he felt sure that she was no longer frightened of Gladstone.

The effect of Farquhar's well-meant confidence was to throw his friend's mind once more into a state of acute distress. If Caroline was no longer frightened of him, much must depend upon the issue of the affair with the third party. Gladstone tried to get a letter from Lady Farquhar to say either that there was a third party and that the field was closed, or that there was not, and that the field was still open :

'The truth is,' he told his father (10 March), 'it is most important that a definite resolution which is to form a basis for future conduct, and which is to be applied to the subjugation of reluctant feelings, should . . . be conveyed in a permanent form.' He had, he said, urged that very strongly on Sir Walter Farquhar, 'and he agreed' ; but he had 'said that he thought his mother's objection to writing was that this matter between her daughter and the third party was so very uncertain in its issue'.

The gulf between Gladstone's mind and Miss Farquhar's was unbridgeable. Two years later, on 13 April (Good Friday), 1838, he summarized, for no eye but his own, his views on the subject of 'Amusements'. He considered it under thirty-nine separate heads, paying particular attention to certain 'indulgences not essentially linked with sin, but opening up many channels of temptation—balls and assemblies, for example'.

28

Gladstone saw no reason why a man should fail in 'carrying his religion into his amusements', and nothing 'in the *essence* of balls and assemblies which . . . so connects sin with that essence, as to render countenance to them in any form, countenance given to sin'. He felt justified, on the whole, in discounting the argument that, by going to balls, 'we are running the risk of making a brother stumble'. After all, Our Lord once attended a wedding-feast, and sat at meat in the house of a publican. It was, he noted, 'a solemn question', but he leaned to the view that even balls might be '*capable* of having the sting taken out of them, at least, as effectually as dinner-parties. Both will undoubtedly remain dangerous. But our whole life is dangerous.'

Those prickly reflections about 'the essence of balls' would have appeared fantastic to Caroline Farquhar, who was an ordinary, light-hearted girl. After a brief engagement she was married, on 26 July, 1836, to the Hon. Charles Grey, a younger son of the former Whig Prime Minister. She was later a woman of the Bedchamber to Queen Victoria, while her husband became a Lieutenant-General, and Private Secretary first to the Prince Consort, and, later, to the Queen.

When the issue was settled, Gladstone penned (10 April, 1836) some private reflections, attributing everything to the wisdom of God, who had seen fit to humble him. He found 'a pungent instruction in the circumstances under which another has been preferred . . . not only under pecuniary disadvantages (as I believe), but also without any presumption of argument about religion. Surely, here is a useful lesson for stubborn and tameless pride! And God be praised!'

But Gladstone was sore. And in the meantime his brothers Tom and Robertson had both married. Gladstone had not at first felt inclined to approve of his eldest brother's choice. After describing himself (10 July, 1835) 'as one who is drawn incessantly not only to the world, and a fallen nature, but to many, at least, of the worst and bitterest of all its evils', he had suggested: 'Marriage may not be in the counsels of God for me—or even for you.'

Thomas, who had already announced his engagement, prepared for battle, but William apologized. He wrote (13 July) that 'It is, in my case, more than ordinarily common to let speculation outrun and distance thought.' When Robertson, however, who was in the family business, became engaged to the daughter of a Unitarian banker in Liverpool, Gladstone made no attempt to conceal his dismay. He spent hours in futile and foolish efforts to draft a form of religious statement which he hoped might prove acceptable to his future sister-in-law, and satisfactory to all parties. Robertson was exceedingly angry, and John Gladstone had to use all his authority to reconcile his sons :

'My dearest William,' he wrote (7 December, 1835), 'I am grieved to say that I concur in this [Robertson's] estimation of the course you deemed it your duty to pursue . . . Robertson is perfectly satisfied with Miss Jones's religious belief . . . He believes that she firmly believes in the fallen state of man and the doctrine of the atonement. . . . He feels, as I think properly, that he is the best judge of his own conduct, as *he* is the responsible party . . . Once more, for God's sake, reflect again on what you may be sowing the seeds of . . . '

After days of heart-searching doubt, Gladstone apologized (26 December) to his father for having adopted 'a course of inconsiderate harshness, a course which I have in the course of my life had too many occasions to regret, and which I well know to lie deep in my character'. But his letter of apology to Robertson (30 December) was qualified and, in part, equivocal. The marriage was celebrated with Church of England rites on 28 January, 1836, and Gladstone was only with difficulty persuaded by his father to attend the ceremony.

The idea of marriage remained in the forefront of Gladstone's mind. But eighteen months passed before he fell in love again. He continued to aim high, and in the summer of 1837 he rather suddenly proposed marriage to Lady Frances Douglas, the eldest daughter of the Earl and Countess of Morton whom he had met for the first time two years previously in Edinburgh, where his father had a town house. He was allowed every opportunity to press his suit, but the girl gave him no encouragement. Her mind was unformed and her character immature, and for some time he was unable to obtain an answer either way.

In his perplexity, Gladstone confided completely in two friends of both families, E. B. Ramsay, Dean of Edinburgh in the Scottish Episcopal Church, and his wife. He told the Dean that he could bear the suspense no longer, and asked him to see the Morton family on his behalf. On 13 November, 1837, the Dean wrote to him :

'I have seen from the tenour of your letter the absolute necessity of a speedy decision . . . and I quite agree with you. The hour of your reading this page is the time for your learning that hope *is damped*. I write this with much and deep feeling of disappointment.

But I am certain that you will not act and feel otherwise than as a man and as a Christian . . . For a mind like yours the whole truth is best told at once. There is the strongest and highest feeling of respect and admiration for your character and attainments . . . expressed by the parents and by the young lady herself as you could have wished . . . They trust that this feeling of respect and regard will not be mistaken for a reciprocation of *feelings* which the mother repeatedly declared were most honourable and gratifying to their immediate object and to " all her belongings ". They . . . will " always be glad of your acquaintance "—I quote their words . . . Well ! Now our dream is past ! The truth is known ! '

Gladstone asked if the decision was final, and the Dean wrote (15 November) : ' The decision is definitive—definitive, not from " repugnance ", but because there is reciprocation of none of those feelings which are required to ground a different verdict.'

On 16 November, Mrs. Ramsay wrote, ' with the sort of interest that a mother may be supposed to feel, and also to give you *the advice of experience* '. Gladstone had, the Dean's wife told him, ' been *precipitate* . . . Another time, dear Mr. Gladstone, be more guarded of yourself . . . A young mind is startled by a proposal of this kind, when she has not had an opportunity even to suspect prefer-ence.' Lord and Lady Morton liked him very much, but they would not influence their daughter: ' The feeling must be spontaneous for *happiness*.'

Gladstone said that he would be willing to consider himself ' fully bound ', if only he could be granted in return the favour of a ' remote encouragement '. But on 7 January, 1838, Mrs. Ramsay told him that there was no hope at all, and that he must brace himself to accept the fact :

' All things are rightly ordered for God's children, dear Mr. Gladstone . . . Believe me, it is best as it is. From the very richness of your mind, your companion for life must be peculiarly gifted, or you will be left alone . . . There is a childlike buoyancy of heart and spirit that seems to set aside all tendency to deep feeling in Lady F.D.'

With indomitable optimism, Gladstone continued throughout the remainder of January to urge the Dean to obtain for him that boon of a ' remote encouragement ' on which he had set his heart. But on 31 January, the Dean told him that the Mortons had said that corre-spondence must cease. On that day Gladstone wrote to his father, and related all the circumstances. He sounded so low that the old man offered to come to London earlier than he had intended :

'Pray do not hurry your coming on my account,' Gladstone told him (2 February). 'For although there was a time when I was not well fit to be alone, I cannot now plead any *special* reason for your accelerating your journey, glad of your arrival as I must be on other accounts.'

On 21 June, 1838, Gladstone wrote to congratulate Lord Morton on the engagement of his daughter, Lady Frances, to Lord Milton, son and heir of Earl Fitzwilliam. Dean Ramsay, very tactlessly, told Gladstone that he had observed with regret the unconcealed exultation with which Lord and Lady Morton had greeted the engagement.

As a result of private preoccupations, Gladstone was less constant in attending the House, less conspicuous in debate, and less animated in the speeches which he made during the autumn of 1835 and the whole of the year 1836. He made amends in 1837, when he was again returned unopposed at Newark at the General Election which followed the accession of Queen Victoria. His father, who stood for Dundee, and his brother Thomas, who stood for Leicester, were both defeated at that Election ; but Disraeli was at last elected at Maidstone. On 14 July, 1837, Gladstone was presented for the first time to the Queen, when he helped to present a loyal address from Oxford University, on her accession.

On 30 March, 1838, Gladstone carried his reputation to a new height by a two-hour speech in defence of the former West Indian slave-owners. He was opposing a motion to cut by two years the period of apprenticeship which had been substituted for slavery in most of the Colonies, in order to prepare the negroes for freedom. He was speaking in a lost cause, for on 1 August, 1838, the apprenticeship system was finally abolished, and the last vestigial survival of slavery disappeared throughout the British Empire. More than once, in the early months of 1838, Gladstone begged his father to allow him to go to the West Indies in order to carry out a personal investigation of conditions on the family properties. The voyage would have helped him to forget the charms of Lady Frances Douglas, but his father, after vainly trying to dissuade him, finally refused his consent with some brusqueness. He knew his son well enough to fear the consequences of an explosive reaction.

Although he continued to specialize on colonial questions, Gladstone's main interest was always the Church. The climate of opinion in which the Reform Act had been passed was anti-clerical, and many people feared that the Church of England would shortly be disestablished and disendowed. Parliament had, however, intervened to save the Church from some of the worst abuses which provoked its critics ; and the clergy themselves were responsible for a spectacular revival of religious activity. One aspect of that revival was manifest in the Oxford Movement. Gladstone was scandalized by the growing emphasis which was being laid on the principle of State intervention in Church affairs, and for that reason he drew ever closer to the High Church party. Because it was no longer possible to mulct the tax-payer to pay for the erection of new churches, he threw himself with fervent enthusiasm into the task of raising funds from private sources. He brooded incessantly over the question of the part which the State Church should play in the life of the nation.

Gladstone was always careful to note the attitude of public men to religion. He was delighted to find that Peel made a habit of reading the works of ' our best Divines ', and that the Duke of Wellington, when he was in London, made a point of attending service every morning at the Savoy Chapel at eight o'clock : ' It is a duty ', the Duke said, ' which ought to be done, and the earlier in the day it is discharged, the better '. Gladstone had a pronounced tendency to hero-worship, but he was a fairly acute observer. The first time he stayed at Drayton in January, 1836, he noted the strange combination in Sir Robert Peel of an elaborate assumption of the manners of a *grand seigneur* with a certain tiresome *gaucherie*. He thought that his host looked splendid in his blue frock-coat, ribboned button-hole, fine boots, and distinctive hat. Peel had, however, a great fund of bawdy stories, and his humour was too ' full blooded ' for Gladstone's taste.

Gladstone struck up a friendship with the poet, William Words-worth, who used sometimes to come to breakfast with him. On one such occasion (8 June, 1836) Wordsworth annoyed his host by arguing in favour of a further instalment of Parliamentary reform. He thought that the country districts should be enfranchised in order to offset the strength of the boroughs. When Gladstone demurred, Wordsworth suggested that the way to strengthen a pyramid was to extend its base. Gladstone at that point changed the subject, and asked whether the new steamboats were fit subjects for poetry. Wordsworth said that they were. Gladstone considered that the poet was very simple and rather dull. He always walked home, when he

33

left, and was careful first to remove his shoes and change his silk stockings for grey worsted ones.

One day, in the autumn of 1837, another poet, Alfred Tennyson, called, by appointment, on Gladstone. They became intimate later; the object of that first meeting was an exchange of reminiscences about Arthur Hallam, whom they had both loved.

On 17 March, 1837, Gladstone recorded at great length a curious conversation with Lord Ashley at the Carlton Club. It arose out of a speech which Gladstone had made two days earlier in the House about Church Rates. "Now I will tell you what, Gladstone," said the future Lord Shaftesbury, as he drew up a chair. "You made a very able speech, but you disappointed me." He accused Gladstone of employing a dangerous and extraordinary argument.

Gladstone had suggested, Ashley said, that the old pagan gods had, like the Hebrew prophets, served a necessary purpose in their day, and had foreshadowed at some points the teaching of the Gospels:

"The notion," Ashley exclaimed, " of the heathen gods producing the same result with the revealed Gospel! I will tell you the remark, my wife made upon it, and I thought it a very sensible one. She said 'Why, if that religion could have produced such effects, they will naturally ask, " Where was the need of Christianity? " ' "

Gladstone, significantly, stood his ground, although it was a truly remarkable attitude for anyone who had begun to consider himself a High Churchman. He had already sensed, at that early date, the need for a principle of universal application reaching back to pre-Christian times and extending beyond the boundaries of Christendom, on which to base more securely the claims of the Anglican religious establishment. He explained that he had found such 'a principle of vigour and of permanence' working through 'many ancient institutions' among which the pagan gods of Greece and Rome were entitled to a place:

"Now, my dear Ashley," he said, " the phenomena presented by them require the assignment of a Gigantic Cause, which alone is adequate."

Twenty years passed before Gladstone sat down to the task of developing those views in greater detail. But, thereafter, most of his leisure for the rest of his life was devoted to working them out with extraordinary virtuosity, and, often, with perverse ingenuity, in a stream of articles and books about Homer. The conversation with Lord Ashley at the Carlton Club ended with an exchange of blessings, as the two young Members of Parliament separated to write letters.

Gladstone was at that time drawing very close to two men whose influence upon him was profound. They were the Rev. Henry Manning, who had been a year senior to him at Oxford, and James Hope, who had been a younger contemporary at Eton and at Oxford, and who was now making a name at the Parliamentary Bar. Hope, who changed his name to Hope-Scott in 1853, after marrying a grand-daughter of Sir Walter Scott, was often described as the best-looking man in England. He had, Gladstone wrote, ' a grace and gentleness of manner which, joined to the force of his inward motives, made him, I think without doubt, the most winning man of his day'. He felt ' an intense affection' for Hope, and admitted that he was ' the man on whom I most relied'. He wrote to him (6 November, 1839) :

' It is possible the world may think well of you from your connection with me, so full is the world of delusions, and so miserably inaccurate are our comparative estimates of men. I think of you much, but I have never told you all I think, and I never shall. May God Almighty ever bless you ! '

The basis of both those intimate friendships was the fact that Manning and Hope-Scott had, like Gladstone, turned from Evangelicalism to a close association with the High Church party in religion. Gladstone wrote to Manning (5 April, 1835) : ' Politics would be an utter blank to me were I to make the discovery that we were mistaken in maintaining their association with religion.' He wrote to Hope-Scott (11 January, 1839) :

' I have been long ago pledged to the service of the Church, and I should be a renegade indeed if the outward form of my present life were to hide from me that which I wish to be the pole star of my existence . . . I am entirely convinced that the movement termed Evangelical, and that which is falsely termed Popish, are parts of one great beneficent design of God, and that, in their substance, they will harmonize and co-operate.'

Since his schooldays at Eton Gladstone had felt an equal urge to express himself in print, and in debate. He had contributed political articles to the Press since he was first elected for Newark. He now felt an imperative need to write a book to explain his view of the right relation between the English Church and the English State.

Gladstone's action was precipitated by a course of lectures about religious establishments which were given in London, in the spring of 1838, by the Professor of Divinity at Edinburgh, Dr. Thomas Chalmers. Among the great and the fashionable, the pure and the intense, the idle and the curious, who flocked to the Hanover Square Rooms to listen to the celebrated preacher, Gladstone sat with a puzzled frown. He felt that the subject was being improperly handled. Chalmers argued that the State was not concerned with matters of doctrinal detail. It was enough if it established and endowed some form of Protestantism, which was the word of God, pure and undefiled, and if it opposed an iron front to Popery, which was the word of God obscured by that of man. To Gladstone that seemed superficial and sorry stuff. He told Manning (14 May, 1838) that he did not believe that Chalmers had ' ever looked in the face the real Doctrine of the Visible Church and the Apostolic Succession, or has any idea what is the matter at issue '.

Gladstone decided that the false impressions disseminated by Chalmers must be corrected at once. He needed an overriding preoccupation at that time, and he worked so hard—twelve hours a day—that he began to have trouble with his eyes. He argued that the State possessed a conscience and had a duty to distinguish between truth and error in religion. Doctrinal differences were, therefore, matters of supreme importance. The Established Church was the conscience of the English State, and that State was bound to give an active, informed, consistent, and exclusive financial and general support to the Anglican religion which was of the purest and most direct Apostolic descent.

The book was finished in July, 1838. It was accepted by Murray and entitled *The State in its Relations with the Church*. Gladstone went abroad in the middle of August, while the book was being scrupulously revised by Hope-Scott. He was still abroad in December, when it was published, and he received his author's copies in Rome.

Gladstone's first object in going abroad was to settle his only surviving sister, Helen, with a companion, at Ems, in Germany. She had been difficult for years, and was subject to nervous attacks and imaginary illnesses. Gladstone noted, a trifle grimly, that one of the misfortunes of ill-health was that it often made self-indulgence appear a duty. From Ems he went on to Florence and Rome, where he joined an English family with whom he had been becoming increasingly intimate. It consisted of Lady Glynne, her son, Sir Stephen Glynne, who sat in Parliament for Flintshire, Sir Stephen's brother, Henry, and his two sisters, Catherine and Mary.

Gladstone and Sir Stephen had been contemporaries at Eton and Oxford, and Gladstone had already stayed once at Hawarden Castle, which was Sir Stephen's home. They all moved to Naples early in October, and from there, on 13 October, Gladstone and the two Glynne brothers went on a tour of Sicily, which lasted until 13 November. Before the tour began, Gladstone found himself deeply in love, once more, this time with Catherine, the elder of the Glynne sisters. All her family knew it, but they pretended not to notice, and called Gladstone by the pet-name, *Gia*.

In Sicily, Gladstone visited the principal towns and temples. At Segesta, their guide, Guiseppe, started to complain about religious doubts. He said they came to him when he was hungry, and saw bad men prospering. Gladstone prescribed an immediate cure. He read him, in Italian, the 37th and 73rd Psalms, and the 12th chapter of the Epistle to the Hebrews.

Gladstone's own faith was fortified by the subterranean rumblings which he heard as he climbed Mount Etna. His account of the mountain found its way into Murray's *Handbook for Sicily*, but his explanation of the purpose of the rumblings was confided to his diary. He supposed that one purpose at least was ' to give a palpable assurance to our faith in the declarations of Scripture concerning the final conflagration of the Heavens and the Earth . . . We see the match, and the combustibles. And nothing is hidden from us but the Hand and the Time which are to bring them together.'

After their return to Naples, the Sicilian party, with Catherine and Mary Glynne, ascended Vesuvius on 29 November. They all left together for Rome on 7 December.

In Rome, Gladstone heard such an unusual number of sermons that even he considered that he owed an explanation to his diary. He ascribed it to the state of his eyes, which made reading uncomfortable. In Rome he met T. B. Macaulay, who had not yet thought about reviewing his book ; and he saw a great deal of Henry Manning. On 29 December he had an argument with the future Cardinal about the case of a woman upon whose hands and feet the stigmata were said to have appeared : ' He believes that those wounds might be produced by a power in the mind. I cannot help thinking it is more simple and more natural to refer to supernatural agency.'

He met and had friendly talks with Dr. Wiseman, the English Roman Catholic leader, to whom he gave a copy of his book as soon as he received a parcel of copies.

In the meantime a worrying letter came from his sister in Germany. Miss Gladstone, who was bored at Ems, had become engaged to Count Léon Sollohub, whose parents were not at all pleased. They insisted that Helen should join the Greek Orthodox Church and live in Russia.

The Sollohubs were a Polish branch of a wealthy and distinguished Russian-Polish family. Helen wrote (6 December, 1838) that Léon possessed a ' delicacy and refinement of mind, almost womanly'. He was aged twenty-six, and ' one of the first things about him that pleased me was his constantly reminding me of you. In face he is somewhat like you, although much fatter '.

The Count had been in the Army, but had quitted it, ' having served in the last Polish Revolution and proved unequal to all its fatigues '. He now hoped to enter the Civil Service. Gladstone did his best, from a distance, to give suitable advice. But his relations with Catherine Glynne had now reached such a critical and delicate stage that it was impossible for him to post to Germany and deal with Helen's affairs.

He was with the Glynnes by moonlight in the Colosseum on 3 January, 1839 ; and he had then an opportunity to speak to Catherine, for a moment, alone. He began to speak of his love, but Catherine would not respond. She moved away, and Gladstone blamed himself bitterly ; he feared that his hopes had all been ruined. He was inhibited by his repressions from folding the girl in his arms, and taking her by surprise, and by storm. He resolved, therefore, to trust to a letter, but he postponed writing it until 17 January, two days before he was due to return home. Its breathless and tortuous style bears witness to the tumult of his emotions. The fact that he emerged more or less successfully from its second paragraph, consisting of one enormous sentence of 141 words and 18 clauses and sub-clauses, is perhaps worthy of remark :

62, PIAZZA DI SPAGNA

17 January, 1839 : Night

I address you, my dear Miss Glynne, in terms below my desires, yet perhaps beyond my right to say in the simple words which I believe will in any event be most acceptable to you, and which no occasion has offered to address to you otherwise than by letter. My heart and hand are at your disposal.

I seek much in a wife in gifts better than those of our human pride, and am also sensible that she can find little in me : sensible that, were you to treat this note as the offspring of utter presumption, I must not be surprised : sensible that the lot I invite you to share, even if it be not attended, as I trust it is not, with peculiar disadvantages of an outward kind, is one, I do not say unequal to your deserts, for that were saying little, but liable at best to changes and perplexities and pains which, for myself, I contemplate without apprehension, but to which it is perhaps selfishness in the main, with the sense of inward dependence counteracting an opposite sense of my too real unworthiness, which would make me contribute to expose another—and that other !

For the substance of what I write I have no apology to offer which can be effectual. As respects its time, my own mind required no postponement, and I could not presume that it would give me any more reasonable hope of access to your affections. I wait your Command with the humility which I owe to a being so far purer and better than my own, and with other feelings which I have not the right to describe in the colours of truth. And, indeed, they are chequered with the consciousness that I ought to wish you a more blessed portion in life than that which alone it is in my power to tender. For pardon, for indulgence, I do not ask. Your own nature will yield me, unsolicited, much more than I desire. But I must cease. May you live, and die, it is not less my anticipation than my desire, from day to day more possessed of the peace which passeth understanding, and of the holiness which is its fountain.

With esteem, with gratitude, suffer me by one more act of boldness to add, with warm and true affection,

I am, Yours,

W. E. Gladstone.

He received his answer the next morning :

Your letter had so completely taken me by surprise, that I feel it is amost impossible to express my sentiments by writing. Although I regard you with great esteem and friendship, you must be aware that warmer feelings are required before consenting to a proposition such as your letter contains. Is it not, therefore, due to you to say that, were an *immediate* answer required (which is only what you ought to have), it must be in the negative ? Should it be any satisfaction to you to see me we shall be at the Porta Maggiore

soon after twelve. I will not enter into the feelings of gratitude I
entertain for your far too good opinion, or dwell upon the compliment you pay me.

Yours very sincerely
Catherine Glynne.

That was distinctly hopeful. Gladstone spent part of that day
with the Glynnes, and he made it clear to Catherine that he did not
ask for an immediate answer. He was given a remote encouragement,
and on that understanding they parted. He packed his things and
left for England the next day, with Sir Stephen and Henry Glynne.
The journey was uneventful except for a single incident which
shocked Gladstone in the coach from Paris to Boulogne (29 January) :

'It was very sad to find two Parisians who . . . were my com-
panions in the "rotonde", gross in their conversation both against
decency and against religion—rank and blasphemous infidelity ! . . .
There was a . . . picture of the *Sunday* balls as the regular occasion
of intrigue, the most unblushing and systematic, which exceeded what
anyone could have supposed ! . . . These men extolled Paris as a
perfect Paradise ! '

Gladstone reached London the next day, and kept his own counsel,
this time, about the understanding which he had reached with
Catherine Glynne.

CHAPTER 3

MARRIAGE AND CABINET OFFICE
1839–1844

THE first business which faced Gladstone on his return to London was the very mixed reception accorded to his book. It was dedicated to Oxford University; and, on the whole, the Universities, and the Bishops, approved. Gladstone's hazy language may have helped, for a time, to conceal the extreme length to which his argument was pushed. The theme was that membership of the Church of England, which possessed a monopoly of religious truth, ought to be the fundamental qualification for membership of the national community. It followed that the Anglican Establishment in Ireland should be maintained at all points, if necessary by force; and that Roman Catholics and Nonconformists should be excluded from civil office throughout the British Isles. Gladstone admitted that his theory was inapplicable in British India, because the native religions were protected by treaties. He did not specify the terms of those alleged treaties, but he condemned the Government's action in assisting Roman Catholic chaplains to minister to the wants of Irish regiments in India. And he implied that the treaty which had established the Presbyterian Church in Scotland was unjustifiable.

Most lay opinion was hostile to those impossible and extraordinary opinions. *The Times*, in particular, was very unkind. A complimentary leading article on 19 December, 1838, was followed by a second favourable notice a week later. Then, on a ' stricter analysis ' of the ' verbal garniture ' in which the author's views were ' muffled ', the tune changed. A leading article on 4 January, 1839, charged Gladstone with infirm judgement, anti-Protestant tendencies, and a Popish kink. A fourth notice on 21 January was positively savage. *The Times* described Gladstone as a menace to the Church, a purveyor of frivolous and irresponsible arguments, and a repository of puerile and discreditable bigotry.

Gladstone was never very sensitive. He told Manning (2 February) that he was convinced that even a year's delay in publishing the book would have been wrong, and he added : ' A good many people say that they found it stiff work. So did I ! ' The fantastic nature of his theory was exposed by Macaulay in pages of pungent comment in the *Edinburgh Review* for April, 1839. Macaulay was more polite than *The Times*, but he accused Gladstone of first deluding himself and of then seeking to delude his readers. He asked why he did not say in plain language that he would like to see Dissenters roasted in front of slow fires. He paid tribute to the author's 'unblemished character' and 'distinguished Parliamentary talents', and he dubbed him, in a phrase which haunted Gladstone for the rest of his life, 'the rising hope of those stern and unbending Tories'.

Gladstone wrote, characteristically, to Macaulay to thank him for the 'candour and single-mindedness' of that review. He was soon forced to admit that his medieval ideal of a Christian society, possessing a monopoly of truth, to which it had a duty to give a permanent and consistent expression in politics, was incapable of realization in that age. His mind, he reflected, had been a dark place into which the light filtered very slowly. He wrote in 1868 : 'Scarcely had my work issued from the Press, when I became aware that there was no party, no section of a party, no individual person, probably, in the House of Commons, who was prepared to act upon it. I found myself the last man on a sinking ship.'

Gladstone soon came to regard the book as one of his mistakes, and he abandoned its theory for practical purposes almost as soon as he had enunciated it. But he never suppressed the book, and it ran into several editions. In his heart he was always rather proud of the blow which he had struck against the increasing dominance of secular motives in the nation's life.

Gladstone had not paused to consider what effect the book's publication might have on his political prospects. He was in no sense a man of the world :

'For years and years,' he wrote, 'well into advanced middle life, I seem to have considered actions simply as they were in themselves, and did not take into account the way in which they would be taken or understood by others . . . The dominant tendencies of my mind were those of a recluse, and I might, in most respects with ease, have accommodated myself to the education of the cloister.'

Gladstone never fully understood that the natural and probable effects of the actions of public men upon the minds of others must often provide the decisive criteria for judging those actions. He long remembered Peel's 'peculiar, embarrassed shyness' the first time he met him after the book came out. And he was inclined to think that he never wholly recovered Peel's confidence. He noted that one day, in June, 1839, Peel passed him 'not rudely', in the street, but without speaking. For once Gladstone's reserve broke down. He ran after Peel and asked what was wrong. His leader then told him for the first time that he regretted the book's publication.

Gladstone at that time sat on no less than ten committees, most of them of a religious character. He was also greatly interested, with his father, Dean Ramsay, and James Hope-Scott, in the project to found Trinity College, Glenalmond, for training young Scotsmen for the Church of England Ministry. His speeches in the Commons were consistently reactionary, and he strongly opposed, on 6 May, 1839, a Government motion to suspend the Constitution of Jamaica. The planter oligarchy in that island had been blocking humane measures for the relief of former negro slaves, but Gladstone argued that to suspend the Constitution would shake the confidence of every British subject throughout the Empire. The Government was so nearly defeated that Lord Melbourne resigned. Peel was asked to form a Conservative Government, but he gave up the attempt when the young Queen tearfully refused to change the Ladies of her Household for Ladies of a Conservative complexion.

So Melbourne returned to office, and that may have been fortunate for Gladstone. He had shaken Peel's confidence, and if a Conservative administration had been formed at that moment, it is possible that no place in it would have been found for him. Gladstone was desperately worried by the slow progress of his courtship of Miss Glynne. He was constantly with her, and with her family, after they came to their town house, 37, Berkeley Square, at the beginning of April, but he was in an agony of introspection and self-reproach. He thought that he had been incorrigibly stupid, and on 6 June he confided everything to his father. He told him that he did not think that he would be able to bear the suspense much longer. Two days later, on 8 June, that suspense was ended.

At a garden party given by Lady Shelley at Lonsdale House, Parson's Green, Miss Glynne agreed to become formally engaged to marry him. They had been strolling together by the river. Gladstone explained to her that he would have preferred to be a clergyman, but that he had dedicated himself instead to a supreme experiment. He wanted to help to make political life truly Christian. Catherine told him that she had copied out many extracts from his book with the object of learning them by heart.

On 17 June Lord Lyttelton became engaged to Catherine's younger sister, Mary, who had refused him a month earlier. The two sisters had been inseparable, and Gladstone, with Catherine, was awaiting developments in a room on the ground floor of 37, Berkeley Square, while Lord Lyttelton was pressing his suit with Mary in the drawing-room. When they came down it was evident that Lyttelton had succeeded. The two sisters fled away for a little, to weep and laugh together, while Gladstone pulled Lord Lyttelton on to his knees and joined him in returning thanks to God. He took Catherine to Lambeth the next day, to be blessed and kissed by the Archbishop.

On 10 June, Gladstone had written to his brother, Thomas, to tell him his news. But Thomas, who was out of Parliament and feeling the want of occupation, was jealous of his youngest brother. He had already complained that William was neglecting him and showing preference for other friends. He accused him now of being secretive, and wanting in brotherly affection. Gladstone told him that he had been ' sore ' about a former occasion when his private affairs had become too widely known. He could, he said, not have attended to his many duties if he had not kept this matter locked in his own breast.

A double wedding was arranged at Hawarden on 25 July, 1839. Contrary to later custom, Gladstone and Lyttelton went to stay there before the event. Rejoicings were unrestrained, and of the two bridegrooms it was agreed that Gladstone looked much the more distinguished. He was in his thirtieth year, tall, upright, pale, resolute, and very clear-eyed. Lord Lyttelton, a boy of twenty-one, despite a massive head and intellectual brow, looked, in comparison, uncouth :

' Well, here we are ! ' Gladstone wrote to Manning, from Hawarden, on 18 July, ' in some considerable glee . . . The only question is, whether we shall ever, at any time, be able to do anything again . . . This holiday of life must be short, and I hope will be short. Its most singular feature to me is its utter novelty. There is nothing in former years with which I can in any way compare it—at least in the years which have elapsed since shedding the name of boy ! '

But Catherine gave herself up completely to her happiness. This ' holiday of life ' was at that moment her whole existence. She wrote to William the day before he reached Hawarden :

So my precious thing does not arrive till to-morrow. I *will* be patient, but somehow I feel a blank ! . . . The foliage is so luxuriant and beautiful . . . The very roses seem to smile, and the whole air is perfumed, and if *you were by my side* to enjoy all

this, it seems to me I should be *too* happy . . . Goodbye my
very very own.   God bless you, and send you safe to

Your *fond*

Joy

who is counting the hours to your arrival.

Gladstone was deeply in love, but his expression was somewhat
inhibited.   He addressed Catherine at this time as ' My own own ',
and signed himself ' Yours affectionately, W. E. Gladstone '.   Not
long after his marriage he began addressing her as, ' My dearest
Cathie '.   He was careful from the first to subscribe his letters, at the
bottom, ' Mrs. W. E. Gladstone '.   But after the death of the last of
his three elder brothers' wives, he at once altered the form of that
subscription to ' Mrs. Gladstone '.

Miss Glynne understood him perfectly, and she possessed great tact.
One day, before they left London, she sent an undated letter to her
' dear old Oak ':

' Now, remember, I wish *you* to appear to great advantage to *our*
Uncle George [1] . . .   You must never call him " Sir ", which I
observe is your habit with your father.   Our family have a prejudice
against it, which I intended to tell you, although it appears so childish
that it is *almost* foolish to mention it.   On the other hand, there being
in it no compromise of conscience, it being a matter perfectly unimportant one way or another, you may as well indulge them.   God
bless you !   Goodnight, my dearest William.'

In the competitive middle-class world to which Gladstone belonged
by birth, it was natural for younger or less securely established men
to address older and established ones as ' Sir '.   But in the Glynnes'
assured patrician world, all men were conventionally on the same
footing.   As a mode of address between friendly equals, ' Sir ' was
ceasing, in some quarters, to be used in the old eighteenth-century
manner, and to the Glynnes it seemed inappropriate to emphasize
distinctions of age or public position.   Gladstone had, in fact, secured
a great prize in every sense, for the Glynnes belonged to a historic Whig
clan.   Catherine's mother, a daughter of Lord Braybooke, of Audley
End, was closely related to four former Prime Ministers—George
Grenville, Lord Grenville, Lord Chatham, and William Pitt.   Miss
Glynne, who was aged twenty-seven in 1839, had long reigned at

---

[1] The Rev. George Neville Grenville (1789–1854 ; Dean of Windsor, 1846–
1854).

Hawarden Castle like a princess. Her father had died when she was a child, but her mother, who idolized her, her two brothers, and her sister revolved around her in their orbits as planets revolve around the sun.

When Hope-Scott wrote to congratulate Gladstone on the grand marriage he was about to make, he felt moved to sound a warning note. He trusted, he said (11 June), that the engagement had been entered upon ' in the fear of God, and with a determination of turning every circumstance of life into an instrument of His honour '. Gladstone replied the same day. He said that he ' loved ' that letter ' far better than merely smooth and thoughtless congratulations. You will, I hope, soon know my wife, and try her by the test you propose . . . I rely much on your friendship. I hope you will never shrink from admonishing me, and that my attachment may grow with your fidelity.'

The double wedding ceremony was performed in Hawarden Church on 25 July by the brides' uncle, the Rev. George Neville Grenville. William and Catherine were married first. Sir Francis Doyle was best man to Gladstone, and he celebrated the occasion in a poem of some merit. At five o'clock on the afternoon of that day, Mrs. Gladstone lay asleep on a sofa at Norton Priory, in Cheshire, which had been lent for the honeymoon by Sir Richard Brooke : ' The beloved sleeps on the sofa,' Gladstone recorded. ' We have read the lessons together. She sleeps gently as a babe. Oh, may I never disturb her precious peace ! '

The next morning they read the Bible together, and resolved to continue that practice throughout their joint lives. Gladstone was able to record his belief that, during the wedding ceremony, his heart had been truly raised ' to a high level according with the spirit of the great mystery of Christian marriage '. Every day, and ' nearly every hour ', he noted, ' convince me of the brightness of my treasure, her pure, enduring brightness '.

On comparing notes after their honeymoons, Mrs. Gladstone and Lady Lyttelton both admitted that it had been a mild shock to find that their husbands, during any waiting-time, were liable to pull books out of their pockets, and to become engrossed in them. Both couples met again at Hawarden a fortnight later, and all four set out (13 August) on a joint tour of Scotland. It was an unusual arrangement, but an extremely happy one. They drove, rode, or walked as they pleased, and they spent a fortnight at Fasque, with John Gladstone, where they were joined by Sir Stephen Glynne. Gladstone and his wife spent the autumn in Scotland, mostly at Fasque ; and from there, on 23 September, Mrs. Gladstone wrote to her sister, Lady Lyttelton, who was staying at Chatsworth, to say that she was expecting a baby. Lady Lyttelton replied that she was expecting one too.

On the way back to Hawarden, for Christmas, the Gladstones visited many houses. They stayed with Lord Rosebery at Dalmeny, and with Lord Morton at Dalmahoy. Gladstone was delighted to find that Catherine was not in the least jealous of Lady Milton, to whom he had proposed marriage two years before, and who was then at Dalmahoy with her husband. He found it necessary to request his father (1 January, 1840) to put a stop to rumours that he had made Catherine consent to abandon some of her old amusement, and that she had warned her, before their marriage, that his views on religion were a great deal stricter than her own. A gossipy old woman who lived at Wrexham had given John Gladstone as her authority for that story.

On 22 January, 1840, the honeymoon period ended, when the Gladstones came to London to stay with John Gladstone at his London home, 6 Carlton Gardens. They had bought for themselves 13 Carlton House Terrace, which was being furnished and made comfortable for them. It was rather a grand house for a young couple, and a part of it was taken by Gladstone's mother-in-law for her private use when in London. John Gladstone, by what his son termed a ' beautiful ' act, chose that moment to divest himself of all his West Indian properties. He divided them among his four sons and left their management in Robertson's hands : ' This increased wealth, so much beyond my needs, with its attendant responsibility, is very burdensome,' Gladstone noted. He used it to initiate a most difficult and extraordinary work, which at once became and remained for the whole of the rest of his life his most important charitable activity. He began to patrol the London streets after nightfall with the object of rescuing and rehabilitating prostitutes.

William and Catherine Gladstone were a wonderfully happy and handsome couple, but although they were in the world they never really seemed to belong to it. Their values were different from other people's and they tended to assume that others, like themselves, cared only for the big things of life. Mrs. Gladstone was tall and slender, and she moved with an indescribable grace. Her eyes were a deep sapphire blue, and capable of expressing every variety of mood. An abundance of thick brown hair waved softly upon her forehead, and she always liked to wear a rose which matched her brilliant complexion. She was brimful of fun, and ready at all times to dismiss intricate details of politics or theology as 'red tape'. But she was completely wrapped up in her husband, and had an intuitive appreciation of anything which, in a large way, affected his career. She was, at times, forgetful, impulsive, and unpunctual, and she was often teased by her husband for her mistakes. She would tease him in return, and tell him, 'what a bore you would have been if you had married someone as tidy as yourself !'

Gladstone adored her ; he told her all his secrets, and his confidence was never once betrayed. But neither was well-suited for the parts they were called upon to play. They consistently neglected those small social duties upon which, in public men and women, the world is inclined to insist. They were kind and courteous to all ; but Mrs. Gladstone was not punctilious in returning calls ; while her husband was indifferent to dinner invitations, and suffered from an inability to remember faces and names. It was felt that they were both too much wrapped up in their private interests to fulfil adequately all the public calls which were constantly made upon them. Their houses were filled with streams of congenial visitors but Gladstone made little effort to entertain or conciliate sufficiently those who, for political reasons, were important to him, and Mrs. Gladstone did not, or would not, check her husband's insensitiveness in such matters.

Gladstone, in 1840, enjoyed a full measure of that admiration which is attached to a young man of proved ability and achievement who may advance to any height. He was widely respected, but little understood, and, in some quarters, mistrusted. It was feared that he was impractical and impulsive. He had, however, secured the ear of the House of Commons, where he radiated, even at that time, a powerful magnetism.

He was a singularly graceful speaker, and his wealth of language appeared to be as inexhaustible as the memory upon which it drew. He was always saturated with his subject. When he warmed to a theme, the mild eyes, beneath the lashes which half veiled them, became replete with fire. The fine head, with its rather prominent brow and crown of jet-black hair set upon the broad shoulders of a superb athletic frame, contributed to the effect which he produced. The complexion was pale, and faintly tinged with olive, but he gave an impression of immense vitality. The strong ascetic jaw, faintly suggestive of a medieval prelate, implied self-mastery. The beautiful hands were perfectly controlled, and used with incomparable dramatic effect while he was speaking.

The most attractive feature of his oratory was the melodious voice, which was much the finest organ of its kind in Parliament. He pronounced some words—e.g. constitootion, or noos—in a fashion peculiar to himself, which the House relished. Highly-strung and contentious at all times, he had learned to introduce little playful touches into his speeches which contrasted well with the dryness of his favourite topics and the habitual gravity of his manner. But a love of splitting hairs, which seemed to grow on him, an excess of moral earnestness, and a capricious sense of proportion, caused him, on occasion, to alienate the sympathies of a certain number of well-intentioned but less-gifted men.

Despite that failing, the outstanding feature of Gladstone's oratory was the way in which it was adapted to its audience. He combined in an unusual degree the arts of exposition and debate. He had an unerring instinct for any weak points in an opponent's argument, and he would swoop upon them, like a hawk. His hearers listened spell-bound as he always somehow managed to extricate himself, with grammar intact, from one reverberating period after another, with their tangle of labyrinthine parentheses. He seldom, as John Bright observed, sailed boldly from headland to headland ; he preferred to hug the coast, and to follow to its source any navigable river which he encountered during his voyage.

Marvellously effective as it was, Gladstone's oratory was never quite of the highest or most enduring quality. It did not, like Chatham's, appeal to elemental passions, which exist independently of the peculiarities of particular audiences. Nor did it appeal, like Burke's, to elemental principles, which hold the fabric of civilization in its place. Elemental passion dismayed Gladstone ; and although he constantly searched for principles of universal validity, he often produced an incongruous effect by applying them to trivialities. He allowed himself to become too much immersed in legislative detail, and he has left few sentences which live in the memory—few passages which would bring a sparkle into the eye of a declaiming schoolboy. Deprived of the magic of his delivery and of his gestures, the printed texts of his speeches lack prophetic inspiration and poetic power. Informed by close reasoning, they appear pedestrian. Their characteristic note is an expression of intellectualized sentiment.

Beneath that smooth expression, an unseen volcano blazed. It erupted at intervals, and shot forth pillars of flame and clouds of smoke. The controls were colossal, but Gladstone's mind was seismic.

Deep inside it, the tensions of the age seethed in molten fury continuously, until, at intervals, the balance of forces at the surface was disturbed. Often the necessary readjustments would be imperceptibly effected. But sometimes a new equilibrium would be established as a result of a mental earthquake, which appeared, to those who did not know, or understand, or like Gladstone, to burst without warning under a clear sky. His mind had experienced one such earthquake already at Naples in 1832. More spectacular examples of its seismic quality were to follow. The impression which Gladstone gave of intense natural vehemence held under tremendous restraint was the secret of the enthusiasm as well of the distrust which he inspired. Once his mind was set in a fresh pattern of conviction he was visited by a sense of infallibility and became an incarnate moral and emotional force. It was, however, impossible to calculate at any moment the nature of the stresses to which his mind might be subject ; like a volcano, it was subject to its own laws, and the risk of earthquakes and explosions was always present.

Grinding toil and prayer were Gladstone's only methods of keeping his dæmonic energy in check. He was never unoccupied for a moment, and even when Parliament was not sitting his day was carefully planned. Whenever he found himself with five minutes to spare, he took up a book and became instantly absorbed in it. His faculty of exclusive concentration was as extraordinary as his energy, and of immense assistance in his work. Fundamentally, in all the relations of life, he was as simple as an unspoilt child. He was guileless, credulous, unsuspicious. When Mrs. Gladstone was not present to protect him he was an easy victim for schemers and bores.

He was so childlike, natural, and just, that in his own family and intimate circle he was not merely loved, but idolized. He was always happiest in his home where his ways were known and understood. He was gay, playful, and excellent company, but even there the blaze inside him was glimpsed at times in his eyes. Friends noticed how when he went up to the nursery, his eye would occasionally flash, and his countenance would grow tense, as he relaxed with one of his children over a game of beggar-my-neighbour.

* * *

In 1840, when he moved into his new home in Carlton House Terrace, Gladstone instituted a daily morning and even session of prayers for his household. At the evening session he would sometimes

ARTHUR HALLAM.
From the pastel at Wickham Court, Kent.

JOHN GLADSTONE AND THOMAS GLADSTONE (LATER, SIR THOMAS GLADSTONE, BT.)—second and third from left—IN THE HOUSE OF COMMONS, 1833.
Detail from the painting by Sir George Hayter.

W. E. GLADSTONE AND MRS. GLADSTONE, 1840.
From the portraits by W. Bradley and F. R. Say at Hawarden.

read a short sermon which he had composed, and nearly two hundred of such sermons are preserved among his papers. On Sundays he attended two Church Services, and taught in a Sunday School attached to St. Martin-in-the-Fields. He was a frequent communicant. He gave up his practice of keeping a detailed daily account of his personal expenses ; but he continued to keep a jejune daily record of the way in which he spent his time.

Socially, when they first married, the Gladstones were in great demand ; and their favourite method of returning hospitality was the breakfast party. Mrs. Gladstone started almost at once a series of weekly breakfast parties at 10 a.m. on Thursdays. Throughout his life Gladstone was always at his conversational best at breakfast, and anyone who had occasion to approach him in a difficulty was most likely to be successful at that hour.

On 17 March, in Gladstone's study which was then only half-furnished, Hope-Scott gave his host a ' heart-stirring ' promise to co-operate to an unlimited extent in any work which Gladstone undertook for the Church : ' I set upon it ', he told Hope-Scott (15 May, 1845), ' a value not to be described.' They discussed Gladstone's personal problem, whether an ' individual whose original covenant has been with the Sacred Ministry, and who has altered its form under the impression that, from peculiar circumstances, the Church required more service in another quarter, would not, upon the unfavourable termination of such an experiment, remain bound by his first plighted troth. All this was spoken with personal application, *and in the strictest confidence.'*

Gladstone was at that moment passing through one of his periodic phases of depression. He cured it, as always, by plunging into fresh work. He felt discouraged by the failure of his book on *State and Church*, and, in consequence, he began for the first, but by no means the last time to think seriously about withdrawing into private life. He was a willing listener, however, when Hope-Scott argued—' I thought even over-strongly,' Gladstone noted—that every Christian had a duty to abide by the calling which he had adopted. Gladstone was always, as he told Lord Lyttelton at that time, ' dependent not so much upon the applause, as upon the assent of others, to a degree which perhaps I do not show, from that sense of weakness and utter inadequacy to my work, which never ceases to attend me '.

The fruit of that intimate conversation with Hope-Scott was two-fold. In the first place, Gladstone brought out a new edition of

State and Church which was twice the length of the original. He knew that the theory was dead, but he was resolved that it should, if possible, be understood. He admitted, in the preface, that his argument had been difficult to follow in detail in the first edition, but the new edition achieved the remarkable feat of being even more obscure than the original. The argument became, virtually, impossible to follow at all.

In the second place, Gladstone wrote a new book called *Church Principles Considered in their Results*. Manning made many suggestions and revised it thoroughly, and by working at very high pressure Gladstone finished it, while staying with the Lytteltons, in August, 1840. The Church of England was depicted as the one true Catholic Church, uniting all that was best in the Roman Catholic and in the Protestant worlds. The theologians received it very coolly and Dr. Arnold pronounced it to be full of ' incredible errors '. The reviewers ignored it, and the author begged Murray in vain to advertise it. It closed the brief chapter of Gladstone's literary crusade on behalf of the Establishment.

In the Commons, Gladstone's warm sincerity and reverential approach were carrying his reputation to fresh heights. It was now generally believed that he would be given Cabinet rank whenever the Conservatives returned to power. He spoke constantly, and he was not afraid, on occasion, to go beyond many members of his Party. On 8 April, 1840, he denounced a war with China into which the Government had blundered because the Chinese sought to enforce their laws against trading in opium. British traders found China a profitable market for opium manufactured in India. The memory of that war is branded indelibly on the minds of all Chinese, and it is the starting point of every history of modern China. Justice, Gladstone declared, was on the side of the Chinese, and ' we, the enlightened and civilized Christians, are pursuing objects at variance both with justice and religion '. He incautiously suggested that the Chinese were justified in retaliating against the British by poisoning wells.

On 3 June, 1840, Gladstone's first child, William, was born. Manning and Hope-Scott were the godfathers. Gladstone had just been elected to Grillion's dining-club, of which he remained a loyal and congenial member for more than half a century ; but he accepted his election under protest, ' because the rules of society oblige me to submit ' ; and he was ashamed, on the first occasion when he attended, to find himself obliged to pay fifty shillings for a dinner.

In the summer of 1841, Lord Melbourne's Government fell. It had proved incapable of balancing a budget. Trade was stagnant ; the lower classes were suffering terrible hardships ; the Chartist movement presented the country with a potential threat of revolution. Wars in China and Afghanistan, and a threat of war with France, imposed a heavy strain on the Exchequer. The only effective means of allaying distress and discontent was to end the trade depression by a root and branch reform of the nation's obsolete fiscal system; but the Whigs seemed incapable of devising a policy. Such measures as they proposed early in 1841 came too late, for Parliament and the people had lost confidence.

On 19 May, 1841, a Government motion to reduce the duty on imported foreign sugar, as part of a plan to bring down the cost of living, was defeated. Gladstone opposed it (19 May) on the ground that it would favour slave-grown sugar from Brazil. He said that he could not be a party to encouraging the slave-trade, that ' monster which . . . while war, pestilence, and famine, slay their thousands . . . from year to year, with unceasing operation, slays its tens of thousands '. Some of his opponents felt that this new Saul was appearing a little too boldly among the Prophets. Lord Howick reminded Gladstone that he lived in a glass-house, and that he would be well-advised to beware of throwing stones.

Lord Melbourne would not resign after his Government was defeated and, on 4 June, Sir Robert Peel carried a resolution of no confidence by a single vote. The House was in an uproar, and Gladstone noted, ' upon looking back I am sorry to think how much I partook in the excitement that prevailed '. With rare obstinacy, Lord Melbourne still refused to resign, but he advised the Queen to dissolve Parliament. Gladstone retired to Newark, where he was opposed at the General Election. He wrote to his father (27 June) that he had given strict orders against ' treating ' :

' There will be no resort to bribery . . . I believe we shall get through without mischief . . . I fear corruption will be tasted to the uttermost in the boroughs. May God control it, and may His spirit, moving upon the face of the waters, cause them, after their manner to bring forth life.'

Gladstone was returned at the head of the poll, and the Conservatives gained a clear overall majority of some 80 seats.

Gladstone had fought the election as an uncompromising protectionist. He described Cobden's Anti-Corn Law League as nothing but a great political fraud: 'Knowing absolutely nothing,' he noted, 'I, as in duty bound, believed everything that was entertained by those in whom I had confidence.' After a brief holiday with his wife at Hoylake, which reminded him of Pæstum, in South Italy, he returned to London on 18 August, and took part in the conferences of the Conservative leaders. On 31 August, Peel sent for him and asked him to take the post of Vice-President at the Board of Trade.

Gladstone was bitterly disappointed. He had stood latterly on such terms with the leaders of his Party that he fully expected to be offered a Cabinet post. But he was better off than Disraeli, who actually wrote to Peel to ask for subordinate office, and was refused. Gladstone felt certain that something untoward had occurred during the few days between the meetings of the Party leaders, which he had attended, and the formation of the Government, to prevent his being offered the Chief Secretaryship for Ireland on which he had set his heart: 'I am distinct in the recollection that there was a shyness in Peel's manner, and a downward eye, when he opened the conversation and made the offer, not usual with him in speaking to me.'

The offer of the Vice-Presidency, however, was made in the kindest terms. Peel said that Gladstone would have his 'unbounded confidence'; and that he would be responsible for trade matters in the Commons. He added that his chief, Lord Ripon, was a master of the subject:

"I consider it," Peel said, "an office of the highest importance."

"Of the importance and responsibility of that office at the present time, I am well aware," Gladstone retorted. "But it is right that I should say as strongly as I can, that I really am not fit for it. I have no general knowledge of trade whatever."

Peel patiently persuaded him to accept. He told him, frankly and in confidence, that he had thought of sending him to Ireland as Chief Secretary, but that objections had been raised on the score of religion. He hinted that the stout Protestants of Ulster might have resented a Chief Secretary who was reputed to belong to the Puseyite 'party'. Gladstone did not pursue with Peel the point about religion. But to his friends he always maintained that he could never be a Puseyite. He was scandalized by the mere suggestion that there could be a 'party' in the Church. He said that 'the first principle of Catholicity in religion' made that idea hateful.

After he had accepted Peel's offer, Gladstone recorded (31 August, 1841): 'It has always been my hope to avoid this class of employment.

On this account I have not endeavoured to train myself for them. The place is very distasteful to me.' He reflected : ' The science of politics deals with the government of men, but I am set to govern packages.' Perhaps no one but Gladstone would have drawn such an absurd distinction. His outlook hitherto had been far too academic. It was most fortunate that he had been forced at last to apply his mind to something practical. He found that Peel's optimistic estimate of Lord Ripon was quite wrong. Lord Ripon, the amiable F. J. Robinson, who had been Prime Minister as Lord Goderich for six months after Canning's death in 1827, was lazy and incompetent. Gladstone noted that although, at the start, his mind had been like ' a sheet of white paper ' he knew ' more about the business ' than Lord Ripon within a month.

The Government was entirely dominated by Peel, who often consulted his favourite, Gladstone, not only on trade subjects, but on general policy. Gladstone worked on trade facts and figures usually for twelve hours a day, but sometimes for fourteen, and occasionally for sixteen hours. He soon found the ground giving way under his feet, and his former opinions on fiscal matters dissolving into air. No-one ever had a more loyal and devoted wife, but even Mrs. Gladstone wrote in her journal :

' He works hard all the time he is at home, and it is a little dreary sometimes.'

The fruits of that work, however, were soon apparent. The Government embarked upon a bold policy of freeing trade and of lowering the cost of living by reducing and revising tariffs ; and of balancing the budget by reviving the income-tax.

Gladstone did not like Peel's idea of reviving the income-tax. He pleaded (November, 1841) in vain for a house-tax instead, but he deferred to the views of his colleagues. Three months later he proved less accommodating. He wanted to reduce the duty on corn further than his colleagues thought prudent. Quite casually, Gladstone told Peel (5 February, 1842) that he was ready to resign if his view were not adopted. ' He was thunderstruck,' Gladstone noted. ' . . . I fear Peel was much annoyed and displeased.' Peel was too well-bred to use angry or unkind words, but ' the negative character of the conversation had a chilling effect on my mind. I came home sick at heart, and told all to Catherine, my lips being sealed to everyone else, as I said to Sir R. Peel, absolutely sealed.'

The next morning, after another talk with his wife, Gladstone sent

Peel a letter of retraction and apology. The Prime Minister 'was all sunshine again'. He told Gladstone, and Lord Ripon, that he would have preferred a lower rate of duty, but that as he had already lost one member of his Cabinet (the Duke of Buckingham), he felt that he could not risk breaking up his Government :

'I, poor fool,' Gladstone noted, '. . . had looked at nothing, and thought there was nothing to look at, but the figures . . . There was no such background of difference between my views and his as to justify the step I had taken. Severances upon narrow grounds would go far to render Government impossible.'

The main burden of the work of tariff revision fell on Gladstone. The budget of 1842, which was passed on 10 June, reinstituted the income-tax, which was fixed at sevenpence, and reduced the duties on corn and on a large number of individual items of raw material. On 16 June, Peel wrote to John Gladstone, to tell him how immensely useful his son had been :

'. . . At no time in the annals of Parliament has there been exhibited a more admirable combination of ability, extensive knowledge, temper, and discretion. Your paternal feelings must be gratified in the highest degree by the success which has naturally and justly followed the intellectual exertions of your son, and you must be supremely happy as a father in the reflection that the capacity to make such exertions is combined in his case with such purity of heart and integrity of conduct.'

Such a letter from Peel who was usually considered cold and reserved was a very remarkable tribute. Gladstone had earned it not only by a vast amount of detailed work in his office and at home, but by his tact in handling a large number of deputations from many trade interests affected by the Government's decisions, and by the high quality of his speeches in the House. He spoke no less than a hundred and twenty-nine times during a single Session. John Gladstone, who had been considering whether to apply for a baronetcy, and been privately advised to wait, was fully reconciled to the delay. Begging Peel to 'pardon the garrulous overflowing of the feelings of an old man', he wrote (17 June, 1842) that his eyes were filled 'with tears of gratitude to Almighty God for giving me a son whose conduct in the discharge of his public duties has received the full approbation of one who, of all men, is so well qualified to form a correct judgement of his merits. William . . . excels his brothers in talent, but not so in soundness of principles, habits of usefulness, or integrity of purpose.' With a merchant's keen eye for the main chance, he ended with a strong hint that he would like a suitable Parliamentary seat to be found for his third son, John, who was on the unemployed list of the Royal Navy.

Gladstone's early admission to the Cabinet was now certain, and many tributes were paid to him. On 9 April, 1842, he was commanded for the first time to dine with the Queen at Buckingham Palace. He told Mrs. Gladstone, the next day, that he had felt as nervous as on the occasion when he had been summoned, at Eton, to Dr. Keate to be flogged. But he was not too shy to lament the absence of a chaplain at table, or the failure to say Grace at dinner :

' Perhaps,' he wrote, ' she will one day supply the omission . . . Majesty can never be perfect, can never put on its most august aspect, without Religion.'

On 18 September, at Hawarden, one month before Mrs. Gladstone's second child was due to be born, Gladstone met with a painful accident. He was shooting partridges with a twin-barrelled muzzle-loader. He had cocked both barrels, and discharged one, when he stood the gun on the ground to reload the empty barrel, without re-setting the full one at half-cock. The gun suddenly went off, and Gladstone lost the top joint of the forefinger of his left hand.

Two operations on the stump were necessary, and the patient bore them with resignation. The remains of the lost joint were retrieved, and preserved in a jam-jar. Fifty-six years later, Gladstone's second son, the Rev. Stephen Gladstone,[1] inserted that missing joint in his father's coffin before it was laid in state in Westminster Hall.

On 18 October, 1842, Gladstone's second child, a daughter (Agnes), was born. Soon after Mrs. Gladstone was well, she and her husband dined at Buckingham Palace. The Queen was most sympathetic about Gladstone's accident. It is worth recording that throughout the remainder of his life, even during his periods of greatest unpopularity, no cartoonist ever took advantage of his deformity, although it was always in evidence when he was using his hands while speaking. The stump was invariably concealed by a black finger-stall.

In May, 1843, the death of the President of the Board of Control gave Peel an opportunity to move Lord Ripon from an office in which he had proved ineffective. Peel wrote to Gladstone (13 May) to offer him the Presidency of the Board of Trade, with a seat in the Cabinet. Gladstone saw Peel at two o'clock that afternoon, and

[1] Private family information.

agreed heartily with the Prime Minister that the Corn Laws, in principle, were no longer defensible. Then, a characteristic difficulty arose.

The Sees of Bangor and St. Asaph had been amalgamated in 1836. Gladstone was pledged to work to undo that amalgamation. Peel was not, at that stage, prepared to pledge himself either way, and Gladstone told him that, in the circumstances, he doubted whether it would be right for him to enter the Cabinet. Whatever Peel may have thought about his favourite's sense of proportion, he discussed the subject with him at length, and gave him three days to make up his mind.

Gladstone walked with his wife in Kensington Gardens, and begged her to pray for him. He called Manning and Hope-Scott into consultation, and argued the matter in all its aspects with them : ' How thankful I am,' Mrs. Gladstone wrote in her journal, ' to be joined to one whose mind is purity and integrity itself ! ' Manning and Hope-Scott strongly urged Gladstone to accept. They said that the point at issue was too narrow to justify the stand which he wanted to take. When Gladstone pleaded that he would be regarded as a traitor by the clergy and laity of the united dioceses, they told him that he must be prepared to face abuse. Gladstone's mind was in agony, but on the third day he went to Peel and accepted : ' I am certain,' he wrote to Lord Lyttelton (30 December, 1845), ' that Hope and Manning, in 1843, were not my tempters, but my good angels.'

So all ended happily, and Peel told his high-minded lieutenant that the Cabinet had been unanimous in inviting him to join it. He said that in all his experience he could not remember a single previous instance of such unanimity.

*　　　　*　　　　*

More than three years before he entered the Cabinet, Gladstone's attention began to be diverted to two separate personal troubles. They became major preoccupations for shorter or longer periods between the years 1840 and 1852, because, busy as he was, Gladstone took upon his shoulders the main burden of dealing with both. The first trouble was the conduct of his only surviving sister, Helen, after her lover, Léon Sollohub, on returning to Russia, had written to say that his parents refused to sanction their engagement.

Miss Gladstone, who found the atmosphere of the Gladstone household much too strenuous and exhausting, had been growing eccentric for some years in her dress, in the hours which she kept, and in the nervous illnesses of which she constantly complained, but of which her family were sceptical. Her maid, Peck, now reported that her mistress had started to take opium. For a time, the report was discounted, but, in the autumn of 1840, Miss Gladstone, from her father's house in Carlton Gardens, began openly to attend services at what Gladstone termed 'Romish chapels'. On 24 May, 1842, John Gladstone told his son that he had heard from Dr. Wiseman that Helen had asked to be received into the Roman Church; and on 6 June, Dr. Wiseman wrote to Gladstone to explain the circumstances in which he had had the happiness to receive Miss Gladstone into that Church. He begged him to intercede with his father to procure 'indulgent treatment' for his sister.

Replying to Dr. Wiseman (11 June) Gladstone said that he 'could not, without shocking you exceedingly, describe' the feelings which had been excited in his mind. He had already, on 30 May, sent a stern letter of rebuke to his sister:

'This delusion is not your first . . . You are living a life of utter self-deception. Not in religion alone, but in all bodily and mental habits, in all personal and in all social relations . . . Five years have elapsed since, in discussing matters relating to your health, I told my father that I regarded you as morally beside yourself, and urged him . . . to put restraint and coercion upon you.' He now told his father that he had seen, in some newspapers, 'the record of our shame', and he drew up a cogent memorandum, under a number of heads (17 June), in which he strongly advised his father to expel Helen from his house and board.

For a moment, John Gladstone hesitated. He told Helen that she must be prepared to leave. Then, on 19 June, 1842, he wrote to his angry son:

'I am sending her away for conscience's sake. If I allow her to go, I throw her upon strangers. She might get ill, and no-one would care for her. I could never forgive myself for having so deserted her. I have struggled hard, but unsuccessfully . . . God has given me many blessings to which she is a counterpoise . . . To turn her away on account of her religion is more than I can bear . . . She is still my child!'

Gladstone went to see his father, and told him he considered that he was acting weakly and wrongly. On 21 June, his father wrote to him: 'I may be wrong, but in this, as in all I do, I study to endeavour to do my duty conscientiously to you *all*, to the best of my frail judgement, such as it is.' He added that he would tolerate no further comment, 'for I am the responsible party—to God and man'. A month later he informed William that Helen was 'a very altered being'. She rose early, was regular in her hours and habits, and took a new interest in life. He hoped that this would last, but said that he was resolved, in any case, 'to continue to be a father' to Helen, to continue to regard her as the mistress of his house, and to require that others should continue so to regard her. On 7 November, 1842, he sent his son a strongly worded rebuke, on his refusal to name his infant daughter after Helen. He said that William and Catherine had subjected Helen to a totally unnecessary slight. Her religion was her private affair. He was satisfied that she was sincere, and no-one, therefore, had any right to condemn her.

But William was unrepentant. He told his father that his daughter's name was an old one in the Gladstone family. It had belonged to an aunt who had died aged only a few months some seventy years before. John Gladstone said that he considered his son's letter and attitude 'extraordinary'.

The improvement in Miss Gladstone's conduct did not prove lasting. Before the next phase arose, however, Gladstone's attention was diverted to a crisis of a different kind. His brother-in-law, Sir Stephen Glynne, owned a small property of between eighty and ninety acres, known as Oak Farm, near Stourbridge. There were valuable seams of coal and ironstone under the land, and in 1835 Sir Stephen had refused an offer of thirty-five thousand pounds for the farm. Urged on by F. Boydell, the agent at Hawarden, he formed a company to develop it ; and, in 1839, Gladstone and Lord Lyttelton each took a tenth share in the undertaking.

It was at about that time, when companies were springing up everywhere like mushrooms, that the father of the Socialist poet, William Morris, made a huge fortune out of 272 shares which he held in a similar company formed to work some copper seams near Tavistock. During six giddy months in 1844 the shares rose in value from one pound to eight hundred pounds each. The Oak Farm Company had a very different history, but Gladstone's hopes were as sanguine. Machinery was installed on the security of Sir Stephen Glynne's estate at Hawarden ; promising relations were established with the Grand Junction Canal Company ; old John Gladstone was conducted round the works. John Gladstone, from the first, distrusted Boydell. He advised the three young partners to keep a close watch on him, and he was not at all pleased when he was asked by his son to assist the Company with credit. Nevertheless, he obliged :

'It is an indifferent business,' Gladstone told his father (18 November, 1841) : ' but it might have been worse, and we ought to be too happy to be under your wing. This, at all events, will be the last drain. It is becoming a serious matter for Stephen, but I hope, with this fresh advance his royalties will be unlocked.'

A year later, Gladstone was writing to tell his father that Boydell was actually trying to pay interest on the shares out of the Company's capital. For two years matters dragged along uneasily, while John Gladstone did his best to supervise Boydell. But he was growing old, and none of the three partners had any understanding of the business in which they were engaged. Boydell, therefore, did much as he pleased, until a new phase arose as a result of the financial crisis of 1847, which broke the Company.

Under the old system of unlimited liability, the outlook had, long before, grown very serious. On 17 November, 1844, John Gladstone advised his son to retire ' at almost whatever sacrifice may be required, or it is impossible to measure or contemplate what may possibly be the consequences, or how distressing they possibly might be to all of you . . . It will never do to quarrel with Boydell . . . Events the most disastrous are *possible*.'

The three brothers-in-law accepted that advice and retired accordingly, by agreement, in exchange for equitable mortgages on the Company. But the credit of the Hawarden estate had been pledged to the hilt. Encouraged by his wife, Gladstone had begun to look on Hawarden, with its two castles—one medieval, one modern—and its thousand acres of parkland, as a second home, and as an indispensable background. William could recover there from the incessant strain of a life which he never really found congenial. And Catherine could continue to reign there as she had done before her marriage. Her brother, Sir Stephen Glynne, was a bachelor and a natural celibate. He spent all his leisure visiting, and writing about, old parish churches —a subject on which he is still considered a leading authority ; and he liked to have his life and affairs arranged for him by others. He called the Gladstones ' the great people ', and was delighted when, a few years later, they reached a financial understanding with him, and came to reside, and inevitably to preside, in his home.

Before that arrangement was concluded, Gladstone had cherished hopes of inheriting Fasque from his father. He wrote to Thomas Gladstone (4 October, 1844) to ask if he really wanted to come into that place : ' My father lately happened to mention what was new to me, though it probably may have been known to you . . . that by his Will, as it stands, you would have Fasque as *constituting* your extra share, and, except for that, would have the same as the other sons.'

Thomas, as the eldest son, was destined to inherit an extra share of his father's estate. But to William's suggestion that, as he did not really love Fasque, he might be willing to take something else in its place, Thomas returned an emphatic ' No ! ' On 31 October, Gladstone forwarded to his wife his brother's letter : ' I enclose you a note from Tom—very private. It only goes to you as into the inner chamber of my own mind. It makes me rather sad.' Two years later, in 1846, Gladstone persuaded his father, on whom a baronetcy had then been conferred, to suggest to Thomas that some property other than Fasque should be attached to the title, since neither Thomas nor Thomas's wife had ever seemed to care much for it. But Thomas replied firmly that, as far as he was concerned, the baronetcy settled the matter. He wanted to inherit Fasque as his father had promised.

That was a great disappointment to Gladstone, who loved the place, and the long health-giving walks over the hills and the heather. He was never likely to be a rich man ; his family was increasing ; he longed for a secure retreat in the country. He was not pleased when, in August, 1848, his father refused to allow him to present a memorial window to the chapel at Fasque as a thanksgiving for his daughter's recovery from a fever. With Tom in mind, Sir John Gladstone said that the chapel window might ' bear a sinister construction '. At that time Gladstone had already flung himself, heart and soul, into the gigantic task of saving Hawarden from being sold, after the failure of the Oak Farm Company had burdened the estate with a debt of upwards of a quarter of a million pounds.

Gladstone's relations with his eldest brother were not very happy. Thomas was consumed by jealousy, and in September, 1841, when he was out of Parliament, he had accused William of being lukewarm in his effort to help him to obtain employment. A year later, through his father, he complained that he was not being invited to Catherine Gladstone's evening parties. He was not mollified by being told to consider himself as possessed of a permanent standing invitation.

A year later, when William was in the Cabinet, Thomas's jealousy and indignation boiled over. He wrote to William (30 October, 1843), to express regret ' at the altered footing upon which we stand as brothers, for I do not think that either your high station . . . or any differences on religious subjects ought to change our relative positions.' He said that he was hardly ever invited to his brother's house in London : ' I am aware that your society is . . . very different from ours, but why should that interfere with our meeting socially, as brothers ? '

To that rather foolish letter, Gladstone sent a characteristic reply. He said he was so busy that he hardly had time to see anyone, but he asked Thomas to let him have a detailed list of all his movements while he had been in town. He said that he would have that list checked methodically, day by day, with the list of his own and Catherine's engagements during that period, with a view to establishing the exact number of times and occasions on which it would have been possible for Tom and his wife to be invited to Carlton House Terrace. A long and inconclusive correspondence followed, and Thomas remained very sore. He bitterly resented being virtually ordered by his father to vote for William at Oxford during the General Election of 1847. He had persuaded himself that William had Roman Catholic sympathies. And in 1853, when his brother was Chancellor of the Exchequer, he wrote vaguely again to complain that William was wanting in ' brotherly affection'.

On 11 November, 1853, Gladstone replied : ' I rarely now read a letter from you on indifferent subjects without more or less deriving the impression that it is written under dissatisfaction, and that I have involuntarily given you some offence.' When Sir Thomas, as he had then become, pressed his point, Gladstone suggested that their correspondence over a number of years should be shown to a disinterested third party, who should be asked for an opinion. Sir Thomas rejected that proposal : ' All is vain ! ' William told him, ' and you need not anticipate my troubling you with more argument or explanation, because whatever I write seems to make matters worse. God knows it is not written with that intention.'

Gladstone sent the entire correspondence to his brothers, John and Robertson, and said that he did not require any comment. From those and other troubles the recreation and happiness which he found at Harwarden became, as time went on, an absolute necessity. He proved that for the preservation of Hawarden in his wife's family there was no limit to the amount of trouble, or risk, that he was prepared to incur.

CHAPTER 4

FAMILY CRISIS—PARTY EXPLOSION
1843–1851

W HEN Gladstone entered the Cabinet at the age of thirty-three, he had already agreed with Peel that free trade and the Corn Laws were in theory incompatible. But he had learned the need for prudence and compromise. On 13 February, 1843, Lord Howick challenged Gladstone to say why he did not apply to corn the free trade principles which he was extending to other commodities. Gladstone retorted that 'the corn trade in this country has been dealt with . . . for a series of centuries, in a different manner from the trade in any other article . . . Burke said that the statesman who refused to take circumstance into his view and consideration, is not merely in error—he is mad ! Stark mad ! Metaphysically mad !'

Between 1841 and 1845, Peel, with Gladstone as his aide-de-camp, launched the country on a great experiment. As Peel had expected, Gladstone took to finance as readily as he had taken to theology. In January, 1843, he published an anonymous article in the *Foreign and Colonial Quarterly*, which he entitled, *The Course of Commercial Policy at Home and Abroad*. In it he stated that distress at home had been caused by 'the paralysis of our foreign trade'. He argued that Britain was better equipped than any other nation to face a conspiracy against her foreign trade. She had 'become the greatest workshop of the world' and was economically far in advance of all other nations. 'If we are to flourish and if we are to live, we must learn . . . to compete with cheaper labour, with lighter taxes, with more fertile soils, with richer mines than our own ; and, if this is to be done, both the working hand, and the material upon which it is to work must, as soon as practicable, be set free. Hence the reduction of duties on raw materials.' He added that England's 'material greatness has grown out of her social and religious soundness, and out of the power and integrity of individual character'.

Until late in 1845, when 'circumstance' made his task almost impossible, Peel managed his Party with great skill. The interest and prejudice of the ruling class were rooted in the policy of agricultural protection. The duties on foreign corn had been imposed in 1815 to protect farmers from a collapse in prices when the home market was exposed once more to an influx of imported foodstuffs after the end of the Great War with Napoleon. But, outside Parliament, the Anti-Corn Law League was crusading for the abolition of those duties. During the General Election Gladstone had described the League as a fraud, and Peel had come out more strongly in favour of protection than he now cared to recollect. After the Election, he let it be known that he did not consider that the Election had been fought on the issue of free trade versus protection.

Gladstone had to perform a very difficult balancing feat which taught him lessons he never forgot. It seemed, at first, a paradox to plain men to expect that a larger revenue would accrue from lower duties. Gladstone always said that, limited as it was, the tariff revision of 1842 cost him six times as much trouble as later efforts in that direction. The revival of the income-tax, which was intensely unpopular, was a minor social revolution. It was said of Gladstone's speeches at that time that all the main clauses were in favour of free trade, while all the sub-clauses favoured protection. But he prided himself that, in all the many speeches which he had made, no serious inconsistencies could be discovered.

The Anti-Corn Law League appealed to popular passions. It had ample funds and an admirable organization, and it was led and inspired by two brilliant orators—Richard Cobden and John Bright. It represented the interests of middle-class manufacturers, and it preached a new era of international peace and understanding, based on the commercial interdependence of nations. The League's speakers denounced agricultural protection in quasi-religious language as a defiance of the will of God, because it tended to make nations independent instead of interdependent, because it benefited the landlords, and because it starved the poor.

Gladstone was made indignant when Richard Cobden and others held up the landlords to ridicule. They called them plunderers and knaves for using the Corn Laws to preserve high rents, and fools for not realizing that such action was unnecessary for that purpose. Gladstone appreciated the force of the protectionist argument that that middle-class campaign for cheap bread was inspired by a selfish desire to save money on wages. The leaders of the Chartist movement, who were also at that time appealing to popular passions on behalf of their political programme of universal suffrage, were by no means sympathetic to the programme of the League. They feared that cheap corn would drive more agricultural workers off the land into the overcrowded urban labour markets. They did not want to see the working-class effort diverted from the campaign to obtain political rights. They believed that the vital preliminary steps towards the realization of social and economic equality were the attainment of universal suffrage and the secret ballot.

Amid that clash of interests and ideas, a single concrete possibility had begun to dominate men's minds. The population had increased, and was increasing, so fast, that one bad harvest might cause disaster. The Anti-Corn Law League made no secret of its hope that a harvest failure would occur, and that it would compel the Government to admit foreign corn free of duty. The harvests of 1842, 1843, and 1844 were good, and they aided Peel. But on 20 August, 1844, Gladstone wrote to Hope-Scott:

' It is a high probability that one bad harvest, or, at all events, two, would break up the Corn Law, and with it the Party. Hitherto it has worked better than could have been hoped, but I cannot deny that it is a law mainly dependent upon the weather.'

That was the main issue before the country. But outside it, Gladstone's mind responded readily to several other problems which faced him at the Board of Trade. He carried, for example, two Railway Acts in 1842 and 1844. The first did little more than enunciate the principle that some supervision of railways by the State was necessary. The Act of 1844, however, was more ambitious. Its most notable feature was a requirement that every Company should run at least one train a day, stopping at every station if required, with good covered seating accommodation for third-class passengers at a maximum charge of one penny a mile. Hitherto, third-class passengers had been treated with contempt. Many trains had carried no third-class accommodation, and third-class carriages, when they were provided, were often open trucks. Passengers were sometimes mixed with cattle, coal, and other merchandise. Gladstone's ' Parliamentary train ', as it was called, earned him the gratitude of third-class passengers, and he characteristically made a point of often travelling third-class himself. He tried to insert clauses into the Bill, empowering the State, in the last resort, to take control of any railway, at the end of a twenty-one year period, if the public had good cause for dissatisfaction with the way in which it was being run. Those clauses, however, excited violent opposition, and had to be dropped.

There was still a great deal of prejudice against railways at that

SIR STEPHEN GLYNNE, BT. (*above*).
From the portrait by J. Saunders at Hawarden.

SIR JOHN GLADSTONE, BT.
Photograph by D. O. Hill & R. Adamson.

HENRY EDWARD (CARDINAL) MANNING (*above*).
  Stipple by F. Holl after G. Richmond.

JAMES HOPE-SCOTT.
  From the portrait by G. Richmond.

time, and William Wordsworth wrote to Gladstone (15 October, 1844) to complain that they were 'injurious to morals' and destructive of the peace of the Lake District. He enclosed an indifferent sonnet in which 'mountains, and vales, and floods' were summoned to greet the engine's 'whistle' with 'the passion of a just disdain'. The mushroom growth of railway Companies was symptomatic of such a wild scramble of speculation, that in 1844 Gladstone carried a Companies Regulation Act. It was the pioneer of a long series of Companies Acts, and it helped to pave the way for the adoption of the limited liability principle.

There was one class of men, employed in the London Docks, whose lasting gratitude Gladstone now earned. The men were employed on loading and unloading coal, and they were engaged and discharged at public houses around the Docks. Their wages were low, and they obtained and held their jobs by buying the publicans' goodwill in the form of money spent on liquor. Gladstone carried an Act to eliminate that practice, by the establishment of a central exchange for the engagement and discharge of hands.

The second great revision of the tariff system in 1845 was always regarded by Gladstone, together with that of 1842, as among the most momentous legislative achievements of his career. But he prepared it under the shadow of a great personal uneasiness; and before the Budget of 1845 was introduced, he had ceased to be a member of the Government.

Peel, in 1844, was trying to pursue a policy of conciliation in Ireland. One of Ireland's principal grievances was the contrast between the Anglican Church Establishment, with its splendid endowments, ministering to a fraction of the population, and the Roman Catholic Church, subsisting on the offerings of the poor, while ministering to the mass of the population. Peel was not prepared to lay hands on the privileges of the Established Church; but he wanted to express his goodwill towards the Roman Catholics. He therefore entered into indirect communication with the Vatican, through the British Ministers at the Courts of Florence and Naples, about methods of conciliating Irish opinion. And he proposed to increase from £9,000 to £30,000 a year the grant which Parliament had voted annually since the Act of Union of 1800 for the Maynooth College in Dublin, where Roman Catholic clergy were trained. He decided, at the same time, to make that grant permanent, and to incorporate the College.

In his book on *Church and State*, Gladstone had attacked the grant of £9,000 which the British Parliament voted annually for the Maynooth College, and he had warned his fellow-countrymen that a mortal danger of corruption must be the consequence of that weak display of tolerance. He knew now that those views were strained and fanciful, and he had no longer any objection to the action which Peel proposed. He had, however, never repudiated his book, and he considered that, if he were to remain a member of the Government after the trebling of the Maynooth grant, his integrity would be compromised.

The desire to avoid an open breach with his colleagues on grounds which it would be distasteful and embarrassing for him to explain in public, betrayed Gladstone into what he was inclined to regard as the silliest action of his life. He sent Peel a letter (12 July, 1844) suggesting that he should be relieved of his office as President of the Board of Trade, and sent to Italy. He said that if it were decided to renew diplomatic relations with the Papal Court, he would like to be appointed British Minister at Rome. In the meantime, he would like to conduct unofficial conversations with the Vatican, through the Ministers at Florence and Naples :

' I can conceive Peel's astonishment,' he noted later, ' on receiving such a letter, and I must own that on this occasion I tried him very hard by a most indiscreet proceeding.'

He had told Peel that if the proposal were unwelcome he would be content to receive no reply ; and he received none. Gladstone was left to wonder by what ' obliquity of view ' he had been led to make his suggestion. He thought that he had been encouraged by Hope-Scott, and tempted by a desire to bring about a more just appreciation, in Vatican circles, of the Catholicity of the Church of England.

By the autumn of 1844, Gladstone's colleagues knew that he meant to resign on the question of the Maynooth grant :

' I have told them ', he wrote (25 November, 1844) to his wife, ' that if I go, I shall go on the ground of what is required by my personal character, and not because my mind is made up that the course that they propose can be avoided, far less because I consider myself bound to resist it . . . They would not assume that it was to be, and rather proceeded as if I had never said a word upon the subject. It was painful . . .'

Gladstone did his best to explain to Peel that his scruples were neither political nor religious. The Prime Minister was kind and patient, but he wrote (3 January, 1845) to Sir James Graham, the Home Secretary, 'I really have great difficulty sometimes in comprehending what Gladstone means.' He complained that although Gladstone's letter was marked 'Secret' it had been posted unsealed: 'It may have been read in every post office through which it has passed.' Sir James Graham replied the next day:

'It is always difficult, through the haze of words, to catch a distant glimpse of Gladstone's meaning. But, though the letter is obscure, the resolution, I am afraid, is taken . . . His loss is serious, and on every account to be regretted . . . Gladstone's omission to seal such a letter was most unfortunate; but the enigmatical style has its advantages. I doubt whether there is a post-master in England who, after reading the letter, would understand one word of it.'

On 10 January, Gladstone spent the week-end at Windsor, where he won 2s. 2d. playing 'Commerce' with the Prince Consort. On 3 February he had an audience at Buckingham Palace to tender his resignation. The Queen said that it was a great loss and that she regretted it very much. The next day he explained his reasons to the House of Commons in a speech which lasted an hour. The sense of his fellow-members was expressed by Richard Cobden, who remarked that he had listened with pleasure, although he was no wiser at the end than he had been at the beginning. Disraeli told his friends that Gladstone's career was finished.

Gladstone remained on excellent terms with his former colleagues. He told his father (27 January, 1845) 'as a symbol of what is material', that the Prime Minister and Lady Peel, the Colonial Secretary and Lady Stanley, and the Foreign Secretary, Lord Aberdeen, had all accepted Mrs. Gladstone's invitation to dinner that evening. But Gladstone's action gave rise to a crop of good-humoured stories about his conscience, which was felt to be tender rather than strong. One of the best was told by the Home Secretary, Sir James Graham. Gladstone, he said, was invited to dine by the chairman of his Election Committee at Newark to discuss the Maynooth Bill which his constituents disliked. Gladstone did not refuse outright, but begged the chairman to consider 'that the day named was the Vigil of St. Simon and St. Jude'. Gladstone admitted, in retrospect, that his resignation was absurd—'fitter for a dreamer, or possibly a schoolman, than for the active purposes of public life in a busy and moving age'.

Sir Robert Inglis, diehard member for Oxford University, begged Gladstone to lead the opposition to the Maynooth Bill. Sir Robert said that he wished that, instead of the Roman Catholic Emancipation Act of 1829, the Duke of Cumberland had been sent to keep the Irish quiet with an army of thirty thousand men. 'As that good and very kind man spoke the words,' Gladstone noted, 'my blood ran cold.' Their effect was the opposite of what Sir Robert had intended. On 11 April, 1845, Gladstone voted in favour of the Maynooth Bill, and said :

'I am prepared, in opposition to what I believe to be the prevailing opinion of the people of England and of Scotland, in opposition to the judgement of my own constituents, from whom I deeply regret to differ, and in opposition to my own deeply cherished predilections, to give a deliberate and even anxious support to the measure.'

Disraeli, whose robust empiricism was as antipathetic to Gladstone as Gladstone's queasy conscientiousness was to him, could make no sense of Gladstone's motives. In opposing the Maynooth Bill, he said that he had once regarded Gladstone 'as the last paladin of principle, the very abstraction of chivalry'. It now, however, appeared that the Right Honourable gentleman had no principles at all. Gladstone was coming round to the view that the extreme and formal claims of the Church of England could not, in that age, be made effective. It would be necessary for the Church to part, voluntarily, with some of her former privileges, and not to attempt to scold the State into an attitude of hostility or indifference. At the same time the Church needed to continue the work of renewing her spiritual life. Gladstone had already, on 6 June, 1844, given proof of the direction in which his mind was moving, when he supported the Second Reading of the Dissenters' Chapels Bill. The object had been to secure the property of Unitarian congregations in their own chapels and endowments.

Soon after his resignation, Gladstone availed himself of two opportunities to assist the Government. In March, 1845, he published an able pamphlet summarizing the benefits of the fiscal changes of 1842. It was entitled *Remarks Upon Recent Commercial Legislation*. And on 15 July he made a four-hour speech in favour of granting preferential treatment to imported colonial sugar. In its advance towards free trade, the Government had been very careful to extend to sugar the exceptional consideration which it accorded to corn. The virtual exclusion of slave-grown sugar from Brazil was regarded as an aspect of the compensation morally owed to the West Indian planters, after the slaves had been emancipated on their estates. The West Indian interest was extremely influential, and Gladstone's father, who remained a diehard all-round protectionist, was its moving spirit. Gladstone, on 15 July, had to answer Lord Palmerston who had argued that preferential treatment for colonial sugar would involve a breach of old treaties with Spain. Gladstone noted that when he sat down, 'Peel, who was one of the most conscientious men I ever knew in spareness of eulogium, said, "That was a wonderful speech, Gladstone!"'

In the mood of intense depression which followed his resignation, Gladstone planned to visit Ireland with Hope-Scott, in order to explore conditions. At the last moment, however, he was diverted another way. He went to Germany instead, in order to deal with a new crisis which had occurred in the affairs of his sister, Helen, who was staying at Baden-Baden.

Miss Gladstone had been sent to Germany, in the summer of 1845, for her health. She had dismissed her companion, after the companion had tried to interfere with her drug-taking habits, and she failed to answer letters from home. Despite all his interests and occupations Gladstone, in a crisis, was always much the most zealous and earnest member of his family. He obtained a letter of authority from his father (19 September, 1845) to go out to Germany and bring his sister home. He obtained another letter (23 September) from Dr. Wiseman, as Miss Gladstone's spiritual adviser, telling her to obey her father.

On 24 September, Gladstone left England. He stopped for a night or two in Paris, where he dined with the French historian, F. P. G. Guizot. In the course of a single memorable conversation, the Frenchman impressed Gladstone's mind so strongly with the view which many foreigners took of England's treatment of Ireland, that a minor but distinct earthquake shock was registered in Gladstone's mind. Twenty-seven years afterwards, he told Guizot that he had never been able to forget that conversation, and that he had pondered deeply and often upon it.

For the moment, Gladstone was absorbed in contemplation of the painful business on hand. He went to Munich, pausing on the way to write a charming rhymed letter to his eldest son, William, describing the place:

> At which I now my pen employ
> In writing to my darling boy.

He called, while he was in Munich, on Dr. Ignaz von Döllinger, and thereby laid the foundation of one of the most intimate of his life's friendships.

Gladstone had never met Döllinger, whom he knew as one of the most liberal of German Catholic theologians. That first meeting was so successful that Gladstone delayed his departure from Munich for a week. On 1 October, he dined with Dollinger and four German professors :

'I never saw men,' he wrote to his wife (2 October), 'who spoke together in such a way as to render one another inaudible, as they did—always excepting Dr. D. . . . He is a much more refined man than the rest. But, of the others, I assure you, always two, sometimes three, and once all four, were speaking at once, very loud.'

On 4 October, before he left Munich, Gladstone had a remarkable conversation with Döllinger about the Eucharist. He always said that his mind had been formed on that subject on that day. Unlike the conversation at dinner, that conversation was conducted in English, and Gladstone kept a full record :

Dr. D. : " . . . If you admit that the Elements become the Body and Blood of Our Lord, it follows that they are not what they were. They have lost their identity . . . So that, if you believe in the Real Presence, you must believe in the cessation of the substance of bread and wine." . . .

W. E. G. : " The objection, as it seems to me, is this. Here is a Sacrament ! We have defined it as consisting of two parts— the outward visible sign, and the inward spiritual grace. If you omit the reality of the sign, you omit the reality of the Sacrament, by destroying one of its essential parts. Now, are bread and wine the signs, or are they not ? And, if so, must they not still be bread and wine ? "

Dr. D. : " It depends upon what you mean by reality. In respect to all that you see and feel, and to all their nutritive qualities, they are as much bread and wine as ever. But with all this, their substratum may be changed."

Dr. Döllinger adduced, in proof of that, the fact that when Our Lord rose from the dead, St. Thomas was able to touch a visible Body which nevertheless possessed the unfamiliar property of being able to glide through closed doors and walls.

W. E. G. : " . . . I can advance no such argument at all. We stand upon the ground that the Elements are declared in Scripture to be bread and wine. Therefore we hold they must be as real and true as other sensible substances. I should set out, from this, that God has given us certain faculties . . . such as are intended, and adequate, to give certain conviction. . . . Therefore . . . we must hold . . . that . . . that which is presented to our senses not only is real, but also is . . . the *essence*."

Dr. D. : " No ! There you are wrong. Independently of doctrine, I believe all physicians and chemists will tell you that there are, in matter, attributes that escape us, and thus, that the whole essence is not presented to us."

W. E. G. : " . . . I should have spoken thus : that the attributes which we perceive, are of the essence, belong to it, and constitute for us the ground of predicating it."

Dr. D. : " . . . It was much happier when the early Church, in the energy of faith could dispense with definitions . . . But heresy arose, and what could the Church do ? "

W. E. G. : " . . . I find the greatest difficulty between the Nicene definition in defence of Our Lord's Divinity, and the definition expressed by Transubstantiation."

At that point, Gladstone noted, the Doctor started to tap impatiently with one foot, and, therefore, ' in a matter so high, I readily refrained from explaining my meaning '.

Dr. D. : " . . . All matter has a spiritual character."

W. E. G. : " A spiritual susceptibility."

Dr. D. : " Yes. It is in that respect that the Elements are changed in the Blessed Eucharist. In another sense they are certainly real."

W. E. G. : " . . . Would it then be allowable to speak thus ? . . . There is a higher region of creation, and there is a lower one, dependent upon it, and receiving life from it. In that lower region, the Consecrated Elements (which are related to both) are still bread and wine. In the higher one, they are no longer such, having spiritually become the Body and Blood of Our Lord."

Dr. D. : " Yes ! "

W. E. G. : " Surely, much would be gained if these things were understood."

Döllinger very heartily concurred, and Gladstone was enchanted by the discovery that the wide-seeming divergence between their views could be so happily reconciled on the basis of a simple proposition about the co-existence of different planes of reality. 'The conversation', he noted, 'was a great comfort to one who views the unity of Christendom as I must do.' It helped him to accept with equanimity in the following month the news of John Henry Newman's reception into the Roman Church: 'God, who made him,' he wrote to Mrs. Gladstone (19 October, 1845), 'can make for us, if need be, others like him.'

While Gladstone was completing his theological education in Munich, Disraeli, in his novel, *Sybil* (1845), was portraying the life of the proletariat in the new industrial cities. He described the 'girl with the vacant face' in Wodgate Yard:

'I be a reg'lar born Christian, and my mother afore me, and that's what few girls in the Yard can say. Thomas will take to it himself, when work is slack; and he believes now in Our Lord and Saviour—Pontius Pilate, who was crucified for our sins; and in Moses, Goliath, and the rest of the Apostles.'

Gladstone tore himself away from Munich on 5 October, and went on to Baden-Baden, where he found his sister in an even worse condition than he had expected: 'On Wednesday,' he wrote to Mrs. Gladstone (9 October, 1845), '. . . she drank off . . . 150 drops of German laudanum, equal to 300 English . . . The consequence was that for some time she was in danger of death ! But she rallied, and is recovering . . . She is poisoned much in body and, more, in mind, by the use of that horrible drug.'

On another occasion, while the door of Miss Gladstone's bedroom was locked against her brother and the doctor, they found that she had drunk the best part of a bottle of Eau de Cologne, mixed with water. Her symptoms were, in part, hysterical, for she often bolted her door against her brother for days on end. Sometimes, when he forced a way in, he found her speechless, and with both arms apparently paralysed: 'Mind and body', he told his wife (28 October), 'play into one another's hands with her in such a way as to make the whole most embarrassing. May God direct me ! '

Occasionally, Miss Gladstone would allow her brother to read to her from her devotional books. Gladstone told his wife that he would then omit only what he was 'absolutely unable to pronounce with sincerity'. His father wrote to insist that Helen should be treated with mildness and consideration. But Gladstone told his wife (1 November) that he looked to nothing 'except the specific we have so often talked of—an engagement to universal obedience.

This would . . . protect her from herself . . . and make to her such disclosures concerning herself as would astonish her.'

Gladstone's bedside manner may have left something to be desired ; and it may be doubted whether, in regard to his sister, he was a sound psychologist. She was terrified of him. Her mind was in revolt against the repressions to which it had been subjected, and she told Gladstone, again and again, that she no longer loved him : ' The channels of common interest and feeling between a brother and a sister are frozen up,' he wrote to Mrs. Gladstone (8 November). ' . . . With her, moral disorganization has reached such a point that it is vain to . . . consider her as a rational agent. . . . Let us pray for her ! "

The doctor, in the meantime, felt it necessary to write Gladstone a letter insisting that, in matters of minor consequence, Miss Gladstone's will must be indulged. Gladstone accepted that view, but he transmitted to his father the doctor's opinion that the only way to wean Helen from opium was to place her for a time in a Roman Catholic convent in England.

Miss Gladstone surrendered at last to an ultimatum from her father (25 October), threatening to cut off her supply of funds, and to leave her to fend for herself. She returned, early in December, to her father's house in Carlton Gardens, accompanied by her doctor, and by a priest. Her brother, during the gloomy weeks which he spent at Baden-Baden, brooded a great deal about the state of religion and politics. He wrote to his wife (12 October, 1845) to express his profound wish to retire from politics for ever. He had, he said, a growing belief that he would never be able to do much good for the Church in Parliament, ' except after having first seemed a traitor to it, and being reviled as such '. He had no ambition to acquire a title, or to found a great family. ' The days are gone by when such a thing might have been possible.' One thing only restrained him from quitting :

' Ireland ! Ireland ! That cloud in the West ! That coming storm ! That minister of God's retribution upon cruel, inveterate, and but half-atoned injustice ! Ireland forces upon us these great social and great religious questions. God grant that we may have the courage to look them in the face ! . . . '

That illuminating passage throws light on a process which was ceaselessly at work in the secret recesses of Gladstone's mind. His mind was convulsed at that moment by a preliminary intimation of the great earthquake which was to sweep away many familiar land-marks a quarter of a century later. But during the intervening years Gladstone appeared to regard Ireland in a mood of consistent and dispassionate detachment. And that fact calls for some explanation.

Gladstone was always seeking relief for a state of chronic mental tension by immersing himself in work which possessed him com-pletely. The exclusive character of that absorption required him to assume a dispassionate and detached attitude to all other subjects, so long as it endured. There was no subject which appealed so much to him as the cause of the oppressed. It enabled him, as it had once enabled Burke, to sublimate certain dark instincts of which he was wholly and happily unaware, but which may have been associated with his superabundant vitality. The cause of the oppressed was, however, the medicine of Gladstone's mind; it was not its daily bread.

Gladstone's iron self-mastery, which held his volcanic energy in check, was operated by his intelligence and by his will. He never gave himself to any subject, whatever attractions it held for him, until he had first convinced himself that the time was ripe for bringing it forward. He believed that his instinct for ' right-timing ', which his enemies called opportunism and greed for office, was his out-standing gift as a statesman. And the seismic way in which that instinct sometimes appeared to operate, was a measure alike of the strength of his self-control and of the vehemence of his nature.

At Baden-Baden, during that rare interval in 1845 when Gladstone had nothing to do except to watch his sister's personality slowly dis-integrate under the influence of drugs, an Irish vent was opened for the first time in the volcano of his mind. The times were not then ripe for bringing forward the Irish question, or for forming a public opinion about it; but it is possible that Gladstone might have convinced himself that they were, if he had not been prevented by the accident of his sister's illness from visiting Ireland, as he had intended. Other interests of an urgent and compulsive character possessed him in swift succession, and the Irish vent in his mind, which Guizot's conversation had helped to open, remained sealed for twenty-three years. When it was unsealed, in 1868, it became at once the funnel of a spectacular eruption, which lasted, with inter-vals, for twenty-six years and transformed the pattern of politics in Great Britain. Before that eruption began, Gladstone had con-vinced himself not only that the times were ripe, but that the odds were at least sufficiently favourable to justify him in courting martyrdom for himself and his Party. In those circumstances, and in those circumstances only, was he willing to dare the uttermost.

When Gladstone returned to England (24 November), in advance of his sister, he found the country in the grip of a major crisis. The harvest had failed at last. Rotten potatoes spelt famine in Ireland, and they convinced Sir Robert Peel that the Corn Laws must be swept aside, not in due course, but at once. Opposition, however, inside the Cabinet, and outside it, was so strong that, on 6 December, Peel resigned.

Lord John Russell, the Whig leader, had already declared for total and immediate repeal; but he and his colleagues lacked the nerve to meet the crisis. In differences among themselves they found a colourable excuse to leave the hateful problem to their opponents. Peel accordingly, on 20 December, returned to office.

All Peel's former Cabinet colleagues except Sir James Graham were opposed to repeal. But the Queen's government had to be carried on, and only one, Lord Stanley, the Colonial Secretary, refused to serve. On 22 December Peel asked Gladstone to take Lord Stanley's place, and Gladstone agreed, after first obtaining the retiring Minister's consent. The Prime Minister expressed his confidence that, despite unfavourable signs, he would be able to carry his measure and hold his Party together. That brave, and necessary, decision saved the country, although it ended Peel's career and broke the Conservative Party.

Gladstone's acceptance of office vacated his seat at Newark. He made no secret of his view that foreign corn must be admitted at once, duty-free, and the Duke of Newcastle, who was a strong protectionist, refused to countenance his standing again. Efforts were made to induce the Duke to change his mind, but they failed. Gladstone said that he would not stand ' upon the basis of democratic or popular feeling against the local proprietary '. But he failed to find another seat. His opponents made every effort to keep him out of Parliament, and although he reviewed the possibilities of eight seats in as many months, he was so sensitive to the difficulties in the way of incurring binding obligations to his constituents that he was without a seat for twenty months. He remained a member of the Cabinet as long as Peel's Government lasted, but it was a difficult and embarrassing position. He had no chance to reply to any of the brilliant and ferocious attacks which Disraeli made upon Peel in the House, and the sense of frustration which resulted whetted the edge of his fierce resentment against Disraeli.

Gladstone spent the New Year with the Queen at Windsor, and was delighted to note the evident favour in which he stood. The Queen wrote (30 December, 1845) to her uncle, the King of the Belgians, ' Mr. Gladstone . . . will be of great use.' On 30 January, 1846, when Gladstone and his wife were dining at Buckingham Palace, the Queen asked Mrs. Gladstone to bring her children to tea on the following Saturday. All four, accordingly—William, Agnes, Stephen, and Jessy—were taken, and the Queen brought her four children into the nursery and watched them play together. She gave the Gladstone children a large white woolly lamb before they left, and kissed them. Mrs. Gladstone told her husband that the Royal children all had ' fat white necks ', which matched the lamb.

Gladstone's brief term of office as Colonial Secretary was only fairly successful. He constantly urged that reliance should be placed not on the exercise of power from the centre, but on the colonists' affections and trust ; but he annoyed Australian opinion by advocating a resumption of the practice of transporting convicts there. He did not handle colonial opinion with sufficient tact, and he had not time to bring down to earth his vague, humanitarian purpose of converting useless British vagabonds into active Australian citizens. The opposition to his policy in New South Wales was headed by Robert Lowe, who, twenty years later, after his return to England, became, for a time, a serious thorn in Gladstone's side, and, later, Chancellor of the Exchequer in Gladstone's first Government.

For one other mistake which he made, Gladstone blamed himself with considerable harshness. He had occasion to recall the Governor of Tasmania, Sir John Eardley-Wilmot, for inefficiency. Of Sir John's inefficiency there was ample proof; but Gladstone added, to his letter of recall, a personal note in which he referred to scandalous rumours about the Governor's private life. Of the truth of those rumours he had evidence which he was debarred from publishing. Its source was a private and confidential letter from the local bishop, and he was involved in considerable embarrassment when Sir John's friends published, with comments, his indiscreet personal note. He recorded that he had shown ' a singular absence of worldly wisdom '.

At the end of the Session, Gladstone was involved in a personal quarrel with Lord George Bentinck who had accused him of uttering a deliberate lie. Gladstone had signed a formal document which declared that a certain judge in India had resigned, whereas, in fact, he had been 'permitted to retire'. Gladstone became so angry and violent that his friends were scarcely able to restrain him. The quarrel was eventually submitted to Lord Stanley, but he failed to compose it, and had to return, with regret, the papers and correspondence. The quarrel was still open in 1848, when Lord George Bentinck died.

The diehard protectionists in the Commons held that Peel had betrayed the Conservative Party. They were led by Lord George Bentinck, and inspired by Disraeli, who had been refused office by Peel and who knew that Peel did not like him. To Disraeli's argument that the Prime Minister had broken his election pledges, Peel was rather insensitive. He held that it was his duty to carry on the Queen's government in the country's best interests as he saw them, but he overrated his power over the Party. Disraeli, who had no strong feeling about the Corn Laws, but who believed firmly in the political and social necessity of a strong landed interest, fanned the resentment of the back-benchers into a flame. He accused Peel of going out of his way to assume responsibility for the Bill through greed for office, and he denounced his Government as an organized hypocrisy.

The lesson of the Reform Act had not yet been forgotten in either House. In the Lords, the Bill for the repeal of the Corn Laws was carried on its Second Reading, by 211 votes to 164 ; its Third Reading was carried without a division on 25 June, 1846. That evening, in the Commons, the protectionists took their revenge. They joined in what the Duke of Wellington called 'a blackguard combination' with the Whigs, Radicals, and Irish, to defeat the Government on an Irish Coercion Bill. Peel resigned at once, although the Duke of Wellington and Gladstone both considered that he should have asked for a dissolution and appealed to the country. Peel was physically exhausted, and in announcing his resignation to the House he paid a glowing tribute to Richard Cobden which most members, including Gladstone, thought was open to serious objection. Cobden had been denouncing the landlords for years as selfish and incompetent monopolists, and Peel's eulogy of Cobden at that moment added fuel to the flame of Conservative discontent. Peel, Gladstone noted in his diary, 'like some smaller men is, I think, very sensible to the sweetness of the cheers of opponents'.

On 6 July, Gladstone delivered up his seals to the Queen, who said she was 'very sorry'. Gladstone thanked her for the baronetcy which she had conferred upon his father among the Resignation Honours. A week later (13 July), he had a talk with Sir Robert Peel, who was laid up with a poisoned toe : 'I led on from subject to subject,' Gladstone noted.

Peel told Gladstone that nothing would ever induce him to take office again : 'He spoke of the immense multiplication of details in public business, and . . . agreed that it was extremely adverse to the growth of greatness among our public men ; and he said that the mass of public business increased so fast that he . . . did not venture to speculate even for a few years on the mode of administering public affairs. He thought the consequence was already manifest in its being not so well done.'

It is likely that Gladstone may have remembered the next part of that conversation, which he recorded, many years later when he was himself in a comparable position :

W. E. G. : "I fully grant that your labours have been incredible, but, allow me to say, that is not the question. The question is not whether you are entitled to retire, but whether, after all you have done, and in the position you occupy before the country, you can remain in the House of Commons as an isolated person, and hold yourself aloof from the great movements of political forces which sway to and fro there."

Sir R. P. : "I think events will answer that question, better than any reasoning beforehand."

W. E. G. : "That is just what I should rely on, and should therefore urge how impossible it is for you to lay down, with certainty, a foregone conclusion . . . that you will remain in Parliament, and yet separate yourself from the Parliamentary system by which our government is carried on."

Sir R. P. : "If it is necessary, I will go out of Parliament."

W. E. G. : "I hope not. The country would have something to say on that, too."

The fall of Peel broke up the Conservative Party and kept it out of power for twenty years ; the feud between the Peelites and the bulk of the Party was too personal ever to be healed. The victory of Cobden's Anti-Corn Law League was a triumph for the middle-class manufacturers ; it inaugurated a period of prosperity and expansion, of emancipation and reform, beneath which the social problem and the bitterness of the unprivileged classes were, for many years, submerged. Political tension was, in consequence, greatly eased. The battle revolved not around principles, but around personalities, and two of the foremost personalities—those of Palmerston and Disraeli—were antipathetic to Gladstone.

The whole of the next sixteen years were spent by Gladstone in searching for a congenial Party connexion. Time and again he found it impossible to come to terms with the conditions that existed, or to establish a working arrangement with the world. He wrote of the five years which followed the repeal of the Corn Laws :

' The whole lifetime of the Parliament of 1847–52 was one during which my political life was in abeyance. In November, 1847, had come the great crisis in the affairs of the Glynne family, and the seemingly all but hopeless struggle to maintain the estate, and repair the disaster, had commenced. The whole conduct of it fell on me. And I should say that, for those five years, it constituted my daily and continuing care, while Parliamentary action was only occasional. It supplied, in fact, my education as Finance Minister.'

★   ★   ★

Before the Oak Farm Company crashed, Gladstone found it neces- sary to make some further arrangements about his sister. He wrote to Mrs. Gladstone from the Carlton Club on 14 December, 1845, to say that he and his brother Thomas had ' licked a scheme into shape . . . It is clear that, without coercion, we cannot shut out opium, as she will bring it herself in her own pocket. Then the only alternative is to put up with it, or to say, " You must go ! "—the latter of these being the very measure from which my father now shrinks.'

Gladstone complained that Helen's affairs absorbed his whole mind and time. His father was being difficult, but he had had ' a lucrative year ', and on New Year's Day, 1846, John Gladstone informed his four sons that he proposed to add a thousand pounds to each of their incomes.

In June, 1846, the Lunacy Commission wrote to say that it had received information that Miss Gladstone had been placed under restraint, and that it wished to send someone to see her. Gladstone told his wife (10 June, 1846) that he had seen Lord Ashley, one of the Commissioners, at the Carlton Club and arranged matters quietly with him. For some time Gladstone continued to advocate draconian measures, while his father pursued a policy of mildness. Gladstone told his wife (12 May, 1846) that Helen was morally destroying herself. He considered that his views must 'either represent a truly awful state of things, or else I am in an error nothing short of monstrous'.

Gladstone constantly told his father that Helen was not 'a *convinced* Roman Catholic'. She was, he thought, 'under a thirst, rather than acting on a distinct idea'. He told all his family that her convictions were emotional and superficial, that 'her connection with the Romish Church is itself most nearly related to the opium, and ranks among its effects', and that his father's management of the case was 'most unhappy'.

Sir John Gladstone allowed his daughter to receive priests in his house, and he yielded to her plea that she should not be boarded in a convent. Gladstone begged in vain that priests should be kept away from her. He considered that her mind should be studied, in order to determine 'whether she was most likely to be brought back to the Church of her youth, and of the sound mind, by a person of one leaning in regard to ceremonial, or another—always taking care to have no-one who was not sound and fast in attachment to the Church of England'.

Miss Gladstone was so terrified of her brother, that in the winter of 1847–8 she herself asked to be allowed to go for a time into a Roman Catholic convent at Leamington. She had refused to travel with her brother between Scotland and London ; and when Gladstone was staying at Fasque she would not communicate with him directly, but only through messengers. Gladstone told his wife that he could only attribute some of her symptoms to *delirium tremens*. From Leamington, Miss Gladstone returned to Fasque, apparently much better, but a relapse occurred during the early autumn of 1848, and she was sent to Edinburgh, to be under the care of a well-known nerve specialist.

In Edinburgh, she was cured of every trace of bodily and mental sickness. None of the symptoms ever recurred, and Miss Gladstone lived happily for the rest of her life. But to her brother's intense indignation and disgust she always attributed her recovery to a miracle.

Dr. Miller, of Edinburgh, in whose charge Miss Gladstone had been placed, sent her brother what he called 'the plain, unvarnished tale' on 6 November, 1848. Miss Gladstone's spiritual adviser, Bishop Wiseman, who was created a Cardinal, and Archbishop of

Westminster, two years later, had been due to see her on 30 October. Before his visit, her jaw was locked, both hands were clenched, and she was calling loudly for chloroform. Miller was convinced that she was perfectly well able to open her jaw and to unclench her hands, if she chose. After Wiseman's visit, she had entirely recovered, and Miller, in jest, had told the bishop that he was a good doctor : ' He smirked and smiled, and seemed to take all my jocular compliments in good part.'

On 3 November, Miss Gladstone wrote an account of the miracle which she alleged that the bishop had performed. The doctor told Gladstone that he had pieced together the background to her story. There had been a week of fasting and praying on the part of a ' bunch of Roman Catholic Ladies '. Bishop Wiseman had arrived at the end of it :

' The party assembled. The folding doors were thrown open between the drawing-room and Miss G.'s bedroom. Paraphernalia were brought from the nunnery. A book-case was converted into an altar (I had noticed a confusion of furniture next day). High Mass[1] was performed. Dr. Wiseman, advancing with a relic (the knuckle bone of some female saint) touched with this relic the jaw ! It flew open. The hand ! The fingers sprang open. The other hand ! It, too, unclosed. Then " Te Deum " was sung by the whole assemblage ! A miracle was, of course, declared !

' This must be very painful to you to read . . . The Catholics . . . are bruiting it all over the town . . . I am glad that I was ignorant of the facts until after Dr. Wiseman left. *With* a knowledge of them, I could not have shown him ordinary respect, for he *must* have known that he was acting the part of a mountebank.'

Dr. Miller said that, after careful consideration, he had decided not to throw up the case. Miss Gladstone was undoubtedly much better, but he feared that her symptoms might some day recur in response to a wish to become again the heroine of such a drama. Rumours of that event reached the ears of Hope-Scott, who wrote to ask Gladstone for details. Very reluctantly, Gladstone complied. He had already had occasion (15 May, 1845) to warn Hope-Scott against the danger of sleeping at his post as ' one of the sentinels of the Church of England on the side looking towards Rome '. He now told him (27 November, 1848) that ' it does not admit of the veriest shadow

[1] Mass must be meant here. High Mass would have required the presence of at least three priests.

of a shade of doubt' that his sister had been the victim of a ' deplorable illusion'. It was 'one of those delusions which seduce some minds into superstition, but which, in the long run, react, and far more powerfully, towards unbelief'. Less than three years later Hope-Scott cut Gladstone to the heart by making his submission to Rome.

Miss Gladstone herself never looked back. On 17 March, 1849, Sir John told his son that ' her considerate and judicious conduct has been everything I could wish. She is anxious to do everything right.' In his extreme old age, Sir John Gladstone became completely dependent upon his daughter, who was thus, at last, able to emancipate herself from the mental climate which had suffocated her and made her ill. But a week or two after her cure, her brother had occasion to administer 'one final rebuke to her for a misdemeanour by which he was most profoundly shocked. He wrote from Fasque (24 November, 1848) :

My dearest Helen,
I write to you with the greatest reluctance on a most painful subject. I have lately been engaged in arranging the books in my father's library . . .

I have this morning seen with my own eyes that which, without seeing, I would never have believed : a number of books upon religious subjects in the two *closets* attached to your sleeping apartments, some entire, some torn up, the borders or outer coverings of some, remaining—under circumstances which admit of no doubt as to the shameful use to which they were put.

I do not enter into any discussion. The subject does not bear it . . . You have no right to perpetrate these indignities against any religion sincerely held.

Gladstone threatened to inform his father, unless Helen gave an undertaking never again to tear up the works of Protestant theologians for use as toilet-paper in the lavatories at Fasque, or Carlton Gardens.

It may be felt that there was a piquant and symbolic quality about the disclosure of that last act of defiance at the moment when Miss Gladstone's physical and mental health was at last re-established. Her religion helped her to renounce opium for a long time, and in August, 1849, Gladstone signalized his reconciliation with his sister, by naming his fourth daughter Helen, after her aunt. That daughter, who became Principal of Newnham College, Cambridge, was throughout her life a model of sanity, sympathy, and understanding. She did not in the least resemble her aunt, who, soon after Sir John Gladstone's death in December, 1851, went to Germany. There, for thirty years, until her death, she lived a life of charity and piety. She was mildly but harmlessly eccentric, and she relished, above everything, the independence of which no-one could ever again deprive her. She corresponded regularly with her relatives at a safe distance. Gladstone often sent her invitations to revisit England and to stay with him at Hawarden. But she never accepted and he never quite understood the reason. After her death, in 1880, he arranged for her body to be brought home from Germany to Fasque, where it was buried with Church of England rites. He first convinced himself, and his brother, Sir Thomas Gladstone, that their sister had ceased to be an orthodox Roman Catholic before her death, and that she had therefore reverted, officially, to the Church of England. He recorded, at that time, his opinion that the matter was important, because of all the women who had seceded to Rome during the previous forty years, his sister had possessed the most powerful mind.

*   *   *

Painful as it was, Gladstone's anxiety about his sister was small in comparison with his agony of mind as the Oak Farm Company slithered into insolvency. It was an advantage to him that he was out of Parliament until the Oxford election of July–August, 1847. Throughout the year, 1847, there was an orgy of speculation on the Stock Exchange ; it culminated in a crash, which reached its peak in October. Share prices fell, often by catastrophic amounts ; credit was virtually unobtainable ; a number of banks stopped payment. The depression was weathered in due course, but the company in which Gladstone and the Glynne family were interested was put into liquidation on the petition of Lord Ward, one of its creditors. The liabilities, which were secured on the Hawarden Estate, were estimated at £450,000.

Every nerve had previously been strained by Gladstone in a vain effort to avert disaster. The Dowager Lady Glynne gave up £1000 a year of her jointure of £2,500, and Sir John Gladstone provided substantial credits. But the mischief had gone too far, and Gladstone's fury vented itself, not without cause, on the head of the Company's managing director—Boydell :

'If the man is sane,' he told his father (2 December, 1847), 'he is a rank scoundrel . . . When I speak of Boydell's sanity, I do not mean that he can be legally mad, but that he is subject to transports of excitement which put him quite past such common-sense as he has.'

Sir Stephen Glynne and Lord Lyttelton gave Gladstone *carte blanche* to do whatever he thought best, and in May, 1848, he attended the bankruptcy proceedings in Birmingham. He described his examination as 'an indecent affair'. Boydell claimed that he had been egged on by Sir John Gladstone : 'I therefore took occasion to mention emphatically,' Gladstone wrote to his father (20 May, 1848), 'that you had no responsibility and took no part except one of sheer kindness . . . Boydell began to brag at one time about his character, upon which I interposed and required that he would be silent on that account so long as I was present, and this had the effect of stopping him.'

A family conclave was held in the library of 13, Carlton House Terrace. The only member of the family who was absent was Sir Stephen Glynne, who, with Gladstone's approval, had taken himself off to Constantinople before the bankruptcy proceedings opened. He was the party most concerned, but Gladstone agreed with his father that Sir Stephen was of no use beyond doing whatever he was told.

Sir John Gladstone opened the proceedings by suggesting that the entire Hawarden property, consisting of rather more than seven thousand acres, should be sold. This would enable Sir Stephen to discharge his debts, and would leave him with a private income of about £4,500 a year. That should be adequate for a bachelor of quiet and artistic tastes, and it should also enable Sir Stephen to continue to discharge some of his hospitable duties as Lord Lieutenant of Flintshire, without undue embarrassment. The family was, however, unanimous in deciding against that course.

It was agreed that Hawarden should be closed and, if possible, let, but that it should, at all costs, be preserved. It was further agreed that Sir Stephen should give up his horses and carriages, that he should live on £700 a year, and that enough land should be sold to produce £200,000. Gladstone was enabled by his father to buy half that land ; the other half was to have been bought by Lord Lyttelton. When Lord Lyttelton found, however, that he could not raise the necessary sum, his portion was bought by Lord Spencer,[1] who was

[1] Formerly Lord Althorp.

an uncle by marriage of Sir Stephen and of Mrs. Gladstone. When those arrangements had been executed, Gladstone, on behalf of his brothers-in-law, bought back the assets of the bankrupt company, the sale of which had been ordered by the Court. After Sir Stephen Glynne had acquiesced without question, a debt of a quarter of a million pounds remained to be discharged.

For some years Gladstone's principal occupation was that of nursing the Hawarden Estate and the Oak Farm Company back to life. He threw his own financial resources, as well as everything which he expected to inherit from his father, into the task. He was convinced, all his life, that that work had been an ideal preparation for the office of Chancellor of the Exchequer, in which he presently achieved such immense distinction. He told Mrs. Gladstone (20 January, 1849) that the work had evidently come to him ' by the ordinance of God ', and that he was dismayed to think how insupportably easy his life would have been if that work had not been sent.

As the situation very gradually improved, it was found possible to reopen Hawarden in a modest way. The place was closed for a short time, but never actually let ; and early in 1852, Sir Stephen was able to return to it with an allowance of about £2,000 a year, instead of £700, for his personal expenses. He never resigned his Lord Lieutenancy. At the same time, Gladstone and his wife entered into a private arrangement with Sir Stephen for their joint occupation of Hawarden on a basis of sharing the expenses. They already had a similar arrangement with Sir Stephen's mother, Lady Glynne, for sharing the expense of running 13, Carlton House Terrace.

Gladstone estimated that, from first to last, he sank £267,500 into the Hawarden Estate. It was natural, therefore, that he should be concerned about the problem of the eventual succession to that property. Sir Stephen was never likely to marry, but his younger brother, Henry Glynne, the Rector of Hawarden—a benefice which was then worth £4,000 a year—had four daughters. After the death of Mrs. Henry Glynne, Gladstone wrote to his wife (24 July, 1851) to say that it was important to consider the future. He warned her that there was ' no subject so delicate as that of succession to properties, in relation to the preservation of unbroken affection in families '. But he considered that, if no heir-male appeared, Sir Stephen might be well-advised to fix the entail upon ' males now living ', instead of leaving the door open for possible, but unknown, future husbands of Henry Glynne's daughters. He added that he was ' quite certain

. . . that it ought not to be done upon any suggestion proceeding, directly or indirectly, from you or me'.

If an entail were fixed on a male 'now living', Gladstone's eldest son, William, would be an obvious candidate. But the position was one of extreme delicacy, because Sir Stephen, who was absorbed by music, and by his antiquarian studies, was too ready to do whatever he was advised. Between 1851 and 1867 much thought was given by Gladstone and Mrs. Gladstone, Lord and Lady Lyttelton, Sir Stephen Glynne and Henry Glynne to the question of the future disposition of the Hawarden property. It was finally agreed that it should be left in trust for one or more of Gladstone's sons, as he should appoint. Two old family friends, the Earl of Devon and Sir Robert Phillimore, conferred at Hawarden from 19–26 October, 1865, at Gladstone's insistence. They were asked to pay especial regard to the interests of the four daughters of Henry Glynne, and the final arrangements were concluded in accordance with their advice.

In 1867, accordingly, Gladstone bought, for £57,000, the reversion to the Hawarden property after the lives of Sir Stephen Glynne and Henry Glynne. The value of the reversion was based on an expectation of joint lives of twenty-two and a half years, but in fact Gladstone only had to wait seven years ; for Henry Glynne died in 1872 and Sir Stephen in 1874. Power had been reserved to either brother to revoke that arrangement on repayment of the principal with interest, but no desire to that effect was ever expressed. Gladstone wrote to his wife (27 September, 1869) that 'in the Providence of God' they had all been welded together into an unusually intimate relationship 'for which I am, and know I ought to be, most grateful'.

A few months after Sir Stephen's death, in 1874, Gladstone transferred the title deeds of Hawarden to his eldest son, William, reserving only to himself an annuity of £3,000 charged on the property. Seven years later he also transferred to his eldest son the land he had bought in 1849 after the Oak Farm smash.

After spending £267,000 of his own money on the Hawarden Estate, and after distributing £120,000 to members of his family during the 1880s, Gladstone was left a comparatively poor man. He spent additional sums of about £83,500 on his rescue work, and £30,000 on founding the hostel and library of St. Deiniol's. At his death, therefore, he left a fairly small sum—about £50,000. He regarded wealth as a trust from God, to be used for His purposes, and he was one of the most generous and charitable men of his generation. He always maintained that hereditary wealth, when it was combined with duty and a tradition of *noblesse oblige*, fulfilled a valuable function with which society could not afford to dispense.

The unusual arrangement whereby Hawarden was shared between the Gladstones and Sir Stephen Glynne for as long as Sir Stephen lived, worked remarkably well. Henry Glynne was Mrs. Gladstone's favourite brother, but both brothers were excellent company. Gladstone occasionally grumbled that Sir Stephen enjoyed choosing topics to fling in people's faces ; and Sir Stephen poked fun sometimes at the solemn ways of the ' Great People ' who had come to make their home in his castle. But it was an extremely happy house, full of children and young people, none of whom held Gladstone in undue awe. It is on record that on one occasion his eldest daughter had to be restrained when she started to address her father as ' Bill '.

The love which Gladstone felt for Hawarden did not stop far short of idolatry. He spent six months there every year for more than half a century, and sank his roots deep into the soil. Before he died, he had reduced the outstanding mortgages on the property from a quarter of a million to ninety thousand pounds. He thanked God, as he lay dying, that he had been permitted to achieve one at least of the great objects of his life. By faith and toil he had preserved the Hawarden Estate. He had kept it in his family. He had paid off the greatest part of the crushing burden of debt with which it had been cumbered when he first made it his home.

CHAPTER 5

LOVE THY NEIGHBOUR
1847–1854

THE bitter feud in the Conservative Party which was caused by Sir Robert Peel's fall in 1846, left Gladstone in an uncomfortable and unfortunate position. He was associated with a group of high-minded men, many of whom were much older than he was, who were united by loyalty to Peel, and by opposition to protection. But the Peelites were not a Party; and they became, in course of time, like a headquarters without an army. Peel was a popular hero, but presently he was dead. Protection was a political bogey, which Disraeli was soon to describe as dead and damned. Nevertheless, the Peelites continued to hang together.

To the nation, the Peelites appeared straight-laced and smug. They commanded a large share of the intellectual capital of Parliament, but they were inclined to parade their principles. Like the Rockingham Whigs, or the Canningites in former times, their display of posthumous loyalty, after the accident of their untimely bereavement, made them slightly absurd. Deprived of half their Conservative associations and all their Conservative friends, they sat glued to the cross-benches, while both sides bid briskly for their services without reaching the reserved price. Lord John Russell made overtures to three of them when he formed his Liberal Cabinet after Peel's resignation. At any moment any or all of them would have been welcomed back into the Conservative ranks, or assimilated into the Liberal ranks, on terms which could have been arranged. But many years passed before the last member of the group either retired or was reabsorbed into the traditional two-Party political pattern.

Two major considerations coloured Gladstone's outlook at that time. In the first place, Liberalism was, in his eyes, infected by the personality of Lord Palmerston, and official Conservatism by that of Disraeli. Palmerston's noisy jingoism disturbed Gladstone's vision of Europe as a community of Christian peoples possessing equal rights and subject to a code of public law which was divinely inspired: Disraeli's apparent levity, and the methods by which that adventurer had pulled Peel down and raised himself to the virtual leadership of the Conservative Party, outraged a moral sense that was rooted in religion.

In the second place, Gladstone's election in 1847 as the junior member for Oxford University hampered his development. Sir Robert Inglis, a diehard Tory, was his fellow-member. Gladstone attached a much too exalted sentimental importance to the honour of representing the University which he loved. He had been dismayed by the prospect of having to seek a popular constituency; he clung desperately to Oxford, and until he finally lost that seat in 1865, he was always haunted by the fear of losing it. In his anxiety to retain it, he sacrificed too much for too long. He found himself representing a constituency which he could never address. His power to sway multitudes, which he possessed in a superlative degree, was scarcely exercised, or even fully disclosed, until he had ceased to sit for Oxford.

Parties, after the General Election of July–August, 1847, were nicely balanced. Gladstone won his election at Oxford by a small majority on 3 August, after declaring that he would never consent to adopt as the test of loyalty to the Church of England, a disposition to restrict the civil rights of those who held different views. During his canvass he approached the venerable President of Magdalen, Dr. M. J. Routh, who was then aged nearly a hundred, and who had known Dr. Johnson. But the old gentleman declined to vote for him.

Thomas Gladstone also refused at first to vote for his brother. He said that William's religious principles were unsound; but he surrendered, after a sharp exchange of letters, to an ultimatum from his father. Nevertheless, Gladstone was soon in trouble with his constituents, and with his father, about the claims of a non-Christian minority. The City of London had returned as its representatives, the Prime Minister, Lord John Russell, and the Jewish banker, Lionel de Rothschild. Rothschild could not take the oath 'on the true faith of a Christian', and Lord John introduced a Resolution to delete those words. To everybody's astonishment, Gladstone, on 16 December, 1847, joined Disraeli in speaking and voting for that Resolution. The Opposition was led by Gladstone's fellow-member for Oxford University, Sir Robert Inglis. The Resolution passed the Commons, but it, and a series of Bills based upon it, were blocked by the Lords until 1858.

Gladstone argued that Parliament had ceased to be an Anglican or even a Protestant assembly. Unitarians 'who refuse the whole of the most vital doctrines of the Gospel' were already admitted; and the tendencies of the age were evidently set in motion by 'the Providential government of the world'. Some of his constituents hissed him on 5 July, 1848, when he visited Oxford, to receive an Honorary Degree, and he was received with cries of ' Gladstone and the Jew Bill ! ' He had, however, greater difficulty with his father.

Sir John Gladstone had strongly resented for some years his son's conversion to free trade. He rebuked him hotly now, not only for seeking to admit Jews to Parliament, but for concealing his intentions and veiling his mental processes. There was some substance in that charge. Gladstone had confided to Sir Thomas Acland his intention to support Lord John Russell's Resolution ; Acland told him that he had decided to oppose it. But he begged Gladstone, in such a matter, to make his meaning crystal clear, and to avoid verbal refinements. He advised him to forget the example of Frederick Maurice, and to speak more in the forthright manner of the Duke of Wellington. Gladstone pleaded with his father that errors and inconsistencies would be much more frequent in public life ' even than they now are ' unless judgement were often held in suspense until the last moment on painful or difficult questions, however plain they might seem to some people. But he pleaded in vain. There were few questions which did not wear an immediate appearance of white or black to Sir John Gladstone. His son said that he would gladly retire from Parliament, if that would save his father annoyance. But the old man laughed at him, and asked what he would propose to do with himself, or for his family, when he retired. Sir John Gladstone was often very difficult as he grew older, but the asperity was only on the surface. He had a profound belief that every man was responsible to his own conscience, and the strong ties of affection which bound him to all his children were never impaired.

During the last flare-up of the Chartist trouble in 1848, Gladstone was called out several times as a special constable. He was on duty on 10 April, when it was expected that a vast socialist mob would converge on the Palace of Westminster. But more special constables than socialists appeared to be on parade, and the affair fizzled out like a damp squib. The event was in the strongest possible contrast with the spectacular outbreaks on the European Continent during that revolutionary year.

In the summer of 1849, Gladstone found time to execute a quixotic mission on behalf of his friend, Lord Lincoln. Lady Lincoln had deserted her husband and gone to Italy, using the name of Mrs. Laurence. There was reason to think that she was accompanied by Lord Walpole, son of the Earl of Orford. Lord Lincoln at first asked

Manning to attempt to find and influence her, and when Manning made difficulties, Gladstone volunteered to go. He went with the full approval of Mrs. Gladstone, who was then expecting another baby, but against the advice of his father, who thought that only ridicule would result. He took with him a moving letter (12 July) from his wife to 'My dearest Suzie', entreating her to listen to Gladstone and to allow him to bring her home.

On 14 July, 1849, Gladstone crossed the Channel, and was, as usual, seasick. He went to Naples, Rome, and Milan, following such clues as he possessed or found, and at last ran his quarry to earth in a villa on the shore of Lake Como. On the morning of 31 July he presented himself at the villa and inquired boldly for Lady Lincoln, or for Mrs. Laurence. He was told that no-one of either name was known, and he was refused admission. He left a note, which remained unanswered.

Late that evening he disguised himself, and entered the grounds of the villa, unobserved. He had learned that a carriage had been ordered for a certain hour. He saw a female figure enter the carriage accompanied by a man. But it was too dark for recognition, and the carriage drove past him with drawn blinds. On making inquiries he discovered that it was bound for Verona. And the next day, 1 August, he followed it.

In Verona, after a day or two, he again ran his quarry to earth. This time he saw Lady Lincoln in daylight, and she coldly repulsed all his efforts to speak to her. Gladstone was, however, able to observe her rounded figure, and the fact that she was with child. So he started, sorrowfully, for home, writing to Mrs. Gladstone from Paris (8 August): 'The same post which carries this, carries also the dagger to Lincoln.'

Some details of that adventure would not have been out of place in a light Italian opera. Sir John Gladstone was so angry when he heard some of them that he threatened to alter his Will. The rôle Gladstone had played, which appeared wildly improbable to those who did not know him well, was publicly disclosed when Lord Lincoln started divorce proceedings against his wife. Lord Lincoln proceeded by means of a private Act of Parliament, and on the Bill's Second Reading in the House of Lords (28 May, 1850) Gladstone gave evidence. He was a good witness, and his transparent unworldliness and integrity protected him from most of the ridicule which other men might have incurred. Stories were circulated, however, that he had gone abroad to collect evidence for a fee, and he had to deny that charge publicly in the House of Commons seven years later. On 26 August, 1849, Sir Robert Peel, who knew his character so well, sent him a charming letter, which referred to his 'unparalleled kindness and generosity' in undertaking that thankless mission for a friend, and to the fact that he had executed it with the utmost delicacy.

On 9 April, 1850, Gladstone's second daughter, Jessy, died of meningitis, and her father was plunged for some hours into such an agony of grief, that his household was seriously alarmed. Then, with extreme suddenness, his controls were reasserted and he became absolutely calm. Under the stress of deep emotion he wrote a moving and intensely emotional account of the child's brief life.

At that time, Gladstone's nerves had been set jangling by two questions. The first concerned foreign policy; the second concerned the Church.

Lord Palmerston, the Foreign Secretary, had declared a naval blockade of the Greek coasts in January. The Greek Government had been dilatory in discharging some of its obligations, and Palmerston had seized a very dubious occasion to bring that Government to heel. He had espoused the cause of a Portuguese money-lender, who claimed that he was technically a British subject because he had been born a member of the Jewish community at Gibraltar. Don Pacifico had owned a house in Athens which a mob had sacked in 1847. He had a claim to some compensation, but that claim was exaggerated to the point of absurdity. Nevertheless, in January, 1850, without consulting France or Russia, who were co-guarantors, with Great Britain, of Greek independence, Lord Palmerston despatched a naval squadron to Greece in the interests of a shady and obscure adventurer.

The French Ambassador was withdrawn from London; and the House of Lords condemned the Foreign Secretary's action (17 June). But Lord Palmerston, who was able, as an Irish Peer, to sit in the Commons, defended his policy in that House in a brilliant five-hour speech on 25 June. He was opposed by Sir Robert Peel, Sir James Graham, Richard Cobden, and John Bright, as well as by Disraeli and Gladstone. Gladstone claimed that he had never before intervened seriously in a debate on foreign affairs, but he forgot the China debate of 1840. He now attacked Palmerston's arrogant claim that a British subject, like a Roman citizen of old, was entitled to privileged treatment. There were no privileged castes or nations in contemporary Europe. All men and all nations were subject to the same rule of law, and if any distinctions were to be allowed, they should be associated with the respect due to feeble nations and to the infancy of free institutions.

Lord Palmerston secured a handsome majority for his jingo views and policy. Gladstone was confirmed in the view that he expressed in a private note to Lord Lincoln (30 January, 1857) after Lord Palmerston had become Prime Minister and Lord Lincoln had succeeded as Duke of Newcastle : ' My dear Newcastle, I think Lord Palmerston the worst and most demoralizing Prime Minister for this country that our day has known. He lives and thrives upon the bad parts of its character, and laughs the good ones to scorn, or passes them by with contempt.'

On the day after the debate ended, Sir Robert Peel was thrown from his horse on Constitution Hill. He was so badly injured that he died in great pain on 2 July, aged sixty-two. Gladstone could not feel that his death was an unmixed calamity, for he had resented Peel's support of Lord John Russell's Government. He considered that his leader had been too much governed by baseless fears that the Conservatives would seek to restore protection. The Great Exhibition, when it opened in Hyde Park in 1851, seemed in one of its aspects to be a carnival dedicated to the principle of free trade. It appeared, at the time, to be a tremendous event, and Gladstone shared the popular delusion that it was destined to inaugurate a new era of international peace, improved taste, and permanent free trade between nations.

The other question which tortured Gladstone in 1850 arose out of a resounding quarrel between the Bishop of Exeter and the Rev. George Gorham on the subject of baptismal regeneration. The Bishop, Henry Phillpotts, had refused to institute the clergyman to a living to which he had been presented by the Crown, on the ground that Gorham had declared baptism to be a mere symbol. The Bishop, naturally and properly, regarded baptism as a means of regeneration ; for if it is only a symbol, what becomes of certain Scriptural texts about the necessity of worthy acceptance ? Gorham employed the Evangelical argument which Gladstone had outgrown before he went up to Oxford, that if baptism is a means of regeneration, how can infants be worthy to receive it ? The controversy produced a great doctrinal crisis.

The Bishop, after examining Gorham for fifty-two hours, declared that he was dissatisfied and that his conscience would not allow him to institute him. Gorham appealed to the Archiepiscopal Court of Canterbury—the Court of Arches—which decided for Phillpotts. He then appealed to the highest ecclesiastical court in the kingdom— the Judicial Committee of the Privy Council, which was composed entirely of laymen.

The Judicial Committee, on 8 March, 1850, decided for Gorham against his Bishop, who was ordered to institute.   The Bishop refused, and Gorham was eventually instituted over the Bishop's head, and in obedience to the decision of a secular court, by a fiat of the Archbishop of Canterbury. The Bishop wrote to Gorham's parishioners to urge them not to attend church.

Gladstone considered that the judgement was an outrage, calculated to manufacture converts to Rome. The State had intervened not only to settle doctrine, but to proclaim heresy. It had denied the efficacy of a Sacrament, and shorn the Nicene Creed of an article. It had impaired the Church of England's claim to Catholicity.   For a time he contemplated resistance. He published a very long letter to the Bishop of London in the attempt to prove that the action of the Judicial Committee was unconstitutional, and he was plunged for many months into a mood of black depression :

' It was ', he noted, ' a terrible time ; aggravated for me by heavy cares and responsibilities of a nature quite extraneous : and, far beyond all others, by the illness and death of a much loved child, with great anxieties about another.'

Before his depression dissolved, Gladstone had abandoned his former belief and hope that the Church of England, by renewing her spiritual life, would be able to win back vast multitudes of Nonconformists into her fold. He realized with astonishment that despite the vast numbers of new churches which had been built up and down the country in recent years, the multiplication of Nonconformist chapels had gone forward on a much greater scale. He had to abandon also at that time, the hope that the Queen would do something for the cause. He was horrified when Lord Aberdeen repeated a remark which she had made about the late Archbishop of Canterbury, William Howley, who had died in 1848. Howley was, she had supposed, ' as good as any of them '. That proved, Gladstone thought, that she cared little for the Church, and that the Prince Consort's influence was bad. Lord Aberdeen warned Gladstone later (22 February, 1854) that the Queen regarded his religious views with considerable suspicion.

Gladstone told his wife (5 September, 1850) that the Church had ceased to be an organized body ; it had become a Tower of Babel. He gradually adjusted his mind to the need for replacing authority by the individual conscience as the inner citadel of the Church. The Church of England would have to learn to live without the aid of the State, and that was a process that would take time. His faith in the Catholicity of that Church remained unshaken, but his two friends, Manning and Hope-Scott, took the opposite view. Their faith in the Catholicity of the Anglican Church was irretrievably broken, and on 6 April, 1851, they both made their submissions to Rome : ' They were my two props,' he wrote in his diary (7 April). '. . . One blessing I have : total freedom from doubts. These dismal events have smitten, but not shaken.'

Manning, too, had no doubts : ' The sun of his Anglicanism ', Gladstone noted, ' set like the sun of the tropics, without a premonitory decline.' Hope-Scott, however, had wobbled for some years. In Manning's case the breach was absolute, and Gladstone and he returned all the letters which they had ever received from one another. Gladstone's feeling for Manning never revived, but his affection for Hope-Scott remained unshaken. He told Hope-Scott's daughter (13 September, 1873) that hardly a day had passed between the date of her father's conversion and the date of his death, on which he had been absent from his thoughts. In the letter he wrote to Hope-Scott immediately after his conversion, Gladstone uttered no word of reproach, and signed himself, ' yours with unaltered affection ', but he removed Hope-Scott's name immediately from the list of his executors and substituted that of his former secretary, Sir Henry Stafford Northcote (later Earl of Iddesleigh).

Thenceforward Gladstone trusted that the principle of freedom, which had already quickened the nation's commercial life, would serve also to quicken its religious life. Thirteen years later he was ready to take another step forward, and to apply the same principle to the nation's political life by admitting to the franchise a substantial section of the working class.

In October, 1850, concern for the health of his daughter, Mary, and the desire to escape for a time from the pain of religious controversy, and from the wearisome details of the Oak Farm Company's affairs, induced Gladstone to take part of his family to Naples, for a holiday. He left Paris on 28 October, noting, with characteristic attention to detail :

'One hundred and twenty miles of railway to Nevers cost 254 francs or £10 3s. for the carriage and ourselves in it : or (about) 13 pence a mile for the vehicle and five third-class passengers . . . We did not quite cover 20 miles an hour.'

It was neither poverty nor meanness, but principle and an innate austerity which prompted him, while travelling with his wife and ailing daughter, to go third-class over a foreign railroad, and to note that the rate was 'dearer than in England'. In the places where they stayed he complained of the difficulty of obtaining particulars about church services and sermons. He thought that it would answer the convenience of travellers if programmes were printed and placed on sale. He managed, however, to attend a fair number.

At Turin, for example, on 1 November, 1850, Gladstone fitted in two sermons. At the Church of San Lorenzo, 'the doctrine was in the coarse and material strain of the popular purgatorial systems—a painful sermon'. At the second, in a church by the Cathedral, he heard 'the same doctrine from an inferior man'. The next day he was unable to find any preaching at all, but he discovered one church where the Offices for the Dead were being celebrated, and he heard them through, with pleasure, to the end. On Sunday, 3 November, he was sadly torn by difficulties of time and geography, but he noted that he had fitted in 'a whole sermon, and two halves'. He made a précis throughout the tour, of every sermon, or part of a sermon, which he heard.

At Naples he again climbed Vesuvius (4 December), but he gave up most of his time to James Lacaita, the legal adviser to the British Legation. Lacaita directed Gladstone's attention to the abominable way in which the political opponents of King Ferdinand II, of the Two Sicilies, were being treated. Gladstone had had no thought of taking any interest in Neapolitan politics, but he attended the trial of a Liberal Minister, Carlo Poerio, who had tried to work a constitution which had been wrung from King Ferdinand two years before in the Revolution of 1848. That constitution had soon been repudiated, and the Government was now engaged in liquidating the last of the men who had upheld it.

Gladstone heard Poerio sentenced to twenty-four years' imprisonment in chains. He was horrified at the way in which the trial was conducted. He succeeded after considerable difficulty in visiting the dungeon in which Poerio was confined, and he satisfied himself that about twenty thousand political prisoners were languishing in conditions of filth and cruelty which no language could adequately describe. But Gladstone did his best, when he wrote to Lord Aberdeen, Peel's former Foreign Secretary :

'It is the wholesale persecution of virtue . . . It is the awful profanation of public religion . . . It is the perfect prostitution of the judicial office . . . It is the savage and cowardly system of moral as well as physical torture . . . This is the negation of God erected into a system of Government.'

Gladstone had, in fact, erupted suddenly, and violently, like Vesuvius. He adduced many supporting details, and he returned to London (26 February, 1851) boiling and seething with indignation. He was met at the station by a messenger from Lord Stanley, the official Conservative leader, who asked if he would be willing to serve— perhaps as Foreign Secretary—in a Government which Lord Stanley was trying to form.

The messenger, Sir Robert Phillimore, was an old friend, but Gladstone could hardly bear to listen to Phillimore. All his conversation was about Naples, and the abominations that were being perpetrated there. He consented, half-heartedly, to see Lord Stanley, but he refused to take any part in the proposed new Government when he was informed that a small duty might be imposed on corn. In the end, Lord Stanley abandoned his attempt, and Lord John Russell returned to office. Gladstone was more than half indifferent ; all his thoughts were concentrated on Naples. He could not rest until he had seen Lord Aberdeen, and written to him at length. He implored him to do something for the cause of human decency in Naples. Lord Aberdeen, who had many European contacts, could not ignore the evidence which Gladstone laid before him ; but he was much embarrassed. He had criticized Lord Palmerston for his Liberal, and even grandmotherly, interventions in European affairs, and he had no wish to see existing European arrangements disturbed. However, he wrote (2 May, 1851) to Prince Schwarzenberg, the Austrian Chancellor, with whom he was on friendly personal terms. He suggested that as Gladstone was in such a state of excitement, it might be worth the Prince's while to avert a scandal by making private representations to the Neapolitan Government.

Prince Schwarzenberg took a long time to reply, and his letter (30 June, 1851) was very cold when it was at last dispatched. He showed that he resented the interference of a British ex-Foreign Secretary in such a matter. He said that he would bring Gladstone's views to the notice of King Ferdinand; but he informed Lord Aberdeen that the British treatment of political offenders in Ireland, in the Ionian Islands, and in Ceylon, had neither escaped his attention nor excited his disapproval.

Before that letter was received Gladstone's patience was exhausted. To Lord Aberdeen's dismay, Gladstone, at the beginning of July, published, as a pamphlet, his *Letter to Lord Aberdeen*. Later that month he published an enlarged edition, with a preface explaining his motives.

A profound sensation was caused, and Gladstone found himself at once a national hero, and a moral force in Europe. He was publicly congratulated by Lord Palmerston, who circulated copies of the letters to all British Missions abroad, and ordered that they should be communicated to foreign Governments. Palmerston rejected the protest of the Neapolitan Minister, which he publicly described, in his jaunty way, as a tissue of lies and coarse abuse. The Press in general, all Liberals, and many Conservatives, gave Gladstone unstinted praise.

The incident inevitably propelled Gladstone some way along the road to Liberalism. But his outlook remained Conservative and wholly undemocratic. All his arguments were addressed to Conservatives, and he found it hard to understand why those who supported, as he did, the established order at home and abroad should be averse from correcting its abuses. He found it equally hard to conceive that the clue to the attainment of effectual reform in Italy might lie in the cause of Italian unity. Guizot wrote to him to point out that the only real choice in Italy was between tyrants like King Ferdinand, and revolutionaries like Mazzini, and that only tyrants could be trusted to safeguard the existing order. Gladstone himself declared (21 June, 1851) that the idea of Italian unity and nationality was a purely abstract proposition, and 'if there are two things on earth that John Bull hates, they are abstract propositions, and the Pope'.

It was not until 1854 that Gladstone was converted, by Italian exiles in London, and particularly by Daniele Manin, from Venice, to the view that the attainment of Italian unity was the essential prerequisite for good government in Italy. And it was not until the 1880s that he became convinced, as he informed the Queen, to her horror, that it was useless to base appeals to the upper classes upon broad considerations of humanity and justice. When he became a

Liberal at the end of the 1850s, it was the Italian question which administered the final shove. When he became, in his old age, a democrat, he recalled the deaf ear which even enlightened Conservatives, like Guizot, had turned to his appeal on behalf of the moral law in Naples.

*　　　*　　　*

After the death of Sir Robert Peel, Lord Aberdeen became the leader of the Peelites. The new Duke of Newcastle, whose ambition exceeded his capacity, coveted the post, but Gladstone told him firmly that Aberdeen was the better man. 'He took no offence,' Gladstone noted. With Lord Aberdeen's approval, Gladstone took a strong line in the House of Commons against the last hysterical wave of anti-Papist feeling which was ever experienced in Britain. It had been sweeping the country since the autumn of the previous year.

The occasion for that outbreak was the Pope's action in dividing England into dioceses bearing territorial titles, and in appointing Dr. Wiseman to be Cardinal-Archbishop of Westminster. The Prime Minister, Lord John Russell, denounced the Pope, on the eve of Guy Fawkes Day, as an insolent and insidious enemy of Great Britain, and said that he looked with contempt upon the mummeries of Roman Catholic superstition. He introduced, and carried, a Bill, which remained a dead letter, to invalidate the assumption of British territorial designations by Papists.

Gladstone, who repealed that Act twenty years later, opposed its introduction. He considered it a Bill against religious liberty, and he told the House during the debate on the Second Reading (25 March, 1851) : 'We cannot change the profound and resistless tendencies of the age towards religious liberty. It is our business to guide and to control their applications. Do this you may, but to endeavour to turn them backwards is the sport of children, done by the hands of men ; and every effort you may make in that direction will recoil upon you in disaster and disgrace.'

It was one of his greatest efforts, but in the division which followed only 95 (all Peelites and Irish) voted against the Bill ; 438 members accompanied the Prime Minister into the lobby.

At the end of that year, on 7 December, 1851, Sir John Gladstone died at Fasque, aged eighty-seven : 'A large and strong nature,' Gladstone recorded, at the end of his life, 'simple, though hasty, and capable of the highest devotion along the lines of duty and love. I

think that his intellect was a little intemperate, though not his character.'
In later years, he tried, unsuccessfully, to persuade Samuel Smiles to
write his father's life.

In the month in which his father died, the first two of the four
volumes of Gladstone's translation of Farini's History of the Papal
States from 1815-1850 appeared. In an article in the *Edinburgh
Review* (April, 1852), Gladstone described the Pope's Government as
'a foul blot upon the face of creation, an offence to Christendom, and
to mankind'. In that month of April, his third son, Henry Neville,
was born.

In the meantime, Lord John Russell's Government had fallen at
last (20 February, 1852), two months after the Prime Minister had
taken the spectacular step of dismissing Lord Palmerston from the
Foreign Office, for indiscretion. A weak Conservative Government
was formed by Lord Derby (formerly Stanley), in which Disraeli was
Chancellor of the Exchequer, and leader of the Commons. There
were several shades of opinion among the Peelites, but Gladstone
exerted all his influence to persuade them to remain independent.
Only Sir James Graham broke away, to the accompaniment of many
expressions of esteem and goodwill, to join the Liberals.

After the General Election which was held in July, the Peelites,
numbering about forty, were left holding the balance between some
300 Conservatives and some 315 Liberals and Radicals. Gladstone
found that his opinions were pulling him towards the left, while his
lingering sympathies, and his Oxford constituents, attracted him
towards the right. His mind was as delicately balanced as the House
of Commons, and he told his friends that he preferred to remain on
the Liberal side of the Conservative Party rather than on the Conservative side of the Liberal Party.

Disraeli made it clear that he had altered his mind about protection,
and that he now accepted the principle of free trade ; but the great
obstacle in the way of Gladstone's co-operation with the Conservatives
was generally understood. It was the inevitable antipathy felt by
Peel's principal political legatee for Disraeli, who had been responsible
for Peel's overthrow. Reflecting upon Disraeli's conduct, Gladstone
noted that he could never hope to enter upon the moral of his 'singular
career'. He added, 'No-one would gratuitously enter upon such a
task, which it would be difficult to execute with fairness at once to
him, to the country, and to public virtue.'

At a party given by Lady Derby on 26 November, the Prime

Minister drew Gladstone aside and began to talk to him about the 'personal considerations' which stood in the way of a rapprochement between the Government and the Peelites. Gladstone found the subject uncomfortable, but said that he and his friends were waiting to see what Disraeli's Budget would contain. He added, as a general proposition, that 'difficulties of a personal nature . . . arising from various causes, present and past relations, incompatibilities, peculiar defects of character, or failure in bringing them into harmony' undoubtedly existed in the new House of Commons.

Disraeli's Budget was introduced on 3 December, 1852. Writing to his wife (6 December), Gladstone described it as 'disgusting and repulsive'. It was an attempt to compensate, at the expense of the small taxpayer, the three most powerful interests which had been injured by the abandonment of protection. Agriculture, shipping, and sugar were to be benefited by the remission of certain taxes and duties, at the expense of the small income-tax payer and of the small householder.

The Budget was badly received, and at 10.20 on the evening of 16 December, Disraeli rose to reply to the attacks which had been made upon it. He appeared somewhat flushed, and Gladstone considered that he had had too much to drink. He made a brilliant speech, however, marred only by some errors of taste, which included a number of violent and sarcastic personal attacks upon his opponents. The House of Commons had not been so excited for many years, and a thunderstorm raged outside, while Disraeli was speaking. When Disraeli sat down at one o'clock in the morning of 17 December, Gladstone rose to answer him.

That was the first of a long series of oratorical duels between Gladstone and Disraeli which were to light up the life of Parliament for many years. As he rose to speak, Gladstone's self-control for once almost failed him. There were moments when his voice became so choked with passion, that he had to pause. But he began by rebuking the Chancellor for the personalities in which he had indulged:

'I must tell the Right Honourable gentleman that, whatever he has learned—and he has learned much—he has not yet learned the limits of discretion, of moderation . . . that ought to restrain the conduct of every member of this House ; the disregard of which is an offence in the meanest among us, but is of tenfold weight when committed by the leader of the House of Commons.'

After tearing his rival's Budget in pieces, Gladstone appealed to the House against the fraudulent chimæras of enchanters and magicians, to the sound moral principles of men of sense and honour, for whom financial policy was grounded in the Christian ethic. The division was taken at 4 a.m., and the Budget was rejected by 305 votes to 286.

That was the greatest triumph as well as the most exciting political passage which Gladstone had yet experienced. His influence and popularity were doubled at a stroke. For once he passed a sleepless night when he returned to Carlton House Terrace. He told his wife (18 December) that he had heard that Disraeli was 'much stung'. He was sorry for that; he had no desire to hurt him; but he wished that he would use his great gifts to better purpose. He added, very characteristically indeed: 'When I came home from the House, I thought it would be good for me to be mortified. Next morning . . . . I *was* mortified.' *The Times*, he wrote, had contained only a garbled version of his speech.

An instinct for self-mortification lay at the root of Gladstone's character. Some years before, when his wife complained that her husband's political duties were keeping them too much apart, Gladstone had told her (21 January, 1844) that they must both sink their individual wills in the will of God. That object was to be attained by two parallel processes:

'The first, that of checking, repressing, quelling the inclination of the will to act with reference to self as its centre: this is, to mortify it. The second, to cherish, exercise, and expand its new and heavenly power of acting according to the will of God . . . until obedience becomes a necessity of second nature . . . Your full triumph . . . will be to find . . . that you would not, if you could, alter what . . . God has plainly willed . . . Here is the path through which sanctity is attained.'

The struggle to keep his feet from slipping on that path was a cardinal object of Gladstone's life. It left him no time at all to relax and pluck flowers on his way. All his letters to Mrs. Gladstone have been preserved, and their tone is extremely significant because, except in the case of his family, and, until 1859, that of one friend (O. B. Cole) who lived in Ireland, he conducted no purely personal correspondences at all. When he was away from Mrs. Gladstone he wrote every day to her, and sometimes twice or even three times in twenty-four hours. The letters are not heavy; they contain playful touches; but they are dominated by a mood of sobriety. In part, that mood reflected the stern repressions which he had imposed upon his volcanic nature. But, equally, it reflected the fervour of that moral and religious revival which imposed a common code of conduct upon all classes during the nineteenth century. Of that code Gladstone became a flawless exemplar. All his words and thoughts reflected it, as well as all his actions.

Respectability was the keynote of that code. Respectability, like Roman citizenship of old, was envisaged as a means of ensuring the stability of society. And like Roman citizenship it seemed to be susceptible of indefinite extension. It was well-suited to an age which is unique in modern history—an age which witnessed the brief economic and political ascendancy of an upper middle class. It set a premium on hypocrisy, however, and it was equally uncongenial to patrician frivolity and plebeian boisterousness.

Women, fortunately, are individualists, and Mrs. Gladstone's letters afford a striking contrast with those of her husband. They are extremely feminine—full of ephemeral gossip and domesticities—and prefaced by terms of endearment which Gladstone, although his love was fully equal to hers, never employed. They would begin, ' My precious darling ', ' My own darling ', or ' My own ', and they would end sometimes with such sentences as, ' I would go to the world's end for you, and *alone*, to do you good.'

Both sides of that delightful and voluminous correspondence are distinguished by one outstanding attribute—an implicit confidence in the permanent and universal validity of certain transcendent values by which it is informed. In both cases, transcendent values were expressed in a practical form. Its most characteristic practical manifestation was the work which Gladstone and his wife undertook for the rescue of prostitutes. That work soon became, and it remained throughout their lives, the principal social and charitable work in which they were engaged.

In 1840, not long after his marriage, Gladstone, James Hope-Scott, and Sir Thomas Acland formed a small lay brotherhood on lines which Gladstone had sometimes discussed while he was at Oxford. The aim was to perform humble and humbling duties, but Acland's interest cooled very quickly, and on 7 December, 1845, Gladstone told Hope-Scott that the scheme was in danger of degenerating into a mere payment of subscriptions. When Hope-Scott failed to respond, Gladstone launched out on his own lines. He made an area bounded by Piccadilly, Soho, and the Thames Embankment his missionary field.

In 1848 Gladstone, with Bishop Wilberforce and Bishop Blomfield, helped to found the *Church Penitentiary Association for the Reclamation of Fallen Women*. In 1854 he and his wife helped to found the *Clewer Home of Mercy*, which still flourishes on the river bank at Windsor. He was on the Management Committee of the *Millbank Penitentiary* to which women arrested on the streets were sent. In 1863 Gladstone helped to found the *Newport Home of Refuge*, in Soho Square, and he helped, two years later, to found the *St. Mary Magdalen Home of Refuge* at Paddington. He often took the chair at meetings of those institutions, and he and Mrs. Gladstone were familiar figures at services held at St. Peter's, Windmill Street, in the same cause.

During the nineteenth century the number of street-walking prostitutes in London, and other big cities, was much greater than it is to-day; and the subject was then veiled under a heavy taboo. Despite all difficulties and remonstrances, however, Gladstone continued that work until he was over eighty years of age. He was helped not only by his wife, but by certain high-minded women, including his niece, Lady Frederick Cavendish, and by Lady Sarah Spencer.

Gladstone's method was to walk the streets by night, alone, on at least one evening a week, armed with a stout stick for protection when he wandered into unfrequented districts. At first, he liked to wait for prostitutes to accost him, and he would then reply with courtesy, simplicity and charm. But he would often accost women himself, and suggest that they should accompany him home, where he told them that they would be treated with respect by his wife and by himself, and that they would be given food and shelter.

He kept a record of every case, but he was scrupulous to treat the women as human beings and not as cases. He spent large sums of money supporting rescue homes, and smaller sums in personal gifts. He felt that he was making a personal contribution towards righting an infamous wrong. He was never unctuous. He did not demand penitence. He looked always to the future. His object was to enable the women to escape from their profession, and, in Victorian phrase, to assist them to redeem themselves. If, after their health had been restored by a spell at the seaside, the women, as often happened, resumed their former occupation, Gladstone never scolded them. He often blamed himself for want of zeal, tact, or charity. He would go after them again and again, and he did not hesitate to pursue them into brothels, preferably in the daytime, but with a supreme, and almost perverse, disregard of worldly considerations.

Many of the police knew what he was doing ; and it is to be feared that some of them misconstrued his purpose. There were times when the Clubs buzzed with gossip, and during his frequent periods of intense unpopularity, or at election times, there was an ever-present risk that a scandal might be written-up and blazoned in the gutter Press. But Gladstone went serenely on his way. The work on which he was engaged touched a very deep chord in his nature. He had schooled himself early in life to sublimate absolutely the tensions which seethed inside him. His rescue work was an important aspect of that process of sublimation. He had experienced a call to enter the Church, and he had not responded to it. He had nursed the ideal of a sacred union between Church and State, and he had watched it dissolve into air. In his rescue work he found a priestly office which he could fulfil as a layman, and in which his duty to God and man could be discharged together. No consideration on earth could have induced him to abandon it until old age had enfeebled him.

It is an unparalleled tribute to the radiant integrity of Gladstone's character that the inevitable effort made during his lifetime, and after his death, to cast doubt upon the purity of his motives, should have been at once so feeble and so ineffectual. His intimate friends were all afraid to warn him of the risk he ran of injuring his Party and ruining his career. In 1882, however, Lord Rosebery volunteered to warn the Prime Minister ; and he, and his friend, Sir Edward Hamilton, who was Gladstone's private secretary, thereafter remonstrated on a number of occasions. Gladstone listened patiently, said little, and for a long time appeared to turn a deaf ear.

In the course of Gladstone's life, some embarrassing incidents occurred, but their number was astonishingly few. The first was in the summer of 1853, when he was Chancellor of the Exchequer. On 10 May, after a division in the House of Commons, he went to Covent Garden to see the last part of the show. While walking home through Long Acre, he was accosted by a young woman at 11.40 p.m. Gladstone was listening to her story, when a youth came up to him, addressed him by name, and threatened to expose him if he did not, as he put it, ' make it right ' with him. He asked for money, or for a job in the Inland Revenue Department.

Gladstone took no notice, but accompanied the girl back to her lodgings which were in King Street, Soho. He was, however, trailed by the blackmailer. The girl ran into the house and the black-mailer again approached Gladstone, and called him a lecher and a hypocrite. Gladstone became exceedingly angry ; he tried to hit the youth with his stick and told him that he was a villainous liar. He looked round for a policeman, but none was to be seen. He walked first to Regent Street, and then to Sackville Street, with the black-mailer following him, sometimes uttering threats but more often begging for favours. In Sackville Street a policeman at last appeared, and Gladstone gave the blackmailer in charge. He announced his name, and appeared at Marlborough Street Magistrates' Court to give evidence the next morning. The youth was committed for trial, and, on 15 June, 1853, he was sentenced at the Old Bailey to twelve months' hard labour. When he had served one half of his sentence, Gladstone asked the Home Secretary, as a personal favour, to release him.

The only other occasion on which Gladstone's rescue work was made the subject of legal proceedings was in 1927,[1] many years after his death. A malignant journalist was annihilated in that year by the just anger and resolute action of Gladstone's two surviving sons.

There were times when Gladstone was involved in almost comic situations. In 1863 he rescued a woman ' at the very top of the tree ', as he informed his wife (30 July). She was aged twenty, and had been provided by her admirer with a house in Brompton Square and a carriage and pair. The vehicle and horses were kept at a neighbour-ing livery stables, and the proprietor was highly indignant when he learned that Gladstone was responsible for the woman's 'redemption'. He threatened to sue Gladstone for the balance of her account.

Much later, in 1882, a member of Parliament, named Colonel Tottenham, who had been a guest at the Athenæum Club, saw the Prime Minister talking to a prostitute on the Duke of York's steps. He dined out, next evening, on the story, and a lady, who had been present at the dinner, prompted by the highest motives, wrote to Sir Edward Hamilton, to report what had happened. After consulting Lord Rosebery, Hamilton showed his chief the letter (9 May). He ventured to say that, in his opinion, Gladstone's conduct was open to the gravest misconstruction. He thought that he had understood the Prime Minister to say that he would give up speaking to women in the streets at night, but he was evidently mistaken. Gladstone himself replied, on a postcard, to the lady who had written to his secretary :

It may be true that the gentleman saw me in such conversation, but the object was not what he assumed, or, as I am afraid, hoped.

W. E. G.

[1] *Wright* v. *Gladstone*.

Four years later, in 1886, at a time when, as Hamilton recorded in his diary (14 July), Gladstone was 'nearly ostracized in society' on account of the Home Rule Bill, Malcolm MacColl, a popular Canon of Ripon, warned Lord Rosebery that stories about Gladstone's rescue work were having a 'baneful effect' in the Metropolitan constituencies. There was reason to believe that poison had been instilled into the ears of the Queen, and that a group of Gladstone's enemies had arranged 'to set spies on him and track his movements with a view to testing the stories about his proclivities in the streets at night, and his visits to certain houses by day'.

Hamilton braced himself at Lord Rosebery's request to warn Gladstone once more. He said that such calumnies could no longer be disregarded, and that even friendly people who heard such stories were at a loss to account for what they heard. He added, or he hoped that he had added, that it seemed incomprehensible that a man in the Prime Minister's position should run such terrible risks.

Gladstone asked for two days to think the matter over. He then said that he feared that there did indeed exist in the world the degree of baseness which his secretary had indicated. He felt constrained, therefore, to admit that the words used by his secretary had been true and wise. He promised, accordingly, never again to speak to women in the streets at night. He added that he felt that his efforts had often been successful, and that there were two cases which he would not undertake to drop altogether. His innocence, simplicity, and candour made the most profound impression upon Hamilton. But even then he could not occasionally resist the urge to speak to prostitutes.

Gladstone never made the slightest attempt to force his stupendously high moral code upon others ; and it was virtually impossible for his enemies to shoot an arrow into his Achilles heel with any hope of success. His childlike integrity had the strength and hardness of a diamond. It was open, however, to anyone whose eyes were blinded by the shining light of Gladstone's example, to discharge his uneasiness and sense of moral inferiority by accusing him of perverse imprudence. It would be hard to exaggerate the imprudence of Gladstone's conduct. But, in truth and soberness, it must be said that words of praise for the work which he performed for nearly half a century in that field must, however carefully chosen and arranged, remain at best so inadequate as to appear tawdry. As a man and as a Christian, Gladstone was in that respect in a class by himself.

Gladstone was well aware of the attempts made to impugn his

motives. He was alive, too, to the danger that his attitude might appear perverse. But he uttered no word of complaint. One day, in 1886, he was kneeling at the Communion Rail in the Savoy Chapel, when the Hon. Mrs. Charles Grey, a woman of the Bedchamber to the Queen, looked up and saw him beside her. Mrs. Grey was formerly Miss Farquhar, whom Gladstone had once wanted to marry. She rose without a second's hesitation and left the church without taking the Communion. Lord Rosebery, who told Sir Edward Hamilton that story (6 March, 1890), said that he had himself experienced a similar instance of prejudice when he was travelling in India in 1886. On 29 December he had wanted to send Gladstone a cable for his birthday. He applied at an Army Telegraph Office, and the officer in charge, coolly, and very formally, assumed full responsibility for refusing to transmit the words, " God bless you ! "

At the end of his life, ruminating unhappily upon the fog of misunderstanding which had darkened his personal relations with the Queen, Gladstone recalled the hints, which had been conveyed to him, that stories about his rescue work had reached her ears. A. C. Benson, son of E. W. Benson who was Archbishop of Canterbury from 1882–96, maintained that Disraeli had discussed the stories ungenerously with the Queen. Gladstone considered that political differences alone were insufficient to account for the harshness of her treatment of him, and that the construction which she had placed upon those stories must, therefore, have been in some degree responsible for the attitude which she had felt it her duty to adopt. Any other man would have had to pay a far greater price, and Gladstone would, in fact, have been content to pay it. All his life, in a spirit of simple and unaffected humility, he did his best to reconcile a nineteenth-century political career with the Gospel and example of his Saviour.

*   *   *

Lord Derby resigned immediately after the rejection of Disraeli's Budget. Gladstone told his wife that Derby's speech in the Lords had been as petulant as Disraeli's, in the Commons, had been admirable and discreet. Lord Aberdeen was summoned to form a Coalition administration, and feeling in the Carlton Club ran high. Gladstone was sitting there, reading quietly after dinner on 22 December, when a group of young men who had dined well began to bait him. They threatened to throw him across the road into the Reform Club, where they told him that he belonged. An account of the incident appeared next day in *The Times*. Gladstone wrote to his wife to assure her that he had taken no harm.

Lord Aberdeen's administration became known as the ' Government of All the Talents '. Lord John Russell, the Liberal leader, was Foreign Secretary ; Lord Palmerston was Home Secretary ; Sir James Graham was First Lord of the Admiralty ; and Gladstone succeeded Disraeli as Chancellor of the Exchequer. On paper, it seemed a brilliant affair, and if it had not stumbled in a very short time into war, it might have lasted for many years.

Gladstone's first contribution was to raise the influence and prestige of the Chancellor's office. Before that time it had not been, as it then became, and has since remained, the second most important place in the Cabinet. In the by-election at Oxford which was caused by his acceptance of office, Gladstone obtained a small majority over a son of Spencer Perceval, the Prime Minister who had been assassinated in 1812.

Gladstone, who was now sitting for the first time in a Cabinet with Liberals, had at once to prepare a Budget to replace that of Disraeli which he had destroyed. He moved into 11 Downing Street, (at that time it was numbered 12) on 3 February, 1853, to the accompaniment of an unhappy correspondence with Disraeli about payments due in respect of official furniture and the Chancellor's robes. The correspondence began quite amicably in the first person, but ended acidly, in the third. On 6 March, 1853, Disraeli wrote with strange discourtesy :

' Mr. Disraeli is unwilling to prolong this correspondence. As Mr. Gladstone seems to be in some perplexity . . . Mr. Disraeli recommends him to consult Sir Charles Wood, who is at least a man of the world.'

Sir Charles was First Commissioner of Works. The next day Gladstone wrote that he had read Disraeli's note ' with regret and pain '. He had, he said, tried ' to observe towards Mr. Disraeli the courtesy which is his due, and he is not aware of having said or done anything to justify the tone which Mr. Disraeli has thought proper to adopt '.

Both men did their best, but their mutual antipathy was ineradicable. Disraeli had a case about the furniture, but no justification at all for his action in refusing to transfer the Chancellor's robes. He clung to them because he believed that they had been worn by Pitt ; and he made them an heirloom in his family.

On 18 April, 1853, Gladstone introduced his first Budget. It was based, like all his Budgets, on a foundation of ruthless economy in all departments of public expenditure. Speaking of his master, Peel, Gladstone once observed, smacking his lips, 'He was a rigid economist! Oh, he was a most rigid economist!' But he was as strict with himself at all times as he was with others. He was scrupulous in making sure that the State paid only its proper share of the expenditure on his official house, even to the smallest items. He used, for example, the same notepaper for his private as for his official correspondence. But he insisted on paying for all the notepaper which he used for any purpose that he did not regard as in the strictest sense official. One of his first actions as Chancellor was to compel the Foreign Office to abandon its practice of using large thick sheets of double notepaper, when single thinner sheets would suffice.

Gladstone was by nature a generous man, but he loathed waste, because he regarded all money as a trust committed by God to man. It is noticeable that even when writing letters from Hawarden, Gladstone did not make use of the fine embossed notepaper on which his brother-in-law, Sir Stephen Glynne, habitually wrote. Mrs. Gladstone once apologized (22 February, 1858) in a letter to her husband, for using it : 'How pompous of me,' she said, 'to write upon this grand paper to you !' As the national prosperity increased, Gladstone constantly expressed his dismay at the growth and spread of personal luxury and extravagance. At Hawarden there was a decent sufficiency, but the place was not run on luxurious lines. Even when he went to stay at Windsor or Balmoral, Gladstone could not sometimes refrain from complaining to his wife, as on 7 May, 1871, about his 'hatred of the fine sheets'.

In his Budget of 1853, Gladstone asked the House to agree to a prolongation of the intensely unpopular income-tax. He planned that it should stand at sevenpence in the pound for two years ; at sixpence for two years after that ; and at threepence for three further years. He said that in 1860 he believed that Parliament would find it possible to dispense with it. He explained his view that the income-tax was, in its essence, immoral. It tempted statesmen to extravagance ; it tempted the taxpayer to practise fraudulent evasions, 'which it would not be possible to characterise in terms too strong'. Its proper use was to serve as a potential reserve in case of war. He intended to continue the income-tax for a period of seven years only, in order to effect another great slash at the customs duties. He proposed to remove the duty altogether on 123 articles, and to

reduce it on a further 133. That would assist the nation's wealth to
'fructify in the pockets of the people'.

Gladstone at the same time persuaded the House to extend the
existing legacy duty to all successions to property, real or personal.
He thereby, for the first time, incurred the hostility and distrust of
the upper classes. The whole Cabinet opposed him when he
announced his intention, but he had worked fourteen hours a day
at his Budget, and his determination carried the day. He forced it
through the Cabinet, and through the House.

That Budget earned Gladstone an immense popular acclaim.
Charles Greville noted in his diary : ' It has raised Gladstone to a great
political elevation, and, what is of far greater consequence than the
measure itself, it has given the country the assurance of a *man* equal
to great political necessities, and fit to lead Parties and direct Governments.' Lord John Russell told the Queen that Gladstone was as
persuasive as Pitt, and that he had delivered one of the most powerful
financial statements ever heard in the House of Commons. The
Prince Consort, writing to congratulate Gladstone (19 April), sent
him a copy of Lord John's letter to the Queen, trusting that his
' Christian humility' would not be hurt. In reply to a letter of
congratulation from Lady Peel, Gladstone wrote that he had been
inspired by a desire to tread, however unequally, in the steps of his
great teacher and master.

The laurels had not yet begun to wither on Gladstone's brow,
when war-clouds appeared ominously and suddenly upon the horizon.
The occasion was trivial—a dispute in Palestine between some Greek
Orthodox and some Roman Catholic monks about the custody of
some Christian shrines. But the cause was a clash between the Russian
desire to expand southward, into the decaying corpse of the Turkish
Empire, and the unformulated but growing feeling of alarm in Great
Britain, with her Indian commitments, at the vast size of the Russian
Empire, which was constantly expanding into Asia, and increasing its
armaments.

The Russians, espousing the cause of the Greek Orthodox monks,
ended by presenting an ultimatum to the Turks. It demanded not
merely satisfaction in Jerusalem, but a virtual protectorate over the
Sultan's Christian subjects in the Balkans.

Gladstone was not a member of the inner circle of the Cabinet,
but he never sought to evade, and, indeed, he rather tended to take
too much to heart, his share of the responsibility for the Crimean

War. Louis Napoleon, the Emperor of the French, who had espoused the cause of the Roman Catholic monks, was anxious, even at the cost of war with Russia, to overcome British suspicions of his dictatorial regime, and to cement an alliance with the power which had overthrown the founder of his dynasty. Gladstone never cared to allow that Great Britain had drifted into war, but Lord Aberdeen was not in complete control of his Cabinet. He was known to be personally favourable to peace at almost any price, and the Russians assumed that he would not interfere. He showed weakness at the outset, when firmness might have succeeded, and he employed threats while the last attempts at conciliation were being made.

War between Russia and Turkey began in October, 1853. Gladstone still hoped that the Cabinet would be able to resist the popular clamour for intervention on the side of the Turks. But the destruction of most of the Turkish fleet off Sinope, on 30 November, raised anti-Russian sentiment in Great Britain to fever-pitch, and the Prince Consort was made the scapegoat of the national hysteria. He was believed to be pro-Russian, and a campaign was waged against him by the Press. Gladstone contributed an anonymous article to the *Morning Chronicle* (16 January, 1854), in the Prince's defence.

On 22 February, 1854, when war was already inevitable, Lord Aberdeen sent for Gladstone. He asked if Gladstone thought that it would be possible for him to resign before war was formally declared. He said, Gladstone noted, that ' all along he had been acting against his feelings . . . He asked, "How could he bring himself to fight for the Turks ? " I said we were not fighting for the Turks, but we were warning Russia off the forbidden ground . . . He said, if I saw a way for him to get out, he hoped I would mention it to him. I replied that . . . I felt such a horror of bloodshed, that I had thought the matter over incessantly . . .'

Gladstone's view, which he explained somewhat imperfectly to the Prime Minister, was that Great Britain had a right, if not a duty, to assume, as a mission, the defence of the Christian peoples under Turkish misrule in the Balkans. That right, and that duty, were both derived from the public law of Europe, which had been perverted and abused when Russia took it into her own hands in pursuit of selfish ends. He would not willingly contribute to a continuance of the anomaly of the rule of a Mohammedan despot over twelve million Christians. But he was prepared to engage in war until the public law of Europe had been vindicated, and not for a day longer.

By a decision which Gladstone said had 'rather stunned' him, the British fleet had been ordered (22 December, 1853) to enter the Black Sea and blockade Sevastopol. Negotiations continued for two months more, but in anticipation of war, Gladstone, on 6 March, 1854, doubled the income-tax. He raised it from sevenpence to one shilling and twopence, in his Budget. He told the House, sternly :

' The expenses of war are a moral check, which it has pleased the Almighty to impose upon the ambition and lust of conquest that are inherent in so many nations.'

That was not a popular argument on the lips of a Chancellor who was responsible for raising money to carry to a victorious conclusion a war for which the nation was loudly calling. And after war was declared on Russia (27 March, 1854), Gladstone was compelled, in an Emergency Budget (8 May), to borrow money on Exchequer Bonds. He did his best to meet the cost by taxes rather than by loans, but he wrote to his wife (28 March) : ' War ! War ! War ! . . . I fear it will swallow up everything good and useful.' He told her the next day : ' We do not yet know the real meaning of the word.'

CHAPTER 6

INTO THE WILDERNESS
1854–1859

GLADSTONE gave generous praise to those who served him well, but he was inclined to plume himself on his ferocity. On 29 April, 1854, he dismissed T. F. Kennedy, Commissioner of Woods and Forests, for bringing discredit upon his office through his inability to manage men, and for an act of injustice towards a loyal subordinate. Lord John Russell thought that the dismissal had been harsh, and it was debated in the Commons on 27 February, 1855. Kennedy was a Privy Councillor, and Gladstone said that he did not doubt his veracity, integrity, or honour ; but the dismissal stood, and the records of the case in the Treasury attest the soundness of Gladstone's decision.

On 3 August, 1854, the House of Commons was told by Sir George Grey, the Secretary for the Colonies, that Gladstone had dismissed his Parliamentary Private Secretary, the Hon. F. Lawley, and that Lawley's appointment as Governor of South Australia, which had recently been announced, was also cancelled. Lawley, a Fellow of All Souls, who was a son of Lord Wenlock and a cousin of Mrs. Gladstone, had been gambling in the Funds. Gladstone admitted in the House that Lawley had made no use of official information, and that he had incurred heavy financial loss, but he insisted that an example should be made because it would be reasonable for the public to suppose that Lawley had made use of secret official information.

Sir George Grey went on to inform the House that Lawley had been addicted to 'the turf', and that he had accepted his secretaryship with Gladstone in order 'to engage himself in higher and more useful pursuits'. He had, at Gladstone's suggestion, applied for and accepted the governorship of South Australia at the age of twenty-nine in order to put himself for a time 'beyond the reach of temptation'. Although Gladstone insisted that Lawley should be publicly broken, he told the House that he still took 'a warm and affectionate interest' in his future. Lawley resigned his seat in Parliament and went at once to the United States as correspondent for *The Times* ; he later joined the staff of the *Daily Telegraph*. He always remained on terms of intimacy with Gladstone's family. Treasury records show that on 29 August, 1854, at Gladstone's request, £300 was paid to Lawley out of the

Secret Service Fund as a reward for his services. He had received £100 a short time before from the same source.

That Gladstone did not always judge harshly is proved by some jingling verses which he circulated at this time among his friends on the fall of George Hudson, the great railroad promoter :

> He bamboozled the mob ; he bamboozled the quality ;
> He led both through the quagmire of gross immorality.
>
> . . . .
>
> The world in its vices is cruel, I wis.
> But the world in its virtue—God save me from this !

Loathing everything that concerned the war in the Crimea, Gladstone sought solace by throwing himself into the causes of University and Civil Service reform. He had strongly opposed Lord John Russell's action in appointing a Royal Commission to inquire into the affairs of Oxford. But after its Report was published (May, 1852), he realized that the government of the University needed to be reconstituted ; and, at some risk to his seat, he undertook to prepare a Bill. He was assisted by Benjamin Jowett, among others, and he preserved copies of no less than 350 letters written in his own hand on this subject between December, 1853, and December, 1854. The Bill was introduced in March, 1854, a few days before the outbreak of war, and it effected a quiet revolution in Oxford life. University and College government became representative ; appointments were thrown open to competition ; power was given to alter trusts, and to require the production of documents and accounts. Religious tests were abolished in respect of candidates for matriculation or for a Bachelor's degree ; but they were retained in all other cases. Gladstone hotly resented the attempts which Disraeli made to sabotage that Bill, and the flippant language which his rival sometimes employed deliberately in order to provoke him.

At the same time Gladstone did his best to throw the Home Civil Service open to competition. He sketched out in some detail a division between what he called the intellectual and the mechanical parts of the Service, and he argued that the time had come to put an end to the practice of filling the ' intellectual ' part of the Service by jobbery. He told Lord John Russell (20 January, 1854) that in open competition the upper class would, on the average, prove superior to the rest of the nation, and that the time had come to give ' a new and striking sign of rational confidence in the intelligence and character of the people '.

On 7 February, 1854, the Queen wrote to ask Gladstone where he proposed that ' the application of the principle of public competition is to stop'. He replied with a memorandum which extorted the Queen's reluctant consent (17 February) after its meaning had been explained to her by the Prince Consort. She begged Gladstone to try to devise some commonsense method of ensuring that candidates should possess practical qualifications, ' besides the display of knowledge which they may exhibit under examination '. She would have preferred a test of character, but Gladstone assured her that :

' experience at the Universities and Public Schools of this country has shown that in a large majority of cases the test of open examination is also an effectual test of character . . . The previous industry and self-denial . . . are rarely separated from general habits of virtue.'

The Indian Civil Service had been thrown open to competition in 1853, but the process of reform in the Home Civil Service was gradual. For some years the right to sit for examinations was restricted to candidates nominated by patronage. Not until 1870, when Gladstone was Prime Minister, was entrance to all major branches of the Service except the Foreign Office thrown open to unrestricted competition.

Gladstone might have been better advised to pay less attention to those two academic subjects, and to think more about the war which was being badly mismanaged by the Government of which he was a prominent member. During the winter of 1854-5 all organization seemed to collapse, and the British Expeditionary Force in the Crimea found itself short of tents, huts, boots, knapsacks, suitable food, and even medical supplies. More casualties were inflicted by scurvy than by the Russians, and the plight of the sick and wounded, despite Florence Nightingale's efforts, was pitiful. There was a rude and prolonged public outcry when the facts became known, and ' the blood-red blossom of war ', which Alfred Tennyson, in his popular poem, *Maud*, had blindly and ecstatically hailed, was proved to be a miserable plant. Among those killed in action were two first cousins of Mrs. Gladstone—Grey and Henry Neville, sons of Lord Braybrooke. The relations between Hawarden Castle and Audley End were so close that they had been more like brothers than cousins.

On 23 January, 1855, John Roebuck, a Radical of Canadian extraction, gave notice of a Motion for a Committee of Inquiry into the condition of the Army in the Crimea, and into the conduct of Government Departments responsible for ministering to its needs. Lord John

Russell told the Prime Minister that, in his opinion, no defence was possible ; and he resigned. Gladstone considered that Lord John had deserted his post, but both men realized that trouble had arisen because the reforming spirit, which had been breathed during recent years into the Church, and into many Departments of State, had left the War Office, and the Horse Guards, untouched. Gladstone was left with a sore conscience about the Crimea for the rest of his life. But he had to undertake the uncongenial duty of replying to Roebuck's Motion, and he made a brilliant debating speech. He described the Motion as mischievous, unprecedented, unconstitutional, and said that the appointment of a Committee would lead to nothing but confusion at home and increased disaster abroad. It was to no purpose, for the Motion was carried by a two-thirds majority. With a sigh of inexpressible relief Lord Aberdeen announced (30 January) his Government's resignation. Gladstone remarked to his chief that they had fallen ' with such a whack ' that ' they could hear their heads thump as they struck the ground '.

The departure of ' poor dear Aberdeen ', as the Queen described him, ' whom I am so deeply grieved to lose ', precipitated a crisis which lasted, with intervals, for a month. Lord Derby tried first to form a Coalition Government, but neither Lord Palmerston nor the Peelites were willing to serve in it, although they undertook to give it ' independent support '.

Instead of trying to form a homogeneous Conservative Government, Lord Derby, to Disraeli's disgust and dismay, asked the Queen to send for someone else. Gladstone considered that Lord Derby had shown a great want of political courage, and certainly his Party paid dearly for that gross blunder during the next two decades. If he had formed a Government, the country would have been united behind him, but he was afraid. Gladstone noted that Derby was too intellectual and unpractical : ' It was not the gambling-table, or the race-course ; it was not even the deer forest or the battue which had charms for his ripening years. His idolatry, if he had one, was an idolatry for blue-books.' He noted also that ' a sentiment of revulsion from Disraeli personally—a sentiment quite distinct from that of dislike, was alone sufficient to deter me absolutely from a merely personal and separate reunion ' with the Conservatives.

That nice distinction was characteristic, but Gladstone understood what Disraeli must be feeling as Lord Derby turned his back on the crisis and cast away his great opportunity. Meeting Disraeli casually in the House of Lords on 1 February, Gladstone put out his hand, which, he recorded, 'was very kindly accepted'.

On that day the Queen sent for Lord Lansdowne, an elderly Whig, who asked Gladstone to see him (2 February). In the course of that interview, Gladstone himself committed what he was inclined to regard as the most gross, although not the silliest, error of his life. He refused to serve in any Government which Lord Lansdowne formed.

Gladstone's judgement was overborne by anxiety about his Tory seat at Oxford. He had alarmed his constituents by his enthusiasm for University reform, and it might have looked odd to accept office from the hands of a Whig immediately after refusing it from those of a Conservative. He recorded that he would have been happy to continue to serve with Whigs and Radicals in a Peelite Government, but that he could not agree to serve, with or without Peelites, in a Liberal Government. He felt that Lord Aberdeen had been roughly treated, and he begged Lord Lansdowne to try to form a homogeneous Liberal Government. He thought that he had understood Lord Lansdowne to say that he would abandon any attempt to form a Government if Gladstone declined to join it.

Three days later (5 February), after Lord John Russell had tried to form a Government and failed, Lord Aberdeen called the Peelites together. He told them that they must put the country's need before their private inclinations, and that they ought to serve with Lord Palmerston, the nation's idol. Very reluctantly, Gladstone consented. But he could hardly bear to reflect upon the evident inconsistency between his refusal to serve with Lord Lansdowne, a man of the highest character, on 2 February, and his acceptance of office four days later, in the Cabinet of a man whom he described to Sir Stephen Glynne as being entirely 'without convictions of duty . . . who systematic-ally panders to whatever is questionable or base in the public mind'. In his distress, he wrote to Lord Aberdeen : 'You are not to be in the Cabinet, but you will be its tutelary deity.' He told Harriet, Duchess of Sutherland (6 February, 1855), the Queen's Mistress of the Robes, whom he had begun to make into a confidante, that he bitterly regretted his severance from Lord Aberdeen, 'whom I love like a father, while I reverence him almost like a being from another world'.

Lord Palmerston, who was then aged seventy-one, carried a breath of the Regency into the evangelical atmosphere of the mid-nineteenth century. He was almost as tough, physically, as Gladstone, and he was destined to remain Prime Minister, with one brief interlude for the next eleven years. Even Disraeli, who was as sore, for a different reason, as Gladstone, at the turn which events had taken, grossly underestimated the quality of the new Prime Minister He told Lady Londonderry (2 February) that Lord Palmerston was an impostor : ' At the best only ginger-beer and not champagne ; and now an old painted pantaloon, very deaf, very blind, and with false teeth which would fall out of his mouth if he did not hesitate, and halt so, in his talk.'

The need to come to terms with the values which Lord Palmerston appeared to symbolize in public life, was a lesson which Gladstone never wholly learned. He quarrelled with Lord Palmerston and resigned from his Government after a fortnight. The occasion was Roebuck's Committee of Inquiry, which Lord Palmerston had hoped to sidetrack by sending, in substitution for it, a Government Commission to the seat of war. Whipped up by Disraeli, the House of Commons insisted upon the formal appointment of a Committee of the whole House within the terms of Roebuck's Resolution. Three Peelites, who held, under Palmerston, the offices which they had formerly held under Lord Aberdeen, resigned, in consequence, on 22 February. They were Gladstone (Chancellor of the Exchequer), Sir James Graham (First Lord of the Admiralty), and Sidney Herbert (Secretary for War). Other Peelites remained at their posts, and the fresh impetus thus given to the gradual disintegration of the group was the only satisfactory aspect of a most ill-judged decision.

With admirable *sang-froid*, Lord Palmerston reconstructed his Government, while Gladstone, in his intense way, explained to the Queen that Parliament's encroachment upon the Executive represented a menace to the Throne. The Queen complained to the King of the Belgians that her three best men had resigned, from the purest of motives : ' The good people here are really a little *mad*, but I am certain it *will* right itself.' It did ; but Gladstone's reputation was, temporarily, blasted. His action was regarded as irresponsible, cowardly, unpatriotic. His speech of explanation made no impression upon the House, and he was accused of running away from the Committee of Inquiry after having helped to mismanage the war. His fall was great, and it was widely celebrated. He appeared to have resigned once too often, and for the first time in his life he found himself so unpopular that he was occasionally insulted by strangers in the streets.

Instead of remaining quiet, and allowing the storm to blow itself out, Gladstone began to agitate for a negotiated peace on the basis of the Czar's offer (in the spring of 1855) to substitute a collective European guarantee of the rights of the Sultan's Christian subjects in the Balkans, for a Russian protectorate.[1] He denounced the Government's decision to continue the war until Sevastopol was stormed and until the Russians were prepared to agree to the neutralization of the Black Sea. He told the Duke of Argyll (21 August, 1855), a Peelite who had remained in the Government, that the music of his cannon was delighting the ears of the middle class which arrogantly called itself the nation. He argued that Russian aggression had been checked ; that the public law of Europe had been vindicated ; and that Lord Palmerston was pandering to a base lust for conquest. Gladstone's voice was joined to those of the Radicals, Cobden and Bright, so that even his intimates became uneasy. Sidney Herbert, who had lately become his most intimate friend, begged Gladstone to remember that the British were a race of flesh and blood, and not a congress of professors of moral philosophy.

Gladstone had no use for such arguments, and he continued to press for peace by negotiation. His influence had almost evaporated, and the Press described him as a traitor, a pious fanatic, or a conceited clown. The Duke of Beaufort made an abortive attempt to procure his expulsion from the Carlton Club. Gladstone was not sensitive, and he wrote (9 August, 1855) to Lord Aberdeen :

' It was a charitable act on your part to write to me. It is hardly possible to believe that one is not the greatest scoundrel on earth, when one is assured of it on all sides on such excellent authority.' He added that he was reading Homer's account of ' the Sevastopol of old time '. He had been driven, for a period, into the wilderness, and in the simplicity of his heart he found an absorbing interest there.

When Sevastopol fell at last, in September, 1855, Gladstone was with his family at Penmaenmawr, on the Welsh coast. He was working on a study of *Homer and the Homeric Age*, which was published in three volumes by the Oxford Press in March, 1858. In

[1] In his innermost heart, Gladstone cherished a hope which had sprung up in many a devout breast, since the start of the Oxford Movement. He longed for a union between the Anglican and the Russian and other Eastern Orthodox Churches. They had much in common, including their denial of the Pope's supremacy ; and although the retention of the *Filioque* clause in the Anglican Creed was one insurmountable bar, the war impeded correspondence and informal conversations which Gladstone relished.

advising his friend O. B. Cole (13 August, 1858) to begin with the third volume, because it was possibly the least unreadable, he said that although he knew that he lacked any true critical faculty he had been driven on by a passion for his subject, and by the belief that he ' might and *should* do good in another way '.

That last phrase is significant. Thereafter, until the end of his life, Gladstone continued to pour out a succession of books and articles about Homer, and about different aspects of Greek history and manners. It is unthinkable that a man with Gladstone's sense of dedication would have permitted himself the luxury of so prolonged a course of work and study if he had regarded it as no more than a scholarly recreation. As such it is practically worthless, for it sheds hardly any light upon Homer. But upon Gladstone's aims and methods it sheds a powerful beam.

Gladstone's main purpose was religious. When he started to write about Homer he ceased to compose sermons for the edification of his household on Sundays at family prayers. He may have felt that 200 sermons provided him with a repertoire sufficient for all emergencies. But it is more likely that he felt that the time had come to widen his field of operations. In his Hellenic studies he tried to analyse the nature of God's Revelation of Himself to the Greeks in Homer, and to relate it to the Revelation which had been vouchsafed to the Jews in the Bible. For that purpose, with daring and wilful ingenuity, and with an extravagant fancifulness which bewildered scholars, Gladstone put the Greeks where the Evangelicals put the Jews, and Homer where they put the Old Testament. He claimed that God had used the Jews to teach man how he should behave towards God, and that He had used the Greeks to teach him how he should behave towards his fellow-men.

In the second volume of his *Homer and the Homeric Age* Gladstone charged the Jews with having hidden the Divine Revelation in a napkin. It was not they who had supplied Christian civilization with laws, arts, science, or with models of greatness in genius or in character : ' The Providence of God committed this work to others ; and to Homer seems to have been entrusted the first, which was perhaps, all things considered, the greatest stage of it.'

With inimitable patience Gladstone laboriously worked out his theory in a large number of published works over a long period of years. He widened his conception of Christianity to embrace not merely the Bible, and the tradition of the Church, but the whole tradition of art, literature, and politics which was mainly Greek in origin, and which had contributed to the Christian Revelation and became inextricably associated with it. The spirit in which he wrote was sublime in some respects, but in others it was reminiscent of the way in which certain individuals try to uncover a Divine message from the details of the architectural construction of the Great Pyramid.

Gladstone conveniently and succinctly summarized his views in an address which he gave on 3 November, 1865, at Edinburgh University, on *The Place of the Greeks in the Providential Order of the World* :

' I submit to you that the true . . . rearing and training of mankind for the Gospel was not confined to that eminent and conspicuous part of it which is represented by the dispensations given to the Patriarchs and the Jews, but likewise extends to other fields of human history and experience . . . It is quite plain that the Greeks have their place in the Providential order, ay, in the Evangelical preparation, as truly and really as the children of Abraham themselves.' The Greek mind was, Gladstone declared, ' the secular counterpart of the Gospel'. Christianity was the salt ; ' the thing salted ' was Greek civilization. Each had its appointed place in God's plan for the world, and Gladstone recommended his audience to fortify its faith by ' tracing the footmarks of the Most High in the seemingly bewildered paths of human history '. He argued that it was wrong to assume that the Jews had been the only chosen people. Was not Balaam, the Moabite, a Prophet inspired by God ? Did not two of the minor Prophetical Books of the Old Testament deal with the affairs of Nineveh ? Were not wise men from the East directed to be the first worshippers of our Saviour ?

Such ingenious and ingenuous arguments provoked smiles in some quarters and irritation in others. Jowett said, impatiently, that a man who claimed to have found the doctrine of the Trinity foreshadowed in Homer must be crazy. Gladstone wrote many scores of thousands of words in an effort to prove that authentic glimmerings of divinity were discernible in the pagan gods of ancient Greece ; and his attempt to catholicize Hellenism and to canonize Homer was a gesture of defiance on the part of a theologian at bay. Gladstone's mind was not profound ; but it was extraordinarily sensitive. He realized that new methods of comparative criticism were tending to emphasize the common elements in all religions rather than the unique aspects of Christianity. He therefore used those common elements to buttress his claim that Christianity was the culminating fact in a perpetual struggle between God and the Devil which pervaded all history and all politics. In that struggle Christianity represented the strategy of God, but every age had its particular tactical needs. Gladstone's contribution to the tactical need of the nineteenth century was to enlist the Olympian deities on the side of Christ. By that means he sought to check the rising tide of unbelief and indifference and to form a common front in which Christians of all kinds could fight side by side with enlightened pre-Christians, and with non-Christians.

In that way Gladstone passed his time in the wilderness. But he also derived very great happiness from his family life. Besides Hawarden Castle, Hagley Hall where his brother-in-law Lord Lyttelton lived was a second home to all Gladstone's family. There were seven Gladstone children and twelve young Lytteltons. Great confluences of the two families used to come together at intervals, and both families lived much as one. The Dowager Lady Lyttelton was a daughter of Earl Spencer ; the Hon. Lady Glynne (mother of Mrs. Gladstone) was a daughter of Lord Braybrooke. Althorp and Audley End were therefore two other great houses within the immediate orbit of the Lytteltons and the Gladstones. The young Lytteltons were effervescent and impatient of restraint ; the young Gladstones were diffident and mindful of authority. But they all loved cricket, and other games ; and they all took an unaffected interest in literature, music, religion, and good works. Above all, they had complete freedom to discuss and criticize all subjects, grave or gay.

Althorp and Audley End were run on luxury lines ; but a note of simplicity, almost amounting to austerity, characterized both Hawarden Castle and Hagley Hall. Neither the Gladstones nor the Lytteltons were very wealthy. Lord Lyttelton, a Fellow of the Royal Society, was almost as fine a classical scholar as Gladstone. He translated *Comus* and *Samson Agonistes* into Greek, and his home was the centre of the social and intellectual life of Worcestershire. During his later years he suffered from bouts of melancholia, during the last of which, in 1876, he committed suicide by throwing himself over the banisters on to the marble floor below. Gladstone always regretted that he had not persuaded his brother-in-law to translate Homer into English verse. He thought that the mental discipline which such a task would have necessitated might have sufficed to avert that disaster.

The Lytteltons and the Gladstones were so numerous and devoted, so quick, eager, and vital, that for many purposes they felt themselves to be self-sufficient. They invented a kind of language for themselves which was formally embodied by Lord Lyttelton, in 1851, in a glossary [1] which was privately printed. It was entitled *Contributions Towards a Glossary of the Glynne Language, by a Student* (*George William, Lord Lyttelton*). In the introduction, the language was described as 'probably indigenous' in the marches of North Wales; and the names of its chief living exponents were given as the Dean of Windsor, Mrs. W. E. Gladstone, The Hon. Lady Glynne, Sir Stephen Glynne, and Lady Lyttelton. The language was in use on such occasions as that described by the Hon. Lucy Lyttelton (later Lady Frederick Cavendish) in her diary for 1857, when she was in her sixteenth year:

Hagley, 1 January, 1857: The whole tribe of Gladstones poured into the house to-day, and we make up the goodly number of eighteen children under 17 . . .

Hagley, 2 and 3 January, 1857. Willy and Stephy [Gladstone] turned up. The dear old house is choked, overflowing, echoing with children. The meals are the fun . . . The noise pervading the room as much from scolders as scolded, from bellowers as bellowed at, from children, boys, women, girls, may be imagined, mingled with clatter of crockery, pouring of tea, hewing of bread, and scrumping of jaws.

Hagley, 4 and 5 January, 1857. Oh, the whirlpool of excitement we are fizzing in . . .'

A few examples will give some idea of the nature of the Glynnese language. A full and formal example is given in the Appendix.

'Bathing-feel'—the state of mind previous to some rather formidable undertaking. *Example*: when Mr. Gladstone was asked in 1841 how he felt on becoming Vice-President of the Board of Trade, he had so far advanced in the language that he was able to reply, '*Bathing-feel*'.

'I died'—a murderous metaphor denoting amusement. *Example*: Mrs. Gladstone: 'William this morning sang a tipsy song to amuse little Mary—I *died*.'

'Quite an old shoe'—an old friend.

'A witch'—half-dressed. *Example*: Mrs. Gladstone: 'Seymour Neville came up and found me *a witch*.'

'Over the moon'—high spirits.

'To shoot'—to discover someone or something rapidly.

[1] It was privately reprinted by John Murray in 1904.

Example : The Dean of Windsor : ' Last night I shot the Bishop of London in a corner at the Queen's party.'
' A face '—an uninvited or self-invited guest.

Gladstone, who loved to hear Glynnese spoken, did not often use that language himself; but Mrs. Gladstone used it on every possible occasion. It is on record that once, when her husband was Prime Minister, she hobbled into the Cabinet Room at Downing Street, as the meeing was breaking up, to announce that she had pulled a muscle in her leg : " Such a quiz, William. I've sprouted a lameness ! "

To all the Lyttelton children Mrs. Gladstone was known as A.P. (Aunt Pussie). But the children of both families were equally devoted to Gladstone. They were impressed, when they were very young, by his great physical strength. He would sometimes carry four of them at a time on his back, even when they had grown quite big.

They all recognized, of course, that Gladstone was exceedingly busy, and that there were many times when he could not be disturbed. But he won children's affection not only because he loved them, but because he treated them naturally and courteously as equals. He earned their confidence by his scrupulous fairness. And, presently, his character, and the strict system upon which his life was regulated, secured their reverence.

That system was based on two fixed principles : conservation of time for the discharge of duty, and avoidance of waste, because extravagance meant squandering a trust from God. Gladstone was sometimes laughed at in his family because he seemed to make an excessive fuss about his health. A minor cold, or a bilious attack, was treated with the utmost seriousness, but that was not because he was a valetudinarian. He considered it his duty to avoid the waste of time which would result if he became ill. And for that reason he wrapped himself up and was cosseted by Mrs. Gladstone all his life. Again, in London, if his carriage were not available, he would practically never take a cab. He would walk, and credit his health account with the loss of time which that exercise involved. His passion for economy extended to quite small details. In every desk which he used, there was always one drawer which contained nothing but half-sheets of notepaper, coiled bits of string, and the edgings of stamps.

At Hawarden, which Gladstone liked to call ' Liberty Hall ', all children enjoyed unfettered freedom to discuss any subject under the sun. Gladstone reproduced the atmosphere which he had enjoyed, as a child, in his father's houses ; and strangers sometimes considered that he was treated with scant respect in his home. He encouraged his children to catch him out, if they could ; and grave and earnest visitors were sometimes disconcerted to hear some chance remark of the great man greeted with childish shouts of, ' A lie ! A lie ! '

Whether there were a house party, or whether the family were alone, Gladstone was always in everything the central figure. But Sir Stephen Glynne, while he lived, was, of course, the nominal host. Most of Gladstone's time, apart from meals, was spent in his library, which was known as the *Temple of Peace* ; and the great object of his children and of his friends was to entice him away from it in the afternoons and evenings. Often those efforts were successful, and Gladstone then invariably became the centre of life and playfulness. In moments of special exhilaration he and Mrs. Gladstone would stand on the hearth-rug with arms round each other's waists, swaying to the words of a chorus which they intoned :

> A ragamuffin husband and a rantipoling wife,
> We'll fiddle it and scrape it through the ups and downs of life.

The absorbing passion of Gladstone's life, and the source of all his strength, was unaffectedly displayed to his household. A big Bible lay open on his dressing table, and he invariably read from it as he dressed and undressed. He did not try to force religion upon his children, but they knew that he liked them to consult him about points of difficulty, and they sometimes did so. Daily family prayers were a part of Gladstone's routine, and on Sundays the whole family went twice to church. When his eldest son, William, left Eton in 1855 and went up to Christ Church, Oxford, Gladstone implored him (11 October) not to allow himself to be upset by the bitter controversies which were raging there as a result of the introduction of ' new and disturbing ideas ' in science and religion. When rightly encountered the spirit of controversy, like that of rash speculation, and of all other evils, could be turned to God's purpose. Controversy should inspire charity ; speculation should deepen faith. It was vital to concentrate at all seasons upon the supreme object of man's journey through the world, ' the recovery of the image of God, as shown unto us in our Lord, Jesus Christ '.

From that height, Gladstone for some years looked down doubtfully and unhappily upon the rival 'infections' of Palmerston and Disraeli. He was completely isolated, and plain men everywhere, as well as acute critics, like Walter Bagehot, began, with growing insistence, to ask whether, despite his splendid gifts, Gladstone was capable of reconciling his delicate mind with political reality, and with the fact that anything so coarse as war could exist. Gladstone considered that each of the two main Parties contained within itself greater diversities than those which divided the more moderate Conservatives from the more moderate Liberals. He longed for office, and for an end to his period of political ineffectiveness. He noted in his diary (31 December, 1856) that he was by no means ready to give up the world if it should please God to call him at that time. Politics and the Church held him in an 'invisible net of pendent steel'. Literature had 'of late acquired a new and powerful hold' upon him. The fortunes of his wife's family still, after nine years, held for him ' with all their dry detail, all the most exciting and arduous interest of romance'. Lastly, his seven children were each day the object of deeper thoughts and feelings, and of higher hopes. The whole difficulty was to discover in politics a possible means of evoking the response which his nature craved. But the time was near when he would have to make up his mind either to abandon his political career, or to come down firmly upon the one side or the other.

In the meantime, like a high-mettled horse, Gladstone shied equally at the prospect of wearing Conservative or Liberal harness. Peace abroad and economy at home were his two political objects. Neither seemed likely to be realized under Lord Palmerston. Early in 1856 Lord Derby made overtures to Gladstone, and those overtures were frequently renewed. Gladstone consulted his friends, Sidney Herbert, Sir James Graham, Edward Cardwell, and Lord Aberdeen ; but the main difficulty was the personality of Disraeli, and the overtures were always rejected. Gladstone's friends felt that Lord Derby had contracted relations with Disraeli which could never be disowned ; that Disraeli could not be dislodged, without his consent, from the leadership of the Conservative Party in the Commons ; and that Gladstone, if he rejoined that Party, would never possess its full confidence or goodwill.

Nevertheless, early in 1857, Gladstone and Disraeli were united in violent opposition to Lord Palmerston's policy in China. On the Canton River, a small vessel, Chinese-owned, but flying, with doubtful legality, the British flag, had been used for smuggling and piracy. It was seized by the Chinese authorities, and twelve Chinese members of its crew were imprisoned. The British Consul at Canton and the Governor of Hong Kong demanded redress and an apology. The vessel and the crew were released, but considerations of 'face' prevented the Chinese from apologizing. The Governor of Hong Kong summoned to his aid a squadron of the Royal Navy which bombarded Canton and killed many Chinese. Lord Palmerston, as soon as he heard the news, expressed satisfaction and accepted full responsibility.

Richard Cobden moved a Vote of Censure in the House of Commons. On 3 March, 1857, Gladstone supported it in a splendid speech which lasted for two hours. He denounced Lord Palmerston in the name of natural justice which was, he declared, older, and more extensive than Christianity, and even deeper than Christianity, because Christianity itself appealed to it. Palmerston retorted by accusing Gladstone of want of patriotic feeling. Had he not, seventeen years earlier, tried to justify the Chinese when they started to poison wells? Lord Clarendon, the Foreign Secretary, attributed Gladstone's action to a rabid lust for office. Cobden's motion was carried by 263 votes to 247 (3 March, 1857), and Lord Palmerston, believing that the middle class would support him, resigned office and appealed to the country. He secured a resounding triumph, and a majority of more than a hundred seats. Gladstone was unopposed at Oxford (27 March) but the pacifists were, for the most part, annihilated. Cobden and Bright were defeated, and even Sir Stephen Glynne lost his election in Flintshire. Gladstone was shocked and disgusted. He had to watch helplessly while a full-scale expedition was despatched to Pekin, where it burnt the Emperor's Summer Palace and extorted terms which were very wounding indeed to Chinese pride.

In July, 1857, Gladstone hurried from Hawarden to Westminster to oppose a Divorce Bill which the Government had introduced. The object was to facilitate divorce for the middle class by establishing a Divorce Court. Gladstone was infuriated on his journey to London by the action of a fellow-traveller in his railway compartment. This man—'more genial than congenial'—first offered Gladstone *The Times*, which was accepted. He then offered a nip of brandy, and finally tobacco. Gladstone's nerves were on edge and he preserved a frigid silence. But he told his wife that having accepted *The Times* in order to avoid conversation, he felt disabled from requesting his companion to refrain from smkoing.

The Divorce Bill kept Parliament in session throughout most of

August. Gladstone used every method, including obstruction, in a vain attempt to defeat the Bill. He argued, with passion, that marriage was indissoluble ; but his action in the affair of the Duke of Newcastle's divorce was brought up once more, and he had to make a personal statement (14 August). Divorce had hitherto been obtained by means of private Acts of Parliament, but Parliamentary time was becoming increasingly restricted. The method, moreover, was expensive, and open only to the wealthy. Gladstone ignored those objections. Years later, when, as Prime Minister, he had to wrestle with an extremely formidable problem of Parliamentary obstruction, the mild methods which he had employed against the Divorce Bill were recalled and flung in his face.

The only concession which Gladstone could extort was a provision that no beneficed clergyman should be required to marry divorced persons. The Bill itself, despite his efforts, became law. Gladstone considered that it had done more to confuse the relations between Church and State than all the Erastian legislation of the previous quarter of a century.

Before the Bill was passed, Mrs. Gladstone's sister, Lady Lyttelton, died (17 August) at Hagley, after the birth of her twelfth child. Private and public grief ate deeply into Gladstone's mind, and for some months he was deeply depressed. One crumb of comfort vouchsafed to him at this time was a friendship which had sprung up between his eldest son, William, and the young Prince of Wales. Willy went several times to stay at Windsor, and he was asked to stay with the Prince near Bonn, on the Rhine, in August, 1857. While he was there, Gladstone was scandalized to hear about ' a little squalid debauch ' in which the Prince had become involved. Forwarding Willy's letter to his wife, he said that it was evident that the Prince of Wales had ' not been educated up to his position . . . kept in childhood beyond his time, he is allowed to make that childhood what it should never be in a Prince, namely *wanton* . . . I rejoice that Willy's soul loathes the tuft-hunting'. Gladstone might possibly have been a happier man if he too had been capable of sowing a few harmless wild oats during his youth.

If it had not been for the Divorce Act, Gladstone would have crossed to the Continent to see his sister. He was gratified when she wrote to say that she had had an audience with the Pope, who had promised to pray for Gladstone ; and he told his brother Sir Thomas (12 June, 1857) that he thought that Helen had at last conquered her aversion from her family. All she needed now was to be roused, by the shock of occasional visits from home, out of her 'self-centred habits, and a kind of indolent indifference'.

On 20 February, 1858, Lord Palmerston's Government fell as a result of a false step by the Prime Minister. An attempt had been made on the life of the French Emperor, Napoleon III; and it was found that the plot had been hatched in England by refugees. The French Ambassador protested in terms which were not merely strong but insolent. Palmerston, however, appeared to feel no resentment. On the contrary, he introduced a Bill to strengthen the law against conspiracy. The patriotic mood, to which he had so often appealed successfully, turned against him overnight. A mob hooted him in Hyde Park; he was denounced in the Commons for truckling to the traditional enemies of his country; and the Conspiracy Bill itself was defeated on its Second Reading by 234 votes to 219. Gladstone voted against the Bill on the ground that it sought to establish 'a moral complicity between us, and those who take safety in repressive measures'. Eighty-four Liberals voted against the Government, and Lord Palmerston at once resigned.

The Queen sent for the Conservative leader, Lord Derby, who asked Gladstone to see him (21 February). But Gladstone would not join his Government. He had no faith in the stability of a Conservative Government, which would be in a minority in the House and, in all probability, in a much greater minority in the country. It could only exist on sufferance, and John Bright wrote to Gladstone (21 February, 1858):

'If you remain on our side of the House, you are with the majority, and no Government can be formed without you. You have many friends there . . . and I know nothing that can prevent your being Prime Minister before you approach the age of every other Member of the House who has, or can have, any claim to that high office . . . You know well enough the direction in which the opinions of the country are tending. The minority, which invites you to join it . . . must go, or wish to go, in an opposite direction . . . Will you unite yourself with what must be, from the beginning, an inevitable failure. Don't be offended . . .'

Gladstone was not in the least offended. He appreciated the force of Bright's letter, and he longed only for a decent opportunity to climb down from the top of the column on which the cartoonists loved to depict him as living like St. Simeon Stylites. He was nearly fifty years old, and it was absolutely necessary that he should make up his mind not only between Palmerston and Disraeli, both of whom were antipathetic to him, but between a practical acceptance of the flesh and the Devil as inescapable aspects of a secular political life, and an unpractical persistence in a scholarly philosophical detachment. Disraeli realized that without Gladstone's adherence, the prospects of Lord Derby's Government were bleak. He therefore offered to resign the leadership of the House of Commons to Gladstone's friend, Sir James Graham, who was aged nearly seventy, if Gladstone would consent to join Lord Derby's Government.

The occasion of that offer was a vacancy in the Cabinet, caused by the resignation, in May, 1858, of the President of the Indian Board of Control. That office, or the Colonial Office, was offered to Gladstone ; but Disraeli's offer to resign the leadership of the House was less magnanimous than it sounded. It was conditional upon Sir James Graham being 'disposed to join the Government', and Sir James was known to be indisposed, on account of his age and opinions, to do anything of the kind. Lord Derby begged Gladstone to consult Lord Aberdeen and Sir James Graham before reaching a decision, and this Gladstone readily consented to do.

Lord Aberdeen leaned to the view that Gladstone should refuse. Sir James Graham thought that, on the whole, he might properly accept. In the meantime, Disraeli, on 25 May, 1858, seconded Lord Derby's offer in a somewhat singular letter, without any conventional beginning or end :

'I think it of such paramount importance to the public interests that you should assume at this time a commanding position . . . that I feel it a solemn duty to lay before you some facts . . .

'Our mutual relations have formed the great difficulty in accomplishing a result which I have always anxiously desired.

'Listen, without prejudice, to this brief narrative.'

Disraeli entered into a lengthy account of his conduct since 1850, and added : 'Don't you think the time has come when you might deign to be magnanimous.'

Disraeli told Gladstone that if he joined Lord Derby's Cabinet he would find it filled with his warm admirers ;

'you may place me in neither category, but in that, I assure you, you have ever been sadly mistaken . . . If Party necessities retain

me formally in the chief post, the sincere and delicate respect which
I should always offer you, and the unbounded confidence which, on
my part, if you choose, you could command, would prevent your
feeling my position as anything but a form.'

For Gladstone's benefit one phrase was interpolated, which was,
perhaps, felt by Gladstone to be not wholly in character : ' There
is a Power, greater than ourselves, that disposes of all this.'

Gladstone's reply, which was dated the same day, expressed veiled
reprobation. It was polished, but cold as ice :

My dear Sir,
    The letter which you have been so good as to address to me will
enable me, I trust, to remove from your mind some impressions
with which you will not be sorry to part . . .
    You have given me a narrative of your conduct since 1850 . . .
and . . . you consider that the relations between yourself and
me have proved the main difficulty in the way of certain political
arrangements. Will you allow me to assure that I have never in
my life taken a decision which turned upon those relations ?

It was distasteful to Gladstone to have to put himself on a level with
this correspondent. But he did his best, and he explained that the
difficulties in the way of his accepting Lord Derby's offer were greater
than Disraeli ' may have supposed '. He concluded :

    You have yourself well reminded me that there is a Power beyond
us that disposes of what we are and do, and I find the limits of
choice in public life to be very narrow.

                                        I am, etc.,
                                            W. E. Gladstone.

Lord Derby laughed when he heard of Disraeli's failure to beguile
the man he termed ' a half-regained Eurydice '. And Disraeli grumbled
that he had done his best with Gladstone : ' I almost went down on
my knees to him.' Gladstone ignored Disraeli when he answered
Lord Derby on 26 May, 1858. He said that he saw no ' prospect of
public advantage or of material accession to your strength, from my
entering your Government single-handed '.

Gladstone's decision on that occasion was a great deal more prudent
than the next one which he was called upon to take. He accepted,
in November, 1858, an invitation from Sir Edward Bulwer Lytton,

the Colonial Secretary, to go out to the Ionian Islands as Lord High Commissioner Extraordinary.

The Ionian Islands had been a British Protectorate since 1815 ; and the islanders were agitating for union with Greece. There had been a number of disturbances, and incidents involving loss of life, and Gladstone was asked to investigate conditions and report. Bulwer Lytton wrote to Disraeli (23 September, 1858) that ' as a Party move ' it would be ' a master-stroke ' if Gladstone could be induced to accept. 'I think I could so put the proposal as to please and propitiate him,' Lytton wrote ; 'if he would consent to be less crotchety, I believe he would suit the occasion better than any other man we could send.'

Disraeli saw no objection. If Gladstone's mission succeeded it might yet provide a means of attaching him to the Conservative Party in a rôle much subordinate to his own. If it failed, Gladstone might be discredited, which would not cause Disraeli any loss of sleep. All Gladstone's friends, except the Duke of Newcastle, advised him to refuse Lytton's offer. But to everyone's surprise, he swallowed the bait. He longed for employment, and the temptation to make an official visit to such places as Corfu and Ithaca, and to extend his knowledge of Homer and ancient Greece, proved irresistible. He loved the Mediterranean, and he thought that he might win fame by restoring the constitutional freedom of a Greek community. Mrs. Gladstone's health, which had suffered after the shock of Lady Lyttelton's death, was an additional motive. The doctors recommended travel and a Southern climate. A last private but characteristic motive was a desire to consult local prelates of the Greek Orthodox Church about the possibilities of union with the Church of England.

Accordingly, on 8 November, 1858, Gladstone left England for Corfu. He was accompanied by his wife and by his eldest daughter, Agnes, and he took with him, as Secretary to his Mission, James Lacaita, whom he had first met in Naples in 1850. Lacaita had since become a naturalized British subject, and Professor of Italian at London University.

There was, from the outset, a touch of comic opera about Gladstone's mission, which was rendered almost abortive before he reached Corfu. A secret despatch from Sir George Young, the Lord High Commissioner of the Ionian Islands, was stolen from the Colonial Office and published in the Press. That despatch recommended the transfer of the smaller islands to Greece, and the outright annexation of Corfu to the British Crown. It could not be known that shortly afterwards Sir George Young had changed that advice, and recommended the maintenance of the *status quo*, and the suppression of representative institutions throughout the islands. But it was wholly impossible either for Gladstone or for Sir George Young to efface the impression which had been produced by the publication of the stolen despatch.

Nevertheless, on his idyllic little stage Gladstone played his part with verve and gusto. Travelling by way of Dresden, Vienna, and Trieste, he embarked on the warship *Terrible*, and reached Corfu on 24 November, 1858. He was delighted, like all civilians, at being received with a salute of guns, but he had no idea how to inspect a Guard of Honour. The General Officer commanding the Garrison stepped briskly forward, thinking that Gladstone was at his side. But he had to return when he looked back and saw the Lord High Commissioner Extraordinary standing perfectly still with a blissful smile on his face, and his hand on his heart.

Gladstone was disconcerted to discover that there were very few copies of Homer in Corfu; and he was scandalized by what he described as the state of 'complete and contented idleness' which he found established there. The inhabitants of Corfu, and the British Garrison, were equally hostile to him. The natives, who were seething with discontent and longing for union with Greece, thought that he had come out to transform their island from a protectorate into a colony and naval base. And the British, who despised the natives, distrusted and ridiculed Gladstone's enthusiasm for everything Greek. With inexcusable discourtesy the Commander of the Garrison never once invited Gladstone to his Mess.

Gladstone was not in the least dismayed by the atmosphere which surrounded him, and he threw himself with the utmost enjoyment into his task. He visited all the islands, as well as Athens and the Albanian coast. At Ithaca he danced at a ball, and at Athens he dined with the Greek Royal Family. He was surprised to find the Acropolis covered with icicles and snow. In Albania he was feasted by the female head of an important clan. He was annoyed with his bodyguard because the men continuously fired their rifles into the air; but he romped boyishly after dinner, and spent the night on the floor of the castle in which he had been entertained, covered by a gorgeous quilt and surrounded by equally gorgeous Albanians. He wondered whether or not the accommodation provided contravened the provisions of

Lord Shaftesbury's recent Lodging-House Act. But in his diary he was content to record that Albania had saddened him :

'It is all indolence, decay, and stagnation. The image of God seems as if it were nowhere. But there is much of wild and pictur-esque.' Disraeli, years before, had written ecstatically of 'a scene equal to anything in the Arabian Nights', and of 'the delight . . . of wearing a turban and smoking a six-foot long pipe'. He had pictured his host as being quite capable of 'daily decapitating half the Province'.

Wherever he went, Gladstone made speeches in Italian. He drew up a draft revised constitution, and arranged that Sir George Young should be recalled, and that he himself should be installed in his place. The Government was delighted, and Lytton telegraphed (11 January, 1859) : 'The Queen accepts. Your Commission is made out.' The Crown lawyers at once pointed out that Gladstone's acceptance of an office of profit under the Crown had vacated his seat in Parliament : 'This I must confess', he telegraphed to Lytton (17 January), 'is a very great blow.' Then, to add to his difficulties, the telegraph system broke down.

A violent outcry arose immediately in England and in Corfu. Gladstone was attacked for supplanting Sir George Young ; *The Times* (13 January, 1859) mocked him for having allowed himself to be tricked by his insidious rival, Disraeli, into abdicating as a statesman and into accepting a fifth-rate mission in order to indulge an inordinate appetite for classical scholarship. Lord John Russell suggested to Lord Aberdeen that Gladstone had been glad of an excuse to escape a forthcoming debate about Parliamentary reform ; Sir James Graham thought that his reputation would never wholly recover ; Lord Palmerston considered him quite incalculable—only partially muzzled by having to represent Oxford : 'Send him elsewhere,' he said, 'and he will run wild.' Even Lord Aberdeen, whom Gladstone worshipped, considered that he was too headstrong and, if possible, too simple and honest. He did not take human factors sufficiently into account. But when Sir James Graham asked Lord Aberdeen whether Gladstone's career might be brought to a premature close, the reply was, 'Ah ! But he is terrible on the rebound.'

Gladstone's friends arranged that a new High Commissioner, Sir Henry Storks, should immediately be despatched to Corfu, in order to relieve Gladstone from the embarrassment in which he had landed himself. That did not save him from the need to face a by-election at Oxford, but he was re-elected (13 February) unopposed, in his

absence. Before he returned to England he presented his scheme of
constitutional reform to the Assembly of Corfu. He spoke in Italian,
and was irritated to find that the Assembly declined to debate his
proposals. It passed a Resolution that it was the unanimous *will* of
the Ionian people that all the islands should be united with Greece ; and
it expressed that demand in a petition to the Queen.

In speech after speech in the Assembly Gladstone drew a characteristic series of fine Socratic distinctions. He pointed out that the *will*
of the Assembly was not the same as its *wish* ; and that the islanders
had failed to distinguish between a right to *request* and a right to
demand union with Greece. He ignored entirely the anomalous nature
of his own position. It was uncertain whether or not he had been
formally superseded as Lord High Commissioner before his successor
arrived (16 February). If he had not been superseded he could not
legally have been re-elected to Parliament in England. If, on the
other hand, he were no longer Lord High Commissioner he had no
title to preside as such during the debates in the Assembly of Corfu.

On 16 February, 1859, the Assembly rejected all Gladstone's
proposals out of hand. Three days later Gladstone started for England,
reflecting, ruefully, that he had entirely failed in his purpose of reconciling the islanders with a continuance of the British connexion. He
did not hurry his journey, and in Turin, on 23 February, he had an
important conversation with Count Cavour.

In Turin, preparations were in evidence on all sides for the start
of the Italo-Austrian war of liberation. Gladstone now sympathized
profoundly with the cause of Italian unity ; and, in that age, to be a
nationalist was to be a Liberal. Foreign affairs were forcing themselves
to the forefront of British politics ; and Conservative support of the
established European order implied sympathy with Austria and
opposition to Italian unity. As he talked with Cavour, the great
Italian leader, Gladstone felt that a light had been vouchsafed to him.
That was a sign that his mind was about to settle in a new equilibrium
by means of the seismic process which was natural to it.

On 8 March, 1859, Gladstone returned to London, and refused an
offer of the Grand Cross of the Bath, or of St. Michael and St. George.
He supported a very mild measure of Parliamentary reform which the
Conservatives were trying to force through Parliament, but he made
a passionate defence (29 March) of the rotten boroughs. He had sat
for one himself, and he argued that they were the proper nurseries
of statesmen. The Bill was rejected by 39 votes on 31 March, when

Lord Palmerston joined Lord John Russell in opposing a Government amendment to lower the franchise qualification in the boroughs. The Liberals opposed the Bill because they had no confidence in the ability of the Conservatives to settle the problem on broad national lines.

Lord Derby appealed to the country, and at the General Election his Party gained some thirty seats ; but it remained in a minority in the House. Gladstone, who had been unopposed, for the last time at Oxford, had no hesitation in refusing an offer to join Lord Derby's Government. He told his friends that the best hope of political stability was a Coalition between Derby and Palmerston, and the removal of Disraeli from the leadership of the Commons.

On 10 June, 1859, the twenty-six-year-old Lord Hartington was put up to propose a Vote of No Confidence in Lord Derby, which was carried by 13 votes. Gladstone's intentions before the Division were a mystery, and many eyes followed him curiously as he entered the Lobby with Disraeli and the Conservatives.

Lord Derby resigned, and Palmerston, aged seventy-five, returned to power. He offered Gladstone any office he cared to name. A year earlier (14 February, 1858) Gladstone, in a private note to Sir James Graham, had complained that no worse Minister than Palmerston had held office in their time. A day or two earlier he had voted with the Conservatives against Lord Palmerston in a critical Division. But now, as he told Lord Acton some years later, ' the overwhelming weight and interest of the Italian question, and of our foreign policy in connection with it . . . led me to decide without one moment's hesitation ' to inform Lord Palmerston that he would be happy to join his Government as Chancellor of the Exchequer.

So the die was cast, and an earthquake silently convulsed Gladstone's mind. The step which he took saved his career, but it was greeted with a chorus of mockery and disapproval. He justified that step by the one word, ' Italy ', and was wholly convinced that he was obeying the call of duty as well as the manifest will of God. His niece, Lucy Lyttelton, noted in her diary (21 June, 1859) :

' Uncle William has taken office under Lord Palmerston as Chancellor of the Exchequer, thereby raising an uproar in the midst of which we are simmering, view [1] his well-known antipathy to the Premier. What seems clear is that he considers it right to swallow personal feelings for the sake of the country . . . There is this

[1] Glynnese for ' having regard to '.

question, however—why, if he can swallow Pam, couldn't he swallow Dizzy, and, in spite of him, go in under Lord Derby ? I don't pretend to be able to answer this.'

The answer is that the outbreak in April, 1859, of the war of Italian liberation had divided public men on an issue of principle for the first time since the repeal of the Corn Laws. Between 1846 and 1859 British politics had hinged on personal factors ; and when that ceased to be the case, Gladstone found that the Conservative outlook on foreign policy was the exact opposite of his. Derby and Disraeli clung to the established order. Palmerston and Gladstone embraced the nationalist cause. Gladstone's motives, which were wholly sincere, were easily misconstrued by his enemies, and in the simplicity of his heart he was much troubled. It was evident that there was no future for him in the Conservative Party, whereas in the Liberal Party his prospects were excellent. He became, at the age of fifty, the youngest member of a virtual triumvirate. Of his colleagues, Lord Palmerston was aged seventy-five, and Lord John Russell, sixty-eight, so that, in the course of nature, Gladstone was certain soon to become Prime Minister. His imagination painted everything, including his motives for the step he had just taken, in grand and glowing colours, but his duty and his interest were coincident and clear. He was conscious of the possession of great powers which he had dedicated to the service of God, in politics. He considered, further, that the Conservatives had no chance of settling the thorny problem of Parliamentary reform which he wanted to see settled. He told his friends that if he had refused Palmerston's offer he could never again have looked any man in the face.

'How could I', he wrote (16 June) to his fellow-member for Oxford University, Sir William Heathcote, ' under these circumstances say "I will have nothing to do with you ", and be the one remaining Ishmael in the House of Commons ? '

So Gladstone returned from the wilderness.

CHAPTER 7

THE PUBLIC PURSE—MENTAL
EARTHQUAKE
1859–1864

ROM Disraeli, Gladstone was thenceforth happy to be divided by what he termed ' longer and larger differences than perhaps ever separated two persons brought into constant contact in the transaction of public business '. But his relations with his new chief, Palmerston, were often near the breaking-point. The Prime Minister's jauntiness set him perpetually on edge ; and he used to say, with a smile, that he had never attended a Cabinet between 1859 and 1865 without taking the precaution of carrying a letter of resignation in his wallet. If it had not been for the accident of the Conservative Party explosion of 1846, and the subsequent dominance of that Party by Disraeli, Gladstone would have continued his work in an atmosphere of Conservatism ; and he would have been a happier man. The Whigs never accepted him ; and he was never really at home in the climate of Nonconformity. He was condemned to spend the rest of his life in an atmosphere which was less natural and congenial to him than the one which he had abandoned.

Mrs. Gladstone had introduced her husband to Whig society ; but that charmed circle was more closely integrated than its Tory counter-part. Gladstone's views about the Church were as unacceptable to it as were the Succession Duties which he had forced through Parlia-ment in 1853. The Whig patricians were almost a family party, and they did not readily admit strangers, or accept their leadership. They made Gladstone feel that he had been bred in a different kennel. Tories and Conservatives, on the other hand, had long been content to adopt strangers and to accept leaders—Canning, Peel, Disraeli— who had been born outside the inner citadel of patrician privilege.

The way in which the Whigs regarded Gladstone was summed up in a phrase which had a wide currency : ' Oxford on the surface : Liverpool underneath.' The same view was uncharitably expressed in a letter from the Hon. Emily Eden to Lord Clarendon in 1860 :

' I daresay he *is* very clever, and he is good-natured, doing his best to bring his mind down to the level of mine ; but he fails. He is always above me ; and then he does not converse—he harangues— and the more he says, the more I don't understand. Then there is something about High Church people that I can't define, but I feel it when I am with them—something Jesuitical—and they never let themselves go. And to complete my list of things, there is an element of parvenuism about him, as there was about Sir Robert Peel—something in his tone of voice, and his way of coming into a room, that is not aristocratic. In short he is not frivolous enough for me. If he were soaked in boiling water and rinsed until he were twisted into a rope, I do not suppose a drop of fun would ooze out.'

Gladstone would, in normal circumstances, have had much less difficulty than Disraeli in securing total acceptance by the patrician Conservatives. His failure to secure such acceptance by the Whigs, with whom he was now allied politically as well as by ties of marriage, deprived him of a response with which his simple nature could not afford to dispense. He was entirely unsnobbish ; but the constant and active support of the dominant influences in every field of activity in which he was engaged was an absolute necessity to him. That need was, perhaps, most perfectly suggested by the tone of his frequent references to the Almighty.

Gladstone had not been a Liberal for more than a few months, when he began to miss the kind of assured support on which he had previously leaned. On 14 January, 1860, in a letter to Richard Cobden, he complained that, for the first time in his life, he had failed to derive satisfaction or help from consultation with Cabinet colleagues, or from ' associates within the narrow circle of those who are, equally with myself, aware of the course of affairs '. He added that he found himself isolated from those of like situation, habits of mind, political training, and connexions. In those circumstances, he began to direct his gaze towards the masses—the source from which Richard Cobden and John Bright had for so long derived their strength. As a result, he presently transformed his position in public life and did much to shift the centre of political gravity in Great Britain.

Gladstone soon came to find Lord Granville, the Lord President of the Council, who was his junior by six years, irresistibly attractive. Lord Granville was everybody's friend ; but Gladstone was, if possible, even more strongly drawn to Sidney Herbert, the Secretary for War, who, with James Hope-Scott, and Arthur Hallam, was one of the three men whom, in the course of his life, he really loved. Of Herbert he recorded : ' A man of his qualities . . . must always be without a rival in his generation. I remember my first sight of him . . . in 1829. The beauty and grace of his appearance, exhibiting

him as one of Nature's nobles, made an indelible impression on me.'
He was gratified, too, by the warm friendship of the Duke of Argyll,
the Lord Privy Seal. If it had not been for those intimacies, Gladstone's position in the Cabinet would quickly have become impossible.
Lord Clarendon told Sir George Lewis (16 July 1860) after a visit to
Osborne, that the Queen thought that the Government would inspire
more confidence if Gladstone ceased to be a member of it, and that
she rather hoped that he would resign. Lord Granville wrote
(26 July, 1860) to his friend, Lord Canning, the Viceroy of India :
  'The Government continues as a whole . . . Gladstone has been on
half-cock of resignation for two months . . . Palmerston has tried
him very hard, once or twice, by speeches and Cabinet minutes, and
says that the only way to deal with him is to bully him a little. And
Palmerston appears to be right. I like Gladstone very much, and
have generally taken his part in the Cabinet. But not to the extent
which Argyll does. The Duchess of Sutherland is miserable at the
attacks made upon him.'
  The cause of those attacks, which were constantly featured in *The
Times*, and in *Punch*, was the fearless stand taken by Gladstone against
a war-scare which had gripped the country. It was believed that
Napoleon III, who had just deserted his Italian allies and annexed
Nice and Savoy, was planning a sudden assault upon Great Britain.
Men in all walks of life joined the Volunteers, and the panic was
fanned by the Press, by the Poet Laureate, Tennyson, and by Lord
Palmerston. Gladstone denounced the panic as a groundless delusion.
He believed, however, that unless prompt action were taken to allay
it, war would probably break out with France of its own accord.
  Gladstone fought the popular agitation on two fronts. He succeeded with great difficulty in persuading the Cabinet to send Richard
Cobden as an unofficial envoy to Paris to negotiate a commercial
treaty. And he dismayed his colleagues, and the country, by the
violence of his opposition to all proposals for increased expenditure on
armaments and fortifications.
  The onset of that controversy deprived Gladstone of most of the
advantage which he would otherwise have derived from the complete
accord between his views and those of his colleagues on the subject
of the Italo-Austrian War. He wrote (15 July, 1859) to his old
acquaintance, Poerio, who had come to England as a refugee, after
being released from his dungeon at Naples :
  'I little thought to have lived to see the day when the conclusion

of a peace should, in my own mind, cause disgust, rather than impart relief. But that day has come.'

The peace referred to was that concluded between France and Austria ; but by October, 1860, the unification of most of Italy had been achieved. Gladstone's six-year-old son, Herbert, wrote to him during that time :

My dear, darling Papa,

Mama . . . has been telling me about good Garibaldi. Did you really go down the dungeon ? . . . I hope Garibaldi will get Naples, because he is good. And I want the King of Naples to go because he is so wicked and shuts up people.

Goodbye, dear Papa,

I am, your little son,

Herbert.

The idea of the French commercial treaty originated with Bright. Cobden pressed it on Gladstone during a visit which he made to Hawarden for that purpose in the second week of September, 1859. Cobden's great personal charm made him an ideal negotiator, and Gladstone forced the project of a treaty upon a doubting Cabinet as ' a great European operation ', and as a union not of Governments, but of hearts. He said that the most effective means of counter-acting the war-passion was to appeal to the sense of commercial interest in the middle class.

Lord Palmerston was partly dependent upon Radical support ; and the new relations into which Gladstone entered with that group as a result of the French Treaty were important. Gladstone, Cobden, and Bright all held that the Treaty enshrined a moral principle which was more valuable than any calculated commercial interest. On New Year's Day, 1861, Bright told Gladstone that his colleagues, Lord Palmerston and Lord John Russell, belonged to a vanished age : ' A new policy, and a wiser and a higher morality are sighed for by the best of our people ; and there is a prevalent feeling that you are destined to guide the wiser policy, and to teach the higher morality.'

Bright's words always carried weight with Gladstone. He told his intimates that it was Bright who had first made him realize that he might one day be Prime Minister. Gladstone did not possess one of those prophetic minds which are capable of peering far into the future ; but his powers of analysis and synthesis were too acute to allow him to rest content with serving as an interpreter of other men's seminal ideas. He reflected a great deal about the reasons which entitled Bright and Cobden to speak with assurance and authority; and in his subconscious mind conditions were prepared for a mental earthquake which rocked the country in May, 1864.

Cobden, in the course of his negotiations in Paris, had found it necessary to promise, in Gladstone's name, a large number. of far-reaching tariff concessions. Those concessions had to be incorporated in the Budget, and that Budget had to be co-ordinated with the signing of the Treaty. For that reason Gladstone advanced his Budget statement by two months—to 6 February, 1860; but he was struck down by bronchitis on the previous day. The knowledge that the free trade movement was about to reach its zenith had aroused widespread excitement. The delay imposed by Gladstone's illness keyed that excitement to concert pitch.

At five o'clock on the afternoon of 10 February, 1860, Gladstone, looking strained and emaciated, introduced his Budget in a four-hour speech. His diary described it as the most arduous Parliamentary operation of his life; but he was radiant with triumph at the close. He refreshed himself frequently while he was speaking with draughts of a mixture of egg and wine, which Mrs. Gladstone had prepared, out of a bottle.

In leaving only 48 articles on the tariff, Gladstone went considerably beyond the provisions of the Treaty with France:

'Our old friend, Protection,' he announced, 'who used formerly to dwell in the Palaces and High Places of the land, and who was dislodged from them some ten or fifteen years ago, has since that period still found pretty comfortable shelter and good living in holes and corners; and you are invited . . . to see whether you cannot likewise eject him from those holes and corners.'

To help pay for those concessions, to meet the cost of providing the Navy with iron-clads, and to finance the expensive luxury of a military expedition to the Chinese capital, of which he disapproved, Gladstone raised the income-tax to tenpence, took advantage of the lapsing of certain annuities, and earmarked the few remaining duties for revenue purposes alone.

The repeal of so many duties helped to reduce the cost of living. When Gladstone was considering the question of a proper allowance for his second son, Stephen, at Oxford in 1864, he was able to write to his wife: 'At the present day, money goes much further in three important items—books, clothes, and journeys.' He said that during his time at Oxford he had never been able to keep within the £250 a year which his father had allowed him, although his father had paid all his bills for horses, and private tutoring, in addition to his allowance. But Gladstone's eldest son was able to live very comfortably on an inclusive allowance of £300 a year ; while his younger sons had £20 less ' by way of preparation for differences hereafter '.

As a result of that great Budget of 1860, Gladstone's reputation soared. Napoleon III telegraphed his congratulations. The Prince Consort told Baron Stockmar that Gladstone, and not Palmerston, was the real leader of the House of Commons, and that his energy and powers of work were ' almost incredible '. Lord Brougham told Gladstone that his peroration had been the best heard in the House since his own speech on law reform in 1828 which, the vain old man could not resist adding, ' has been so much talked about '.

The laurels on Gladstone's brow soon withered in a sultry atmosphere of controversy. He had proposed to repeal, at a cost of one and a quarter million pounds a year, the excise duty on paper, which his new Radical friends had long denounced as a tax on knowledge. Books, pamphlets, and newspapers would all be cheapened if that measure went through, but substantial sections of the upper class complained that that measure was too democratic. The paper manufacturers, and the proprietors of expensive periodicals who feared competition from a cheap Press, strongly opposed it. It was widely believed that Gladstone was making a bid for Radical support ; and while the controversy was at its height he quietly resigned (30 March) from the Carlton Club.

At that time it was the practice to make every tax the subject of a separate Bill. The Paper Bill was only carried in the Commons by a majority of nine ; it was rejected by the Lords on 21 May. Lord Palmerston had detested it from the first ; he regarded it as one of Gladstone's tiresome fads. Before it went to the Lords he took the extraordinary step of writing to the Queen to express his hope that the Lords would reject it. On 22 May he informed her that the Bill was ' lost like Sir John Franklin '. The Lords might, he added, have exceeded their constitutional functions in throwing out a Money Bill, but ' the opinion of the great majority of the public is that they have done a right and useful thing '. The Queen informed the King of the Belgians that the rejection of the Paper Bill was ' *a very good thing* ', and that it would save a good deal of revenue. Gladstone,

GLADSTONE, c. 1859.
otograph by Maull & Pullyblank.

GRANVILLE GEORGE LEVESON-GOWER,
2ND EARL GRANVILLE.
Mezzotint by T. Atkinson after G. Richmond.

SIR ROBERT PEEL, BT.
Mezzotint by G. R. Ward after F. Gr

GEORGE HAMILTON GORDON,
4TH EARL OF ABERDEEN.
Engraving by D. J. Pound from a photograph
by Mayall.

SIDNEY HERBERT
(LORD HERBERT OF LEA).
Mezzotint by G. R. Ward after F. G

she said, had threatened to resign and might carry out his threat :
'He is terribly excited.'

Gladstone had no knowledge of the Prime Minister's light-hearted
correspondence with the Queen. He flung himself into the struggle
and thanked God for the strength. His diary recorded (23 March)
that he had worked a 16½-hour day. He characterized the action of
the Lords as ' a gigantic innovation on the Constitution ', and he varied
his frequent threats to resign by uttering dark threats about his intention to bring the Lords to heel. In July the Commons passed three
Resolutions asserting the exclusive right of the Commons to decide
questions of finance and taxation. Lord Palmerston, who moved
them, seemed, nevertheless, to affirm his sympathy with the Lords.
He said that the controversy over the Paper Bill was closed. Gladstone showed plainly that he meant to continue the struggle ; he said
that he reserved the right to enforce the privileges of the Commons by
deeds, and not by words. He was wildly applauded by the Radicals,
but by no-one else ; and the Conservatives were delighted by the
spectacle of the Prime Minister and the Chancellor of the Exchequer
wrangling on the floor of the House of Commons. Disraeli and
Lord Derby twice approached Lord Palmerston with offers of support
for any provisional administration which he might form in case
Gladstone should break up the Government.

Gladstone's friends thought that he was killing himself by overwork. He looked pale and ill, and Sir Robert Phillimore noted
(12 August) that he needed ' air, rest, and generous living '. Gladstone's violence and obstinacy excited a measure of social unpopularity ;
but the firm stand which he took against the Lords on the Paper Bill
earned him for the first time the fervent admiration of the masses.

Gladstone told his friends that his difficulties inside the Cabinet were
such that he came to the House for refreshment and recreation.
His hold over the House was wonderful, but on 20 July his diary
recorded : ' Lost my Savings Bank Monies Bill—my *first* defeat on a
measure of finance in the House of Commons.' His instinct for
self-mortification made him add : ' This ought to be very good for
me. And I earnestly wish to make it so.' Inside the Cabinet he was
locked in a bitter struggle with his colleagues on the subject of the
Service Estimates.

Gladstone described his principal colleagues as ' captains-general
of the alarmists '. They believed that Napoleon III might at any time
launch a sudden blow at Great Britain ; and they read a sinister

meaning into his interest in cutting a canal through the Suez isthmus. Again and again Gladstone protested against 'the powerful influence and infection of national emotion' upon otherwise generous and sympathetic minds (letter to Sidney Herbert ; 28 November, 1859). He argued that England was a difficult country to invade ; that the Channel was a much better barrier than the Rhine ; and that the Commercial Treaty with France would quickly lessen the tension.

A Royal Commission on National Defence had recommended the expenditure of eleven million pounds on fortifications. Gladstone told the Prime Minister (7 February, 1860) that he would regard any loan for such a purpose as a betrayal of his public duty ; but he found almost no support in the Cabinet. Lord Palmerston explained frankly that he was an old man, with only two public objects left in life. The first was to suppress the last remnants of the trade in negro slaves ; the second was to leave Britain in a proper state of defence. Gladstone wrote memorandum after memorandum in the effort to show that the national danger was greatly exaggerated. There was no evidence that the French were a Godless nation, or even that they were inveterately hostile. Why had they not struck during the crisis of the Indian Mutiny, when every available soldier had been rushed across half the world to smash the rebels ?

The Whigs were at one with the Conservatives in holding that Gladstone was a menace to his country's safety. His name was as much hated at Brooks's as it was at the Carlton Club. Lord Palmerston told the Queen that Gladstone's resignation would be a serious blow to the Government, but that it would be better to lose Gladstone than to risk losing Portsmouth or Plymouth. The main public reason why Gladstone failed to make good any of his frequent threats to resign was very frankly given in a letter marked 'Most Private' which he addressed to the Prime Minister on 26 February, 1860. He explained that, over and above certain personal motives, he was determined to force his Paper Bill through Parliament against the opposition of the House of Lords : 'I desire', he wrote, 'to be in at the death, even if it should be my own.'

Among Gladstone's private motives were, firstly, the arguments of his Radical friends that he could do most good by remaining at his post ; and, secondly, the intense pleasure which he derived from his personal relations with the Secretary for War, Sidney Herbert, although their views were often diametrically opposed. Herbert was always willing to meet Gladstone half-way, so that Gladstone, too, became willing to accept a series of compromises. He was not afraid, on occasion, to allow his heart to rule his head a little, and he recorded that Herbert's kindness had been extraordinary. He had found that public life could not be all that he had hoped, and he had no desire to return to the wilderness. He rehearsed his agony in his diary, and gave the verdict against himself nearly all the time. But as he wrestled in prayer with his Maker he felt justified in claiming that his prayers had been abundantly answered.

So Gladstone accepted an arrangement which was negotiated by the Duke of Somerset (First Lord of the Admiralty). Much was conceded, but much, too, was saved. In 1860 the national expenditure stood at nearly £73 millions, excluding a small loan for fortifications, which was finally extorted from Gladstone. It had stood at £56 millions in 1853. In 1862 it again fell below £70 millions, and to below £68 millions in 1863. The French panic died away; the revenue responded to the free trade measures of the Great Budget of 1860; thereafter, every year yielded its surplus, and, out of that surplus, Gladstone distributed fresh remissions of taxation. But the Prime Minister and the Chancellor of the Exchequer continued to be separated by an unbridgeable gulf, as the moral intensity of the mid-nineteenth century faced the jaunty patrician assurance of the Regency period: 'Wait 'till I'm dead!' Palmerston used to say: 'If Gladstone gets my place, you'll see some strange doings!'

Gladstone was convinced that the real wealth of nations was the product of individual thrift and industry. Thrift and industry were moral qualities, which would be killed by public or private extravagance. All extravagance, therefore, was a great moral evil. Gladstone remembered so well the time when poverty had been embittered almost to the point of revolution by the spectacle of public funds frivolously squandered on pensions and sinecures, that his devotion to the cult of ruthless economy was unshakable. He declared at Edinburgh (29 November, 1874):

'It is the mark of a chicken-hearted Chancellor when he shrinks from upholding economy in detail . . . He is not worth his salt if he is not ready to save what are meant by candle-ends and cheese-parings in the cause of the country.'

Gladstone's long-term object was to raise the moral standards and ideals of the people by improving their material conditions. He had no trust in the efficacy of State action to achieve that end. His method was to remove all restrictions upon trade, and to extend its area. All taxation, in his view, operated in restraint of trade, and therefore, in order to reduce prices, and to secure full employment, it was necessary to keep taxation and public expenditure to a minimum. For that reason he was tireless in pursuit of opportunities to reduce the numbers of Civil Servants alike in the highest and in the lowest grades. Individuals might suffer hardship, but he was certain that the permanent interest of the mass of the people would thereby be served.

Gladstone enjoyed devoting time to replanning processes of work with a view to executing small-scale staffing economies. He did much to curb and mortify that spirit of extravagance which is present in all bodies which administer public funds ; but he sometimes showed a want of proportion. At Greenwich, for example, on 28 October, 1871, when he was Prime Minister, he thought it worth while to begin a full-scale survey of his Government's record in every field of its activity, by announcing proudly that 1,463 superfluous clerks and workmen had been sacked from the Dockyards ; and that he had abolished one post worth £1,200 a year in the Board of Inland Revenue, and amalgamated two posts, each formerly worth £1,200 a year, in the Board of Customs. Again, during the Midlothian Campaign, it was noticed that he sometimes began his eloquent denunciations of the record of Disraeli's Government in every corner of the globe, by accusing Disraeli of having created an unnecessary Civil Service Commissionership, worth £2,000 a year, for the convenience of an elderly and impecunious friend (Lord Hampton).

Periodical sackings of clerks in good times as well as in bad earned Gladstone a measure of unpopularity. But occasionally he did himself real harm. An example occurred in February, 1886, when he was forming his first Home Rule Cabinet. Much hinged at that time upon his personal relations with Joseph Chamberlain, who already felt that he had been slighted. Preoccupied as he was with many grave and urgent problems, Gladstone went out of his way at that inopportune moment to reduce from £1,500 to £1,200 a year the salary of Jesse Collings, who was not only Chamberlain's Parliamentary Secretary at the Local Government Board, but also his most intimate friend. When Chamberlain protested in the strongest possible terms, Gladstone rebuked him with harshness, and was only induced to alter his decision after much correspondence, and the strenuous intervention of Sir William Harcourt.

Many other examples could be cited ; but one more incident must suffice. When he was on his mission to Corfu, Gladstone issued orders that the labels on the official bags sent to him by the Colonial Office should not be wasted. The address was to be scratched out, so that the labels could be used again. One day, while his secretary was saving a fraction of a penny in that way, an officer of the Garrison whom Gladstone had expressed a wish to see and who had, accordingly, been summoned urgently from Trieste, where he had been on leave, entered the room. Gladstone was scandalized to learn that the officer had chartered a special steamer at a cost of several hundred pounds.

Gladstone's passion for finance was matched by an astonishing power of making its dry details intelligible and exciting to the man in the street. His annual Budget statements were awaited with the utmost eagerness by the whole country. He delivered them with the air of a master-chef who has created some incomparable dish; and his boyish air of satisfaction at the elasticity of the revenue never failed to delight and amuse the House of Commons. His virtuosity in the field of finance was at least equal to that displayed by Macaulay in popularizing the art of writing history.

In introducing the Budget of 1861 (11 April), Gladstone told the House plainly that it must choose whether it wished the country to continue to be governed extravagantly at an annual cost of £70 millions plus, or whether it would be content to revert to a more modest annual expenditure of between £60 and 62 millions. In the latter case he would be happy to abolish the income-tax. He did not conceal his view that the spirit of extravagance would never be successfully exorcised from Whitehall, as long as the income-tax remained.

In 1861, Gladstone reduced the income-tax from tenpence to ninepence by taking advantage of the delay in repealing the Paper duty. With great difficulty, he compelled the Cabinet to include once again a provision for the repeal of that duty in the Budget. He recorded that on one occasion, while the subject was being discussed in the Cabinet, Lord Palmerston lost his temper, and that the meeting broke up in disorder.

A much more important point which Gladstone secured was an arrangement that in 1861, and in every successive year, all financial legislation, necessitated by a Budget, should be incorporated in a single comprehensive Finance Bill. By that means he won a total victory over the House of Lords. He forced through the repeal of the Paper duty, because the Lords did not dare at that time to reject an entire Budget out of hand. Their memories of the dangerous quasi-revolutionary agitation during the 'twenties, 'thirties, and early 'forties were still too vivid. When, after Gladstone's death, they plucked up courage to reject the Budget of 1909, the Parliament Act of 1911 was their reward.

Gladstone was justified in claiming that the rise of a cheap Press, as a result of the repeal of the Paper duty, had opened a new epoch in the lives of the poor. He believed that it had contributed much towards what he called their moral enfranchisement, by giving them a fresh interest in public affairs, and a fresh attachment to their country's institutions. The association of Gladstone's name with that measure helped to wind up his own past, and to open a channel of loyalty and affection between himself and the masses. His victory over the Lords, after the resolute stand which he had taken, greatly enhanced his prestige in the House of Commons. Although he was never able to dispense with the income-tax, all his worst troubles, except one, were now over ; and his later Budgets swung majestically down the tideway of an ever-increasing national prosperity.

By 1866 Gladstone had reduced the national expenditure to £66 millions, and the income-tax to fourpence. But three years before that, in his Budget speech of 1863, he was able to announce an increase of twenty per cent in the national income between 1853 and 1861. If the rich had been growing richer, the poor had been growing less poor. There was no parallel, Gladstone claimed, in any age or in any country, to the addition which had been made during the past twenty years to the real wealth of the average British labourer. He did not add that his own reforms had contributed much to that result ; but the facts were well known, and his reputation continued to advance.

The one serious trouble which Gladstone could do nothing to avert sprang suddenly out of a clear sky over his native Lancashire in 1861. Civil war broke out in the United States, and tens of thousands of cotton workers were thrown out of employment as a result of the Northern blockade of the ports of the Southern States from which the cotton had been exported to the Lancashire looms. Gladstone had early imbibed a strong prejudice against Americans—' a dishonest, unprincipled people', he had dubbed them in a letter to his father (3 June, 1844). He felt an especial contempt for the money-grubbing Northern Yankee tradesmen and farmers, and he shared the prejudiced view held generally by the English upper class, that the Southern planters, with their cultivated drawl, were the nearest approach to gentlemen that America could show. He noted, however, that he did not share Lord Palmerston's secret opinion that a permanent division of the American Union would be greatly to the advantage of Great Britain.

As the bloody struggle continued, the carnage sickened Gladstone, and he begged Lord Palmerston and Lord John Russell to mediate. He had formed the view that the North would never be able to restore the Union by force of arms, and he considered that diplomatic recognition should be accorded to the Southern Confederacy if the North continued to reject the good offices of the British Government.

Throughout the summer of 1862 Gladstone and his wife did their best to provide relief work on the Hawarden estate for cotton operatives who had been thrown out of employment. Gladstone's mind was full of their sufferings when he visited Newcastle-on-Tyne on 7 October, 1862, at the start of a triumphant political tour of the industrial North-East. He found himself hailed for the first time as the Parliamentary hero of the masses, and the popular refrain ran :

> Honour give to sterling worth.
> Genius better is than birth !
> So here's success to Gladstone !

If the Whigs chose to reject him, the masses at least were eager to take him to their hearts. The applause for once went to his head, and on the first day of the tour, at a banquet in the Town Hall at Newcastle, on 7 October, he committed another of the cardinal blunders of his life. He let fall the words :

' We know quite well that the people of the Northern States have not yet drunk of the cup . . . which all the rest of the world sees they nevertheless must drink. We may have our own opinions about slavery. We may be for or against the South. But there is no doubt that Jefferson Davis, and other leaders of the South have made an Army. They are making, it appears, a Navy. And they have made—what is more than either—*they have made a Nation.*'

That statement reverberated round the world and caused a profound sensation. Everyone supposed that it implied that Great Britain was about to recognize the Southern Confederacy, and the American Minister wondered if he ought to ask for his passports. Gladstone's colleagues were generous, and they helped to repair the damage. But the form of reply which Gladstone's secretary was instructed to send to indignant correspondents who wrote to complain about his words, was couched in his worst manner. It was long and almost unintelligible ; a part of the last sentence ran :

'. . . and, generally, Mr. Gladstone desires me to remark, that to form opinions upon questions of policy, to announce them to the world, and to take, or to be a party to taking, any of the steps necessary for giving them effect, are matters which, although connected together, are in themselves distinct, and which may be separated by intervals of time, longer or shorter according to the circumstances of the case.' Gladstone's more genial critics may have laughed out loud when they received that communication. But the dour and embittered ones were probably much irritated.

Many people were puzzled by Gladstone's attitude towards the Civil War. Bright wrote to Charles Sumner (10 October, 1862) : ' He is unstable as water in some things ; he is for union and freedom in Italy, and for disunion and bondage in America. A handful of Italians in prison in Naples without formal trial shocked his soul . . . but he has no word of sympathy for the four million bondsmen of the South ! ' Gladstone, of course, detested slavery, but he saw no object in denouncing it at a time when he thought that the anti-slavery cause was lost. If he had taken up the cause of the ' bondsmen of the South ' his temperament would have required him to lay every other interest aside. He was not willing, without first-hand experience of American conditions, to frame an indictment against an entire people which he conceived to be in process of becoming an independent nation.

Gladstone would have done better to remain silent, but his record made it certain that whether he spoke, or held his peace, he would be criticized. As always, he was his own sternest critic. He described his offence as one of ' incredible grossness ', and he commented on his incapacity for viewing problems all round ' in their extraneous as well as internal proportions '. He admitted wryly, that without that power it was hard to know sometimes ' when to be silent and when to speak '. His indiscretion caused some harm to Anglo-American relations for many years ; but the unexpected victory of the Northern States had an important effect upon Gladstone's outlook. All trace of his former prejudice was slowly dissolved, and he presently came to regard the American democratic experiment as one of humanitys' supreme achievements.

In the following year, 1863, Gladstone experienced a signal rebuff as a result of an extraordinary proposal which he had included in the Budget. He tried to subject the incomes of all charities to income-tax. The public outcry was loud and prolonged, and on 4 May Gladstone, at the Treasury, received an indignant deputation headed by the Duke of Cambridge, which included the Archbishops of Canterbury and York, the good Earl of Shaftesbury, and many leaders of the nation's life in every field.

That evening, in the Commons, Gladstone made a most eloquent speech in defence of what was generally regarded as a monstrous proposition. His passion for perfection had led him to regard the exemption of charities from taxation as an injustice to the rest of the community. He calculated that it cost the nation £216,000 a year. He argued that all money was a trust from God, and that therefore, so long as an income-tax existed, it was fair that all money should be taxed alike. Nineteen out of every twenty charities were the product of testamentary bequests. He had little use for such deathbed gifts ; the motives behind them were not always laudable. Money should be given away during a man's life ; and when it was so given it had already paid tax. It was grossly illogical that money given away after a man's death should pay no tax ; and the law ought to be changed.

Turning to the nature of existing charities, Gladstone described a number of scandals and abuses which masqueraded under the name of charity. Parliament and the Press, he declared, knew almost nothing about them : ' It is too much to suppose that hospitals are managed by Angels and Archangels, and that their Governors do not, like the rest of mankind, stand in need of supervision and occasional rebuke.' A public grant to deserving institutions would be very much more satisfactory than the existing omnibus exemption of every species of so-called charity from taxation. Such grants would make the public a party to the management of such institutions, and the effect would often be extremely salutary.

But Gladstone had gone too far ; countless vested interests were disturbed and alarmed ; the country was resentful ; and even his family protested. His proposal was decisively rejected by the House of Commons. Lord Palmerston said that Gladstone was a dangerous man, because he was capable of persuading himself of anything. Gladstone had, however, spoken with such heartfelt conviction, that the House, in a way, felt proud of him. His courageous, not to say reckless attack upon the way in which some charities were run caused some abuses to be brought voluntarily to an end.

The loss, by death, of old friends to whose prudent counsel he had often harkened, was partly responsible for Gladstone's temerity on that occasion. It was partly responsible also for his opposition to Lord Palmerston's action in returning the Ionian Islands to Greece in 1863. The rest of the Cabinet was virtually unanimous for that course ; but, for a time, Gladstone argued against it. He held that the Greeks did not want to be bothered with the islands, and that the cause of constitutional freedom would be better served by a temporary continuance of the British connexion.

The friends who died were Lord Aberdeen in the winter of 1860, Sidney Herbert in the summer of 1861, and Sir James Graham in the autumn of that year. Gladstone wrote (26 October, 1861) to the Duchess of Sutherland : ' The remainder of my political career . . . will be passed, in the House of Commons, without one old friend who is *both* political and personal. This is the gradual withdrawal of props, preparing for what is to follow.'

Aberdeen and Graham were old men, but Sidney Herbert, who had been created Lord Herbert of Lea when he became ill, died of cancer at the age of fifty-one. Behind his formidable reserve, Gladstone was always emotional. He seldom cared to admit to anyone how deeply, during the years which followed, he missed the companionship of Herbert's ' beautiful and sunny spirit '. Sir Robert Phillimore called to see Gladstone at breakfast on 3 August, 1861. He found him alone, and became the recipient of his confidence. All the time he was speaking about Herbert, Gladstone's voice was choked by sobs ; no-one—not even Lord Granville—was ever able quite to fill the place which Herbert had held in his affections.

One other loss which Gladstone suffered was that of the unlucky Duke of Newcastle who died in 1864. Gladstone recorded that he had been a wonderful and valuable friend, but that it would be best that no-one should ever attempt to write a life of the Duke. He was delighted by the office, which devolved upon him, of acting as executor and trustee. Newcastle had indulged a passion for building, and had told his friends that he was a ruined man. Gladstone found that that idea had been a delusion, and that the trust property alone, rightly handled, yielded more than £30,000 a year. Two of the sons presented him with an unfamiliar problem :

' Both ', he wrote to Mrs. Gladstone (29 October, 1864), ' are in danger of arrest for debt . . . and the latter [Lord Albert Pelham-Clinton] of trial, by Court-Martial ! He is, however, as cool as a cucumber ! I cannot yet make him out at all. He lost six thousand pounds at billiards, all in one night, to a youth named Wilbraham.'

The Duke had left his affairs in a state of chaos, but Gladstone, despite his preoccupations, spent long periods at Clumber, and found recreation and interest in reducing to order everything which came within his reach. He took ' unhappy Albert' in hand, after he had been dismissed from the Royal Navy, ' without any declaration of disgrace', and persuaded him to go up to Oxford with a firm resolve to work hard and to do right.

In December, 1861, the Prince Consort died. Three months later, on 19 March, 1862, Gladstone obeyed the Queen's command to wait upon her at Windsor. He had first been carefully coached by the Duchess of Sutherland, but he admitted that he felt uneasy about the way in which he should behave ' to one who was at once my Sovereign, and a widowed fellow-creature'. He remained standing throughout a long interview, while the Queen sat.

The Queen began by asking about Mrs. Gladstone, and then inquired about the state of the nation. Gladstone told her that the cotton famine had caused great distress, and that he was immensely impressed by the patience and understanding that were being shown by the unemployed. They had made such extraordinary moral and social progress, that they were now using their enforced leisure to improve their minds by reading.

The conversation was then turned by the Queen to foreign affairs, and Gladstone became eloquent on the subject of the Greek Church. The Queen intervened at one point only to ask whether the Greeks did not have confession, ' like the Roman Church ? ' :

' I said, " not like the Roman Church at all ! " They had none of the same assumption to direct the conscience ; none of the same interference with family relations ; that the Greek priest, being a family man, was in all respects a citizen, quite as much as the clergyman of this country, nay, perhaps, more so, because their religion was so intimately associated with the preservation of their national life during their degradation.'

He might have said a great deal more about the Greek Church, but his note of the interview shows that at that point the Queen warmly assented to all his views and changed the subject.

' She now looked down for a moment, and, changing the theme, said that the nation had been very good and kind to her in her time of sorrow. She struggled not to give way while she spoke this artless appeal, but, as she spoke, she seemed the most womanly of all the women in her dominions. The splendour and the majesty were as though they were not. She spoke as the heir of our common flesh and blood . . .

'She spoke of the formidable aspect of the future, and said that hers was not a mind gifted with . . . elasticity . . . She said that if ever woman had fondly loved a man, she had fondly loved the Prince.' As the Queen relieved her mind by speaking about the Prince, and about his extraordinary combination of gifts, Gladstone was slightly startled to hear her 'naming his personal beauty among them'. The Queen said that she intended to do her best, 'but she had no confidence in herself'.

Gladstone observed that he was 'not sorry to hear her use that language'. Over-confidence was a vice; and lack of it was often a virtue. In saying that, he made a psychological error. It was the woman and not the Queen who was asking to be positively reassured that she had no grounds for her lack of confidence. She had already promised to do her best, and Gladstone's words were cold comfort. He did not do badly, but he would have done better to remember the woman at that moment, and to relegate the majesty, temporarily, to the background.

The Queen went on to say that she was 'irascible' by nature, and that she had often fretted and worried the Prince. 'The sun and light of her life' were departed; no-one could fill the Prince's place. Gladstone warmly assented, but he blamed himself afterwards for not having 'gone a little further in the language of hope'.

The Queen was pleased with the interview. She noted that Gladstone had been 'very kind and feeling', and that he had spoken 'with unbounded admiration of my beloved Albert, saying no-one would ever replace him'. Gladstone recorded his astonishment at her humility, and his admiration for her elasticity of mind, dignity, and strength of character. He was to find that the strength of character had its drawbacks, and that the humility and elasticity were illusory.

Gladstone's personal relations with the Queen were at their closest at that moment. Thereafter, they gradually diverged through misunderstanding to open distrust and dislike. On 28 April, 1862, she wrote him a heartbroken letter of thanks for a speech about the Prince which he had made at Manchester. It ended:

'HER *only* wish is to get soon to her own darling again. Every day seems to increase the intensity of a sorrow which *nothing, nothing* can alleviate, as there never was *love* and devotion like hers! Every source of interest or pleasure causes now the acutest pain. *Mrs.*

Gladstone, who the Queen knows is a *most* tender wife, may, in a faint manner, picture to herself what the Queen suffers.'

To that letter Gladstone sent (29 April) a moving and compassionate answer :

'. . . It is impossible for human hands to carry to Your Majesty the consolation that such a bereavement requires . . . One who, rare as is Your Majesty's sorrow, sorrowed and suffered more, can in His own time and way, either lighten the burden, or give strength to bear it, or bring the conflict gently to an end. Unable to see into the future, we believe, Madam, that He can choose for You the best of these ; and that He will.'

That passage, so characteristic of its writer, may be compared with an equally characteristic passage from a letter which Disraeli wrote to the Queen, about the Prince, a year later (25 April, 1863) :

' The Prince is the only person, whom Mr. Disraeli has ever known, who realized the Ideal. None, with whom he is acquainted, have ever approached it. There was in him an union of the manly grace and sublime simplicity of chivalry, with the intellectual splendour of the Attic Academe . . . As time advances, the thought and senti-ment of a progressive age will . . . cluster round the Prince ; his plans will become systems, his suggestions dogmas, and the name of Albert will be accepted as the master type of a generation of pro-founder feeling, and vaster range, than that which he formed and guided with benignant power.'

The Queen was enchanted by Disraeli's ' most striking and beautiful letter '. But Gladstone, who saw her frequently at this time, was incapable of flattery. It never even occurred to him to use different language to his Sovereign from that which he was normally accus-tomed to use ; and he therefore failed to gain her ear. He stayed nearly two months at Balmoral in the early autumn of 1863, as Minister in Attendance. But there was always a feeling of constraint. He objected strongly, in common with the Archbishop of Canterbury, and the Deans of Westminster and Windsor, to the Queen's habit of taking communion in the Scottish Kirk. And although he kept that opinion to himself, the Queen, on one occasion, resented his action in using a Royal carriage to attend a Scottish Episcopal Church service some fifteen miles from the Castle. He wrote to Mrs. Gladstone (27 September) : ' I do not think Sunday is the best of days here. I in vain inquired, with care, about Episcopal Services.'

He went for very long walks, covering sometimes as much as

twenty-five miles, and returning 'as fresh as a lark'. He enjoyed himself on the whole, and told Mrs. Gladstone : 'The Household life is really very agreeable, when one comes to know them. One way and another, they have a great deal in them.' He was, however, increasingly dismayed to find that whenever the Queen quoted ' an opinion of the Prince, she looks upon the matter as completely shut up by it, for herself, and all the world'. He considered that it was his duty to speak seriously to the Queen, and a perfect opportunity presented itself on 11 October, when they were at Holyrood House together, in Edinburgh. But although ' I did not find myself timid, yet I could not manage it at all to my satisfaction . . . She said all her habits and wishes were formed on the Prince's wishes and directions, and she could not alter them.'

On 18 November, 1863, Gladstone wrote hopefully to his wife, after he had returned to London. 'I only saw the Queen for a moment . . . Her voice I thought was more like the old voice of business.' He ought to have known that it was not upon a purely business level that the relations between a future Prime Minister and a widowed, moping, female Sovereign could most profitably be conducted. Mrs. Gladstone, at any rate, knew better, and she often urged her husband to keep more in mind the human side of that relationship. She wrote to him as early as October, 1862, when he was about to start for Windsor : ' Now, contrary to your ways, do *pet* the Queen, and for once believe you can, you dear old thing.' Unhappily, Gladstone never learned the way.

For nearly two and a half years after the Prince Consort's death, the Queen continued to like and trust Gladstone, because her husband had done the same. On 11 May, 1864, however, her confidence was severely shaken. Gladstone was speaking in the House on the Second Reading of a Liberal Private Member's Bill to lower the franchise qualification in towns. Lord Palmerston, who was absent from the House, had particularly asked Gladstone, in writing, to be careful not to commit himself, or the Government ; but that afternoon an earthquake convulsed the Chancellor's mind. He astonished the House, and the country, by a single sentence :

' I venture to say that every man who is not presumably incapacitated by some consideration of personal unfitness or of political danger, is morally entitled to come within the pale of the Constitution.'

Gladstone went on to introduce a number of refinements and qualifications, and he later annoyed his critics by his bland manner of drawing attention to them. He had said, for example, that ' of course, in giving utterance to such a proposition, I do not recede from the protest I have previously made against sudden, or violent, or excessive, or intoxicating change'. But he had clearly told the House of Commons that the qualities needed for the franchise were ' self-command, self-control, respect for order, patience under suffering, confidence in the law, regard for superiors'. And he had equally clearly stated that, in his view, the upper section of the working class was now in possession of those qualities. Plain men everywhere considered that he had advocated something very like universal suffrage. The Bill was rejected by 272 votes to 56, but the effect of Gladstone's dramatic intervention could never be effaced.

Disraeli declared that the Chancellor had evidently been converted overnight to the doctrines of Rousseau and Tom Paine. The Queen told Lord Palmerston (15 May) that she was ' deeply grieved at this strange, independent act of Mr. Gladstone's . . . The Queen sincerely trusts that this imprudent declaration may not produce the agitation in the country which it is calculated to do.' Lord Palmerston himself was horrified. He wrote to Gladstone (12 May) : ' You lay down broadly the Doctrine of Universal Suffrage, which I can never accept. I entirely deny that every sane and not disqualified man has a moral right to vote . . . your Speech may win Lancashire for you, though that is doubtful, but I fear it will tend to lose England for you.' He ended by rebuking Gladstone for another part of his speech. Gladstone had recounted a warning that he had given to a trades union deputation that had recently waited upon him. He had told it that if it wanted Parliament to enfranchise the working class it must take care to bring pressure to bear on Parliament. The Prime Minister took leave to observe that ' The Function of a Government is to calm, rather than to excite Agitation '.

The earthquake which convulsed Gladstone's mind on the afternoon of 11 May, 1864, in the House of Commons, was the culmination of a very slow process of thought. It appears to have been finally pre-cipitated by a deputation from the Society of Amalgamated Engineers, which he had received on the previous day (10 May) at the Treasury. It had asked Gladstone to modify the rules of his Post Office Savings Banks with a view to enabling it to place the Society's ample funds in the safe keeping of the Government. Such confidence, a generation earlier, would have been unthinkable, and the Chancellor was effectu-ally conquered.

In the course of an acrimonious correspondence with Lord Palmerston, Gladstone showed himself unrepentant. He thought that his speech had been talked into importance, but he said that the best course now open to him was to publish it in pamphlet form. He brushed aside the Prime Minister's objections, and told him frankly (21 May) that although publication was certainly intended to be ' in the nature of a justification of what I said . . . its principal purpose is to get rid of the strange misconstructions of which it has been the subject '. He instructed Murray, accordingly, to print a large edition of the speech at once. He wrote a preface, couched in his woolliest vein, which showed that his mind needed a little time in which to settle down in its new equilibrium. But it was clear that his standing in the country had been radically transformed.

The Radicals were of course delighted, and they heaped praises on Gladstone's head. But his outlook was different from theirs. They regarded the vote as a natural right, which it was the duty of the masses to demand. They wanted to give power to the proletariat because they nourished the superficial belief that wars and misgovernment would then cease. Gladstone had no such illusions. He argued only that government would become more efficient and more stable if a vote were given to every person who was morally fit to exercise the privilege. The franchise was not, in his eyes, a natural right to be demanded ; on the contrary, it was a privilege to be earned. In that way he translated a rather dreary agitation into a triumphant affirmation of principle.

In the House of Commons (27 April, 1866), Gladstone compared the silent changes, which had been taking place in the minds of the working class, with the movements of the earth's crust. The process was constant, undeniable, resistless ; but too slow to be observable in detail. The metaphor was well-chosen. In the early 1840s the structure of English society had seemed to be in danger of collapse. At that time it had been built on a treacherous bog of poverty and discontent ; but Sir Robert Peel, and Gladstone, had put in hand, before it was too late, the necessary work of drainage and repair. As the threat of violence died away, a sense of thankfulness began to pervade all classes ; it was pithily expressed in the phrase, ' England is satisfied with her institutions '. The revolutions which convulsed the Continent in 1848–9 left the island kingdom untouched ; and Englishmen felt that they could well afford to sympathize with oppressed peoples in Italy, Poland, and elsewhere.

GLADSTONE, 1879.

zotint by T. A. Barlow from the portrait by Sir John Millais.

LORD JOHN RUSSELL
(1ST EARL RUSSELL), 1861.

JOHN BRIGHT, c. 1875.

SPENCER COMPTON,
MARQUESS OF HARTINGTON
(8TH DUKE OF DEVONSHIRE), 1

HENRY JOHN TEMPLE
(3RD VISCOUNT PALMERSTON), c. 1861.

Mezzotint by C. A. Tomkin
after H. T. Munns.

The reform movement, however, remained as active as it had ever been; the difference was that it had ceased to be revolutionary. In every big town, and in every important trade, an urgent and spontaneous desire existed that the franchise should be extended. Parliamentary opposition was too strong to enable any Bill to be carried, but between 1849 and 1866 five different Cabinets discussed Parliamentary reform, and six Speeches from the Throne referred to it. The working class, nevertheless, remained convinced that its just aspirations could and would be realized through Parliament in the end, so that the new phase of the reform movement was peaceful, constitutional, and respectable. That fact made a deep impression on Gladstone.

The urban proletariat had now allied itself with the middle class. It aimed at assimilating its cultural and economic standards with those of the bourgeoisie, so that Karl Marx was almost in despair. As he worked long hours unnoticed every day in the British Museum, he bitterly complained that 'in England, prolonged prosperity has demoralized the workers ... The ultimate aim of this most bourgeois of lands would seem to be the establishment of a bourgeois aristocracy and a bourgeois proletariat, side by side with the bourgeoisie ... The revolutionary energy of the British workers has oozed away ... They totally lack the mettle of the old Chartists.'

The workers' energies were unimpaired, but they were flowing into new channels as a result of improved economic and cultural standards. Economic standards were being raised by the action of the trades unions in winning for the workers a share in the increasing national prosperity; cultural standards were being raised by numerous working men's clubs and colleges, public libraries, and mechanics' institutes, which were springing up in towns throughout the country. The artisan class in the towns was beginning to live, and not merely to exist; and what the municipalities failed to provide was often made good by the workers themselves. *Self-Help*, by Samuel Smiles, which was published in 1859, was for many years a best-seller, and Smiles's later works, *Character*, 1871, *Thrift*, 1875, and *Duty*, 1880, all enjoyed great popularity and influence. Vast numbers of artisans, whose fathers had dreamed about manning the barricades, were now passionately eager, even in times of unemployment and distress, to devote their spare time to the sober task of improving their minds by reading. Gladstone had commented about that to the Queen when he saw her for the first time after the death of the Prince Consort.

Gladstone's view was that the working class had earned a right to vote at Elections because it had submitted itself to a preliminary process of moral self-enfranchisement. He familiarized himself with the conditions and outlook of that class by personal observation in his native Lancashire. Speaking at Crosby, near Liverpool, on 13 November, 1868, he said that 'the noble, the heroic conduct of the Lancashire operatives during the cotton famine' had finally turned the scale with him. He had felt it to be 'a shame and a scandal that bodies of men such as those should be excluded from the Parliamentary franchise'. By a similar empirical test, when universal adult suffrage was conceded in 1918, it was felt to be intolerable that men such as those who had fought and died on the Somme, and at Passchendaele, should be excluded.

Holding those views, it was, of course, impossible that Gladstone should continue to represent mid-Victorian Oxford. When the University rejected him at the General Election of 1865, he was, for once, almost unmanned by grief, but he was able to glory in being, as he said, at last 'unmuzzled'. There was, in that age, a grand simplicity about the terms of the democratic argument into the midst of which Gladstone now plunged. The Victorians were inhibited in some directions, but they were wholly uninhibited in giving large and lofty expression to idealistic views about progress, liberty, justice, and similar abstractions. Gladstone had found it hard to believe that the cause of popular democracy could prevail in North America. He had never imagined that anything so apparently dull and drab could rise to the height of Abraham Lincoln's Gettysburg Address. The praise of government of the people, by the people, for the people, was clothed in language as majestic and imperishable as that which Thucydides had put into the mouth of Pericles, two thousand four hundred years before. The proud words crossed the Atlantic, as the proud words of Pericles crossed the intervening centuries, to fall upon ears that were attuned to the message they conveyed. They strengthened men's confidence in themselves and lent the hues of romance and enchantment to the concept of popular democracy.

The whole heat and energy of Gladstone's intense nature soon closed around that concept. His nature was always frustrated unless it could operate on the widest scale and on the most exalted plane. There was nothing exalted about Lord Palmerston, and Gladstone, in consequence, felt frustrated for some years after he had saved his career, in 1859, by joining Lord Palmerston's Government. He was thankful when at last he found an opportunity to overcome that frustration by summoning the masses to his aid.

Thenceforward he used the masses to provide himself with the response which his nature craved, but which he had ceased to find in the social world in which he moved. He rewarded the masses, and, for a time, he satisfied them, by appealing not to their self-interest, but to their self-respect. He invested them with the quality of a supreme tribunal before which the greatest causes could be tried. And by that means he completed, in the political field, the work of spiritual emancipation which Wesley had begun.

The zest and aptitude for platform work which Gladstone first evinced in the early 1860s was considered grossly undignified by many of his Parliamentary colleagues. Until 1886 he never lost, in any degree, his hold on the House of Commons, but from 1865 onwards, he was happiest when addressing great popular audiences in provincial halls. As early as 19 October, 1864, he recorded, in his diary, after a provincial tour :

' So ended, in peace, an exhausting, flattering, I hope not intoxicating circuit. God knows, I have not courted them. I hope I do not rest on them. I pray I may turn them to account for good. It is, however, impossible not to love the people from whom such manifestations come, as meet me in every quarter . . . Somewhat troubled by dreams of halls, and lines of people, and great assemblies.'

The mobs, which Gladstone addressed, understood him no better than he understood them. They were incapable of rising to the height of the idealized vision which he had formed about them ; and they imagined, quite wrongly, that he was the champion of many aspirations which they had only half-formulated and of which he was wholly unaware. He was hardly at all interested in the bread-and-butter problems with which they were increasingly concerned. But Gladstone and the vast crowds which flocked to hear him felt their statures enhanced and their spirits enriched as hour after hour his magical voice called down from Heaven the lightning of poetry and passion to discharge itself in the air and flash sparks from mind to mind.

The mood which Gladstone kindled was one which priests, orators, poets, and artists have sought to kindle throughout the ages. It is the mood in which mortal men are made to feel that they are somehow ' greater than they know '. Gladstone's oratory was utterly sincere, and it appealed successfully to the untutored instincts of those who listened to it. He shared with the masses a glowing, childlike faith in the perfectibility of human nature ; and he had no illusions about the imperfect nature of the art which he practised. He had discussed the limitations of the orator some years earlier, in the third volume of his *Homer and the Homeric Age* :

'His work . . . is an influence principally received from his audience (so to speak) in vapour, which he pours back upon them in a flood . . . He cannot follow nor frame ideals. His choice is to be what his age will have him, what it requires in order to be moved by him, or else not to be at all.'

Gladstone was resolved 'to be'. And because he accepted the limitations inherent in his means, he acquired the chameleon-like qualities of a superlative advocate. He came to believe that he could best divine God's purpose by consulting the uncorrupted minds and hearts of men in masses everywhere. That was the secret of his ascendancy, and it was also the secret of the intense distrust which he later inspired. He became as necessary to the masses as they became to him : and the fervent Christian temper of British popular democracy was the offspring of their marriage of convenience.

CHAPTER 8

THE PEOPLE'S WILLIAM—PRIME
MINISTER
1864–1868

IN the autumn of 1864, Lord Palmerston, who was aged eighty, came again into acute conflict with Gladstone over the Service Estimates. Gladstone wrote from Balmoral (7 October) to his wife about a letter which he had sent to the Prime Minister. He said that his differences with Palmerston had haunted him 'like a nightmare' for months, and that unless he obtained some satisfaction he might resign before February.

In his letter to the Prime Minister Gladstone said (6 October) that public opinion called loudly for reduced expenditure, and he compared the current Service Estimates with those for 1858–9. Lord Palmerston, in the beautiful handwriting which Gladstone always said was the best he had ever seen, retorted (19 October) that the comparison was meaningless : 'As civilization advances, one generation is not satisfied with the arrangements that suited their forefathers. Gentlemen's houses are better, and more extensively provided . . . In the same way our new barracks are immense improvements upon the old ones—much to the advantage of the soldier . . . and I am sorry to say much remains to be done.'

Gladstone had been justly criticized for neglecting and injuring the soldiers' health by his refusal to find money to provide reasonable accommodation and sanitary arrangements. He had been unmoved by the argument that the cost of maintaining a convict exceeded that of maintaining a soldier, and by the fact that the urinal tubs, which stood in the barrack rooms at night, had to be emptied in the morning and used for washing. But Lord Palmerston had more to say. He told Gladstone that a revolution was taking place in the construction of ships of war. Such ships were useless now, unless they were armour-plated at prodigious expense ; naval as well as military guns of all kinds were becoming more efficient and more costly. The Prime Minister warned Gladstone that public opinion was dominated by two overriding sentiments : 'the one—a disinclination to organic changes in our representative system ; the other—a steady determination that the country shall be placed and kept in an efficient condition of defence'.

On receipt of that rebuke Gladstone openly hinted (22 October) at resignation. He said that the Prime Minister was making use of his personal popularity to keep the Defence Estimates at an unnecessary and inflated level. But Lord Palmerston replied (7 November) that Gladstone was confusing cause and effect. He could no longer, he said, tolerate Gladstone's claim to be allowed to dictate policy to the entire Cabinet on the ground that ' his honour ' required that his views should be blindly adopted. The Foreign Secretary and the heads of the Service Departments knew a great deal more than the Chancellor of the Exchequer about ' those transactions and schemes of policy of the other nations and governments of the world upon which our course must from time to time necessarily depend '. He added that if Gladstone disagreed in principle, his resignation would be accepted, with regret.

Although his bluff was thus called, Gladstone felt that he could do more for the cause of public economy by remaining at his post, than by resigning. He continued, nevertheless, to worry his colleagues. On 20 January, 1865, Palmerston informed the Queen that Gladstone had ' been as troublesome and wrong-headed as he often is upon subjects discussed in Cabinet. He objected strongly to fortifying Quebec, and insisted upon a considerable reduction in the number of men for the Navy. The whole Cabinet, however, was against him, with the exception of Mr. Milner Gibson, who feebly supported him, and the Duke of Argyll, who put in a word or two in his favour.'

If he had seen that letter, Gladstone would have objected strongly to the principle of allowing the Sovereign to be made aware of the views expressed by individual Ministers at Cabinet Meetings. He told his wife (21 January) that Lord Palmerston and Lord Russell [1] were ' old women ' ; and even Lord Granville thought that in some respects there was a little more to be said for Gladstone's attitude than ' the two old boys ', as he called them, would admit. Although it is impossible to defend Gladstone's blindness to the need for keeping abreast of contemporary developments in the art of war, he was right in thinking that an Anglo-French *entente*, which could easily have been arranged, might have safeguarded the peace of Europe at that time. He argued for such a policy in vain.

Neither Lord Palmerston, who had served at the War Office

[1] Lord John Russell was created Earl Russell in 1861.

for six years during the Great War against Napoleon, nor Lord Russell could bring themselves to trust Napoleon's nephew. The Defence Estimates were directed against France. No-one yet appreciated the menace to European tranquillity which Bismarck's Germany had begun to represent; and, thus, except in the case of Italy, the Government's handling of foreign affairs was unhappy.

In 1863, Lord Palmerston helped to throw Russia into the arms of Prussia by lecturing the Czar for his manner of suppressing a rebellion in Poland. A few months later, Lord Russell, in rejecting a French proposal for a European Conference, took occasion to lecture the French Emperor in such a cold and haughty spirit as to rule out any prospect of collaboration. Bismarck had helped the Czar in Poland, and before long he reaped his reward. When in February, 1864, he seized from Denmark the Duchies of Schleswig and Holstein, no-one interfered to stop him. Austria was his ally; Russia preserved a benevolent neutrality; France and England were not in harmony or prepared to take joint action. Six months before Danish territory was invaded Lord Palmerston had told the House of Commons that if war broke out over the problem of Schleswig-Holstein, ' it would not be Denmark alone with whom the aggressors would have to deal '. Gladstone recorded that the Cabinet was not consulted about that important statement, and that ' owing to the exhausted state of the Session ', little public notice was taken of it. He thought that he had himself been unaware of it at the time. Nevertheless, the Danes, in their extremity, appealed to Britain for the support which had been promised.

Palmerston and Russell pleaded in the Cabinet for war, provided that the French could be induced to join on the British side. Napoleon III was sounded, but his answers were unsatisfactory, and Gladstone delighted the Queen by throwing his influence on the side of peace. There was widespread public sympathy for the Danes, but no desire for a single-handed war against Prussia and Austria. While Danish resistance was being crushed, Palmerston and Russell were fiercely attacked in Parliament and the Press for their policy of ' meddle and muddle '. Disraeli moved a Vote of Censure in the Commons which Gladstone answered at Palmerston's request. Gladstone had hoped that Great Britain and France together would have been in a position to enforce a settlement ' on judicial grounds '. He argued for ninety minutes on 4 July, 1864, that the guarantee upon which Denmark had relied had been a joint obligation upon the Powers, and that it became automatically inoperative when other Powers declined to act. The Motion of Censure in the Commons was defeated by only eighteen votes ; a similar Motion in the Lords was carried by a majority of nine. So ended an unsatisfactory episode which launched German militarism on a long career of aggression, and cost Great Britain, for a time, much of her influence in Europe.

As the dissolution drew nearer, Gladstone became extremely uneasy about his university seat at Oxford. He valued his newly-won popularity with the masses, and he now began to extend his influence in the country by cultivating personal relations with leaders of the Nonconformist Churches to which many members of the lower middle and working classes belonged. For a time he still toyed with the hope of effecting a religious reunion, but his main desire was to wean Nonconformists from their social and cultural isolation. They seemed at that time to be set apart from their fellow-citizens as self-conscious, if not defiant, 'witness-bearers'. Gladstone told a Unitarian friend (2 January, 1865) that, devoted as he was to dogma, he could no longer imagine how he could ever have believed that salvation depended upon the reception of any one particular creed : 'Long, long ago have I left those weeds behind me.'

Gladstone's frequent appearances at Nonconformist tea-parties were much publicized ; and they caused bewilderment at Oxford. That bewilderment was increased by a speech which he made in the House of Commons on 28 March, 1865, about the Anglican Church in Ireland. A Radical member had moved a Resolution which called, in effect, for that Church's disestablishment. Gladstone opposed it on the sole ground that the time was not yet ripe. He said that the position of that Church was profoundly unsatisfactory, because it catered for only a fraction of the Irish people. As a Missionary Church it was an obvious failure, because the proportion of Protestants to Roman Catholics had been greater during the sixteenth century than it was during the nineteenth.

Gladstone had intended to speak as a private member, and had privately declared his intention to denounce the Church of Ireland as a menace to religion, to civil justice, and to peace. Happily, news of his intention had reached Lord Palmerston in time, and Gladstone was firmly reminded that he must speak as a member of the Government. He had, however, said enough to make Oxford feel that the effort required to understand Gladstone was becoming too tedious, and at the General Election of July, 1865, he lost his seat to Gathorne

Gathorne-Hardy, afterwards first Earl of Cranbrook. The figures were :

Heathcote :	3236	elected
Gathorne-Hardy :	1904	elected
Gladstone :	1724	

Gladstone might conceivably have retained the seat if the privilege of voting by post had not been accorded for the first time at that election. Clerical graduates all over the country registered their indignation at the attitude which he had disclosed towards the Irish Church.

The event, although foreseen, was the most bitter and grievous political blow which Gladstone suffered in the whole course of his life. Palmerston prophesied that nothing would now restrain Gladstone from running amok. Gladstone noted in his diary : ' A dear dream is dispelled. God's will be done ! ' He repeated over and over again to himself the sixteenth verse of the eighty-sixth Psalm : ' O turn unto me, and have mercy upon me ; give strength to thy servant, and save the son of thine handmaid.' He had, however, previously taken practical steps to save himself, and to secure his retreat in case of need. He had reserved a nomination for South Lancashire.

By sitting first for a pocket borough and then for Oxford University Gladstone had hitherto been spared the necessity for wooing on his own behalf the votes of a popular constituency. He had, however, assisted his father, his brothers Thomas and John, and his brother-in-law, Sir Stephen Glynne, to fight normal seats, and he had found the experience disagreeable. He had disliked particularly his experience in the county of Flintshire, where he had helped Sir Stephen to contest every election between 1837 and 1857. Before 1837 Flintshire had been represented for a century and a half by members of the Mostyn family ; in that year, however, the Hon. M. L. Mostyn, who had been unopposed in the three previous elections, was narrowly defeated by Sir Stephen. In 1841 Mostyn defeated Sir Stephen by means which Gladstone characterized as ' bribery, faggotry, abduction, personation, riot, factious delays, landlords' intimidations, partiality of authorities'. Gladstone on that occasion incurred a portentous rebuke from a member of the Grosvenor family for a breach of etiquette in canvassing Lord Westminster's tenants. He was informed that interference between a landlord, with whose opinions he was acquainted, and his tenants, was an unjustifiable breach ' of those laws of delicacy and propriety ' which were generally considered binding in such cases.   Mostyn, in 1841, was unseated in favour of Sir Stephen on a petition, but he was returned at the two following elections. In 1857 Sir Stephen was again defeated by another member of the Mostyn family.   Gladstone was thankful that he was spared for many years what he regarded as the inescapable indignities to which so many of his colleagues were exposed.   Even in his most radical moods he continued to regret the disappearance of pocket boroughs, and to look back wistfully to Oxford.   However, when at last he was compelled to accept the inevitable, he cast his former scruples away, and dedicated himself to the task of turning his necessity to gain.

To Manchester, accordingly, Gladstone sped on 18 July, after learning, the night before, that his defeat at Oxford was virtually accomplished.   His opening words in the Free Trade Hall were greeted with shouts of applause from an audience of six thousand persons :

" At last, my friends, I am come amongst you.   And I am come . . . unmuzzled."

Those words were widely reported and their significance was appreciated throughout the country.

That evening, Gladstone went on to Liverpool, where he addressed at eight o'clock another great meeting of five thousand people.   He told them frankly that he was broken-hearted at leaving Oxford. He said that he had clung to that seat with ' desperate fondness ', but that he had always done his best ' to unite that which is represented by Oxford with that which is represented by Lancashire '.   He was returned by a small majority, and in thanking the electors at Newton, where the Poll was declared on 22 July, he said :

" If I came here a wounded man, you have healed my wound . . . I have seen nothing at all said against me . . . except this—that I am an erratic politician ; and that is a thing, gentlemen, that I have been accustomed to hear said of me as long as I have lived."

Gladstone was indignant when Archbishop Manning wrote to warn him against the risk of adopting extreme views, and of losing his self-control in ' the new and larger field ' which he had entered. He told Manning (21 July) that he knew well that he was sadly lacking in self-control, but that the caution about extremism was quite unnecessary.   He complained (25 July) to the Bishop of Oxford (Samuel Wilberforce) that Manning had ceased to be human : ' No shirt-collar ever took such a quantity of starch.'

PEGASUS UNHARNESSED

PUNCH, July 29, 1865

Gladstone had previously told Wilberforce (21 July) that in his political life he had experienced two great 'deaths'. The first, 'very slow', had been the breaking of his tie with the Conservative Party; the second, 'very short and sharp', had been the breaking of his tie with Oxford: 'There will probably be a third, and no more.' When the Bishop inquired the meaning of that 'oracular sentence' Gladstone said that it had better remain 'in its proper darkness'. In fact, the mood of depression which visited him after the emotional strain through which he had passed, had made him toy once again with the idea of retiring from politics and devoting the rest of his life to religion.

The elections had given the Government a slightly increased majority, but before the new House met, Lord Palmerston died just before his eighty-first birthday. Gladstone was at Clumber, carrying out the duties, which he rather relished, of a trustee of the Newcastle properties. Mrs. Gladstone was at Fasque, staying with Sir Thomas Gladstone, who was, she told her husband, 'as grim, and low, and silent as can be'. Sir Thomas had a boil in an inconvenient and uncomfortable place, and Gladstone did his best to console his wife. He said that his sister-in-law, Lady Gladstone, would have made a 'grand barbarian' in the dawn of history, and added (18 October) that Lord Palmerston's death had destroyed all prospect of a quiet life: 'To-day was a good preparation, with a beautiful and absorbing Service of 3½ hours in Church.'

After church, Gladstone wrote to Lord Russell. He assumed, he said, that Russell would be Prime Minister, and he added:

'I am sore with conflict about the public expenditure, which I feel that other men would have either escaped, or have conducted more justly, and less fretfully. I am most willing to retire. On the other hand . . . I am quite willing to take my chance under your banner in the exact capacity I now fill.'

The Times had suggested Gladstone's name as Prime Minister (19 October), while Delane, its editor, had been out of town. Delane, who disagreed with that suggestion, hurried back and called (20 October) for Lord Russell, and on that day the Queen sent for Russell, who was aged seventy-three. Lord Russell was loved by his friends, whom he entertained with an endless flow of anecdotes, but to the public he appeared cold and aloof. He was a shy man, very short, and frail, and he spoke with an exaggerated drawl, using old-fashioned expressions such as 'ooman for woman, and obleeged for obliged. Many people were surprised that he should take office again, but the King of the Belgians wrote (28 October) to Queen Victoria : 'These politicians never refuse ! ' Lord Russell at once asked Gladstone to lead the House of Commons—a duty which he had never before had to undertake.

After waiting some weeks, the Queen wrote (19 February, 1866) to congratulate Gladstone on the way he had begun his task. She said that she had heard good accounts of him on all sides. In fact, however, many doubts were current about Gladstone's ability to lead. He was thought to be dictatorial, irritable, impulsive, and lacking in judgement and tact. He was often described as 'the white elephant '—a liability to any Government which he joined. On the other hand his personality was magnetic ; he might inspire love, or hate, but never indifference ; and the moral power which he wielded was a weapon of incalculable potency.

As the masses emerged from passivity into ever deepening political consciousness, they trailed ' clouds of glory ' for a time, like children. In that mood, Gladstone's glowing intensity and earnestness appealed very strongly to them ; and to Scotsmen, particularly, he appeared somewhat in the character of George Meredith's first love :

> Boldly she sings, to the merry tune she marches,
>   Brave is her shape, and sweeter unpossessed.
> Sweeter, for she is what my soul first awaking
>   Whispered the world was—morning light is she !

The masses were for a long time disposed to reject the sophisticated view that politics are a choice between a number of courses of varying degrees of expediency. On the contrary, their hearts responded to Gladstone's reiterated assurances that all important political questions involve clear-cut moral issues. Gladstone expounded and universalized those issues in the exalted light of his personal religion, and, as he did so, Disraeli loved to accuse him of cant and humbug. To Disraeli, the prime duty of a British statesman was to advance British interests and uphold British honour, and his methods were avowedly empirical. Gladstone said more than once that such words as ' interest ' or ' honour ' were meaningless unless they were equated with the causes of humanity, justice, civilization, and religion. He constantly urged ' the pursuit of objects which are European by means which are European, in concert with the mind of the rest of Europe and supported by its authority ' (29 March, 1878). He prayed constantly for guidance, and believed that he received answers to his prayers. In those circumstances he was apt to confound with moral obliquity, any arguments or convictions which ran counter to his own.

In the House of Commons, Gladstone did his utmost to be circumspect, and he even sometimes appeared too modest and deferential ; but he continued to arouse mistrust. Sir Thomas Acland, playing the part of the candid friend, wrote on 28 January, 1868, to tell Gladstone some of his faults. He said that he was taking a great liberty, but that he had heard so much grumbling that he felt it a duty to write.

There was, Sir Thomas said, a widespread impression that Gladstone cared too much about Homer, and religious controversy, to read the newspapers or keep in touch with his rank and file : ' One man personally complained that, when you sought his opinion, you spent the whole interview impressing your own view upon him, and hardly heard anything he had to say.' Sir Thomas complained that Gladstone's *entourage* was narrow, and that parts of it were second-rate. He begged him to cultivate the strong men, and the rising men ; to drop into the smoking room of the House of Commons sometimes, as Lord Palmerston had done, and to make himself agreeable to the small fry. He thought that it might be an advantage if Gladstone were to join the Athenæum Club, where he would meet many men whose goodwill would be useful to him, because their influence upon opinion was considerable.

Sir Thomas Acland had good grounds for writing in that way. Lord Russell, when he was about to resign the Liberal Party leadership, wrote to Lord Clarendon (8 October, 1867) to complain that Gladstone obstinately refused to do any political entertaining : ' I shall ask you and about 15 other peers to dine with me on the 18th. A glass of wine and a friendly greeting can do no harm. Gladstone says he cannot keep abreast of me in this respect ; but I think he is wrong. He ought to ask Bright . . .' During a crisis of the Reform Bill debate in March, 1866, when every vote counted, Lord Granville, who was in process of becoming the most loved and trusted of all Gladstone's friends, found it necessary to warn Gladstone that he had needlessly offended a possible supporter. He begged him to ' take him into a corner, and then tell him that he is a fool, and that he smells disagreeably, or any other not very secret fact '. It would really hardly matter what Gladstone said, if only he would take some notice of the man. In Parliament there was often no other effective way of influencing individual votes.

Gladstone tried hard to learn, but he made little progress. He thanked Acland (30 January, 1868), but said that after thirty-six years in public life he thought that he himself must be allowed to be the best judge of ' how to husband what little energy of brain, and time for using it, remains to me '. He admitted that he found literature seductive, but ' change of work is the chief refreshment of my mind ' ; he added that he only wrote about religion on Sundays. He was, he said, so busy that he could not undertake to do more than try ' to be thoroughly open to all Members of Parliament who seek me, while my seeking them must of necessity be limited '. He refused to join the Athenæum Club, because there were professional and other men there who might feel that they had some claim on his time and attention. He preferred the United University Club, where he was more likely to be left in peace, and he remained a member of it from 1854 until he died. Although he grew restive in a self-consciously professional atmosphere, Gladstone was always gregarious ; he greatly enjoyed the select company at Grillions, and at ' The Club ', an older and equally distinguished dining society, to which he had been elected in 1857. The fact that Disraeli never belonged to ' The Club ' may possibly have enhanced the attraction of its dinners. On the whole, the best comment upon Gladstone during the 1860s was made by Benjamin Jowett, who said that no-one of such great simplicity had ever before been found in so exalted a station.

*   *   *

Gladstone enjoyed much more cordial relations with Lord Russell than he had done with Lord Palmerston. He sympathized warmly with Lord Russell's desire to force a new measure of franchise reform through Parliament, and he toiled night and day at the task of preparing a Bill. Lord Russell could never forget that he had been the hero of the great Reform Act of 1832, and the subject of reform was now the only public interest which he had left. He wrote to Gladstone (25 January, 1866) : ' If I bring in, or contribute to bring in, a measure, it will be to me a satisfactory close of my political life, whether carried or defeated.'

In introducing the Representation of the People Bill on 12 March, 1866, Gladstone admitted that ' the limbo of abortive creations ' was ' peopled with the skeletons of Reform Bills '. He proposed to lower the property qualification from a rental of £10 a year in the boroughs and £50 a year in the counties, to £7 and £14 respectively. It was calculated that some 400,000 voters might be added to the electorate, as compared with upwards of 800,000 in 1832, and it was as at once evident that a political storm of the first magnitude had arisen.

The Bill was opposed not only by the whole of the Conservative Party, but by a section of the Liberals as well. Its foremost Liberal critic was Robert Lowe (afterwards Viscount Sherbrooke), an albino, who had practised law in Australia and taken part in politics in New South Wales. Lowe had acquired in the Antipodes a pathological loathing for democracy, and in organizing the Liberal revolt he acquired a position of personal supremacy which had never, in Gladstone's view, been surpassed. It lasted for one year only, but that was sufficient to wreck Gladstone's hopes. It was characteristic of Gladstone that he should have later pressed the Queen to recognize Lowe's achievement. In recommending him for a viscountcy in 1880, he told the Queen that Lowe had soared to such heights for a few months in 1866 that he ought never to be lost ' in the common ruck of official barons '.

John Bright compared Lowe, and the dissident Liberals, to the distressed Biblical figures whom David had gathered round him in the Cave of Adullam. They became known, in consequence, as the ' Adullamites ', or the ' cave-men '. As the contest grew hotter, Gladstone became more and more excited ; he was much provoked on 28 March by an ungenerous speech by Lowe, in which the working classes were described as the ultimate repository of venality, ignorance, drunkenness, and of impulsive and unreflecting violence. Those words caused great bitterness in the country, and Gladstone at once retorted that the members of the working class were ' our fellow-subjects, our fellow-Christians, *our own flesh and blood*, who have been lauded to the skies for their good conduct '. He compared the opposition to the enfranchisement of a section of them with that which it would have been appropriate to offer to a hostile invading army. Lord Cranborne, who as Lord Salisbury was presently to be Prime Minister for an even longer period than Gladstone, described Gladstone's speech as sentimental claptrap. Did he really think that he could see a moral principle in a £7 borough rental ? Were not tramps, paupers, and lunatics also our own flesh and blood ? Where did he suppose that his argument would lead ?

On 6 April, 1866, at Liverpool during the Easter Recess, Gladstone staked the existence of the Government on the passage of the Reform Bill. He said that Ministers had crossed the Rubicon, blown the bridges, and burned their boats. He denounced the two greatest magnates in Lancashire—Lord Grosvenor, an Adullamite, and Lord Stanley, Lord Derby's heir—as a pair of selfish aristocrats who were conspiring to defeat an act of justice to the people. Such language gave great offence.

During the debate on the Second Reading, Disraeli said (27 April) that the Bill was conceived in the spirit of the American rather than in that of the British constitution. He taunted Gladstone with the speech which he had made at the Oxford Union thirty-five years earlier, in 1831, against the great Reform Bill, and he received a stinging rebuke :

'As the Right Honourable gentleman has exhibited me, let me exhibit myself. What he has stated is true. I deeply regret it. But I was bred under the shadow of the great name of Canning. Every influence connected with that name governed the politics of my childhood and my youth. With Canning I rejoiced at the removal of religious disabilities and at the character which he gave to our policy abroad ; with Canning I rejoiced at the opening which he made towards the establishment of free commercial interchanges between nations. With Canning, and under the shadow of the yet more venerable name of Burke, I grant that my youthful mind and imagination were impressed with the same idle and futile fears which still bewilder and distract the mature mind of the Right Honourable gentleman. I had received that fear and alarm of the first Reform Bill in the days of my undergraduate youth at Oxford which the Right Honourable gentleman now feels ; and the only difference between us is this—I thank him for bringing it out—that having those views I moved the Oxford Union Debating Society to express them clearly, plainly, forcibly, in downright English while the Right Honourable gentleman does not dare to tell the nation what it is that he really thinks, and is content to skulk under the shelter of the meaningless amendment of the Noble Lord. . . .'

After comparing his reception into the bosom of the Liberal Party with that which Virgil's Queen Dido had accorded to the ship-wrecked Aeneas, Gladstone ended with a fine peroration :

'You cannot fight against the future. Time is on our side. The great social forces which move onward in their might and majesty and which the tumult of your debates does not for a moment impede or disturb . . . are against you. They are marshalled on our side. And the banner which we now carry in this fight, though perhaps at some moment it may droop over our sinking heads, yet it soon again will float in the eye of Heaven, and it will be borne by the firm hands of the united people of the three kingdoms, perhaps not to an easy, but to a certain and to a not far distant victory.'

Gladstone noted in his diary that he had spoken from one until half-past three in the morning, 'a toil much beyond my strength, but I seemed to be sustained and borne onward, I know not how'.

In the Division which followed, an Opposition amendment to postpone the Second Reading until the Government should produce a Redistribution Bill was defeated by a bare majority of five. For a moment the Cabinet considered giving way, but Lord Russell and Gladstone stood firm.

The debate, which lasted for several weeks, was interrupted on 3 May by the Budget. Gladstone repealed the duties on timber and pepper, and made other minor concessions. He took occasion to warn the House that the British coalfields might be exhausted by 1966, and that the consequent diminution of the nation's productive powers might be catastrophic. He deduced the characteristic conclusion that more serious efforts should be made to redeem the national debt in good time, and to curb expenditure.

A few days later (7 May) the Queen asked Lord Russell whether he would like her to scold Gladstone for his tactless conduct of the Reform Bill debate. Lord Russell said that he considered that to be unnecessary, but Lady Frederick Cavendish (formerly Lucy Lyttelton) noted in her journal (31 May) : 'I suppose Uncle William is wanting in tact ; for there is treason through the camp, and the oddest combination and fermentation of parties against him.'

The end came on 18 June, when an Opposition Motion to take the rateable value instead of the rent of a house as the basis of the franchise was carried against the Government by eleven votes. When the result was declared, the House was in an uproar, and Gladstone recorded : 'There was shouting, violent flourishing of hats, and other manifestations, which I think novel and inappropriate.' They may have appeared inappropriate but they would not have been novel to anyone who remembered the Reform Bill debates of 1832.

That was not the first defeat which the Government had suffered, and the Cabinet had decided two days earlier that the disputed clause need not necessarily be treated as vital. The Queen told Lord Russell on 19 June that it was his duty to remain in office in view of the outbreak of war (18 June) between Austria and Prussia ; and Lord Russell had no wish to resign. He had reached the last phase of his career, and the prospect of its abrupt termination dismayed him. He would have liked to seek a general Vote of Confidence from the House, or to seek a retrial of the adverse vote on the disputed clause. Gladstone, however, supported by Lord Granville, argued strongly in the Cabinet that both those courses would be discreditable. Either might, he rightly thought, lay Ministers open to the reproach of clinging to office.

Two other courses were open to the Cabinet. It could appeal to the country ; or it could resign and abandon the Bill. Gladstone was so afraid that the Cabinet might seek to cling to office in deference to the wishes of the Queen, the Prime Minister, and *The Times*, that he advocated immediate resignation. He thought afterwards that a dissolution followed by an appeal to the country would have been best : ' Such an appeal,' he considered, ' unhesitatingly made, would have evoked a response similar, though not equal to, that of 1831.' Bright strongly advised Gladstone (24 June) to press for a General Election, but the Government Whips believed that an appeal to the country would be unpopular and unsuccessful. After a week's hesitation the Cabinet decided (25 June) for immediate resignation without asking for a dissolution.

On the following day (26 June) Lord Russell and Gladstone had separate audiences with the Queen at Windsor. The Queen thought that Gladstone looked ill and harassed ; he told her that Parliamentary government had been discredited by previous miscarriages on the issue of franchise reform. The Queen begged Lord Russell to reconsider his decision to resign, and the Cabinet was summoned, but it refused. At six o'clock on 26 June, after a telegram had been sent to Windsor, Gladstone accordingly announced the Government's resignation to the House of Commons. He noted : ' I kept to facts without epithets, but I thought as I went on that some of the words were scorching.' Lord Derby took office at once, although he was in a minority in the Commons ; he formed a Conservative Government without the aid of the Adullamites who refused to join him, and Disraeli succeeded Gladstone as Chancellor of the Exchequer and leader of the Commons.

The provocative language used by Lowe in opposing the Reform Bill had excited much bitterness and class-feeling. Its full extent was not immediately realized, but it was exacerbated by an economic crisis which developed after the failure, in May, 1866, of the great financial house of Overend and Gurney. In the subsequent financial panic many enterprises collapsed; for three months the Bank of England found it necessary to raise its discount rate to ten per cent; and a popular agitation against upper-class mismanagement was revived after a long period of quiescence. In London there were meetings and riots, and as early as 27 June a large crowd marched from Trafalgar Square to Gladstone's house in Carlton Gardens, chanting, 'Gladstone and Liberty!' Gladstone was dining out, but Mrs. Gladstone was at home. At the request of the police she appeared on the balcony with her daughters, and bowed to the mob, which cheered loudly and then peacefully dispersed. *The Times* (29 June) and some other newspapers took Gladstone to task for courting the mob after the manner of John Wilkes and Lord George Gordon. Mrs. Gladstone, understandably, was delighted at the people's tribute to her husband.

On 23 July there was a more serious demonstration when the authorities closed the gates of Hyde Park against a reform meeting at which Gladstone had been invited to speak. He had refused the invitation, but in doing so he had said that in the hour of defeat he had 'a presentiment of victory'. The mob tore down the railings of Hyde Park over a length of some 1,400 yards, and trampled the flower beds which were overlooked by the mansions of Park Lane. The Life Guards were summoned to assist the police, and a number of heads were broken. Many more meetings and protest marches were held, and Conservative opinion began to veer round to the view that franchise reform could not be much longer postponed. Spencer Walpole, the somewhat feeble Home Secretary, burst into tears when an indignant deputation from the Reform League called on him by appointment to protest against the closing of Hyde Park; the amusement which he thereby caused helped a little towards blunting the edge of the widespread popular resentment.

Gladstone, who was now feeling mentally as well as physically exhausted, decided to take a holiday abroad. He complained that he was being persecuted by a mass of suggestions and solicitations which poured in upon him by every post, and he thought that the split in the Liberal Party which Robert Lowe had caused, could best be left to 'the healing powers of nature'. Accordingly, on 28 September, 1866, he left England with Mrs. Gladstone and his daughters, Agnes and Mary, for Rome, where they were joined by Sir Stephen Glynne.

Before he left London, Gladstone unfortunately irritated the Queen

by refusing her request, conveyed to him through her secretary—
General Grey—to support a Motion in the House of Commons for
the purchase of a small amount of gun-metal for the Prince Consort's
statue (the Albert Memorial) in Kensington Gardens. Replying
to General Grey (24 July) Gladstone pointed out that £50,000 had
been voted in 1863 for the Memorial to the Prince, and that the work
would not be finished for some years :

'It is contrary to the rules of good administration to ask money
from Parliament for a particular work without intimating that more
will be required, and then to ask for more for the same purpose. And
in the rules of good administration none has so deep an interest as the
Crown . . . Nothing should ever be put into Supplemental Estimates except that which could neither have gone into the original
Estimates, nor be postponed to next year. This satisfies neither
condition . . . You will see after what I have said that I can give no
pledge to support the proposal.'

For three years Gladstone had persistently opposed the Queen's
frequently expressed desire for an inconsiderable additional vote for
the purchase of gun-metal for her husband's statue. He was always
willing to move or support votes to provide generous incomes for
members of the Royal Family, and their connexions, but he would not
compromise upon a matter which he regarded as one of principle,
however small. After much correspondence between the Court and
Ministers he had won Palmerston round to his view. The question
of the Prince's statue touched the Queen very closely indeed, and she
deeply resented Gladstone's attitude. On 25 July, Disraeli, as Chancellor of the Exchequer, had no difficulty in securing the assent of the
House of Commons to the proposal. He was rewarded (26 July)
by a very warm letter of thanks. The Queen told him that she well
knew how truly he at least had appreciated ' her dear, great husband '.
Gladstone's inflexible adherence to principle was everywhere appreciated. On that occasion, however, he would have done well to
be less rigid ; his intransigent attitude was unavailing, and it appeared
unfeeling and unkind.

Before Gladstone started for Rome, Archbishop Manning advised
the Pope to treat his distinguished visitor with every consideration.
Gladstone could, he said, easily be turned into a friend, but he could
be a most dangerous enemy if wrongly handled. Accordingly,
on 22 October, when Gladstone had the first of two private audiences
with Pius IX, he was made to sit down, in spite of his protest that in

all his long experience he had never once been invited to sit by Queen Victoria. Gladstone was received in Rome as the representative of British democracy, and the Pope assented politely to a proposition by Gladstone that 'the general tendency of these days is towards democratic government'. His Holiness was, however, careful to explain that in Italy the character of the people made free elections unthinkable and Gladstone was too polite to pursue that subject. Three of Gladstone's former colleagues, Edward Cardwell, Lord Clarendon, and the Duke of Argyll, were in Rome at that time. Gladstone was delighted when he heard the Pope's pithy summary of his impressions of all four, and he never tired of repeating it :

'Mr. Gladstone I like but don't understand. Mr. Cardwell I understand but don't like. I like *and* understand Lord Clarendon. The Duke of Argyll I neither like *nor* understand.'

Gladstone in Rome was unwearied in flitting from church to church, not to study their architecture, but to hear and comment upon as many sermons by as many varieties of priests and friars as possible. He felt very much drawn to Lord Clarendon, who came out on 30 October. Clarendon was covertly amused by Gladstone, and he wrote to Lady Salisbury (24 November) : 'Italian art, archæology, and literature, are G.'s sole occupations. Every morning at 8 he lectures his wife and daughters upon Dante, and requires them to parse and give the root of every verb. He runs about all day to shops, galleries, and persons, and only last night he told me that he hadn't time for the reading room, and hadn't seen an English newspaper for three or four days.' Lord Clarendon's tongue, which was constantly running away with him, caused him presently much embarrassment with the Queen, whom he had nicknamed 'the Missus'. His nickname for Gladstone was 'Merrypebble', and he told his friends in Rome that although mental and physical restoration had made Gladstone appear moderate in his opinions, he was liable to become violent again when he returned to his old haunts and habits in England.

When Gladstone returned home at the end of January, 1867, after dining on 27 January with the French Emperor in Paris, the political situation was considerably changed. John Bright and other Radicals had roused the Midlands and the North against Robert Lowe's suggestion that the wage-earners were the moral and intellectual inferiors of the bourgeoisie. At Birmingham, Leeds, Manchester, Glasgow, and Edinburgh, monster meetings had been held, at which trades unionists had marched past Bright for hours on end, carrying banners, and pledging themselves to work for franchise reform. The gentlemen of England, with the unerring instinct which never deserts them, noted the signs. They cared little about foreigners, but some of them were aware that Bismarck, in the new Constitution which he had framed for Germany, had based his Reichstag on a system of universal and secret franchise.

Disraeli saw that a new Reform Bill had become inevitable, and he had always wished to re-establish Conservatism on a popular basis. He had thought out no plan ; he cared little for detail or consistency ; but with his hand all the time feeling the pulse of the House of Commons as well as that of the country, he produced a bewildering series of proposals with what Gladstone termed diabolical cleverness and unexampled rapidity.

Disraeli took over from Bright the catchword, 'household suffrage', and he cleverly and characteristically called Bright into consultation. He adopted a rating instead of a rental qualification for the franchise, and conciliated the Conservative back-benchers by introducing a number of safeguards which were discarded when they had served their purpose. Disraeli proposed, for example, to exclude all those whose rates were paid by their landlords, and to give extra votes to large taxpayers, to holders of funds in savings banks, and to all university graduates.

Gladstone denounced this Bill with its checks, safeguards, and counterweights as a 'gigantic engine of fraud'. Only a small minority of householders paid rates personally, and it seemed to Gladstone therefore that Disraeli was advocating a lottery as well as a fraud. Gladstone argued that when the time for household suffrage was ripe, 'it ought to be a real household suffrage'. He urged that, for the present, true household suffrage went beyond the wishes and needs of the time, and that a straightforward and moderate measure was required, which should perform all that it promised.

The House of Commons, which had rejected a moderate measure of reform in the previous year, had been greatly impressed by the subsequent agitation in the country and was now in a perplexed but malleable mood. Disraeli, the leader of the House, and Gladstone, the leader of the Opposition, were both distrusted by their Parties, and the Conservatives were in a decided minority ; but Disraeli was as skilful in handling his followers, as Gladstone was stiff and obstinate. Gladstone failed to appreciate that the phrase ' household suffrage', once Disraeli had aired and advertised it, was bound to prove irresistible. In an indifferent and cynical House, Gladstone argued about minutiæ with high-minded and enthusiastic intensity. But the lax temper of the House gave Disraeli his chance to effect a reform in which he sincerely believed, and Gladstone suffered a resounding rebuff. At a Party meeting in his own house, 11, Carlton House Terrace, on 21 March, 1867, Gladstone had a hostile reception and failed to secure support for his policy of an outright attack upon the Bill on its Second Reading. Deeply humiliated, he proceeded instead by way of detailed amendments aimed at wrecking it in Committee.

The effect of those amendments, most of which were carried, was to give the country household suffrage on a democratic basis in place of the modest measure which had first been proposed. Disraeli accepted the changes with his eyes open, and although three members of the Cabinet—Lord Cranborne, Secretary for India, Lord Carnarvon, Secretary for the Colonies, and General Peel, Secretary for War— resigned (2 March, 1867), the bulk of the Party stood firm. In 1846 Peel had taken the Conservatives by surprise, and had thereby broken up the Party. In 1867 Disraeli was careful to draw the Party gradually towards the end which he desired, and he could afford therefore to laugh at Lord Cranborne's taunt that his conduct represented 'a political betrayal that has no parallel in our Parliamentary annals'. Gladstone's loathing for his rival's brilliant tactics was so strong, that he often became more heated in debate than was good either for his reputation or for his health. On 26 March Disraeli raised a loud laugh against Gladstone by congratulating those on the Government front bench on the security which they derived from the presence of 'a good broad piece of furniture' between themselves and the leader of the Opposition.

On 12 April Gladstone made a great effort to destroy the Bill at its weakest point, by attacking the provision that those whose rates were paid by their landlords should be excluded from the franchise. He had done everything which he could think of to conciliate his mutinous followers, but he found himself in a minority of twenty-one. Forty-three Liberals voted with the Government ; about twenty more abstained ; Gladstone noted in his diary that this was 'a smash perhaps without example', and he told Sir Robert Phillimore that he thought of retiring to a back bench and giving up the leadership. Mrs. Gladstone who was seen to turn ' white to the very lips as the tellers came in, or even a little before ', told Lady Frederick Cavendish that William, when he came home, ' could hardly speak '. She had never, she said, seen him so ' knocked down '. Disraeli, after looking in at the Carlton Club, where he was loudly cheered in the crowded coffee room, went home in triumph to his wife. At 93, Park Lane, at three o'clock in the morning, Mrs. Disraeli had ready a pie from Fortnum and Mason's, and a bottle of champagne, already open : " My dear," Disraeli exclaimed, as he drank the champagne and dug his fork into the pie, " you are more like a mistress than a wife ! " The contrast between the sphinx-like nonchalance of Disraeli's face, and the furrowed gloom of Gladstone's, excited comment.

Gladstone was in a quandary which tortured him. He appreciated the force of Robert Lowe's argument that both Parties were con-ducting a ' Dutch auction ' in which the Constitution was being sold to the highest bidder ; but he felt bound to do his best, in the interest of public morality, to bring the reality of Disraeli's Bill ' into corres-pondence with its great professions '. In so doing he delivered himself into his opponent's hands. Disraeli knew that he could afford to sit back and to allow the House to take control. He made concession after concession, and rejoiced in the success of his tactics. On 27 May, for example, after winning round his colleagues, he accepted an amendment by a little-known back-bencher which, in effect, conceded the point on which Gladstone had been so signally defeated on 12 April. The franchise was granted to tenants whose rates were paid by their landlords, and the Conservatives remained in full control of the battle : ' Never ', Gladstone noted, ' have I undergone a stronger emotion of surprise than when, as I entered the House, our Whip met me and stated that Disraeli was about to support Hodgkinson's Motion. But so it was, and the proposition was adopted without disturbance, as if it had been an affair of trivial importance.'

The upshot was that when the Bill was finally carried, a million new voters were enfranchised in place of the four hundred thousand who would have benefited from Gladstone's abortive measure of 1866. In the boroughs, household suffrage was conceded, and occupiers of lodgings of £10 annual value were also enfranchised. In the counties, the franchise limit was lowered to cover occupiers of houses rated at £12. Provision was made for a long overdue redistribution of seats for the first time since 1832. Disraeli claimed with justice that he had educated his Party ; he had achieved an extraordinary triumph, and there was no-one capable of behaving to him as he had once behaved, on a similar occasion, to Peel. Lord Derby admitted that the Bill was a leap in the dark, but he remembered that as a young man, when he had been called the 'Rupert of debate', he had helped to carry the great Reform Act. He told Lord Granville that he was delighted to have 'dished the Whigs', and he said in public that he felt the greatest confidence in the sound good sense of his fellow-countrymen. After a good deal of grumbling the Lords accepted the Bill, which they would certainly have rejected if it had been sponsored in the first instance by Gladstone, whose strategic objective was now secured. It became law on 15 August, 1867.

The vehemence of Gladstone's speeches at that time was noted by all. It was observed that he often spoke with a kind of suppressed and bitter laugh, gesticulating with both arms and glaring from side to side. He allowed himself the luxury of speaking to his family about his hatred of and contempt for Disraeli—'the one man', Lady Frederick Cavendish recorded, 'of whom he does not think better than he deserves'. He allowed himself to think that Disraeli was debauching Parliament and driving all ideas of honour out of public life. He admitted that his rival's diabolical cunning had achieved 'for the purpose of the hour' an astonishing success which was 'in a tactical sense highly damaging to us'; but he failed to understand the cause of his defeat. Acclimatized too exclusively to a rarified atmosphere of intellectual controversies, abstract propositions had gradually revealed themselves as Gladstone's political ideals. Most members of the House of Commons had been bred among the wholesome realities of country life, and the temper of the House as a whole was earthy and matter-of-fact. Order and strong government were regarded as the essential foundation of liberty, justice, and every other good.

Gladstone's ends did not differ materially from those of his opponents, but his concentrated self-absorption and inflexible adherence to an exalted conception of politics as an aspect of moral and religious truth made it hard for him to adjust his means to his ends. There were moments when he seemed to confuse the two, and to ignore the fallen state of man. His failure to make adequate use of those arts and stratagems which statesmen must employ, if parties and events are to be successfully controlled in an imperfect world, made Gladstone's leadership appear ineffective. He was always in danger of allowing the best to become the enemy of the good.

It was as dangerous and rash for Gladstone to demand a plain, straightforward Bill in 1867, when Parliament was in a thoroughly confused and unstraightforward mood, as it would have been for a military commander to order a frontal attack upon a well-prepared and naturally strong enemy position. Gladstone was ingenuously surprised not only by Disraeli's tactics, but by the satisfaction which those tactics gave to most members of the House of Commons, and to the nation. As a result Gladstone was reduced temporarily to a disgusted silence, and Samuel Wilberforce, the Bishop of Oxford, acknowledged that Disraeli had almost taught the House of Commons to ignore Gladstone. Small boys invented the riddle, 'Why is Gladstone like a telescope?' The answer was, 'Because Disraeli draws him out, looks through him, and shuts him up!'

In his hour of triumph Disraeli would have been wise to remember, what others had learned from experience, that Gladstone could be 'terrible on the rebound'. Gladstone's conduct of the reform debates had caused many members of Parliament to distrust his powers of leadership; it had, however, firmly established his position among the less sophisticated rank and file of the Party in the constituencies. Disraeli, 'the Lord High Conjuror', found, when the General Election was held, that it was useless to tell the new voters that they owed their votes to him. They felt that in fact, if not in form, they were in-debted to Gladstone, and when they cast their votes they expressed that feeling.

At Christmas, 1867, Lord Russell, who was aged seventy-five, announced that he would not continue to lead the Liberal Party at the General Election, which could not be long delayed. Gladstone was his inevitable successor, and Mrs. Gladstone wrote to her husband (31 March) begging him to cultivate 'great dignity, great patience, but not too much humility, and to guard against too much eagerness or violence one moment, and then too much civility and modesty another'. He needed, she said, to be and to appear more calm. At that moment Gladstone was still wrestling with the subject of reform, and he was plunged in a mood of deep depression. As he emerged from it he made no secret to his intimates and to his family of his intention to seek a drastic means of restoring the fortunes of the Liberal Party. He discovered that means in Ireland, and within a short time his mind was exclusively absorbed by the Irish problem. As a result he reached the premiership by way of a furious assault upon the Irish Church establishment which he had once conceived it to be his most sacred duty to seek to preserve unimpaired at any cost.

Gladstone had never visited Ireland, but for a moment in 1845 he had felt passionately about the Irish question.[1] He had then deliberately averted his gaze because other interests engrossed him, and because he knew his temperament sufficiently well to be at least half-conscious that a mental earthquake would have convulsed his mind if he had permitted it to dwell for long upon Ireland. In those circumstances all other interests would have had to be swept aside. Gladstone considered that his sense of timing was his most valuable political gift. He noted at the end of his life that the most 'striking gift . . . entrusted to me . . . is an insight into the facts of particular eras and their relation to one another, which generates in the public mind a conviction that the materials exist for the formation of a public opinion and for directing it to a particular end'. He claimed that his proposal of religious equality for Ireland in 1868 was an important illustration of the exercise of that gift ; and an entry in his diary (31 December, 1868) may have been intended as an explanation of his long neglect of the Irish problem :

'I feel like a man with a burden under which he must fall if he looks to the right or left, or fails from any cause to concentrate mind and muscle upon his progress step by step. This absorption, this excess, . . . is the fault of political life, with its insatiable demands which do not leave the smallest stock of moral energy unexhausted and available for other purposes . . . Swimming for his life, a man does not see much of the country through which the river winds, and I probably know little of these years through which I work and live.'

Gladstone's enemies were prompt to equate the gift for 'right-timing' on which he plumed himself, with opportunism and greed for office. Even his friends were surprised and sometimes amused to find that he always repudiated any suggestion that he was ambitious. Neither friends nor enemies really understood the degree of difference which separated Gladstone from themselves. He was impelled by different motives and guided by different influences and beliefs. Many misunderstandings and disappointments arose from that cause.

Gladstone's opportunism and sense of timing were at the service of a passionate sense of duty. That sense of duty constantly impelled him to devote the great powers which he was well aware that he possessed to purposes which seemed to him to involve the moral issues for the sake of which he had entered politics. In general he was much too fond of the right to be capable of pursuing the expedient,

[1] See pp. 75–76 above.

and as a Party leader that was often a disadvantage. Nevertheless there were occasions, particularly towards the end of his life, when he was able to persuade himself that an expedient course was a right one. Whenever that happened Gladstone was visibly troubled, and he was liable unconsciously to discover some preternaturally subtle excuse to which few plain men would have cared to subscribe.

Gladstone's true interests were outside politics, and as he grew older politics disgusted him more and more. He became increasingly anxious to retire and to devote his powers to a defence of the cause of orthodox religion which was being hard-pressed by the rising tide of indifference and by the arrogant assaults of the scientists. When he spoke of his heartfelt desire to withdraw from political life and to possess his soul for a few years before he died, most of his friends and all his enemies believed that he was consciously or unconsciously a hypocrite. They were utterly mistaken, for he was radiantly simple and sincere. Only an overpowering sense of duty, joined to the pressure of his followers, kept him from realizing his longing for retirement until he was aged eighty-four, to the detriment of his reputation and the heartfelt regret of those who knew him best and loved him most.

Because politics were to Gladstone always primarily a duty, while his real interests lay outside them, he failed not only to master the minor political arts, but also to overcome certain faults of temperament which militated against the success of the policies which he advocated with splendid and infectious enthusiasm. He often misjudged individuals because he persistently overrated their goodness and intelligence. He sometimes misjudged events, partly because his prepossessions were so vehement that it was hard for him to be dispassionate, and partly because the subtlety of his intellect was liable to lead him to discover reasons for or against a given cause which were in reality almost worthless.

Once he had convinced himself of the rightness of a cause Gladstone became incapable of moderation. He told John Bright (10 December, 1867) that he had hesitated for a long time to attack the Irish Church because it was a subject which ' may again lead the Liberal Party to martyrdom '. At Southport, on 19 December, 1867, when he announced his intention of reforming not only the Irish Church but the Irish land and educational systems as well, he openly boasted of the first martyrdom to which he had led his Party over the question of reform in 1866 :

" We knew perfectly well," he cried, " that if we retired from office, the triumph of reform was absolutely certain. We were firmly convinced that the blood of an administration would be the seed of the success of Parliamentary Reform."

Gladstone wrote to his sister in Germany (3 January, 1868) that he was aware that he could not expect to 'live politically to see the Irish question settled'; he had taken up that question in the name of 'the God of truth and justice'. It was clear that despite his sense of timing, the moral aspect of that question meant everything to him, and that political considerations counted in comparison for little.

That messianic mood was wholly alien to the Whig temperament, and by no means congenial to important sections of the Liberal rank and file in the House of Commons, where it evoked distrust and bewilderment. In many parts of the country, however, and particularly in the North, it excited admiration and enthusiasm. On 16 March, 1868, a month after Disraeli, aged sixty-four, had succeeded Lord Derby, who was crippled by gout, as Prime Minister, Gladstone openly proclaimed in the House of Commons his intention to disestablish the Irish Church.

With that war-cry Gladstone summoned the Liberals to battle. On 23 March he gave notice of a series of Resolutions, and Disraeli told the Queen that the situation was serious. He said, however, that he thought on the whole, that 'Mr. Gladstone has mistaken the spirit of the times and the temper of the country'. He added that English hatred of Popery, and of the Irish, would probably prove strong enough to wreck Gladstone's plans.

On 30 April, 1868, amid scenes of heartening enthusiasm, Gladstone carried his first Resolution on the subject of the Irish Church by a majority of 65 : "This", he told the Duchess of Sutherland, "is a day of excitement—almost of exultation. We have made a step, nay a stride, and this stride is on the pathway of justice, and of peace, and of national honour and renown." Disraeli saw that he would not be able to continue to govern the country through a minority in the House of Commons, and he advised the Queen to dissolve Parliament as soon as the new electoral registers were ready. They were expected to be ready in November, and Disraeli incurred some odium by appearing to wish the House to believe that the Queen was unwilling to dispense with his services as Prime Minister.

Parliament was dissolved on 11 November, while Gladstone was conducting an electoral campaign in South-West Lancashire,[1] in the course of which he made fifteen major speeches. At Wigan on 22 October he led up to a peroration which was long remembered. He compared the Protestant ascendancy in Ireland with :

'Some tall tree of noxious growth, lifting its head to Heaven and poisoning the atmosphere of the land so far as its shadow can extend. It is still there, gentlemen, but now at last the day has come when, as we hope, the axe has been laid to the root [Loud Cheers]. It is deeply cut round and round. It nods and quivers from top to base [Cheers]. There lacks, gentlemen, but one stroke more—the stroke of these Elections [Loud Cheers]. It will then, once for all, topple to its fall, and on that day the heart of Ireland will leap for joy, and the mind and conscience of England and Scotland will repose with thankful satisfaction upon the thought that something has been done towards the discharge of national duty, and towards deepening and widening the foundations of public strength, security, and peace [Loud and prolonged applause].'

The result of the General Election was a triumph for Gladstone. The Liberals were returned to power with a majority of some 112 seats. Gladstone himself was rejected by his rigidly Protestant constituency of South-West Lancashire, but in anticipation of defeat there he had already been nominated for Greenwich where he had a comfortable majority. His eldest son, William, was returned for Whitby. On 1 December, 1868, Gladstone was cutting down a tree in the park at Hawarden, when a telegram was delivered. It informed him that the Queen's secretary, General Grey, would arrive from Windsor that evening. 'Very significant,' was Gladstone's comment, as he took up the axe and resumed his attack on the tree. After a few minutes he ceased, and resting on the handle of the axe, he exclaimed to his guest, the Hon. Evelyn Ashley, a son of Lord Shaftesbury, in a voice of deep earnestness and with an intense expression : 'My mission is to pacify Ireland.' He then turned once more to the tree and said not another word until it was down.

General Grey's visit had been preceded by a letter (27 November, 1868) from Gerald Wellesley, the Dean of Windsor, in anticipation of what he termed 'the crisis'. There had been rumours, as Lord Clarendon told Lady Salisbury (1 December), that Gladstone was 'utterly repugnant' to the Queen. Using the freedom of a former

[1] Somewhat altered in shape from the constituency of South Lancashire which Gladstone had won in 1865 after his rejection by Oxford University.

Eton contemporary, Wellesley now offered Gladstone a word of advice. He did not conceal the fact that the Queen was afraid of Gladstone, but he assured him that she had ' a great regard and esteem ' for him, and warned him that she was a woman, and that she would need to be treated as such :

' Everything depends on your manner of approaching the Queen. Her nervous susceptibility has much increased since you had to do with her before, and you cannot show too much regard, gentleness, I might even say tenderness towards her. Where you differ, it will be best not at first to try and reason her over to your side, but to pass the matter lightly over, with expression of respectful regret, and reserve it, for there is no-one with whom more is to be gained by getting her into the habit of intercourse with you. Put off, until she is accustomed to see you, all discussions which are not absolutely necessary for the day . . .'

Wellesley told Gladstone that the Queen disliked his Irish Church policy, that she would probably say so frankly, but that ' she fully understands that you are pledged to the principle before Parliament and the country, and . . . she will give you her usual loyal support in carrying on the Government as long as you can do so.'

In reply (29 November, 1868) Gladstone wrote :

' Every motive of duty and interest that can touch a man should tend to make me study to the best of my small powers the manner of my relations with H.M. She is a woman, a widow, a lover of truth, a Sovereign, a benefactress of humanity. What titles ! . . .

' I have plenty of besetting infirmities. Among others, I am a man so eager upon things as not to remember always what is due to persons. And I have another great fault in the unrestrained, or too little restrained manifestation of first impressions, which I well know is quite a different thing from the virtue of mental transparency . . . Few things would be more painful to me than the thought in retrospect that I could at any time have caused H.M. one moment of gratuituous pain or trouble . . .'

So Gladstone was well prepared for General Grey's visit, which was made mainly for the purpose of impressing upon Gladstone the Queen's objection to appointing Lord Clarendon as Foreign Secretary. Clarendon, who had been Foreign Secretary throughout the Crimean War, was competent and experienced, but he had offended the Queen by his flippant and casual ways. Grey was surprised to discover that Mrs. Gladstone was completely in her husband's confidence about the Queen's objection to Lord Clarendon and, as far as he could see, about all other matters.

On 3 December, 1868, Gladstone had his first audience, as Prime Minister, at Windsor. He undertook, in the Queen's words, to tell Lord Clarendon 'as from himself . . . how necessary it was that *all* the Ministers should consider my feelings'. He promised that he would try to induce Clarendon to refuse office on grounds of ill-health, and 'if he found this impossible, that he would take care to prevent my being annoyed with him . . . he should be brought as little into personal contact with me as possible'. The Queen hotly resented the nickname which Lord Clarendon had given her, of 'the Missus', and Gladstone agreed that it 'was his *own* fault, not to be more cautious with his tongue'.

Lord Clarendon took office as Foreign Secretary despite his Sovereign's displeasure, and Gladstone, surmounting that first hurdle, found him a 'delightful' colleague. While the Prime Minister was forming his Cabinet, Algernon West, a professional civil servant, who was appointed Gladstone's principal private secretary, wrote a charming description of his chief. West was called to 11, Carlton House Terrace on 24 December, 1868, and found the Prime Minister seated at his desk wearing a dark frock-coat with a flower in his button-hole. Gladstone wore brown trousers with a stripe down them after the fashion of the 1840s. His neckcloth was slightly disordered, and his collar, which was the cartoonists' delight, was enormous. The amputated forefinger of his left hand was covered, as always, by a black finger-stall. As West walked into the room Gladstone's eye flashed with annoyance at the interruption, but when Mrs. Gladstone explained who West was, her husband's face relaxed into a kindly smile.

When Disraeli became Prime Minister for the first time, in February of that year, he had responded to congratulations with the jaunty comment: " Yes ! I have climbed to the top of the greasy pole." The spirit in which Gladstone entered upon his task was confided to his diary on his fifty-ninth birthday (29 December, 1868) :

'This birthday opens my sixtieth year . . . I ascend a steepening path, with a burden ever gathering weight. The Almighty seems to sustain and spare me for some purpose of His own, deeply unworthy as I know myself to be. Glory be to His name !'

CHAPTER 9

IRISH RHAPSODY
1868–1873

ALTHOUGH Gladstone candidly told Lord Granville (11 April, 1868) that for some years he had been 'watching the sky with a strong sense of the obligation to act with the first streak of dawn', he had done little to prepare public opinion when that dawn broke in Ireland. Two bomb outrages perpetrated in England by Irish Fenian conspirators in September and December, 1867, had impressed Gladstone, without unduly influencing him. The second outrage, at Manchester, cost a dozen lives, and Gladstone told the House of Commons (31 May, 1869) that it had helped to convince him that further delay would be dangerous. He believed that it might yet be possible to reconcile the Irish to a continuance of British rule.

Gladstone was not popular in Ireland because of his action in 1853 in extending to that country the income-tax which Peel had withheld. When he formed his Government in 1868 he had no experience and no real knowledge of the Irish problem, and his ignorance was shared by the whole of his Cabinet and by the mass of the British people. He had no suspicion that in the cause of Ireland he was destined to lead the Liberal Party to martyrdom, or that the whole of the rest of his life was to be devoted to that cause. If he had known, he would have been horrified, for he took office with the firm intention of accomplishing his mission within a year or two, and of retiring subsequently to Hawarden in order to devote himself to religion.

It was due in great measure to Lord Granville (known to his intimates as 'Puss') that Gladstone found his first Cabinet the pleasantest and easiest to handle of the four over which he presided. The very warm friendship which sprang up between Gladstone and Granville excited comment because the two were so different in character, habits of life, and fundamental convictions. Lord Granville, who became Colonial Secretary, was a popular social figure, devoted to every kind of sport and amusement. No-one but he could have dragged Gladstone to Epsom in June, 1870, to see the Derby, leaving the principal private secretary in Downing Street to record his disgust, 'thinking it', Algernon West noted, 'out of his line, and not altogether a dignified thing' for Gladstone to do. No-one but

Granville would have habitually begun his letters to the Prime Minister : ' My dear G.' With his indolence and extravagance, Lord Granville possessed great charm and tact ; he had a sense of perspective, as well as the rare and invaluable gift of being able to relieve the tensions in Gladstone's mind. Their intimacy was most fortunate for the Liberal Party. After Lord Granville had apologized on one occasion for having addressed the Prime Minister disrespectfully at a Cabinet meeting, Gladstone wrote to him (24 July, 1870) :

' to ask for an understanding between ourselves that when, amid the many and complex movements of the wheels, any one goes wrong, we two shall first talk it over together ; for it is impossible for any man to talk over a difficulty with you and not to find himself nearer to a solution . . . I am almost ashamed to make any request of you, of whom all my recollections, were our political relations to end to-day, would be absorbed in one, that of your inexhaustible and overflowing kindness.'

The substance of the mildly astringent advice which Lord Granville tendered was usually less important than its quality of acceptability. Gladstone had always needed an echo to the sound of his own voice, and he opened his mind again and again to Lord Granville as he never did to any other friend. For example, in an uninhibited review (9 September, 1873) of the conduct of Robert Lowe, the Chancellor of the Exchequer, Gladstone wrote : ' I think it well to deposit this explanation with you—with no-one else.' Again, on 7 August, 1874, after his Government had fallen, he confided to Granville his opinion of Sir William Harcourt who, after being Solicitor-General, had opposed his former chief on the Public Worship Bill :

' Even his slimy, filthy, loathsome eulogies upon Dizzy were aimed at me . . . It is quite plain that he meant business, namely my political extinction . . . I feel for those who are to come after me in regard to their dealings with him. I am not angry with him, I do not respect him enough to be angry . . . Forgive this piece of amicable confession.'

It is worth noticing that in writing to his wife (5 August) on that subject Gladstone was much more restrained. Mrs. Gladstone often urged her husband to remain calm, and Gladstone was content to tell her that he had had ' a *mauvais quart d'heure* ', a ' frantic tirade from Harcourt extremely bad in tone and taste and chiefly aimed at poor me . . . I have really treated him with forbearance before, but I was obliged to let out a little to-day.'

Before he took office, and after he had made up his mind to dis-establish the Irish Church, Gladstone found himself troubled by the inconsistency between his present views and those which he had expressed in his ill-fated book on *State and Church* thirty years before. He therefore composed *A Chapter of Autobiography* which Murray published on 23 November, 1868. Proofs were sent to Lord Granville who wrote to Gladstone (14 October) : ' I never read anything which delighted me more. So candid, so simple, and so clear ! It is per-fectly unanswerable.' It was, and if further proof were needed of Gladstone's delightful simplicity, it was given when he invited Richard Trench, the Archbishop of Dublin, and leading members of the Anglican hierarchy in Ireland, to come to London in order to discuss round a table the disestablishment and disendowment of their Church. Gladstone's invincible faith in the efficacy of reason and argument led him to think that he might be able to obtain their voluntary consent, and he was greatly dismayed to find himself denounced at diocesan conferences throughout Ireland as a brigand and an enemy of God.

In his *Chapter of Autobiography* Gladstone admitted that his view of the Church of Ireland in 1868 was ' the direct opposite ' of what it had been in 1838. He admitted further that he had completely mis-judged the future alike of the Anglican Church and of English Non-conformity. He had formerly sought to apply theoretical tests to Church Establishments ; he now realized that practical tests only were valid. He argued that by voting for the Maynooth grant after resigning from Peel's Cabinet in 1845 he had regained complete liberty of action with regard to the Irish Church which he had once sought to defend. He had, at Oxford in 1847, refused to pledge himself to maintain that Church, although he had desired ' with an almost passionate fondness ' to represent that University in Parliament. He had never subsequently believed in the claims of the Irish Church, and no-one had any right to criticize him because he had not at once started to agitate for its overthrow : ' It is one thing to lift the anchor ; it is another to spread the sails.'

The Queen, who was no cynic, and a majority of her subjects, believed that Gladstone was deceiving himself when he argued that he was not inspired primarily by a desire to rally the Liberal Party when he launched his campaign against the Irish Church. Gladstone's conscience, however, was clear ; he had exposed it to the world ; and it seemed evident that he was right in holding that the time was ripe.

Within two months of taking office he sent the Queen (21 January, 1869) two lengthy and closely-written papers outlining his proposals. The Queen asked Theodore Martin, her husband's biographer, to analyse the fog of words and far from lucid sentences, and to make a précis for her. She then told Gladstone (31 January) that although she hardly yet understood the subject, she greatly regretted that he had committed himself to so sweeping a measure.

Gladstone had already formed two plans for associating the Royal Family more closely with Ireland. The first envisaged the acquisition of a royal residence in that country, to which he wanted the Queen to go sometimes, instead of to Balmoral. The second envisaged the abolition of the Lord-Lieutenancy, and the appointment of the Prince of Wales as Viceroy with a responsible Secretary of State at his side. As soon as he became Prime Minister, Gladstone obtained the offer of a royal residence from a Dublin banker, John La Touche, and he begged the Queen to give the subject her earnest and immediate attention. Disraeli, who had once favoured a similar plan, had dropped it when he found that it was unwelcome. The Queen did not now reply, as she might have done, that Gladstone had never thought it worth while himself to visit Ireland. She replied cautiously (8 January, 1869) through General Grey, who said that the offer was ' very liberal, and indeed noble ', but that Balmoral was necessary to the Queen's health, and that nothing could take its place in her affections.

For the moment Gladstone was content to leave that matter in abeyance, and he was dismayed on 3 February, 1869, when the Queen's doctor, Sir William Jenner, called to see him with an intimation that the Queen declined to open Parliament in person, not entirely on account of health reasons but ' from an anxiety to avoid any personal interference in the great question pending with respect to the Irish Church '. The Queen suggested (4 February) that Gladstone might inform the Press, if he liked, that the Queen had been ' more than normally suffering from severe headache '. That proposal infuriated Gladstone. He had many talks with General Grey, who assured him (1 June, 1869) that ' Princess Louise is *very* decided as to the ability of the Queen to meet any fatigue, and is most indignant with Jenner for encouraging the Queen's fancies about her health '. Grey wrote again (5 June) : ' Dismiss the thought of there being any weight of work from your mind, and this the Princess *emphatically* repeats.'

Thus encouraged, Gladstone said (7 June) that he intended to get at the whole truth. He considered that 'will', or wilfulness, lay 'at the root of many human, and especially of many feminine complaints'. Grey cordially agreed. He told Gladstone (9 June) :

'I am fairly persuaded that *nothing* will have any effect but a strong— even a peremptory—tone. In spite of Sir William Jenner I believe that neither health nor strength are wanting, were inclination what it should be. It is simply the long, unchecked habit of self-indulgence that now makes it impossible for her, without some degree of nervous agitation to give up, even for ten minutes, the gratification of a single inclination, or even *whim*'. He warned Gladstone (12 June) that any 'postponement of the fight, which *must* come, will make it seem more painful and difficult'.

The Queen's continued neglect of her public duties was causing widespread and increasing discontent. Gladstone felt that, as Prime Minister, he had a duty to interfere. He had already begun to brood over what he privately termed 'the Royalty question' before he introduced his Disestablishment Bill to the Commons on 1 March, 1869, in a great speech which lasted three and a half hours. In his peroration Gladstone confessed that he understood very well :

'the punishments that justly fall upon those Phætons of politics who, with hands unequal to the task, attempt to guide the chariot of the sun.'

He may, conceivably, have recollected those words in 1886 and again in 1893 when he enacted Phæton's rôle while introducing his first and second Home Rule Bills.

The Disestablishment Bill, which embodied an ecclesiastical revolution, passed its Third Reading in the Commons, on 31 May, and the Queen, who shared her subjects' nervousness about the temper of the new electorate, did her utmost to avert a clash between the Commons and the Lords. All her influence was used in favour of conciliation, and Gladstone, in thanking her (9 June, 1869), ventured to improve the occasion :

'It can never', he wrote, 'be the duty of one who has the honour to serve Your Majesty to close his eyes against facts : and Mr. Gladstone has not a doubt that at the present moment the exertions which Your Majesty's wisdom has spontaneously prompted to avert a collision between the two Houses of Parliament would carry yet greater authority had it happened that they could have been made on the spot.'

He begged the Queen to return to London and to attend more to the duties of her high office; he said that he knew, without consulting them, that all his colleagues were of a like mind.

Before the Bill became law on 26 July there were many anxious moments, and it looked occasionally as though it might have to be abandoned. On 22 July, when the worst was over, Gladstone was 'absolutely overcome'. He came home exhausted, saying character-istically not that he wanted to go to bed, but that he wanted 'to go straight to Church'. He was extremely grateful to Archibald Tait, the Archbishop of Canterbury, who had fought down a strong antipathy to a measure which deprived the Irish Church of a quarter of its revenues and turned it into a self-governing corporation.

Recuperating at Hawarden, and at Walmer Castle where Lord Granville lived as Lord Warden of the Cinque Ports, Gladstone at once turned his mind to the more difficult and serious problem of Irish agrarian discontent. Granville had warned him (26 May) that that question might well break up the Government. At least four of its members, Lord Clarendon (Foreign Secretary), Robert Lowe (Chancellor of the Exchequer), Edward Cardwell (Secretary for War), and the Duke of Argyll (Secretary for India), were hostile, while the rest of the Cabinet were politely sceptical. Even John Bright (Presi-dent of the Board of Trade), whose health was bad, was too much wedded to an impracticable scheme of State land purchase, to be of use in relation to any other plan. Gladstone had no plan of his own at first, but he warned Bright (22 May, 1869) that land bought and resold by the State would soon be found concentrated in a few hands again, and that any such scheme could in any case only benefit a few favoured Irish tenants.

As Gladstone studied the problem its outline gradually became clear to him. Irish industry had been restricted by hostile English legislation, so that the mass of the population depended for its livelihood upon the land. That land had passed into the hands of absentee Protestant English conquerors as a result of a series of confiscations, and those landlords' title-deeds were popularly regarded as scraps of paper.

Economists had always argued that Ireland needed to be cleared of its superfluous inhabitants, and the great famine of 1845–7 had done much to forward that result. Three-quarters of a million people had died of starvation and two millions had emigrated, but the population was still too large, and pressure upon the land, which was uneconomic-ally worked, encouraged landlords to extort high rents. It is true that after the famine about a third of the landlords were ruined, but the British Government had seized its opportunity to pass the Encumbered Estates Act of 1849 with what Gladstone now termed 'lazy, heedless, uninformed good intentions'. Those intentions were to increase food production by facilitating the sale of land to those who possessed the capital to make it productive. In furtherance of that policy two more Acts were passed to make evictions easier, and as a result another two hundred thousand persons were driven off the land. Most of the new landlords were competent but hard-fisted Irish capitalists who wanted to clear the best land for grazing.

Although there was no effective Irish Party in the House of Commons until 1874, Irish members had tried to revive and foster a custom which had grown up in Ulster, and occasionally elsewhere, whereby landlords in fixing rents were required to take into account improvements effected by their tenants. Those tenants claimed the right to sell the goodwill, or increment, which their improvements had added to the value of the land. Parliament did its best after the famine to stamp out that tenant-right custom because it impeded the free sale of land to those who had the capital and the knowledge to make the best use of it. Lord Palmerston, an Irish peer and landlord, coined the phrase : 'Tenant's right is landlord's wrong.' An Act of 1860 expressly debarred tenants from receiving compensation for improvements when they were evicted, and it is hardly surprising that an unappeasable sense of wrong which had been burned into the hearts and minds of the Irish people should have begun to find expression in a series of outrages.

The difference between agrarian custom in England and Ireland was thus very wide. The law in both countries was the same, but custom was more important than the law. In England, squire, parson, and tenant-farmer formed a closely-knit community of interest and sympathy which was undreamt of in Ireland. Irish tenants were men of straw, barely distinguishable from agricultural labourers, rack-rented and living in constant dread of eviction. In consequence the idea of property, which in England was popularly associated with the unquestioned rights of the landlord, was associated in Ireland with the alleged wrongs of the cultivator of the soil.

After concentrating for three months on that problem in the winter of 1869-70 Gladstone decided to introduce a Bill to protect tenants in Ireland from unfair treatment. The Bill extended to the whole of Ireland the old Ulster tenant-right custom, and it established a scale of compensation not only for improvements but for disturbance as well. Courts were empowered to revise exorbitant rents, but the Courts dispensed class-justice by construing that term in the interest of the landlords, and the Irish tenant failed to obtain security of tenure or effective security against being rack-rented. When a great agricultural depression began in 1875, many tenants ceased to be able to pay their rents. The Act was then found to be virtually useless, and Gladstone came to realize that a stronger measure was required.

Cardinal Manning and the Roman Catholic hierarchy warned Gladstone of the defects of his Bill, but in the prevailing climate of English opinion no more liberal measure was possible. Gladstone himself told Chichester Fortescue, the Irish Chief Secretary, on 6 December, 1869, that he was 'a good deal staggered at the idea of any interference with present rents'. The Land Act was passed with no great difficulty because its full implications were not understood. It established the far-reaching principle that property in land was not absolute, and that principle made possible an agrarian revolution in the 1880s. In 1870 neither Parliament, nor the Cabinet, nor Gladstone himself, who believed, for a time, that he had solved the Irish agrarian problem, were prepared to go further. It became necessary in that year to apply coercive measures to stamp out crime in Ireland, and after Gladstone had at the end of the year released some political criminals from prison, Disraeli was able to raise a cheer by charging the Prime Minister (27 February, 1871) with shaking property to its foundations, consecrating sacrilege, condoning treason, making government ridiculous, and sowing the seeds of civil war.

* * *

Between 1869 and 1874 there was enough work to satisfy even Gladstone's appetite, and in W. E. Forster's Education Act of 1870 the Prime Minister took only a lukewarm interest. Gladstone was never a zealous educationist; his chief concern was that children should continue to be taught the meaning of the Christian religion. Having resigned himself to the need for accepting some sort of distasteful compromise in order to meet the views of those who favoured an unsectarian system of national education, Gladstone was agreeably surprised to discover that Forster's Act was nearer to his views than he had at first dared to hope.

The catchword, 'We must educate our masters', which had been fathered by Robert Lowe after the second Reform Act, was on everyone's lips. A National Education League had been founded in Birmingham by Joseph Chamberlain and others to demand universal, free, compulsory, unsectarian primary education. Those who sought to uphold the principle of religious education in voluntary Church schools formed a National Education Union. Forster's Act, which passed its Third Reading on 9 August, 1870, was a compromise between those rival views. While it did not make education generally free or compulsory, it established a system of elective school boards which were designed to fill the gaps in the existing voluntary system.

The school boards were empowered to levy rates, build schools, provide teachers, and to insist, if they thought fit, upon the attendance of children who were receiving no other form of instruction. They were also empowered, if they thought fit, to pay the fees of necessitous children in board schools or in voluntary schools. That last provision infuriated the Nonconformists because it was used in some cases to subsidize Church schools out of rates. In the board schools, which were all open to inspection, no form of denominational religious teaching was allowed. Gladstone eased his mind by doubling the State grant to those voluntary denominational schools which accepted inspection and were pronounced satisfactory.

Harassed as he was, the subject of Church appointments was ever in the forefront of Gladstone's mind. He told the Home Secretary, H. A. Bruce, in February, 1870 : ' If you read in the papers some morning that I have been committed to Bedlam, and that a straight waistcoat is considered necessary, please to remember it will be entirely owing to the vacancy in the see of St. Asaph.' In that year he completed the work of throwing open to competitive examination all departments of the Civil Service except the Foreign and the Education Offices. He also, characteristically, took great pride in the inauguration of the halfpenny postcard of which he proceeded to make a lavish use because it appealed to his sense of economy.

In 1871 Gladstone forced through Parliament a Bill abolishing religious tests at the Universities. He told the Solicitor-General, Sir John Coleridge, that the measure was ' beyond anything odious ' to him, but, once he had made up his mind that it was necessary, he fought for it with all his strength. He carried also through Parliament a Bill to give trades unions a satisfactory status, and to legalize strikes. In approving that measure it did not occur to Gladstone that there was any need to legalize peaceful picketing during strikes. He thereby offended the working class, whose material

204

needs he never understood, because, without peaceful picketing, strike action could not be made effective. In 1875, when the Conservatives were in power, Disraeli seized his chance to buy working-class votes by legalizing peaceful picketing.

In foreign affairs, Gladstone incurred criticism for his ' starry-eyed ' manner of handling the three most important crises which came his way. He defined the main principle on which his foreign policy was based in a letter (17 April, 1869) to General Grey. Great Britain should seek ' to develop and mature the action of a common, or public, or European opinion . . . but should beware of seeming to lay down the law of that opinion by her own authority '. He claimed that the Crimean War, and the offer to Denmark in 1863, ' when we could get no-one to join us ', proved that we were willing to go to war in defence of that opinion. Great Britain's fund of strength and credit, however, needed to be thriftily used. International law, or opinion, could not ' be sustained by physical force alone, still less by the physical force of a single Power '.

In furtherance of that policy Gladstone made a vigorous but futile attempt to persuade Bismarck to abandon his decision to annex Alsace and Lorraine after the overthrow of France at the battle of Sedan in September, 1870. Lord Granville, who became Foreign Secretary in July, after Lord Clarendon's death from overwork, warned Gladstone that Bismarck would not be moved. Nevertheless, with invincible optimism, Gladstone begged his colleagues to enlist the support of the neutral powers in an attempt to reason with Bismarck. Gladstone published his views anonymously in an article entitled *Germany, France, and England*, in the *Edinburgh Review* (October, 1870). He was naïve enough to believe that his authorship might remain a secret, but the veil of anonymity was pierced at once. Lord Granville begged Gladstone not to run the risk of antagonizing the new Germany in a lost and hopeless cause, but Gladstone made a last fruitless approach to Bismarck through a private channel in February, 1871, before he was finally compelled to accept the accomplished fact. Bismarck often described the Prime Minister contemptuously as ' Professor Gladstone ', and Gladstone told Granville that Bismarck's violent and unjust annexation of two provinces of France marked the beginning of a new and unhappy phase of European history.

In October, 1870, Russia, encouraged by Bismarck, seized the opportunity presented by the Franco-Prussian War to denounce the clauses in the Treaty of Paris of 1856 which had closed the Black

Sea to Russian warships. British opinion was strongly anti-Russian, but France was prostrate, and Gladstone, who was always troubled by his share of the responsibility for the Crimean War, was helpless. A conference which met in London in January, 1871, legalized an action which it was powerless to revoke ; it tried to save its face by issuing a declaration that treaties could not be abrogated without the consent of all the signatories. That solemn platitude was greeted, in the circumstances, with derision, and Gladstone and Lord Granville were made to appear weak and ineffective.

Gladstone and Lord Granville earned much unpopularity in another case, which concerned the United States. In July, 1862, during the American Civil War, by a gross act of negligence a disguised warship had been allowed to escape from Liverpool Docks to the open sea where she had hoisted the Southern colours. Her crew was largely British, and for nearly two years, until she was caught and sunk, the *Alabama* had preyed on the commerce of the United States. She had done much damage, and it was obvious that large compensation would have to be paid by Great Britain. Both sides, however, were proud and sore. Alfred Tennyson, for example, wrote to Gladstone (5 February, 1872) : ' If you let those Yankee sharpers get anything like their way in the *Alabama* claims, I won't pay my ship-money, any more than old Hampden.' Irresponsible American claims assessed the indirect damage arising out of the prolongation of the war at fantastic sums, running into hundreds of millions of pounds, and the dispute, which dragged on for years, envenomed Anglo-American relations. Gladstone determined to assert the rule of international law by bringing the matter before a tribunal of arbitration. That vitally important assertion of principle succeeded despite great difficulties caused by intransigence on both sides, and it was one of the great achievements of Gladstone's career.

In September, 1872, five arbitrators at Geneva awarded the Americans three and a quarter million pounds in damages. Gladstone who had been greatly helped by the conciliatory and statesmanlike attitude of the American member of the arbitration tribunal, Charles Francis Adams, thought the sum rather large, but he told the Chancellor of the Exchequer to look cheerful, and to ask for a cash discount in return for an immediate payment. Gladstone had shown great moral courage, and the wisdom of the course he pursued has been fully endorsed by posterity. *The Times* applauded his action, but important sections of British opinion looked back wistfully to the great days of Lord Palmerston, and blamed the Government for a blow to British prestige. Unfair complaints were heard in some quarters that Gladstone was unfit to handle foreign affairs.

Gladstone had firmly decided to retire from public life as soon as he had solved the Irish problem. Another problem, however, had now arisen which he regarded for a time as of even greater importance although, as it concerned the Queen personally, he kept it a profound secret until the day he died. He described the 'Royalty question' succinctly in a letter to Lord Granville on 3 December, 1870 : 'To speak in rude and general terms,' Gladstone wrote, 'the Queen is invisible, and the Prince of Wales is not respected.' Accordingly he addressed himself with all his habitual intensity to the task of ensuring that the Monarchy should fulfil adequately the rôle for which he considered that it had been designed by God. The Queen never forgave him, and she believed that in Gladstone's mind the will and purpose of God were identified with the interest and policy of the Liberal Party.

Gladstone's handling of the Royalty question affords much the best insight into his character and methods during his first administration. During 1871 the Queen was at the lowest ebb of her temporary unpopularity owing to her continued seclusion and neglect of her public duties, and to her constant demands on Parliament for money for her growing family. The fall of the French Monarchy precipitated a republican agitation, and when Prince Arthur (later Duke of Connaught) came of age in 1871, there was a public demonstration in Trafalgar Square against 'princely paupers'. Sir Charles Dilke in the House of Commons demanded an inquiry into the Queen's finances, and Joseph Chamberlain told cheering crowds at Birmingham that a republic was inevitable. Some fifty Republican Clubs were established in Birmingham, Cardiff, Aberdeen, Norwich, Plymouth and other towns. The situation had been made worse when the Prince of Wales was cited as a co-respondent in a divorce suit which opened on 16 February, 1870. He was quite innocent and his name was cleared, but his pleasure-seeking way of life gave offence in some quarters and he was insulted at the theatre and hissed on the racecourse.

Gladstone wanted to make the Queen do her duty, as he saw it, and to find suitable employment for the Prince of Wales by remodelling the government of Ireland and sending the Prince there as Viceroy. The more liberal Gladstone became, the more fervent became his attachment to the Crown as the most venerable of all the nation's institutions. For that reason he was never tempted to criticize the Monarchy in public as he loved, later, to castigate 'the upper ten thousand', and 'the West End of London'. He was always happy to help the Queen to obtain Parliamentary grants of money for her numerous dependent relatives, and he profoundly influenced the future course of English radical opinion by rebuking and suppressing every species of criticism which was directed at any time against the Throne. He was, however, as incapable of making the necessary imaginative effort to understand and make allowance for the human weakness of royalty, as the Queen was incapable of making the intellectual effort needed to understand Gladstone. The Prime Minister regarded the Queen in too institutional a light, and the Queen regarded her devoted Prime Minister in a manner which was too feminine and personal. Before long the two most representative figures of the Victorian age had become mutually antipathetic.

General Grey, in urging Gladstone to take a firm line with the Queen, assured him (1 June, 1869) that all her children were worried at her growing unpopularity. The Queen, unfortunately, had little confidence in Grey, who became ill and died early in 1870. Her confidence was given in the first instance to the Dean of Windsor, and then to Henry Ponsonby, who succeeded Grey in the secretary's office. Ponsonby was a convinced Liberal and a faithful admirer of Gladstone ; he shared Grey's opinion about the Queen's health and habits, but for some years he felt far from secure in his new office.

Gladstone's plan, which envisaged the abolition of the Irish Lord-Lieutenancy, and the installation of the Prince of Wales as permanent Viceroy of Ireland, would have required the Prince to reside in Ireland for some months in every year. The Chief Secretary would have become a Secretary of State with full responsibility for the government of Ireland. Gladstone outlined that proposal in a long letter to Lord Granville which he despatched from Hawarden on 3 December, 1870. It was shown at once by Granville to Lord Bessborough, the Lord Lieutenant of Ireland, who characterized it (6 December) as 'the wildest and most visionary . . . I ever heard of'.

Gladstone's plan for settling the Royalty question had now taken shape and it went a good deal further than this Irish plan. He never lost an opportunity of urging the Queen to stay in London, and to perform public and ceremonial duties. He constantly made inquiries about her health, and expressed scepticism about her alleged headaches and nervous attacks. At an audience at Windsor on 25 June, 1871, at which he outlined the Irish part of his proposals, Gladstone noted that he repeatedly warned the Queen that:

' it was to be regarded by no means as an exclusively Irish question, but as likely to be of great utility in strengthening the Throne under circumstances that require all that can be done in that sense, if indeed we can make it the means of putting forward the Royal Family in the visible discharge of public duty.'

The plan, however, Gladstone ruefully noted, ' did not seem to find favour ', and the Queen appeared particularly resentful of Gladstone's remarks about the Prince of Wales. She said that it was a stupid waste of time to try to connect the Royal Family with Ireland, since ' Scotland and England deserved it much more '. She complained that the climate of Ireland was uncongenial to her [1] and that it would be bad also for the Prince of Wales.

Early in August, 1871, Gladstone made a determined effort to persuade the Queen to delay her departure for Balmoral, and to prorogue in person the Parliamentary Session which had been prolonged by debates on the Ballot Bill and Army reform. He told her that it was her duty to do it, and she became greatly distressed. She told Lord Hatherley, the Lord Chancellor (10 August), that the attempted ' interference with the Queen's personal acts and movements ' was ' really abominable . . . What killed her beloved Husband ? Overwork and worry ! What killed Lord Clarendon ? The same ! . . . And the Queen, a woman no longer young, is supposed to be proof against all and to be driven and abused till her nerves and health give way with this worry and agitation and interference in her private life.' She said that ' she must solemnly repeat that unless the Ministers *support* her and state the truth she *cannot* go on, but must give her heavy burden up to younger hands '.

On 15 August Ponsonby told Gladstone that the Queen did not fully understand the case. She thought that she was being urged to stay in London ' for a political purpose—in order to help the Government '.

---

[1] During a visit to Ireland in August, 1861, the Queen had been accompanied by the Prince Consort, the Prince of Wales, and Prince Alfred. The Prince Consort was the object of hostile demonstrations on account of an incautious comparison which he had drawn between Irish and Polish discontent. The Queen never forgot or forgave that insult offered to her husband less than six months before he died.

Gladstone, on receipt of that letter, became exceedingly angry. He wrote to Ponsonby (16 August) :

'Upon the whole I think it has been the most sickening experience which I have had during near forty years of public life.

'*Worse* things may easily be imagined : but smaller and meaner cause for the decay of Thrones cannot be conceived. It is like the worm which bores the bark of a noble tree and so breaks the channel of its life.'

Gladstone was intensely worried not only by the Queen's unpopularity, but by her apparent unwillingness or inability to make the small sacrifice of habit and convenience which was needed to satisfy public opinion. Sir William Jenner, whom Gladstone dubbed 'a feeble-minded doctor', begged the Prime Minister not to drive the Queen too hard ; her nerves might give way ; her grandfather, George III, had died mad. Grey and Ponsonby were both convinced that Jenner's influence was pernicious and Gladstone, therefore, continued to do his best to stimulate the Queen's sense of duty. The Queen thought that to yield to popular clamour, when no really important principle, as it seemed to her, was at stake, would expose her to an endless series of demands which would disrupt her routine, exhaust her strength, and leave her no peace. She hotly resented Gladstone's constant pressure, and Gladstone wrote sadly to Lord Granville from Balmoral on 1 October, 1871, when he was taking his turn as Minister in attendance:

'The repellent power which she so well knows how to use has been put in action towards me on this occasion for the first time since the formation of the Government. I have felt myself on a new and different footing with her . . . On account of her natural and constant kindness, as well as of her position, I am grieved ; and this much more because of what is to come. For the question gathers in gravity, as we may judge from the visible signs which so frequently recur. And an instinct tells me that much will have to be said about it ere long ; more probably with reference to putting forward the Prince of Wales than to forcing duty upon her, against which she sets herself with such vehemence and tenacity.'

Gladstone's vehemence and tenacity were fully equal to the Queen's, and he at once entered into confidential discussions with the Duke of Cambridge, the Dean of Windsor, and Lieut-Colonel Ellis, one of the Prince of Wales's equerries. He was warned by Princess Louise that he was attempting the impossible, but he saw his duty clearly and nothing could now deflect him from the course on which he had embarked. After the Prince of Wales's recovery in December, 1871, from a severe attack of typhoid which had at one time seemed likely to prove fatal, Gladstone made up his mind that the subsequent mood of thanksgiving had given him, as he told Lord Granville (22 December), 'the last opportunity' to act before it was too late : 'We have', he wrote, 'arrived at a great crisis of Royalty', and he told his sister, in Germany (1 January, 1872), that the Royalty question was now the one remaining consideration which deterred him from quitting public life.

Ponsonby was tireless in encouraging Gladstone : 'I feel', he wrote (23 December, 1871), 'that I am not the person to have raised the question, but if no-one will say anything, matters will go on in the old rut, and a deep and nasty rut it is !' Gladstone complained that the Prince of Wales was exercising a disastrous influence on society. He made enquiries about his unsatisfactory money affairs, and said that he wanted to see the Court as pure as King Arthur's Round Table. At that point, Ponsonby sounded a cautionary note. He remarked (24 December, 1871) that he knew little about King Arthur but that he had learnt from Tennyson's poem that even the Round Table had fallen short of perfection.

In the first week of March, 1872, Gladstone again laid before the Queen his plan for the employment of the Prince of Wales in Ireland. He described the plan, in a private memorandum, as being aimed 'at improving the relations between Monarchy and Nation by forming a worthy and manly mode of life, *quo-ad* public duties, for the Prince of Wales'. He noted that the Prince was being ruined because he was condemned by his mother to lead an utterly purposeless existence, but the Queen inevitably found it hard to dissociate Gladstone's concern for the interests of the Throne from the mission to pacify Ireland which was the professed object of his Government. Her reaction could hardly have been worse, and on 8 March, 1872, Ponsonby told Gladstone that the plan was unacceptable to the Queen and to the Prince. The Prince had expressed a wish to be attached instead successively 'to each of the great public offices, where he would learn habits of business in general and the work of the Department in particular'. Gladstone made no attempt to conceal his poor opinion of that scheme.

The Prime Minister did not despair. He warned Ponsonby (9 March) that the issue was a 'weighty' one, and that the Queen's attitude afforded 'further matter for grave consideration' ; and he conferred secretly with the Prince of Wales's secretary, Francis

Knollys, as well as with the equerry, Colonel Ellis. Warmed by the sunshine of the Prime Minister's confidence, Arthur Ellis poured out his heart on 7 June, 1872, in a letter which he begged Gladstone to keep secret from every eye save his own. He urged the Prime Minister not only to press forward with the plan for sending the Prince to Ireland as Viceroy, but also to obtain authority for the Prince and Princess of Wales to hold Courts in London and to deputize for the Queen at ceremonial duties during a part of every summer : ' Buckingham Palace ', Ellis wrote, ' is untenanted from year's end to year's end . . . There is only one great capital in Europe where the Sovereign is not represented, and that capital is London.' The Prince's frivolity was entirely the result of his enforced idleness : ' Whatever he has hitherto been asked to do, he has done fairly well.'

That was just what Gladstone wanted to hear ; it supplied an echo to his thoughts. Thus encouraged, he embodied his full proposals in a very long letter to the Queen, which he despatched on 5 July, 1872. He proposed that in future the Prince of Wales should spend four to five months every year, between November and March, serving as Viceroy of Ireland ; that he should spend the months of April, May, and June in London deputizing for the Queen ; that he should spend one month in the autumn with the Army, another month at Sandringham, one at Balmoral, ' with occasional fractions of time for other purposes '.

Defending his proposal that the Prince should take over the Queen's ceremonial duties in London, Gladstone wrote :

' This is a portion of the subject which Mr. Gladstone can only approach with the utmost delicacy and reserve . . . He can hardly find words to express his sense of the weight of the social and visible functions of the Monarch, or of their vast importance alike to the social well being of the country, and to the stability of the Throne . . . In the latest years Your Majesty had found it necessary, from considerations of health, to adopt altered plans of residence, and to place the discharge of these visible functions on a contracted scale. Mr. Gladstone is anxious in the highest degree that the fund of strength and credit which Your Majesty stored up for the Monarchy in the affections of the people, should not be diminished. But he bears in mind that its maintenance depends less upon memory, and upon reason, than upon habits, which require to be sustained by visible signs almost from day to day.' He begged the Queen to ascribe ' his prolixity to the depth of his anxiety for the interests involved ' ;

reminded her that it had been most painful to him on several occasions to have had to urge the Queen to undertake 'what Your Majesty felt could not be undertaken'; and warned her that the Prince's recent illness had 'given to the present juncture the character of a noble and priceless opportunity from which the greatest benefits may be extracted, but which, if it be let slip, can hardly recur'.

The Queen's reply showed that Gladstone had given deep offence. It was written from Osborne on 12 July, and it was very brief:

'As the Queen has so much to write and do—she has made use of Colonel Ponsonby's pen in answering Mr. Gladstone's long Memorandum in which he submits his proposals on the Prince of Wales, and sends it herewith.'

Ponsonby, instructed by the Queen, said that she would 'not at present enter into the details of the plan which seem to be full of objections, but will simply remark that it does not seem to be desirable to introduce violent changes into the Government of Ireland at a moment when that country appears to be in a state of fermentation . . .' With regard to the proposal that 'the Prince and Princess of Wales should represent the Queen on occasions of Court and public ceremonial during the months of April, May, and June', and with regard to a suggestion from Gladstone 'that the Queen might call on the Prince and Princess of Wales to exert an influence on Society for its moral and social benefit', the Queen took leave to remind her Prime Minister that she did 'her utmost' to fulfil her duties 'as far as her health will permit', and that she considered that modern society was far better than that which existed 70 or 80 years ago. She was, however, willing to discuss the subject with the Prince of Wales. The letter ended with the remark that the Queen considered that that part of Gladstone's letter was 'a question which more properly concerns herself to settle with the members of her family as occasion may arise'.

At that stage it would have been evident to anyone but Gladstone that the subject had been pressed as hard as the circumstances warranted. It is not wise to endanger the good by concentrating too exclusively upon the best. Lord Granville begged Gladstone to let the matter drop, but Gladstone told him (16 July, 1872) that for once he could not accept his advice. He had 'no wish to irritate', but the country and the Queen herself had suffered too much in the past 'from want of plain speaking'. He said that he could not feel that he had yet discharged his full responsibility in the matter.

Accordingly, on 17 July, Gladstone again sent the Queen a long letter in which he said that he would attempt to distinguish between the paramount importance of the end which he had in view, and the secondary importance of the means which he suggested for the attainment of that end :

'That which Mr. Gladstone would venture to call the fundamental proposition is that it is highly requisite to provide the means of remodelling (so to speak) the life of the Prince of Wales, by finding His Royal Highness that adequate employment from which, without any fault, he has hitherto been debarred. And the considerations which recommend the proposition may, as it seems to Mr. Gladstone, be summed up under two heads ; the first that which relates to the Prince of Wales personally and for his own sake ; the second that which embraces the general interest of the Monarchy, and the importance of increasing and husbanding its strength.'

Under the second head Gladstone ventured to observe that :

'Were a Nation a being formed to act by pure and dry reason, without doubt it might be shown' that the Queen's unfortunate seclusion was due to 'the state of Your Majesty's health . . . and in no degree to an alteration of will on Your Majesty's part. But a Nation seems to be affected more powerfully and practically by other forms of motive than by mere reasoning. It is perhaps more acted upon by signs than by proofs ; it ceases fully to believe in what it does not see.'

He added that his career was near its close, and that he was not writing 'with reference to any interest personal to himself or peculiar to the present Government'. His plan was 'in the nature of an experiment ; and must be tried by the working'. It had been formed 'to supply a public want'.

It was difficult for the Queen, who was not used to such plain speaking, not to see a connexion between 'the public want' to which Gladstone referred, and the Irish policy to which he assured her that his plan for the Prince of Wales had no reference. In any case the Queen was no more 'a being formed to act by pure and dry reason', than the British nation was. She was dismayed by a memorandum, enclosed with Gladstone's letter, which analysed her previous objections to his plan under six main separate heads, in an attempt to prove them unfounded. The Queen replied non-committally and in some evident perplexity on 21 July, but on 5 August she said firmly that:

'Mr. Gladstone put forward this plan merely in the nature of an experiment, and the Queen cannot avoid repeating that she does not think Ireland is in a fit state at the present moment to be experimented upon . . . The Queen therefore trusts that this plan may now be considered as *definitely* abandoned.'

Gladstone noted at once in a private memorandum that the Queen's letter was 'a very grave one . . . Only one thing I cannot do. I cannot regard this reply as bringing the matter to a state in which it is to be put by, for I think it is of the weightiest character.' He considered that the Queen was exercising undue influence on the Prince of Wales, and he tried unsuccessfully to obtain her permission to approach the Prince directly himself. However, the use of the term 'experiment' in the Queen's letter gave him the further opening which he desired.

After very careful consideration, he sent the Queen another long letter on 28 August, 1872, in which he explained that he had 'spoken of his plan as an experiment in immediate reference not to Ireland but to the Prince of Wales'. He asked again that he should be permitted to explain directly to the Prince 'any points . . . on which Mr. Gladstone may not have enabled Your Majesty to place His Royal Highness in full possession of his meaning'. He enclosed another memorandum in which he said that he had attempted, under five main heads, to mitigate or remove the Queen's objections as he now understood them.

It was all to no purpose, and on 2 September in a brief note the Queen informed Gladstone that it was 'useless to prolong the discussion'. She advised the Prime Minister to consult 'such of his colleagues who best know the Prince of Wales' and to devise some scheme for teaching him methods of business in the India Office, or some other Department of State. She told Lord Granville that her mind was made up, and that when, as in the present case, 'she had the strongest conviction' on a subject 'she generally found she was right'. Gladstone was, of course, equally convinced that he was right, but he told Lord Granville (6 September) that he had formed the view that 'it would not be right for me to resign upon the matter, as it would do more harm than good'.

On 15 August Gladstone had accepted a command to stay at Balmoral in the middle of September. On 6 September he wrote with icy courtesy to inquire 'whether as matters now stand it will still be Your Majesty's desire to see him there, and he will assume, unless he hears to the contrary, that Your Majesty has no occasion

to command his presence'. He added an expression of his deep grief
at finding his views 'so unequivocally disapproved by Your Majesty
in a matter of so much importance, either way, to the interests of
the Monarchy'. With equal courtesy the Queen replied (11 September) that while she would have been happy to see the Prime
Minister 'for 2 nights' at Balmoral while he was staying with the
Duke of Sutherland at Dunrobin, 'if there is nothing very special
to communicate, the Queen dislikes to urge Mr. Gladstone to put himself to the inconvenience and fatigue of coming over'. Relations
had now reached a point at which Lord Granville found it natural
to pass Gladstone a note during a meeting of the Cabinet (July,
1873) :

'Which do you and Mrs. Gladstone dislike the least—to dine
with the Queen on Wednesday at Windsor, or to go down for a
Saturday and Sunday to Osborne ?'

Gladstone chose the former alternative, and he always relied on
Granville to help him to save his relations with the Queen from
breaking down in form as well as in fact. It is possible that Gladstone's instinct for self-mortification was in some subconscious way
stirred and quickened by the failure of his attempt to mould his
Sovereign to his will. He brooded about it a great deal, and near
the end of his life he noted :

'My attempt to bring about an altered attitude on the part of the
Royal Family towards Ireland may have been a daring one, but I
think it was right, although it also involved, as I framed the scheme,
important changes in England. It was not . . . an exclusively Irish
proposal. Since the death of the Prince Consort, the Court (properly
so-called) had virtually dropped out of existence . . . It has always
been my belief that the Prime Minister had particular responsibilities
of his own, little shared by his colleagues, in advising the Sovereign
on matters of general policy and conduct, when the public interest was
concerned. On this principle I proceeded, and I did not consult in
this matter with my colleagues except, probably, with Granville.'

He added that he had 'kept the matter profoundly secret for a quarter
of a century, and the time has not yet come for divulging it, though
come it must . . . It has its proper place in any account of our relations with Ireland. My way, as will be seen, was absolutely blocked
by Her Majesty, and the case was one in which this obstacle was insurmountable. I thought also that she much misliked the English part
of the arrangement as an interference, which it undoubtedly was, with

her personal conduct, and the new and less beneficial framework of her public life.'

Despite his persistence, it is only fair to say that Gladstone gave up the struggle to find suitable employment for the Prince of Wales before either the Queen's or the Prince's private secretaries were content to see him let it alone. As late as 8 December, 1872, after Gladstone had stayed at Sandringham with the Prince, Knollys wrote to Ponsonby :

'I should have written to you directly after Mr. Gladstone had left here, had anything as regards the question of employment resulted from his visit. But he did not even mention the subject to the Prince, and the latter said nothing to him. G. will never again have so good an opportunity, and the whole thing is too disheartening.'

Knollys added that the Prince had been 'quite ready and prepared for the subject'.

Gladstone was completely disheartened by the failure of his plan to solve satisfactorily the 'Royalty question'; and eight months later, in August, 1873, when Gladstone was at Balmoral as Minister in attendance, Ponsonby noted : 'I sometimes think him rather mad—earnestly mad, and taking up a view with an intensity which scarcely allows him to suppose there can be any truth on the other side.'

Gladstone had spoken of his intention to retire. He had complained that he was thwarted on every side, and that the composition of the House of Commons had been adversely affected by Parliamentary reform—'Statesmen on the old lines are becoming impossible'. Ponsonby commented :

'Looking back on his visit here, although he was physically well and although he was in good spirits, he was not he same man that he was two years ago. He seldom or never spoke of the political future. He was looking back, not forward. There was no keenness about future measures, and he made little or no stand against anything which the Queen insisted on. He gave way. There was a sort of want of interest in the political future which was not like his old self . . . He was most pleasant and agreeable, and talked to me very openly on most matters.'

The Queen also noted Gladstone's complaisance, and Lord Granville, who succeeded his chief as Minister in attendance, wrote to Gladstone (20 September) : 'The Queen told me last night that she had never known you so remarkably agreeable.' Gladstone was, however, profoundly depressed and afflicted with a deep sense of failure. The

217

Queen's real view, moreover, was expressed in a characteristic letter to General Ponsonby, dated 18 November, 1874 :

'she must say to General Ponsonby, tho' he may hardly like to believe it, that *she* has felt that Mr. Gladstone would have liked to *govern* HER as Bismarck governs the Emperor. Of course not to the same extent, or in the *same* manner ; but she always felt in his manner an overbearing obstinacy and imperiousness (without being actually wanting in respect as to form) which she never experienced from *anyone* else, and which she found most disagreeable. It is the same thing which made him so unpopular to his followers, and even to his colleagues.'

Ponsonby pointed out, the same day, that Gladstone, unlike Bismarck, was 'honest and true' ; he asked the Queen to believe that Gladstone was entirely loyal and devoted to her. The Queen agreed (19 November) that Gladstone was 'loyal and meant to be so'. She complained, however, that he was, as Lord Palmerston had said, '" a very dangerous man ". No-one can be sure for a moment what he may *persuade himself* to think right, and hence the impossibility to place confidence in him.' She complained that he was 'often very harsh and, as the Queen said yesterday, very dictatorial, and wished the Queen to do what *he* liked, and would listen to *no* reasoning or argument'.

In the Queen's eyes Gladstone stood for democracy and for radical changes in many fields. He represented new tendencies which the Queen did not understand and which she therefore disliked ; and he was incapable of explaining things simply to her. Disraeli, on the other hand, was coming forward as an ardent champion of the two simple ideas which inspired the Queen's political creed. As early as 24 June, 1872, four months after an abortive attempt on the Queen's life had precipitated a reaction in her favour, Disraeli had exalted the Crown as the focus of the new imperialism in a famous speech at the Crystal Palace. Imperialism was a middle-class reaction to the steady increase in the wealth and armaments of the Continental Powers which threatened Great Britain's prestige ; and it constantly gained support as the century drew towards its close. The Queen's concern for the position of the Crown was her instinctive response to everything which she failed to understand in the changing spirit of the times ; and by her personality and longevity she succeeded before she died in vastly strengthening the Crown's position. Disraeli spoke and wrote to the Queen in what was virtually basic English, spiced with delicious absurdities. He professed a profound reverence for her mature wisdom and experience, and indulged to an unlimited extent in flattery of a kind which disgusted Gladstone. By that means Disraeli restored the Queen's self-confidence which always wilted in contact with Gladstone.

Disraeli had no need to create a personal prejudice against Gladstone by deliberately disparaging him to the Queen. There is no evidence that he ever tried to do so, and the Gladstone family was probably mistaken in supposing that he did. It is clear, however, that Gladstone's position was weakened by Disraeli's unscrupulous encouragement of the Queen's partisan tendencies which were very feminine but quite unconstitutional. He showed cunning, later, in devising irregular means for maintaining direct communication with her while his rival was in office.

The Queen's dislike of Gladstone began in political disagreement and became personal. Gladstone was greatly troubled by the early phase of that unhappy development throughout the year 1872. Preoccupied in that way, he found it increasingly difficult to keep his natural vehemence under control. His mind was distracted by an overmastering private desire to quit politics, as soon as the Irish and the Royalty questions were out of the way, and to devote his declining years to the defence of religion against what he described to the boys of Liverpool College on 22 December, 1872, as 'the insufferable arrogance' of such men as Herbert Spencer, who 'assumed airs of unmeasured superiority over former ages', who claimed that they were wiser than the Fathers of the Church, and who had 'challenged all religion, but especially the religion we profess, to the combat of life and death'. He told his sister (31 December, 1872) that his life had always been a double one :

'The welfare of my fellow-creatures is more than ever at stake, but not within the walls of Parliament. The battle is to be fought in the region of thought, and the issue is belief or disbelief in the unseen world, and in its Guardian, the Creator-Lord and Deliverer of Man.'

The Prime Minister was particularly anxious to be free to challenge the Decree of Papal Infallibility which Pope Pius IX had pronounced on 18 July, 1870. Gladstone could never truly relax, and he told his sister (13 October, 1874) that that Decree had made her Church 'the most effective, I do *not* say conscious ally of the great unbelieving movement'. It was, he said, necessary to prove to the world that the Church of Rome had turned its back upon freedom, reason, and history, and thereby caused all the enemies of God to rejoice. On his birthday (29 December, 1870) he begged God in his diary to give him ' a lawful opportunity of escape from the present course of daily excess which is, for me, inseparable from my place and calling '. Without it, he considered that his life would never attain ' its just balance '. He told his wife (5 January, 1871) that he had been going through his accounts to see what money they would have to live on when he retired. He found that he had only £4,800 a year apart from his salary, and he described that position as ' worse than it has been for a good many years . . . It shows pretty plainly the propriety of giving up art purchase, and viewing the possession of the present house as likely to terminate with the period of official life.'

The ' present house ' was 11, Carlton House Terrace where Gladstone had chosen to live as Prime Minister in preference to 10, Downing Street, which he used as an office. He often told his family that the present age was much the most important and interesting since that of Christ's Advent ; and it tortured him to think that his hands were tied while others fought the vital battle of orthodox religion. He would have greatly liked also to be able to devote more time to his Homeric studies. He had bewildered his contemporaries in August, 1869, within a year of becoming Prime Minister, by publishing *Juventus Mundi, The Gods and Men of the Heroic Age*, which partly summarized and partly developed his fantastic speculations. The book, which had been written before he took office, attempted to show, amongst much else, that Christ had been foreshadowed by Apollo, the Virgin by Latona, Satan by Ate, and the Trinity by a combination of Zeus, Poseidon, and Hades. No man can bear to remain sensible and serious at all times, and the tensions which seethed in Gladstone's mind, deprived of any comparatively harmless vent, began to provoke minor faults of temper and judgement in the conduct of his private as well as in that of his public life.

On 7 April, 1872, for example, even Mrs. Gladstone was moved to protest against her husband's suggestion that their son Herbert (later Viscount Gladstone of Lanark ; 1854-1930) should be removed from Eton on account of a school report that was less good than usual. Gladstone had written that ' with all his charm and all his merits, he doesn't yet know what strong effort and hard work are '. Mrs. Gladstone pointed out that Herbert had suffered from ill-health :

' I don't say he has *your* energy, or *your* ability, but I do say he has done his best, and worked up to his powers. Do you not think, if I may say so, that your words are too strong ? . . . Let Willy [William Henry Gladstone, their eldest son ; 1840–1891] read this . . . I am half-afraid you won't have time ; but be assured I uphold to Herbert *your* opinion ; and do my best to carry out your wishes, and act as a spur. Had it not been for . . . the fact of your incessant and *never*-ending hard work, which of course prevents your thinking so much of home interests and pleasures, and studying Herbert as you would wish, *I* should not have ventured my opinion against yours.'

Herbert Gladstone, after obtaining First Class Honours in Modern History at Oxford, served as Home Secretary under H. H. Asquith and later governed South Africa with distinction. In common with his three brothers and three sisters he always worshipped and was utterly devoted to his father.

In his public life Gladstone's impatient temperament occasionally tempted him to take short cuts to achieve his ends, and to justify them in a manner which to plain men appeared perverse. An example occurred in the summer of 1871, when Edward Cardwell's proposals for Army reform were held up by violent opposition to a Government proposal to abolish the system whereby anyone who desired to make the Army his career had to buy a commission. Gladstone resolved the difficulty by persuading the Queen to end that system by means of a Royal Warrant. It was by that means that the system had been sanctioned by the Queen's grandfather, George III. The Queen rather relished that arbitrary exercise of her Royal authority, but she was unpopular at the time, and the Prime Minister incurred criticism from Radicals and Conservatives alike for his lack of scruple and discretion. Faced with obstructive tactics in the Commons and the certainty of defeat in the Lords, it had become clear to him that his object was unattainable by normal Parliamentary means. His old Peelite colleague, Edward Cardwell, was breaking down as a result of overwork, and Gladstone would never admit that he had been wrong on that occasion to by-pass Parliament by making use of the ancient prerogative power of the Crown. He claimed that the Lords had acted illegally by rejecting what was in effect a measure of finance, and he was proud of the smart victory which he had gained. The Liberal historian E. A. Freeman, however, expressed a widely-held view when he wrote in the *Pall Mall Gazette* (12 February, 1874) : ' The thing did not look well . . . This is one of those cases in which a strictly conscientious man like Mr. Gladstone does things from which a less conscientious man would shrink.'

Another instance of perversity occurred in October, 1871, when Gladstone appointed Sir Robert Collier, the Attorney-General (later Lord Monkswell), to the Judicial Committee of the Privy Council. Collier reminded Gladstone that such appointments were restricted to those who had sat on the judicial bench in England or in India. Against the Lord Chancellor's advice, Gladstone impatiently arranged for Collier to be appointed a High Court judge at once, and to sit for two days, in order to satisfy the requirements of the statute. The whole body of judges resented the Prime Minister's cavalier action, and Chief Justice Cockburn protested in very strong language about the manner in which Collier's appointment had been rigged. Gladstone brushed Cockburn's letter aside, and in February, 1872, the matter was raised in Parliament, while Collier, whose qualifications were never in dispute, begged in vain to be allowed to withdraw from a position which had become unhappy and embarrassing. The affair was pressed to a division in both Houses, and a Government majority of twenty-seven in the Commons was followed by a majority of two in the Lords.

Before those votes were taken, Gladstone had further damaged his reputation by provoking another totally unnecessary quarrel. He appointed to a Crown living, at Ewelme, a graduate of Cambridge who possessed every qualification except the statutory one for that particular appointment of being a member of Convocation at Oxford. Gladstone, when that was pointed out to him, reacted for no reason at all with a violence which amazed his friends and delighted his enemies. The clergyman (the Rev. W. W. Harvey) was personally unknown to the Prime Minister ; he was a Conservative and not a Liberal ; but he was an excellent man who had written a number of books, and Gladstone refused to retreat or even to hear reason. He arranged for Harvey to be technically incorporated as a member of Oriel College, and admitted to the Oxford Convocation after the statutory forty-two days' residence, for the sole purpose of enabling him to be presented to the living. A storm broke out at once, and on 8 March, 1872, Gladstone was called upon to defend his wanton act of high-handed folly in the Commons. Less than a month had passed since he had had to defend, on 19 February, his action in the case of Sir Robert Collier. The Prime Minister argued that although Oriel College had acted in response to his known wishes, he had no control over the University and no statutory requirement had been broken.

Gladstone's enemies did not scruple to express their belief, or at least their hope, that the Prime Minister was going crazy. His friends were forced to admit that he was beginning to show signs of overwork and strain. In the meantime the Government's popularity continued to suffer a progressive decline, and some vivid metaphors used by Disraeli at the Free Trade Hall at Manchester on 3 April, 1872, were repeated from lip to lip. The Conservative leader had compared the Treasury Bench to :

' one of those marine landscapes not very unusual on the coast of South America. You behold a range of exhausted volcanoes. Not a flame flickers on a single pallid crest. But the situation is still dangerous. There are occasional earthquakes, and ever and anon the dark rumbling of the sea.'

CHAPTER 10

TALKING TURKEY

1873-1878

THE last year of the Government's life was not a happy one for Gladstone who seemed to be almost everywhere losing ground. He was in his sixty-fourth year and he had begun to speak of himself as an old man. On 13 February, 1873, after some three months' preparation, he opened in the House of Commons the third round of his first public attack upon the Irish problem when he introduced his Irish University Bill. In a speech lasting three hours he outlined a complex proposal for establishing a new university in Dublin, which Roman Catholics would be able to share with Protestants on equal terms. Roman Catholics had, with few exceptions, refused to allow their sons to attend Trinity College, and Gladstone, in a characteristic phrase, informed the House that hitherto, in the field of higher education, the position of Roman Catholics was ' miserably bad. I go further, and would almost say that it is scandalously bad.'

Unhappily, Gladstone's Bill did not meet the aspirations of Roman Catholics who wanted the new University to be as Catholic as Trinity College was Protestant. His speech made a great impression, but criticism fastened on two points. In the first place there was to be no teaching of theology, moral philosophy, or modern history, because those subjects were controversial ; in the second place, any teacher could be suspended or dismissed if he offended the religious suscepti-bilities of his students. Archbishop Manning did his best to persuade Cardinal Cullen and the Roman Catholic hierarchy to accept the Bill, but his efforts were unsuccessful : ' This ', he told Gladstone (12 March), ' is not your fault, nor the Bill's fault, but the fault of England and Scotland and three anti-Catholic centuries.'

When Gladstone received that letter his Government had been defeated by three votes on the Bill's Second Reading. The end came at two o'clock on the morning of 12 March, when the figures were 287 to 284. Gladstone made what was, by general consent, a fine speech in a lost cause, and on 13 March he announced that his Government would resign without asking for a dissolution. A curious negotiation followed. The Queen sent for Disraeli, who refused to take office or to recommend the Queen to dissolve Parliament. He calculated that his chances at the polls would be improved if the Government could be made to incur increased odium by remaining in office a little longer. Gladstone argued that Disraeli, after the Government had resigned in consequence of a defeat in the House of Commons, was constitutionally bound to take office. Disraeli contemptuously rejected that suggestion and appealed to the Queen. Gladstone was as unwilling as Disraeli to advise a dissolution of Parliament at that moment, and since it was necessary that the Queen's government should be carried on, Gladstone agreed (18 March) to resume office. Disraeli said that Gladstone's resignation had been foolish, impulsive, and unnecessary, and Gladstone found that defeat, resignation, and return to power had sadly weakened his position.

The situation was made worse during the summer by the disclosure of irregularities in the administration of the Post Office. Post Office revenue and savings bank balances had been used for capital expenditure on telegraph services without Parliamentary sanction. In private, Gladstone made no attempt to conceal his mortification; but in public he was unusually cautious. He transferred Robert Lowe, the Chancellor of the Exchequer, to the Home Office, and he assumed the office of Chancellor himself, combining it with that of Prime Minister. He permitted William Monsell, the Postmaster-General, to resign, but promised to submit his name for a peerage in the Dissolution Honours List.

Gladstone always loathed personal cases, and he was embarrassed and exhausted by another such case at that time. A. S. Ayrton, the First Commissioner of Works, had been tactless and overbearing in an office which brought him into contact with Royalty owing to his responsibility for the upkeep of the Royal palaces. Gladstone admitted to the Queen (15 August, 1872) that Ayrton had caused great and constant trouble through his rudeness and want of tact :

' To few probably has he given more trouble than to Mr. Gladstone ; but Your Majesty will be the first to feel that this does not absolve Mr. Gladstone from an obligation to judge him justly. Mr. Gladstone is indeed himself reputed to be a person singularly subject to illusions : but he is quite sure that he has no illusions with respect to Mr. Ayrton.'

Nevertheless Gladstone rightly retained Ayrton in his post for fear of compromising the Queen who had tried to veto his inclusion in the Government. If dropped, the bitter-tongued economist would openly have attributed his dismissal to the part he had played in resisting the Queen's extravagant demands for greater public expenditure on the royal palaces—thus provoking renewed criticism of the Queen's neglect of her duties and renewed speculations about the size of her private fortune, which Gladstone wished to avoid. He argued therefore that Ayrton's industry, ability and fundamental integrity were more important than his unfortunate personal qualities. But he persuaded Ayrton to move in August, 1873, making him Judge Advocate-General, an office which might again have involved personal contact with the Queen, who protested strongly and only gave her consent on condition that she would never be required to see or speak to Ayrton.

Those worries probably helped to account for an action which caused some resentment after John Stuart Mill died in May, 1873. Gladstone had greatly admired Mill, and he allowed his name to be associated with those of the Duke of Argyll, Lord Derby, Lord Salisbury, and others, in sponsoring a public memorial. Unfortunately, it was suggested in the course of a correspondence in The Times that Mill had, as a young man, advocated birth control. Gladstone was scandalized, and he at once withdrew his name from the list of sponsors, although the Duke of Argyll implored him to take time to reflect, and assured him that the allegation was misconceived. Gladstone said that he had no wish to pass judgement or to cause controversy, but he might have been expected to see that the impulsive and ostentatious withdrawal of the Prime Minister's name was bound to involve both.

Gladstone's decision to dissolve Parliament was taken impulsively during a temporary mood of depression which visited him at the time of the marriage of his eldest daughter, Agnes, to the Rev. E. C. Wickham (27 December, 1873). The marriage, which was entirely unworldly, delighted Gladstone, but the preparations for it distracted and exhausted him. On 8 January, 1874, Gladstone told Lord Granville that the Government had been reduced to impotence. He added that he could see only one remote possibility of benefiting the country and of restoring at the same time the fortunes of the Liberal Party. He explained that he was considering an appeal to the country on the basis of a spectacularly popular budget. For that purpose the Government would have to use the large surplus which it had accumulated ; it would have to enforce a further instalment of ruthless economy in every department of expenditure ; and it would finally need to liquidate immediately a tiresome war with the Ashantis which was being waged on the Gold Coast.

At Gladstone's request Parliament was dissolved on 26 January, 1874. The Liberal Party's appeal to the electorate was based on a pledge to abolish the income-tax. To achieve that object it would have been necessary to slash once more the naval and military estimates, and immediately before he resigned Gladstone was involved in painful and heated controversy with C. J. Goschen at the Admiralty, and with Edward Cardwell at the War Office. The Prime Minister trusted that the country would give him a mandate to overrule the objections of the Service chiefs.

Gladstone was involved at the same time in a personal embarrassment about his Parliamentary seat. Some lawyers held that he should have offered himself for re-election at Greenwich in September, 1873, when he had assumed the additional office of Chancellor of the Exchequer. Before 1919 members of Parliament had to offer themselves for re-election whenever they accepted any office of profit under the Crown. Gladstone was advised by the Law Officers that, as he was already Prime Minister, no by-election was necessary at Greenwich; but strong legal arguments were also advanced on the other side. The matter was widely discussed, and it was known that the Opposition intended to stage a debate when Parliament reassembled after the Christmas Recess. One result of Gladstone's sudden decision to dissolve was that he escaped the unpleasantness of that debate.

On the day before he resigned the Queen sent Gladstone a hectoring letter on the subject of the appointment to ecclesiastical office of men with leanings towards Rome. She warned Gladstone to be on his guard, and added that she considered ' this especially necessary on the part of Mr. Gladstone who is *supposed* to have *rather* a bias towards High church views himself '. Gladstone habitually took such immense pains over ecclesiastical appointments that even a minor one was liable to disrupt the routine of his office for days on end. He was, however, as always, willing to be mortified, and on 22 January he humbly acknowledged ' the very mild and circumspect terms of the allusion to himself '. In a letter of great length, for which he apologized, he assured the Queen that he had never at any time been guided ' in matters of ecclesiastical patronage, by so poor and unworthy a standard as his own impressions or belief in Religion '. He pointed out, however, that there were undoubtedly some modern clergymen who were barely distinguishable from atheists, and he referred Her Majesty to a recent ' masterly survey ' of the present state of the Church of England by his old Roman Catholic friend, Dr. Döllinger.

In framing his appeal to the country Gladstone wore the spectacles of a Chancellor of the Exchequer instead of those of a Prime Minister. He reflected at the end of his life that the electorate had been no more interested in his promise to repeal the income-tax, which then stood at threepence, than it had been in his call for economy. The country was bored, and Gladstone's rigid financial doctrine made no appeal to it. It wanted a more colourful foreign and imperial policy, and a measure of social reform at home, rather than in Ireland. Disraeli's election address was not much less dreary than Gladstone's. It did, however, promise rest from 'incessant and harassing legislation'; and it undertook to restore Great Britain's influence in Europe, and 'to support by every means her imperial sway'.

The General Election gave the Conservatives a majority of about fifty over all other parties. A new Home Rule Party which, as a result of the Ballot Act,[1] made its appearance in Ireland for the first time was one of the causes of Gladstone's defeat. Other causes were the Government's colourless record in foreign affairs, which was considered inglorious; the unpopularity of the Education and Licensing Acts; and the refusal to allow peaceful picketing during strikes.

Gladstone himself put most of the blame on the brewers. He told his brother Robertson (6 February, 1874) that he had been 'borne down in a torrent of gin and beer. Next to this has been the Education Act of 1870, and the subsequent controversies.' He never ceased to lament his failure to abolish the income-tax which he liked to call 'a tangled network of mantraps for conscience' and a menace to public and private morals. He noted in 1896 that:

'The dissolution of 1874, with its result, cost the country scores of millions, and may yet be found to have cost it hundreds . . . Since the year 1874 the repeal of the income-tax has been wholly out of reach; and we have actually, without war, raised it to a higher point (8^d) than that at which (7^d) it was fixed by Sir Robert Peel in 1842 !'

Sickened by his defeat, Gladstone went to Windsor on 17 February to resign. He told the Queen, in her own words, that his downfall was 'the greatest expression of public disapprobation of a Government which he ever remembered', and that he intended to quit politics because 'wrangling discussion in the House of Commons, after the

[1] Secret voting relieved tenants from the fear of reprisals if they chose to cast their votes against the known wishes of their landlords.

position he had held, was not a fit thing for people in old age'. The Queen noted that she would have liked to tell Gladstone that he owed his defeat 'to his own unpopularity, and to the want of confidence people had in him'. She contented herself, however, with chaffing him about his wish for retirement ; 'I said this was all very well, but that for a person in his position to decide this beforehand was almost impossible. Sir Robert Peel had said the same but, if he had lived, he could not have carried it out.' Gladstone should have remembered that he, too, had said much the same to Peel in 1846.

The mood of depression which settled on Gladstone was much slower to lift than usual. He was in his sixty-fifth year—older than Peel had been at his death in 1850. Gladstone would have been utterly astonished to know that over twenty years of active political struggle still lay ahead of him. The narrow margin of votes (403) by which he had escaped defeat in his constituency at Greenwich rankled in his mind, and he told Lord Granville (12 March) that he reserved his freedom to divest himself of the leadership 'at no distant time'. He considered that he was incapable of restoring the fortunes of his Party and that, in religious matters especially, he was hopelessly out of touch with Liberal thought. He longed for an interval of quiet between Parliament and the grave, and he told Mrs. Gladstone (6 April) :

'The anti-Parliamentary reaction has been stronger with me even than I anticipated . . . In London I think we were too much hustled to speak leisurely or effectually of the future. It will open for us by degrees . . . There is one thing I would like you to understand clearly as to my view of things . . . I am convinced that the welfare of mankind does not now depend on the state of the world of politics : the real battle is being fought in the world of thought, where a deadly attack is being made with great tenacity of purpose and over a wide field upon the greatest treasure of mankind, the belief in God and the Gospel of Christ.'

It was for that reason that Gladstone wished to quit politics, and throughout 1874 he attended the House of Commons infrequently. He had refused a peerage ; he had retained his seat in the Commons ; but rumours of his impending retirement were widely current. Few people seriously believed that he would be content to spend the remainder of his life at Hawarden, arranging his papers, cutting down trees, and indulging in the exquisite delights of religious and scholarly controversy. While the issue remained in doubt, however, the

Party rank and file complained that Achilles was sulking in his tent, and Mrs. Gladstone was extremely uneasy. Despite her forgetfulness and disorderly methods, she was exceptionally shrewd, and she wrote to her husband (8 January, 1875):

'I know full well your whole soul is bent upon doing right. You would go to the death in a righteous cause. Who could hold you when the battle-cry sounded? I expressed myself so badly in the hurry of parting . . . Remember there are those who can speak more frankly to me than to you, and who desire your honourable course of action. Is there not something to be said against your own point . . .? Great Church questions may arise when your power and influence may be valuable. Would you have the same power, by a sudden rush, to fight after *putting the reins upon others*? The Party would naturally be at sea. Is there no medium course? . . .' She warned her husband that the world thought that he cared 'only about *fights*'. She would like the world to see him 'so patient, so good, sacrificing your own wishes and only helping others, accepting the position and meeting it'. If only he would retain the leadership there would be no need to attend the House often: 'Who would expect it? Could you not take it quite easily?' She said that her nephew, Edward Talbot (who became Bishop of Winchester in 1911) had pointed out that many people would attribute Gladstone's retirement to 'religious mania' which must do his reputation harm. She thought that 'by proving you can *calmly* attend to political business in Opposition you would double your influence when needed'.

Calmness was not one of Gladstone's attributes, and medium courses were uncongenial to him. He wrote to his wife (11 January, 1875):

'I am obliged to stand to my conclusions for many reasons. Among them the Church reason is one of the most serious, and the other, the undefined and prolonged character of the service if now undertaken . . . I am indeed sorry that you and I have not been able to take the same view of this important subject, but you know that I am acting on convictions long entertained, and will I am sure believe that I have probed myself deeply and used all the means in my power to get at a right conclusion.'

He told her that Lord Hartington would succeed to the Liberal leadership in the Commons, and added that a report from his doctor, Andrew Clark, had made it impossible for him to plead ill-health. There was nothing wrong with him at all except a slight tendency to diarrhœa.

Mrs. Gladstone replied the next day (12 January) :

'It is a great deal too much to say that you and I take different views of this important question of the leadership . . . But I did consider it my duty to lay before you the drawbacks . . . Perhaps I am too sensitive in the feeling of anything like running away when the road is dark and hopeless . . . However my poor opinion is so little worth having, perhaps I need not have said anything.'

She thanked God for Clark's excellent report ; added, a little inconsequently, that there could be no safer vent than diarrhœa ; and said that what she most desired to see was ' less high pressure, *calmness* in work, and more allowance of relaxation '.

Gladstone's colleagues did all they could to persuade their chief to retain the Party leadership. Lord Granville urged (5 January) that Gladstone's reputation was so great and his hold on large sections of the country so strong that ' secession will not affect your power of resuming your Parliamentary position when you choose to do so. But you would grievously disappoint the Liberal Party, with the exception, perhaps, of William Harcourt.' He admitted that the question of overwork was serious, but added that Gladstone could depute much of the work to others. He asked pointedly, ' with your extraordinary mental activity, and fecundity, and with your temperament, will you ever find yourself in a position in which you will not strain your physical strength ? '

Gladstone's reply, dated 13 January, 1875, was published, together with Lord Granville's regretful acknowledgement, in all the newspapers:

My dear Granville,

. . . I see no public advantage in my continuing to act as the leader of the Liberal Party . . . At the age of sixty-five, and after forty-two years of a laborious public life, I think myself entitled to retire on the present opportunity. This retirement is dictated to me by my personal views as to the best method of spending the closing years of my life.

I need hardly say that my conduct in Parliament will continue to be governed by the principles on which I have heretofore acted : and whatever arrangements are made for the treatment of general business, and for the advantage of the Liberal Party, will have my cordial support. I should perhaps add that I am at present, and may for a short time be, engaged on a special matter which occupies me closely.

The draft of that letter had been shown previously to Lord Granville who had begged that the last sentence should be omitted as an irrelevant complication. Gladstone characteristically refused. The 'special matter' was a sudden attack which he had launched against the Roman Catholic Church in the *Contemporary Review* for October, 1874, and which he was now pursuing in a violent war of pamphlets.

In Gladstone's absence, the Liberal leadership was divided between Lord Hartington in the Commons and Lord Granville in the Lords. To Lord Hartington, who was reluctant to accept the ungrateful charge, Gladstone strongly urged (2 February, 1875) the great principle of *noblesse oblige*, and paid tribute to the 'manhood' which Lord Hartington had always displayed. In the Commons, Gladstone continued to sit on the Opposition front bench, where his occasional appearances and unheralded interventions became a source of some embarrassment to the Party. In July, 1874, for example, when Disraeli was engaged in a campaign to suppress ritualism in the Church of England, the Liberals refused to support Gladstone's demand that the Government should be required to consult representatives of the Church before introducing ecclesiastical legislation. In the autumn of that year many Radical eyebrows were raised when Gladstone, at Hawarden, gravely but successfully rebuked a deputation of striking miners for an offence against liberty in demanding a 'closed shop'.

Gladstone's conception of the nature of Party discipline dated from an earlier age. He had, however, done more than anyone else to mould the Liberal Party out of disparate elements, and it is strange that he should have failed to appreciate the embarrassment which his independent actions caused. His campaign against the Roman Catholic Church was certainly not calculated to bind the new Irish Party to the Liberal side. Gladstone had chafed all his life against the cramping effects of narrow political considerations, and he believed that the third and final phase of his life had begun. He had broken his tie with the Conservatives ; his tie with Oxford had been broken ; he felt that he had now broken his tie with politics altogether in order to atone as far as possible to his conscience for his failure to answer the call he had heard in his undergraduate youth to take Holy Orders —a call which he could never wholly forget.

* * *

The first fruit of Gladstone's leisure after the fall of his Government was a series of three articles on Homer which appeared in the *Con-*

temporary Review. The last article (July, 1874) sought to clear Homer of the charge that he had been a war-monger. Gladstone found that the Trojan War had not been a war of aggression. It had served ' the worthy, nay the paramount end of establishing on a firm and lasting basis the national life, cohesion, and independence' of the Greeks. Bismarck had privately justified the Franco-Prussian War on similar lines, but Gladstone's object was to clear Homer's reputation before putting forward a fantastic theory about the connexion between the *Iliad*, the *Odyssey*, and the Book of *Genesis*. He gave the clearest expression to that theory in an article in the *Contemporary Review* for April, 1878, which was entitled, *The Iris of Homer and Her Relation to the Book of Genesis*. Gladstone proved to his own satisfaction that the Greeks ' stand among the descendants of the persons who are named in the Book of *Genesis* as survivors of the Flood '. He found that ' the beautiful and benevolent Iris of Homer '—the messenger of the Gods—traced her descent directly from the rainbow mentioned in the ninth chapter of the Book of *Genesis*. From that and other evidence Gladstone claimed that he had established ' beyond all reasonable doubt the derivation of an important part of the Olympian scheme of Homer, from Hebrew sources '.

With far-fetched fantasies of that kind Gladstone sought to counter the inroads which science was making upon the foundations of orthodox religion. He did not understand science, but he firmly believed that its revelations could and should be used for the glory of God. Just before his Government fell he found time (12 January, 1874) to assure Herbert Spencer in a long letter that ' to treat a man as an enemy of science is to treat him as an enemy to God ', and he told Stanley Jevons, more specifically (10 May, 1874), that ' the doctrine of evolution, if it be true, enhances in my judgement the proper idea of the greatness of God, for it makes every stage of creation a legible prophecy of all those which are to follow it '. Gladstone's faith that the revelations of science would ultimately prove to be reconcilable with those of religion was more in accord with the spirit of a later age than it was with that of the nineteenth century. Scientists during the nineteenth century were not gifted with humility ; they had to fight too hard to secure acceptance for their theories.

Gladstone considered that the Decree of Papal Infallibility had placed a deadly weapon in the hands of the materialists, and strengthened everywhere the hands of the enemies of religion. One of his motives, accordingly, in visiting Germany during the summer of 1874 was to

clear his mind, in conversation with Dr. Döllinger, before he renewed
his attack on the Roman Catholic Church. Gladstone took with him
his eldest son, William, to whom he was about to transfer the Hawarden
property. That property had fallen to Gladstone at last on 10 July,
1874, when Sir Stephen Glynne collapsed and died suddenly while
exploring the antiquities of Shoreditch. Gladstone told the Duke of
Argyll that Sir Stephen's death had profoundly changed ' the outward
form ' of his life at Hawarden. In substance, however, the change
made little difference. Sir Stephen's personality had been completely
submerged by that of ' the great people ', as he had always dubbed his
sister and her famous husband, and Gladstone told his wife that Stephen's
willingness to allow others to arrange his life for him had been positively feminine. Sir Stephen's bachelor life at Hawarden had been
lived so modestly and quietly that it was not always easy to remember
that he was the real owner of the place, and the Lord-Lieutenant of
his county.

At Munich Gladstone spent most of his time with Döllinger who
had recently been excommunicated by the Archbishop of Munich for
his refusal to accept the Infallibility Decree. Gladstone described
to his wife (12 September, 1874) how he and Döllinger had passed
the Archbishop in the street. He said that as they were both,
fortunately, hatless, the encounter caused no embarrassment. On
his way home Gladstone called on his sister, and did his best to
persuade her to return to Hawarden and to abandon the Roman
Catholic religion. Miss Gladstone sympathized with Döllinger, and
Gladstone told her that the sympathy which she felt was equivalent
to a call to exercise her private judgement. He warned her of the
paralysing effects of inertia, and said that he needed her help in a
pamphlet which he intended to write against her Church. Miss
Gladstone said that she was so worried that she felt ill, but Gladstone
told his wife (19 September) : ' Her walking is simply wonderful—
29 miles in one day, including a high pass, with no real fatigue, and quite
fresh the next morning.' The Gladstones were a tough breed, and
Mrs. Gladstone felt certain that her husband would never succeed
with his sister. She became, for once, extremely impatient, and
begged her husband (23 September) to leave Helen alone and to
return home at once. Gladstone was puzzled, as always, by his sister's
attitude, but he left her and returned to Hawarden.

As soon as he was settled in his library, Gladstone sat down to renew
his attack upon the Church of Rome. He composed in a few days

a pamphlet entitled, *The Vatican Decrees in their Bearing on Civil Allegiance*, which was published in November by Murray. By the end of the year 150,000 copies had been sold, earning Gladstone £2,000. The Pope helped to advertise it by denouncing Gladstone as ' a viper attacking the bark of St. Peter '. Murray at once pointed out that the Pope's acquaintance with the language of the Billingsgate fish-market proved that he could claim at least a nominal connexion with St. Peter.

Gladstone declared in his pamphlet that he rejoiced to be rid of the official ties which had formerly restrained him from running the risk of ' stirring popular passions '. The Roman Church, by turning its back on freedom and on history, had placed every loyal British Roman Catholic in an intolerable position ; his loyalty to the Crown and his duty to the State were at the mercy of the whim of an Italian priest. Gladstone urged his Roman Catholic fellow-citizens to assert their integrity by opposing the Decree of Papal Infallibility as their ancestors had opposed the Spanish Armada.

Gladstone was delighted by the success of his pamphlet ; he told Lord Granville (2 November, 1874) that his motive had been to defeat a world-wide Roman Catholic conspiracy ' to direct European war to the re-establishment of the temporal power ; or even to bring about such a war for that purpose . . . The whole circumstances have vividly recalled to me the trouble of mind I went through before publishing the letters to Ld. Aberdeen about Naples—another difficult case in which I was obliged to act because no-one else could have the same point of view.' He added (7 December) that the overwhelming success of his pamphlet should tend ' to strengthen and *hearten* the Party generally '. Lord Granville, who was travelling in Italy, replied with tact and circumspection. He said that Gladstone's letters were ' charming ', but that he would prefer to wait to talk the matter over with him rather than to enter into a ' long catalogue of pros and cons that occur to me '. He expressed the hope that ' the enormous profits ' which Gladstone must be earning by his pen would make it unnecessary for 11, Carlton House Terrace to be sold.

By the beginning of February, 1875, 21 printed replies covering more than 1,000 pages, including 200 pages by Manning, had been collected by Gladstone. Working all day and half the night in his library, Gladstone composed a second pamphlet which he sent to Murray on 20 February. It was entitled, *Vaticanism : an Answer to Reproofs and Replies,* and he wrote : 'May the peace and blessing of God go with the work !' It was much more violent than the former pamphlet, but the public was already bored and the sales were disappointing.

In the second pamphlet, Gladstone described the Church of Rome as 'an Asian monarchy : nothing but one giddy height of despotism, and one dead level of religious subservience'. Pope Pius IX wanted to extinguish the rule of law, to enthrone an arbitrary tyranny in its place, and to conceal his crimes against liberty beneath a suffocating cloud of incense. Cardinal Cullen, the Primate of Ireland, ordered prayers to be said for Gladstone in all churches to the end that he might be made sensible of his errors, and of the wrong which he was seeking to do to the Pope and the Catholic Church.

Although Gladstone found such controversy extremely congenial, his desire for action remained unsatisfied. He again felt depressed after the publication of his second pamphlet, and it was then observed that he was seen rather more frequently in the House of Commons. On 16 March, 1875, he intervened in a debate on a Regimental Exchanges Bill, and Disraeli told the Queen (17 March) : 'Mr. Gladstone not only appeared, but rushed into the debate . . . The new Members trembled and fluttered like small birds when a hawk is in the air.'

Gladstone was uneasy in his mind about that impulsive intervention, and on 30 March he confided to his diary his 'views about the future and remaining section of my life', which he noted that he had done his best to explain orally to his wife :

'In outline they are undefined, but in substance definite : the main point is this : that setting aside exceptional circumstances which would have to provide for themselves, my prospective work is not Parliamentary . . . But there is much to be done with the pen, all bearing much on high and sacred ends, for even Homeric study, as I view it, is in this sense of high importance . . . God has in some measure opened the path for me ; may He complete the work !'

That is not the language of clear-cut conviction. Gladstone constantly prayed for light, but he was far from certain of the direction in which he was going. He told his wife (19 May) that he was 'feeling his way' and that he could only hope that it would clear for him by degrees. He complained constantly that he was out of touch with opinion in the House and in the country, and it seemed plain to the rank and file of the Party that the gulf which had opened between Gladstone and many aspects of British Liberal thought was growing wider. Joseph Chamberlain, for example, pointed out in the *Contemporary Review* for October, 1875, that an ex-Prime Minister who devoted his leisure to ' a critical examination of the querulousness of an aged priest, is hardly in touch with the robust common sense of English liberalism'. On that occasion Chamberlain underestimated, as he was often to do later, the extent to which liberalism, as a dynamic and malleable creed, was capable of taking whatever stamp was impressed upon it by the mind and mood of the man who had done most to mould it and to translate it into action.

In March, 1875, Gladstone disposed of 11, Carlton House Terrace together with a number of pictures and much porcelain which he had been at pains to collect. He felt that he must retrench in order to provide for his children, and he told his wife (28 February) that no-one else in Carlton House Terrace had an income of less than £20,000 a year. Gladstone's action in taking a cheaper house at 73, Harley Street was widely regarded as significant of his intention at some time to re-enter active political life.

For another sixteen months Gladstone remained free to stroll round his park at Hawarden, cutting down trees, and explaining to his family how the story of the Redemption had been divinely ' hinted at' in Homer. He came fairly frequently to London where he indulged a passing interest in spiritualism by attending séances. He was deeply mortified to discover, when his brother Robertson died on 23 September, 1875, that the firm of Gladstone and Co., of which Robertson had been the nominal head, had dwindled almost to nothing. Robertson had been a mere cypher in the hands of a man named James Wyllie, who had originally been a creature of Sir John Gladstone ; and Wyllie's first action after Robertson's death was to push Gladstone's third son, Henry, into the street. Henry Gladstone was soon settled in a post with Gillanders, Arbuthnot, and Co. of Calcutta,[1] which Sir John Gladstone had also founded ; and he enjoyed an exceedingly distinguished career in commerce. Gladstone was, however, sickened by what he conceived to be Wyllie's treachery in swallowing up the Gladstone firm. He told Sir Thomas Gladstone (27 December, 1875) that their father had been ' no common man. His name was an honour to the commerce of England. And the more I think of the man, the more I revolt against the

---

[1] The home firm was Ogilvy, Gillanders, and Co. Both names are unchanged.

extinction of his name.' Gladstone sent to Sir Thomas some lines which he had composed on Robertson's death :

> He lay in noble guise along the bed ;
> The flowing locks of youth still decked his head.
> His features spoke of manhood's prime and pride,
> And still his three score years and ten belied.

From those and other moody distractions, Gladstone was recalled by the extraordinary consequences of a peasants' revolt in Bosnia (part of the modern Yugoslavia) which then formed part of the Turkish Empire. The revolt which started in 1875 could not be suppressed. Aggressive Russian sympathy for the oppressed Southern Slavs clashed with British distrust of Russia and with Disraeli's desire to raise British prestige and to play a commanding rôle in Europe and the world. A great war was avoided by the narrowest of margins, and Gladstone, more furious than Achilles after the slaughter of Patroclus, returned to the political arena.

Early in 1876 it became clear that the flame of rebellion in the Balkans was spreading like a forest fire. The only political alliance on the Continent of Europe at that time was the League of the Three Emperors (Germany, Russia, and Austria) which proposed that the Turks should be coerced into granting better conditions to their Christian subjects. Disraeli rejected that proposal out of hand. He argued that it masked a conspiracy on the part of Russia and Austria to partition Turkey ; and he sent a fleet to anchor off the Dardanelles as a warning to Russia. Joint intervention by the Great Powers was made difficult by that independent action ; and the Turks, relying on British support as at the time of the Crimean War, were encouraged to adopt an intransigent attitude towards Russia.

The Three Emperors League was not hostile to Great Britain, but it saw no good reason why Great Britain should interfere in Eastern Europe. Disraeli, much influenced by considerations of prestige, had already, in pursuit of a colourful and active foreign and imperial policy, acquired control of the Suez Canal ; and he was at that time forcing through Parliament a Bill to proclaim the Queen as Empress of India. The Queen herself was unhappily about to throw to the winds the wise restraint which she had hitherto shown. Influenced equally by distrust of Russia and dislike of Gladstone she became as violent a ' Jingo ' as any man or woman in the land.

In April, 1876, the Bulgarians revolted against the Sultan, and during May some 12,000 Bulgarian men, women, and children were massacred by Turkish irregular troops. The news gradually filtered through, and Disraeli was questioned about it in the House of Commons for the first time on 26 June. Two generations later, when the public had grown accustomed to horrors on an incomparably greater scale, British opinion might have been less deeply stirred. In 1876, however, statesmen were in a position to draw to almost any extent upon vast untapped reserves of moral indignation. Lord Derby, the Foreign Secretary, was profoundly moved by the 'Bulgarian Horrors'; even the Queen was dismayed for a time by Disraeli's apparent sympathy with the Turks. Disraeli had little feeling for oppressed Christian peoples struggling to be free. He thought that the Turks would have done better to bribe than to massacre the rebels, and he was afraid lest the Russians should use the atrocities as an excuse for seizing Constantinople. From there they might have been in a position to threaten the new British naval base at Alexandria. He therefore affected to discount the atrocity stories, and he somewhat shocked public opinion by giving a flippant reply to W. E. Forster in the House on 10 July, 1876. The Prime Minister took leave to doubt whether ' torture has been practised on a great scale among an oriental people who seldom, I believe, resort to torture, but generally terminate their connexion with culprits in a more expeditious manner'.

Gladstone waited for nearly two months in a mood of very dangerous calm. He noted twenty years later that he had been ' slow to observe the real leanings of the Prime Minister'. As an ex-member of the Cabinet which had embarked upon the Crimean War in 1854, Gladstone felt a weight of personal responsibility towards the Christian minorities in the Balkans. The rights which Russia had formerly possessed to protect those minorities had been annulled after the Crimean War. The Treaty of Paris, 1856, had substituted a European guarantee of protection which the Powers had failed to enforce. Gladstone had a right, therefore, to claim that Great Britain was bound by international law to extend to the Christian minorities of the Turkish Empire the degree of succour and protection which Russia proposed to offer from motives which he optimistically held to be mainly Christian and humanitarian.

On 31 July, 1876, Gladstone asked Disraeli, in the House, to institute inquiries about the massacres. He urged that the Crimean War had substituted ' a European conscience expressed by the collective guarantee and concerted action of the European Powers ' for the rights which Russia had formerly possessed to intervene in Turkish affairs on behalf of the Christian minorities. He said that the only alternative to the 'European Concert' was a 'European convulsion'. Disraeli retorted by dismissing exaggerated accounts of the atrocities as 'coffee-house babble'. He said that it was futile at that late date 'to enter into the politics of the Crimean War'.

Thenceforward, as the crisis deepened and thrust every other issue into the shade, Disraeli's empirical realism was exposed to a constant and relentless flow of moral precepts from Gladstone. Disraeli, supported by the Queen, society, high finance, the most powerful section of the Press, and by what was left of the rough, happy, ignorant mass of merry England, took his stand on a rather narrow conception of British imperial and strategic interests. He identified those interests with the maintenance of Turkish integrity, and was only held back at the last moment from embarking on a war, which would have been as useless as the war in the Crimea, by a combination of ill-health, Cabinet dissensions, and popular discontent. When Disraeli discovered at Berlin that British prestige could be better secured by throwing over Turkish integrity, he did so without a qualm. He then received the credit for a settlement which embodied, not his ideas, but those of Lord Salisbury, Prince Bismarck, and Count Shuvalov.

Robustly opportunist as it was, Disraeli's policy throughout the crisis reflected the mood of the fashionable world. As Queen Sophie of Holland wrote on 7 September, 1876, to her intimate friend, Lady Derby : 'I cannot feel any sympathy with Servians and Bulgarians, and think them as bad and cruel as their enemies.' Disraeli tended to regard Turks and Christians as pawns in an exciting struggle which was being waged between Great Britain and Russia for a dominant position in the Mediterranean. To his mind, British interests were the sole test of policy, and in Gladstone's view, his interpretation of those interests excluded considerations of justice, or of humanity.

As the last round of the long duel between Gladstone and Disraeli opened, Gladstone, deriving his chief support from intellectuals, Nonconformists, and hosts of upright, God-fearing men and women many of whom had only recently been enfranchised, took his stand squarely on the moral issue. In that age his resolute insistence on that issue made his ultimate return to power inevitable. His greatest service, however, was his appreciation of the truth that the choice confronting Great Britain did not lie between support of Russia and support of Turkey. It lay between a continuance of Turkish misrule, and the adoption of the principle of national self-government in the Balkans. Gladstone constantly pointed out that the Balkan Christians were not seeking alliance with Russia, but delivery from oppression. He argued that, if Disraeli had his way, all the Christian peoples of the Near East would be driven into the arms of Russia.

Gladstone was far from being an unreserved champion of Russia. He sought to contain Russian expansion not by shoring up the decaying corpse of the Turkish Empire, but by calling into existence a string of independent Christian States from the Adriatic to the Aegean and the Black Sea. He did not want to allow Russia to become the sole champion of the principle of nationality in the Balkans; he repeatedly urged that the matter should be taken out of Russian hands and made a common European responsibility. Gladstone's approach to the problem was more realistic than Disraeli's. The future was on his side, as it had been also in the matter of the *Alabama* arbitration. instead of identifying British interests with the integrity of Turkey, which could not, in the long run, be maintained, Gladstone identified them with the principle of nationality in the Balkans, and through that principle with the causes of Christian civilization, justice, and humanity.

Disraeli's attempt to discount the 'Bulgarian Horrors' provoked an outbreak of protest meetings during the month of August, 1876, throughout Great Britain. That popular indignation gave Gladstone his opportunity to direct public opinion towards the end which he desired. He wrote calmly to Lord Granville on 7 August: 'As a Party question this affords no despicable material, but there are much higher interests involved.'

Gladstone was scandalized on 11 August when Disraeli, in the last speech which he made in the Commons before taking his seat in the Lords as Earl of Beaconsfield, argued that: 'There is nothing to justify us in talking in such a vein of Turkey as has been, and is being, at this moment entertained. . . . What our duty is at this critical moment is to maintain the Empire of England.'

Gladstone was about to talk of Turkey in a vein which succeeded in troubling momentarily, at any rate, the quietest waters of sophisticated apathy; on 29 August, after a consular report had been published which confirmed some of the worst details of the atrocities, he asked Lord Granville whether he would be shocked to hear that he proposed to write a pamphlet:

'Good ends can rarely be attained in politics without passion, and there is now, the first time for a good many years, a righteous passion.'

241

Gladstone confided to his wife (5 September) that Granville had been lukewarm, but he added, 'he could not persuade me to hold it back'.

Gladstone at that moment was crippled by lumbago, but he wrote his pamphlet at white heat in four days. As he wrote, his mind was convulsed by the most violent earthquake which it had yet experienced. He laid aside a large bundle of notes, entitled *Future Retribution*, on which he had been working, labelling the wrapper : 'From this I was called away to write on Bulgaria.' On Monday, 4 September, 1876, his daughter Mary recorded : 'Papa rushed off to London on Sunday night, pamphlet in hand, beyond anything agog over the Bulgarian horrors which pass description. The whole country is aflame—meetings all over the place.'

Never had Gladstone's instinct for right-timing been more perfectly exemplified. *The Bulgarian Horrors and the Question of the East* was published by Murray on 6 September, and by the end of the month some 200,000 copies had been sold. Gladstone declared that the Turks ' are, upon the whole, since the black day when they first entered Europe, the one great anti-human species of humanity '. Disraeli had shamelessly condoned outrages so vile ' that it passes the power of heart to conceive or of tongue and pen adequately to describe them '. British and French blood and treasure, poured out like water during the Crimean War, had served only to afford the Turks this opportunity to indulge ' abominable and bestial lusts ' and to enact scenes ' at which Hell itself might almost blush '. Women and children had been violated, roasted, and impaled ; no refinement of torture had been spared ; and Gladstone concluded :

' Let the Turks now carry away their abuses in the only possible manner, namely by carrying off themselves. Their Zaptiehs and their Mudirs, their Bimbashis and their Yuzbachis, their Kaimakams and their Pashas, one and all, bag and baggage, shall, I hope, clear out from the province they have desolated and profaned. This thorough riddance, this most blessed deliverance, is the only reparation we can make to the memory of those heaps on heaps of dead ; to the violated purity alike of matron, of maiden, and of child . . . There is not a criminal in a European gaol ; there is not a cannibal in the South Sea Islands, whose indignation would not arise and overboil at the recital of that which has been done, which has too late been examined, but which remains unavenged ; which has left behind all the foul and all the fierce passions that produced it, and which may again spring up in another murderous harvest, from the soil soaked and reeking with blood, and in the air tainted with every imaginable deed of crime and shame . . . No Government ever has so sinned ; none has proved itself so incorrigible in sin or, which is the same, so impotent for reformation.' He called upon the Concert of Europe, which Disraeli had done his best to disrupt, ' to afford relief to the overcharged emotion of a shuddering world '.

Gladstone's overcharged emotion gained only a momentary respite as a result of the publication of that fulminating pamphlet. On 9 September he addressed a great open-air meeting of his constituents at Blackheath, in pouring rain. He said that he had lived long in public life, that he had witnessed ' many vivid movements of the popular mind ', but that he had never witnessed ' one to compare with that which during the past fortnight has taken its commencement and which has swollen with such rapidity to the dimensions of a movement truly national '. He said that the question at issue had ' a breadth and a height and a depth that carries it far out of the lower region of party differences, and establishes it on grounds, not of political party, not even of mere English nationality, not of Christian faith, but on the largest and broadest ground of all—the ground of our common humanity '. He called upon the Russians to drive the Turks out of Bulgaria :

' I, for one, for the purposes of justice, am ready as an individual to give the right hand of friendship to Russia when her objects are just and righteous, and to say, in the name of God, " Go on and prosper ! " '

At Aylesbury, on 20 September, Disraeli accused Gladstone of using sublime sentiments for the furtherance of personal and party ends. He described him as worse than any Bulgarian horror, and was rebuked by *The Times* for bad taste. Gladstone was goaded almost beyond endurance by such language. Disraeli was toying with the idea of occupying the Dardanelles in order to forestall a Russian invasion of Turkey, and at the Guildhall, on 9 November, he not only made a bitter attack on Servia and Montenegro which had declared war on Turkey ; he threatened Russia openly with war if she failed to stop the flow of ' volunteers ' into those countries. The language which Disraeli used inspired a famous music-hall refrain :

We don't want to fight, but by Jingo if we do,
We've got the ships, we've got the men, we've got the money too !

Gladstone described that provocation as ' almost incredible '. He told the Duke of Argyll that the Jews of the East had always hated the Christians, and that he could only suppose that Disraeli was motivated by that hatred. The Duke cordially agreed. He assured Gladstone that Disraeli's 'Judaic feeling' was the only genuine motive left in his mind since Lady Beaconsfield's death, and that he would be willing to sacrifice everything to it. He made Gladstone read Disraeli's favourite novel, *Tancred* (1847), in which much of the action is laid in Palestine. The theme is the corruption of Western material civilization, and the author pleads for the establishment of a new Eastern Empire, under British suzerainty, which should be guided and inspired by the mystical genius of the Hebrew race.

Gladstone always denied that he had actually loathed Disraeli, but those who knew him best were agreed that at that time his sentiment towards his rival became that of black hatred. He read in *Tancred* how the hero was advised by an Eastern potentate to 'magnetize' the British Queen. Tancred was told that all he need do was to use his 'beautiful voice', to whisper 'fine things' into her ear. Gladstone was alarmed by the constitutional dangers which might arise as a result of the ascendancy which Disraeli had acquired over the Queen. He would have been still more alarmed if he had known the full extent to which the Queen's views had become unbalanced; before long she was urging the Cabinet to go to war, and threatening to abdicate if it ignored her outbursts.

Gladstone made no attempt to conceal his view that whatever had been objectionable in Lord Palmerston's policy had received a 'tenfold development' in Disraeli. Immediately after Disraeli's death in April, 1881, Lord Acton, in a letter to Edward Burne-Jones (7 May, 1881), put Gladstone's opinion of his rival into words which 'cannot be employed in public'. He imagined Gladstone saying that he thought Disraeli's doctrine 'false, but the man more false than his doctrine . . . that he demoralized public opinion, bargained with diseased appetites, stimulated passions, prejudices and selfish desires, that they might maintain his influence; that he weakened the Crown by approving its unconstitutional leanings, and the Constitution by offering any price for democratic popularity . . .' That was a moderate representation of Gladstone's opinion of Disraeli while the Eastern crisis lasted, and Disraeli reciprocated Gladstone's hatred. He gleefully told Lady Bradford (December, 1876) that the Queen really loathed Gladstone, and that she thought him mad. He told Lord Derby (October):

'Posterity will do justice to that unprincipled maniac, Gladstone
—extraordinary mixture of envy, vindictiveness, hypocrisy, and superstition ; and with one commanding characteristic—whether preaching,
praying, speechifying, or scribbling—never a gentleman ! '

It was fortunate that the Conservatives and the Liberals were both
divided among themselves at that time. Lord Salisbury, Lord Derby,
and Lord Carnarvon all sympathized more than Disraeli did with
the aspirations of the Christian peoples in the Balkans, and they
managed to exert a restraining influence over their chief's pro-
Turkish policy. On the Liberal side, Lord Granville and Lord
Hartington both considered that Gladstone was being much too
unguarded in his encouragement of Russia, and that he did not take
sufficiently into account the difficulties in the way of bringing about
self-government throughout the Balkans. Lord Hartington told Lord
Granville (18 December, 1876) that if Gladstone went much further,
'nothing can prevent a break-up of the Party'.

Gladstone cared little about such risks, but his family was troubled.
Lady Frederick Cavendish noted in her Journal (8 October, 1876) that
'Uncle William' was too headstrong. He had rebuked Lord Frederick
Cavendish for meeting Turkish diplomatic representatives at dinner,
and had described them as untouchable 'symbols of iniquity'.
Gladstone complained constantly that the upper classes had betrayed
their responsibility : 'When did the Upper Ten Thousand ever lead
the attack in the cause of humanity ? Their heads are always full of
class interest and the main chance.'

' Of one thing ', Lady Frederick recorded, ' I am as certain as I have
been all my life—that there is no personal ambition, or any motive
but love of justice and mercy (and utter disbelief in Dizzy, I allow)
in his present course.'

In fashionable circles, Gladstone was now so intensely unpopular
that lying stories about his rescue work in the London streets by night
were freely circulated, and his family treated with contempt a spate of
anonymous letters. After the breakdown of a conference at Constantinople (8 December, 1876, to 20 January, 1877), the unparalleled
vehemence with which Gladstone, taking to the platform, began
slowly but inexorably to arouse the indignation of the British masses
against Disraeli, excited animosities which were very slow to die
down. The political atmosphere remained uncomfortably heated
for years, with the result that, until Gladstone's final retirement,
no important issue could be debated in a dispassionate mood. The

tone of moral outrage which Gladstone used with complete sincerity in talking about Turkey between 1876 and 1880 was borrowed by his opponents and often used artificially during the succeeding decade when Ireland had replaced Turkey as the principal object of Party contention.

On 24 April, 1877, after long forbearance, Russia declared war on Turkey and started an all-out drive on Constantinople. Gladstone, who had noted in his diary (15 April) that he felt it ' a holy duty ' to write an article in praise of Montenegro for the *Nineteenth Century*, considered that Russia had good reason for her professed resolve to discharge single-handed a duty which the European Concert had shirked. The Cabinet as a whole exercised a restraining influence over the pro-Turkish ardour of the Prime Minister and the Queen ; and the Government adopted a policy of conditional neutrality for so long as no threat developed to a specified list of vital British interests.

Lord Granville and Lord Hartington set themselves the task of restraining Gladstone's pro-Russian ardour. The views of some of the Liberal rank and file were expressed in a letter from Sir William Harcourt to Sir Charles Dilke (10 October, 1876) : ' Gladstone and Dizzy seem to cap one another in folly and imprudence, and I don't know which has made the greatest ass of himself.'

The outbreak of the Russo-Turkish War divided public opinion on an issue of foreign policy more acutely than at any period since the French Revolution, and excitement was intense when Gladstone, against the wish of all his principal colleagues, gave notice that he would move five Resolutions in the Commons on 7 May, defining his policy in the Russo-Turkish War.

The first Resolution censured Turkey for failure to fulfil her treaty obligations ; the second declared that the Turks had lost all claim to British moral or material support ; the third recommended self-government in the Balkans ; the fourth recommended that pressure should be brought to bear on Turkey by the Great Powers ; the fifth recommended the first four Resolutions to Her Majesty's Government. As soon as Gladstone's intention was known, Disraeli's Cabinet, which had been in a ferment, rallied round its chief, while Lord Granville and Lord Hartington complained that Gladstone, after formally renouncing the leadership, was threatening to split the Liberal Party and to make their position impossible. Lady Frederick Cavendish, who loved her uncle very dearly, noted in her Journal (11–17 February,

246

1878) that her husband had been made ill with worry on account of the tension between his brother—Lord Hartington—and Gladstone :

'They are 2 men so utterly unlike in disposition and mode of viewing things, and Uncle W. having been driven by the very nature of this great question to take a leading part (he has felt a special responsibility as the only surviving compos [1] statesman who conducted the Crimean War and was a party to the Treaty of Paris) has necessarily been prominent, though no longer leader . . . I am come round to the conviction that he should either have continued to lead the Party, or withdrawn from Parliament altogether, or taken a Peerage. It is immensely to the credit of both him and Cavendish [2] that they have pulled together at all, and is due to the perfect honesty and sense of duty of both.'

Lord Hartington made it clear to the House on 7 May, 1877, that he was not willing to support Gladstone's third and fourth Resolutions, and that he considered them inopportune. Gladstone, in speaking to the first two only, admitted frankly that the disclosure of such differences of opinion ' must have had a dissipating effect on the mind of the House '. He argued that ' we have improperly allowed the vindication of the great cause in the East to pass into the hands of a single Power ' ; and he pleaded that coercion should be applied to Turkey by a united Europe after the manner in which it had been applied in the 1820s, when Greece was struggling to be free :

' But that was a policy that had no more the approval of what I may call the West End of London than the Christian cause has now. That portion of England does not express the true sentiments of England. Looking over all the great achievements that have made the last half century illustrious, not one of them would have been effected if the opinions of the West End of London had prevailed.'

Gladstone rejoiced to proclaim ' the knell of Turkish tyranny ' :

' So far as human eye can judge it is about to be destroyed. The destruction may not come in the way or by the means that we should choose ; but come this boon from what hands it may, it will be a noble boon, and as a noble boon will gladly be accepted by Christendom and the world.'

A future Prime Minister, Arthur James Balfour, who was then aged twenty-nine and intimate with Gladstone's family, listened to

[1] *Compos mentis,* or in possession of his faculties. Lady Frederick forgot Lord Granville and the Duke of Argyll.
[2] Lord Hartington.

that speech from a Government back bench. The House, when Gladstone began, was hostile and impatient, and at first members streamed out of the House. Then, as reports reached them that a major eruption was in progress, they poured back until the Chamber was crowded. Balfour said that he could never erase from his memory the impression which Gladstone's speech had made on his mind. As a feat of Parliamentary eloquence, endurance, and skill, he believed that it had never been equalled. In his diary Gladstone was content to record: 'Such a sense of solitary struggle I never remember ... I rose on the main question nearly in despair ... I spoke 2½ hours, voice lasting well. House gradually came round ... Never did I feel weaker or more wormlike.'

Replying to the debate on 14 May, Gladstone spoke with moderation. He described the Russian Emperor as 'a Christian gentleman', and the Russians as a people 'as capable of noble sentiments as any people in Europe'. He said that if Russia succeeded, 'as an Englishman I shall hide my head, but as a man I shall rejoice'. Gladstone's Resolutions, which in fact constituted a plea for the coercion of Turkey, were lost by 253 to 354 votes. But for the loyalty of Lord Hartington it is likely that the figures would have been much more adverse, for contemporary estimates suggest that there were no more than sixty or seventy avowed coercionists in a House of 658.

Loyal as Lord Hartington was, he felt extremely uncomfortable. He wrote to Lord Granville (25 May, 1877):

'Mr. G. says that he has never been able to comprehend the cause of the late split, and under those circumstances it seems to me very likely that it will occur again. . . . While we remain responsible for the management of the Party in Parliament, Mr. G. cannot expect that we should entirely subordinate our own opinions and judgement to his, and unless we do, it seems inevitable that one section of the Party will follow his lead, and the other ours. . . . I think that we have some right to ask Mr. G. to look at the facts, as they exist. . . . He does not cease to be the leader of the Party by merely saying that he will not be the leader. If, as he has done since the autumn, he takes the lead, he *is* the leader, and all that he can do is to disclaim (for I do not think that he can really divest himself of it) the responsibility which naturally attends upon leadership.'

Lord Granville laid that letter before Gladstone without eliciting any response, but his tact helped to ease a delicate situation. He would have been consoled a little if he had known the extent to which

Disraeli's Cabinet was torn by dissensions as the Russian armies advanced. In a letter to the Queen, dated 3 November, 1877, Disraeli outlined seven distinct shades of opinion in his Cabinet, from those who wanted immediate war with Russia to one member (Lord Derby) who stood for peace at any price.

The Turks put up a brave but hopeless resistance, and early in January, 1878, the Russians, after liberating the Balkans, surged almost up to the walls of Constantinople. In that month the excitement in Great Britain was quite as intense as at the time of Napoleon's escape from Elba. A storm of anti-Russian feeling swept England south of the Trent. It was impossible in London, and difficult elsewhere, for meetings to be held in favour of peace ; and Gladstone, who had his windows in Harley Street smashed by a mob, was a constant object of hostile demonstrations and a liability to the police who were responsible for his safety. He was hustled on one occasion with Mrs. Gladstone, in the streets, and even hooted (12 April, 1878) by fellow-members in the lobby of the House of Commons. He noted in his diary (11 March) :

' Went to the Levée. The Princess [of Wales] for the first time received me drily. The Duke of Cambridge, black as thunder, did not even hold out his hand. Prince Christian could not but follow suit. This is not hard to bear.'

Gladstone was anathematized by society, and deeply hurt on 11 January, 1878, when he was publicly described by the Duke of Sutherland, the son of his old confidante, Harriet, Duchess of Sutherland, as a Russian agent. Throughout the industrial North, however, and in Scotland, the masses had begun to hang upon every word he uttered, and to reverence him almost as a god.

On 24 January, 1878, the British Mediterranean fleet was ordered to sail through the Dardanelles to the Turkish capital. The orders were temporarily cancelled at the request of the Turks who were anxious that the Russians should be given no excuse for breaking off negotiations for an armistice ; but Gladstone was stung to fury by the provocation which Disraeli offered. Speaking at Oxford on 30 January he denounced the orders to the fleet as ' an act of war, a breach of international law'. He admitted that he had become an agitator, and said that he had been driven to it by Disraeli :

' When you speak of the Government you mean Lord Beaconsfield. . . . Not one man in the Government has a tenth part of his tenacity of will and patient purpose . . . My purpose has been . . .

to the best of my power for the last eighteen months, day and night, week by week, month by month, to counterwork as well as I could what I believe to be the purpose of Lord Beaconsfield.'

Two days later, writing to Lady Bradford, Disraeli commented:

' The mask has fallen, and instead of a pious Christian, we find a vindictive fiend who confesses he has for a year and a half been dodging and manœuvring against an individual—because he was his successful rival.'

On 1 February, 1878, an armistice was signed, and on 13 February orders were finally issued that the British Mediterranean fleet should sail through the Dardanelles into the Sea of Marmora. There was no opposition, but on 3 March, by the Treaty of San Stefano, which ended the Russo-Turkish War, Russia obtained far-reaching concessions from Turkey, including an outlet into the Mediterranean. Provision was made for the creation of a vast autonomous Bulgaria, which was to include Macedonia and to be under Russian tutelage. That and other provisions of the Treaty appeared unacceptable to the British Cabinet, and when the terms were made known on 22 March there was a panic on the Stock Exchange, and a shrill and prolonged public outcry.

Disraeli, who had identified his country's interests with the maintenance of Turkish integrity, was greatly concerned about prestige. Gladstone repeatedly denounced prestige as a miserable delusion, but to it, in that crisis, Disraeli appeared willing to sacrifice much. If, however, he could avoid ' losing face ' he was as happy to retreat from his original position and to countenance a partition of Turkey, as he would have been to comply with the Queen's hysterical desire for a useless war with Russia if he could have induced his Cabinet to agree. Disraeli wished to make Great Britain the arbiter of Europe, and on 28 March Lord Derby resigned from the Foreign Office in protest against a decision to call out the reserves, and to move Indian troops through the Suez Canal to Malta. Lord Salisbury, who succeeded Lord Derby, pressed at once for a Conference in order to resolve the deadlock between Great Britain and Russia. A deepening trade depression in Great Britain, and Russian internal unrest, provided a stimulus to agreement, and after preliminary Anglo-Russian conversations in May, a Conference opened at Berlin on 13 June, 1878, under the chairmanship of Bismarck who saw no prospect of any advantage to Germany from a European war at that moment.

Disraeli and Lord Salisbury represented Great Britain at Berlin, and

'DOCTORS DIFFER!'

William G. 'I warn you, Mr. Bull, your constitution is being seriously impaired by that—a—person's treatment.'

Benjamin D. 'My dear Mr. Bull, your constitution is perfectly safe in my hands.'

PUNCH, June 1, 1878

by 13 July a practical compromise was ready for signature. The swollen Bulgaria of San Stefano was split into three parts, of which one—Macedonia—was returned to Turkey without any guarantee of better government. In the main, however, the settlement was based on the abandonment of the principle of Turkish territorial integrity. Many wide provinces were amputated in order to satisfy the claims of Turkey's neighbours. By a separate Anglo-Turkish convention Great Britain received the island of Cyprus, and a pledge of good government was extorted from the Turks in return for a guarantee of the future territorial integrity of Turkey in Asia.

Crippled with gout, but beaming, and leaning on Salisbury's arm, Disraeli returned to London on 16 July saying that he brought ' Peace with Honour '. He received an unprecedented acclaim. The Queen wanted to make him a Duke, but he would only accept the Garter. In the Gladstone family the wish was expressed that he might be made Duke of Jericho and despatched to administer his duchy ; and Gladstone's first public reaction to his rival's apotheosis was silly, petulant, and ill-considered. Speaking at Southwark on 21 July, three days after Disraeli had defended the Berlin settlement in the House of Lords, Gladstone denounced it far too strongly. The country was overjoyed that the threat of imminent war had been removed, and the Treaty had much to recommend it. Gladstone's strongest abuse was reserved for the Cyprus convention, which he described as ' insane . . . an act of duplicity not surpassed and rarely equalled in the history of nations '.

On 27 July, Disraeli delivered a crushing retort at a fashionable banquet at which he and Lord Salisbury were entertained in the Riding School at Knightsbridge. After making the sound point that the Crimean War could have been avoided by vigorous action before its outbreak, he said that Gladstone's talk about insanity could only have proceeded from ' a sophisticated rhetorician inebriated with the exuberance of his own verbosity, and gifted with an egotistical imagination that can at all times command an interminable and inconsistent series of arguments to malign an opponent and to glorify himself '.

The Times scolded Disraeli mildly the next day for his ' curious little burst of irritation ' ; Gladstone made light of it to friends, saying that he could never ' condescend ' to notice Disraeli ' in a personal way ' because there was no ' foundation of good faith ' or ' anything serious or sincere in any of his utterances, however vehement '.

Disraeli was, however, determined on that occasion to score a personal point against Gladstone, if he could. On 29 July he complained to the House of Lords that he had been described by Gladstone as 'a dangerous and even a devilish character', and that Gladstone was constantly employing offensive personal expressions about his conduct and character.

Gladstone felt it necessary to write to Disraeli on 30 July to ask for details. He began his letter 'Dear Lord Beaconsfield', and begged that he might be supplied with a detailed list of the times and places at which he had used the offensive and personal expressions to which Disraeli had taken exception. Disraeli was now treading on air. He had angled for that opportunity to snub Gladstone, and he replied coldly, in the third person, on the same day, that the necessary researches would take time, and that he was busy.

The matter was carried no further. As Lord Granville told the Queen (24 April, 1880) :

'Lord Beaconsfield and Mr. Gladstone are men of extraordinary ability ; they dislike each other more than is common among public men. Of no other politician would Lord Beaconsfield have said in public that his conduct was worse than the Bulgarian atrocities. He has a power of saying in two words that which drives a person of Mr. Gladstone's peculiar temperament into a great state of excitement.'

Gladstone had learned slowly and very painfully the need for tolerance and compromise, but he was too simple, passionate, and high-minded to accept the world as it is. He never fully appreciated the limitations which are imposed by human nature upon all work that is performed by human hands, and the process of achieving a modest degree of good by reconciling a host of selfish interests was always hateful to him. Edmund Burke, in a famous passage,[1] had deified 'prudence and conformity to circumstances' as 'the god of this lower world'. Gladstone was always himself capable of both prudence and conformity, but in his opponents, and especially in Disraeli whose personality grated on him at almost every point, he was inclined to confound those qualities with depravity, and to treat them as tokens of the Beast in *Revelation*.

Disraeli's bluff had magnificently succeeded, but Lord Salisbury admitted some twenty years later that 'the wrong horse' had been backed at Berlin. The country had been led to the brink of war, and if Disraeli's gamble had failed, his fame, which is unassailable in

[1] Letter to the Sheriffs of Bristol, 1777.

some other fields, would have been sadly tarnished. After throwing many provinces of Turkey to the wolves as well as to the lambs, Disraeli lacked the will, and the means, to carry to its logical conclusion the policy that he had been constrained to accept in place of his own. Cyprus had been acquired ostensibly as a base from which Great Britain would be in a position to implement what was virtually a single-handed guarantee of Turkish territorial integrity in Asia against further Russian aggression, in return for a promise of better government. That promise and guarantee proved unenforceable in face of Turkish resentment at her desertion by Great Britain. Russia's ambitions received a severe check, but she retained some of her conquests in Asia and in Europe. Only a British protectorate over Asia Minor, which was impossible ; large-scale money grants, which were not forthcoming ; or a truly popular Turkish revolution, for which the time was not then ripe, might have availed at that period to effect the regeneration of Turkey.

So great was the relief that war had been averted, that Disraeli's slogan, ' Peace with Honour ', delighted the British people. Together with the charming acquisition of Cyprus, it helped to conceal the fact that the Turkish problem in Europe had been solved to a great extent in the only possible way, by the adoption of the principle of self-government for oppressed national minorities. That was the principle which Gladstone had advocated throughout the crisis, and it was the opposite of the policy of maintaining intact the territorial integrity of Turkey which Disraeli had upheld until the last possible moment. Gladstone's hatred and distrust of Disraeli, and his delicate moral scruples about Cyprus, the acquisition of which was in many respects a brilliant coup, led him to do much less than justice to the merits of the Treaty of Berlin. It realized, at least in part, many of Gladstone's objects, and its substance was more important than the means by which it had been obtained. Gladstone had seen fit on a number of occasions to apologize publicly for his wish to make use of Russia in order to achieve his aims ; his dismay at seeing those aims so unexpectedly realized by Disraeli, and the fierce language which he used, made him seem factious and inconsistent. Even the dubious arrangements about Turkey in Asia represented a fairly honest attempt in very difficult circumstances to secure reforms for which Gladstone had strongly pressed in European Turkey.

Despite the obloquy which he incurred in fashionable quarters, it is an astonishing tribute to the moral sway which Gladstone exerted over the masses whose material needs he never understood, that within eighteen months of Disraeli's apotheosis at Berlin, Gladstone should have succeeded in injecting into the minds of a majority of the British electors a potent dose of his intense, scorching conviction about the ' infection ' of Disraeli's personality, and the flagrant immorality of the policies which Disraeli had pursued.   Thereafter, he never ceased to proclaim his faith in the political efficacy of what he called ' righteous indignation ', and the Queen, who thought him crazy, never forgave him.   He stumped the country invoking the wrath of Heaven like some ancient Hebrew prophet ; and at the General Election of 1880, when he enjoyed his finest hour, he was wafted back to Downing Street—against his innermost desire, as he was sometimes almost half inclined to believe—by the spirit of a nation which had never before been summoned from its depths by a call so heartfelt and so clear.

CHAPTER 11

HIS FINEST HOUR
1878–1881

IN his diary on 28 December, 1878, Gladstone noted that he had been passing through an unexampled political crisis :

'I profess to believe it has been an occasion when the battle to be fought was a battle of justice, humanity, freedom, law, all in their first elements from the very root, and all on a gigantic scale. The word spoken was a word for millions, and for millions who for themselves cannot speak. If I really believe this, then I should regard my having been morally forced into this work as a great and high election of God.'

The vastness of the scale on which the battle was being fought made it easier for Gladstone to believe that he had been called by God to play his part in it ; but he added that he craved three boons of God, 'over and above all the bounty which surrounds me'. The first was 'escape into retirement' ; the second, 'that I may speedily be enabled to divest myself of everything resembling wealth' ; the third, that 'when God calls me, He may call me speedily. To die in Church appears to be a great euthanasia, but not at a time to disturb worshippers.'

On 29 December—his 69th birthday—Gladstone noted : 'Why has my health and strength been so peculiarly sustained. All this year, and more, I think, I have not been confined to bed for a single day. In the great physical and mental effort of speaking, often to large audiences, I have been, as it were, upheld in an unusual manner ; and the free and effective use of my voice has been given to me to my own astonishment. Was not all this for a purpose ? And has it not all come in connexion with a process to which I have given myself ?' He added that this 'appears to me to carry all the marks of the will of God'. It is a great strength to any man, once he has embarked upon a course of action, to believe that he is executing God's will. It is, however, difficult in such circumstances to do justice to the motives of opponents.

Disraeli was irritated by Gladstone's insistence that all important political questions involved clear-cut moral issues. He considered that, in an imperfect world, the choice must lie between policies of varying degrees of expediency. Gladstone considered that men who thought like that were corrupted by the insolence of wealth and privilege ; and it was for that reason that he wished to divest himself of both. For the remainder of his life he directed his stormy and emotional appeal over the heads of 'the upper ten thousand' to the moral and religious instincts of the masses. He always insisted, however, that he was no leveller. John Ruskin, when staying at Hawarden in December, 1878, accused his host of being numbered among those who think 'one man as good as another' :

'Oh dear, no !' Gladstone replied. 'I am nothing of the sort. I am a firm believer in the aristocratic principle—the rule of the best. I am an out-and-out *inegalitarian*.'

Ruskin clapped his hands with delight when he heard that confession.

Gladstone was convinced that the rule of the best could be secured through the free play of unrestricted competition between individuals, interests, and ideas. That theory suited an age in which the sky alone seemed to set a limit to the continuous expansion of markets, increase of wealth, and surcease of obsolete restraints. During the late 1870s, however, industrial competition from the newly-unified German Empire, and agricultural competition from the American Middle West, helped to bring about a great, widespread, and prolonged depression, with its accompaniment of strikes, unemployment, and agitation for better conditions. Public opinion, in consequence, began to grow increasingly critical of the *laisser-faire* policy which had served the country so well. During the 1870s the centre of gravity of international power shifted from Western to Central Europe ; compulsory military service was adopted by all the Great European Powers except Great Britain ; and year by year a larger proportion of the wealth of nations was spent upon armaments. The British felt a desire on the one hand to see their national and imperial interests more strongly defended and more vigorously asserted than Gladstone thought proper, and on the other to examine the methods by which Bismarck was seeking to strangle socialism in its cradle by exerting a growing measure of State interference in German industry, commerce, and social questions. An age was dawning in which the use and distribution of wealth would be felt to be of equal importance with its production, and in which wealth itself and competition would ultimately be less highly esteemed than welfare and security.

Gladstone was alive to the challenge of socialism, which he met by appealing to the first principles of his own liberal creed. He was deeply interested all his life in the problem of the right use of wealth, and he expressed his outlook with remarkable clarity in an article which he contributed to the *Nineteenth Century* in November, 1890, about the millionaire American ironmaster, Andrew Carnegie. Gladstone accepted Carnegie's opinion that unless men had the opportunity to make colossal fortunes, industry would not be able to flourish, and he warmly commended the American's argument that wealthy men should themselves take action to narrow the widening gulf between classes, through charity during their lifetimes. He rejected, however, Carnegie's conclusion that inheritance was bad, and that heavy death-duties were the wisest of all forms of taxation. Gladstone considered that inherited wealth was on the whole ' a good and not an evil thing ', and he thought that sons should succeed to their fathers' responsibilities not only as landowners, but in banking, industry, commerce, and other fields.

Gladstone pleaded that rich men should all follow Carnegie's example in distributing a substantial portion of their wealth during their lifetimes. He argued that during his own lifetime the vast majority of rich men had failed to give away any ' adequate or becoming portion of their incomes ', and he expressed very strongly an opinion, which he had always held, that charitable bequests made by will were a demoralizing fraud, involving ' the danger of serious moral evils . . . What is wrested from me by the gripe of Death I can in no true sense be said to give . . . It is dangerous enough when we are taught to plume ourselves upon virtues that are real . . . But to have sham virtues set up in our own personal image is the worst kind of image-worship that I know.'

Gladstone ended by appealing to rich men to ' subscribe an engagement having no legal force ; and no moral sanction . . . except the action of the private conscience ' to give away during their lifetimes a minimum fixed proportion of their incomes from all sources. He said that at his age (eighty-one at that time) ' the work of correspondence necessary to organize the plan, and set it going, would be altogether beyond my power to undertake. At the same time, I am ready to be the careful recipient of any assents to the general proposition which there may be a disposition to tender ; and (without any other pledge) I should hold myself bound to make such endeavours towards a practical beginning as would at least prevent good intentions thus conveyed from falling to the ground.'

Gladstone was expressing optimistically and ingenuously the simple faith which underlay his liberal creed. Without faith in the existence of human goodwill and a strong sense of individual responsibility, there can be no secure foundation for the belief in freedom of trade, worship, thought, and speech ; in equality for men and nations before an impartial and clearly-definable law ; and in the right of every morally qualified man to a voice in government. Gladstone worshipped the principle of liberty, and he saw no reason why individual action and initiative should not suffice to add freedom from want and freedom from fear to those other freedoms which the masses had already learnt to enjoy. Throughout his life Gladstone invariably gave away a substantial annual portion of his own income, and he calculated that if everyone were to do the same, ' the surplus property of the few will be a treasure administered for the common good '. By that means Gladstone hoped that the rich and the poor could be reconciled ; but the world wars which occurred during the twentieth century upset his reckoning, and helped to show that in some directions he had overestimated human nature, and underestimated the material cost.

Under suitable conditions no limits can be set to the heights to which human nature will rise. Gladstone's efforts, accordingly, were concentrated on the means of implementing the liberal experiment. It was with that object that he undertook at the end of November, 1879, his famous Midlothian campaign, nearly twenty-one years after he had formally become a member of the Liberal Party. That astonishing and never-to-be-forgotten fortnight, during which Gladstone erupted with greater effect than at any other period of his life, may be regarded in one of its aspects as a popular celebration of the coming-of-age of the liberal experiment.

Gladstone's choice of Midlothian was significant. He needed a conspicuous eminence on which he could light a beacon for the entire country in preparation for the General Election whenever it should occur ; and he had made up his mind that he would never again contest his ungrateful constituency at Greenwich. During the remainder of Gladstone's life the Liberal Party was driven increasingly to seek its principal support on the periphery of the British Isles ; and after his death it maintained its hold upon the Celtic fringe for some time after its hold upon the country as a whole was lost.

The sitting Conservative member for Midlothian, Lord Dalkeith, son and heir of the Duke of Buccleuch, was dismayed when he heard who his opponent was to be. Gladstone was adopted in January, 1879, and his principal sponsor was Lord Rosebery, proud, handsome, brilliant, and perverse, who was aged thirty-two. As a result of the campaign which followed Lord Rosebery's hold over the Scottish Lowlands, and Scottish national sentiment, began to match that which the Duke of Argyll had long before acquired over the Scottish Highlands and the Scottish academic world as a result of his impressive character and eloquence.

Before going up to Midlothian, Gladstone took a holiday in Germany. He went with Mrs. Gladstone and their children, Herbert and Mary, to stay with Lord and Lady Acton at Tegernsee, the beautiful home of Lady Acton's sister, Baroness Arco. The Gladstones stopped on the way at Cologne (15 September), where they dined with Gladstone's sister at 5 o'clock. Mary Gladstone noted that the evening seemed endless. Miss Gladstone was 'beyond words contrary at first, and I shall never forget our reception, nor will Herbert'.

On Friday, 19 September, after rowing across the lake, Mary Gladstone walked back with Lord Acton, leaving Gladstone and Dr. Döllinger, who was a fellow-guest, to follow at a leisurely pace behind. Lord Acton, who was twenty-five years younger than Gladstone, and a stepson of Lord Granville, embarked on a panegyric on Mary's father, which he later elaborated in the form of a letter. He said that Gladstone united the highest qualities of Chatham, Fox, Pitt, Canning, and Peel, without their drawbacks. In wealth, depth, and force of mind, Burke was his only possible rival. He regretted that Gladstone had wasted so much time writing books and articles which did not, as in Burke's case, equal his speaking, still less, as in Macaulay's, surpass it. He regretted also that Gladstone's judgement of men was fallible. That, Lord Acton thought, would explain to posterity Gladstone's 'lofty unfitness to deal with sordid motives . . . his inability to sway certain kinds of men, and that strange property of his influence which is greatest with multitudes, less in society, least at home'. He thought it would also explain why Gladstone formed no school and left no disciples, and why his colleagues followed him unwillingly, as they had once followed Palmerston, because he had the power to move the masses. Lord Acton regarded two of Gladstone's mental gifts as outstanding.

The first was 'the vigour and perpetual progress of his mind' which was as open and lively as a boy's ; the second was the perfect marriage within that mind of theory and policy. Lord Acton was always frustrated by his inability to prevent the Roman Catholic Church, in the necessity for which he believed, from denying certain principles of liberty which he could never bring himself to abandon. Gladstone had the power to relieve that sense of frustration. To Lord Acton, liberty was justified ultimately by the manner in which it was used, and the process whereby Gladstone developed the conscience of the community by appealing to it, appeared to provide that justification. Lord Acton, therefore, saw Gladstone as the incarnation of a rational Providence which was shaping the pattern of history towards the goal of the triumph of liberty, and his feeling for Gladstone fell not far short of idolatry. Lord Acton was inclined to exaggerate the permanent appeal of Gladstone's oratory after the voice and gestures were stilled and only the written record remained. And he underestimated the significance of Gladstone's neglect of social problems. It is greatly to be regretted that he never employed his vast learning to compose an exposition of the intellectual premises of liberalism, which is one of the twentieth century's most conspicuous wants.

After staying in Cortina, Venice, and Paris, the Gladstones returned home on 22 October. A month later, on 24 November, 1879, Gladstone went up to Dalmeny to stay with Lord Rosebery at the start of a fortnight's tour of the county of Midlothian in preparation for the General Election. At numerous stations between Liverpool and Edinburgh, crowds of working men gathered to cheer Gladstone as he passed. He made his first speech at Carlisle station, and he spoke again at Hawick and Galashiels. Night had fallen after a beautiful, sunny day, when the train pulled into Edinburgh where Lord Rosebery was waiting with a four-in-hand and many outriders to drive the great impresario to Dalmeny. Bonfires blazed on the hills and fireworks cascaded in the sky : ' I have never ', Gladstone noted, ' gone through a more extraordinary day.'

On the next day, Tuesday, 25 November, Gladstone drove into Edinburgh to deliver at the Music Hall in George Street his first Midlothian Address. He began by describing his opponent, Lord Dalkeith, as a model nobleman, who ' sets to us all an example in the active and conscientious discharge of duty, such as he believes duty to be '. He added that he had sat in Sir Robert Peel's Cabinet with Dalkeith's father. He next denounced the Government for financial profligacy in pursuit of ' false phantoms of glory ' ; it had annexed the Transvaal ; it had annexed Cyprus ; it had established, in conjunction with France, a virtual protectorate over Egypt ; it had made war upon the Zulus ; it had assumed impossible single-handed commitments in the whole of Turkey in Asia, ' including the principal part of Arabia'; it had by 'the most wanton invasion of Afghanistan broken that country into pieces'. Gladstone appealed from the Government and from Parliament to the conscience of 'a great and free and powerful people'. He concluded:

'Let every one of us resolve in his inner conscience, before God and before man, let him resolve . . . that he will do his best to exempt himself; ay, that he will exempt himself from every participation in what he believes to be mischievous and ruinous misdeeds . . .'

On 26 November Gladstone spoke amid what was described as 'a perfect storm of applause' at the Corn Exchange, Dalkeith. He ended his speech by proposing that a measure of home rule should be conferred upon 'the different portions of the United Kingdom' in order to relieve Parliament of an overwhelming weight of business. Nothing should be done to 'compromise the authority of the Imperial Parliament . . . But subject to that limitation, if we can make arrangements under which Ireland, Scotland, Wales, portions of England, can deal with questions of local and special interest to themselves . . that, I say, will be the attainment of a great national good.'

From the Corn Exchange, Gladstone moved on to the Foresters' Hall, where a presentation was made to Mrs. Gladstone. In acknowledging it, Gladstone said that he loathed war with his whole heart, and he begged his wildly cheering audience never to 'suffer appeals to national pride to blind you to the dictates of justice'. He reminded it that:

'The errors of former times are recorded for our instruction, in order that we may avoid their repetition . . . Remember the rights of the savage, as we call him. Remember that the happiness of his humble home, remember that the sanctity of life in the hill villages of Afghanistan, among the winter snows, is as inviolable in the eye of Almighty God as can be your own.'

Multitudes of torchbearers were drawn up in serried rows to illuminate the streets as Gladstone quitted the town.

On 27 November, when Gladstone visited West Calder, triumphal arches had been erected all the way along the route from Dalmeny, and the popular excitement was intense. The town itself was decorated with arches and the streets were illuminated with multitudes of fairy lanterns at night. Gladstone spoke about the agricultural depression, warning his hearers against the seduction of quack remedies, such as protection. In foreign affairs he claimed that Disraeli had violated every canon of morality, that he had inflicted great injuries upon his country, and that he had endangered world peace 'and all the most fundamental interests of Christian society'.

Every word that Gladstone spoke was reported all over the country by newspapers which had not then learnt to devote the main part of their space to sport and other non-political subjects. People flocked to Midlothian from all parts of Scotland, including the storm-vexed Hebrides, to hear the magic voice, to watch the eagle eye, to enjoy the superb gestures, and to share in what Disraeli called a 'pilgrimage of passion' and Gladstone a 'festival of freedom'. On 29 November Gladstone spoke to 4,700 people in the Corn Exchange at Edinburgh about finance. The first rule of finance, he declared :

'is that the Chancellor of the Exchequer shall boldly uphold economy in detail ; and it is the mark, gentlemen, of . . . a chicken-hearted Chancellor of the Exchequer when he shrinks from upholding economy in detail . . . No Chancellor of the Exchequer is worth his salt who is not ready to save what are meant by candle-ends and cheese-parings in the cause of his country . . . He is under a sacred obligation with regard to all that he consents to spend.'

He could not, he said, emphasize too strongly that 'resistance in detail to jobbery and minute waste and extravagance is the first of all sound financial rules.' Yet one of Disraeli's first acts on taking office was to create a £2,000 a year post for Lord Hampton as a Civil Service Commissioner 'to do what had been admirably done without that office before, and has not been, and nobody pretends that it has been, one bit better done since.'

As soon as that speech was finished Gladstone went with Lord Rosebery to the Waverley Market to address an audience of over 20,000 working men and women. It was said that the enthusiasm reached a height which had never been equalled in Scotland : 'It is no light cause,' Gladstone began, 'that has brought together . . . this great ocean of human life.' He told his audience that he regarded it as 'a festival of freedom', and as he reviewed conditions in Austria, Turkey, Russia, and the Balkans, he enchanted his hearers by making them feel that they truly were the final court of Christian morals. From Midlothian, Gladstone travelled via Dunfermline and Perth, where he made two minor speeches, to Taymouth Castle, to stay with Lord Breadalbane. Everywhere he was received with addresses of welcome and votes of confidence. On 1 December, his daughter wrote : 'It has been the same story over and over again . . . And here it is so much more stirring than in England, because the faces are so intelligent . . . All Scotland is panting for a look at him.' On 5 December, Gladstone enjoyed what he himself called 'an over-powering day'. He addressed the students of Glasgow University as Lord Rector in the morning, and in the late afternoon he made a political speech to 6,000 people in St. Andrew's Hall, Glasgow.

Gladstone commended to his University audience 'the intellectual dignity of the Christian Ministry'. He urged them to fight the rising tide of materialism and unbelief, and reminded them that morals and civilization, if divorced from faith in God and a future life, must perish. He poured scorn on an aphorism of Disraeli, who had delivered the previous Rectorial Address, that 'Nothing succeeds like success' :

'Effort, gentlemen ; honest, manful, humble effort succeeds, by its reflected action upon character, especially in youth, better than success . . . Work onwards and work upwards ; and may the blessing of the Most High soothe your cares, clear your vision, and crown your labours with reward.'

That afternoon, in St. Andrew's Hall, from which thousands of people had to be turned away because all places were filled, Gladstone began by again denouncing Disraeli for creating an unnecessary Civil Service Commissionership to accommodate his friend, Lord Hampton. He spoke a great deal about Cyprus, which he described as a ' valueless encumbrance'. The Anglo-Turkish Convention by which that island was annexed was 'a gross and open breach, or rather a gross and manifest breach, of the public law of Europe'.

Gladstone went on to describe the Queen's assumption of the title of Empress of India as theatrical bombast and folly, and the war with Afghanistan as a crime against God. Moneys voted for the relief of famine in India had been used to drive Afghan ' mothers and children forth from their homes to perish in the snow'. Disraeli's policy was ' pestilent' in every corner of the globe. What was the crime of the Zulus ? Ten thousand had been slaughtered ' for no other offence than their attempt to defend against your artillery with their naked bodies, their hearths and homes, their wives and families . . . To call this policy Conservative is, in my opinion, pure mockery, an abuse of terms. Whatever it may be in its motive, it is in its result disloyal, it is in its essence thoroughly subversive.' Disraeli was trying to lead the people along a road ' which plunges into suffering, discredit, and dishonour'. Gladstone called upon his hearers to take another road, ' which slowly perhaps, but surely, leads a free and high-minded people towards the blessed ends of prosperity and justice, of liberty and peace'.

In the whole Midlothian campaign Gladstone made no more than five great major indoor political speeches, two lesser ones, and a large number of brief incidental outdoor ones, delivered hatless in the frosty air. In that happy and glorious fortnight, however, he did much to swing public opinion round into distrust and dislike of Disraeli, and he impressed his personality upon a body of liberal thought and doctrine which meant much more for mankind at large in the future than it did for the electoral prospects of the British Liberal Party in 1880. Gladstone still felt, rather perversely, that he was free to speak his mind because he had divested himself of the responsibility of leadership; and he had not previously consulted the Liberal leaders about what he intended to say. He ignored the fact that he had chosen to lead since 1877, and for the first time in his life he spoke without qualification and with only occasional indulgence in verbal distinctions and refinements. His main themes were few, and although they were developed with an abundance of detail, they were expressed with a grand and limpid simplicity. The torrent of his indignation overwhelmed his hearers and bore them towards the goal which the speaker desired. Whether or not they were, or felt themselves, really competent to pronounce judgement upon the issues which Gladstone raised, their manhood kindled at his words, and it became unthinkable to them that an appeal launched with such searing intensity of conviction could be made in vain.

On 8 December, 1879, Gladstone returned to his Temple of Peace, at Hawarden. He was received at Chester, and elsewhere on his route, with frantic enthusiasm. At Hawarden a house-party was assembled, and Lady Frederick Cavendish noted that while Mrs. Gladstone collapsed and took to her bed, Uncle William was 'as fresh as paint'. For the first time in her experience 'the Great Man' appeared to be 'a little *personally* elated':

'It has always hitherto been the cause, or the moment, or the circumstances, or *something*, that he thinks he is the mere mouthpiece of; but this unheard-of enthusiasm for his name, in his own country (for he is a pure-bred Scotchman), and after the long time of abuse and loss of influence, has deeply moved him.' In London, Disraeli told Lady Bradford that he had not read a line of Gladstone's 'wearisome rhetoric' which had been planned 'on the wild assumption that Parliament was going to be dissolved'. In fact, Disraeli said, he did

THE COLOSSUS OF WORDS

PUNCH, December 13, 1879

not propose to dissolve until 1881. At Balmoral the Queen told Lady Ely that nothing would ever induce her to accept Gladstone as Prime Minister again. Gladstone himself told John Bright (28 November) that he could not wholly exclude the possibility that there might be an irresistible popular demand that he should resume the Liberal leadership. He added, however, that he knew the Queen's feelings and that he would never force himself upon her ; and he told his son Henry, in India, that it was out of the question that he should show any disloyalty to Lord Granville and Lord Hartington who were the leaders of the Party.

It was generally felt that public opinion would decide the issue, and Bright advised Gladstone (12 December) to pursue a course of ' masterly inactivity.' In the meantime Gladstone appreciated at last the extent to which he had exposed others as well as himself to embarrassment by his action five years before in resigning the leadership. It was fortunate that Lord Granville and Lord Hartington were men of scrupulous honour and good sense.

In the middle of January, 1880, Gladstone was summoned to the deathbed of his sister Helen, in Cologne. He went out with Sir Thomas and Lady Gladstone, and found Miss Gladstone suffering from paralysis of the bowels. Her constitution was magnificent, but the doctor told Gladstone that it had been undermined by continuous indulgence in enormous doses of morphia. Before she died on the evening of 16 January, Miss Gladstone spoke about religion ; it was evident that she was much troubled, and she asked Gladstone why he had come to tease her.

Gladstone and his brother resolved that their sister's body should be brought home to England, and buried at Fasque with Church of England rites. But Gladstone found it necessary first to convince himself that what they proposed to do was a moral duty. His method was characteristic. He noted : ' I felt myself under the most sacred obligation to proceed judicially, and to exclude from my mind, to the best of my ability, everything in the nature of sectarian or ecclesiastical prepossession. I have done what I think an upright Roman Catholic brother would have been bound to do—namely, in the absence of a direct statement of her wishes, to examine the evidence.'

The evidence consisted of a large stock of novels, sundry other books, and a few journals and calendars. There was also Gladstone's awareness of his sister's sympathy with Dr. Döllinger, who had been excommunicated. The novels were examined by Gladstone and by

267

Sir Thomas, and none proved to be specifically Roman Catholic, nor, so far as they could see, was there one written by a Roman Catholic author. On the contrary, there were a large number published by the Society for Promoting Christian Knowledge, which is, of course, a Protestant body.

There were, unfortunately, 'sundry other books' that were undeniably of a Roman Catholic complexion. Those, however, had mostly been published before the Decree of Papal Infallibility was issued. Those which had been published later did not, in Gladstone's considered judgement, 'bear the marks of having been used'. A volume of the Prayers of St. Anselm, with an introduction by Cardinal Wiseman, gave Gladstone some trouble, because it looked so new. He felt, however, that it would be fair to set against that an English Psalter, from the Anglican Prayer Book, which was unquestionably 'dog-eared'. It did not appear that Miss Gladstone had regularly received any Roman Catholic journals; on the other hand she had regularly received *The Guardian*, a Church of England newspaper. It did not appear, finally, that she had used a calendar which could be described as distinctively Roman Catholic since 1871.

After weighing that evidence with scrupulous and extraordinary solemnity, Gladstone felt justified in deciding that his sister had ceased to be a Roman Catholic and that she had therefore reverted automatically to the Church of her youth: 'I believe,' he wrote to Mrs. Gladstone on 17 January, before he had assembled all the evidence, 'that she would have asked to be buried in the Church of England, but I cannot prove it.'

The next day, however, Gladstone wrote again to his wife, enclosing a summary of the evidence, and delivering his considered judgement upon it: 'Is not all this most extraordinary, and a perfect and substantial proof that she lived and died in unity with us?'

In a private memorandum Gladstone added: 'I opened my mind to my brother as follows. "It is my conviction," I said, "that in loyalty to her we are absolutely bound, when we take her remains to England, to exclude any interposition by a Roman Catholic."' Sir Thomas, who had from the first felt no doubt about the matter, expressed his cordial agreement; and Gladstone then said: 'There would be a different case for consideration if there were any Church of those termed "Old Catholics" in England or Scotland, but, there being no such Church, the occasion does not arise.'

In conclusion, Gladstone noted that his sister had possessed the most powerful mind of all the women who had seceded to Rome during the past forty years. For that reason, he wrote, the question of her religious belief was one of considerable importance.

It is doubtful whether Miss Gladstone's muddled and troubled mind could fairly have been described as powerful, and it is much more open to doubt whether Gladstone in that matter was capable of acting as an impartial judge. However, he did his best, and although he deceived himself a little, his sister was at last at peace. On 27 January, 1880, her remains were laid to rest with Anglican rites in the family vault at Fasque. *The Guardian* published a report that she had died a Roman Catholic, and Gladstone asked the Editor, through a friend, to contradict that statement. He was profoundly thankful, when all was over, that there had been no controversy.

★   ★   ★

At the end of February, at a by-election at Southwark, the Conservatives won a seat which had been traditionally Liberal. Encouraged by that and other false signs, Disraeli on 8 March, 1880, startled the country by announcing that Parliament would be dissolved at once. He had mistaken the mood of the Court and society for that of the nation. In the Election manifesto which he published on behalf of his Party the next day, he declared that peace depended on England's ascendancy in the Councils of Europe, and that the agitation for Home Rule in Ireland was a menace 'scarcely less disastrous than pestilence and famine'.

On 16 March, Gladstone left London to begin his second Midlothian campaign. Rather selfishly, he proposed to leave Mrs. Gladstone behind, but her vigorous protest was seconded by their daughter Mary, who knew that her mother would have been 'wretched and forlorn' if she were left behind. A crowd of 2,000 people cheered Gladstone as he arrived at King's Cross Station. In Midlothian, Gladstone described the enthusiasm as 'ungovernable' and his return as 'a moral certainty'. He told the electors that a great State Trial was proceeding in which the constituencies were being asked to return verdicts of 'Guilty !' against Disraeli and the late Government. His speeches were addressed to the nation at large, as at West Calder (2 April):

'I am sorry to say we cannot reckon upon the aristocracy ! We cannot reckon upon what is called the landed interest ! We cannot reckon upon the clergy of the Established Church either in England or in Scotland !. . . . We cannot reckon upon the wealth of the country, nor upon the rank of the country ! . . . In the main these powers are against us . . . We must set them down among our most determined foes ! . But, gentlemen, above all these, and behind all these, there is the nation itself. And this great trial is now proceeding before the nation. The nation is a power hard to rouse, but when roused harder still and more hopeless to resist . . .'

The Elections were spread over a fortnight, and on the next day, 3 April, Gladstone refreshed himself by cutting down trees in Lord Rosebery's park : 'It seemed', he noted, 'as if the arm of the Lord had bared itself for work that He has made His own.' He was referring to news of Election victories which kept coming in. On the evening of 5 April the figures for Midlothian were announced. They were :

> Gladstone, 1,579
> Dalkeith, 1,368

Of Gladstone's sons, William was returned for East Worcestershire, and Herbert, after failing for Middlesex, was returned unopposed for Leeds which had been reserved for his father's use in case the Midlothian election had ended after all in defeat.

By 7 April it was clear that the Liberals had gained a decisive victory, and Gladstone noted : 'The triumph grows and grows ; to God be the praise !' On 10 April, Lord Wolverton informed Gladstone at Hawarden that he had reason to think that Lord Granville and Lord Hartington would both insist that Gladstone should resume the Party leadership and take office as Prime Minister : 'I am stunned,' Gladstone noted, 'but God will provide.' On 12 April he told the Duke of Argyll that 'the downfall of Beaconsfieldism is like the vanishing of some vast magnificent castle of Italian romance'. An authoritative contemporary estimate of the final result gave the Liberals 347 seats, against 240 Conservatives and 65 Irish Nationalists.

The Queen, who was at Baden-Baden, was overcome with surprise and mortification. As early as 4 April she sent a note about Gladstone to Sir Henry Ponsonby : 'She will sooner *abdicate* than send for or have anything to do with that *half-mad fire-brand* who would soon ruin everything, and be a *Dictator*.' She said that she would never submit to his 'democratic rule'.

On 9 April the Queen wrote to Disraeli that she would take no notice of Gladstone and that she hoped that the Liberal Party—

'this shamefully heterogeneous union'—would soon dissolve into its component parts. She told Disraeli that he was to write to her in future, in the first person, upon public as well as upon private subjects 'without anyone knowing about it'.[1] Her one hope, she said, was 'that the Conservatives will come in stronger than ever in a short time'. She ordered Ponsonby (8 April) to warn Lord Granville and Lord Hartington that Gladstone would be unacceptable to her as Prime Minister, 'for she considers his whole conduct since '76 to have been one series of violent, passionate invective against and abuse of Lord Beaconsfield'. She considered that Gladstone had 'caused' the Russo-TurkishWar. Ponsonby begged her not to commit herself until she had seen Disraeli who, he said, would probably feel bound to advise her to send for Gladstone. But Disraeli saw no reason why he should smooth his enemy's path. Characteristically he told the Queen that there was no reason why she should hasten her journey home, and she did not arrive until 17 April. Disraeli went to Windsor to see her the next day, and he then advised her to send for Lord Hartington. Hartington, he observed, was a Conservative at heart, a gentleman, and very straightforward. Disraeli added that he had 'every confidence in Hartington', but that Lord Granville was less disinterested and too much devoted to Gladstone. Disraeli said that he proposed to resign at once without waiting for Parliament to meet ; he resigned formally on 21 April.

On 22 April, accordingly, the Queen sent for Lord Hartington and asked him to form a government. He replied that no government could be formed without Gladstone who would be unwilling to serve in any subordinate capacity. He suggested that the Queen should send for Gladstone at once. The Queen asked what authority Lord Hartington had for saying that Gladstone would not serve under him, and she ordered him to tell Gladstone that he would never again enjoy her confidence. Lord Hartington said that he must leave his friend to explain and defend his own conduct in resigning the Liberal leadership, but he admitted that he, personally, thought that Gladstone had made a bad mistake. In return he forced the Queen reluctantly to admit that Gladstone's personal loyalty was and had always been above reproach. He then went off to consult Lord Granville and to ask Gladstone, specifically, at the Queen's request, whether or not he would be willing to accept a subordinate position in the new Liberal Government.

[1] That was a most rare privilege at that time.

Lord Hartington saw Lord Granville first, and accepted his advice not to repeat to Gladstone what the Queen had said about her want of confidence, in case it should cause Gladstone, for whom the country was clamouring, to withdraw a second time. He then called on Gladstone at Harley Street and asked formally if he would be willing to take a subordinate office. Lord Hartington said that he would not have asked such a question if he had not been ordered to do so by the Queen. Gladstone, who had previously authorized Lord Wolverton to state his views to Lord Granville and Lord Hartington, said that he had not changed them. He would only take office as Prime Minister, but he would, of course, be willing to give all the support in his power to any government which Granville or Hartington might form.

Gladstone added, rather strangely, that he had resigned his ' trust ' to Granville, not to Hartington who had been elected, subsequently, to the leadership of the Party in the House of Commons. The Queen, in Gladstone's view, had wrongly by-passed Lord Granville when she sent for Lord Hartington. Gladstone considered that it was her duty to send for the leader of the Opposition. His messianic view that the Party leadership was in his gift as a trust from God to dispose of as he thought fit had been expressed on a number of previous occasions ; and it was a potentially dangerous delusion. It helps to account for the way in which he appeared to cling to office, as he grew older and ever more contemptuous of the colleagues by whom he was surrounded. On the present occasion the issue was academic and it was settled with good feeling and good sense ; Lord Granville, and Lord Hartington, were both convinced that the national interest required Gladstone's immediate return to office as Prime Minister, and Gladstone agreed with them.

On 23 April Lord Granville and Lord Hartington went together to Windsor, and Lord Hartington reported the result of his interview with Gladstone. He told the Queen frankly that he had not repeated to Gladstone what she had said about her want of confidence, because no man could tell how he would have taken it. He added that the nation was evidently resolved that Gladstone should again be Prime Minister. Lord Granville joined Lord Hartington in begging the Queen not to delay, but to send at once for Gladstone, and not on any account to start by saying that she could not trust him. Lord Granville suggested that she might say that she regretted his violence, and many of the expressions which he had recently used in public, and that it was her wish that he should regard Disraeli's territorial acquisitions as accomplished facts. They consoled her a little by saying that they did not believe that Gladstone would be able to bear the strain of office for very long.

The Queen agreed to send for Gladstone, and Lord Granville and Lord Hartington returned to London to summon him to her presence. Gladstone expressed his 'sense of the high honour and patriotism with which they had acted', and apologized to them both at last for the embarrassment which he had caused by resigning the leadership five years before. He said that he had acted in good faith, believing that quiet times lay ahead, and added that he had only been drawn out of his retirement by compulsion. To that they made no reply. Gladstone at once offered Lord Granville the Foreign Office, which was accepted, and Lord Hartington the India Office. Lord Hartington said that he would require a little time for consideration, but that in principle he was willing to be a member of the Government.

Gladstone then left for Windsor, asking his wife to pray for him. He saw the Queen at 6.50 p.m. and accepted her commission to form a Government. After a brief discussion about the claims of certain candidates for office, the Queen told Gladstone that she meant to be frank. He had used expressions in public which had caused her alarm and pain. Gladstone admitted that he had 'used a mode of speech and language different in some degree from what I should have employed had I been the leader of a party or a candidate for office'. He said, however, that violence and bitterness now belonged to the past, and that he looked to 'a personal retirement comparatively early'. He noted that the Queen observed 'with some good-natured archness' that he would have to bear the consequences of the strong language he had formerly used. He assented, and recorded that the Queen had been 'natural under effort'. The Queen told Disraeli that evening that Gladstone looked 'very ill and haggard, and his voice feeble'. She was amazed when Gladstone told her that he intended to combine the office of Chancellor of the Exchequer with that of Prime Minister.

That action had a disastrous effect on Gladstone's outlook, for it focused his attention on a mass of petty detail at a time when it should have been free to range broadly over the whole political field. On the three other occasions when he took office, in 1868, 1886, and 1892, he had a definite constructive purpose in view. In 1880 he was to some extent at sea. He conceived that he could conform best with

the will of God by exorcizing in the shortest possible time the mora
and political legacy of 'Beaconsfieldism', and afterwards by retiring in
order to cultivate what he described in his diary on 29 December, 1879
(his seventieth birthday), as 'the poor little garden of my own soul'.

In order to exorcize Beaconsfieldism it seemed to Gladstone that a
start would have to be made at the Exchequer. He was in doubt
where to begin and he fumbled, characteristically, for a mission there.
He was obsessed by the deficit of eight million pounds which Disraeli
had bequeathed in place of the surplus of six millions which he had
inherited from the Liberals. The country had shown unmistakably
in 1874 that it was bored by Gladstone's rigid financial doctrine, but
Gladstone ignored that lesson in 1880. Even more serious was the
fact that he took office in utter ignorance of the calamitous state of
Ireland. More than four years later in Edinburgh on 1 September,
1884, he frankly admitted that he had been taken entirely by surprise
by 'the severity of the crisis that was already swelling upon the
horizon, and that, shortly afterwards, rushed upon us like a flood'.
Incredible as it may seem, Gladstone only once visited Ireland during
the whole course of his life. He spent three weeks there in October–
November, 1877, when he received the Freedom of Dublin, but the
visit taught him nothing. Disraeli never once visited Ireland. At
the General Election of 1880 Gladstone coldly dismissed Disraeli's
reference to the dangerous condition of Ireland as a barefaced attempt
to divert attention from his Government's guilt elsewhere. The
result was that Gladstone's second Government never gave the impression of controlling events; it seemed to be at their mercy.

As soon as the new House met (29 April), the Speaker, H. B. W.
Brand, noted that the Liberals were likely to prove a difficult team
to drive and that many individuals seemed determined to go their
own ways in spite of Gladstone. There was manifested in the House
generally an undertone of bitterness and violence which was caused
in part only by the Irish members. Much of it was due to the feverish
atmosphere which Gladstone had himself created while he was engaged
in the task of rousing the masses against Disraeli. That atmosphere of
strain was made worse by the patent ineffectiveness of Sir Stafford
Northcote, the leader of the Opposition.

Sir Stafford Northcote was an amiable old gentleman who seemed
never able to forget that he had been Gladstone's private secretary
at the Board of Trade. The younger members noticed that Northcote
was afraid of Gladstone, and they were provoked accordingly into

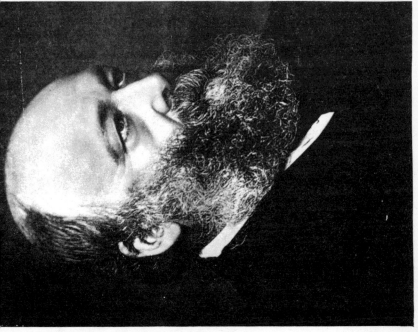

AMIN DISRAELI (EARL OF BEACONFSIELD) (*above*).
otograph by W. & D. Downey, *c.* 1873.

ERT ARTHUR TALBOT GASCOYNE-CECIL, 3RD MARQUESS OF SALISBURY.
otograph by Russell & Sons, *c.* 1898.

'THE PEOPLE'S WILLIAM.'
By 'Spy', *Vanity Fair*, 1 July, 1879.

taking into their own hands the business of baiting the great man. Northcote, when Gladstone glared at him, felt sometimes as James Stuart Blackie, the Professor of Greek at Edinburgh, had felt on a recorded occasion when he and Gladstone were disputing about Homer. Sir Joseph Boehm, the sculptor, was present, and he described how Blackie, in his excitement, jumped out of his chair at one moment in order to contradict one of Gladstone's more extraordinary theories. Gladstone made no movement of any kind, but his outer eyelids expanded like those of a bird of prey when it is making ready to paralyse the nervous system of a prospective victim. That baleful glare was concentrated for a full minute upon Blackie, whose tongue stumbled. He flushed and looked confused and sank back speechless into his chair. So Northcote sometimes felt on the Opposition front bench ; he quailed beneath the eye of the Prime Minister.

The lightning in the House, therefore, found no suitable conductor in the person of the leader of the Opposition, and it began to discharge itself in the form of an inexhaustible series of gay, brutal, audacious, irresponsible, and brilliant attacks upon Gladstone by members of the ' Fourth Party '—Lord Randolph Churchill, Sir Henry Drummond Wolff, and John Gorst. Disraeli, from behind the scenes, urged them on ; he told them that Northcote represented ' the respectability of the Party ', but that he well understood their impatience with Northcote ' because I never was respectable myself ! ' Gladstone also gave the Fourth Party involuntary encouragement, for with his invariable courtesy he constantly paid his high-spirited young critics the compliment of demolishing their wildest arguments at considerable length with the aid of all the formidable weapons of debate in his incomparable armoury.

Tension existed in Gladstone's Cabinet as well as in the House of Commons ; it was difficult for Whigs and Radicals to work in harmony. In forming his Government, Gladstone took great pains to conciliate the Whig patricians to whom the demagogic methods which he had employed in Midlothian and elsewhere had been highly distasteful. Whig patricians, accordingly, filled most of the major Offices of State. Lord Granville was Foreign Secretary ; Lord Spencer, Lord President of the Council ; the Duke of Argyll, Lord Privy Seal ; Lord Hartington, Secretary for India ; Sir William Harcourt,[1] Home Secretary ; Lord Northbrook, First Lord of the

[1] Sir William Harcourt, although a Whig by birth, held Radical opinions and was regarded by the public as a moderate Radical.

CABINET-MAKING

Head Carpenter. 'I hope Your Majesty likes the new Cabinet. It's been har[d]
  work—such a quantity of material !'

The Queen. 'I see most of it is well seasoned—let us hope the new wood wil[l]
  stand well !'

PUNCH, *May 8, 1880*

Admiralty; Lord Kimberley, Secretary for the Colonies. Two Radicals only were given places in the Cabinet. John Bright, whose radicalism was dimmed by age, became Chancellor of the Duchy of Lancaster, and Joseph Chamberlain, whose radicalism was presently to be transformed into jingoism, became President of the Board of Trade. In his heart Gladstone did not believe in Chamberlain's integrity and he never liked or understood him. He was bored by the agitation for social reform and local government with which Chamberlain's name was associated, and he could never work happily with him as he had learned to do with John Bright and was later to do with John Morley. Chamberlain, who was Lord Mayor of Birmingham, had contributed to Gladstone's victory by means of the National Liberal Federation which he had created. That Federation had proved efficient enough to win 60 of the 67 seats which it contested, and Chamberlain felt that the Radicals were inadequately represented in the Government. At the same time he resented Gladstone's insensitiveness to the social problem, and his gestures of goodwill towards Russia, whose despotic government was a bugbear to all Radicals.

The independent temper of the new House of Commons was apparent from the start. When, for example, the Government introduced a Bill to enable tenant-farmers to protect their crops by destroying ground game (hares and rabbits), the Conservatives successfully carried an amendment for local option. Shortly afterwards, to the Queen's disgust, the Radicals succeeded in negativing a Government proposal to erect a memorial to the Prince Imperial who had fallen in the war against the Zulus. Much the worst embarrassment which the Government suffered, however, arose out of the case of Charles Bradlaugh, the Radical member for Northampton.

Bradlaugh stood for much that Gladstone detested. He was an avowed atheist, an advocate of contraceptives, and a reputed republican. As an atheist he claimed the right to take the Oath of Allegiance by affirming, since the words ' So help me God ' in the prescribed form of oath had no meaning for him. That claim was considered by a Select Committee and rejected.

Bradlaugh at once offered to take the oath in the prescribed form, but the House was angry and out of hand, and many members objected. In an attempt to save the situation Gladstone persuaded the House to appoint another Select Committee to inquire whether the House had a right to interfere in order to prevent a member from taking the oath in the prescribed form. That Committee reported that Bradlaugh, having no religious belief, was incapable of taking the oath. It recommended, however, that he should be allowed to affirm. Nevertheless, despite all that Gladstone could do, a motion to that effect was defeated by 275 votes to 230 at one o'clock in the morning of 23 June, 1880. Gladstone told the Queen that, when the result of the division was announced, the House was convulsed by 'an ecstatic transport of excitement' which exceeded anything he ever remembered. An Opposition motion to debar Bradlaugh from affirming or from taking the oath was then carried amid a storm of cheering.

Gladstone thought as badly of the man as he did of his opinions, but he considered that Bradlaugh had an incontestable right to comply with the law and to take his seat. The spectacle of Gladstone defending the rights of such a man gave the Fourth Party its opportunity. Lord Randolph Churchill made his name by his brilliantly witty efforts to identify Gladstone with the causes of atheism, blasphemy, and contraceptives. Bradlaugh had invited persecution, and the insidious process could not be abandoned once it had been begun. It gave too much secret pleasure to too many people, and above all it gave the Opposition an irresistible excuse to bait Gladstone and his hard core of Nonconformist supporters in the names of religion and morality. By that means the Opposition gained a measure of revenge for the impassioned attacks which Gladstone, in the names of religion and morality, had delivered against Conservative policy during the Midlothian campaign.

During the five years which followed, Bradlaugh, like John Wilkes during the previous century, was repeatedly expelled from the House of Commons, to be re-elected every time by his constituents at Northampton. The scandal became one of the most tiresome of Gladstone's preoccupations, and in the hope of bringing it to an end he gave notice, in April, 1881, of a Bill to legalize affirmation. At that time the temper of the House was such that he took no further action, but two years later, in April, 1883, he noted that he took 'the bull by the horns' by winning round the Archbishop of Canterbury to his view. As a result of their conference he introduced a Bill to enable unbelievers to affirm as Quakers and Jews were already entitled to do. Gladstone's speech on the Second Reading (26 April, 1883) made ostensibly on behalf of a man he detested, with a section of the Liberal Party in open revolt, was one of his noblest performances. He argued that the distinction insisted upon by the House between those who were willing to take the oath in the form prescribed by law, and those who were not, was worthless. The oath implied no more than a tepid Deism ; and such indifference, which was far more common than ' blank atheism ', and which was in fact the supreme ' mischief of the age ', remained untouched by the law. Gladstone argued that the continued persecution of Bradlaugh in the name of religion must damage the cause it purported to serve :

' Unbelief attracts a sympathy which it would not otherwise enjoy, and the upshot is to impair those convictions and that religious faith, the loss of which I believe to be the most inexpressible calamity which can fall either upon a man, or upon a nation.'

Four days later Gladstone's Bill was lost by three votes after Lord Randolph Churchill had begged the House to remember ' the effect on the masses of the State recognition of atheism ' at the time of the French Revolution. Bradlaugh, accordingly, was arbitrarily prevented from taking his seat until a new Parliament was elected in 1885. In 1888, Bradlaugh himself was permitted to pilot an Affirmation Bill successfully through a Conservative House of Commons. Three years later, in 1891, when Bradlaugh lay on his deathbed, Gladstone successfully supported a motion which expunged from the Records of the House the unjust Resolution of 23 June, 1880, whereby Bradlaugh had been debarred from swearing or affirming.

One other irritant was to trouble Gladstone as long as he lived and to cause him periods of black depression. The Queen would have no more to do with him than she could help. A year earlier (13 March, 1879) Gladstone had been bitterly hurt when the Queen pointedly omitted to invite him and Mrs. Gladstone to the Duke of Connaught's wedding. He received many letters expressing indignation, and a few foolish ones expressing sympathy, but he replied to none and maintained a loyal and dignified silence. The Queen repeated back to Disraeli a phrase which Disraeli had taught her. Gladstone, she complained, ' is not a man of the world '. She told Disraeli (20 September, 1880) that she dealt with the Government mostly through Lord Granville,' for I never write except on formal *official* matters to the Prime Minister . . . I look always to you for ultimate help.' Gladstone blamed Disraeli for turning the Queen into a partisan, and he made one good joke about him, which was widely repeated, when Montagu Corry, Disraeli's secretary, was made a peer (Lord Rowton) in the Dissolution Honours. Gladstone did not consider that Corry had earned a peerage, and he said that nothing comparable had been seen since Caligula made his horse a consul.

In March, 1881, Disraeli's last illness began. 'May the Almighty be near his pillow!' Gladstone wrote in his diary on 29 March. When the end came on 19 April, Gladstone incurred much odium for not attending the funeral. He had at once offered a State burial in Westminster Abbey, which he imagined would have been to Disraeli's taste. Disraeli had, however, left directions that he should be buried in the churchyard at Hughenden in the same grave with the wife to whom he had owed so much and been so devotedly attached. The service at Hughenden was attended by the Prince of Wales and other members of the Royal Family, by foreign Ambassadors and Ministers, and by the leading statesmen of the day, including Lord Hartington, and many other Liberals. Disraeli's executors sent Gladstone an invitation, but he pleaded pressure of work and stayed away.

For some days thereafter, Gladstone's passion for sincerity caused him mental anguish which brought on a sharp attack of diarrhœa. He could not decide what he should say, when the House reassembled after the Easter Recess, in proposing that a national memorial to Disraeli should be erected in Westminster Abbey. Instead of giving notice of that Resolution himself, he deputed Lord Richard Grosvenor to do it for him. He prayed earnestly for light, which was happily vouchsafed to him, and his speech on 9 May fulfilled the highest expectations of friends and opponents. It did not say that Disraeli had left a blank in the political world, or that his loss was greatly to be deplored, but the speech was, nevertheless, a masterpiece of dignity and tact, and critical chatter was stilled. Gladstone praised Disraeli's unique career, his loyalty to his race, his devotion to his wife, and his absence of rancour. He praised also certain qualities which the dead statesman had possessed 'in a degree undoubtedly extraordinary . . . his strength of will; his long-sighted consistency of purpose . . . his remarkable power of self-government; and, last but not least, his great parliamentary courage—a quality which I, who have been associated in the course of my life with some scores of Ministers, have, I think, never known but two whom I could pronounce his equal'.

The two Gladstone had in mind were Sir Robert Peel and Lord Russell. He felt, however, very uneasy about the affair. He could not bring himself to believe in the sincerity of Disraeli's desire for a quiet burial in a country churchyard, and he thought that it was one more pose. He grumbled to his secretary, Edward Hamilton: 'As

he lived, so he died—all display, without reality or genuineness.'
He said that he doubted whether anyone would succeed in portraying
in its true colours Disraeli's 'extraordinary career'. He considered
that Disraeli's most striking characteristic was 'the utter absence of
any love of liberty'. His Eastern policy had been so scandalous that
he felt bound to assume that it was conditioned, like that of the
proprietor [1] of the *Daily Telegraph*, by prejudices and antipathies
associated with the Judaism which they had both discarded.

[1] Edward Levy-Lawson (Lord Burnham), 1833-1916.

CHAPTER 12

THE RESOURCES OF CIVILIZATION

1880–1884

THE private secretaries [1] in Downing Street were worried, even before the Government was completed, by Gladstone's concentration upon finance. He seemed to be interested in nothing but a plan which he had formed to win the farmers' vote, and thereby to complete the Conservatives' discomfiture, by repealing the malt-tax in his forthcoming supplementary budget. On the day his Government was completed (29 April, 1880) Gladstone gave a financial dinner to discuss means of achieving that result. One personal matter which annoyed him at the outset was the strongly-expressed indignation of the Austrian Ambassador at some expressions used by Gladstone during his election campaign about the Emperor Francis Joseph and Austrian policy in the Balkans. Lord Granville with difficulty persuaded Gladstone to write a letter for publication (11 May) withdrawing words which he had spoken 'upon secondary evidence' while 'in a position of greater freedom and less responsibility'. The last phrase caused some unkind laughter, but Gladstone held up his letter until he had received private assurances from the Ambassador that Austria had no further ambitions in the Balkans.

Gladstone installed his nephew, Lord Frederick Cavendish, at the Treasury as Financial Secretary. Lord Frederick was a poor speaker, but he possessed charm and integrity and he constantly smoothed relations between his brother—Lord Hartington—and Gladstone. Gladstone came to rely upon Lord Frederick as much as he did upon John Bright and only a little less than he did upon Lord Granville, and he conceived for him an almost doting affection. Lord Fred-

---

[1] There were four private secretaries—(Sir) Arthur Godley (Lord Kilbracken) ; (Sir) Edward Hamilton ; Horace Seymour ; and (Sir) George Leveson-Gower (who lived until 1951). Sir Edward Hamilton, G.C.B., who was afterwards Permanent Secretary to the Treasury, and was known as 'The Cob' on account of his cheerfulness and strong, compact little figure, kept a personal diary which is in the British Museum but not open to inspection until 1956. Gladstone, and Lord Rosebery with whom Hamilton was very intimate, figure largely in its pages. The kindness of the Trustees of the British Museum—in the sympathetic exercise of their discretion—in allowing me to make use of Hamilton's diary has been helpful in this chapter, and in some others.

erick's first task was to help his uncle to prepare the budget which Gladstone presented to the House in a two-hour speech of unusual simplicity on 10 June. The House was astonished to learn that the malt-tax, which the Conservatives had long wanted to repeal but had never dared to touch, was to go. It had produced eight and a half millions a year, but Gladstone said that he was resolved to help the farmers at a time of cruel agricultural depression. He proposed to recoup the loss by raising the income-tax from fivepence to sixpence, and by slightly increasing the tax on beer. He was boyishly delighted by the success of his budget, and he told his friends that he had cut the ground from under the Tories' feet.

A few weeks later, when dining with the Dean of Windsor, Gladstone complained that the combined strain of the two offices which he held was almost intolerable. The Dean asked, naturally, why he did not give up the Chancellorship of the Exchequer. ' Because I have not sufficient confidence in the financial judgement of my colleagues,' was the startling reply. Gladstone had, in fact, a perfectly competent candidate in H. C. E. Childers, the Secretary for War, to whom he resigned the Chancellorship at last in December, 1882. He generously described Childers subsequently as a better Chancellor than himself.

The task of switching into reverse the pro-Turkish policy which Disraeli had followed almost until the last was at once taken in hand by Lord Granville. The Treaty of Berlin had provided for the cession by Turkey of a small, barren, but precisely-defined piece of territory to Montenegro, and of a large but undefined area of Thessaly to Greece. Gladstone habitually described the ' Montene*greens*' as ' the most wonderful race alive ', and as the Sultan made no move to implement those clauses of the Treaty, Gladstone organized a naval demonstration off the coast of Albania in September, 1880. He obtained the co-operation of the Concert of Europe, but the French, German, and Austrian Admiralties made no secret of the fact that their warships had been ordered in no circumstances to open fire. Bismarck joked boisterously about ' Professor ' Gladstone in shining armour ; the Queen was furious ; and Gladstone admitted that the demonstration was reduced to a farce. He was indignant to learn that Conservative ex-Ministers were going up to Balmoral in relays in order to soothe the Queen, and he sent Lord Granville to explain the situation to her verbally on 20 September. Lord Granville was less successful than Gladstone had hoped.

The failure of the naval demonstration caused Gladstone to urge that the Powers should send an expedition to seize Smyrna, on the coast of Asia Minor, and to sequestrate the customs revenues of that important harbour. The question whether Great Britain should act alone if the Concert of Europe declined to co-operate was left undecided. Russia and Italy were agreeable, but France, Germany, and Austria opposed the plan and refused to help. Bismarck said contemptuously that his prayers would accompany the expedition.

The Turks, fortunately, were unaware of the differences among the Powers, and Gladstone was immensely relieved to learn on 10 October that the Sultan had taken fright. He wrote on that day to his wife that he was awaiting a confirmatory telegram from Constantinople, and that the European Concert was working 'for purposes of justice, peace, and liberty, with efficiency and success . . . That has always been the ideal of my life in foreign policy : and if this goes forward rightly to the end it will be the most conspicuous instance yet recorded, the best case of success yet achieved.'

Gladstone said that ' most probably, though not certainly ' Smyrna would have been attacked even if the Turks had discovered that France, Germany, and Austria had refused their aid, and if in consequence the Sultan had refused to yield. He noted in a subsequent memorandum that the Turks had yielded ' not to a threat of coercion from Europe, but to the knowledge that Great Britain had asked Europe to coerce . . .' In his letter to his wife he quoted the first verse of the hymn, ' Praise to the Holiest in the height ! ' And Mrs. Gladstone replied ecstatically (11 October) :

> ' We praise Thee and will praise Thee,
> We bless Thee and will bless,
> We give thanks to Thee and will give thanks.

' And you, dearest own, who have mercifully been permitted to take part in such mighty operations ! What shall I say ? . . . The " ideal of your life " in foreign policy ! God only grant it may be all right ! . . . We shall be all ready for you to-morrow.'

11 October was ' a day of darkness and doubt '. No telegram was received from Constantinople, and Gladstone had to remain in London. He told his wife : ' One way or another I believe the Almighty will work it out.' On 12 October the eagerly awaited telegram from Constantinople arrived at the Foreign Office, and as soon as it was deciphered Lord Granville hurried off to 10, Downing

Street.   He arrived at noon and found Gladstone at his desk, absorbed
in a letter he was writing and oblivious of the presence of Lord
Granville, Arthur Godley, and Herbert Gladstone in his room.
Lord Granville proceeded to execute a *pas de joie*.   He danced very
gracefully upon his toes, waving his arms in the air and brandishing
his copy of the telegram.   At last Gladstone looked up, and the
Foreign Secretary for a full minute continued to dance and to enjoy
the Prime Minister's gaze of utter stupefaction.   Then he handed
him the message :

"God Almighty be praised ! " Gladstone exclaimed. "I can
catch the 2.45 to Hawarden."

In November, accordingly, the Montenegrins received the district
they had been promised, and in May, 1881, after anxious negotiations, Thessaly was ceded to Greece—the biggest change in a European frontier to be effected by peaceful means during the nineteenth
century.   On 21 March, 1881, Gladstone was delighted to receive
from the Princess of Wales, who was also a Princess of Greece and
Denmark, a jewelled pencil-case, in the shape of an axe, with a
charming inscription :

'From the Princess of Wales to the great People's William,
because of the many trees he has axed, and of the many questions
he has been "axed", and in the hope that he will not cut down
the Greek frontier by another yard.'

Gladstone would have liked to cede Cyprus to Greece, but he
reluctantly allowed himself to be persuaded by Lord Granville that
the state of public opinion made that impossible.   Gladstone reversed,
however, Disraeli's forward policy in Afghanistan by withdrawing
the British garrison from Kandahar ; and he also withdrew the
'military consuls' whom Disraeli had started to infiltrate into Asia
Minor.   A more difficult problem faced him in South Africa.

During the Midlothian campaign, Gladstone had denounced the
annexation of the Transvaal in such scathing terms that the Boers
naturally expected that he would take immediate steps to restore
their independence.   Since the overthrow of the Zulus—their
strongest local enemy—the Boers had felt more confident than ever
of being able to defend their independence unaided.   Gladstone
hesitated, however, because he was preoccupied with financial and
other problems, and also because he was afraid of precipitating a
clash between Britons and Boers on a sub-continental scale.   He
considered that the best means of averting such a clash would be to

frame a comprehensive scheme of South African federation. Months slipped by while different schemes were being examined, and Gladstone infuriated the Radicals by waiting until August, 1880, to recall Sir Bartle Frere, the Governor of the Cape, who had been responsible for the Zulu War. Gladstone argued that as Sir Bartle could hardly be expected to start another war, his rare personal charm, and knowledge of South African problems, might be profitably employed in preparing a scheme of federation.

The Transvaal throughout 1880 seethed with discontent, and Gladstone, in order to play for time, decided to show a bold front. On 6 January, 1881, he announced that an immediate grant of self-government was out of the question, but he found soon that he had to eat his words. The Boers rose in revolt, and on 27 February Major-General Sir George Colley, the Governor of Natal, was defeated and killed at Majuba Hill. Less than a hundred Britons died, but the news of a humiliating reverse touched off an explosion of that Jingo sentiment which Gladstone was doing his best to exorcize. The Queen, the Opposition, and powerful organs of the Press, called loudly for reinforcements and revenge.

Negotiations with the Boers were in progress while the battle of Majuba Hill was being fought. Gladstone had now to decide whether to concede from weakness what he vainly wished he had conceded earlier from strength, or whether to break off negotiations and yield apparently to popular pressure by concentrating sufficient strength to crush the Boers. He never lacked courage, and he chose the harder course.

By the Convention of Pretoria (2 August, 1881) independence was restored to the Transvaal, subject to British supervision of its foreign relations with powers other than the Orange Free State. The Transvaal recognized the Queen's suzerainty but that formality was dropped three years later. The public outcry against Gladstone was exceedingly bitter, and the Queen wrote (7 August) to accuse him of breaking his promise to recognize ' accomplished facts '. The Boers received the impression that they could do with the British what they pleased, and that delusion was an important contributory cause of the war of 1899–1902 which Gladstone had hoped to avert. He blamed himself much for the incautious expressions which he had permitted himself formerly to use, and in consequence his speeches became even more than usually filled with those nice qualifications and distinctions which always irritated his opponents.

At Leeds, for example, on 7 October, 1881, Gladstone concluded a long argument about the way in which the Conservatives had sullied 'the fair name of England' in Afghanistan and elsewhere, with the words : 'And so, gentlemen, I say that while we are opposed to imperialism, we are devoted to the empire.'

Gladstone protested repeatedly against what he called 'the new form of Jingoism' which seemed to him to entail a general grabbing of land by Great Britain whenever another nation showed its face in anything like proximity to a British possession, as in New Guinea, the New Hebrides, and on the east and west coasts of Africa : 'Nothing', he told Edward Hamilton on one occasion, 'will induce me to submit to these colonial annexations . . . I don't mean to be pedantic . . . but I would welcome the Germans as our neighbours in South Africa, and even as neighbours in the Transvaal.'

Gladstone never understood that high moral principles, in their application to foreign policy, are often more destructive of political stability than motives of national self-interest. In that respect he was at a disadvantage in not being a man of the world. It must be said, too, that he was at an even greater disadvantage in possessing a mind which was conditioned to search at all times for high moral principles in order to justify the vagaries of his volcanic temperament. A startling instance of that quality of Gladstone's mind was provided in July, 1882, when in defiance of all laws of superficial probability he ordered the bombardment of Alexandria and a single-handed occupation of Egypt by a British army.

The political importance of Egypt, which was still a province of the vast Turkish Empire, had been greatly increased after the opening of the Suez Canal (1869) which had been built by French engineers with French capital. Gladstone had disliked the daring coup whereby Disraeli had secured control of the Canal in 1875, and he had prophesied almost from the first (House of Commons : 6 March, 1876) that financial control would ultimately lead to political control. In Midlothian (25 November, 1879) he had described the subsequent process whereby France and England had established a joint control over the bankrupt and mismanaged Egyptian Treasury, in order to safeguard their interests, as one of Disraeli's 'mischievous and ruinous misdeeds'. He acknowledged that 'we have assumed jointly with France the virtual government of Egypt', and he found, after he came to power, that the policy had gone too far to be reversed. On 12 February, 1884, he told the Commons :

'I affirm, and I will show, that the situation in Egypt is not one which we made, but one that we found. I shall show that we have never had an option [cries of Oh! Oh!] . . . It would not have been in keeping with the propriety of things to reverse the attitude which we found occupied by the British Government in Egypt.'

The Egyptian crisis which faced Gladstone was precipitated by a nationalist revolt at the end of 1881, which was directed against foreigners and headed by Colonel Arabi. Fifty foreigners were massacred during a riot in Alexandria on 11 June, 1882, and the British consul suffered injuries. The system of dual control by Great Britain and France was gravely imperilled, and, on the forts protecting Alexandria, Arabi started to mount guns which were intended as a threat to the Royal Navy.

Gladstone vainly attempted to induce the Concert of Europe to intervene and restore order, but he had no success. His scruples excited Bismarck's contempt: 'Let the Powers interested settle it as they please,' he told the German Ambassador at Constantinople, 'but don't ask me how, for I neither know, nor care.' The Powers most interested were Great Britain and France, but the French refused to act. France was rocked by an unexpected political convulsion, caused by fear lest there might be a sinister motive behind Bismarck's apparent desire to see French troops locked up in Egypt, in addition to those which were already committed in Tunis and Algeria. In consequence the French fleet sailed away at the last moment from Alexandria, and left the British on their own.

Gladstone was now faced with the decision which might have faced him eighteen months earlier in the case of the Montenegrin and Greek boundary claims. Should Great Britain act alone, or should she, as in the case of Schleswig-Holstein (1864), draw back in the absence of material aid from any other European Power? Gladstone, on this occasion, did not draw back. He was appalled equally by the threat which Arabi represented to political morality by seeking to establish an arbitrary tyranny, and to financial morality by seeking to repudiate his country's lawfully-incurred debts to foreign bond holders. Gladstone told the Commons on 22 July, 1882, after operations had begun:

'We should not fully discharge our duty if we did not endeavour to convert the present interior state of Egypt from anarchy and conflict to peace and order. We shall look . . . to the co-operation of the Powers of civilized Europe . . . But if every chance of

GLADSTONE INVADING EGYPT

obtaining co-operation is exhausted, the work will be undertaken by the single power of England.'

On 10 July the British Admiral was instructed to deliver an ultimatum to Arabi, ordering all work on the fortifications of Alexandria to cease within twelve hours. No answer was received, and at daybreak on 11 July the British fleet opened fire. Rioting and anarchy ensued, and Gladstone on 24 July asked Parliament for a Vote of Credit of £2,300,000, and raised the income-tax from 5d. to 6½d.[1] He informed the Sultan of Turkey (30 July) that a British army was on the way to restore order in Egypt ; and on 19 August the troops, commanded by Sir Garnet Wolseley, were successfully disembarked at Port Said.

That resolute action was too much for old John Bright, who resigned from the Cabinet in protest, and never held office again. Bright told Lord Rosebery (13 July) that Gladstone's conduct was 'simply damnable—worse than anything ever perpetrated by Dizzy'. He told the House of Commons (15 July) that he had resigned because the intervention in Egypt was 'a manifest violation of international and moral law'. Gladstone felt sharp regret but no resentment. In private he continued to speak with great affection of Bright— 'splendid old fellow !', 'sound as a roach !', 'such a grand moral tone !' On one occasion he remarked : 'Just compare his high principles with those of Chamberlain and Dilke and the new style of Radicals, who are *all opportunism* !' To the Queen, however, Gladstone wrote (15 July) that he was 'obliged to admit that he does not clearly comprehend Mr. Bright's present view'.

The army in Egypt fulfilled the highest British hopes. The enemy was brought to battle on 13 September, 1882, and annihilated at Tel-el-Kebir. Arabi was taken prisoner and handed over to the young Khedive of Egypt for trial and punishment ; the British were sole masters in Egypt. Gladstone refused Bright's request that he should intervene with the Khedive to save Arabi from being hanged, and it was not due to Gladstone that the nationalist leader was permitted to expiate his crimes by a long period of banishment to Ceylon. He told Sir Thomas Gladstone (23 July, 1882) that Arabi had shown himself to be 'one of the greatest villains alive' ; and when the news of Tel-el-Kebir was known, Gladstone, on his own initiative, ordered salutes of guns to be fired in Hyde Park and elsewhere in honour of

[1] It was raised to 8d. for the half-year in which the whole of the increase was to be collected, which was the equivalent of 6½d. for the year as a whole.

. GLADSTONE AND MRS. GLADSTONE, *c.* 1870.

THE LOBBY OF THE HOUSE OF COMMONS, 1886.

the victory. His secretaries were unanimous that they had never seen him in such extraordinary spirits. On 15 September he was moaning like a child because he had recollected an engagement at Hawarden which would prevent him from staying to hear the victory salute in London. He was full of praise for the generals, the admirals, the officers, and the men, and for the first time since he came into office he accepted an invitation to stay at Balmoral. He even remembered to write a line of congratulation to Lord Cardwell, who had served in his previous Government as Secretary for War, oblivious for the moment of the fact that Lord Cardwell was out of his mind and would not therefore be in a condition to appreciate the attention.

Gladstone's spirited handling of the Egyptian crisis afforded his Government a fillip of which it stood greatly in need. He soon found, however, that the settlement of Egypt was a matter which required time, patience, heavy expense, and which caused serious embarrassment. Gladstone hoped at first that the period of occupation might be short, but he was quickly undeceived. He never doubted the rightness of his decision to invade Egypt, but his momentary elation soon yielded to a mood of profound depression. In October and November, 1882, he expressed heartfelt regret that he had not made up his mind to quit politics a year earlier, before ' three special circumstances '—the Egyptian and Irish entanglements, and the problem of Parliamentary obstruction—had arisen to stay his hand. The degree of intense personal interest which he showed in intimate conversations with friends and colleagues, in the details of the Government's reconstruction after his retirement, seemed to some of them to be inconsistent with the liberty of choice which his successor was certain to require.

Gladstone's staff considered that their chief's moods of mental depression were liable to be most pronounced at times when he was physically most resilient. The black moods seem also to have been associated with the reaction that followed the taking of any important and especially of any violent decision. Between April, 1880, when he took office, and December, 1882, when he resigned to Childers the Chancellorship of the Exchequer, the question of retirement was constantly in the forefront of Gladstone's mind. But he spoke about it most during the two periods of depression which visited him in the autumn of 1881, shortly after he had ordered the arrest of Charles Stewart Parnell, the leader of the Irish Nationalists in the House of Commons, and in the autumn of 1882, shortly after he had smashed, by force, Arabi's nationalist movement in Egypt. In both cases the periods of depression exceeded considerably in length the periods of elation which they followed.

On 4 November, 1881, less than three weeks after the arrest of Parnell, Gladstone had a long conversation about retirement with Lord Frederick Cavendish at Hawarden. He said that his emergence from retirement at the time of the Bulgarian Horrors had been accidental, conditional, and temporary. The specific purposes for which he had subsequently taken office were for the most part accomplished. The Berlin Treaty had been carried out; Afghanistan had been evacuated; the Transvaal had been settled; above all, finance had been put on a satisfactory footing. Two matters only made Gladstone hesitate at that moment—the state of Ireland, and the problem of Parliamentary obstruction. He thought, however, that those might soon be settled and that he might retire at Easter, 1882.

Gladstone said that he wanted in any event to give up the Chancellorship of the Exchequer. He only hesitated to do that because he was afraid that such action would have the effect of binding him to remain on as Prime Minister for an indefinite time. In conversation with Gladstone some months later (20 April, 1882) Edward Hamilton drew from his chief the fact that pressure of work was only one reason why he wished to give up the Chancellorship. Another was the impossibility of framing a satisfactory budget in a world in which ' economy and retrenchment ' had altogether ceased to have the force of a religious creed. In matters of economy, Gladstone exclaimed, ' I am an old mouldy landmark on a desert shore '. He had managed in his budget of 4 April, 1881, to reduce the income-tax from sixpence halfpenny to fivepence, but he complained that in his thirteenth and last budget—that of 1882—there was nothing to be done. No clear call for ruthless economy was to be heard in any corner of the land.

Gladstone gave Lord Frederick Cavendish three reasons for his urgent wish to quit politics. In 1882 he would celebrate the fiftieth anniversary of his first entry in Parliament. At the same time his relationship with the Queen was ' intolerable ', ' greatly worse than I ever anticipated '; he had to wage an almost daily battle with her ' on the side of liberty as opposed to Jingoism '. Lastly, he felt that he was standing in Hartington's way. He said that he wanted to be fair to Hartington, and he implied, without embarrassing Lord Frederick by stating the case too precisely, that he knew that his action in renouncing the leadership in defeat, and then resuming it after victory, had not, although he had himself contributed so largely to that victory, worn an appearance of generosity.

Lord Frederick said that his brother would again be placed in an impossible situation if Gladstone were to retire while still in possession of his full powers. No one but Gladstone could lead; the country would be always clamouring for him; the only possible course, if he were irrevocably bent on retiring, would be to take a peerage. Gladstone said that he would be very reluctant to do that. He admitted that he was continually astonished at his own powers of physical endurance—he was sleeping perfectly again, like a child. He added that he was reluctant to make the mistake which the Duke of Wellington and Lord Palmerston had made in clinging to office for too long, and he said that he would have another talk with Lord Granville.

Lord Granville was so often the recipient of Gladstone's confidence on the subject of retirement that he took the trouble to consult Gladstone's doctor, Sir Andrew Clark, about the Prime Minister's health. Sir Andrew told him that Gladstone was not only sound from head to toes, but built in the most beautiful proportion he had ever seen of all the parts of the human body to each other—head, legs, arms, and trunk, all without a flaw, like some ancient Greek statue of the ideal man. He added that of all the persons he had treated, Gladstone, with his careful habits, had the best chance of living to be a hundred.

Thus reassured, Lord Granville constantly poured cold water on Gladstone's suggestions that the time was at hand when he ought to retire: 'Your case is not normal,' he told him (22 October, 1882). 'Your bodily and mental strength are exceptionally strong . . . The hold you have on the country is extraordinary; the power you have to confer further advantages on it is exceptional. It may seem unfriendly to you . . . but I cannot aid or abet you in striking such a blow on the Liberal Party, and one which they would so deeply deplore, and I fear resent.' That was the 'echo to his own voice' which one part of Gladstone's nature desired to hear. For a time the issue still occasionally seemed doubtful, and Lord Hartington blithely informed Sir Henry Ponsonby on 10 January, 1883: 'We have great difficulty to prevent his bolting.' Gladstone was then about to go to Cannes for six weeks' rest, and the Queen, after consulting Lord Granville, hopefully offered her Prime Minister a peerage. She told Lord Granville (8 February), after Gladstone's refusal, that she was thankful that he had taken the offer so well. From the beginning of 1883, however, after he had resigned the Chancellorship of the Exchequer and returned from a long holiday in the South of France, Gladstone only talked of retirement in order to refresh his mind. He now conceived that he was tied to politics by a divine summons to make a Christian response to a series of political challenges. As he grew older he came to regard the character of that response as of far greater importance than any practical or immediate results which it might achieve. He no longer hoped to live to see many such results, but he was increasingly convinced that, among the statesmen of the age, he alone could be trusted to make the lofty but humble moral response which he regarded as essential if civilization were not to be submerged beneath the rising materialist tide.

At the end of Gladstone's life some of his closest friends and admirers were inclined to regret that he had not resigned in 1882 on the fiftieth anniversary of his entry into public life. If he had done so, however, he would have been false to his nature, and he would have deprived posterity of the spectacle of a great man's unconquerable mind triumphing until the last in the highest sense over hostile and uncongenial circumstances. Gladstone was willing if necessary to lead the Liberal Party to martyrdom in the cause of Ireland. Unless, however, he had proved that willingness by virtually incurring martyrdom, a false impression might have been left to the world. Whenever he was convinced that he heard the call of duty, Gladstone was willing to dare the uttermost. He loathed the bombardment of Alexandria, but he told the Commons (12 February, 1884) that the British task in Egypt was :

'one which we are executing not alone, on our own behalf, but on behalf, I may say, of civilized mankind. We undertook it with the approval of the Powers of Europe—the highest and most authentic organ of modern Christian civilization ; but having undertaken it at their invitation, or with their concurrence, we must fulfil it as we received it from them.'

The attempt to make the Powers of Europe fulfil their rôle as 'the highest and most authentic organ of modern Christian civilization' was worthy of Gladstone's gifts. His temperament would never have allowed him to rest. Remembering the sudden attack which he had launched on the Roman Catholic Church from the purest motives, as he saw them, in 1874, before he was distracted by the Bulgarian Horrors, it is impossible to regret that he continued until the end of his life to play his part on the grandest possible scale

—the only one which could satisfy him—in the field of politics to which his mind was never more than half reconciled but to which it had long been wholly conditioned.

*   *   *

A revolutionary situation in Ireland had been growing steadily worse since 1877, when the catastrophic fall in agricultural prices, due to competition from the New World, began to make it impossible for Irish tenant-farmers to pay their rents. Their straits, and those of the peasantry, from whom they were often barely distinguishable, became desperate, and as the tide of evictions mounted, so did that of every species of outrage directed against the landlords, their agents, and their property. It was exceedingly difficult to obtain evidence against perpetrators of agrarian crimes, and juries commonly refused, in any case, to convict. The passionate hopes and loyalties of the masses of the Irish people were embodied in the person of Charles Stewart Parnell, who was aged thirty-four in 1880. He worked to induce all Irish revolutionary elements to co-ordinate their political and terroristic programmes in a single realistic movement directed by himself. His goals were Home Rule and the transfer of the ownership of the soil from the landlords to the farmers. He became President of the Land League which was founded in Dublin in 1879 to enforce those ends by fair means or by foul.

Parnell enforced his leadership on the Irish Nationalist Party in the House of Commons after the General Election of 1880. It might have seemed as unlikely that he should command the almost idolatrous love of the Irish masses, as it was that Gladstone should command that of vast sections of the British masses, or Disraeli that of the remnants of 'Merrie England' and of the British upper class. All three were utterly different from their followers in character and in background. Parnell was a Protestant, and a landlord from Wicklow, who had been educated at Cambridge; he knew little and cared nothing about Irish history or culture. He was, however, a born leader of men. Proud and reserved, he possessed the cold intelligence and masterful character which command involuntary respect; ignorant and reckless, he possessed also the arrogance which springs from the hereditary possession of land in a country where the owners are distinguishable racially from the tillers of the soil. Some acid in his mind drove him into unconventional paths; he loathed the English, and he inherited from an American mother, whom he worshipped, a bitter contempt for the English upper class. Unlike most Irish members of Parliament, he had no trace of an inferiority complex ; he believed that men should be ruled through their weaknesses, and he was betrayed in the end through his own.

Parnell's first task was to carry the art of Parliamentary obstruction to a point at which, until the rules of debate were altered, it became impossible for business to be conducted in the House of Commons on any subject except that of Ireland. Opportunities of obstruction at that period were almost unlimited. The House's traditional rules had grown up gradually with the object of allowing private members to question the executive as much as they pleased ; and Gladstone, during the Divorce Bill debates in 1857, and 'the Colonels' during the debates on Army reform in 1870, were held to have somewhat overstepped the limits deemed suitable among gentlemen.

The Irish members had no ambition to be considered gentlemen, and every intention of making unworkable the traditional Parliamentary procedure which had answered the needs of their oppressors. That was the situation which faced Gladstone in 1880 ; he was at first bewildered by it, and he played for time. He knew, however, that it was impossible, when people are on the verge of starvation, to apply the conventional laws of property, and he scandalized the Whig patricians by introducing, as a stopgap measure, a Bill to compel Irish landlords to compensate tenants in certain circumstances when they evicted them.

In the Commons twenty Liberals voted against that measure, and many more abstained from voting. Lord Lansdowne, a great Anglo-Irish magnate, resigned in protest from his office as Under-Secretary for India. Gladstone forced the Bill through the Commons but the Lords rejected it on 3 August, 1880, by 282 votes to 51. In that year the number of evictions in Ireland rose to some 10,500 (compared with some 2,200 in 1877) and the Land League adopted the weapon of the boycott. It started when Captain Boycott, the agent of Lord Erne, was treated as a leper ; his servants departed ; shopkeepers, stablemen, laundresses, refused to serve him ; postmen mislaid his letters ; his crops remained unharvested ; no-one would answer when he spoke. The movement spread like wildfire through the Irish countryside ; it was applied to anyone who accepted a holding from which a tenant had been evicted, as well as to landlords and their agents.

Gladstone resolved to introduce a new Land Bill which would, he hoped, remedy the defects of the Act which he had carried in 1870. It was so complicated that it was said that no-one could understand it except Gladstone and Sir Henry Thring, the Treasury Counsel, who helped him to draft it. That measure for some weeks absorbed almost the whole of Gladstone's time, but great pressure was brought to bear on him, while he was preparing it, to suspend habeas corpus in Ireland and to pass a new and drastic Coercion Act. W. E. Forster, the Chief Secretary for Ireland, and Lord Cowper, the Lord-Lieutenant, insisted that unless law and order were restored, the Land Bill's prospects in Parliament would be fatally prejudiced. Gladstone noted that he yielded reluctantly, bearing in mind:

'the special commission under which the Government had taken office. It related to the foreign policy of the country, the whole spirit and effect of which we were to reconstruct. This work had not yet been fully accomplished, and it seemed to me that the effective prosecution of it was our first and highest duty. I therefore submitted.'

Gladstone had no love for the hirsute and graceless Forster whom he considered 'a very impracticable man'. Forster was known as 'Buckshot', because he had advocated its use as a means of dispersing mobs. In December, 1880, Gladstone was exasperated to hear reports that Forster had been conducting himself wildly at the Athenæum Club—behaving, Hamilton recorded, 'more like an inebriated or demented man than one merely who has lost his nerve'. The Coercion Act, which virtually gave the Viceroy power to lock up anyone he pleased for as long as he pleased, was passed by the Commons on 1 February, 1881, after a sitting which had lasted 41 hours. The obstructive tactics of the Irish members were only ended by a *coup d'état* on the part of the Speaker which had been concerted previously with Gladstone. The debate was closed when the Speaker put the question from the Chair on his own responsibility. When his ruling was challenged the next day he said that he had acted out of a sense of the duty which he owed to the House ; he was rewarded by a storm of cheering in which no-one joined more lustily than Gladstone. With characteristic impulsiveness, Gladstone begged the Speaker to permit his name to be submitted to the Queen for the immediate award of a G.C.B. The Speaker had to excuse himself on the ground that he was expected to appear impartial.

On 3 February Gladstone gave notice of a Resolution for altering the House's rules of debate by the introduction of a compulsory closure. It was carried after most of the Irish members had been suspended, and the new device was subsequently greatly extended in order to preserve the machinery of Parliament from breaking down in new conditions. Many remedies were tried from time to time in order to overcome the obstructive tactics of the Irish members, and nothing in Gladstone's career caused him more uneasiness, except the Queen's continued harshness and hostility. Gladstone worshipped the ancient institutions of his country with a fervid intensity which it would be difficult to exaggerate. The breakdown in the traditional Parliamentary procedure strengthened his moody wish for retirement, and weakened his confidence in every field. In a confidential talk with Sir Henry Ponsonby in March, 1881, Gladstone said:

'My day is drawing to a close and when a man gets worn out he gets gloomy. Formerly I saw no reason why Monarchy should not go on here for hundreds of years, but I confess the way Monarchy has been brought to the front by the late Government in political and foreign affairs has shaken my confidence . . . Some of those you live with probably accuse me of being a radical. I am not. . . . But when I am gone, younger men who take my place will either be far more advanced than I ever have been, or will be forced on by the extreme liberalism of the masses. I dread this . . .'

With the aid of the closure, the Coercion Act was carried; and on 7 April, 1881, after paying that price, Gladstone introduced his Land Bill in regard to which Parnell had not been consulted. It conceded to Irish tenants what came to be known as 'the three Fs'—fair rents, fixity or security of tenure, and the right to sell freely their holdings when they wished. Power was taken to set up judicial tribunals to review rents, and to prevent any tenant from being evicted so long as he paid a rent fixed by a tribunal.

Although it was calculated that over 100,000 tenants who were in arrears with their rent were excluded from the benefits of the Land Bill, a resounding blow was dealt, nevertheless, to entrenched doctrines about the sanctity of property, and the Duke of Argyll resigned from the Cabinet in protest:

'You think you have the Cabinet behind you,' he wrote to Gladstone (13 April, 1881). 'I wish you had heard the talk when you went off to see the Queen and left us mice without the cat . . . The Cabinet has submitted to what they think political necessity—one main ingredient in which has been your authority in proposing *anything.*'

The Queen used her great influence to avert a clash between the two Houses, and the Bill became law on 22 August, 1881. The issue had been doubtful until the last, and the Queen grudgingly admitted to Lord Granville that Gladstone had for once laid aside his 'high-handed dictator style'. Before the Bill passed the Commons it had occupied 58 sittings and Gladstone had personally fought its battle, clause by clause. *The Times* remarked on 22 July that it was only occasionally, at official banquets, that the public was reminded that the Cabinet contained other members, besides the Prime Minister.

The way was thus prepared for the creation of that landowning peasantry which after a long period of troubles has proved to be the basis of a revived Irish national life. The Irish Nationalists, however, did what they could to wreck the Act. They tried, without much success, to prevent members of the Land League from making applications to the rent tribunals, on the ground that rents due to alien landlords were contrary to natural justice. They argued that further concessions could only be extracted from the Government if terroristic outrages were to continue. In a speech at Leeds on 7 October, 1881, Gladstone issued a clear warning to Parnell:

'For the first time in the history of Christendom a body—a small body—of men have arisen who are not ashamed to preach in Ireland the doctrines of public plunder . . . I take as a representative of the opinions I denounce the name of a gentleman of considerable ability— Mr. Parnell, the Member for Cork . . . He desires, gentlemen, to arrest the operation of the Land Act . . . We are determined that no force, and no fear of force, and no fear of ruin through force, shall . . . prevent the Irish people from having the benefit of the Land Act . . . If . . . there is still to be fought a final conflict in Ireland between law on the one side, and sheer lawlessness on the other . . . then, I say, gentlemen, without hesitation, the resources of civilization are not yet exhausted.'

Parnell retorted by denouncing Gladstone as 'this masquerading knight-errant, this pretending champion of the rights of every nation except those of the Irish nation'. The Prime Minister, he said, had 'thrown off the mask', and revealed himself as a man 'prepared to carry fire and sword into your homesteads unless you humbly abase yourselves before him and before the landlords of your country'. The Cabinet met on 12 October to consider that challenge, and decided that 'the resources of civilization' should forthwith be called into use. Parnell was arrested under the Coercion Act the next morning and thrown into gaol; Gladstone announced the news to a wildly cheering audience at the Guildhall where he had gone to receive the Freedom of the City of London.

The Land League declared a rent-stike and was proscribed by the Government; its leaders were arrested and imprisoned. Gladstone declared at Liverpool (26 October) that the League was seeking to march 'through rapine to the dismemberment of the Empire'. In Ireland there was in consequence a sharp increase in political crime, and a number of extremist secret societies sprang up which alarmed Parnell because they jeopardized his leadership. For that reason, and for another very private reason, Parnell became anxious to negotiate. He wanted to leave prison in order to reassert his authority, and he wanted also to be reunited with his mistress, Mrs. O'Shea, the wife of one of his followers in the House of Commons, with whom he had fallen in love with all the passionate intensity of his pent-up, lonely nature.

In April, 1882, accordingly, an understanding was negotiated with Parnell by Joseph Chamberlain on Gladstone's behalf through two channels. One channel (Justin McCarthy) was reputable; the other (W. H. O'Shea, the husband of Parnell's mistress) was not, and its use was to prove unfortunate. Gladstone was unworldly, and in perfect innocence he was content to negotiate with Parnell through O'Shea and through Mrs. O'Shea, although Lord Granville had written casually to him as early as 24 May, 1882, that Mrs. O'Shea [1] was said to be Parnell's mistress. O'Shea's sole motive was to obtain ministerial office, and Gladstone persisted in thinking that he was under obligations to O'Shea.

As a result of those secret conversations, Parnell and two other Irish members were released from Kilmainham Gaol on 4 May, 1882, on condition that Parnell would support the Land Act, and on the understanding that Gladstone would introduce a Bill to extend the benefits of that Act to tenants who were in arrears with their rent. W. E. Forster resigned from the Cabinet in protest, and was replaced as Chief Secretary for Ireland by Lord Frederick Cavendish, whom Gladstone loved like a son. Lord Cowper, the Lord-Lieutenant, resigned at the same time on grounds of ill-health, and was succeeded by Lord Spencer, who was given a seat in the Cabinet.

[1] She was Catherine Page Wood, a niece of Lord Hatherley who had been Lord Chancellor in Gladstone's first Government, and a sister of Field-Marshal Sir Evelyn Wood, V.C.

GLADSTONE COMMITTING TREASON

Treaty of Kilmainham, April, 1882

Lord Frederick was so little known to the public that his appointment was received with derision ; but the laughter was swiftly hushed. He crossed to Dublin on 5 May and was stabbed to death by terrorists the following afternoon while walking in Phœnix Park with his permanent under-secretary, T. H. Burke, who was also murdered. The terrorists had no idea who Lord Frederick was ; they killed him because he tried to protect his companion whose life they had resolved to take.[1]

Gladstone and his wife were dining that evening at the Austrian Embassy. Mrs. Gladstone had gone on to a party at the Admiralty, while her husband walked home alone to Downing Street. At the Admiralty Mrs. Gladstone was asked to return at once to Downing Street where Hamilton broke the news to her. As he did so, Gladstone arrived, so that it was impossible to break the news to him by degrees. Mrs. Gladstone and her husband went down on their knees in the inner hall and prayed together for a few moments. Then they drove to 21, Carlton House Terrace, where Lady Frederick Cavendish lived. They arrived shortly before one o'clock in the morning, and were received by Lord Hartington who said that his sister, Lady Louisa Egerton, had already broken the news. Lord Granville arrived a few minutes later.

In her journal Lady Frederick Cavendish wrote :

'Uncle William . . . his face . . . like a prophet's in its look of faith and strength . . . came up and almost took me in his arms, and his first words were, "Father, forgive them, for they know not what they do." Then he said to me, "Be assured it will not be in vain," and across all my agony there fell a bright ray of hope, and I saw in a vision Ireland at peace, and my darling's life-blood accepted as a sacrifice for Christ's sake, to help to bring this to pass . . . I said to him as he was leaving me, "Uncle William, you must never blame yourself for sending him." He said, "Oh no, there can be no question of that." ' Gladstone was never adroit at expressing deep personal feeling, but Lady Frederick said, after he had left, 'He is like an oak to lean against.' She recorded her belief that God had 'sent Uncle William with a message straight from Him, which alone at that moment could give me strength . . . the assurance that my darling's life was not given in vain'.

The murder of Lord Frederick Cavendish, like the recall of Lord

[1] The terrorists were tracked down two years later and brought to trial. Four were hanged ; others were imprisoned for life.

Fitzwilliam in 1795, put an end to any hope of immediate reconciliation between the English and the Irish peoples. W. E. Forster had already created an atmosphere of suspicion on 5 May while explaining to the House of Commons his reasons for resigning. He had then accused the Government of submitting to blackmail. He made that atmosphere worse ten days later, when the House was debating Gladstone's unofficial deal with Parnell. Gladstone was challenged to produce documentary evidence of Parnell's willingness to support the Land Act, and with the Prime Minister's consent Parnell rose to read a copy of the letter he had written to O'Shea from prison on 28 April, and which he had asked O'Shea to lay before the Government.

Parnell had obtained a copy of that letter from O'Shea. After he had read it, Forster rose to inform the House that an important sentence had been omitted from the copy of the letter which Parnell had read. That sentence expressed Parnell's willingness ' to co-operate cordially for the future with the Liberal Party in forwarding Liberal measures and measures of general reform '.

The next day (16 May) Gladstone was subjected to severe cross-examination about a statement which he had made to the effect that no compact of any kind existed between the Liberal and the Irish Parties. He held firmly to that statement, but Arthur Balfour wounded him very deeply indeed by saying : ' I do not believe that any such transaction can be quoted from the annals of our political or parliamentary history . . . It stands alone in its infamy.' He, and his uncle, Lord Salisbury, in the House of Lords, accused Gladstone of staging a shabby political manœuvre, of prevaricating about it, and of trying to pass it off as an honourable transaction. Gladstone described Balfour's speech as intolerable and disgraceful. Chamberlain explained that O'Shea, in originally communicating Parnell's letter to him, had asked leave to withdraw the controversial sentence ; the incident had, however, made so little impression on his mind that he had not even noticed that that had been done when Parnell read his letter to the House.

The Conservatives suspected that Gladstone was bidding for Irish support in order to strengthen his hands in framing radical legislation in defiance of the Whig section of the Liberal Party. Gladstone had in fact offended the Radicals by his policy of coercion in Ireland, by his neglect of social reform at home, and by sending Lord Frederick Cavendish—a Whig—to Ireland ; and he was anxious now to appease them. He appointed George Otto Trevelyan, an indubitable Radical, to succeed Lord Frederick, but he was compelled, in deference to public opinion, to introduce (11 May) an even more drastic Coercion Bill. The Opposition's attempt to read a sinister meaning into the Kilmainham agreement did Gladstone some harm, but Balfour's motion that the House should adjourn in order to give the Government an opportunity to explain its actions in greater detail was not pressed to a division.

To balance the new Coercion Act, which was applied with rigour and success, Gladstone introduced (15 May) an Arrears Bill, which had the effect of cancelling arrears of rent in cases when tenants occupying land worth less than £30 a year were unable to pay. The opposition was almost hysterical, and there was again, for a time, a danger of a constitutional crisis, for Gladstone threatened to appeal to the country if the Lords rejected the Bill. Many Irish landlords, however, felt that it was better to receive some rent than none, and Lord Salisbury, who continued to the last to denounce the Bill as an act of robbery and confiscation, was deserted by most of his followers. The Arrears Act became law on 10 August, 1882.

It was calculated that Gladstone had reduced rents in Ireland on the average by twenty per cent. The situation remained dangerous, but on 30 August, 1884, Gladstone was able to announce at Edinburgh that whereas in 1881 there had been 4439 reported agrarian crimes in Ireland, in 1883 the number had dropped to 870. Parnell was now content to bide his time and to watch for opportunities of extorting a measure of Home Rule by exploiting Party differences in England. Gladstone turned to face his difficulties in Egypt, and to consider what steps he could take, under pressure from Joseph Chamberlain, to satisfy radical opinion at home.

On account of lack of time, Gladstone postponed regretfully but indefinitely his plans for establishing a system of local government in the countryside, and for reforming the government of London. In April, 1883, however he pleased the Radicals by countenancing a Bill for putting down corrupt practices at elections. In the same month he gave Government support to a Resolution condemning the system of licensed brothels which had been established by the Contagious Diseases Acts of 1864, 1866, and 1869 in eighteen ports and garrison towns. At the same time he arranged to prepare and to pass through Parliament early in 1884 another large-scale extension of the franchise.

The Corrupt Practices Act of 1883 was almost as important as the Ballot Act of 1872 ; but in its case Gladstone, for the first time while serving as Prime Minister, took no part in the drafting of a major Bill. He was content to give warm praise and encouragement to Sir Henry James, the Attorney-General, to whose hands he entrusted the measure. Gladstone felt, if possible, even more strongly about the question of licensed brothels, but he left the Resolution to be drafted and introduced by (Sir) James Stansfeld, a Radical Non-conformist. The Resolution was carried, but it was not converted into law until three years later, when the Acts which had established a system of licensed and regulated prostitution in certain localities were repealed without debate to Gladstone's heartfelt satisfaction.

Between 1882 and 1886, malicious stories about Gladstone's rescue work in the streets of London by night were being circulated more freely in society than at any previous period in Gladstone's career. Lord Granville, Lord Rosebery, Edward Hamilton, and Herbert Gladstone (who was an unpaid Lord of the Treasury) did their utmost on a number of occasions to impress upon the Prime Minister the nature and gravity of the risks he ran. On 10 February, 1882, Lord Granville and Lord Rosebery actually spun a coin to decide which of the two should undertake the delicate and disagreeable task of remonstrating with Gladstone. Lord Rosebery lost the toss but he achieved nothing. For years Gladstone refused, perversely, to recognize the need to change his ways. He always listened, and sometimes said that the night walks, in which he had indulged for half a century, were the mainstay of his health. One peculiarly delicate matter which caused anxiety in Gladstone's entourage was his friendship with Mrs. Langtry, ' the Jersey lily ', who was probably the loveliest ' professional beauty ' of the day. Lord Rosebery alone among Gladstone's friends had the courage to speak openly to him about that acquaintance.

Mrs. Langtry was a friend of the Prince of Wales, and rightly or wrongly her reputation was such that at that period few houses would receive her. The Prince of Wales was always charming to Gladstone, and often paid him little attentions ; and Gladstone, since the failure of his efforts on the Prince's behalf in the early 1870s, had felt a very warm sympathy with the Prince. He loved to dine at Marlborough House, and he enjoyed staying at Sandringham ; it was noticed that whenever he did so he would lay aside his lifelong prejudice against smoking, and that he would exhale cigarette smoke slowly and reflectively through his nostrils, as the Prince did. Gladstone knew that the Prince desired that Mrs. Langtry should be received and not cold-shouldered in society, and in his ingenuous and simple way he decided to call on her himself. He found her charming. He gave her his favourite 'goody' books to read and allowed her to make social capital out of the acquaintance. With his habitual unworldliness he also gave her the code-sign which enabled a very few privileged people to send him, when they wished, letters enclosed in double envelopes which escaped being opened by the private secretaries. Mrs. Langtry alarmed the secretaries greatly by the use which she made of that privilege.

Gladstone only saw Mrs. Langtry occasionally, but he was visibly and invariably refreshed by the society of pretty women. Mrs. Langtry was so extraordinarily beautiful that crowds used to surround her wherever she drove or walked in London. Gladstone's imprudence would have been dangerous to a man in his position at any time, but it was especially dangerous in view of the malicious gossip which was then so widely current. It is another tribute to the radiant integrity of his character that despite the anxiety of his intimates, no harm resulted from that wholly innocent indiscretion.

*   *   *

Before he prepared his Representation of the People Bill, Gladstone, with his wife and his daughter Mary, went for a short cruise in the *Pembroke Castle* (4,000 tons) as the guest of the owner, Sir Donald Currie. Among his fellow-guests were the Tennysons, Sir William Harcourt and his son, 'Lulu', the beautiful Laura Tennant, Sir Andrew Clark, and others. Gladstone informed the Queen that the plan was to visit some of the islands in the Hebrides, and then to sail round the British Isles. The weather was, however, so perfect and the sea so calm (Gladstone was a poor sailor), that a proposal by Alfred Tennyson that the yacht should cross the North Sea to Norway and Denmark was immediately and unanimously adopted. It was noticed that the Prime Minister and the Poet Laureate were as jovial as boys together; and the unheralded arrival at Copenhagen of two such famous men made a considerable stir. On 17 September the Gladstones dined with the King and Queen of Denmark; they met at dinner, among others, the Emperor and Empress of Russia, the King and Queen of Greece, and the Princess of Wales. A party was given for all the Royalties on board the yacht the next day, at which

Tennyson read some poems, and Gladstone made a speech. The Prime Minister was warmly congratulated by the Empress of Russia on the stand which he had made on behalf of Montenegro. Three days later (21 September) the yacht put into Gravesend, and Gladstone disembarked with the feeling that he had enjoyed a more than usually agreeable holiday. He had had long talks with Tennyson about Homer and Dante, and he had succeeded in persuading the poet to accept a peerage. Gladstone had written to the Queen from Copenhagen to explain the circumstances in which he had gone abroad without seeking her permission, and to apologize. He had been critical on a number of occasions of the Queen's lack of consideration in spending long periods abroad without appointing Councillors of State to act for her in her absence, and in his own case he anticipated no trouble.

The Queen was, however, as she informed Lord Granville (18 September) 'very indignant'. The Prime Minister, she wrote, 'and especially one not gifted with prudence, is not a person who can go about *where* he likes with impunity . . . The Queen believes everyone is much astonished at this escapade.' She told Gladstone (20 September) that she gave him full credit for not having reflected, and that she believed that he had avoided all political discussions with foreign Sovereigns :

'But she doubts the public believing this . . . The Prime Minister of Great Britain cannot move about (especially when every step he takes is reported—she knows not by whom, or whether a Reporter was on board with him ?) as a private individual, and any Trip like the one he has just taken will lead, as she has above observed, to Political speculations which it is better to avoid.'

Gladstone for once told Lord Granville (22 September) that the Queen's letter was 'somewhat unmannerly'. He resented especially the rude and unfounded question about the press reporter. He replied to the Queen on the same day, acknowledging his responsibility and regretting that he had not anticipated her displeasure :
'Increasing weariness of mind under public cares for which he considers himself less and less fitted, may have blunted the faculty of anticipation, with which he was never very largely endowed.' He told Hamilton that the Queen was jealous of the deference paid to an old man of whom she strongly disapproved, while she herself lived to a large extent withdrawn from public view. He could not, however, put the incident out of his mind. A root cause of the

Queen's jealousy was her rigid adherence to the old-fashioned view that all questions involving foreign policy and national prestige were the peculiar preserve of the Sovereign and of the patrician governing class. She considered that Gladstone's ostentatious action in submitting such questions to the untutored judgement of the masses in Midlothian and elsewhere was not merely democratic, but crazy: 'Such conduct', she had written to Sir Henry Ponsonby (16 April, 1880), 'is *unheard-of*, and the only excuse is—that he is not quite sane.' Lord Granville had caused Gladstone great disquiet at Christmas, 1880, by incautiously repeating to him a hint which he had received from Ponsonby about the reasons for the Queen's dislike of Gladstone. Lord Granville had written to the Queen in November to congratulate her upon inviting Gladstone to Balmoral, and the Queen had considered that letter presumptuous. She wrote to Ponsonby (November, 1880):

'Tho' *never personally* liking Mr. Gladstone . . . the feeling which is uppermost in her mind . . . is the feeling of great *displeasure* for the great harm he did *when out* of office, which told against the late Government and brought all the present difficulties upon us: and this feeling must be lasting . . . Sir Henry could perhaps give Lord Granville a hint *as from himself entirely* about this.'

Gladstone himself thought that the Queen's partisan conduct would end by bringing the Throne into disrepute. The notes which he made of his Cabinet meetings contain frequent references to the Queen's intolerable and ill-judged attempts at interference, and to her inadmissible desire to be told the views of individual Ministers. Gladstone complained to Lord Rosebery at Hawarden (5 January, 1883) that 'the Queen alone is enough to kill any man'. He told Hamilton (3 December, 1883) that the best method open to him for strengthening the Throne was to extend the base of the pyramid of which it was the apex by widening the franchise. To that task, accordingly, Gladstone's best efforts were directed strenuously for the next twelve months. He was, however, distracted throughout by a crisis in the Sudan, which arose directly out of his intervention in Egypt.

The Sudan, which had been under Egyptian rule for sixty years, was disturbed in 1881 by a revolutionary movement of its own. Gladstone considered that he had no responsibility for the Sudan, and he made an ingenuous distinction between Arabi's nationalist revolt in Egypt and the Mahdi's nationalist revolt in the Sudan, which wore a cloak of religion.   Gladstone, who had crushed Arabi, described the Sudanese as a people 'struggling rightly to be free'.   Nevertheless his Government did not stop the Egyptian Government from making an attempt to reconquer the Sudan; and that attempt involved Great Britain.

In November, 1883, an Egyptian army, ten thousand strong, commanded by an Englishman, Colonel Hicks, who held the rank of General in the Egyptian Army, marched into the Southern desert to meet the Mahdi.   It was annihilated on 5 November, and there were virtually no survivors.   The Sudan was at the Mahdi's feet.   The Queen and the Opposition considered that such a blow to British prestige ought to be avenged at once.   The effect on Mohammedan opinion in India had to be taken into account: 'These are wild Arabs', the Queen wrote to Gladstone (9 February, 1884), 'and they would not stand against regular good Troops at all . . .   We have taken a great deal of responsibility upon us in Egypt—but not enough . . .'   She added that the British name would be indelibly disgraced and that public opinion would never forgive Gladstone, if the Sudan were not liberated as soon as possible from 'murder, and rapine, and utter confusion'.

Gladstone considered that Great Britain had already taken on too much responsibility.   He was willing, however, to admit that the British had a moral duty to aid the Egyptian Government in withdrawing the scattered Egyptian garrisons in the Sudan, which were all in danger of being massacred by the Mahdi's fanatical followers.

Hitherto, responsible Conservatives had found it difficult to attack Gladstone's Egyptian policy, because, in the main, they approved of it.   It had been left to Lord Randolph Churchill, the leader of 'the Fourth Party', to throw away all inhibitions.   He had unblushingly expressed sympathy with Arabi's nationalist movement in Egypt and had described the Egyptian war as a surrender to alien stock-brokers and money-lenders.   A good example of his method is seen in a speech which he made at Edinburgh, on 18 December, 1883, in the heart of Gladstone's constituency of Midlothian.   He accused Gladstone, 'the leader, the idol, the demi-god of the Liberal Party', of an act of criminal aggression against Egypt, and demanded that he should be thrown out of Egypt 'bag and baggage':

'He came among them with his armies and his fleets; destroyed their towns; devastated their country; slaughtered their thousands; and flung back those struggling wretches into the morass of oppression, back into the toils of their taskmasters. The revolution of Arabi was the movement of a nation ; like all revolutions it had its good side, and its bad. You must never, for purposes of practical politics, criticize too minutely the origins, the authors, or the courses of revolutions . . . Would you undo the French Revolution because of the Reign of Terror ? Would you undo the Revolution of Naples because Garibaldi might not be altogether a man to your mind ? You know you would not. You know that those revolutions were justified by atrocious governments.'

Such cynical brilliance and superb patrician insolence exasperated Gladstone, who attributed Churchill's attitude to the demoralizing legacy of Disraeli. He was, however, firmly resolved to undertake no fresh adventures in the Sudan. The Government knew nothing about the details of the military situation there, and in an unhappy hour Gladstone acquiesced in a decision taken jointly on 18 January, 1884, by Lord Hartington, Lord Granville, Lord Northbrook, and Sir Charles Dilke (President of the Local Government Board since December, 1882) to send Charles Gordon, C.B., a Major-General of Engineers, to the Sudan. General Gordon was given no formal directive, but he was ordered to go out and report on the best means of evacuating the Egyptian garrisons.

Gladstone, who had never met Gordon, was resting at Hawarden when that decision was taken ; he telegraphed his concurrence the next day. Lord Salisbury, when he read the announcement, thought that the Government had taken leave of its senses, for Gordon was a famous warrior and the last man who was likely to be willing to conduct an inglorious retreat from a country of which he had already acted once as Governor, under the Khedive, between 1877-1879.

Like 'Lawrence of Arabia', Gordon exercised an extraordinary fascination over his fellow-countrymen. Sword in hand and Bible in pocket he had enjoyed a romantic career of warfare in China, Africa, India, and the Crimea. Fearless, erratic, brilliant, perverse, always notoriously undisciplined, Gordon's power of self-deception matched that of Gladstone and his religious fanaticism matched that of the Mahdi. It was an inexcusable error to send such a man on such a mission.

The Government believed for a week or two that it had found a convenient way out of a temporary difficulty, and Lord Granville wrote jubilantly to the Queen (15 January, 1884) : ' He is a genius and a splendid character.' The Queen cordially agreed, and only wondered why Gordon had not been appointed 'long ago'. The Press hailed the announcement with a whole-hearted satisfaction, which probably masked a hope, in some quarters, that the unpopular policy of evacuation might now be reconsidered on the spot. General Gordon was seen off from London at Victoria Station by the Duke of Cambridge, by Lord Granville, and by Lord Wolseley, the victor of Tel-el-Kebir. Every schoolboy's heart beat faster at the thought of that famous knight-errant speeding towards the desert—to adventure of a kind utterly at variance with the prosaic mission which he had been sent to accomplish—to a fate which was to convulse nation and Empire and to bring down on Gladstone's unbowed but by no means blameless head an elemental cataract of ridicule, hatred, and contempt.

CHAPTER 13

STRUGGLING TO BE FREE

1884-1886

WHEN Gladstone on 28 February, 1884, introduced his Representation of the People Bill to the House of Commons within six weeks of General Gordon's departure for the Sudan, he was already aware that he had inadvertently committed his Government's fate into Gordon's hands. He cut out and preserved a cartoon from *Punch* (6 February) which showed him being carried on Gordon's back, and he told his family ruefully that Gordon would probably cause the death of his Government. As early as 9 February, 1884, the Queen wrote to warn Gladstone that she 'trembled' for Gordon's safety and that the consequences of any disaster would be catastrophic. Gladstone's attention appeared to be exclusively given to the franchise problem, and to the dangers which threatened when the Lords opposed the Bill, and when Chamberlain and others raised the cry, 'Peers versus People'. Gladstone never, as Chamberlain noted, seemed to 'bend his mind' to the issue which confronted him as a result of Gordon's defiance of the orders which he had received.

Instead of proceeding as he had first intended to the Red Sea coast of the Sudan, Gordon called at Cairo where he arranged matters to his liking with the British Consul-General, Sir Evelyn Baring (Lord Cromer), who was the real ruler of Egypt. Lord Granville weakly acquiesced in Gordon's formal appointment as Governor-General of the Sudan. Gordon argued that the tribes would obey him if he were to resume the appointment which he had held five years before, and that his mission would in consequence be accomplished more easily. That mission was, in fact, transformed. Disdaining an escort, Gordon proceeded at once to Khartoum which he reached on 18 February. His dangerous journey was followed at home with breathless excitement. As soon as he was installed in the Palace at Khartoum, Gordon began to bombard the authorities at home and in Cairo with a variety of plans for smashing the Mahdi and for settling the future of the Sudan.

Gladstone bitterly resented the continuous storms of jingo emotion which Gordon's conduct and situation provoked, and which the Opposition exploited to the full. Gordon threw to the winds

GETTING A LIFT!

OR ' THE GRAND OLD MAN OF THE [RED] SEA '

PUNCH, February 2, 1884

whatever plans of evacuation he may previously have started to form. He considered that Gladstone did not understand the code of military honour which forbade him to retreat; he preferred to think of himself as the man on the spot, in sole charge of a vast country and of a difficult war. With refreshing candour he confided to his Journal (19 September, 1884):

'I own to having been very insubordinate to Her Majesty's Government and its officials, but it is in my nature and I cannot help it. I fear I have not even tried to play battledore and shuttlecock with them. I know if I was chief, I would never employ myself, for I am incorrigible.'

The Queen cared nothing and public opinion cared very little about the details of the orders which had been issued to General Gordon. The nation's affection went out to the beloved figure of the lonely hero at his post of danger, and Gladstone's unwillingness to send an expedition to his support or rescue, outraged men's patriotic pride. As the Mahdi's forces closed in on Khartoum during March, 1884, communications became precarious. The Cabinet was, however, convinced that Gordon was in a position to withdraw if he so desired, and on 26 March it decided that the date and mode of withdrawal must be left to Gordon's discretion. Gladstone told Lord Granville four years later (12 March, 1888) that it would have been 'madness and crime' to comply with Gordon's demand for reinforcements: 'It was his absolute duty to withdraw; and I have never heard his power to do so disputed.'

Gladstone continued to hope in vain that Gordon would presently retreat in compliance with the orders which he had received, and he did his best to be reasonable without altering his basic policy. He had to take into account the feeling of a large section of the Radical group in Parliament that a relief expedition was wrong in principle.

One of Gordon's first actions on reaching Khartoum was to ask for the despatch of a notorious slave-trader, named Zebehr, to help him with his task. Gladstone tried to induce the Cabinet to agree, but he had to desist in face of the adamant hostility of the Radicals and of the anti-slavery enthusiasts who found a Parliamentary mouthpiece in W. E. Forster. Lord Granville, who was now thoroughly alarmed, suggested that Gordon should be recalled. Gladstone, however, begged Granville not to press that demand, which would have had no chance of being endorsed by a majority of the Cabinet.

At the War Office, where Lord Hartington had succeeded Childers in December, 1882, as Secretary for War, the comparative advantages of different routes for a relief expedition were being exhaustively examined. As late as 29 July, Lord Hartington informed the Cabinet that it was impossible to say whether or not General Gordon was in a position to leave Khartoum without assistance ; he urged, however, that preparations should be expedited in case an emergency should arise. Gladstone minuted two days later that ' to send an expedition . . . at the present time would be to act in the teeth of evidence which, however imperfect, is far from being trivial, and would be a grave and dangerous error '.

Public opinion in the meantime was growing extremely agitated, and the Queen was deeply concerned. As early as 13 May the Government's majority on a Motion of Censure dropped to 28 in the Commons. On that occasion Gladstone declared that an expedition would involve ' a war of conquest against a people struggling to be free. [Oh ! Oh !] Yes, those people are struggling to be free, and they are rightly struggling to be free.'

The ingenuous distinction, which Gladstone's statement implied, between the nationalist movement in Egypt which he had smashed with a clear conscience in 1882, and the nationalist movement in the Sudan which he now appeared to welcome, was incomprehensible to many even of his warmest admirers. Forster, in his blunt way, told the House that everyone except the Prime Minister was convinced that Gordon was in danger, ' and I attribute his not being convinced to his wonderful power of persuasion. He can persuade most people of most things, and above all he can persuade himself of almost anything.'

It is impossible to discount the force of that gibe. Gladstone manifested his power of simple, honest self-deception more frequently towards the end of his life than he had done at its beginning. One perfect instance of it occurred in a speech which he made at Penmaenmawr on 3 October, 1882, when he was drawing a distinction between his own action in ordering the invasion of Egypt, and the many flagrant acts of imperialist aggression which had been perpetrated by Disraeli. He declared in all sincerity : ' We have carried out this war from a love of peace, and, I may say, on the principle of peace.'

By the beginning of August, 1884, it was obvious that public opinion would tolerate no further delay. Pressed by Lord Hartington and Lord Selborne—and faced with gentle pressure even by Lord Granville, as Gladstone dolefully recorded—the Prime Minister asked the House of Commons on 5 August for a grant of £300,000 to enable operations to be undertaken for the rescue of General Gordon in case of need. He grumbled to Hamilton that that would probably mean 2*d*. on the income-tax in the long run. An expeditionary force was mobilized in Cairo, and Lord Wolseley arrived there on 9 September to take over the command. Strong enemy opposition was expected and emphasis was therefore laid upon caution rather than upon speed. It was not until 5 October that a force, ten thousand strong, began its 1,600-mile advance up the Nile to Khartoum, while Gladstone groaned inwardly at the manner in which his hand had been forced. He considered that Gordon had defied him, and that nothing could avail now to expiate the General's insubordination except some supreme success 'like Nelson at Trafalgar', which should bear a manifest token of the blessing and sanction of the Almighty. Far away, in the Palace at Khartoum, Gordon was vastly amused by Gladstone's dilemma. He noted in his Journal (26 September) that anyone who had ventured to predict that Gladstone would despatch two armies into Egypt would have been scouted as a madman : 'I like to take things in a light-hearted way,' Gordon wrote, with an almost audible chuckle. '. . . Man proposes—God disposes.'

*　　　*　　　*

Against that darkening background, Gladstone fought to reward the multitudes who had hailed him in Midlothian, and who often at that period decorated their tables with sweet-williams in his honour. He proposed to increase the electorate from some three millions to some five millions by extending to country-dwellers the principle of household suffrage which had been conferred upon townsmen in 1867. He told the Commons (28 February, 1884) that he made the proposal in fulfilment of his Parliamentary mission, and that he took his stand on the broad principle that the strength of a country is increased in proportion to the number of capable citizens who enjoy the vote. He argued that the cause of liberty could not have triumphed during the American Civil War except 'in a nation where every capable citizen was enfranchised and had a direct and energetic interest in the well-being and the unity of the State'.

The Bill passed the Commons without great difficulty on 27 June, but on 8 July the Lords decided not to pass it unless a measure for redrawing the electoral map of Great Britain were incorporated with it. As Gladstone had promised to introduce a Redistribution Bill as soon as possible, the difference between the Houses was not wide ;

but tempers were frayed. Gladstone was unwilling to delay because he was afraid of imperilling his Reform Bill. The Lords did not care to deliver a frontal attack upon the principle of reform ; they were, however, resolved that the electoral interests of the Conservative Party should be adequately protected in the necessary scheme of redistribution. Gladstone warned the Peers on 26 June that a collision between the two Houses would end in the defeat of the Lords and that it might jeopardize the existing form of the Constitution. He was rebuked by the Queen (28 June) for his language, and asked to adopt a more conciliatory tone.

Gladstone wished to be conciliatory, but he had to manage his Radical followers, and he was provoked when the Queen informed him (15 July) that the House of Lords reflected the ' true feeling of the country ' better than the House of Commons. Gladstone told Lord Granville (16 July) that it was useless to quarrel with ' Her Infallibility ', but he was seriously concerned about his power to control the Radicals. He had helped to overcome Lord Hartington's opposition by threatening to resign and to request the Queen to send for Lord Hartington. He had less control over Chamberlain, who menaced the Peers openly at the Devonshire Club on 23 July, and who subsequently, in a series of violent speeches, called upon them to mend their ways or take the consequences. The reports of all those speeches were read by the Queen with scrupulous care ; she constantly abused Gladstone on Chamberlain's account, and called upon him (25 July) to restrain his ' wild colleagues and followers ... and not allow Agitators and Demagogues to mislead the people '. In reply to a further outburst from the Queen (10 August), Gladstone told her that while he had felt able to ask his Radical colleagues for an assurance that they would not ' at this stage of the controversy ' raise ' questions of organic change in the House of Lords ', he had obtained no promise that they would maintain silence ' as to its past and present working '.

When Gladstone went up to Midlothian on 27 August for a tour of his constituency, which was, as always, superbly stage-managed by Lord Rosebery, he was careful to keep a guard upon his tongue. He was impressed by the aplomb of his host's head-coachman when one of the carriage horses fell down and died of heart-failure. In reply to Gladstone's expression of regret, the man coolly remarked, " We have four more of the same colour at Mentmore."

Gladstone sent the Queen a memorandum on the constitutional

issue which impressed her (26 August) by its 'fairness and impartiality'. He went over one day to see her at Balmoral, when he was staying in the neighbourhood, and she told the Duke of Argyll (7 October) : ' Mr. Gladstone was plausible and amiable when *here*, but as soon as he got among his foolish adorers, all was forgotten.' She complained to Ponsonby (16 September) of ' his *constant* speeches at every station, without which the country *would not* be *excited* . . . The Queen is *utterly* disgusted with his *stump* oratory—so unworthy of his position —almost under her very nose.' The Queen's alarm was shared by the Poet Laureate, Lord Tennyson, who sent Gladstone on 25 October, soon after the new Session opened, a somewhat uninspired poem which began :

> Steersman, be not precipitate in thine act !

The Queen, in the meantime, had circulated Gladstone's excellent and conciliatory memorandum among the Opposition leaders, and at her suggestion secret negotiations were opened between the Liberals and the Conservatives in order to avert a constitutional crisis of the kind that had nearly caused a revolution in 1832. The question of redistributing constituencies on a large scale was bound to be extremely delicate, for each side in such a case must always suspect the other of being biased, if only unconsciously, in its own interest.

Over tea at 10, Downing Street on 22 November, 1884, after preliminary meetings on 14 and 19 November, Lord Salisbury and Sir Stafford Northcote conferred in secret with Gladstone, Lord Hartington, and the Radical Sir Charles Dilke who had become President of the Local Government Board in December, 1882.

On 22 November, Mary Gladstone, passing the door of her father's room, noted that the two loudest voices were those of Lord Salisbury and Sir Charles, and that ' Papa ', when he emerged, appeared to be ' extremely cheerful '. The negotiations went well, and on 27 November an acceptable compromise was reached. The Liberals agreed to introduce a Redistribution Bill at once on the basis of abolishing all the remaining small boroughs with less than 15,000 voters, and of dividing most of the old two-member constituencies in town and country. In return, the Conservatives undertook that no further opposition would be offered to the Franchise Bill in the Lords.

The Radicals were delighted that, at the suggestion of the Conservatives, the two-member constituencies were to be split ; it meant an end to the old system of running a Whig and a Radical in double harness against a pair of Conservatives ; and the Radicals judged rightly that the Party machine would be controlled increasingly by its left wing. The Whig magnates in consequence were more discontented and mistrustful than before of Gladstone's leadership which they repudiated within two years. The Conservatives were satisfied because they calculated rightly that they would gain in the long run from the traditional conservatism of the newly enfranchised voters in the countryside. Parnell, despising Liberals and Conservatives with complete impartiality, was delighted to find that the Irish vote had been trebled at a stroke. He resolved to make full use at the first opportunity of the strength which had been added to his arm, and which seemed to make the attainment of Home Rule at last a practical possibility.

Compliments were at once exchanged between the Party leaders and the Queen. At lunch, on 27 November, Gladstone, Hartington, and Dilke behaved like boys out of school, with, Mary Gladstone observed, ' a sort of devilish twinkle in their eyes '. At tea, after a final conference with Lord Salisbury, Gladstone was ' splitting and chuckling '. He wrote on that day to thank the Queen ' for that wise, gracious and steady exercise of influence on Your Majesty's part which has so powerfully contributed to bring about this accommodation and to avert a serious crisis of affairs '. The Queen told Gladstone (1 December) that Lord Salisbury and Sir Stafford Northcote had expressed warm appreciation of his ' very conciliatory tone and manner '.

Gladstone was tired, and he was also much worried by a personal case of a kind which always tormented him. Lord Rosebery, to whom he was under obligations for many services and much kindness, was extremely discontented. Through Lady Rosebery and Mrs. Gladstone he had let Gladstone know that he wanted a seat in the Cabinet which should be combined with exclusive responsibility for Scottish affairs ; but Gladstone had fobbed him off with undersecretaryships, one of which, at the Home Office, he had filled from August, 1881, to June, 1883. Gladstone would have served his Party well if he had found a place for Lord Rosebery in his Cabinet when the Duke of Argyll resigned in April, 1881, but he was too much imbued with the notion that young men ought to work their ways up the ladder of promotion to appreciate, as Disraeli would have done, that Rosebery was no ordinary young man. He was the rising hope of Scotland and already a force in England, and he possessed the rare quality of magnetism which attracts and moves currents of opinion. His prickly sensitiveness made Gladstone's task more difficult, but the Prime Minister's cavalier treatment of a brilliant young patrician who had no great love for politics might have resulted in Lord Rosebery's services being lost to the Liberal Party. Gladstone carelessly planted hopes of promotion in Rosebery's breast which he proceeded, with equal apparent carelessness, to disappoint. The Prince of Wales expressed surprise (25 July, 1884) that Gladstone had found no place for Lord Rosebery in the Cabinet.

At the beginning of September, 1884, Gladstone did try to induce the not very competent Lord Carlingford to quit the offices which he held of Lord President of the Council and Lord Privy Seal, but Lord Carlingford refused to resign, or to accept the Embassy at Constantinople which was held out to him as a bait. On 25 September Lord Granville chivalrously offered to resign in order to make room for Lord Rosebery, but Gladstone would not hear of that. Gladstone explained his difficulties to Rosebery on 11 October, and on 8 November he asked him to become First Commissioner of Works, with a seat in the Cabinet. Lord Rosebery refused, on the ground that Gladstone had not taken a firm enough line in the Sudan. His real reasons were, however, that he disliked the office which he had been offered and that he thought that Gladstone should have found means to give him one of Lord Carlingford's two offices, with a specific responsibility for Scottish affairs. Rosebery told Lord Granville (12 November) that the Office of Works was a paltry employment, ' having neither dignity nor importance ... being only a sort of football for contending connoisseurs '. The restless and impatient state of mind which inspired that petulant letter did Rosebery much harm in Gladstone's eyes, but there were faults on both sides. Lord Rosebery's exaggerated sensitiveness encountered in Gladstone an unusual degree of insensitiveness ; the older man could have handled the younger more wisely as well as more kindly, and the outcome of that phase of their relationship was perhaps rather more fortunate than Gladstone deserved.

During the first weeks of 1885 the thoughts and hopes of the nation went out to General Gordon as he waited in Khartoum for the delayed relief of which his famished garrison was now desperately in need. On 28 January an advanced detachment of Lord Wolseley's expedition arrived within sight of the town, and came under fire from the Palace. Khartoum had fallen two days before ; six hours of massacre had followed ; General Gordon was dead. Lord Cromer expressed the truth when he declared in his book on *Modern Egypt* (1908) :

' The Nile expedition was sanctioned too late, and the reason why it was sanctioned too late was that Mr. Gladstone would not accept simple evidence of a plain fact which was patent to much less powerful intellects than his own.'

Gladstone and Lord Hartington were staying with the Duke of Devonshire at Holker when the news was received in England on 5 February. On his way to London Gladstone was handed a telegram from the Queen which read :

' These news from Khartoum are frightful, and to think that all this might have been prevented and many precious lives saved by earlier action is too fearful.'

By the Queen's command, that telegram, with its peculiar grammar, was not ciphered, as was customary, but left open to the world for anyone to read through whose hands it passed. Gladstone was exceedingly angry, and he wondered if he could continue in office after receiving a public rebuke from his Sovereign. He replied to the Queen with dignity and at considerable length :

' Mr. Gladstone has had the honour this day to receive Your Majesty's telegram *en clair* . . . stating that it is too fearful to consider that the fall of Khartoum might have been prevented and many precious lives saved by earlier action.

' Mr. Gladstone does not presume to estimate the means of judgement possessed by Your Majesty, but so far as his information goes he is not altogether able to follow the conclusion which Your Majesty has been pleased thus to announce to him. . . . '

The Queen wrote to inform Gladstone the next day that she could not trust herself to write more, and Ponsonby was unable to persuade her to express regret for the open telegram. The Queen was so overwrought that she became physically ill for a time. Hamilton noted that the gloom and rage of London knew no bounds, and that Gladstone had made matters, if possible, worse, by his thoughtless and injudicious action in keeping an engagement to go to a theatre on the night of 10 February. When he was reproached for it, he said, characteristically, that Gordon's death had not been confirmed at the War Office, and that he might be merely a prisoner-of-war.

On 8 February, 1885, three days after the news of the fall of Khartoum was received, and while the Government was being deluged beneath a cataract of universal execration, Lord Rosebery's pride prompted him to inform Gladstone that his services were now unreservedly at the Prime Minister's disposal. Lord Rosebery accepted the vacant office of First Commissioner of Works which was sweetened, at Lord Granville's suggestion, and with Lord Carlingford's acquiescence, by that of Lord Privy Seal.

The spectacular accession of so notable a magnate, and of one who evidently had a great future before him, at the moment when Gladstone's reputation had touched the lowest point in his whole career, was remarkable. Gladstone's private view of the man who was ultimately to succeed him as Prime Minister was, however, characteristically restrained. He observed that Rosebery was one of the ablest as well as one of the most honourable men he had ever known, but that he doubted whether he really possessed common sense.

For some months Gladstone tried to persuade himself, and the House of Commons, that Khartoum had fallen as a result of treachery, which might have occurred at any time, and not as a result of starvation. He was, however, vulgarly denounced throughout the land as Gordon's murderer; and in the Music Halls, the initials 'G.O.M.'—Grand Old Man—were reversed to read 'M.O.G.'—Murderer of Gordon. One popular refrain ran:

> The M.O.G., when his life ebbs out,
> Will ride in a fiery chariot,
>   And sit in state
>   On a red-hot plate
> Between Pilate and Judas Iscariot.

The mood of hysteria, which drew crowds every day to Westminster in the hope that they might have an opportunity to hoot at the Prime Minister, lasted for about three weeks. It denoted a fundamental change in the climate of contemporary thought. The mid-Victorian public, in the first flush of its emancipation and enfranchisement, had responded readily to Gladstone's flattering appeals to its reasoning faculties, and Gladstone's main strength had been based on that response. In politics, however, as in finance, bad coinage drives out good, and the late-Victorian public seemed to grow less responsible and more excitable every day. It was much more accessible to emotional than it was to rational appeals, and Gladstone in his old age was haunted increasingly by the fear that the masses might in the end prove to be just as corrupt and irresponsible as the classes which, in his view, had succumbed long ago to the temptations of wealth and power.

During the mood of depression which settled upon him after the momentary elation caused by the success of his Franchise Act had dissolved, Gladstone again made up his mind to retire at the General Election. Lord Acton begged Gladstone to consider (2 February, 1885) that ' the traditional character of the State ' could not be preserved during a period of crisis unless he were to remain in harness. Gladstone replied (11 February) that there was ' no crisis '—only ' a chronic distemper ' which threatened to bring about a decline of standards by ' a process of slow modification and development in directions which I view with misgiving '. He did not think that his retirement would make any difference. The favourite idea of the Conservatives was Lord Randolph Churchill's ' Tory democracy ', which :

' is no more like the Conservative Party in which I was bred than it is like Liberalism. In fact less. It is demagogism, only a demagogism not ennobled by love and appreciation of liberty, but applied in the worst way to put down the pacific, law-respecting, economic elements which ennobled the old Conservatism, living upon the fomentation of angry passions, and still in secret as obstinately attached as ever to the evil principle of class interests.'

Modern Liberalism, he pointed out, was less debased than modern Conservatism, but : ' its pet idea is what they call construction— that is to say, taking into the hands of the State the business of the individual man.' Gladstone said that he could never accept that idea. He could only hope that his franchise reform would call out the highest qualities in the new electorate, and that ' the sense of justice, which abides tenaciously in the masses, will never knowingly join hands with the fiend of Jingoism '.

Gladstone was realist enough to appreciate that some compromise with ' the fiend of Jingoism ' was necessary on the morrow of the fall of Khartoum. Accordingly, when the Cabinet met on 7 February, 1885, he announced that for reasons of prestige—which he despised —particularly among the Mohammedans in India, and in order to protect the peace and security of Egypt, it would unhappily be necessary to crush the Mahdi in the Sudan. That policy was so distasteful to him that when he announced it on 19 February to the House of Commons he was feeble and ineffective. His daughter Mary noted that he left Downing Street amid a storm of hisses and groans, and that his speech ' utterly failed to cheer or strengthen or comfort any human being'. He dashed the expectations of friends and opponents alike by his omission to say one word in praise of General Gordon.

On the Vote of Censure in the Commons on 27 February Gladstone's majority dropped to 14. The Cabinet sat all the following day (Saturday) to discuss the question of resignation. At one moment Gladstone held out alone for continuance in office; he appealed to the 'manhood' of his colleagues, and his indomitable attitude carried the day. He considered that he was rewarded by God two months later for his fortitude, when a dramatic and unforeseen crisis in Anglo-Russian relations afforded him an excuse, which he seized with ingenuous delight, to reverse his previous decision to crush the Mahdi.

The Russian Government had been extending its dominion for many years in Central Asia. It seemed now to the Russians that while British attention was concentrated in the valley of the Nile, the time might be ripe for an advance in the valley of the Oxus. Accordingly, on 30 March an experimental incident was staged at the village of Penjdeh, a few miles inside the frontier of Afghanistan. After a brisk and sanguinary engagement the village was occupied by Russian forces, and Russian threats were uttered which seemed to menace the independence of Afghanistan. Innumerable newspaper articles and political speeches purported to show that Penjdeh was a gateway to India.

The Afghans, who had suffered worse things at Disraeli's hands, were not much perturbed. The Indian Government, however, was alarmed, while a wave of anti-Russian sentiment convulsed Great Britain and produced a panic on the Stock Exchange. The country wondered darkly how Gladstone would meet the crisis; and to almost everyone's surprise he reacted with a vigour that Disraeli might have envied. He asked the House of Commons (27 April) for a Vote of Credit of eleven million pounds, and announced that all the forces of the Empire would be concentrated immediately in readiness to meet the threat which seemed to proceed from the Russian act of wanton and high-handed aggression. He said that there could no longer be any question of a fresh campaign in the Sudan. Circumstances had changed. 'It is a paramount duty incumbent upon us to hold our forces in the Sudan available for service wherever the call of duty and honour may summon them in the service of the British Empire.'

In face of that unexpectedly resolute attitude the Russians drew back at once, and agreed to submit the incident at Penjdeh to arbitration. On 1 May Gladstone wrote to his wife that there was a ray of hope :

' As to all the later history of this Ministry, which is now entering its sixth year, it has been a wild romance of politics with a continual succession of hairbreadth escapes and strange accidents pressing upon one another . . . Russia and Ireland are the two *great* dangers remaining.'

The next day (2 May) he wrote : ' The answer came from St. Petersburg this afternoon—the Cabinet was summoned at a moment's notice. . . . Praise to the Most High.'

Gladstone at bay had been in a dangerous mood. He adhered now inflexibly to his decision to abandon the Sudan to the Mahdi. Believing firmly that God had inspired the Russian crisis with that end in view, he was unmoved by taunts that he had made an unscrupulous use of it in order to reverse the policy which he had previously announced in regard to the Sudan. Gladstone had, in fact, begun previously to madden the Queen by his attempts to modify that policy in detail. As early as 3 March, 1885, the Queen had written to Lady Wolseley :

' In *strict confidence* I *must* tell you I think the Government are *more incorrigible* than ever, and I do think your husband should use *strong* language to them, and *even* THREATEN to resign, if he does not receive strong support and liberty of action . . . But it *must never appear*, or Lord Wolseley *ever let out*, the *hint* I give you ! '

The Queen wrote to Lord Wolseley himself (31 March) begging him ' to *resist* and strongly oppose *all* idea of retreat ', and ' to *destroy* this letter as it is so *very confidential* '. It was indeed fortunate that Gladstone was unaware that his Sovereign, behind his back, was endeavouring to persuade the Commander-in-Chief in Egypt to imitate Gordon in bidding defiance to the Prime Minister.

On 13 April, after securing the approval of the Cabinet, Gladstone formally told the Queen that he had reversed his policy in the Sudan, which would now be abandoned to the Mahdi. A prolonged exchange of angry telegrams followed. The Queen was at Aix-les-Bains, and she ordered Gladstone (14 April) to ' do nothing without Lord Wolseley's advice, which you *must* follow, at any rate, in military matters '. On 17 April she gave her consent, as a constitutional Sovereign, to the new policy, but she warned Gladstone that his ' *total reversal* of the policy declared two months ago, without any hint or sign of warning to her' would have a disastrous effect in India. She added :

'She emphatically *protests against* the argument that as the Sudan War was undertaken when the *enthusiasm* of the *English people demanded* it, it should *now be abandoned because* that *enthusiasm* has has [*sic*] subsided ! ! *NO* war and indeed *no Government can* be carried on if Ministers have *no fixed principles* by which they are prepared to stand or fall, or if they change their policy according to every breath of popular opinion ! '

Gladstone's cogent arguments were detailed at great length ; public opinion was, however, as dissatisfied as the Queen. It may have been prudent to wait to reconquer the Sudan until Sir Evelyn Baring had had time to restore Egyptian finances and to reconstitute an efficient Egyptian Army, but that motive was not the primary one which caused Gladstone to abandon the Sudan. His loathing for anything resembling Jingoism prevented him from appreciating as clearly as he should have done that Egypt could never enjoy security until the Sudan was liberated and governed on civilized lines.

The problem of the Sudan was a torture to Gladstone, as he told Bright (2 March, 1885). He was willing to regard Gordon as 'a hero of heroes', but he felt that he had claimed a 'hero's privilege by turning upside down and inside out every idea and intention with which he had left England, and for which he had obtained our approval'. He told Lord Granville (12 March, 1885) that 'a great but greatly excusable' blunder had been made. 'The cause was insufficient knowledge of our man.'

Insufficient knowledge of human nature, and insufficient appreciation of the vital importance of sentiment in politics, were the fundamental causes of Gladstone's catastrophic failure in the Sudan. He understood passion well but sentiment hardly at all; his reputation never recovered from the reproach that he had trampled upon the flag and tarnished his country's honour. The patriotic youth of the nation felt that its interests were no longer safe in Gladstone's hands ; it was inexcusable that he should have found no words of praise for all that the Nile Army had endured in vain.

Lord Wolseley wrote to the Queen (22 March, 1885) : 'A few cheering words to these soldiers ... would have cost him nothing ... However, if the Queen is satisfied with the conduct of her troops, I don't think our men care very much what Mr. Gladstone thinks of them. *They* certainly don't think much of *him*.'

There was no need for Gladstone to have exposed himself to such criticism, and his insensitiveness did him harm. Much more serious, however, was the criticism directed against his settlement of the Egyptian debt problem which involved his country in grave and prolonged diplomatic embarrassment. Gladstone sought to lighten his conscience by placing the ultimate responsibility for the administration of Egypt in the hands of the Concert of Europe, instead of leaving it in those of Great Britain. Accordingly, on 20 March, 1885, after three years of negotiation, the control of Egyptian finance was entrusted to a Board on which the six great European Powers— Great Britain, France, Germany, Austria-Hungary, Russia, and Italy— enjoyed equal representation.

The French never ceased to regret that they had taken no part in the bombardment of Alexandria and in subsequent operations in Egypt. They bitterly resented the position which the British had gained in a country which had formerly been regarded as a French sphere of interest. Accordingly, as the French and Russians worked in harness on the Board, any British proposal was liable to be out-voted unless Germany and Austria-Hungary, who also worked in harness, voted on the side of Great Britain. British foreign secretaries, therefore, had constantly to purchase German support with concessions in different parts of the world in order to secure the good government of Egypt.

Gladstone, supported by Lord Granville whose powers were failing, concluded that unfortunate settlement from the highest motives. He intended thereby to emphasize the unity of Europe, but in fact he unwittingly increased disunity, and upset international stability. The settlement helped to keep Great Britain and France apart for nineteen years, and Gladstone concluded it without having appreciated Bismarck's motive in giving it enthusiastic support. Gladstone was unaffected by the criticism which that settlement provoked, partly because of his fervid conviction that men and nations are bound by the same moral code in conducting all their affairs. He bluntly informed the electors of Midlothian (17 September, 1885) that ' we have, according to my conviction, from the very first . . . committed by our intervention in Egypt a grave political error '. He continued :

' The consequence which the providential order commonly allots to such error is . . . retribution . . . Until we shall have been enabled to quit Egypt we shall, I fear, remain liable in a hundred ways to be thwarted and humiliated through the numerous rights secured there, by international arrangements, to other Powers.'

Gladstone regarded those unfortunate and almost unworkable arrangements as an aspect of a moral and providential order against which it would be impious to appeal. Abuse did not daunt him, but it handicapped his work for Home Rule. He continued fearlessly, but with increasing anxiety, to address the masses as the highest court of Christian morals on earth, while Lord Salisbury, the Conservative leader, proclaimed with equal conviction (*Quarterly Review*; October, 1883) his belief that 'the people, as an acting, deciding, accessible authority, are a myth'. In the bright noonday of intellectual liberalism, Gladstone had purchased the people's love with coin of the purest gold. That coinage was debased by his competitors, and in the auction which followed the currency was recklessly inflated. In the early days of that auction, Lord Randolph Churchill learned much from the arts which Gladstone practised in Midlothian; and he made a corrupt use of what he learned. Randolph Churchill reached out a hand to Lloyd George, and Lloyd George exchanged a nod with Adolf Hitler on the trail from Midlothian to Limehouse and from Limehouse to the Nuremberg Rally.

* * *

During the last months of the Government's life the Cabinet was torn by dissensions and misunderstandings. Lord Spencer, the courageous and high-minded Irish Lord-Lieutenant, and Henry Campbell-Bannerman who had succeeded G. O. Trevelyan as Chief Secretary for Ireland, pressed strongly for a renewal of the Coercion Act of 1882 which was due to expire. Joseph Chamberlain and Sir Charles Dilke hated coercion, and would have preferred to conciliate Irish opinion by means of a comprehensive scheme of local self-government on a county basis, culminating in a central board. There was no suggestion of a separate Parliament, but to Gladstone's chagrin the local government plan was outvoted in the Cabinet on 9 May, when all the peers, except Lord Granville, opposed it, and all the commoners, except Lord Hartington, favoured it. Chamberlain and Dilke, who hoped that the next Parliament would be more radical, now wished that all Irish legislation should be deferred; they thought that its prospects would be prejudiced if it were introduced during the last months of the Government's life. Gladstone, however, after announcing (15 May) that he intended to renew some parts of the Coercion Act, gave notice (20 May) of his intention to introduce a scheme of State land purchase.

A LETTER TO THE QUEEN

Gladstone, during the early morning of 9 June, 1885, writing to inform the
Queen of the defeat of his Government, which had just occurred.

Chamberlain and Dilke somewhat impulsively resigned, and their resignations were only suspended and not withdrawn when the Government was unexpectedly defeated on the Budget (8 June, 1885) by a combination of Conservatives and Irish Nationalists which was on that day put into operation for the first time amid wild cries of 'Coercion !' and 'Buckshot !' The voting was 264 to 252, and Gladstone resigned the next day. He had been planning, if necessary, to reconstruct the Cabinet and to carry on the Government without Chamberlain and Dilke.

No General Election was possible until the winter, because the new electoral registers could not be ready before then ; Lord Salisbury therefore hesitated to form a minority Government. He was, however, less cautious than Disraeli had been in March, 1873, and on 23 June he agreed to form a Government after failing to extort anything more than a vague pledge of tolerance from Gladstone pending a dissolution of Parliament. The Queen, who remained at Balmoral while the crisis lasted, rebuked Gladstone sharply for not going north to see her. He pleaded pressure of work, and begged her in vain to return to London or Windsor.

In his diary Gladstone noted that the fall of the Government was a great personal relief to him ' including in this sensation my painful relations with the Queen, who will have a like feeling '. The Queen nevertheless wrote Gladstone a kind letter (13 June) begging him to accept an earldom. In declining that offer (14 June), Gladstone told the Queen that he was ' fully alive to all the circumstances that give it value ', and said that he would treasure her letter as an heirloom. He sent the Queen's letter to Lord Granville, remarking that ' it must have cost her much to write ', and that it had both moved and upset him. The grounds of his refusal were that a peerage would keep him chained to politics until the day he died ; that he could do most good in the Commons until the time came for him to retire ; and that he was too poor to be an earl.

The seven months of Lord Salisbury's first Government (June, 1885, to January, 1886) were to Gladstone the most perplexing and embarrassing which he ever experienced. Since Christmas, 1884, he had not concealed from Mrs. Gladstone, from his sons, or from Lord Granville, the fact that he believed that it would prove necessary to give Ireland a separate Parliament. He had sympathized whole-heartedly with the cause of nationalism in Italy and in the Balkans, recognizing instinctively that nationalism in its essence was an expression of social

RESIGNING THE LEADERSHIP

" A position of greater freedom and less responsibility."—*W.E.G.*

11 *May, 1880*

and political maladjustment. He applied liberal principles with the zeal of a convert, and as he brooded over the problem he could not conceive how a policy which was right abroad could be wrong at home. His faith in self-government was not founded, like Chamberlain's, on any practical results which it might be expected to achieve in fields such as health, housing, and education. It was founded on the principle that men must love the highest when they see it. The highest in that context meant to Gladstone a policy which enhanced men's dignity and self-respect, and which stimulated—to use a phrase which was very often upon his lips—their manhood. He finally made up his mind to fight the cause of Home Rule during a brief holiday which he took in the Norwegian fiords on Sir Thomas Brassey's yacht, the *Sunbeam*, from 8 August to 1 September, 1885. Gladstone found in Norway a small people living happily in a spirit of democracy, and the effect upon his mind was comparable with that of his visit to Naples in the winter of 1850–1. He loved what he found in Norway, for it touched one of the deepest chords in his nature.

To Gladstone the cause of Home Rule was an end in itself. He made it clear to his sons that he was not willing merely to continue to fight the battle of Liberalism versus Conservatism. If that were all, he would prefer to retire. Herbert Gladstone explained to Edward Hamilton (7 August, 1885) that his father was faced with an almost insuperable difficulty in deciding about the tactics which he should adopt. He had hoped to advance to Home Rule by stages through the application of liberal principles of self-help and individual effort. Those principles ought to have led already to the institution of a system of local government in Ireland, but that road had been blocked by the fatal Cabinet vote of 9 May, 1885. It seemed useless now to undertake the struggle without an assurance from Parnell that a reasonable measure of Home Rule would be accepted by his people as 'a practical solution'.

Gladstone, accordingly, was careful to inform himself constantly of the latest trends of Catholic and of Irish opinion by maintaining contact with Cardinal Manning and with Parnell. Communications with Parnell had been conducted by the Chief Liberal Whip, Lord Richard Grosvenor, through Mrs. O'Shea. Lord Richard's strong prejudice against Parnell and against Home Rule made him possibly an even less satisfactory channel than the lady who was held by rumour, to which Gladstone paid no attention, to be Parnell's mistress.

During the summer of 1885 relations between the Conservatives and the Parnellites became so close that, as Herbert Gladstone told Hamilton on 7 August, 1885, Mrs. O'Shea, ' Parnell's spokeswoman or speaking-trumpet ', had ceased to provide any useful information. Gladstone became so impatient that he adopted the undesirable expedient of writing to the lady himself. He sent her eight letters in 1885, making it clear that he sought nothing at all, except factual information. He may have remembered how he had been unjustly reproached in May, 1882, for seeking a corrupt political compact with Parnell at the time of the Kilmainham agreement. It was apparent now that the Conservatives were straining every nerve to obtain Parnell's support at the forthcoming General Election. Parnell was only concerned to obtain the best terms he could for the cause which he represented. He repeatedly begged Gladstone for a statement of his views or intentions, and he left the door open until the last minute. But Gladstone resolutely declined to give Parnell the slightest hint. The Irish must first state their minimum demands, and Gladstone would then frame his policy and announce it when he thought fit. He told Mrs. O'Shea on 8 August, 1885 : ' It is right I should say that into any counter-bidding of any sort against Lord R. Churchill I, for one, cannot enter.'

To that high-minded and hyper-sensitive position Gladstone adhered inflexibly, despite the increasingly strong pressure which was brought to bear on him by his family as the General Election drew near. Herbert Gladstone, who sat for Leeds, used every argument he could think of to induce his father to change his decision, but he made no impression at all. Gladstone's lips were sealed completely against Parnell and almost completely against all his colleagues except Lord Granville who failed to give wise advice. Gladstone held that his honour as well as his interest were involved.

Gladstone rightly considered that it would be shameful as well as dangerous to inform Parnell privately, without consulting his colleagues, about his conversion to Home Rule. He could not, however, either consult his colleagues or announce his conversion publicly without breaking up the Liberal Party, and without appearing to bid for the Irish vote. Gladstone realized, moreover, how greatly his reputation had been damaged and his strength impaired by the disasters at Majuba Hill and at Khartoum and by the angry passions which his policies and conduct had aroused. He told Lord Rosebery (13 November, 1885) :

' The production at this time of a plan by me would not only be

injurious, but would destroy all reasonable hope of its adoption . . .
I well know from a thousand indications, past and present, that a new
project of mine, launched into the air, would have no *momentum*
which could carry it to its aim.'

In those circumstances Gladstone's mind reverted to the past. He
remembered the parts which the Duke of Wellington and Sir Robert
Peel had played in 1829 in connexion with Roman Catholic emancipation. He remembered Sir Robert Peel's action in 1845-6 on the
question of the Corn Laws. He remembered how Disraeli had
carried the Second Reform Act of 1867, and how he himself had,
by private arrangement with Lord Salisbury, overcome the Lords'
opposition to the Third Reform Act of 1884. As he contemplated
those various precedents in the light of the contemporary Irish problem,
Gladstone saw only one tolerable solution. The Conservatives, who
had abandoned coercion and who were dependent for their continuance
in office upon the Irish vote, would need to go one step further and
introduce a measure of Home Rule themselves. Gladstone imagined
that the Conservative right wing would probably peel off, and that
the Ulster representatives might revolt, but he presumed that the
bulk of the Conservative Party would remain loyal to its leader.
Gladstone would himself, in those circumstances, have been delighted
to support Lord Salisbury with a fervid and embarrassing intensity.
He imagined that he might have to sacrifice some congenial Whigs
as well as some uncongenial Radicals, but he presumed that enough
of the Liberal Party would remain loyal to him to ensure the success
of the Home Rule policy. That would be a fitting climax to his
career. He would, moreover, have had it in his power to convince
himself at any moment that Lord Salisbury was growing lukewarm
in the cause, and that it was his duty, therefore, to oust the Conservatives
and to take over the helm himself in obedience to the will of God as
well as that of the people.

With habitual simplicity and naïveté Gladstone continued for some
months to hope and to believe that Lord Salisbury, whom he liked
and admired and with whom he had sometimes stayed at Hatfield,
would perceive and execute his duty as Gladstone saw it. There
were solid grounds for hope in the very remarkable reversal of
Conservative policy towards Ireland which had already taken place
since Lord Salisbury came into office. Even before the fall of Gladstone's Government, Lord Randolph Churchill, who now sat in
Lord Salisbury's Cabinet as Secretary for India, had pretended to be

scandalized (St. Stephen's Club, 20 May, 1885) by Gladstone's announcement that some parts of the Coercion Act would be renewed. Lord Randolph had described that statement as 'an insult to the feelings of our brothers on the other side of the St. George's Channel' and as an extraordinary travesty of liberal principles. As soon as Lord Salisbury took office the newly appointed Lord-Lieutenant of Ireland, Lord Carnarvon, abandoned his predecessor's system of repression ; he announced that Ireland would be governed in the same way as England, and he did everything possible to conciliate Irish opinion.

Gladstone, therefore, was careful to do nothing and to say nothing which might have had the effect of making Lord Salisbury's task more difficult. Gladstone's conception of Lord Salisbury's aim was a noble but preposterous delusion, because it was founded on a too-exalted idea of human nature and political reality. Lord Salisbury, with his habitual common sense, gave careful consideration to the practical implications of the rôle for which Gladstone had cast him. His Lord-Lieutenant, Lord Carnarvon, was personally in favour of Home Rule, and with the Prime Minister's knowledge he held secret talks during the summer with Justin McCarthy, another of Parnell's agents. On one occasion (1 August, 1885) Lord Carnarvon even met Parnell secretly in London in order to discuss tentatively the subject of Home Rule. He made a full report to the Prime Minister whom he had previously consulted, and although the Cabinet was not informed, the Irish problem was discussed between Lord Salisbury and Lord Carnarvon with frankness and freedom. The Prime Minister appreciated the Lord-Lieutenant's desire to pursue a bold forward policy and he allowed him ample latitude. He soon made up his mind, however, that he was in no position to play the part which Peel had played in 1829, or in 1846.

In the cause of Home Rule, Gladstone descried the sacred tokens of a compulsive and universal moral principle. He drew an inflexible distinction between principle and details ; searched constantly for the former ; and was willing, and even eager, in the last resort, to incur martyrdom in a great cause. Lord Salisbury, on the other hand, cultivated a cool patrician detachment. He once informed the House of Lords (22 February, 1884) that 'there are no absolute truths or principles in politics' ; and he explained to his son that the distinction commonly drawn between principles and details was illusory : 'In practice, everything is done by the arrangement and execution of the

335

details.' He admitted that he felt no personal wish to satisfy Irish national aspirations, and that he was more interested in the many delicate problems which came to him as Foreign Secretary than he was in the Irish problem which confronted him as Prime Minister. He held those two great offices at once.

Lord Salisbury was willing to believe that there might be much theoretical virtue in Home Rule. In so hopelessly unpractical a cause, however, he saw no virtue in breaking up the Conservative Party as Sir Robert Peel had done in 1846 on the question of the Corn Laws. Lord Salisbury understood that political parties are not composed of scrupulous metaphysicians but of men of human clay with worldly and divergent ambitions. He remembered that in 1867 he had himself maintained to the last a diehard but unsuccessful opposition to Disraeli's Reform Bill. He was Prime Minister now in a minority government which was also his first, and in 1885 he was by no means securely seated in the saddle. Just below him, Lord Randolph Churchill, whose rise had been meteoric and whose reputation was at its zenith, was modelling his career on that of Disraeli. Churchill was evidently aching for a chance to overthrow the 'Old Guard' in the interest of 'Tory democracy' by playing the part which Disraeli— with no family connexions to help him—had once played successfully against Peel. It seemed to Lord Salisbury that the duty which he owed to his Party would have made it an act of criminal folly to give Churchill that chance.

The only problem facing Parnell was to decide whether Gladstone or Lord Salisbury had most to offer. Parnell had many Irish followers in the towns of England, Scotland, and Wales, and they would vote as he ordered at the General Election. Gladstone's love of liberty, his passionate sympathy with the cause of oppressed nationalities, and his vehement and enthusiastic temperament, possessed obvious and attractive possibilities. Without passion it would be hard to carry a constitutional revolution to completion, and Lord Salisbury was so alarmingly cold-blooded as to appear at times almost cynical. It was true that some sections of Gladstone's Party might refuse to follow its leader, but Lord Salisbury also was subject to that risk. On the other hand, if Lord Salisbury could be induced to adopt Home Rule it would be much easier for him than it would be for Gladstone to manage and appease the Conservative backwoodsmen in the House of Lords. High hopes, which were destined to be blasted, had been raised in Parnell's breast by his communications with Lord

Carnarvon. Lastly Parnell had to consider that the Conservatives were numerically the weaker of the two Parties, and that his position as arbiter would be destroyed if either side were to secure an independent majority.

Before making up his mind, Parnell did his utmost to elicit a plain statement from Gladstone. He obtained nothing, however, but evasive and hypothetical generalities. On 9 November, 1885, Gladstone declared in a speech at Edinburgh that it would be disastrous if the General Election failed to return to Parliament ' a Party totally independent of the Irish vote '. After that exhibition of high-mindedness Parnell hesitated no longer. The Elections were due to begin on 23 November. On 21 November all Irishmen in England, Scotland, Wales, and Ireland, were instructed to vote Conservative, and Gladstone was denounced with unnecessary acerbity as the man who had coerced Ireland, deluged Egypt with blood, menaced religious liberty in the schools, and attacked freedom of speech in Parliament. The best expert opinion estimated that Parnell's action resulted in the loss outside Ireland by the Liberals to the Conservatives of between 25 and 40 seats.

The final results of the General Election gave the Conservatives 249 seats, the Liberals 335, and the Irish Nationalists—a solid phalanx united under Parnell's virtual dictatorship—86. The Conservatives and Irish together had the same number of seats as the Liberals— 335 in each case. So long, therefore, as the Salisbury-Parnell alliance held firm, the result was a dead heat, and Lord Salisbury very properly continued in office.

Until 12 January, 1886, when the new Parliament was due to meet, Gladstone remained at Hawarden cutting down trees and brooding about the past and the future. He was the object of widespread speculation. Many visitors came to stay and they noticed that, as always, their host was at his conversational best at breakfast. He created jealousies by being more open with some of his former colleagues than he was with others, but he disclosed his mind fully only to God, his family, and Lord Granville.

Gladstone still cherished the vain hope that Lord Salisbury would call him and Parnell into conference for the purpose of settling the Irish problem on non-Party lines through the introduction of an agreed measure of Home Rule. He and Lord Salisbury had, however, both made up their minds. Lord Rosebery told Hamilton, after a visit to Hawarden, that the grand old man had Ireland on the brain, and that, if Lord Salisbury shirked his duty, nothing would prevent Gladstone from turning him out of office and introducing a Home Rule Bill himself 'regardless of the consequences'. On 14 December, unknown to Gladstone, Lord Carnarvon's plea for a Conservative Home Rule Bill was laid before the Cabinet and decisively rejected. The Lord-Lieutenant, who found himself in a minority of one, allowed himself to be persuaded by his colleagues to postpone his resignation until the new Parliament met.

On the next day, 15 December, Gladstone's increasing anxiety and impatience drove him at last to make an overt approach to Lord Salisbury. Without consulting any of his colleagues, he drove over to Eaton Hall, where the Duke of Westminster was entertaining a house-party, and called Arthur Balfour, Lord Salisbury's nephew, aside. He said that he had reason to believe that unless Home Rule were granted at once the Irish would resort to violence and assassination in England as well as in Ireland. He confirmed what he said in a letter (20 December), and added that:

'It would be a public calamity if this great subject should fall into the lines of party conflict. I feel sure the question can only be dealt with by a Government, and I desire specially, on grounds of public policy, that it should be dealt with by the *present* Government.'

Gladstone indicated that his 'desire would be' to support Lord Salisbury 'in a proposal for settling the whole question of the future government of Ireland . . . reserving, of course, necessary freedom'.

Balfour undertook to bring Gladstone's suggestion to the notice of Lord Salisbury who laid it before the Cabinet. It was rejected out of hand. Gladstone's action was attributed less to naïve unworldliness than to a sinister wish to split the Conservative Party before the Liberal Party was disrupted.

At that moment the danger of an explosion in the Liberal Party was great; rumour and confusion reigned supreme. Isolated at Hawarden, Gladstone seemed virtually to have abdicated; he gave no leadership, no guidance, no encouragement of any kind. The violent terms of abuse which Parnell had employed against the Party at the General Election had infuriated Liberals of all shades of opinion, from extreme Whigs to extreme Radicals. Many had pledged themselves to their constituents to have nothing more to do with the Parnellites. Although Gladstone concealed his views, his intentions were guessed in some quarters, and they caused consternation. The principal Whigs, except Lord Granville and Lord

Spencer, as well as the principal Radicals, were strongly opposed to Home Rule, and in the absence of any hint from Gladstone the tone of the Liberal Press was hardening against Ireland. Old John Bright had no use for Home Rule, and Chamberlain had come away from a visit to Hawarden (7–8 October) without reaching a satisfactory understanding with Gladstone. Gladstone had disliked almost as much as the Queen the radical programme of social reform which Chamberlain had enunciated in a series of fiery speeches before the General Election in an endeavour to supplement the more tepid programme which Gladstone favoured.

Mrs. Gladstone's feminine jealousy of the new position which Chamberlain had made for himself was evident to Gladstone's intimates, and the Queen wrote (2 October) imploring Gladstone to teach his Radical followers that ' *liberalism* is not *Socialism* and that *progress* does not mean *Revolution* '.

Gladstone gladly did his best, but his powers were limited, and Chamberlain and Dilke were now known to be toying with the idea of breaking away from Gladstone's leadership and creating an independent Radical group in Parliament which would be opposed to Home Rule and untroubled by the passions and prejudice which such a policy would be sure to arouse.

Although Chamberlain was an enthusiast for local government, because of the material benefits which it had produced in Birmingham and elsewhere, he was opposed in principle to Home Rule. He had no belief in the ethical and spiritual advantages which Gladstone thought it would produce ; he grudged the time and effort which a Home Rule Bill would divert from the problem of social reform at home which he considered much more urgent ; and he thought that the Home Rule policy had no chance of being endorsed by the British masses, or of being carried through Parliament.

In those unpropitious circumstances, Herbert Gladstone, on his own initiative, went up to London from Hawarden on 14 December, 1885, with the intention of rallying Liberal opinion by giving the Liberal Press a strong hint about his father's views, and about the dangers which threatened the Party. He had long been a convinced Home Ruler ; he thought that his father, whom he worshipped, was the only man capable of securing Home Rule ; and he knew that his father would retire if the Liberal Party failed to adopt that policy. In a series of interviews, which were headlined on 17 December, Herbert Gladstone broadcast the news of his father's conversion, and added a few incautious and pungent comments of his own about the attitude of the Whig and Radical leaders.

That disclosure was overdue and its effect, on the whole, was salutary, although it could, with advantage, have been less ineptly made. Herbert Gladstone took insufficient care to explain that he was speaking ' off the record ' in order to give much-needed guidance to the Liberal Press, and that he was expressing his personal views. Most of what he had said was printed as a direct expression of his father's opinions.

Gladstone at that critical moment was characteristically occupied in a violent controversy with T. H. Huxley ; he was trying to defend the literal truth of the account of the Creation, given in the *Book of Genesis*, against the attacks of contemporary science. In an article entitled, *Proem to Genesis*, which he posted to the *Nineteenth Century* on 17 December, 1885, Gladstone set out to prove that ' the five origins, or first appearances, of plants, fishes, birds, mammals, and man, are given to us in *Genesis* in the order of succession in which they are also given by the latest geological authorities '. Those ' astonishing anticipations ' so ' entirely transcended, in kind even more than in degree, all known exercise of human faculties ' that they must be regarded as ' manifestly God-given '.

Recalled to mundane questions by his son's indiscretion, Gladstone was not unduly disturbed. He had in fact told his son that he was at liberty to state at any time his personal impressions of his father's views. The storm broke with such violence, however, that even Gladstone was for once driven to prevaricate. He issued a disclaimer which read :

' The statement is not an accurate representation of my views but is, I presume, a speculation upon them. It is not published with my knowledge or authority ; nor is any other, beyond my own public declarations.'

He told Lord Hartington (17 December) that nothing was changed and that he still considered that it was Lord Salisbury's duty to satisfy Ireland's demands. ' A Tory Government can do it more easily and safely than any other . . . My earnest recommendation to everybody is not to commit himself.'

Lord Hartington, in common with plain men everywhere, was excessively irritated by Gladstone's continued attempt to deny, on purely formal grounds, the palpable facts that he and the Liberal Party were now in practice committed to Home Rule, and that Ireland had been dragged into the forefront of Party politics. As late as

24 December, 1885, Gladstone told Mrs. O'Shea that he still hoped that the Conservatives would ' propose some adequate and honourable plan' and that nothing in the meantime should be done to endanger the alliance between the Conservatives and the Irish Nationalists. ' It is useless', Lord Hartington wrote to Lord Granville (2 January, 1886), ' to expect him to be intelligible . . . Did any leader ever treat a Party in such a way as he has done?' In opposition to Gladstone, Lord Hartington had on 21 December publicly reaffirmed his refusal to accept any policy of Home Rule.

On 21 January, after the new House had met, the Speech from the Throne announced that the legislative union between Great Britain and Ireland would be preserved, and that a new Irish Coercion Act might prove necessary. Gladstone announced that he reserved his freedom of action, and that speaking ' as an old Parliamentary hand' he advised new members to wait until he should give the signal ' to make a movement forward'. The tone in which those words were uttered gave bitter offence to some sections of the House ; it was considered arrogant, and for some days there was a hushed sense of expectancy.

The storm broke on 26 January when the leader of the House, Sir Michael Hicks-Beach, gave notice of the Government's intention to introduce a new Coercion Act. All Gladstone's hesitations were instantly dissolved, and he stood forth again as an inspired, not to say reckless, leader. He went to Sir William Harcourt and explained that he intended to turn out the Government at once, before the House became bogged down in a debate about coercion.

"What!" Sir William exclaimed. "Are you prepared to go forward without either Hartington or Chamberlain?"

"Yes!" Gladstone retorted. "I am prepared to go forward without anybody!"

Gladstone noted: ' This was one of the great imperial occasions which call for such resolutions.'

That evening, accordingly, the Government was defeated on a motion by Jesse Collings regretting the absence from the Queen's Speech of measures for benefiting rural labourers. That was the policy for which Chamberlain had fathered the slogan ' Three acres and a cow!' and that was the first occasion on which Gladstone announced his support of it. The division was taken at one o'clock on the morning of 27 January, when the Government was defeated by 331 votes to 257. The Irish Nationalists voted with Gladstone, but 18 Liberals, including Lord Hartington, G. J. Goschen, and Sir Henry James, voted with the Government. Lord Salisbury resigned the next day (28 January) and soon after midnight on the morning of 30 January, Gladstone, who was now aged seventy-six, received from Sir Henry Ponsonby the Queen's verbal commission to form his third administration. The Queen told Ponsonby (24 January) that:

' She does not in the least care, but rather wishes it should be known, that she has the greatest possible disinclination to take this half crazy and really in many ways ridiculous old man—for the sake of the country.'

Ponsonby and Hamilton both hinted to Gladstone that he had undertaken a task which would have been too much even for a man in the prime of life. Gladstone retorted that no-one except an old man could hope to be of use. Everyone was violent and excited about Home Rule, but his white hairs, and the fact that he could have no personal ambition, would command involuntary respect.

PUNCH, January 30, 1886

THE GRAND OLD HAND AND THE YOUNG 'UNS.

' I stand here as a Member of the House, where there are many who have taken their seats for the first time upon these benches, and where there may be some to whom possibly I may avail myself of the privilege of old age to offer a recommendation. I would tell them of my own intention to keep my counsel, and reserve my own freedom, until I see the occasion when there may be a prospect of public benefit in endeavouring to make a movement forward, and I will venture to recommend them, as an old Parliamentary hand, to do the same. (Laughter.)'

From Gladstone's Speech (January 21, 1886)

CHAPTER 14

THE CHARIOT OF THE SUN
1886–1887

WHEN Gladstone took office on 30 January, 1886, it was too early to say how far the Liberal revolt against his leadership might spread. Only 18 Liberals had voted with the Conservatives on 27 January, but 76 had been absent from the division. Gladstone's first action was to draw up a short memorandum which he sent or showed to everyone whom he invited to join his Government. It stated that he proposed ' to examine whether it is or is not practicable to comply with the desire widely prevalent in Ireland . . . for the establishment of a legislative body to sit in Dublin, and to deal with Irish as distinguished from imperial affairs ; in such a manner as would be . . . calculated to support and consolidate the unity of the Empire on the continued basis of imperial authority and mutual attachment'.

Lord Hartington declined that offer at once :

' I am unable ', he wrote (30 January), ' to attach great importance to a distinction between examination, and the actual conception and announcement of a plan . . . Parliament or the country may reject a plan ; but the Government which has undertaken to enter into such an examination can scarcely stop short of proposing a policy founded on it.'

Lord Hartington was glad not to have to meet Gladstone in order to discuss the matter. He had complained to Lord Granville as recently as 8 August, 1885, that he never could understand Gladstone in conversation. He was content now to explain that he could no longer risk compromising his integrity for the sake of Party unity.

Other prominent Whigs who followed Lord Hartington were Lord Derby, Lord Northbrook, Lord Selborne, and Lord Carlingford, who had all been members of the previous Liberal Cabinet. The Duke of Argyll, Sir Henry James, G. J. Goschen, and John Bright also refused to serve. Thus was accomplished the great schism in the Liberal Party which Gladstone rightly regarded as an event of social as well as political and historic importance. Before 1868, when Gladstone first became Prime Minister, Liberal policy had been shaped by the great Whig families and their connexions ; even after 1868 that policy had been greatly influenced by them. After 1885–6 the

343

Whigs ceased to dominate the Liberal Party, and most of them were gradually absorbed into the Conservative ranks under the name of Unionists.

Unlike Sir Robert Peel, forty years earlier, Gladstone was not left in the position of a general without an army. Lord Granville remained faithful, and he was followed, with varying degrees of reluctance, by Lord Spencer, Lord Rosebery, Lord Kimberley, Lord Ripon, and Sir William Harcourt. The action of Lord Spencer in climbing after Gladstone into the chariot of the sun was extraordinarily fortunate for his leader. Lord Spencer's name was so widely associated with repression and coercion that his unexpected conversion astonished the country. He was not particularly intelligent, but he was high-minded, experienced, and sound. He was a popular master of the Pytchley Hunt, and his character compelled respect. He became Lord President of the Council, and without his adherence the prospects of Home Rule would have been darker even than they already were.

Joseph Chamberlain also agreed (30 January) to take office and ' to give an unprejudiced examination ' to Gladstone's proposals ' with an anxious desire that the result may be more favourable than I am at present able to anticipate '. He made it clear that he did not believe that it would prove possible to reconcile the security and unity of the Empire with the establishment of a legislative body in Dublin, and that he would have preferred ' a more limited scheme of local government coupled with proposals for a settlement of the land and perhaps also of the education questions '. Chamberlain's friend, and fellow-Radical, Sir George Trevelyan, joined the Cabinet on similar terms. Sir Charles Dilke, who was perhaps the ablest of the three, was unfortunately not available. He was involved in an unsavoury divorce suit, and was for a time in such danger of being prosecuted for perjury that his friends were vainly urging him to flee the country for a time.

The task of drafting, in three months, the Home Rule and Land Purchase Bills would have proved an intolerable strain to most men in the prime of life. To Gladstone, however, who undertook it in his seventy-sixth year amid a storm of execration and ridicule, the effect was tonic, and he was in excellent spirits. It was evident that even if Home Rule could be forced through the House of Commons, it would be rejected by the Lords, and many moderate Liberals dreaded a constitutional crisis in a cause for which public opinion had not been adequately prepared. Gladstone was too ingenuous to understand that more than half the nation believed that he had sold himself to Parnell for the sake of another spell of office ; and he was too single-minded to have time to spare for doubts or gloomy foreboding. He convinced himself that, in the last resort, the Lords would never dare to resist what he described to Lord Rosebery (13 November, 1885) as 'a mighty heave in the body politic' after the Home Rule policy had been shown to be 'the fixed desire of a nation, clearly and constitutionally expressed'.

Gladstone was, as Hamilton noted, 'nearly ostracized' in society ; the light in which he was regarded is well illustrated in a letter written by (Sir) Dighton Probyn, V.C.,[1] a member of the Prince of Wales's Household, to Sir Henry Ponsonby. Probyn was trying to sting Sir Henry, whose Liberal sympathies were well known :

'Don't talk to me about Gladstone. I pray to God that he may be shut up as a Lunatic at once, and thus save the Empire from the Destruction which he is leading her to. If he is not mad, he is a Traitor.

'I am worried about Lord Spencer. I have always looked upon him as being an honest Englishman, and a Gentleman . . . But he has fallen into that Traitor's clutches, and is lending a helping hand to a fearful Civil War . . . A man of that sort advocating Communism shakes my belief in anything mortal.'

As Gladstone's spirits rose, there was a most unfortunate recrudescence in his street-walking activities by night on behalf of prostitutes. Lord Rosebery warned Gladstone that stories had been instilled like poison into the Queen's ear, and that a few Conservative M.P.s, among whom a Colonel Tottenham was prominent, had resolved to track the Prime Minister's movements by setting spies on him. After a talk with Lord Rosebery, Edward Hamilton sent his former chief a strongly worded letter of warning, and Gladstone, in consequence, agreed at last (16 July, 1886) to abstain for ever from his rescue work in the streets. Even then, however, he reserved his freedom to pursue two cases which he said that he felt unable to drop entirely, and he was in correspondence about cases until the end of his life. With childlike innocence, Gladstone said that he was compelled reluctantly to recognize the degree of baseness which existed in human nature.

Similar characteristic innocence had caused Gladstone to cling for

[1] He was, later, Comptroller to Queen Alexandra.

too long to the hope that Ireland's demands would be met by Lord Salisbury on non-Party lines. He had once again allowed the best policy to become the enemy of the good, and he had failed to educate his Party at a time when the tide of intellectual liberalism was already on the ebb. Ten years earlier, at the time of the Bulgarian Horrors, nearly all the middle-class intellectuals had stood at Gladstone's side. But now their influence was thrown into the scales against him— Huxley, Tyndall, Tennyson, Browning, Matthew Arnold, Froude, Goldwin Smith, Martineau, Jowett, and Herbert Spencer, all openly opposed Home Rule.

If Gladstone had been capable of leading his Party with a greater degree of worldly wisdom, he would have called a conference of his principal supporters in the early autumn of 1885, and taken them into his confidence. Prospects of unity would still have been badly impaired as a result of past faults of temper and understanding which Gladstone had displayed, but the situation would have been less dark than it was during the spring and summer of 1886. Gladstone would, at the least, have been spared the reproach, which he incurred in June, 1886, that the scales had been turned against Home Rule by the seats which Parnell had handed to the Conservatives at the General Election of 1885, after failing to elicit from Gladstone any hint about his intentions.

By the autumn of 1885 it was too late to prevent a split of some kind from developing in the Liberal Party whenever Gladstone chose to commit it to Home Rule. The alternative would have been Gladstone's retirement, and that would have involved the abandonment of his policy. As Mrs. Gladstone told Hamilton, however (26 March, 1886), no consideration on earth would have prevented her husband in the last resort from attempting to implement that policy himself, because he believed that it was a duty owed by man to God. He desired no personal credit, Mrs. Gladstone said, and would be content to fail if he could only contrive to lay the foundations of an eventual settlement.

Those foundations would have been more securely laid if the Home Rule Bill of 1886 had passed the House of Commons. The verdict of the country when Gladstone appealed to it at the General Election of 1886 would have been, at the least, much less adverse if it had fallen to the Lords instead of to the Commons to reject the Bill, and if, after the secession of the Whigs, a Radical secession could have been averted. By treating his colleagues and supporters with more tact and consideration, and less apparent contempt, Gladstone could have kept the inevitable Liberal split within much narrower bounds. Sir Henry James, for example, who had been Attorney-General in Gladstone's previous Government, retained a warm feeling for his former chief, which was reciprocated. When Gladstone was forming his Cabinet in 1886 he asked Sir Henry to be Lord Chancellor, despite the fact that he had voted on 27 January with the Conservatives. In different circumstances Sir Henry would have jumped at the Woolsack, but the violent attacks made upon him by the Irish Nationalists at the General Election of 1885 had provoked him into declaring that he would have nothing more to do with Parnell. He agreed now with Gladstone that Home Rule had become inevitable, but he refused to join the Government because he felt that his integrity would be compromised if he were to repudiate, for the sake of office, words uttered in the heat of combat. Other less notable Liberals found themselves similarly situated as a result of Gladstone's inept and too scrupulous approach to an unhappy chapter in British history ; and a considerable majority among the rural masses whom Gladstone had recently enfranchised was readily persuaded that the grand old man was an unscrupulous politician avid for power.

After losing the main body of the Whigs, Gladstone's failure to conciliate the Radicals was an added misfortune. Chamberlain could have been kept loyal if he had been more wisely handled. Gladstone would have had to acknowledge openly the position which the Radical leader had earned for himself in the country, and to acknowledge tacitly the strong claim which Chamberlain had established to succeed to the leadership of the Party. He would have had also to make further concessions in good time and by easy stages to the Radical demand for social reform at home. None of this should have been unduly difficult. Chamberlain's position was a fact, and Hartington's secession made the succession problem much easier of solution. Even if, by some miracle, Lord Hartington had remained in the fold, his strong claims to succeed to the leadership could have been left to be adjusted with Chamberlain, after Gladstone's retirement, in an atmosphere from which the Celtic intensity radiated by the grand old man had been banished in favour of cool, unemotional, English good sense. Once Lord Hartington had gone, there was no reason why the Liberal Party should not have been reconciled with the need for social reform. Disraeli had not failed to reconcile the Conservatives with that need, and only a few years later, in 1891,

Gladstone allowed himself to be pushed, almost without protest, into the radicalism of the Newcastle Programme for the sake of winning votes at the General Election of 1892.

Gladstone's patent inability to come to terms with human nature would have impaired an ordinary man's title to the name of statesman. It is clear that Chamberlain's price in 1885-6 would not have been prohibitive, for his radicalism was already undermined by worldly success. The reasons which Chamberlain gave (30 January, 1886) for adhering to the Government, although honest and unequivocal, were less robust, and less intelligent, than the reasons which Hartington gave, the same day, for his refusal to join it.

Gladstone noted those signs, and was scandalized by the opportunism of a man he disliked, distrusted, and undervalued. It never occurred to him that for the sake of Ireland it might be his duty to play Chamberlain like a fish. When Chamberlain resigned (26 March, 1886) Gladstone, in a mood of blissful irresponsibility, told Lord Rosebery that nothing that had happened since the Government was formed had given him comparable satisfaction. Edward Hamilton left in his diary an inimitable sketch of the great Radical in the jubilee summer of 1887, after watching him narrowly at a party given by the Duchess of Manchester at her house in Great Stanhope Street. The Duchess, a daughter of Count von Alten, of Hanover, was and for years had been, as Gladstone and all the great world knew, Lord Hartington's mistress. She married him quietly in the summer of 1892 as soon as possible after her husband's death. In the privacy of his family Gladstone had frequently complained that she was pulling her lover in a Conservative and Jingo direction. At her house, on 13 July, 1887, Hamilton noted that Chamberlain was absent from the room in which the Princess of Wales was dancing tirelessly and with inimitable grace. He found the famous Birmingham screw-manufacturer, with his eye-glass, and with the inevitable orchid in his coat, in a room in which baccarat was being played for high stakes. There, the great demagogue, partnered by Lord Randolph Churchill, was keeping the bank against the Prince of Wales and a group of gilded youths. It would have been hard, as Hamilton commented, for ' all the major and minor prophets ' to have foretold the social apotheosis of Joseph Chamberlain.

The ways of the great world had always been uncongenial and in some respects incomprehensible to Gladstone. He was utterly different from all his contemporaries, and the pattern of nineteenth-century history would have been incomparably poorer and more commonplace had it been otherwise. Nevertheless, for the purposes of the day, Gladstone's obtuseness was disastrous. He had no idea how to manage men. He had long ceased to make any adequate attempt to fulfil the social duties which were expected of him in London, and he used often to say that it was 'monstrous', at his time of life, that he should be expected to entertain his colleagues and supporters. He complained that one hour at a party was more exhausting than four at the House of Commons. He despised the minor arts by which supporters are conciliated and encouraged, and the great world heartily reciprocated Gladstone's indifference. It happened that the Prime Minister's article, *Proem to Genesis*, was published in the *Nineteenth Century* in January, 1886. Few people bothered to read it, but for a time it was a stock jest to ask, " Have you read Gladstone's *Genesis* ? ", and to answer, " I'm waiting for his *Exodus* ! "

In those circumstances, amid the incredulous jeers of his opponents, Gladstone appealed more loudly than ever before from the corruption of ' the upper ten thousand ' to ' the upright sense ' of the masses. In a Home Rule address to the electors of Midlothian on 1 May, 1886, the Prime Minister declared that he found arrayed against him : ' in profuse abundance, station, title, wealth, social influence, the professions, or the large majority of them—in a word, the spirit and power of Class, and the dependents of Class '.

He said that for the past sixty years ' the Classes ' had ' fought uniformly on the wrong side ', and that in the end they had always been beaten ' by a power very difficult to marshal, but resistless when marshalled—by the upright sense of the nation . . . The heart, the root, the beginning and ending of my trust, is in the wise and generous justice of the nation.'

It was because Gladstone believed that Chamberlain was an insincere careerist that he received him coldly when he called (31 January) to ask what office the Prime Minister wished him to fill. Chamberlain suggested the Colonial Office, and, according to Sir Charles Dilke, Gladstone exclaimed, in a tone of surprise, ' Oh ! A Secretary of State ! ' Gladstone had reserved that office for Lord Granville whose powers were now rapidly failing, and whose return to the Foreign Office had been very properly vetoed by the Queen. Lord Granville needed the salary because he had recently suffered heavy pecuniary loss. Lord Hartington had hoped, for a moment,

349

that he might carry Lord Granville with him, and Gladstone's affectionate gratitude when that hope was disappointed, overbore his judgement. He asked Chamberlain, therefore, to return to the Board of Trade. Chamberlain said that he would prefer a change, but that he would take any post that Gladstone cared to suggest. Gladstone asked for time to reflect, and the next day he offered the Presidency of the Local Government Board, which Chamberlain accepted.

Having fobbed off with a comparatively unimportant office, the man whom he would have done well to treat as his principal lieutenant, it might have been expected that Gladstone would at least have been careful to pay Chamberlain minor attentions and respect. What followed would have been almost incredible had any other man than Gladstone been concerned. Chamberlain asked that Jesse Collings, the spokesman of the agricultural labourers, who had proposed the amendment on which Lord Salisbury's Government had been ousted, should be appointed Parliamentary Secretary to the Local Government Board. The relation in which Collings stood to Chamberlain was about midway between that in which Patroclus had stood to Achilles, and that in which Sancho Panza had stood to Don Quixote. Gladstone grudgingly consented, but added, as an afterthought, that the salary attached to Collings's office would have to be reduced from £1,500 to £1,200 a year.

Chamberlain was so amazed and exasperated that he threatened to resign and told Collings not to reply to Gladstone's offer. Gladstone himself was occupied on 2 February in giving away his daughter Mary, who was married on that day at St. Margaret's, Westminster, to the Rev. Harry Drew, a penniless curate of great personal beauty who combined extremely high principles with a keen sense of fun. The young couple began their married life as inmates of Hawarden Castle where Gladstone's son-in-law acted as a kind of domestic chaplain.

As Gladstone drove to St. Margaret's he was not thinking of Chamberlain or even of Ireland. The Queen, on the previous day, had found him ' intensely ' and ' almost fanatically ' in earnest in his belief that he was sacrificing himself for Ireland ; he had appeared ' dreadfully agitated and nervous ', and had estimated the odds against him at about 49 to 1. The next day, however, he looked as though he had not a care in the world. Among those who signed the Register were two future Kings and two future Prime Ministers—

Edward VII and George V ; Lord Rosebery and Arthur Balfour. At the luncheon, after the ceremony, Gladstone casually asked Sir Algernon West (Chairman of the Board of Inland Revenue) who ought to be appointed Chancellor of the Exchequer. West at once said 'Chamberlain', but Gladstone, who had already offered the post to Sir William Harcourt, said that Chamberlain would terrify the City of London. West said that Chamberlain would make an excellent Chancellor after a few weeks' experience, and Lord Rosebery, who had just become Foreign Secretary at the Queen's wish, was, later, inclined to regret that Chamberlain had not been given the Exchequer instead of Harcourt.

Sir William Harcourt was ambitious to be Lord Chancellor, and Chamberlain, in happier circumstances, would have much preferred the Chancellorship of the Exchequer to the office which he had accepted. It is certain that if, in 1886, it had happened that the Liberal Party had been led for some years past by a man possessing half Gladstone's moral earnestness and twice his knowledge of human nature, Chamberlain's genuine objections to the principle of Home Rule could have been overcome. By 1886 the two men were so incompatible that it was too late. Chamberlain resented Gladstone's unwillingness to retire, and confused his power of honest self-deception with hypocrisy. Gladstone misread Chamberlain's crisp self-assurance, and confused with insolence and unprincipled ambition the legitimate pride which the younger man took in the influence and popularity he had acquired in circles which the Prime Minister viewed with indifference or contempt.

That incompatibility may help to explain, although it cannot excuse, Gladstone's conduct. On receipt of Chamberlain's protest about Jesse Collings's salary, the Prime Minister, with bland impatience, sent the Chief Liberal Whip, Lord Richard Grosvenor, to beg Chamberlain to be less petty, and to consider the public interest. Chamberlain asked Sir William Harcourt to see Gladstone on his behalf. He wrote to Harcourt (5 February, 1886) :

'Damn ! Damn ! ! Damn ! ! ! Collings has got him more votes than all his peers put together, and this is his reward. The offer has been refused. Grosvenor was sent to me by Mr. Gladstone to induce me to relent . . . He has failed, and I have requested him to tell Mr. Gladstone that his action makes me doubt whether he attaches any importance to the presence of either Collings or myself in his Government, and that I wish to reconsider my position. Is it possible to act an ungracious part in a more ungracious way than Mr. Gladstone has done ? '

There was no element of malice in Gladstone's desire to slash Collings's salary. It was an act of the purest stupidity. Gladstone wanted to save £600 a year by slashing the salaries of the Parliamentary Secretaries to the Local Government Board and the Board of Trade [1] as a lesson to Sir William Harcourt that a paramount need for ruthless, cheese-paring economy existed in every field of expenditure. With considerable trouble, Harcourt at length induced Gladstone to give way. Gladstone told Sir William (8 February) that he would submit to Chamberlain's obstinacy, and not to his worthless arguments, on condition that Harcourt, as Chancellor, could reconcile the matter with his conscience. Gladstone told Collings what he had done, and also wrote rather pathetically to Chamberlain (6 February) :

' I have written to Collings about the salary . . . As for me, in these matters, I am like Lot's wife, solitary and pickled on the plain of Sodom.'

The next day Chamberlain wrote to Harcourt, with mock solemnity :

' Mr. Gladstone has given way about Collings, *subject to your consent !* Ferocious Economist, I beseech you not to dock poor Collings of his scanty pittance ! '

Chamberlain was instructed to prepare a Local Government Bill on which he set to work at once. He prepared a scheme of parish, district, and county councils throughout the British Isles, but Gladstone took no interest whatever in that vitally important measure, and none of its intended provisions came before the Cabinet. The whole of the Prime Minister's attention was devoted to Ireland, as, with the assistance of a Radical journalist, John Morley, who sat in the Cabinet as Chief Secretary for Ireland, he hammered the Home Rule and Land Purchase Bills into shape. The Land Purchase Bill was the first to be discussed in Cabinet (13 March). It provided that Irish agricultural landlords should be given an opportunity to withdraw from Ireland if they so desired, and that their tenants should be assisted to become the proprietors of their holdings, by means of a gigantic loan of up to some one hundred and twenty million pounds, at 3 per cent, secured on British credit.

It was proposed that a loan of fifty million pounds should be floated

---

[1] Henry Broadhurst, the only ' working class ' member of the Government, was Parliamentary Secretary to the Board of Trade.

forthwith, and Chamberlain asked whether that sum was to be advanced to a part of the United Kingdom, or to what might become a practically independent nation. Gladstone was forced to disclose some part of the outline of his Home Rule Bill, and Chamberlain said that he would never consent. He and his fellow-Radical, Sir George Trevelyan, who sat in the Cabinet as Secretary for Scotland, professed to regard the plan as a monumental aberration on the part of the grand old man, which must involve the indefinite postponement of all domestic schemes of social reform.

The two resignations were allowed to stand over until 26 March, when the Cabinet met to discuss the Home Rule Bill. Chamberlain then learned that Irish representatives would cease to sit at Westminster, that the Irish Parliament would possess powers of taxation, that the Irish would appoint their own judges and magistrates, and that the Irish Parliament would have authority in every matter not specifically excluded by the Act. After announcing their resignations, Chamberlain and Trevelyan left the Cabinet room ; and Gladstone made no effort to call them back. It was subsequently arranged that both Ministers should make their explanations to the House after Gladstone had introduced the Home Rule Bill on 8 April, 1886.

On 8 April, accordingly, Gladstone drove from Downing Street to Palace Yard amid thunderous cheers from his admirers who had gathered along the route, undeterred by torrents of rain. The scene inside the Chamber was without parallel in living memory ; every inch of floor-space from the mace to the bar was crowded with chairs and extra benches, on which members had secured places at daybreak. Mrs. Drew noted that ' the air tingled with excitement and emotion '. Mrs. Gladstone, accompanied by her three daughters, and by Lady Frederick Cavendish who was listening to a debate for the first time since the assassination of her husband, watched from the gallery. As Gladstone entered the Chamber at 4.30 p.m. his supporters rose in a body to greet the aged impresario with round upon round of applause. He spoke for three hours and a half, and was heard throughout with deep and anxious attention : ' Voice, and strength, and freedom ', he noted, ' were granted to me in a degree beyond what I could have hoped. But many a prayer had gone up for me, and not, I believe, in vain.'

The speech was severely factual and there were few oratorical flourishes. Gladstone sought to prove that he was a preserver and not a destroyer of the true unity of the kingdom and empire. Among subjects reserved to the Imperial Parliament at Westminster were matters affecting the Crown, foreign policy, defence, customs and excise, religious establishments, posts, and coinage. The thorny question of Ulster was left open :

'I cannot allow it to be said that a Protestant minority in Ulster is to rule the question at large for Ireland . . . But I think that the Protestant minority should have its wishes considered to the utmost practicable extent in any form which they may assume.'

The Bill provided that Ireland should pay a fair contribution towards the expenditure of the United Kingdom on such Imperial necessities as defence, and the service of debt. As Irish customs and excise were also to be fixed by the Parliament at Westminster from which Irish representatives were excluded, the Opposition at once raised the time-honoured cry, 'No taxation without representation!' Gladstone was in a quandary, for he felt that to admit Irish representatives to Westminster, where they had made themselves intensely disliked, might mean permitting Irishmen to decide the fate of future British Governments in relation to issues which did not concern Ireland and which were within the competence of the Parliament at Dublin.

Gladstone's thoughtful speech set the tone for the entire debate which was conducted on an unwontedly high level on sixteen days during the following two months. Gladstone delivered five major set speeches during that time. In one of them (16 April) he introduced the Land Purchase Bill which had a very bad reception and was quietly laid in its coffin like a still-born child. The Radicals thought that it treated the landlords too tenderly ; the landlords declared that they would neither accept Home Rule nor quit their properties ; the Irish Nationalists claimed that they were insulted by a proposal that the interest on the loan for land purchase should be passed through the hands of a British Receiver-General ; and many moderate men felt that Gladstone was too careless of property rights ; that he was seeking, for his own ends, to play ducks and drakes with British credit ; and that he was beginning to develop into a destructive and incalculable engine of revolution.

For moderate men the situation was coloured not only by the apparent suddenness of Gladstone's changed attitude towards Parnell, but by the fear that he was liable to be equally incalculable in regard to other fundamental issues. Certain phrases in an address which

Gladstone had issued to the Electors of Midlothian on 17 September, 1885, had been widely discussed for months. He had written about the reform of the House of Lords, and about the existence of ' a case to justify important change ' in its constitution ; he had, furthermore, used ominous words about the possibility of disestablishing the Church of England, with the approval of the nation, after the matter ' shall have grown familiar to the public mind by thorough discussion '. He had added that he did not consider that the Church's spiritual life need be adversely affected by disestablishment.

Gladstone's cryptic utterances and volcanic methods excited intense disquiet, and that disquiet strengthened the hands of Sir Michael Hicks-Beach, Lord Hartington, and Joseph Chamberlain when they attacked the Home Rule Bill with rare eloquence and relentless cogency. Gladstone failed to make allowance for the emotional appeal made by Protestant Ulster, and Lord Randolph Churchill was inspired to coin the damaging slogan, ' Ulster will fight, and Ulster will be right ! ' In moving the Second Reading of the Home Rule Bill—the first was allowed to pass unopposed—Gladstone admitted (15 May) that the Bill bristled with difficulties, ' which only require goodwill and patience to deal with, and different men feel them in different degrees '. From that time forward he embarked on a policy of appeasement.

On 20 May, for example, Gladstone suggested that Irish members should be admitted to take part in the proceedings of the Parliament at Westminster when proposals were made there for altering Irish customs or excise. A week later he went further. He summoned his Parliamentary supporters to a meeting at the Foreign Office, and asked them to vote for the Bill in principle, with the understanding that it would be amended later in Committee. He said that he would be willing either to defer the Committee stage until the autumn, or to wind up the Parliamentary Session after the division on the Second Reading, and to introduce a new and revised Bill in October. He indicated that the Cabinet favoured the latter proposal.

Parnell protested strongly against the suggestion that the Bill should be withdrawn, and Gladstone's control gave way for a moment when he received the Irish leader's letter. The next day (28 May) Sir Michael Hicks-Beach challenged Gladstone to state his intentions ; he said that, if the Bill were to be withdrawn and subsequently remodelled, the vote on the Second Reading would be a farce—a badly disguised vote of confidence in the Government.

Gladstone replied majestically that he would not stoop to discuss the suggestion that he was concerned about his continuance in office. The conflict would be fought to a finish :

'The Right Honourable Gentleman says that . . . the Bill is to be remodelled. I think that happy word is a pure invention. I am not aware that there is a shadow or shred of authority for any such statement.'

At that point Lord Randolph Churchill interjected the word 'reconstructed'. Gladstone admitted that the word 'reconstructed' had been used, but asked : 'Does the Noble Lord dare to suggest that it was used with respect to the Bill ?'

Lord Randolph Churchill, with good reason, replied, 'Yes !', and Gladstone exclaimed with some heat, 'Never ! Never ! [cheers]. It was used with respect to one particular clause of the Bill.'

The words 'Never ! Never !' proved fatal. Under the sting of a Parliamentary gadfly Gladstone's conciliatory attitude had suddenly hardened into one that was as plain as it was uncompromising. The Bill as a whole would not be altered ; only the clause about Irish representatives at Westminster would be reviewed.

On 31 May, Joseph Chamberlain summoned a meeting of dissentient Liberals which was attended by 55 members. A letter from John Bright was read, in which the veteran Radical announced his intention to vote against the Second Reading. Bright had previously written to Gladstone (13 May) to explain the reasons for his dislike of the Bill. He mentioned the case of Ulster, to which Gladstone was strangely blind, and added that the Prime Minister had failed to prepare Parliament or 'the intelligence of the country' for so violent a constitutional upheaval. Bright said that Gladstone had no adequate grounds for his apparent belief that the Irish would rest content with Home Rule. Their leaders were men without principle :

'Your policy of surrender to them will only place more power in their hands, to war with greater effect against the unity of the three kingdoms with no increase of good to the Irish people.' Surrender in Ireland ; surrender in the Sudan ; surrender in the Transvaal— that word, 'surrender', pursued Gladstone throughout the long and exhausting debate. He had, in truth, made insufficient allowance for the reluctance of a spirited, privileged, and as yet unchastened ruling class to concede anything more to terrorism and intimidation. That was much the strongest prejudice which Gladstone had to overcome, and he never understood its power.

When Gladstone rose on 7 June to close the debate, he wore a white carnation in his coat, and his pallor matched that of the flower. He knew then that defeat was almost inevitable, but he was determined to go down with all his guns firing. Gladstone denied that he had ever said that the Bill would be reconstructed : 'A person who has not promised that a Bill shall be reconstructed, is free to reconstruct it but is not bound to do so. I hope I have made a clear distinction.' That distinction was not very clear, but it was characteristic, and the Prime Minister added, above the tide of mocking laughter : ' I take it to be absolutely beyond dispute, that that which is voted upon to-night is the principle of the Bill, as distinguished from the particulars of the Bill.'

The Protestants of Ulster, Gladstone roundly asserted, were not the only people capable of loyalty in Ireland. They were loyal because they had nothing to complain about. It was necessary to produce a state of affairs in which the Roman Catholics would feel themselves similarly carefree : 'It is *our* policy that tends to union, and *yours* to separation.' This was one of the ' golden moments ' of history.

Gladstone denied that he was seeking to repeal the Act of Union of 1800, but he deplored the abominable way in which Ireland had been treated by England since the Union as well as before it. That treatment was ' a broad and black blot ' upon the British record :

' Ireland stands at your bar, expectant, hopeful, almost suppliant . . . She asks a blessed oblivion of the past, and in that oblivion our interest is deeper than even hers . . . Think, I beseech you, think well, think wisely, think, not for the moment, but for the years that are to come, before you reject this Bill [Loud and prolonged cheers].'

Gladstone sat down soon after one o'clock on the morning of 8 June, and the division was taken at once. 93 Liberals voted against the Second Reading, and the Bill was thrown out by 343 votes against 313—a majority of 30. At about 2 a.m. the grand old man sat down alone in his room at the House of Commons to write his account for the Queen. There his friends found him, bent, and for the first time almost crushed, beneath the weight of his burden.

In Cabinet later that morning (8 June) Gladstone was pale as death, but utterly unrepentant and undaunted. He brushed aside the suggestion that the Government should resign and make way for the Conservatives. He reeled off twelve cogent reasons for an immediate appeal to the country against the decision of Parliament, and his

357

resolute attitude was unanimously endorsed. The Queen was asked to dissolve Parliament immediately, and the election campaign which followed was fought with unprecedented bitterness.

The Liberals made play with an unhappy phrase used by Lord Salisbury on 15 May at St. James's Hall. The Conservative leader had suggested that some peoples—Hottentots, for example, and Hindoos—were incapable of self-government. Liberal speakers everywhere reminded the people that the Tories set Irishmen and Hottentots on a level. The fiercest abuse which Gladstone had to endure, issued from Lord Randolph Churchill. In his address to the electors of South Paddington (19 June), Lord Randolph wrote :

' Mr. Gladstone has reserved for his closing days a conspiracy against the honour of Britain and the welfare of Ireland more start-lingly base and nefarious than any of those other numerous designs and plots which, during the last quarter of a century, have occupied his imagination . . . This design for the separation of Ireland from Britain . . . this monstrous mixture of imbecility, extravagance, and political hysterics, is furnished by its author with the most splendid attributes, and clothed in the loftiest language . . . but . . . the united and concentrated genius of Bedlam and Colney Hatch would strive in vain to produce a more striking tissue of absurdities . . .

' For the sake of this . . . farrago of superlative nonsense . . . all business other than that which may be connected with political agitation is to be impeded and suspended . . . all useful and desired reforms are to be indefinitely postponed, the British constitution is to be torn up, the Liberal Party shivered into fragments.

' And why ? For this reason and no other : to gratify the ambition of an old man in a hurry . . .

' The negotiator of the *Alabama* arbitration, the hero of the Trans-vaal surrender, the perpetrator of the bombardment of Alexandria, the decimator of the struggling Soudan tribes, the betrayer of Khartoum, the person guilty of the death of Gordon, the patentee of the Pendjeh shame, now stands before the country all alone, rejected by a democratic House of Commons . . . He demands a vote of confidence from the constituencies.

' Confidence in what ?

' In the Liberal Party ? No ! The Liberal Party, as we know it, exists no longer : in his Irish project ? No ! It is dead . . . In himself ? Yes ! . . .

' Gentlemen, it is time that someone should speak out . . . At this moment, so critical, we have not got to deal with a Government, or a Party, or a policy. We have to deal with a man ; with a man who makes the most unparalleled claim for dictatorial power which can be conceived by free men. It is for that reason that I have deliberately addressed myself to the personal aspect of the question . . .

' Mr. Gladstone, in his speech at Edinburgh on Friday, recommended himself to the country in the name of Almighty God.

' Others cannot and will not emulate such audacious profanity . . . '

That was superb invective, and there was enough mischief in the phrase about the old man in a hurry, to strike home and do damage. It was taken up all over the country, and it helped to gain for Lord Randolph, at the age of thirty-seven, the appointments of Chancellor of the Exchequer and leader of the House of Commons when the Elections were over. It may have helped to inspire the unprecedented violence of the language employed by *The Times* not only against Gladstone's policy, but against his character and motives.

Finding himself unopposed at Midlothian, Gladstone was tireless in addressing public meetings elsewhere. He informed the Queen (22 June), who had protested strongly, that he was only following ' a rule of popular agitation' which had been established by Lord Salisbury since 1880. In forwarding that ' strange letter' to Sir Henry Ponsonby the Queen said that it was ' grievous' to see a man of Gladstone's age ' behave as he does, and lower himself to an ordinary demagogue . . . If only he could be stopped ! '

There was no stopping Gladstone now. He was at Glasgow on 22 June ; at Manchester on 25 June ; at Liverpool on 28 June. He noted at Liverpool : ' Seven or eight hours of processional uproar and a speech of an hour and forty minutes to five or six thousand people . . . I went in bitterness, in the heat of my spirit, but the hand of the Lord was upon me.'

While the results were coming in, early in July, Gladstone stayed at Hawarden, without his secretaries : ' I cannot', he told Mrs. Gladstone (2 July), ' see the advantage of being in London. The absolute work may be nearly the same, but I have dead quiet at night, and the Church in the morning is an immense advantage.' During the rest of the day Gladstone despatched innumerable letters and telegrams to candidates, some of which were rather wildly and unhappily worded. They were all published day by day in the Press, and as Mrs. Drew noted (25 July), they gave ' the whole world (and no wonder) a mistaken impression ' of her father's mental condition.

'No-one', she continued, 'thinks more strongly than he does that it was a mistake writing those, but . . . , as he had no secretaries, each was dashed off without reflection, in the heat of the moment.'

Much feeling was caused by an attack which Gladstone made on the Duke of Westminster for his action in helping to bring about the defeat of the Liberal candidate at Chester. In a consolatory letter (9 July) to his unsuccessful follower, Gladstone said that the Duke had struck 'a *fresh* blow at the aristocracy'. The Duke retorted by turning out of Eaton Hall the finest of the many portraits of Gladstone which Millais painted. It was bought by Sir Charles Tennant who presented it later to the National Gallery.[1] A typical example of Gladstone's language at that time was contained in a letter which he wrote (17 July) to his former secretary, George Leveson-Gower, after his defeat for North-West Staffordshire. Gladstone said that he was 'amazed at the deadness of vulgar opinion to the black-guardism and baseness—no words are strong enough—which befoul the whole history of the Union'.

The Times had already pointed out (10 July) that Gladstone had been acquainted with the history of that Union for half a century, and that he had 'never found it infamous until he needed an excuse for throwing himself into the arms of the Parnellite faction'. It informed its readers that it was impossible to keep pace with the mental evolutions of an unscrupulous politician in search of office. On 17 July *The Times* frankly charged Gladstone with the enormous offence of having changed his mind about Ireland from base motives of ambition; it suggested that the Prime Minister was unfit ever again to be trusted with affairs of state : 'Great as is Mr. Gladstone's fall measured by numerical standards, it is altogether eclipsed by the tremendous moral descent . . . which we venture to think cannot be paralleled in English history.' The masses, whom he had enfranchised, had been grossly betrayed ; they were unversed in political arts, and Gladstone had set out deliberately to take advantage of their ignorance by clouding and revolutionizing their minds : 'We do not know where to look for anything to match the extraordinary collection of letters, telegrams, and speeches emitted by him during this shameful struggle for unworthy ends.'

The Queen, Sir Henry Ponsonby, Lord Rosebery, and Gladstone's private secretaries consulted together about means of stopping the flow of excited letters and telegrams from Hawarden. The Queen

[1] It hangs in the National Portrait Gallery.

complained to Ponsonby (6 July) that the Prime Minister was ' trying to revolutionize the country and to ruin his own reputation '. Ponsonby told her the next day that as the Elections were ending, the worst was presumably past, and on 8 July, when he returned to Downing Street, Gladstone was quite calm again. He greeted his son with the words, ' Well, Herbert, dear old boy, we *have* had a drubbing, and no mistake ! ' The final results gave 316 Conservatives and 78 Liberal Unionists a combined majority of 118 over 191 Gladstonian Liberals and 85 Irish Nationalists.

The Elections had been turned by Gladstone into a virtual plebiscite on Home Rule, and that issue was too novel and academic. The rural electorate, more particularly in Southern England, disappointed of its hopes of social reform, voted solidly Conservative. Large sections of the urban electorate, however, outside London and Birmingham, remained loyal to Gladstone. The Queen had written to Gladstone (4 July) to express regret at his incessant attacks on ' the wealthy and educated classes ', and to invite him to recognize in his opponents an honesty of purpose equal to his own. Gladstone replied (8 July) that he had ' expressly and repeatedly ' recognized his opponents' honesty, ' but those recognitions are lost in the length of his interminable speeches which it cannot be expected that anyone should read '.

He admitted ' with great sorrow ' his defeat, but pointed out that many years had passed since he had first had occasion to draw attention to ' the singular fact that for a long series of years, on all the greater questions dependent mainly on broad considerations of justice and humanity, wealth, station, and rank had been wrong, and the masses had been right '.

On 20 July Gladstone submitted his Government's resignation to the Queen, and with a sigh of unspeakable relief she turned to her Unionist friends.

Lord Salisbury asked Lord Hartington to become Prime Minister in a joint Unionist Government, but Lord Hartington declined. He stated publicly (5 August) that he still hoped for a Liberal reunion after the rump of the Party had abandoned the aberration of Home Rule. His real reasons, however, were different. They were confided (24 July), in substance, to Lord Salisbury and to G. J. Goschen.

Lord Hartington considered that if he were to take office as Prime Minister he would be ruled by Lord Salisbury, and that Chamberlain with his followers would be driven back into Gladstone's arms.

Lord Salisbury and Joseph Chamberlain were unwilling to sit together in the same Cabinet. Lord Hartington also considered that he would probably be defeated by a Gladstonian Liberal at the by-election in his constituency which his acceptance of office would necessitate.

Lord Salisbury was therefore left to form a purely Conservative Government. Gladstone was left to reflect that while he had, like Peel in 1846, smashed up his Party, he was deprived of the consolation which Peel had enjoyed of watching his policy succeed. It was perhaps fortunate that Gladstone could not know that, as a result of his precipitate ineptitude, the Liberal Party would, with one brief interlude, be out of office for nineteen years.

On 23 July Mrs. Gladstone sent her husband from Hawarden a letter for their wedding anniversary :

My own own,

We are away from each other, but not in spirit. My mind travels back to the 47 years of blessed memory with a thankful heart. Thank you for all you have done, for all you are, and for the lovely example you have been to me, in sorrow, or in joy ! And Almighty God strengthen and help you more and more, and lift you up *continually*, so that if further work and further toil and anxiety be yours, the same Hand which has so mercifully sustained you, may still lead you along the earthly path, until it leads to the Heavenly Habitation of rest and bliss, to the shadowless light of the full day.

Darling old thing, I long to give you such a kiss. We are just going to Church, and the best thing of all will be to pray for you, and to thank God for the extraordinary mercies which for 47 years have been given to us.

Till tomorrow,
Your loving
Wifie.

In the serene happiness of his home, all Gladstone's troubles dissolved, and he toiled cheerfully at a pamphlet on the Irish question which was published on 22 August, 1886. Ireland, he wrote, had only to persevere for a few years of 'constitutional and peaceful action, of steady and free discussion', and the 'walls of Jericho' would presently fall 'not in blood and conflagration, but at the trumpets' peal'. The pamphlet breathed confidence and serenity.

On 30 July Gladstone went to Osborne for his farewell audience with the Queen. He noted that the conversation 'was filled up with nothings' and that the Queen sedulously avoided 'anything which could have seemed to indicate a desire on her part to claim anything in common with me'. He found the occasion 'rather melancholy. But on neither side, given the conditions, could it well be helped'.

While he was at Osborne, Gladstone told Sir Henry Ponsonby that he had been writing letters while in office and with the aid of his secretaries, at the rate of about 25,000 a year. In a letter to his wife (31 July), Ponsonby gave an amusing account of a conversation with the fallen Minister as he prepared to leave Osborne on 31 July in order to catch the boat. Ponsonby came to say goodbye, and Gladstone, who had not mentioned Ireland to the Queen, began on that subject at once. The dialogue went as follows :

W. E. Gladstone : "Now about Ireland. I cannot for the life of me see that any other plan, generally speaking, is practicable besides that which we have put forward."

Sir Henry Ponsonby : "And which was rejected because it gave Ireland an existence separate from England."

W. E. G. : "Good Heavens no ! In what way ? "

Sir H. P. : "It gave Ireland a Parliament—"

W. E. G. : "A Statutory Parliament for the management of her own affairs."

Sir H. P. : "But co-equal, so far, with the Parliament of Westminster."

W. E. G. : "Not co-equal ! The power of all the Governments possible could not create a co-equal Parliament."

Sir H. P. : "But you destroyed the Imperial Parliament—the governing body of the United three Kingdoms."

W. E. G. : "No ! No ! No ! A hundred times no ! The Imperial Parliament remained in complete enjoyment of all its powers."

At that moment a footman reminded Gladstone that the carriage was ready to start. Gladstone took no notice, and continued talking to Ponsonby.

W. E. G. : "Yes ! Yes ! I tell you, of all its imperial power."

Sir H. P., raising his voice to the pitch of Gladstone's : "Minus that of the independent Irish government."

W. E. G. : "It wasn't to be independent in that sense."

363

At that moment the footman warned Gladstone that he might miss the boat. Gladstone replied impatiently, "Yes! Yes!" and continued talking to Ponsonby.

W. E. G.: "No! I say if there had been a repeal of the Union, a restoration of Grattan's Parliament—"

Ponsonby and the footman, after exchanging glances, managed between them at that moment to push Gladstone into the waiting carriage; he went on speaking out of the open window.

W. E. G.: "that *might* have been an independent Parliament, but what we demand is a statutory body for the management of Irish affairs, which we have failed to manage from Westminster, and this is what—"

The rest was lost as the coachman whipped up the horses and the carriage drove off: "Most unfortunate," Ponsonby commented, "I think I was getting the best of it."

Ponsonby returned to the Queen who wanted his advice about a letter she had drafted to send to Gladstone. She had ended it by asking Gladstone not to encourage the Irish to expect that they would ever have Home Rule, as that was now impossible. Ponsonby considered that the Queen ought not to say that to the Opposition leader, and that Gladstone would certainly retort that Home Rule was a probability rather than an impossibility. In the end the Queen wrote (31 July):

'On the occasion of Mr. Gladstone's visit yesterday, the Queen did not like to allude to the circumstances which led to his resignation—but she would wish to say a few words in writing.

'Whatever Mr. Gladstone's personal opinion as to the best means of promoting peace and contentment in, and restoring order to Ireland, the country has unequivocally decided against his plan, and the new Government will have to devise some other course—in due time . . .' The Queen said that, in the circumstances, she trusted that Mr. Gladstone's 'sense of patriotism may make him feel that the kindest thing he can do *for* Ireland is to abstain from encouraging agitation by public speeches'.

Gladstone assured the Queen that he would never encourage violence. He said, however, that the only threat to the peace and contentment of Ireland which he recognized came from the Protestants of Ulster 'under deplorable instigation from this side of the Water'.

He noted, privately, 'Poor Ireland ! It has but a small place in her heart.' He felt desperately tired, and on 25 August he went again to Tegernsee, in Bavaria, to spend a holiday with Lord and Lady Acton and Dr. Döllinger. Mrs. Gladstone was unhappy at being left behind.

Dr. Döllinger was now aged eighty-seven, but Gladstone still found him a tolerable walking companion. On 7 September, 1886, the two old men walked seven miles together over a hill which separated Tegernsee from the next valley towards the East. Döllinger disagreed with Gladstone's views about Home Rule, but he refused to discuss the subject because he said that Gladstone was impervious to argument and 'clad in triple steel'. Gladstone was, however, gratified to find that the subject had aroused great interest in the Catholic monasteries of Bavaria. He visited several of them, and had long discussions about Home Rule with the monks.

As soon as he came home (19 September), greatly refreshed by his holiday, Gladstone plunged into a new controversy. He turned suddenly on Lord Tennyson, and accused him of marring 'by tragic notes' the happiness of Queen Victoria's jubilee. The Poet Laureate had published a sequel to his early poem, *Locksley Hall*, and Gladstone disapproved of the note of pessimism and disillusionment which had crept into it. He preferred, he said in an article which was published in January, 1887, in the *Nineteenth Century*, the 'ample vitality' of Tennyson's youth to the 'stilted vitality' of his age. After cataloguing the long series of reforms which had helped to set the individual free during the previous half-century, Gladstone said that he could see no grounds for disquiet at all, except only in two directions. He foresaw trouble if the State were ever to try to work out the individual's vocation for him, instead of leaving him to his own devices, as God intended. And he foresaw further trouble in Ireland 'although for the purposes of this paper I regard it as forbidden ground '.

That boundless, bracing optimism helped to make Gladstone the supreme representative of an age of shallow-rooted thought, and of pullulating and uninhibited activity in every field. It helped also to make him superior to life's accidents. His philosophy found characteristic expression in an article entitled *Universitas Hominum* which he contributed to the *North American Review* in December, 1887. He said that history, ' complex and diversified as it is, and presenting to our view many a ganglion of unpenetrated and perhaps impenetrable enigmas, is not a mere congeries of disjointed occurrences, but is the evolution of a purpose steadfastly maintained, and advancing towards some consummation . . .'

That consummation was 'the Christian scheme'. The reason for the existence of other religions 'less favoured than our own' must 'wait for final elucidation at the hands of the All-just and All-wise'. The final consummation of that Christian scheme was not, at present, fully discernible ; 'yet it does offer a mass of net results . . . of which I will select two, the most comprehensive in their character. First, that in the precinct of Christendom is found the actual mastery of the world, where all that exists, exists in the main by its permission, or under its control. Secondly, that whereas other ruling powers and paramount forms of civilization have had, following upon their maturity, their " decline and fall ", . . . the great Christian civilization presents many and perhaps conclusive signs of a progressive, though a chequered growth, without any decree set forth against it of a boundary or an end.'

That, Gladstone wrote, was the pattern of history which it was every man's duty to reflect in his thought and in his work. A fire of inspiration should drive him forward, 'and its warmth will be part of his reward'. Of that inspiration and that warmth Gladstone possessed his full share. He wrote in his diary on his seventy-seventh birthday (29 December, 1886) :

'It has been a year of shock and strain. I think a year of some progress ; but of greater absorption in interests which, though profoundly human, are quite off the line of an old man's preparation for passing the River of Death. I have not had a chance given me of creeping from this Whirlpool, for I cannot abandon a cause which is so evidently that of my fellow-men, and in which a particular part seems to be assigned to me.'

Such was Gladstone's creed, simple, vulnerable, positive. It gave him courage to recognize now the need for patience. He was no longer in a hurry, and as the Government disclosed its hand he watched the tide of events swing slowly round to his advantage.

In September, 1886, the Government rejected Parnell's plea that Irish landlords should be prohibited from evicting tenants who paid up half their arrears of rent. The continued fall in agricultural prices was causing such widespread distress that the Government was forced to adopt that plan in August, 1887, after some landlords had behaved in a manner which was as legal as it was abominable. Lord Clanricarde, for example, an eccentric bachelor and multi-millionaire, whose annual rent-roll in Ireland alone exceeded £25,000, obtained from the Irish Chief Secretary, Sir Michael Hicks-Beach, the use of 500 constables. With their aid he proceeded to effect a large number of pitiless evictions among the 1,900 tenants of his 52,000 Irish acres against the advice of his agent and without visiting his estates.

GLADSTONE UNDER WAY

The Irish responded by setting the law at defiance and adopting what they called the Plan of Campaign. They combined to refuse to pay a higher rent than local opinion considered reasonable. That opinion was expressed through unauthorized associations of ignorant and desperate peasants. There was a renewed wave of outrage and terrorism, which was answered by a drastic Coercion Act, and while Gladstone raised his voice in denunciation of the Government, Arthur Balfour, aged thirty-eight, was sent to Ireland to restore order, as Chief Secretary, on the resignation of Sir Michael Hicks-Beach through ill-health on 5 March, 1887.

Balfour filled the place in the affections of his uncle, Lord Salisbury, which Lord Frederick Cavendish had once filled in those of Gladstone, who was his uncle by marriage. And Balfour's appointment, like that of Lord Frederick, was greeted with derision. Balfour was regarded at the outset by the Irish as an effeminate dilettante, and was nicknamed ' Clara ', but he quickly showed his claws. Before long he was being denounced as ' Bloody Balfour ' on both sides of St. George's Channel. The new Coercion Act became law in August, 1887, and the prisons were soon overflowing. It began to look as though Ireland might be deprived of Parliamentary representation at Westminster after all, as her M.P.s were flung, one after the other, into gaol, where they were treated as common criminals.

Balfour's Coercion Act did not pass the Commons without encountering serious opposition. With the object of smoothing its passage, The Times had, on 7 March, 1887, begun to publish a series of articles entitled, Parnellism and Crime. Those articles tried to prove that the Irish leaders were privately sympathetic towards crimes which in public they found it expedient to denounce ; but they attracted little notice.

The Times was not an impartial newspaper. Its editor, G. E. Buckle, hated Gladstone, and it had departed, during Gladstone's third administration, from its traditional policy of giving fair support to the Government of the day. Its reputation, however, stood so high that the political and social worlds were convulsed when, on 18 April, 1887—the day fixed for the Second Reading of the Coercion Bill—The Times printed in facsimile a letter which Parnell was alleged to have written (15 May, 1882), expressing qualified approval of the murders of Lord Frederick Cavendish and T. H. Burke :

' To denounce the murders was the only course open to us . . . But . . . though I regret the accident of Lord F. Cavendish's death, I cannot refuse to admit that Burke got no more than his deserts.'

A sulphurous leading article reiterated a previous challenge to Parnell to bring an action if he dared, and Lord Salisbury went out of his way to point an obvious moral. All Gladstone's enemies were now able to indulge the delicious hope that the grand old man deserved to be treated as a moral leper. Had he not allied himself with Parnell from motives which were manifestly disgraceful ? And was it not clear that his ally, Parnell, had criminally connived at the assassination of Gladstone's favourite nephew ?

CHAPTER 15

WHEN THE BOUGH BREAKS
1887–1892

A^T the moment when *The Times* launched its attack upon Parnell's personal integrity, a formal attempt to reunite the Liberal Party had just broken down to the accompaniment of useless recriminations. That attempt was precipitated by the impulsive resignation, on 23 December, 1886, of Lord Randolph Churchill, who overreached himself and ruined his career. Joseph Chamberlain seized the opportunity, that night, to make a gesture of conciliation to Gladstone in a speech at Birmingham. Chamberlain feared that the Government without Lord Randolph might become so reactionary that he would have difficulty in supporting it.

On the eve of Christmas the call for reconciliation was well-timed, and Sir William Harcourt responded with alacrity and enthusiasm. Gladstone gave his blessing to the idea of a conference, but Lord Hartington was afraid of compromising himself if he were to consent even to discuss Home Rule. He declined, therefore, to take any part in the experiment of a round-table conference which met twice in mid-January and once in mid-February, and which was never repeated. The Gladstonians were represented by Sir William Harcourt, Lord Herschell, and John Morley ; the Liberal Unionists by Joseph Chamberlain and Sir George Trevelyan. The only result was that Sir George Trevelyan unconditionally rejoined the Gladstonian camp. An interview between Gladstone and Chamberlain took place on 5 April, but it proved as abortive as the wider conference.

Gladstone hoped that, as the situation in Ireland continued to deteriorate, English opinion would swing slowly and decisively in his favour. Chamberlain thought that Gladstone might be back in power in 1888. For nearly three years a kind of guerilla warfare raged in Ireland, and Gladstone did everything he could to depict the Conservatives as the friends of privilege and as the oppressors of the downtrodden Irish peasantry. He told a meeting of Yorkshire Liberals on 17 March, 1887, that until the Irish problem was settled, it would be impossible for any useful business to be transacted in Parliament, and he seldom spoke himself at that period on any other subject. He constantly claimed, as at Cardiff on 7 June, that the civilized world had already pronounced judgement in his favour.

On 9 September, 1887, during a riot at Michelstown, in County Cork, the police fired into a mob. Three lives were lost and a coroner's jury returned a verdict of 'wilful murder' against the police, whom Arthur Balfour had previously congratulated. At Nottingham (18 September), Gladstone coined the phrase 'Remember Michelstown !', and it was quite effective on Liberal platforms for many years. The jury's verdict against the police was quashed by the High Court on a technical point of law.

The Queen's Jubilee in June, 1887, helped the Government by releasing a wave of imperialist and patriotic emotion. Gladstone himself on one occasion (27 May) was persuaded to entertain a party of visiting colonials. He was living at Dollis Hill, near Willesden, in an attractive Regency villa with its farm buildings behind and 500 acres of fields around it which had been lent to him by Lord Aberdeen. Mrs. Gladstone had characteristically sent out her invitations too late. Few guests, therefore, arrived, and those who did were regaled by a substantial tea with meat sandwiches laid out on the lawn on a coldish afternoon. Gladstone, who seemed in excellent spirits, told his guests that it was absurd to imagine that other countries might be so base as to envy the wealth or power of Great Britain, or that they might ever scheme to attack and despoil her. He astonished them by saying that he had never in his life dined at the House of Commons until once, quite recently, when he had felt too exhausted to return home without refreshment. After the visitors had departed, Gladstone turned to Edward Hamilton, and said solemnly in a low voice which vibrated with intensity :

'If I were in a dying condition, I confess I should have one great apprehension in my mind—what I conceive to be the great danger to my country. It is not Ireland. That difficulty will be solved. It is not the character of future measures. The good sense of the people will take care of those. It is the *men* of the future—personalities of the stamp of Randolph Churchill, and Chamberlain !'

Gladstone made a great fuss before the Queen's birthday (24 May) about sending a letter of congratulations. He wondered if it would be acceptable, or in accordance with precedent, and he would not post it until Mrs. Gladstone had first consulted Sir Henry Ponsonby : 'Please be quite honest,' Mrs. Gladstone wrote (21 May). 'I never can make him think he is a great man ! . . . Please, one line, directed to *me tonight*.'

Other factors besides the Jubilee were helping the Government at that time. G. J. Goschen, a Liberal Unionist, who succeeded Lord Randolph Churchill as Chancellor of the Exchequer, W. H. Smith, the great newsagent and stationer, who succeeded as leader of the Commons, and Arthur Balfour who succeeded Sir Michael Hicks-Beach as Chief Secretary for Ireland, all proved outstandingly successful in office and in debate. Arthur Balfour in particular, without in any way abandoning his air of fashionable elegance, astonished the House by the proof which he repeatedly gave of his ability to stand up to Gladstone on equal terms. Gladstone told the Liberal 'Eighty' Club (19 April, 1887) that the Government's 'adamantine majority' could best be undermined by platform work outside the walls of Parliament. He urged his hearers to inform the minds and enlighten the consciences of the masses in the constituencies, and on 29 July, with unwonted levity, he told a large audience in the Memorial Hall, Farringdon Street, that after being apparently extinguished twelve months before, he found that he was now everywhere 'popping up again'.

The charges brought by *The Times* against Parnell helped for a time to prejudice the Home Rule cause. On the day (18 April) that the facsimile letter appeared in print, Parnell informed the House of Commons that it was 'an audacious and unblushing fabrication'; but he disregarded the challenge of the editor of *The Times* that he should vindicate his character by bringing an action for libel. Parnell's position was difficult, for if he had sued in Ireland and obtained a verdict there, that verdict would have carried no weight in England; while if he had sued in England he would have had little chance of obtaining a verdict, and he would have been exposed to a dangerous and damaging cross-examination about his whole career as a revolutionary agitator, before a hostile Middlesex jury, in a matter which had already been publicly prejudged by Lord Salisbury, the Prime Minister. Caring for nothing except Home Rule, and Mrs. O'Shea, Parnell decided to ignore *The Times*. His pride may have derived some satisfaction from that public display of his contempt for English opinion.

It is disagreeable to have to admit that Parnell was probably well-advised to take no action, but his silence infuriated his enemies, and inspired them with a fierce determination to force him by hook or by crook into a court of some kind. There appeared to be no better effective prospect of stopping the flow of Home Rule successes at by-elections, and great excitement was, therefore, aroused when

Parnell was brought to bay at last through the action of an eccentric Irishman, F. H. O'Donnell. O'Donnell had sat in the previous Parliament ; he, too, had been attacked by *The Times* ; and he brought a belated action for libel in July, 1888.

The Times briefed the Attorney-General, Sir Richard Webster (Lord Alverstone), and the jury returned a verdict in its favour without troubling to leave their box. Before they did so, however, Sir Richard read a number of fresh letters which Parnell was alleged to have written, some of which contained open incitements to murder. Convinced that he would be unable to obtain justice from any English jury, Parnell made (6 July, 1888) a personal statement in the House of Commons. He denied that he had written or authorized the writing of any of the alleged letters, and demanded that a Select Committee of the House should be appointed to inquire into the forgery.

Infected by the troubled and excited state of public opinion, the Government refused that reasonable demand. It offered instead, and finally, against Parnell's wish, arbitrarily and unfairly insisted upon, the appointment of a ' special commission ' of three judges, all of whom were outspoken Unionists, to inquire not merely into the question of the letters, but into the whole substance of the charges brought by *The Times* against members of Parliament and others. One result was, as Gladstone pointed out in a speech at Hawarden (20 August), to threaten Parnell at the least with financial ruin. The commission of judges was, in effect, ordered to inquire into the whole course of Irish history during recent years. So long as it sat Parnell would be under the necessity of briefing counsel of approximately the same rank as the Attorney-General. There was, Gladstone declared, gross inequality in the procedure which the Government had ordered, for *The Times* was a wealthy newspaper, and if it were convicted of fraud, or proved to have been deceived, it would probably lose few subscribers, whereas if Parnell were convicted of lying he would be a broken as well as a bankrupt man.

The Government had its way, and Parnell, against his friends' advice, began separate proceedings against *The Times* for libel at Edinburgh, with the object of diverting attention from the judges' commission which began its sittings on 18 September, 1888, in London. Parnell briefed Sir Charles Russell (Lord Russell of Killowen), and *The Times* was again represented by Sir Richard Webster. Seventeen months passed before the judges reported, and during that time some 98,000 questions were addressed to some

450 witnesses on 128 days. The question of Parnell's alleged letters was not reached until 14 February, 1889.

Under brilliant cross-examination by H. H. Asquith, a young Liberal member of Parliament who made his name on that occasion, the manager of *The Times*, J. C. Macdonald, was forced to admit that no adequate steps had been taken to establish the authenticity of the letters, and that the notorious facsimile had been printed by the editor, G. E. Buckle, with much misgiving. On 20 February a disreputable journalist, Richard Pigott, who had forged all the letters and sold them to *The Times*, entered the witness-box. He collapsed under cross-examination by Sir Charles Russell. The cross-examination was not concluded at the close of the day's sitting on Friday, 22 February, 1889, but Pigott had had enough. Over the week-end he fled to Paris, leaving two discrepant confessions behind, one of which was signed in the presence of Henry Labouchere, M.P., the editor of *Truth*. Pigott was traced to Madrid, where the Spanish police ran him to earth on 1 March with a warrant for his arrest. He shot himself dead as they burst into his room, and that desperate act helped greatly to emphasize the innocence of Parnell.

The Irish leader became a popular hero overnight. The British sense of fair play kindled on his behalf into a blaze, and a tremendous fillip was given to the Home Rule cause. Lord Salisbury did himself little good by reminding the public that the judges' commission was still sitting and that the letters were of minor importance, since they only proved that one disaffected Irishman had forged the writing of another from squalid motives. The commission continued for another year to try the Irish cause, but public opinion had made up its mind, and *The Times* on 27 February, 1889, unreservedly withdrew all charges against Parnell which had been based on letters obtained from Pigott. At Edinburgh, Parnell's libel action had been dismissed with costs on 5 February. Notice of appeal had been given, and *The Times* was fortunate to be able to compromise the action by an immediate payment of £5,000—a sum of which Parnell was greatly at that moment in need. Scottish opinion was much disturbed, and the Irish leader was accorded the Freedom of Edinburgh. From first to last the case cost *The Times* over £200,000 and greatly damaged its reputation. *The Times* lost many readers to the new popular Press as a result of the disproportionate amount of space which it had felt it to be its duty to devote day by day to the boring details of the proceedings of the commission.

When Parnell entered the House of Commons on 1 March, 1889, for the first time after his vindication he received an extraordinary ovation. Gladstone rose in his place and bowed low to him, and the Liberals, Liberal Unionists and Irish Nationalists stood and cheered until they were hoarse, some waving their hats and others clapping their hands. While the Opposition demonstrated like schoolboys, most, but not all, Conservatives remained seated and made no sign. Lord Hartington, who still sat with Joseph Chamberlain in piquant proximity to Gladstone on the Opposition front bench, was the only man who remained seated on that side of the House.

Parnell received the ovation standing, with a countenance which appeared expressionless to some, contemptuous to others. When silence was restored he made an unemotional speech of about twenty minutes on the Government's Irish policy, which the House had been debating, without a single warm sentence or personal allusion of any kind. Members felt as though they had been subjected to a douche of ice-cold water, and doubts were expressed in the smoking-room as to whether Parnell was really human or even perhaps wholly sane. Nothing could, however, extinguish the effect of the exposure of the forgery, and Gladstone set the seal upon Parnell's rehabilitation by inviting him at the end of the year to stay at Hawarden. Mrs. Drew noted (18 December, 1889) that, at forty-three, the Irish leader looked ' more ill than any other I ever saw off a death-bed '. His manner was ' refined and gentlemanlike ' ; he spoke with calmness and apparent frankness in a voice that was 'low and weak'; he radiated a mysterious magnetism, and his deep piercing eyes seemed to ' look bang through, not at, yours '.

The judges' report, when it finally reached Parliament (13 February, 1890), exposed involuntarily the way in which sentiment and passion had caused the ordinary processes of opinion, administration, and even law to be abused. Parnell was completely exonerated, but many of his colleagues, and the Irish Nationalist cause in general, were severely implicated by the judges' findings. Nobody cared, and the report came as an anti-climax. The public remembered only that Parnell, after being accused by *The Times* and by the Prime Minister of disgraceful conduct, had been shown to have been the victim of an impostor. It concluded, therefore, quite mistakenly, that the Irish leader was a spotless hero who had been the victim of a sinister and far-reaching conspiracy. At the same time the executive was discredited because it had overreached itself by invading the sphere

374

of the judiciary in order to make party capital out of Parnell's misfortune. Even the fair name of British justice was seen to have been slightly tarnished, not only by the judges' action in lending their aid and countenance to the Government's plans, but by Parnell's avowed and, as events at Edinburgh had proved, but too well-founded reluctance to trust the impartiality of a British jury.

When W. H. Smith on 3 March, 1890, moved the adoption of the judges' report, Gladstone, in a magnificent speech, appealed to members as ' individuals, man by man ', to express their detestation of the iniquitous outrage to which Parnell had been subjected by *The Times* and by the Government. He appealed, however, in vain. The report was adopted without qualification or amendment ; and only one man, as the debate ended (11 March), broke clean away from the solid if somewhat uneasy ranks of the Conservatives. Lord Randolph Churchill, with the first marks of the fatal disease that was later to destroy him beginning already to be stamped upon his features, denounced the Government for its unfair treatment of the Irish leader and for its arbitrary behaviour :

' What has been the result of this uprootal of constitutional practice ? What has been the one result ? Pigott ! A man ! A thing ! A reptile ! A monster ! Pigott ! Pigott ! ! Pigott ! ! ! Pigott ! ! ! ! '

*　　　*　　　*

Gladstone was very well satisfied, on the whole, with the outcome of the affair of the forged letters, for the nation appeared to be rallying behind him in a way which even his warmest admirers would hardly have dared to anticipate. By the end of 1890 the Government had suffered a net loss of 12 seats at by-elections, and a General Election in the spring of 1890 would have resulted in an overwhelming majority for Home Rule. The political barometer seemed to forecast the sunniest weather, and Gladstone could not possibly foresee the crippling blow which fate was waiting to deal him. He told Dr. Döllinger (13 July, 1889) that unless he himself were suddenly to die, or, ' which would be worse ', unless Parnell were to be removed, the success of the Home Rule cause seemed assured.

Gladstone was convinced that he would soon be in office again, and that God was preserving him for that purpose. He was 80 on 29 December, 1889, but he still cut down trees in his park at Hawarden, and presented chips to the hordes of admirers from all parts of the kingdom who flocked thither to stare at him. He laughed at Sir Andrew Clark who had been asked by Lord Granville and Lord Spencer to warn him that such violent exercise was very risky at his age, and that 'something might snap at any moment'. When he finally gave up tree-felling in October, 1890, he devoted many strenuous hours instead to rearranging the 28,000 books in his library. Mrs. Gladstone rounded very sharply on Edward Hamilton, one evening (30 June, 1888), when he hinted that her husband might be too old to undertake again the office of Prime Minister. The colour rushed to her face as she said that she and her husband were convinced that the call would come 'sooner than people expected', and that, if it were not answered, her husband would be guilty of a breach of trust, and of 'working now under false pretences'. Mrs. Gladstone added that she would much prefer that her husband should die in harness, and in the act of attempting to translate his words into deeds, than that he should run away from his duty, as he had once appeared to do in 1875.

When the Gladstones on 25 July celebrated their golden wedding, many tributes were paid to the perfect example of married bliss which they had presented for half a century to the world. The Queen sent a somewhat chilly telegram of congratulations, but the Prince of Wales sent a massive silver-gilt inkstand, and Lord Rosebery, whose touch was always happy, sent a gold-topped walking-stick for 'the old parliamentary hand'. The women of the three kingdoms gave a new portrait of Gladstone, with his little grandson, painted by Millais, and a most affectionate letter was sent to Mrs. Gladstone by the aged Cardinal Manning.

On his golden wedding day Gladstone made an eloquent speech in the House, which was greeted rapturously by the Conservatives, in support of the report of a Select Committee which had been appointed to consider the question of additional grants for the main-tenance of the Royal Family. Gladstone had been a member of that committee, and his speech offended the Radicals. He was opposed by John Morley and Sir Edward Grey, as well as by Henry Labouchère to whose opinion he was often, unaccountably, willing to defer.

The Queen showed no appreciation of Gladstone's loyal attitude, and Edward Hamilton noted that Gladstone's language about her, in private, became for a time 'unmeasured'. He was bitterly offended when she refused an invitation to Hawarden in August, 1889, while she was making a tour of Wales. She went instead to the home of her husband's biographer, Sir Theodore Martin, near Llangollen. Gladstone sometimes complained to Lord Granville about the Queen's hostility which filled him, he said (12 March, 1888), not with regret or annoyance, but with ' disgust '.

A far more serious private trouble arose at this time, when Gladstone's eldest son, William, collapsed on 1 March, 1889, from what appeared to be a stroke, accompanied by paroxysms and followed by sickness, partial paralysis, and loss of speech. Cancer of the brain

GLADSTONE IN THE HOUSE OF COMMONS, 1893, BY PHIL MAY

was not diagnosed until much later, and William Gladstone lingered for more than two years, before dying on 4 July, 1891, while under-going an operation. He had possessed great physical strength and had been an enthusiastic mountaineer. Although he had spent many years in Parliament and had held minor office, William Gladstone was without ambition, and he had given up a great amount of time to music. He was idolized by his mother.

By comparison with that blow, the deaths of Sir Thomas Gladstone (22 March, 1889), John Bright (27 March, 1889), Dr. Döllinger (10 January, 1890), and Lord Granville (31 March, 1891) were lesser griefs. Gladstone never made a parade of his emotions, and he

377

incurred criticism, when his brother died, because he did not remember to wear mourning. He was invariably preoccupied, and like a commander in the field he had no time to spare in which to lament the loss of comrades. He had been campaigning all his life and he saw, at last, the prospect of a crowning victory before his earthly mission was completed. He awaited the event with courage and high hope, as, wearing his years lightly, he relaxed in the society of his friends.

Friendship for friendship's sake had never formed any significant part of Gladstone's strictly regulated scheme of life. That life to him meant the service of God, and he was too simple to understand that many men were eager to take advantage of him. When, for example, he felt the need to relax with increasing frequency in his old age, he was perfectly happy to take favours from such men as Sir Donald Currie, the shipowner, and from Sir Edward Watkin, who wanted Gladstone's support for the Channel Tunnel Company in which he had a controlling interest. Gladstone was a convinced believer in the desirability of a Channel tunnel, and he hotly resented the arguments which were constantly brought against it on grounds of military security. Gladstone's advocacy might, however, have carried more weight if it had not been common knowledge that Watkin occasionally arranged Gladstone's holidays abroad and sent couriers to assist his journeys, and that he had extended a branch railway to Hawarden for Gladstone's convenience (1890). As long as he had a congenial audience Gladstone was content, and rightly or wrongly, parts of his entourage were regarded as second-rate. He was too guileless to be always a good judge of men and too ingenuous to see that he would have been wise to choose carefully those from whom he was willing to accept favours.

His two most intimate private friends at the end of his life were Stuart Rendel [1] (1834–1913), a wealthy engineer and armament manufacturer, whose daughter, Maud, married Gladstone's third son, Henry, on 30 January, 1890, and George Armitstead [2] (1824–1915), a wealthy financier. Both were stalwart back-benchers who often put the Gladstones up for long periods in London and entertained them for short periods abroad. George Armitstead, in particular, acted

[1] He had been at Eton, and Oriel College, Oxford, and became Lord Rendel on Gladstone's recommendation in 1894.

[2] He was born in Russia and educated privately; he became Lord Armitstead on Sir Henry Campbell-Bannerman's recommendation in 1906. He lived in complete privacy and retirement after Gladstone's death in 1898. The fact that he had married unsuccessfully was unknown to Gladstone.

for some years as Gladstone's unofficial travel agent. In that way
Gladstone's enemies were given an excuse to accuse him of sponging,
but Gladstone himself was much too unworldly to care or even
to understand. He occasionally took a furnished house in London
for a few months, but he was convinced that he would soon be
back in Downing Street and he therefore divided most of his time
in London between Stuart Rendel's houses at 4, Whitehall Gardens
(which had once belonged to Sir Robert Peel) and, later, 1, Carlton
Gardens, and at the villa at Dollis Hill which had been lent to him
by Lord Aberdeen. He devoted to charity as much as possible
of the money which he saved in that way. Gladstone was exceedingly
generous as well as unworldly, and he carried out his resolve to divest
himself of all superfluous wealth before he died.

Towards the end of Gladstone's life some of those who knew him
best began to record their impressions of his conversation and habits.
He was never seen to better advantage than during the period around
his eightieth birthday, when he appeared to enjoy a kind of St. Martin's
summer. His confidence in the coming triumph of the great cause
which he had espoused matched his deep reverence for the heroes
of the past and helped him to overcome his distrust of the men of the
future. A few samples of those records may be of interest.

Lord Rosebery loved to tell a story about a visit which he had
paid to Hawarden when Lord Ripon and John Morley were fellow-
guests. All three were sitting with Gladstone in the library one
evening, when their host rose rather suddenly and bundled Lord Ripon
and John Morley into another room, leaving them with a solitary
candle between them. Gladstone had recollected that it was the hour
of family prayers, and in his view the banishment of Lord Ripon,
who was a Roman Catholic, was indispensable. The presence of
John Morley, who was an agnostic, would have been tolerated, but
he too was banished to save Lord Ripon from feeling lonely. Both
men would have been happy to stay behind with Rosebery, who
assured them, the next morning, that they had only themselves to
blame. Lord Ripon had been banished for believing too much;
John Morley for believing too little.

On 26 December, 1888, when the Gladstones were staying for two
months with the George Rendels at their villa in Naples, Gladstone
argued after dinner that occasional drunkenness, when it was solely
due to ' social feeling and temptation ', deserved to be treated with
indulgence. Later that evening, Gladstone sat alone reading a

theological book in German by Dollinger, in a small study which had been fitted up for him by his host. Stuart Rendel, watching his brother's guest through a chink in the door, could see the book firmly held up to the candle. Unwilling to go to bed before the guest, Rendel was making up his mind to disturb Gladstone, when he suddenly noticed the great arch of Gladstone's head so situated that it was obvious that he had dropped on to his knees, and was deep in prayer, bending low over the seat of the arm-chair in which he had been reading. Ten minutes passed, while Rendel waited, and then the light suddenly disappeared. Gladstone had slipped out by another door, 'shunning, I suppose,' Rendel noted, 'any break in his thoughts and acts by his usual bidding of me goodnight.'

Gladstone's tolerance of drunkenness was remarkable in one so austere. Hating a teetotal dinner, but having no temptation to drink hard, during his later years he appeared greatly to relish stories which hinged upon drunkenness. On the other hand, his repressions made any stories which hinged even remotely upon sex, virtually incomprehensible to him. Intimate friends occasionally tried to explain such stories to him in vain. Cynicism and irony invariably disgusted Gladstone, and his sense of humour was notoriously capricious. There were, however, two rather surprising stories which Gladstone could sometimes be persuaded to tell when he was in the right company, and in the right mood.

One concerned an Englishwoman in the Scottish Highlands who expressed regret when a local chieftain arrived at a party in Lowland dress, with trousers :

" Na, na, Lady ! I never put on a kilt nowadays—except when I have taken physic."

The other concerned a fellow-member of the House of Commons who had once been a guest with Gladstone of the Duke of Argyll at Inveraray. This man loved his liquor, and his host noticed one evening that he was flushed and excited although the port had only been round twice. The Duke promptly asked the men if they wished to retire before they joined the ladies, and Gladstone's fellow-guest could not restrain his indignation at being deprived of the third glass of port on which he had been counting :

" Na, na, Duke ! It will be a long time before Your Grace makes any of us p—— in this house."

Speaking of the Army, Gladstone said at Naples that he could not help resenting the pretensions of an exclusive caste, which was too closely associated with the Court. He did not think that the Navy was separated from the nation in quite the same way. He spoke of the terrible evening when the news of Lord Frederick Cavendish's murder was known in London. Lord Hartington had been quite useless at his niece's house : 'However much he felt, he had nothing to say.' Lord Granville, on the other hand, had been splendid. Before they all dispersed he had embraced everyone, including Gladstone.

On a later occasion, in December, 1891, when he was staying as the guest of George Armitstead at an hotel in Biarritz, Gladstone spoke with evident relish about Döllinger as a man 'purged of self' and about Manning as a man in whom 'the flesh was extinct'. Shortly afterwards (31 December) Gladstone had to spend a day in bed after a surfeit of wild strawberries. He said that he had never encouraged his sons to enter politics because politics pandered to the passions and gave too much scope to the 'natural man'. Ideals in politics could never be realized ; he had been forced to recognize that truth. It was, however, vital to feed constantly and to fan the flame of 'righteous indignation'. For all the deterioration which had occurred during his time in public life, he blamed one man only— Disraeli. Palmerston had had faults, but he had had also many sound principles and genuine liberal convictions. Disraeli had had no principles or convictions of any kind, except on the subject of the Jews. Gladstone said that he had not, he thought, personally disliked Disraeli ; he had, on the contrary, found plenty to admire in him ; but he had intensely disapproved of the man who had corrupted and debauched the public life of England.

Disraeli, Gladstone declared on another occasion, must bear the blame for the demoralization of Randolph Churchill, Joseph Chamberlain, and even Arthur Balfour who had become the most unscrupulous man in public life. Gladstone dreaded the day when John Morley, 'with his lofty and high-souled integrity', would be left alone to face such adversaries. He added that he did not believe that modern man was improving as a type ; 'he is not so big, so grand, so heroic as he has been'.

Gladstone overvalued Morley as he had overvalued Lord Granville, because they both tended to say smooth things to him and to give him the support and comfort which he liked. In John Morley's letters, however, there is occasionally a sycophantic note, which is wholly absent from Lord Granville's. Mrs. Gladstone begged Morley

(1 January, 1892) not to be afraid of putting unpleasant points some-times to her husband : " The perturbation from what is disagreeable only lasts an hour," she assured him. She tried to persuade her husband that Morley was 'deepening'—i.e. that he was becoming a 'believer'—but Gladstone was not convinced. Gladstone considered that Morley was 'as great morally as he is intellectually'; he added that he could only regret that he nevertheless lacked magnetism and the gift of leadership.

Speaking of some of his former colleagues, Gladstone said that Peel's most tiresome fault was a tendency to sulk. John Bright was as unselfish a man as he had ever known, but he could not, unfortun-ately, endure chaff. He said that at an early stage in his relations with the Queen he had vainly tried to induce her to meet his old friend, Dean Ramsay, of the Scottish Episcopal Church. The Queen had then told him that she 'was not much of an episcopalian'. She was, he knew, unreasonably prejudiced against Scottish Episcopalians, and he was afraid that she had little feeling for the Church of England either. He had always resented the fact that she took Holy Com-munion in the Church of Scotland, though he believed that she did so only once a year. He had ascertained that she only communicated twice a year in the Church of England.

As Gladstone grew older, the repressions of a lifetime were in-sensibly lifted a little, and he found it possible to relax simply and naturally in the presence of young, pretty, and vivacious women. Margot Tennant,[1] for example, left Hawarden just before Parnell arrived for his one visit. After she had left, Gladstone sent her (17 December, 1889) a poem which in quality is well above his average as a versifier :

Margot

When Parliament ceases, and comes the Recess,
And we seek, in the country, rest after distress,
As a rule upon visitors, place an embargo
But make an exception in favour of Margot.

For she brings such a treasure of movement and life,
Fun, spirit, and stir, to folk weary with strife.
Though young, and though fair, who can hold such a cargo,
Of all the good qualities going as Margot?

$$\bullet \quad \bullet \quad \bullet \quad \bullet \quad \bullet \quad \bullet$$

[1] A daughter (1864-1945) of Sir Charles Tennant; married (1894) H. H. Asquith (1852-1928), Prime Minister, 1908-16, Earl of Oxford and Asquith, 1925.

Gladstone was rewarded by a letter (19 December) beginning ' Very dear and honoured Mr. Gladstone '. Despite the appeals of many women friends, however, he set his face against all proposals that women should be given the vote. He told Samuel Smith, M.P. (11 April, 1889), that he had too much respect for the difference between the sexes, to seek ' to trespass upon the delicacy, the purity, the refinement, the elevation ' of women's nature.

On 30 January, 1890, Gladstone went up to All Souls College, Oxford, of which he was an Honorary Fellow, to spend ten days as an ordinary member of that society. He derived immense pleasure from his visit, and it may safely be said that there were few weeks in his life which he enjoyed so well. His ostensible purpose was to verify certain references in connexion with some articles about the Old Testament which he had in hand. The articles appeared in *Good Words* between March and November, 1890 ; they were republished in book form in December, 1890, and entitled *The Impregnable Rock of Holy Scripture*. Gladstone's unavowed purpose, however, was the recovery, in his eighty-first year, of some portion of the impressions of his youth in preparation for a fourth term of office as Prime Minister.

Gladstone pleased All Souls quite as much as the College pleased him : " Ah, Professor ! " he said, on the afternoon of his arrival to one diehard Tory who had previously declared a conscientious resolve to avoid any traffic with the Liberal iconoclast. " It is one of the great charms of Oxford that one meets at every moment someone with whose name in some branch of learning one has long been familiar." The Professor surrendered at once, and was soon trotting about after Gladstone with a cream-jug and sugar-bowl.

From first to last that visit was an extraordinary success : ' I am reading the Lessons,' Gladstone wrote to his wife (2 February), ' and all sorts of things—such pranks ! ' He conquered the hearts of the Oxford Tories by his exquisite courtesy and simplicity, by his childlike delight in their company, and by a fascinating combination of complete sincerity and a seemingly unbounded faculty of self-deception. He deplored in conversation the increasing slackness of University dress and ceremonial ; regretted the disappearance of the gold tuft of the nobleman-commoner, which he said, quite wrongly, that he had always considered ' a valuable element ' in the social life of Oxford ; and, although his youngest daughter, Helen, became Principal of Newnham College, Cambridge, he made it clear that to him personally the invasion of the University by women students was profoundly distasteful. As the days passed he seemed to become more and more possessed by the genius of the place, so that Tory sentiments poured from his lips with increasing frequency: " I view," he declared, " with the greatest alarm, the progress of socialism at the present day . . . Whatever influence I possess will be used in the direction of stopping it." He defended the pocket boroughs, and said that the Duke of Wellington had been perfectly right when he said, in 1830, that the Constitution was incapable of improvement. The country, Gladstone roundly affirmed, had never been better governed than it was in the days before the great Reform Act; he argued that the unreformed House of Commons would have been perfectly competent to carry all the really worthwhile reforms between 1830 and 1880, and he recalled with pleasure that the first reformed House of Commons, to which he had been elected in 1832, still contained one member who habitually wore a pigtail, and two who did so from time to time.

No Fellow of All Souls, however junior, had ever within living memory made use of a prefix in addressing another, however old or eminent. And Gladstone, when he found himself addressed by a junior Fellow—a beardless youth—as ' Mr. Gladstone', said, "Surely it should be Gladstone here ! " But an exception had to be made because no-one felt that it would be natural or appropriate to take him at his word. Gladstone's characteristic humility was felt occasionally to be overdone. He revelled in all the attentions that were paid to him, but he caused some amusement when he was heard to remark, at a tea-party given by a professor's wife, that he felt sure that if he were to slip quietly away without saying goodbye his absence would not be noticed.

One night, in response to an invitation, Gladstone strolled into the hall of the Union Society, and addressed the bewildered undergraduates, who had wanted something political, on the connexion between Homeric and modern Assyriological studies. The undergraduates submitted in silence, but they woke up after the vote of thanks, when he gave them, at last, ten minutes of genuine oratory. He praised the good old days, and his voice appeared to break at the end when he said that he would almost be willing to kiss every stone in the ancient walls of Oxford.

It was noticed that Gladstone frequently dragged Andrew Carnegie's ' gospel of wealth' into his conversation. He did so in order to make the point that anyone who postponed his charitable duties until after his death was a mean and contemptible creature. Testamentary bequests, Gladstone repeatedly declared, did not deserve the name of charity. It was every man's duty to follow Carnegie's example in giving away during his lifetime all the money he could spare. Gladstone was always careful to add that he strongly disapproved of the 'levelling' tendencies of the American millionaire's social and political creed.

Gladstone several times described himself as a lover of every species of lawfully constituted authority : 'I am the most conformable of men,' he would say. Oblivious of the fact that he was destined shortly to declare himself in favour of the disestablishment of the Church of Wales, he observed with great emphasis that any proposal of that kind would be a crime against God. He explained that he was an unrepentant dogmatist and denominationalist.

Gladstone did not appear at all pleased when Mrs. Gladstone arrived unexpectedly to stay for two nights with Sir Henry Acland, the Regius Professor of Medicine, in order to see, as she put it, that her husband did not damage his health by over-exerting himself. When they were together, however, their devotion to one another impressed everyone. When Mrs. Gladstone first appeared, her husband, with delightful inconsistency, was loudly lamenting the threat to which the peace of Europe had constantly been exposed as a result of Russia's aggressive designs on Turkey. The genius of the place must have caused him temporarily to forget that he had spent a large part of his political life in characterizing that alleged threat as a typical piece of Tory hypocrisy, and as an invention or delusion of Disraeli. Gladstone broke off at once when he saw his wife, and he was soon launched into an eloquent defence of the old, unreformed Oxford, and into a vindication of the claims of Eton, 'the queen of schools', to take pride of place above all others.

★   ★   ★

Throughout most of 1890 the tide of popular opinion continued to flow uniformly in the direction which Gladstone desired, and Lord Salisbury's Government appeared to be in danger of foundering. Its majority sank to four (17 June) on the Local Taxation Bill, and its licensing proposals had to be ignominiously withdrawn. It failed in its proposal that business should be carried over to an autumn session. On 28 December, 1889, however, a cloud 'no bigger than a man's hand' had appeared on the distant horizon. A year later it had become a thundercloud which threatened to overwhelm the Opposition, and to destroy the Liberal-Irish alliance on which all Gladstone's hopes depended.

W. H. O'Shea had filed a suit for divorce against his wife, and cited Parnell as co-respondent. The case came up for trial in November, 1890, and John Morley was sent to Brighton to interview the Irish leader in his rooms at the Hotel Metropole on 10 November. After a long discursive talk about the political situation, Morley brought up the question of the divorce : "There's one point on which I have no right to speak to you, and if you don't like it, you can say so. But it's important that we should know whether certain legal proceedings, soon to come on, are likely to end in your disappearance from the lead for a time."

Parnell, while Morley spoke, was toying with the prongs of a fork, and a smile slowly overspread his face :

"My disappearance ! Oh, no ! No chance of it ! Nothing in the least leading to disappearance, so far as I am concerned, will come out of the proceedings. The other side don't know what a broken-kneed horse they are riding."

Morley, whose ' high-souled integrity ' had won Gladstone's fervent admiration, concluded that there would be no adverse decree. He congratulated Parnell, and said that the Home Rule cause could not succeed without him. Parnell, coolly, agreed :

"The Irish people," he said, "are very slow to give a man their confidence, and they are still more slow to withdraw it."

The conversation was switched at once to less delicate ground, and Morley felt justified in reporting to Gladstone (13 November) that there was reason to think that Parnell would emerge as triumphantly from the divorce court as he had done from the special commission. Two days later (Saturday, 15 November) the case opened and there was found to be no defence. O'Shea was granted a decree *nisi* on 17 November and the judge saw fit to speak scathingly about Parnell. Gladstone had, on the previous day, reached the conclusion that Parnell should apply at once for the Chiltern Hundreds and resign his leadership of the Irish Party ; and *The Times* on 18 November enjoyed its revenge.

Referring to the precedent of Sir Charles Dilke, *The Times* pointed out that ' no statesman aspiring to control a powerful Party could survive the blow of having such a charge proved against him ' as had been proved to the hilt against Parnell. Parnell's disgraceful

386

conduct was on a par with the tenour of the whole of his previous life :

'Domestic treachery, systematic and long-continued deception, the whole squalid apparatus of letters written with the intent of misleading, houses taken under false names, disguises and aliases, secret visits and sudden flights, make up a story of dull and ignoble infidelity untouched, so far as can be seen, by a single ray of sentiment, a single flash of passion, and comparable only to the dreary monotony of French middle-class vice, over which the scalpel of M. Zola so lovingly lingers.'

To Gladstone the scandal came as an utter surprise, although he had heard rumours about an alleged liaison between Parnell and Mrs. O'Shea as early as May, 1882. Detectives had dogged Parnell's footsteps during the Irish troubles of that year, and Sir William Harcourt, who was notoriously indiscreet, had, as Home Secretary, read their reports and gossiped with Lord Granville and others. Throughout Queen Victoria's reign, however, the stigma attached to adultery was sufficient to blast the careers of public men. For that reason a useful and powerful taboo existed at that time against hearing or repeating scandal. Gladstone had always been particularly scrupulous to observe that taboo, and his mind did not register gossip. The nature of Parnell's private life had been known to, or strongly suspected by, many leading politicians for some years. But as long as no public scandal resulted, Parnell's liaison with Mrs. O'Shea did no more harm, politically, than, for example, did Lord Hartington's equally famous liaison with the Duchess of Manchester.

Once the scandal became public, however, the circumstances were altered, for the public mind was conditioned by the evangelical conscience of the age. During the last fortnight of November, 1890, the nation was convulsed by an hysterical ferment of reprobation, and Gladstone was expressing a sound political judgement when he used over and over again the Scottish expression, 'It'll na dee!' The Irish Party, and its principal newspaper, appeared still to stand solidly behind Parnell. But the Liberal Party, with its solid core of upright, narrow, respectable, Nonconformist voters, leapt into spontaneous revolt. Letters and telegrams poured into Hawarden Castle threatening Gladstone with a withdrawal of support unless he took immediate positive action to sever his alliance with a branded adulterer.

Gladstone rightly refused to make any overt move. He hoped that Parnell would retire voluntarily as soon as it was plain that the country had made up its mind. When Gladstone came up to London on 24 November to stay at Stuart Rendel's house at 1, Carlton Gardens, he resisted all attempts which were made to persuade him to woo the Nonconformist conscience by censuring publicly Parnell's immorality: " What ! " Gladstone exclaimed indignantly to Sir William Harcourt, who should not have exposed himself to the rebuke : " because a man is what is called the leader of a Party, does that constitute him a censor and a judge of faith and morals ? I will not accept it. It would make life intolerable."

Nevertheless, Gladstone was forced to admit that he had been occupied for the past five years in rolling ' the stone of Sisyphus ' —or the cause of Home Rule—to the top of the hill, and that now, unless Parnell consented to retire, it was obvious that that stone would crash down again to the bottom. In those circumstances Gladstone reluctantly allowed himself to be persuaded by his colleagues on the night of 24 November to compose a friendly letter of warning to John Morley, which Morley was asked to show to Parnell. In that letter the operative paragraph read :

' Notwithstanding the splendid services rendered by Mr. Parnell to his country, his continuance at the present moment in the leadership would be productive of consequences disastrous in the highest degree to the cause of Ireland. I think I may be warranted in asking you so far to expand the conclusion I have given above, as to add that the continuance I speak of would not only place many hearty and effective friends of the Irish cause in a position of great embarrassment, but would render my retention of the leadership of the Liberal Party, based as it has been mainly upon the prosecution of the Irish cause, almost a nullity.'

Gladstone in that letter had based himself fairly upon political and not upon moral grounds. The letter embodied an entirely proper confidential hint from a man whose duty required that he should do no less to a man whose duty it was to subordinate himself to the interests of the people whom he professed to serve. Gladstone hated writing that letter, and in the first draft he actually omitted the vital sentences which have been quoted. His friends insisted that they should be inserted, as had been agreed, and Gladstone, without complaint, walked over to the writing table and amended the draft.

So far no mistake had been made, and Lord Spencer was the only one of Gladstone's colleagues who was inclined to think that even Parnell's temporary withdrawal might prove fatal to the cause of

Home Rule. In fact, however, Parnell's voluntary and temporary withdrawal at that time would have been the one means of saving that cause. The full fury of the tornado would then have been given time in which to exhaust itself; the Liberal Party would have been returned to power at the next General Election with a decisive majority; many facts in palliation of Parnell's adultery could have been allowed to become widely known; and Parnell, in due course, would have resumed his leadership. The advice cabled by Cecil Rhodes from South Africa to Parnell was as wise as it was succinct: " Resign—marry—return ! "

Unfortunately, Parnell was too arrogant to take that advice. He despised the hypocrisy of the English, and he bared his teeth and prepared to fight. He had been too bitter and too proud even to ensure that his conduct should be fairly represented by the evidence which came out at the trial, and the case against him was made to appear, at the trial, much blacker than it really was. The ludicrous and squalid details, over which *The Times* and the public gloated, gave an entirely misleading impression of the facts. Parnell was as indifferent to public opinion as he was contemptuous of the strictures which the garrulous judge had unhappily considered it to be his duty to pronounce.

The divorce suit was undefended, but in fact Parnell's liaison had been condoned by O'Shea who had been consistently unfaithful to his wife, and who had behaved in a mean and far more reprehensible way than Parnell. O'Shea's objects were to obtain political office through his hold over Parnell, and to continue to extort money from his wife by blackmail. The O'Sheas were entirely dependent, financially, on a rich old aunt who paid Mrs. O'Shea a large annual allowance, and who, on her death in 1889, left her niece a fortune of nearly £150,000. The will was contested by other relatives, including Mrs. O'Shea's brother, Field-Marshal Sir Evelyn Wood, V.C.

O'Shea, an ex-officer of Hussars, who had been living extravagantly on his wife for twenty years, had been disappointed of his hopes of intriguing himself into office. He was now threatened with financial ruin through the action of his wife's relatives, and he had no hope of obtaining anything from Parnell whose estates had been mortgaged to the hilt in order to pay the legal expenses caused by the special commission. When O'Shea set out deliberately to ruin Parnell in 1889–90 he was an embittered man who felt that he had nothing more to lose and that the only consolation left to him was revenge.

Even after he had enjoyed that revenge, he managed to find another characteristic method of extorting money by blackmail from his former wife. The divorce had left him with a legal right to the custody of the two surviving children whom Mrs. O'Shea had borne to Parnell while she was still, ostensibly, living with O'Shea. O'Shea renounced that right in return for an annual allowance.

Parnell only wanted to be allowed to live openly with the woman he loved. He was sick of false beards and false names, and he refused any longer to compromise. That refusal led Gladstone impulsively to commit another of the cardinal blunders of his life. Gladstone's blunder was precipitated by Morley's failure to run Parnell to earth on the morning of 25 November, 1890, before the Irish Party met at 2 p.m. to elect its leader for the new Parliamentary Session.

Morley's object was to show Parnell a copy of the letter which Gladstone had written on the previous evening, but Parnell was adept at concealing his tracks and hiding when he so desired. The Irish Party met, therefore, and re-elected Parnell as its leader in total ignorance of the views of the Liberal leaders. When that meeting had broken up, soon after 3 p.m., Morley found Parnell at last in the centre of an excited group of his supporters. Parnell came forward with a smile, and held out his hand ; he apologized for having failed to make an earlier appointment to meet Gladstone's emissary.

Morley asked Parnell to come at once to Gladstone's room for a talk. On the way, Parnell, with an air of studied ingenuousness, mentioned casually that he had just been re-elected to the leadership of his Party. Morley made no comment until they were closeted alone in Gladstone's room. He then said that he was sorry to hear about Parnell's re-election, because he had something important to say which might still, he hoped, make a difference. He then read the text of Gladstone's letter, and noted that Parnell's face hardened.

When Morley had finished, Parnell said that he had no intention of retiring, temporarily or permanently. The outcry against him was a mere ' storm in a teacup '. Morley pointed out that a temporary retirement was indispensable if the Home Rule cause was to be saved. Parnell said he did not agree, that his mind was made up, and that he would not discuss the matter further. The interview was brief, and as he rose to leave, Parnell said : " Of course, Mr. Gladstone will have to attack me. I shall expect that. He will have a right to do that."

A few minutes later, Gladstone entered his room. Without waiting to remove his hat, and without sitting down, he asked Morley with great eagerness what had happened. " He is obdurate ! " Morley said, and for some instants Gladstone stood dumb and incredulous by the table. Then Gladstone's mind was convulsed, as it had been convulsed often on previous occasions, by a spasm of excitement which caused a fatal decision. He said that his letter must be sent to the Press immediately and published in all the newspapers.

Morley pleaded for discussion, or at least for a little delay, and the two men walked together into the House where they were joined on the Opposition front bench by Sir William Harcourt. A whispered colloquy followed, and Sir William agreed with Gladstone that the letter should be sent to the Press at once. Morley was despatched to do the deed after first warning Parnell. Parnell was at that moment in his usual place in the House, and Morley went into the lobby and called him out. Parnell, as soon as he was told, said simply :

" Yes ! I think Mr. Gladstone will be quite right to do that. It will put him right with his Party ! "

Parnell's tone was dry and restrained, but there was bitterness in his heart. On that day, after betraying his mission, he had sacrificed his people on the altars of his passion and of his pride. Gladstone, too, made an irretrievable blunder. By sending to the Press the letter which he had addressed to Morley he turned a friendly and timely private expostulation into a hostile and untimely public ultimatum which led to instant war. The alliance between the Liberals and the Irish, which had been the central fact in the political situation, was changed overnight into fratricidal strife, and the Home Rule cause was fatally prejudiced. Such fierce passions were aroused that little chivalry was shown. Even Lord Hartington, who might have been expected to be capable of feeling some semblance of sympathy with Parnell, told the Queen—' in his curious, gruff way ', she noted (29 November)—that ' I never thought anything in politics could give me as much pleasure as this does.'

Gladstone's sense of right-timing appeared to have deserted him, and he had behaved once more like an old man in a hurry. His position was exceedingly difficult, but he ought at least to have waited until public opinion had been allowed ample time in which to bring its full weight to bear, for it might, in the end, have proved strong enough to undermine Parnell's authority and position. It was foolish of Gladstone to take so openly upon his own shoulders the odium which, with more tact and finesse, he might have laid much more conveniently to the account of English middle-class hypocrisy. Gladstone should, for a time at least, have been able to satisfy the hard core of his Nonconformist followers, by arranging that his private opinion should be widely circulated, and that the difficulties of his position should be publicly and repeatedly emphasized by his principal colleagues.

The course which Gladstone adopted was more straightforward but far less expedient. In consequence the crisis was precipitated with terrible suddenness, and moderate counsels were given no opportunity to relieve the confusion or to blunt the bitter edge of controversy. The Irish Party was faced with a choice between deposing, at Gladstone's dictation, the commander whom it adored, or sacrificing the prospect of Home Rule at the moment when its triumph seemed at last to be assured. It failed to reach a decision, and for that reason both disasters were incurred. Parnell was deposed ; Home Rule was lost ; and, in addition, the Irish Party was torn in two and rent by debilitating feuds.

On 29 November Parnell issued a manifesto to the Irish people in which he appealed to the wildest and most irresponsible nationalist elements. He accused Gladstone of having taken up the Irish cause for selfish personal ends, and of subsequently betraying it. Parnell falsely declared that Gladstone had informed him at Hawarden that he was unwilling to meet Ireland's minimum demands. Gladstone had tried, Parnell claimed, to destroy the independence of the Irish Party by bribery.

It was clear to Gladstone, as it was also to responsible Irishmen and to the political world generally, that Parnell had lost his head. The Irish Catholic hierarchy had hitherto kept silence, but on 30 November it intervened against Parnell, and its action turned the scales. After twelve days of stormy debate in committee room 15 at the House of Commons, the Irish Party split into two warring factions. One faction, 26 strong, including John Redmond under whom the Party was eventually reunited, adhered to Parnell. The larger faction, 44 strong, seceded under Justin McCarthy.

The result was that Gladstone's second Home Rule Bill was presented to the country in 1893 without having been previously concerted with the accredited leaders of the Irish nation. It was framed against a background of internecine strife which alienated and disgusted British opinion, and it was deprived of the glamour and prestige

GLADSTONE BY HARRY FURNISS

which would have belonged to it if the grand old man of English politics and the darling of the Irish nation had come forward together to lay it upon the table of the House.

Some share of the responsibility for driving Gladstone forward against his better judgement must rest upon the shoulders of Sir William Harcourt. Day by day Sir William tried to persuade his aged and troubled chief to appease the Nonconformist conscience by treating the Irish leader as an offender against the moral code. Gladstone would never do that, but Harcourt's influence was felt when Gladstone issued his fatal order that Parnell should, in effect, be cashiered. Harcourt's influence was felt again, after Parnell had issued his reckless manifesto, when Gladstone unwisely declared that he would have nothing more to do with the Irish Party as long as it continued to be led by Parnell. That refusal was a mistake, for it appeared harsh in itself, and it was resented as a fresh provocative act of wanton interference in Irish affairs.

Parnell, like Lord Randolph Churchill, possessed the nature of a spoilt child ; each was the author of his own ruin. After marrying his mistress in June, 1891, Parnell died heartbroken and exhausted at Brighton on 6 October. During the last months of his life he had sown such feuds among his followers that his Party remained for years in a ferment ; and in Ireland a most unhappy legend gained currency, that Gladstone had set himself the task of breaking Parnell after changing his mind about the possibility of conceding all the demands which he had once promised. The truth was utterly different, but Gladstone's impulsive action in first cashiering Parnell, and afterwards refusing to treat with him even in secret, cost him much of the fame, affection, and gratitude among Irishmen everywhere which he had so richly earned.

The fall of Parnell was the heaviest political blow which Gladstone had sustained since the loss of his seat at Oxford : " You have no regrets," he asked Morley wistfully (17 December, 1890), " at the course we took ? " " None ! None ! " Morley replied. " It was inevitable. I have never doubted." Gladstone doubted, however, and Morley reported to Edward Hamilton on Boxing Day that he had never in his life seen the grand old man so depressed.

*　　　*　　　*

The General Election was drawing near, and for the first time in modern British history the line of cleavage between two main Parties was found to be based to a great extent upon class. Gladstone was deserted by almost all the patricians and by the great majority of the upper middle class. In those circumstances, in order to win the Election, he was pushed into radicalism against his will, but that radicalism was of a kind which looked as much to the past as it did to the future. Many Radicals in Southern England had already been attracted to socialism. Many more, in the Midlands and elsewhere, had been drawn off by Chamberlain, who had broken finally with Gladstone, and those were later either absorbed, like Chamberlain, into the ranks of the Conservatives, or recuited to the socialist creed. Gladstone's radicalism, therefore, became predominantly an expression of the centrifugal instincts of the ' Celtic fringe ' in Scotland, Wales, and Cornwall, where the masses vainly resisted for a time the centripetal tendencies of the age. The centripetal principle triumphed, and except on one occasion in 1906, after Gladstone's death, the Liberal Party never regained its hold upon England. As the years passed its light failed steadily ; between 1918 and 1939 it ceased to be an effective political force and was pushed ever further into the extremities of the island, where the Atlantic Ocean breaks against Land's End, and moans in the Pentland Firth and Cardigan Bay.

Collectivism, ' construction ',[1] socialism, were all anathema to Gladstone until the end of his life. His measures had aimed at the fulfilment of great moral ideas rather than at the distribution of small material gains. He had invariably appealed to broad abstract principles, with the object of making men worthier citizens by enhancing their capacities. When, as at the time of the repeal of the Corn Laws, he had fought for the material good of the workers, he had not been animated by considerations of shillings and pence, but by a love of liberty and justice. It was that love which inspired Gladstone's devotion to the cause of Home Rule, but in 1891 that cause was in eclipse. Serious unemployment riots in February, 1886, and November, 1887, and the great London dock strike of 1889, when Cardinal Manning had quickened the conscience of the nation, had focused the attention of increasing numbers of liberal-minded men and women upon the social problem at home.

Joseph Chamberlain, from his position outside the Government, had helped to educate the Conservative Party towards an acceptance

---

[1] ' Construction ' was a favourite word with Gladstone. He used it to describe a compound of socialism and social reform, undertaken by the State or by public bodies.

of broader views and more democratic way. The establishment in 1888 of rural self-government by county councils, the creation of the London County Council, and the abolition in 1891 of all fees in elementary schools, had been steps in that direction.

In those circumstances, Gladstone on 2 October, 1891, took a step which was out of harmony with the tenour of his previous career. He announced at Newcastle-on-Tyne—where he had not stayed since his disastrous speech in favour of Jefferson Davis in 1862—a number of policies which had been crudely designed to provide a practical answer to the social problems which were agitating the public mind, and to offset the reverse inflicted on the Liberal Party by the quarrel with the Irish Nationalists.

The 'Newcastle programme' wore the appearance of a demagogic hotch-potch which had been hastily compiled with the object of attracting as many votes from as many different sources as possible. The staple diet of Home Rule was garnished by such items as church disestablishment in Scotland and Wales, 'one man, one vote', triennial parliaments, and local vetoes on the sale of intoxicating liquors. Power was to be taken to acquire land for allotments and other public objects; district and parish councils were promised; and employers were to be made liable for accidents to workers. There were vague hints about further limitation of hours of work, and about payment of members of Parliament; and a warning to the House of Lords against the consequences of any interference with a Home Rule Bill.

Much of that was extremely distasteful to Gladstone, and he made no attempt to digest some parts of it at all. He became a little negligent in his old age about the means which he employed to achieve his ends. He had so much still to do, and so little time. He was nearly eighty-two years of age. It was noticed at Newcastle that while he was attacking the House of Lords, his arms were raised higher and higher, as though they sought to invoke the wrath of Heaven, while his knees sagged lower and lower, until it seemed as though they must end by touching the boards. The performance was not one over which he would have wished his biographer to linger, and he did not linger long over it himself. He seldom referred to it, and forgot it as soon as possible. Lord Hartington, speaking at Lord Salisbury's side at Liverpool on 25 November, 1891, said that he had now renounced the last hope of Liberal reunion. Three weeks later, on 15 December, Gladstone left England to spend two and a half months as George Armitstead's guest in the South of France.

396

When the Gladstones returned to London on 29 February, 1892, the air was full of rumours about an early dissolution of the Parliament which was then six years old. The Opposition spent its energy in deriding a Government proposal to extend local government to Ireland by means of county councils. On 24 May, Gladstone bitterly attacked a proposal by Arthur Balfour, who had become leader of the Commons on the death of W. H. Smith in October, 1891, that two Irish judges should have power to dissolve any Irish county council which had misconducted itself. On a number of occasions Gladstone scouted the idea that there was any need to accord separate treatment to Ulster in any scheme of Home Rule which a Liberal Government might introduce.

Parliament was dissolved on 29 June, 1892, a fortnight after Gladstone had told a deputation from the London Trades Council (16 June) that he declined to take up the question of a legal working day of eight hours. Ireland, he said, had the first claim upon his time. While he was speaking at Chester on 25 June, four days before the dissolution, Gladstone's eye was cut and damaged by a piece of gingerbread. The injury caused him great pain, but he refused to prosecute the woman who had thrown it.

While the Elections were in progress the Gladstones stayed with Lord Rosebery at Dalmeny. The Liberal Party managers had predicted a comfortable majority of at least a hundred, and if it had not been for the Parnell catastrophe that result would have been attained. The Queen, from the first, was pessimistic. She wrote to Sir Henry Ponsonby (4 June) that 'the idea of a deluded excited man of 82 trying to govern England and her vast Empire with the miserable democrats under him is quite ludicrous. It is like a bad joke!'

Gladstone emerged victorious, although he was mortified to find that his majority in Midlothian (13 July) was reduced to 690. The final results gave 273 Liberals, 81 Irish Nationalists, and 1 Labour member, a majority of 45 over 269 Conservatives and 46 Liberal Unionists. Lord Salisbury waited to meet Parliament and was defeated on 11 August, 1892, on a vote of no confidence moved by H. H. Asquith. The Government resigned at once, and on 13 August Sir Henry Ponsonby conveyed to Gladstone the Queen's commission to form his fourth administration. Gladstone begged Ponsonby to explain to the Queen that Home Rule was a profoundly conservative measure; it would bring peace and contentment to Ireland, and would turn the Irish into loyalists, and probably into Tories.

Gladstone's friends were dismayed by the smallness of the Liberal majority; the new Government was entirely dependent upon the Irish vote, and the result was just sufficiently favourable to make it inevitable that the Home Rule Bill would pass the Commons with the virtual certainty that the Lords would subsequently reject it with the tacit approval of about half the electors and almost all the dominant influences in Great Britain. It was not a cheerful prospect but Gladstone's spirit rose to meet the challenge. His fourth administration was an epic contest against hopeless odds which lasted for just under a year and a half.

At Biarritz, during the previous December, Gladstone had been visited by his old friend and former secretary, Sir Algernon West, G.C.B. West was due to retire during 1892, on attaining the age of sixty, from his post as chairman of the Board of Inland Revenue; and it was arranged that, in the event of a Liberal victory at the General Election, West should act as the unofficial head of Gladstone's secretariat and give his aged chief all the help in his power: " You have attached yourself to a corpse," Gladstone told him, " and for so short a time ! "

Accordingly, on 15 August, 1892, when Gladstone went to Osborne to kiss hands as Prime Minister, he was accompanied by Sir Algernon West, who had resigned from the Board of Inland Revenue on 4 April. The Queen awaited Gladstone's visit with the utmost apprehension. Lord Salisbury had warned her (2 July) that Gladstone had ' entirely outlived his judgement, though his eloquence to a great extent remains and his passions have become more imperious '. The Queen took the extraordinary step of announcing in the *Court Circular* that she had received Lord Salisbury's resignation ' with regret ', and she noted privately that Gladstone was ' greatly altered and changed, not only much aged, walking rather bent, with a stick, but altogether; his face shrunk, deadly pale, with a weird look in his eyes, a feeble expression about the mouth, and the voice altered '.

Gladstone's impression of the Queen was equally unfavourable. He told Hamilton (19 August) that he had noticed a sad deterioration; her intellect had grown sluggish and her judgement was impaired. He told Sir Algernon West that the interview had been as dismal as that which might have taken place between Marie Antoinette and her executioner, and he noted: ' not one sympathetic word, or any question, however detached '.

At dinner at Osborne on 15 August, Gladstone sat far away from

398

the Queen, next to Sir Henry Ponsonby's daughter, Mrs. Montgomery. Guests usually spoke in hushed tones at the Queen's table, but Gladstone ate heartily of everything that was put before him, and talked loudly throughout the meal about the necessity of Home Rule. When the ladies had retired, the Queen asked Mrs. Montgomery what Gladstone had been talking about with such animation. "Home Rule, Ma'am!" "I know! He always will!" When West went up to Gladstone's bedroom to see if he was comfortable, he found that it contained a cheap print of Disraeli, with other 'lodging house daubs'. For some time, while he was trying to get to sleep, the Prime Minister was disturbed by a Maid of Honour strumming on a piano in the adjoining room.

(*See page 401.*) John Morley vetoed Lord Aberdeen's appointment. Morley had been Chief Secretary when Aberdeen was Viceroy of Ireland in 1886 ; and they had then worked on terms of equality. Morley was now resolved not merely to be, but to appear to be, in undisputed control. He therefore insisted, despite Gladstone's fervent support of Lord Aberdeen, upon the appointment of a different Viceroy ; and Lord Houghton (later Lord Crewe) was accordingly appointed.

CHAPTER 16

THE GRAND OLD MAN
1892–1894

I N forming his fourth and last administration at the start of the thirteenth Parliament of the Queen's reign, Gladstone complained that he was ' beset right and left '. He had a number of difficult personal cases on hand of a kind which always set his nerves on edge. Foremost among those was the case of Lord Rosebery.

At Dalmeny during the General Election, Lord Rosebery had been irritated by Mrs. Gladstone. He thought that she had begun to interfere too much, and Gladstone himself had given offence by confiding more in John Morley than in Lord Rosebery. Lord Rosebery knew that his return to the Foreign Office was desired by Gladstone and considered indispensable by the Queen. But he went away on his yacht in order to make himself inaccessible, and he displayed a spirit of prickly independence which almost goaded Gladstone to despair. Lord Rosebery refused to take office on the ground that he suffered from insomnia. He said also that he desired solitude, and that all ambition had been buried with his wife who had died in November, 1890.

Gladstone told Lord Spencer that in public life Lord Rosebery was ' a perfect Bismarck '. He admitted that there was no-one from whom in private he had received more affection and generosity, but he would not see that Rosebery needed to be treated differently from other people. After a final abortive interview between Gladstone and Lord Rosebery on 11 August, the Prince of Wales successfully intervened on 15 August. Rosebery called on Gladstone during the afternoon of 15 August and said that if it had not been for the Prince he would never have consented to join the Government.

Gladstone told Lord Rosebery ' with intense passion ' that he had been through a terrible week. Sir William Harcourt, in particular, had treated him ' brutally '. Sir William had no belief in Home Rule, and had tried to dictate terms to Gladstone, who had reminded him that he, and not Sir William, was Prime Minister : " But it is for us to consider whether we will join you," Sir William had retorted. Gladstone told Lord Rosebery that he thought that he had never before been addressed so rudely, and he asked Lord Rosebery not to repeat what he had said ' to a living soul '. Sir William accepted

office as Chancellor of the Exchequer, but many personal relation-
ships were turned rancid by the bitter, unsparing tongue of that
warm-hearted, overbearing mountain of a man.

Lord Rosebery, Sir William Harcourt, John Morley who became
Chief Secretary for Ireland, and Lord Spencer who became First
Lord of the Admiralty, were all in the running for the succession to
the leadership whenever the time should come for Gladstone to
retire. Most of Gladstone's colleagues considered that he overvalued John Morley and Lord Spencer. Morley was as sensitive as
Rosebery, although in a different way. He was thought to be fussy
and old-maidish ; Lord Spencer was thought to be deficient in
initiative and intellectual force.

Henry Labouchère and Lord Acton strongly desired to enter the
Cabinet, and Lord Aberdeen wanted to go to Ireland as Viceroy.
All three were disappointed. The Queen could not tolerate
Labouchère's republicanism, and Gladstone, with his usual high-
minded loyalty, shielded the Queen by taking the responsibility for
his exclusion upon himself. He liked Labouchère, and did not in the
least resent a very widely-quoted remark which Labouchère had
made. Labouchère had said that while he had no objection to
Gladstone's habit of concealing the ace of trumps up his sleeve, he
did object strongly to his reiterated claim that it had been put there
by Almighty God. When he was refused office, Labouchère asked
for the Washington embassy as a consolation prize. The Americans
would have been pleased, and Gladstone wished him to have it, but
that appointment was in the hands of the Foreign Secretary, and Lord
Rosebery, who had been pilloried in *Truth*, had no love for Labouchère.

Gladstone deputed Sir Algernon West to break to Lord Acton
the news that there was no place for him in the Cabinet. Lord
Acton ' took it beautifully ' at the United Service Club, and Gladstone
was ecstatic in his praise. He offered to make Lord Acton Captain
of the Gentlemen-at-Arms, and Sir William Harcourt laughed loudly
at the idea of a half-German professor being placed in command of
the Beefeaters. Lord Acton may well have seen the humour of it,
but he wanted a post at that time for financial reasons. He had suffered in some speculations of his stepfather, Lord Granville, and in the
end he was glad to accept a Lordship-in-Waiting to the Queen.

Lord Aberdeen was seen by Gladstone himself. He had set his heart
on the Irish viceroyalty,[1] and Gladstone, who liked him immensely,

[1] See note on page 399.

told Hamilton that his behaviour had been 'angelic'. Lord Aberdeen was promised Canada, subject to the Queen's consent, and he went to Ottawa as Governor-General in September, 1893, when the term of office of Lord Stanley of Preston was ended.

The Cabinet contained seventeen members, and Gladstone described that number as 'outrageous'. He would have liked to cut the salaries of all Secretaries of State. He said later that he did not think that he would thereby have lowered the quality of candidates for the highest offices, and that he would have set a much-needed example of the 'minutely conscientious administration of public expenditure'. He thought that he could have made a good case for cutting the salaries of High Court judges at the same time; he did not, he said, believe that a modest cut would have impaired the future quality of the judicial bench. Gladstone contented himself, however, by making a rule that no member of the Cabinet should be a director of any public company. Lord Salisbury subsequently rescinded that rule, and Gladstone was confirmed in the opinion which he had once (24 February, 1888) expressed to Lord Acton that there was 'apparently' in Lord Salisbury, 'and in his nephew, Balfour, who is like him in much (bolder but less brilliant and incisive), an indifference on certain questions of honour that I cannot understand. I cannot describe it otherwise than as the exact opposite of the sensibility that Burke nobly described—that " which feels a stain like a wound ".'

The two members of the Cabinet who proved most successful were both newcomers and Nonconformists. H. H. Fowler (Lord Wolverhampton), aged sixty-two, had entered Parliament late in life; he had been Financial Secretary to the Treasury in 1886 and he now became President of the Local Government Board. H. H. Asquith, aged forty, had never held office before; he became the best Home Secretary of the century. One Cabinet appointment gave the Prime Minister peculiar satisfaction. (Sir) Arthur Dyke Acland, the son of Gladstone's oldest surviving Oxford friend, Sir Thomas Acland, became Vice-President of the Council. He did good work for education, but held Gladstone in such awe that he seldom opened his lips in the Cabinet.

The Government was hardly formed when the Prime Minister's career was nearly ended by a wild heifer which had escaped into the park at Hawarden. During the late afternoon of 29 August, Gladstone was taking a solitary stroll when the brute saw and attacked him. It knocked him down and stood over him. Bruised and

W. E. GLADSTONE INTRODUCING THE SECOND HOME RULE BILL.

W. E. GLADSTONE, MRS. GLADSTONE, AND THEIR GRANDDAUGHTER (DOROTHY DREW
    HAWARDEN, 1894.
  Photograph by Robinson & Thompson.

HAWARDEN CASTLE, c. 1885.

shaken, the Prime Minister retained his presence of mind. He lay quiet, pretending to be dead, until the cow's attention was distracted for a moment. He then picked himself up, dodged behind a tree, and escaped. Returning to the house the eighty-two-year-old Prime Minister was half-way through dinner before Mrs. Gladstone noticed that he seemed unwell. He said that he felt stiff and sore, and in answer to questions he explained what had happened. He was put to bed at once and bandaged, and the heifer was shot next day. The Queen made inquiries and wrote a letter of sympathy to Gladstone, who felt the effects of the accident for about three weeks. A beautiful and elaborate wreath was received at Hawarden, with a card attached, ' To the memory of the patriotic cow which sacrificed its life in an attempt to save Ireland from Home Rule '.

Divergencies inside the Cabinet arose almost at once. The great province of Uganda was run by the British East Africa Company, which was no longer able to pay its way. The Company proposed, therefore, to evacuate Uganda, and Gladstone, supported by most of the Cabinet, saw little objection. Lord Rosebery, however, would not hear of evacuation. He threatened to resign if Uganda were not annexed, and pointed out that Germany or some other power would inevitably seize control of it.

Gladstone could not afford to lose Rosebery, but he sighed for the days of Sir Robert Peel. Peel, he said, was a rigid economist, and a pacifist who did not suspect the intentions of foreign powers. Peel had had no desire to see the boundaries of the Empire constantly and unreasonably enlarged. A compromise was arranged whereby the Government gave the Company financial aid, and after Gladstone's retirement, Lord Rosebery proclaimed a protectorate over Uganda. Gladstone, who had been intensely excited by the dispute, noted that of all the blunders which he had ever committed, the one for which he had the least excuse was the appointment of Lord Rosebery as Foreign Secretary : ' Again and again he resisted my overtures.' Gladstone added :

' The fatal element in this appointment was his total and gross misconception of the relative positions of the two offices we respectively held, and secondly his really outrageous assumption of power apart from both the First Minister and from the Cabinet.'

Lord Rosebery sulked for a time when Gladstone received Waddington, the French Ambassador, and indicated that he would be happy to discuss the Egyptian problem. The Foreign Secretary considered that he should have been first approached, and the proposed discussions were never held. For those reasons during the autumn of 1892, Gladstone was exceedingly depressed and he began once more to tell his intimate friends that he was counting the days to his retirement. For some weeks he appeared to lose almost all interest in public affairs ; he could hardly bring himself to undertake any work on the preparation of the Home Rule Bill ; and he flatly refused to attend the Lord Mayor's Banquet, which was invariably graced by the Prime Minister's presence. Gladstone's principal attention was given to the preparation of the first Romanes memorial lecture which he had promised, many months before, to deliver on 24 October, 1892, in the Sheldonian Theatre at Oxford.

Gladstone's discourse, which was entitled *An Academic Sketch*, was distinctly nebulous. It dealt with the history of the idea or ideal of a university education. The speaker's passionate love of Oxford was, however, manifest throughout, and the grand old man was rewarded by a storm of cheers.

After Lord Tennyson's death on 6 October, 1892, the Prime Minister took considerable interest in the question of the succession to the office of Poet Laureate. The Prince of Wales urged A. C. Swinburne's claims, but Gladstone told Sir Henry Ponsonby (20 October) that after giving the matter full consideration he had reached the conclusion that Swinburne was ' *absolutely* impossible'. Gladstone had previously (7 October) told Lord Acton that Swinburne's *Poems and Ballads* (1866) were so ' bad and horrible ', that they disqualified their author : ' Wordsworth and Tennyson have made the place great. They have also made it extremely clean.'

Gladstone appeared at one time to consider that Ruskin's incipient insanity might be less of a bar than Swinburne's uncleanness. He told the Queen (13 October) that although Ruskin had only written a few poems, he was ' a poet in prose '. Arthur Acland had previously tried to obtain a K.C.B. for Ruskin, who felt himself neglected. After much correspondence, the Laureateship was left vacant until 1896 when Lord Salisbury appointed Alfred Austin, a Conservative journalist and poetaster.

Gladstone sat down seriously to work on the Home Rule Bill during the first week of November. It occupied almost the whole time of a cabinet committee which consisted of Gladstone, John Morley, Lord Spencer, Lord Herschell (Lord Chancellor), Henry Campbell-Bannerman (Secretary for War), and James Bryce (Chancellor of the Duchy of Lancaster) who was also the Regius Professor of Civil Law at Oxford and the author of *The American Common-wealth* (1888).

One difficulty which faced Gladstone was the invincible hostility of Sir West Ridgeway, the Civil Service head of the Irish Office, to the Home Rule cause. After Ridgeway had been induced to quit his post, Gladstone authorized Morley (20 November, 1893) to pay him £1,800 on the Secret Service account.

In the interests of Home Rule Gladstone had previously made two well-meant approaches to the Queen, whereby he hoped to bring about a more tolerant atmosphere. On 9 October he offered to send her to read all the letters which he had received more than sixty years before from Arthur Hallam, whom he and Tennyson had both loved. He added that he had seen Tennyson for the last time just after Robert Browning's death in December, 1889 : ' Tennyson said to him, " I have no doubt he is a great genius, but " (rather loudly) " I can't read him " ! ' The Queen replied that she would be glad to read Arthur Hallam's letters to Gladstone.

On 28 October, Gladstone struck a less happy note. He sent the Queen ' on his own responsibility ' a long memorandum about the political situation and the growing danger of a class war.

' At the present juncture ', Gladstone explained, ' the views of Your Majesty's actual advisers . . . are hardly at all represented, and as Mr. Gladstone believes are imperfectly known, in the powerful social circles with which Your Majesty has ordinary personal intercourse . . .

' The leading fact to which he would point . . . is the widening of the gap, or chasm which . . . separates the upper and more power-ful from the more numerous classes of the Community . . .

' This evil has been aggravated largely by the prolongation and intensity of the Irish Controversy . . .

' For the first time in our history we have seen, in the recent Elec-tion, a majority of the House of Commons, not indeed a very large, but also not a very small one, returned against the sense of nearly the entire peerage and landed gentry and of the vast majority of the upper and leisured classes . . .

' The moderate Liberal (and by moderate Liberal Mr. Gladstone means such a person as Lord Granville or Lord John Russell) has not quite become, but is becoming a thing of the past. There is to a large extent not only a readiness but a thirst for conflict with the House of Lords.'

After that alarming introduction Gladstone argued that the best means of saving the country from the dangers of a class war was the speedy settlement of the Home Rule controversy :

'Though Mr. Gladstone is firmly convinced that Home Rule is conservative, he is far from contending that it must of necessity always remain so . . . the longer the struggle is continued, the more the Liberal party will verge towards democratic opinion.' Gladstone ended what the Queen described as this ' very curious ' document by reiterating his ' firm conviction ' that ' the proposal of Home Rule is a proposal eminently conservative in the highest sense of the term '.

On Ponsonby's advice the Queen sent a purely formal acknowledgement. On 16 November, however, she pointed out that as she was entirely ignorant about the contents of the proposed Home Rule Bill she ' found it impossible to follow the argument used ' in Gladstone's memorandum. She added : ' He surely cannot mean that all are bound to support his policy without knowing the details of the measure, which, if the Queen rightly reads his Memorandum, is a conservative one . . . '

Gladstone was perplexed by the literal manner in which the Queen had construed his use of the term ' conservative '. He explained (18 November) that ' when he has spoken of Home Rule as a conservative measure, he has principally meant that, as he believed, it would tend powerfully to establish harmony between the several portions of the United Kingdom, and to attach some millions of Your Majesty's subjects far more firmly to Your Majesty's throne, and to the laws and constitution of the country '. He went to see the Queen at Windsor on 26 November, but he described the audience as ' sterile '. Lord Rosebery had previously advised his Sovereign by telegram to talk to Gladstone about Poets Laureate.

Gladstone went to Hawarden at the beginning of December ; and he received on 3 December, at very long last, the freedom of his native city of Liverpool. Lord Rosebery and Sir Algernon West began at that time to allow themselves to become irritated by Gladstone's family ; they considered that its members were too eager to interfere. Lord Rosebery complained (7 December, 1892) that they were becoming unmanageable, and even Hamilton noted unkindly (3 August, 1892) that Mrs. Gladstone and her daughter Helen were ' waylaying everybody, and scheming this and scheming that ; intercepting letters and almost listening at keyholes. I pity poor Algy West, who naturally complains with some bitterness.' On

7 December Hamilton noted again that, to Lord Rosebery's intense annoyance, the family were 'actually telegraphing to Armitstead, who is in Russia, about arranging the projected expedition for them to Biarritz . . . It is extraordinary how utterly wanting they are in any sense of dignity or self-respect.'

Gladstone was occasionally so overwrought that such difficulties were inevitable. He was suffering from insomnia, and was worried by the gradual failure of his hearing and by the threat of cataract in his left and best eye. He was not always considerate, but he was loved and venerated by his intimate circle. The little jealousies which surrounded him in his old age are no more significant than those which surrounded Napoleon—whom Gladstone professed to admire greatly in many ways—during his exile at St. Helena.

As time went on, Sir Algernon West found that his task grew no easier, and he complained sometimes that Gladstone's family wanted to dictate to him. On 14 December, 1893, for example, Hamilton found West bewailing the domestic situation in Downing Street: 'Mr. G.', he said, 'was becoming more and more the mere tool in Mrs. G.s hands, and she was less and less scrupulous about plans. If she wanted Mr. G. to go away, he went, regardless of all public calls ; and there was more and more sponging on Armitstead. It was Armitstead to do this, and Armitstead to do that, without apparently any thought of the expense to which this good-natured creature was exposed.'

None of that was unnatural. Gladstone was simple and unworldly, and he was frequently exhausted. On 18 December, 1892, the Queen gave Gladstone leave to go abroad, and, with the Cabinet's approval, he left England, with Mrs. Gladstone and Miss Gladstone, on 20 December to spend Christmas, his eighty-third birthday (29 December), and New Year, as George Armitstead's guest at Biarritz Armitstead came over to England to chaperon his guests on their journey.

Relaxing in the sunshine, Gladstone discoursed with rather more than his wonted vehemence on his favourite topics. He censured Archbishop Cranmer for moral weakness before he reached the stake, Shakespeare for excessive adulation of the Tudor despotism, Sir Walter Scott for 'silly' Toryism, and servility to 'that creature', George IV, Lord Salisbury for having made T. H. Huxley a privy counsellor, the English people for panicking at the suggestion of a Channel tunnel, and the human race for losing its 'sense of sin'.

Gladstone returned to London greatly refreshed on 10 January, 1893, and stoutly resisted Lord Rosebery's proposal that the army in Egypt should be reinforced in order to overawe the new and youthful Khedive who was resentful of British control. Gladstone told Sir William Harcourt (20 January) that such proposals made him 'fearful about the future', and he added :

'My life is a perfect burden to me. I would as soon set a torch to Westminster Abbey as send more troops to Egypt. It can't be . . . I can see nothing for it but for Lord Rosebery to resign.'

The Queen ordered Gladstone (21 January) to remember 'the terrible case of Khartoum and the cruel fate of Gordon !' She said that her letter was to be read to the Cabinet. Lord Rosebery did not resign. He promised Lord Cromer, in Egypt, the troops for which he had asked, and said that he would delay making any announcement as the moment was inauspicious. The new Parliament met for the first time on 31 January, and the Queen's speech contained a reference to events in Egypt which had necessitated the strengthening of the British army of occupation. A troopship on its way home to England from India had been ordered to disembark at Suez.

The Queen's speech announced also that the Government would introduce a 'Bill to Amend the Provision for the Government of Ireland'. Gladstone had entitled it a 'Bill for the Better Government of Ireland', but on 29 January the Queen flatly refused to allow the words 'Better Government' to be put into her mouth. On 13 February, 1893, Gladstone was ready to introduce that Bill. He rose at 3.45 p.m. in a crowded House after an almost sleepless night. His voice was good, though low, and he spoke for two hours and a half.

The main difference between the second and the first Home Rule Bills was a provision that 80 representatives from Ireland should sit at Westminster. They were to speak and vote only on matters which affected the Irish nation, and Gladstone estimated that, although the subject was 'full of thorns and brambles', that would include '9-10ths, or 19-20ths, perhaps 99-100ths' of the business which came before the Imperial Parliament. Representative Irish peers would continue to sit in the Lords, and each House would be responsible for construing the provisions of the Act in so far as they related to Irish representation at Westminster. In his peroration Gladstone appealed for peace between the British and Irish nations :

'If it were with my latest breath I would entreat you to let the dead bury the dead, and to cast behind you every recollection of bygone

WRITING THE QUEEN'S SPEECH

evils, to cherish and love and sustain one another throughout all the vicissitudes of human affairs in the times that are to come.'

The First Reading was allowed to pass without a division.

On 23 February, when the Opposition divided the House on a Welsh Suspensory Bill, which Asquith introduced, with the object of preparing the way for the disestablishment of the Welsh Church, the temper of the House was shown by the taunts which Lord Randolph Churchill flung at Gladstone. Lord Randolph accused the Prime Minister of selling the Welsh Church in order to buy votes for Home Rule :

' On behalf of the Irish policy nothing must be spared—not even the Established Church in Wales. Votes ! Votes ! Votes ! That is the cry of the Right Honourable Gentleman, and that is the political morality which he preaches . . . An English Government has never yet been conducted on such principles—better suited to a Whitechapel auction than to the conduct of our State.'

It was Lord Randolph's last throw before his strange illness destroyed him. Gladstone retorted that he accepted ' the monosyllabic invocation of the noble Lord, and I say " Vote ! Vote ! Vote ! " for both Welsh Disestablishment and Home Rule.'

The Queen was almost incoherent with rage. She told Gladstone (25 February) that he had taken :

' the *first step towards* the *disestablishment* and *disendowment* of the *Church* of England ! ! . . . this measure is *in reality directed against* the *whole Church* . . .

' The Queen *trusts* Mr. Gladstone may *yet pause* before taking so *disastrous* a step as to *attempt* to *disestablish* part of the English Church of which *she* is the *Head* ; and of which she *always* thought Mr. Gladstone was a *loyal member.*'

Gladstone's reply to the Queen was cogent and comprehensive : he sent (27 February) her letter to Asquith with the comment : ' The Queen's studies have not yet carried her out of the delusive belief that she is still by law the " head " of the Church of England.' Asquith was given leave to introduce his Bill by 301 votes to 245, but the measure was subsequently dropped.

On 28 February, to everyone's surprise, Gladstone found himself momentarily the idol of the City of London. In a lucid and brilliant speech he tore to pieces a proposal that the gold standard should be replaced by a bi-metallic standard. He argued that gold would always be stable and that silver could never be satisfactory.

THE GRAND OLD MARIONETTE; OR THE HOME-RULE DANCE

PUNCH, *February 18, 1893*

The Second Reading of the Home Rule Bill was carried on the night of 21/22 April, 1893, by 347 votes to 304, and when the House went into Committee on 8 May the Prime Minister took personal charge. He was alert and tireless ; he hardly ever left the House ; like some hero in Homer he gloried in every episode of the battle, and his performance, at the age of eighty-three, must be ranked among the supreme achievements of his life. For days on end he was able to forget the sombre certainty that the Bill would be rejected by the Lords, and the strong probability that the country might be too indifferent to raise the cry, ' Peers versus People ', on that issue.

One evening at that time Lord Randolph Churchill, in his warm-hearted, impulsive way, accosted Albert Grey, a Liberal Unionist, and exclaimed : ' And that is the man you deserted ! How could you do it ? ' He said that he could never bring himself to resume his ' unscrupulous attacks ' on Gladstone, who had really caused his political ruin. Lord Randolph added that he could have left Lord Salisbury and joined the Opposition, where he would have felt more at home, if Gladstone had not taken up Home Rule : ' But I can never countenance Home Rule, no matter what happens.' Gladstone had a certain regard for Lord Randolph who often visited him at Dollis Hill. In his ingenuous way he was grateful to Lord Randolph for having mortified him at times.

Gladstone made speech after speech on almost every amendment that was suggested, and at the end of June a new guillotine procedure, known as ' the gag ', had to be introduced. A time limit was set for the debate on blocks of clauses in order to overcome the Opposition's tactics of obstruction. Gladstone made no concessions to Ulster, and he called upon the Protestants of the North to unite ' in a noble and glorious unity ' with their Catholic fellow-countrymen in the South. He did, however, make three concessions as the debate proceeded.

On 16 May he accepted an amendment which expressly reserved the supremacy of the Imperial Parliament. On 12 July he accepted another which permitted Irish representatives at Westminster to speak and vote on all subjects. On 18 July Gladstone promised to review in six years' time the financial provisions of the Bill, and to set up a Royal Commission to study the whole subject of past and future Anglo-Irish relations.

On 11 April Gladstone told the Queen that Joseph Chamberlain was his most formidable antagonist ; the duel between them was marked by a number of incidents. On 21 April, a few days after the young Austen Chamberlain had delivered his maiden speech, against the Bill, Gladstone turned to Joseph Chamberlain and said that that speech 'must have been dear and refreshing to a father's heart'. All agreed that Chamberlain had never appeared so deeply moved. He rose in his place and bowed low to the Prime Minister. A fortnight later, however, when the members of the London Stock Exchange marched in procession through the City, Chamberlain addressed them in front of the Guildhall and made a fiery attack on Gladstone while a copy of the Home Rule Bill was being ceremoniously burned. The City of London had complained that Gladstone had caused a catastrophic fall in the values of Irish railway stock and bank shares, and that Ireland might find it impossible to raise credit unless her finances were controlled from London.

On 25 July Gladstone accused Chamberlain of using 'language of habitual, gross, and enormous exaggeration'. Next day Chamberlain replied to what he called that 'ferocious' speech, and on 27 July the atmosphere in the House was sultry and electric. Chamberlain renewed his attack on Gladstone, who, he said, behaved 'like a god', calling white black, or black white, as he chose. He continued: 'Never since the time of Herod——'

At that moment a shrill cry of 'Judas!' arose from the Irish benches, and it plunged the House into an uproar which the weak Chairman of Committees was unable to control. A mob was formed on the floor of the House and in an instant blows were being exchanged. The Speaker was sent for, and he arrived in about three minutes; his presence and dignity restored order at once, but the incident was regarded as disgraceful for many years. The Queen suggested to Gladstone (30 July) that the Bill itself, so repugnant to the feelings of the majority of the British nation, and desired only by a disaffected body of Irishmen, must bear the blame.

Gladstone kept Parliament sitting throughout the whole of that summer; it was not adjourned until 21 September. On the night of 1/2 September, however, the Third Reading of the Home Rule Bill was carried by 307 votes to 267. A week later, on 8 September, after the Duke of Devonshire (formerly Lord Hartington) had moved the Bill's rejection in the Lords, Lord Salisbury wound up the debate:

'If you allow this atrocious, this mean, this treacherous revolution to pass, you will be untrue to the duty which has descended to you

from a splendid ancestry ; you will be untrue to your highest traditions ; you will be untrue to the trust that has been bequeathed to
you from the past ; you will be untrue to the Empire of England.'

The division was taken and the Lords rejected the Bill by the
crushing majority of 419 to 41.[1] It was said that not a dog barked
from John o' Groat's to Land's End. The country was bored ; the
subject was exhausted ; many of Gladstone's colleagues were secretly
relieved. The mood of the country appeared to be adequately
expressed by the ripple of restrained hand-clapping with which an
awed and respectful crowd greeted the peers as they climbed into
their carriages after the division.

Gladstone immediately asked his colleagues to agree to a dissolution, in which the appeal to the country would have been that
which was used in 1910—'Peers versus People'. His colleagues
refused, but the Prime Minister remained undaunted. He persuaded
himself that they would agree presently, after the Lords had over-
played their hand by rejecting a few more Liberal measures, and he
announced publicly at Edinburgh (27 September) that Home Rule
would again appear upon the waves during the next session. Before
that time arrived a dispute of the gravest character arose between
Gladstone and his colleagues, and it led directly to his resignation.

The Parliamentary Session was resumed on 2 November, 1893,
and on 19 December an Opposition motion, calling for an expansion
of the British Navy, was proposed by Lord George Hamilton, who
had been First Lord of the Admiralty from 1886-92. Strained relations with France and heavy recent increases in expenditure upon
armaments by foreign powers had aroused widespread alarm in
Great Britain. Gladstone regarded that alarm as hysterical and he
treated it with contempt. He described Lord George's motion as
'unconstitutional', and stated that the responsibility for the nation's
safety and defence belonged solely to the Government which was
not prepared to share it with the Opposition.

Public opinion was profoundly disturbed. The Queen, the
Opposition, and the most powerful section of the Press, considered
that Gladstone's assurances were worthless. Almost all Gladstone's
colleagues were convinced of the urgent need to strengthen the Royal
Navy. The crisis had hardly dawned when a charming incident
occurred, which is not undeserving of record.

[1] The voting strength of the Lords (exclusive of princes of the blood) was
560. Over 82 per cent of that strength voted in the division.

On 16 December, during the continuance of the seemingly interminable session which had already lasted eleven months, and which allowed a break of only four days at Christmas, Gladstone received at Downing Street a letter in a childish hand, written between pencilled lines. It was from a son of Lord Pembroke:

Dear Mr. Gladstone,
   I am sorry we cannot go to Ireland for Christmas, as you have only given Father four days holiday. And I hope you will give him some more after this letter.
Yours sincerely,
George Sidney Herbert.

Gladstone replied the same day:

My dear Boy,
   It is very sad. I feel for you. And I feel with you. As you cannot get to Ireland, so I cannot get home, to my only home, at Christmas. And you, I hope, will have many, very many, very happy Christmasses. But I, having had eighty-three already, feel that I am taking one of my last chances.
   Can anything be done? Not by me. But I think your Father could do something, if he thought it right to ask some ten or a dozen of his friends to abate a little the number and length of their speeches. For they are so fond of him that I believe they would do it. But I could not expect them to do it for my asking. If they did it for him, there is no saying whether it might enable you to go to Ireland.
   With best wishes for Christmas, Easter, and all other times.
Ever Yours,
W. E. Gladstone.

On the day that letter was written Gladstone had a long discussion with Lord Spencer about the Naval Estimates. Lord Spencer had great charm of manner but, after a fortnight of intermittent discussion, Gladstone found that the man in whom he hoped that he had found a second Granville had surrendered to what the Prime Minister termed a 'conspiracy' on the part of the Sea Lords: 'He accepted', Gladstone noted, 'the monstrous scheme of the Admirals in a reduced form, content to have cut it down from something yet more monstrous. It would have been better to bring it to the Cabinet in all its nakedness, when it would, perhaps, have encountered an effectual smash.'

There was no chance of that. Gladstone stood practically alone against all his colleagues. Ship design, gunnery, and armour, like so much else within contemporary experience, had begun to take on the appearance of a series of dissolving views. Battleships were already costing over a million pounds apiece, and existing British battleships were in danger of being outclassed by those of foreign powers. A recent disaster in the Mediterranean had shown how narrow was the margin of safety on which Great Britain relied. On 21 June, 1893, the two best British battleships had been in collision : one sank, the other was seriously damaged.

It was no longer a question of building one or two new units. Whole new classes of warships, incorporating the latest developments in the art of naval warfare, were certain to be required at intervals during the future in order to maintain British naval supremacy. On that supremacy the safety of the Empire and the peace of the world depended. Sea communications were of paramount importance to Great Britain, and it was obvious to almost everyone less high-minded than Gladstone, that the richest empire on earth would soon be attacked and plundered if it were not appropriately armed for defence. In those circumstances the strain on the budget was bound to be severe ; but Gladstone continued to think in terms of the Crimean War, Peelite finance, and the anti-militarist and free trade idealism of the 1850s.

Naval supremacy at the time of the Crimean War had rested upon wooden ships which often lasted for sixty years. Great Britain had accumulated such quantities of those that no foreign power was in a position to outbuild her. The new conditions were unfavourable to Great Britain ; but the defensive element in the naval arm, upon which British manpower and British financial power were concentrated, was more manifest than it was in the great conscript armies of the continental powers. Great Britain was the only great European power which had no military conscription.

Europe, during the 1890s, was dividing itself into two rival armed camps. Gladstone told West (3 January, 1894) that the proposed increase in the British Naval Estimates would be regarded as an act of defiance which ' would end in a race towards bankruptcy by all the powers of Europe '. That danger existed, but Gladstone's proposed remedy appeared fatuous and unrealistic. The threat to the emotional foundations of the liberal creed which he professed was far more immediate than the threats of bankruptcy or even war.

For a few weeks Gladstone's colleagues expected that in due course he would give way, as he had done in the cases of Uganda and Egypt. On those occasions, however, he had been angry and argumentative ; on the present occasion he was mostly quiet and pathetic. He said that it was a question of principle, and of opposition to militarism, and instead of scolding his colleagues he seemed to be concerned mainly to see as little of them as possible.

On 9 January, 1894, Gladstone addressed his colleagues for nearly an hour with scarcely a pause in cabinet, but he convinced no-one, except the First Commissioner of Works, J. G. Shaw-Lefevre. Harcourt and Morley expressed sympathy with their chief, but both urged that Gladstone would be better advised to accept the estimates than to resign on that issue. Gladstone was so indignant that he moved his chair and turned his back on Harcourt. He said that he would resign if his colleagues so desired, and that he would base his reasons upon the state of his hearing and eyesight. He added that he intended to leave for the South of France in four days' time.

Gladstone convinced himself that Sir William Harcourt's conversion to the policy of increased Naval Estimates was due to his being ' charmed ' with the idea of raising the money by means of a graduated death duty. The Prime Minister regarded that proposal with disgust, and described it as ' the most radical measure of my lifetime '. He added that he found it ' too violent. It involves a great departure from the methods of political caution established in this country, where reforms, particularly financial reforms, have always been considerate, and even tender.' He considered that real estate deserved to be handled with especial tenderness, on the ground that it ' has more of presumptive connexion with the discharge of duty than that which is ranked as personal '.

Gladstone was impervious to argument. Overstrain was making him senile, and he cherished the hope that his colleagues would find that he was indispensable, and would therefore recall him from Biarritz on his own terms. He told Lord Rosebery (10 January) that the dead were with him—' Peel, Cobden, Bright, Aberdeen ! ' He told West (11 January) that the admirals had ' got their knife ' into him, and that their proposals were ' mad ! mad ! mad ! No statesman that ever lived, perhaps excepting Palmerston, would have given way.' When Gladstone left for Biarritz with Mrs. Gladstone,

Mrs. Drew and her child, Lord Acton, and George Armitstead on 13 January, he ordered that no cabinets should be held in his absence. His colleagues now knew what it was to have to deal with an old man. They all loved and admired him, but when the Prime Minister quitted England, leaving everything in confusion, Lord Rosebery observed that Palmerston had once prophesied that Gladstone would wreck the Liberal Party and die in a madhouse.

At the request of the Cabinet, Sir Algernon West left London on 18 January, 1894, to see Gladstone and, if possible, to bring matters to a head. West found his chief conducting an acrimonious, unprofitable, and unnecessary controversy with the Queen about an honour for Lord Lansdowne, the retiring Viceroy of India. The Queen wanted to make Lord Lansdowne a duke, or to confer the garter upon him if he preferred to remain a marquis. Gladstone firmly refused to offer anything more than a G.C.B., although the Queen had written that such an offer would be 'almost an insult'. The Queen had reminded Gladstone that the Sovereign and not the Prime Minister was 'the fountain of honour'. Gladstone retorted (17 January) : 'It is true, indeed, as Your Majesty observes, that the Sovereign is the fountain of honour ; but it is also true that the Sovereign is the fountain of law.'

West did his utmost to persuade Gladstone to accept the increased Naval Estimates for the sake of Ireland, the Liberal Party, and his own reputation. He pointed out that Lord Spencer was only asking for an additional three million pounds. Gladstone said that his duty to Europe was paramount over all other claims, and he argued, perversely, that when, in 1859–60, he had been at loggerheads with Lord Palmerston on the subject of expenditure on armaments, there had been imminent danger of war. Gladstone had, in fact, at the time, scoffed at that danger, but he was now so angry and excited, that it was difficult for West to follow, in its entirety, his argument. The Prime Minister ended the discussion by saying that his mind was composed : 'You might as well try to blow up the rock of Gibraltar.'

West left Biarritz for London on 22 January, after asking Gladstone whether he might take any crumb of comfort home to the Cabinet. At that moment the Prime Minister almost lost his self-control : 'The plan is mad ! And who are they who propose it ? Men who were not born when I had been in public life for years.' Gladstone had been in public life for more than sixty-one years, and to him all men were now beginning to wear the appearance of remote and ineffectual

. GLADSTONE.
otograph by John C. Murdoch.

W. E. GLADSTONE, 1894.

shadows. He added that the Chancellor of the Exchequer had neglected his duty as custodian of the public purse.

Gladstone had committed his views to writing, but he could not find the paper when he wanted it. It was discovered in a pocket of an overcoat after West had left, and a summary of it was posted to West by Hans Shand, who had been West's secretary at the Board of Inland Revenue and who was now acting as Gladstone's personal secretary at Biarritz. When West received Shand's letter it was clear that no possible loophole remained.

Gladstone wrote that Lord Spencer's proposal exceeded public expectation. It was unprecedented. It would pander to the aggressive instincts of professional warmongers. It would blast the pattern of his political career and tear to shreds every tradition which he had inherited from former colleagues who had been his teachers. Above all, it was an act of barefaced provocation which had even less excuse than German, French, and Russian militarism. Peace was the nurse of liberty and England's duty was to cherish both. The admirals' policy was the enemy of both.

After showing that paper to the Cabinet, West left for Biarritz again on 25 January. Gladstone asked at once if the Cabinet now believed that he meant to abide by what he had said. West replied that they did, and that they thought that he would resign from Parliament as well as from the Government. The Prime Minister took that better than West had expected. He said that he would need time for reflection, and that he would wish to consult his constituents.

West stayed at Biarritz until 4 February, 1894, while rumours appeared in the Press that Gladstone intended to retire. Those rumours were not quieted by a carefully qualified denial. On the day that West left Biarritz, Gladstone shook from his sleeve a card which he hoped might be accepted as the ace of trumps. It proved, however, to be only the joker. In a letter to Edward Marjoribanks (Lord Tweedmouth), the Liberal Chief Whip, Gladstone suggested that Parliament should be dissolved at once, and that the Party should appeal to the country against the House of Lords.

Gladstone indicated that the grounds of that appeal would be the action of the Lords in rejecting the Home Rule Bill, in fatally mutilating an Employers' Liability Bill, and a Bill to establish parish councils, and in shelving a Bill for the taxation of land betterment values. Gladstone noted that the Lords had afforded him ' one of the finest opportunities ever offered to statesmen'. They had 'in their intemperance, committed themselves to a hopeless position'. He was convinced that 'the appeal to the nation would have worked as it did in 1831', and he added that he had no idea of any plan for reforming the House of Lords. He was anxious only 'to restrain its legislative powers'.

That plan was by no means fantastic, but time and preparation would have been needed before it could have been presented to the country with any hope of success. The House of Lords had recovered from the qualms which had made it cautious for many years after the first Reform Act ; its Conservative partisanship was now even more open and undisguised than the Queen's, and its popular rejection of the Home Rule Bill had done much to bolster its morale. Nevertheless, what Gladstone termed 'the cup of wrath' was as yet by no means filled. It should have been obvious that nothing could be attempted until the Government's attitude on the naval estimates had been made clear. The Liberal Party was not even ready for a General Election at that moment, and some items of the Newcastle programme, which Gladstone had proclaimed, remained unfulfilled. It is in the highest degree unlikely that Gladstone's appeal would have been successful in 1894.

Gladstone's colleagues construed his resilient courage as senile optimism. Sir William Harcourt called Gladstone's plan 'the act of a selfish lunatic', and Lord Kimberley (Lord President of the Council and Secretary for India) summoned a meeting of all the Ministers in London. West reported that Gladstone was now inclined either to treat all matters with levity, or to fulminate against all his colleagues as 'criminals'. The assembled Ministers sent Gladstone a telegram which read simply :

'Your suggestion is impossible.'

Four days later, on 10 February, Gladstone reappeared in Downing Street. He asked West to dine with him, but West noted that he 'could not face it'. The danger that Gladstone's great career might end in pathos and burlesque was very real. Everyone tried to be kind and patient, but Gladstone was extremely difficult : 'I am not angry,' he would say, 'I am quite calm.' But he frequently described the proposed naval estimates as 'mad and drunk', and said that he might retain his seat in Parliament after he had resigned, in case he could be of use.

On 17 February, 1894, Gladstone held a Cabinet dinner at Downing

Street. His colleagues expected that he would take that opportunity to announce formally his resignation, which was now taken for granted, and when dinner was over, Lord Rosebery asked, somewhat portentously, whether the doors should be locked : " Certainly ! " Gladstone replied. " If anyone has any topic to raise, it might be done now ! " No-one spoke and the anti-climax seemed absurd. Gladstone was seething inwardly with rage, and at that moment he despised all his colleagues. He could not force himself to speak to them. They knew his views ; they had rejected his suggested dissolution ; they would have to rest content with that for a few days more.

On 23 February, at Gladstone's request, Sir Henry Ponsonby called at Downing Street. Gladstone asked him to ask the Queen if he might write to her in confidence. That request was unnecessarily mysterious, and the Queen thought that the Prime Minister meant to ask for a dissolution. She professed to fear that he might intend to face the country with an appeal for the abolition of the House of Lords, and she refused to be bound to secrecy in advance on a matter about which she might wish to consult her friends.

Rumours again appeared in the Press that Gladstone's resignation was imminent. Gladstone replied by telegram to one inquiry (25 February) : *Rumours such as described wholly unknown in Downing Street and without foundation. Private Secretary.*

On 27 February Ponsonby called at Downing Street to inform West that the Queen was greatly agitated. He needed to know at once what Gladstone had in mind.

West went to see Gladstone while Ponsonby waited. The Prime Minister was furious at the Queen's want of confidence, and West was unable to obtain any coherent instructions. He returned therefore to Ponsonby and told him in confidence that Gladstone intended to resign, and that he wanted to inform the Queen in his own way and in his own time. West, therefore, suggested that Ponsonby should say that the Prime Minister's eyesight was getting rapidly worse. The Queen would be able to guess the rest.

Later that day (27 February) Gladstone wrote to the Queen to convey ' the preliminary intimation ' of his intention to resign office ' when the business of the present Session, and any matter immediately connected therewith, shall have been disposed of . . . He reserves all explanation of particulars until the day, perhaps a very early one, when he humbly proposes to carry his intention into effect.' Gladstone indicated that his resignation, whenever it was tendered, would be ' on physical grounds '.

On 28 February Gladstone visited the Queen and noted sadly : ' She was at the highest point of her cheerfulness . . . Any fear that the intelligence I had to give her would be a shock to her, has been entirely dispelled . . . She said she was sorry *for the cause* which brought about my resignation.'

Gladstone had not yet resigned or set a definite date for his resignation. He held his last Cabinet on 1 March, and informed his colleagues of his resolve. Lord Kimberley began an impromptu valedictory address, but he broke down and could not continue. Gladstone, who seemed as hard and upright as a rock, was about to reply, when Sir William Harcourt called, ' Stop ! ' He had been forestalled by Lord Kimberley, but he now pulled a manuscript from his pocket and began to read a formal valedictory address, gulping at intervals and dabbing his eyes with his handkerchief. Gladstone, in thanking his colleagues, spoke for about four minutes. He ended with the words, ' God bless you all ! ' He then went out at one door while the rest trooped out of the other. Lord Rosebery thought that he was disgusted, but Gladstone was, in truth, more than half indifferent. He noted : ' a really moving scene ', but he liked afterwards to refer to ' that blubbering Cabinet '.

Later that afternoon, Gladstone made his last speech to the House of Commons. Few members knew that he was addressing them for the last time. He attacked the House of Lords for its attitude towards the Parish Councils Bill. He said that the relations between the two Houses had become intolerably strained, and that the controversy between them would have to be pushed to a conclusion. The next day (2 March) he diverted himself by completing a verse translation of five of Horace's love odes, for the *Nineteenth Century*.

On the afternoon of 2 March, Gladstone went down to Windsor with Mrs. Gladstone to dine and sleep. His reception at Windsor caused a mental and spiritual wound which remained open until he died. He brooded over it constantly, and wrote, at intervals, a number of memoranda about it. He occasionally dreamed that the Queen invited him to breakfast, alone, at ten o'clock—' a circumstance ', he was careful to note, ' which I never remember to have heard of in regard to anyone, and which was not accordant with what is known as to H.M.'s (very judicious) habits with reference to the early part of the day.' But no Queen, no breakfast, and no ten

o'clock ever materialized, and Gladstone drew the reluctant conclusion that the Queen's unkindness had more deeply affected his
mind ' down at the root ' than he realized, on the surface. He added
that he had striven ' to keep down that regret, and to set it, as it were,
behind me, and to attain, as near as I could, to indifference '.

Gladstone was surprised when the Queen failed to consult him
about his successor. He would have suggested Lord Spencer, on
grounds of seniority, but the Queen was resolved to send for Lord
Rosebery, and she did not consult Gladstone. There was no constitutional need for such consultation. Sir Henry Ponsonby asked
Gladstone, on the morning of 3 March, whom he had in mind :

' I replied to him that this was, in my view, a most serious matter.
All my thoughts on it were absolutely at the command of the Queen.
And I should be equally at his command if he inquired of me from her,
and in her name : but that otherwise my lips must be sealed. I knew
from him that he was in search of information to report to the Queen,
but this was a totally different matter.'

Gladstone was not a light man, and he was very deeply offended
indeed by the casual way in which his resignation appeared to be
handled. His formal resignation letter was elaborately composed at
Windsor on the morning of 3 March and presented by Gladstone in
a box to the Queen before luncheon. The Queen, however, quietly
assumed that his resignation had already been tendered, either in the
' preliminary letter ' which he had written on 27 February in order
to break gently to Her Majesty the shock of his intention, or at the
audience which she had given him on 28 February. In acknowledging
Gladstone's formal letter of 3 March, the Queen wrote (the same day) :

' Though the Queen has already accepted Mr. Gladstone's resignation, and has taken leave of him, she does not like to leave his letter
tendering his resignation unanswered. She therefore writes these
few Lines to say that she thinks, after so many years of arduous labour
and responsibility, he is right in wishing to be relieved at his age of
these arduous duties, and she trusts he will be able to enjoy peace and
quiet, with his excellent and devoted wife, in health and happiness,
and that his eyesight may improve.

' The Queen would gladly have conferred a Peerage on Mr. Gladstone, but she knows that he would not accept it.'

On that letter, Gladstone's comments were bitter and understand-
able. He had arrived at the supreme moment in his career. He
noted, in the first place, that the Queen had stated that the letter was

'not written for the purpose of accepting my resignation, as this had previously been done. But the facts stand thus. There was no tender of resignation by me until I wrote out at Windsor, on Saturday afternoon, the letter in which it was contained . . . I put it into a box and carried . . . it to the Queen, and told her it contained my tender of resignation . . . Then followed the short conversation . . . Not one word was said of resignation : and it seems that, if it was accepted, it was in some way accepted *before* it was tendered.'

The conversation itself, Gladstone noted, was 'neither here nor there. Its only material feature was negative . . . Was I wrong in not tendering orally my best wishes ? I was afraid that anything said by me should have the appearance of *touting*.' No reference was made by the Queen to the future, or to the past. He received not one syllable of thanks for all his years of faithful and honourable service, and the Queen's letter was so curt as to be almost insulting. He wrote to Ponsonby (5 March, 1894), in reply to a generous letter, that he had found it necessary to harden his heart 'into a flint'.

But that heart refused to harden, and on 2 January, 1896, Gladstone placed on record in his diary :

'my strong desire that after my decease my family shall be most careful to keep in the background all information respecting the personal relations of the Queen and myself during these later years down to 1894, when they died a kind of natural death. Relations sad in themselves, though absolutely unattended with the smallest ruffle on their surface. It was the kind and generous farewell from Ponsonby which had to fill for me the place of a farewell from my Sovereign.'

A few days later, in a private memorandum, he wrote :

'Granted that the absence of any act and word of regard, regret, or interest, is absolutely deserved. But then I have a wife. Of her, H.M., in her concluding letter wrote in terms (which conveyed some implication of reproach to me) of warm interest and praise.' He thought that the Queen might have presented her portrait to Mrs. Gladstone or 'some voluntary offering . . . But there was nothing of the kind. For I cannot reckon as anything what appeared to be a twopenny-halfpenny scrap, photographic or other, sent during the forenoon of our departure by the hand of a footman.'

The Queen noted in her Journal (3 March, 1894) that she saw Mrs. Gladstone after breakfast. 'She was very much upset, poor thing, and asked to be allowed to speak, as her husband " could not speak ". This was to say, which she did with many tears, that whatever his errors might have been, " his devotion to Your Majesty and to the Crown were very great ". She repeated this twice, and begged me to allow her to tell him that I believed it, which I did ; for I am convinced it is the case, though at times his actions have made it difficult to believe . . . I kissed her when she left.'

That was all. The Queen made no effort to conceal her unutterable relief. Gladstone felt that he could justly compare himself with an undemonstrative but not inefficient mule which had served him faithfully in Sicily during a tour in 1831 :

'I had been on the back of the beast for many scores of hours. It had done me no wrong. It had rendered me much valuable service. But it was in vain to argue. There was the fact staring me in the face. I could not get up the smallest shred of feeling for the brute. I could neither love nor like it.'

Gladstone made some efforts to persuade himself that the Queen had had a kind intent in conveying a message to him while he was at Windsor during that last visit. Ponsonby had remarked ' apropos of nothing' that the Queen had respected but never liked Sir Robert Peel. Gladstone felt that that statement had been made to him by command, and that the Queen believed it to be true. But he felt sure that the Queen had once liked Peel. He considered that it would have been against nature for anyone to like both Peel and Disraeli, and that ' the admiring attachment which the Queen formed to Lord Beaconsfield, between 1874 and 1880, so darkened her older sentiment toward Sir Robert Peel, that it became incapable of recognition'.

Why, then, he asked, ' was the statement made to me ? I think out of the compassion due to her general kindliness of nature . . . She might say to herself, " He could not suppose himself qualified to stand as Lord Beaconsfield stood in my estimation. But I will give him this comfort, that that was a position to which even Sir Robert Peel never attained, and which accordingly he may with less pain forego." '

The random reflections of a retired Titan in impotent old age on a subject which caused him acute disquiet must be judged with sympathy and caution. Gladstone never understood the nature of the temperamental incompatibility which had caused a gulf to open between him and the Queen, and he was inclined, in the end, to attribute it to foul stories about his rescue work among prostitutes. He told his sons that, if she really believed those stories, he was surprised that she should have treated him so well, but he noted, in 1897 :

'I do not speak lightly, when I state my conviction that the circumstances of my farewell, which I think were altogether without parallel, had serious causes, beyond the operation of mere political disagreements, which no doubt went for something, but which were insufficient to explain them. Statements, whether true or false, must have been carried to her ears, which in her view required (and not merely allowed) the mode of proceeding which was actually adopted.'

It is in the highest degree unlikely that foul stories about Gladstone's rescue work had seriously affected the position. It is true that numerous stories were current, that some reached the Queen's ears, and that they persisted until the case of *Wright* v. *Gladstone* in 1927 put an end to them for ever ; but few responsible persons, even among Gladstone's bitterest enemies, gave them credence. In his relations with the Queen, far more than in his conduct of the Home Rule controversy, Gladstone experienced his most dismal failure. By a curious paradox, however, his most enduring success as Prime Minister sprang ultimately directly from it.

Throughout the nineteenth century, constitutional conventions governing the relationship between the Sovereign and the Prime Minister were fluid. Gladstone's mind also, to the last, remained open to fresh impressions, and he employed all his intense earnestness in the attempt to acclimatize Monarchy to the shifting conventions of an increasingly democratic age. The Queen fought him because her mind had been set hard at the time of the death of the Prince Consort. Bewildered by the gradual onset of democracy, she clung to the belief that it was her duty to hand down, unimpaired, her heritage to her successors. There remained, throughout the century, a wide and dubious borderland in which it was open to the Queen to assert her authority whenever she chose. She was encouraged to assert it by Disraeli's flattery, which fortified her self-confidence, and precipitated her reversion to Hanoverian type. Thereafter she remained unashamedly partisan. Electoral hazards to which the Sovereign is not subject, and the immense prestige which attached itself to the Queen's long tenure of 'the noblest office upon earth', ruined Gladstone's attempts to secure the Queen's acceptance, during their lifetimes, of a new pattern of constitutional monarchy. The Queen rejected it, but the nation adopted it, and all subsequent British Sovereigns and Prime Ministers have followed the pattern which Gladstone cut. That new pattern involved the final abandonment by the Sovereign of all power to impede the will of the people constitutionally expressed and interpreted. It transformed the Crown politically into a rubber stamp, but it enhanced to an incalculable degree the force of its moral and emotional appeal. During the twentieth century, which has witnessed the overthrow of so many historic dynasties and ancient supporting traditions, the House of Windsor and the British monarchical tradition have constantly renewed their strength. They have continued, amid a mælstrom of conflicting material and intellectual motives, to symbolize the primacy of spiritual and imaginative factors. As the most venerable and significant of the nation's institutions, Gladstone laboured to ensure that the monarchy should serve a purpose for which he conceived that it had been designed by God. Throughout the long unhappy record of his personal relationship with the Queen, he held consistently to that high aim. In consequence, the main share of the credit for cutting the modern pattern of British democratic kingship is due to Gladstone, and that imponderable achievement was a work of far greater value and deeper import than he could foresee.

CHAPTER 17

EPILOGUE
1894–1898

FLOWERS poured into Downing Street when the news of Gladstone's resignation was known. Mrs. Drew said that her father had 'all the love, and honour, and glory that Death brings, without any of its terrors and horrors'. Gladstone himself kept repeating that it was like a funeral, and he insisted that he had no regrets. He told Sir Edward Hamilton (5 March) that his watchword throughout had been 'Europe'; and that the Cabinet, by insisting on a fantastic increase in the Naval Estimates, had shown that it wished to destroy that idea. It had taken a step on a road which must lead to war, and Gladstone said that he would be perfectly content to stand alone, against the entire world, in defence of the principle that the nations of Europe were a community designed by God to uphold together the highest standards of civilization.

Gladstone was glad to be able to obtain a peerage for Stuart Rendel and a privy counsellorship for West, and he found that Mrs. Gladstone felt his retirement more than he felt it himself. She had gloried in the thought that she had lived, as she put it, 'inside the mainspring of history', and she sometimes had difficulty in repressing her tears. Gladstone never entered the Palace of Westminster again after his last speech on 1 March, 1894, attacking the House of Lords, but he retained his seat until the General Election of July, 1895, in which he took no part, and in which the Conservatives gained an overwhelming victory.

Most of the last four years of Gladstone's life were spent at Hawarden; on his infrequent visits to London he stayed usually at Lord Aberdeen's villa at Dollis Hill. There, on 24 May, 1894, he underwent a successful operation for cataract.

After he had returned to Hawarden, Gladstone noted (13 September) that in the field of religion much work awaited him ' if it please God to give me time and vision'. He wrote an article entitled ' The Place of Heresy and Schism in the Modern Christian Church', which appeared in the August number of the *Nineteenth Century*. He argued that although the Christian Church was 'no longer entitled to speak with an undivided and universal authority', its 'inner citadel' remained impregnable. 'That citadel is, and ever was, the private conscience', which deserved to be called 'the vice-regent of God on earth'. Through the private conscience 'within the sacred precinct of the Church', God would continue to guide the onward march of mankind.

That was Gladstone's faith. He noted (1 October) that he had been compelled to break 'a Hawarden practice of fifty years' by ceasing to attend early morning service every day 'because I may not rise until ten at the earliest'. Two evening services—one at five, the other at seven—afforded him 'a limited consolation'.

By June, 1895, Gladstone was sufficiently recovered to visit Kiel and Hamburg for the opening of the Kiel Canal. He was the guest, with Mrs. Gladstone, Mrs. Drew, and Herbert Gladstone, of Sir Donald Currie on the *Tantallon Castle*. When Gladstone saw Kaiser Wilhelm II sail in dazzling sunshine through the line of German battleships (21 June) on the yacht *Hohenzollern*, he remarked coldly to those standing near him : "This means war !" He was presented by Prince Bismarck with a young oak tree from Friedrichsruhe, which he planted at Hawarden, very close to the house, on the West, as soon as he returned home. It is to-day a fine tree.

Gladstone now had two main preoccupations. The first was a new edition of the works of Bishop Butler, whom he had always loved ; it was published in February, 1896, and was followed by a volume of subsidiary studies. The second was the foundation of the Library of St. Deiniol's, Hawarden, to which he contributed £30,000. That institution was rebuilt, its endowment was greatly increased, and a hostel was provided, after Gladstone's death. Its purpose was to promote 'divine learning' and to combat unbelief.

Twenty thousand volumes from Gladstone's private collection formed the nucleus of the library of St. Deiniol's. Gladstone helped to arrange many of the volumes on the shelves of their new home, and he was mortified to discover that some three per cent of all the books which he had purchased were duplicates.

Gladstone regarded politics as the principal secular reflection of religious truth. He had once thought that that truth could only be realized on earth within an exclusive community, specifically dedicated to its service. He no longer had any fear of subjecting that truth to the rigours and to the stimulus of open competitive examination ; and he, therefore, expressly provided that the hospitality of St. Deiniol's 'and its conveniences and advantages should, as far as possible, be made available to persons outside the pale of the Anglican Church, or even of the Christian religion '.

When Hamilton visited Hawarden early in October, 1894, he noted that it was probably one of the last layman's houses in England where grace was said, as a matter of course, before and after meals. Gladstone grumbled about the extent to which the country was class-ridden, and said that he wondered how long the masses would continue to put up with it. Formerly, one party had vied with another in measures of economy ; now, each vied with the other in devising extravagant schemes for the purpose of buying votes. Free education already cost three millions a year, and Gladstone prophesied that there would be no end to the expenditure which it would ultimately entail. He was certain that Lord Salisbury did not really believe in free education, although he had conceded it. Gladstone added that he did not believe in it himself.

The massacres of Armenians which occurred in Turkey during the autumn of 1894, brought Gladstone out of his retirement. He was most profoundly stirred, and he told an Armenian deputation at Hawarden on his eighty-fifth birthday (29 December, 1894) that the Turkish Empire deserved to be rubbed off the map. He said that it was a disgrace to civilization and that it had long been a curse to mankind. Gladstone addressed great public meetings at Chester (6 August, 1895) and at Liverpool (24 September, 1896) to protest against the massacres, and he published articles and letters in the Press. The speech at Liverpool which he delivered at the age of eighty-six, lasted for an hour and twenty minutes. It was the last great public speech of his life, and it evoked round upon round of applause. Gladstone denounced the Sultan of Turkey as ' the great assassin ', and argued that under international law, and, more specifically, under the terms of the Anglo-Turkish convention whereby Disraeli had acquired Cyprus, Great Britain had a duty to intervene, if necessary alone.

Lord Rosebery, the leader of the Opposition, agreed with Lord Salisbury, the Prime Minister, that the peace of Europe would be imperilled if Great Britain were to act alone. The Turkish Ambassador protested in strong terms against Gladstone's abuse of the Sultan, and not one of the great powers was prepared to act. Gladstone demanded that the Turkish Ambassador should be handed his passports, and many Liberals supported that demand against the more cautious policy which the Government was pursuing and which Lord Rosebery had endorsed.

Until his health failed, Gladstone continued to do his utmost to compel the Government, at any cost, to bring its policy into line with the Christian ethic. He told his sons that he wished only that God would give him the strength to lead a new crusade, and to arouse the British nation against the unspeakable Turk and the supine policy of Lord Salisbury. Gladstone's action in the Armenian question was the last and most important of a long train of causes which prompted Lord Rosebery to announce on 8 October, 1896, his resignation from the leadership of the Liberal Party.

On 7 October, 1896, Lord Rosebery sent Gladstone an affectionate letter of reproach and explanation:

' I wish you to know from myself that I have resigned the leadership of the Liberal Party—that is, if I ever held it, of which I am not quite sure !

' I will not disguise that you have, by again coming forward and advocating a policy which I cannot support, innocently and unconsciously dealt the *coup de grâce* ; by enabling discontented Liberals to pelt me with your authority.'

Gladstone replied by return of post that that letter as ' a receipt for a stab under the fifth rib ' was ' not only kind, but kindness itself '. He added : ' Our political relations have been tragical enough : but you have prevented their carrying any infection into the personal sphere. Will it surprise you when I tell you that my first knowledge of a difference between us was when I read the letter stating that sole action meant European war ? '

Lord Rosebery had never concealed his view that Gladstone's policy of intervention was likely, if adopted, to lead to a European war. In a speech on 9 October, Lord Rosebery described Gladstone as ' our leader ', and pointed out that Gladstone would always be in a position to lead the Liberal Party whenever he desired.

Gladstone repeatedly declared that his sole desire was repose ; but he could never rest from controversy. He was much concerned in the summer of 1896, about a Vatican decree which impugned the validity of Anglican Orders. With unquenchable faith in the efficacy of reasoned argument, Gladstone addressed a letter (1 June, 1896) to Cardinal Rampolla, the Papal Secretary of State. He argued the Anglican case with cogency and moderation at considerable length, before referring, at the end, to ' Papal utterances . . . charged with an ineffable emptiness ' that ' pass us by like the idle wind '. He accused the Pope of mutilating the Sacraments, imprisoning the

431

Bible, exalting Aristotelian metaphysics into definitions of faith, and of transferring to a human tribunal an allegiance which is due to God alone.

Friends often visited Hawarden, and Gladstone sometimes spoke very freely to them. He hoped that the Queen would abdicate after the Diamond Jubilee of 1897, in order to make way for the Prince of Wales ; he thought that the armaments race in Europe was certain to end in war ; he said that he no longer feared either science or democracy—materialism and militarism would be the Devil's agents during the twentieth century. Gladstone amused himself at times by drawing up lists of names of men who had severely censured him. Lord Shaftesbury, Thomas Carlyle, A. C. Swinburne, Pope Pius IX, and John Ruskin were included in those lists, and he was careful to note that the Pope had spoken ' officially', and that Ruskin had ' changed'. He considered that, despite all their abuse, his political opponents had treated him with unexampled generosity, and he indulged his instinct for self-mortification by recording : ' Nothing could have united such a body of independent witnesses as this, except that what they said was the truth.'

The last three winters of Gladstone's life were spent in the South of France, and at Cannes on 26 March, 1897, Gladstone and the Queen met for the last time. The Queen was resting in preparation for her Diamond Jubilee, and Princess Louise arranged the meeting. Gladstone told the Princess that he would not come unless the Queen herself commanded it, but the Princess overcame that difficulty by inviting the Gladstones to tea in the hotel at which the Queen was staying. After tea, the Queen sent for Gladstone, and he noted : ' We were shown into a room, tolerably but not brilliantly lighted, much of which was populated by a copious supply of Hanoverian royalties.'

The Queen shook hands with Gladstone—' a thing . . . which had never happened with me during all my life '—but ' to speak frankly, it seemed to me that the Queen's peculiar faculty and habit of conversation had disappeared'. A few days later the Gladstones returned to Hawarden, where Gladstone, in preparation for death, addressed his mind to the future of the Hawarden property.

On 6 June, 1897, the old man who was regarded by the Queen and half the country as a wild and dangerous radical, wrote a letter which was to be given to his grandson and heir, William Glynne Charles Gladstone, as soon as he was old enough to understand it. The boy was then aged twelve, and he had already come into the Hawarden property on his father's death in 1891:

'In the small county of Flint', Gladstone wrote, 'the Hawarden estate ranks as a leading influence. Should it be possible, through favouring influences, to reunite to it the lands which it has lost, or other lands, I contemplate such a contingency with satisfaction. Society cannot afford to dispense with its dominant influences.'

Large properties, Gladstone continued, were much more socially beneficial than small ones : 'The influence attaching to them grows in a larger proportion than mere extent, and establishes a natural leadership, based upon free assent, which is of especial value at a period when the majority are, in theory, invested with a supremacy of political power which, nevertheless, through the necessities of our human nature, is always in danger of slipping through their fingers.'

Gladstone related at length the history of 'the great smash' of 1847, when the boy's great-uncle, Sir Stephen Glynne, had been ruined. He described the struggle which he had waged for half a century, and the sacrifices which he had gladly made, to salvage and restore the estate. As a result of those efforts, the Hawarden property now consisted of some 7,000 acres and some 2,500 souls. It produced an annual income of between £10,000 and £12,000, and the outstanding debt had been reduced to about £90,000 :

'Your uncle, Henry, who is thoroughly competent to deal with the subject, now anticipates that if and when you come to full age [1906], the debt will have been substantially extinguished, and you will come into possession of an inheritance substantially corresponding with that which your grand-uncle held when he came of age seventy years ago.'

Gladstone continued :

'Early in the nineteenth century, Miss Austen, a popular writer of the time, has occasion to describe, in one of her novels,[1] the position of the young heir to a landed property who is in proximate expectation of succeeding to his inheritance : "He was just entering into life, full of spirits, and with all the liberal dispositions of an eldest son who feels born only for expense and enjoyment."

'Relatively to the law as it then stood, and presuming the youth not to be perplexed by any problems of conscience, this is a just description.'

Gladstone pointed out that Sir William Harcourt's scheme of

[1] *Mansfield Park*; the character is Tom Bertram.

death duties in 1894 had entirely altered the position. Under that Act, 'a person succeeding to the estate of Hawarden, if I am near the truth in valuing it with all its incidences and free of debt at four hundred and fifty thousand pounds, would be called upon to pay a sum of not less than 25 or 30 m.[1]

'This law affects you only in a minor degree, since you are already in legal possession, and would only have to pay on my death a duty amounting to a very few thousand pounds on an annuity of three thousand a year which you are charged with on my behalf. But your successor would be liable for the charge in full, and no-one can answer for the duration of each successive life . . . This presents to us a state of things very different from that of Miss Austen's heir-apparent.'

Gladstone considered that 'in times to come, the emoluments of landlords may run some risk of diminution through legislation devised in the interests of occupiers. Not that there is any substantial ground for apprehending injustice to owners of property in this country. But the landlord will not have things all his own way, as he had in former times . . . And undoubtedly, I think, opinion will, and ought, to be more exacting as to the fulfilment of the duties attaching to landed ownership than it has been heretofore.

'What I have sought to bring into view is the change of circumstances since the days when Miss Austen wrote. It is a melancholy fact that even when unjustly favoured by the State in point of taxation, our landowners, *as a body*, have not proved able to keep their expenses within their proper means, and hence have saddled their estates with a mass of mortgages. A free and well-conducted proprietary body is a mainstay of the State : a crippled and embarrassed one constitutes a grave public danger.'

Gladstone begged his grandson to remember that a mortgage was another name for a fraud : 'A mortgaged man retains all the signs of full ownership when he has lost the substance.' It would be immoral to pay death duties by means of a mortgage, and a grave objection to Sir William Harcourt's drastic law was the temptation to which, in that respect, landlords had been exposed.

Gladstone begged the boy to remember always that he belonged 'to a race which bears upon it the taint of sin, from which it is the highest and most essential business of life to escape' ; he begged him also to treat the Hawarden property 'as a kind of sacred trust. It

[1] i.e. *milia* = thousands.

has been only by much care and labour redeemed from alienation, and handed down to you and to coming generations with its traditions unbroken.' Every man on this earth was required to do his duty ' according to the particular lot in life to which it may have pleased the good God to call us '.

In conclusion, Gladstone wrote that a landlord must never regard ' possession as a means simply of expense and enjoyment ; he must look upon it as a serious call . . . which provides him with an opportunity of showing both his Christianity and his manhood . . . He will learn in it the secret and satisfaction of independence : the multiplication of our wants is the multiplication of our chains ; and simplicity of life is no small part of the pleasure of life.'

That grandson, about whom the old man's hopes were centred, was killed in action on 13 April, 1915, near Laventie, during the first World War, while serving as a subaltern with the Royal Welch Fusiliers. He was then aged thirty, and was Lord-Lieutenant of Flintshire, and member of Parliament for Kilmarnock Burghs.

★   ★   ★

On 2 August, 1897, Gladstone made his last speech. He was addressing the members of the Hawarden Horticultural Society, and he advised them to continue to cultivate their gardens. Shortly afterwards his last illness began. He was attacked by cancer behind the cheekbone, and the earliest symptom was an unpleasant kind of catarrh. The malignant growth slowly extended its hold downward, but many months passed before its true nature was recognized. Gladstone went to Cannes on 26 November, 1897, to stay with Lord Rendel, and he began then to be torn by paroxysms of pain. He returned to Hawarden on 18 February, 1898, and for the first time in his life he found himself unable to concentrate.

A year or two earlier, when Gladstone had stumbled in the dark and sustained a deep cut on his arm, the doctors were astonished that the wound should have so quickly healed. Gladstone was told that such resilience, at his age, was almost incredible. He had replied that the matter might be very serious for him, and that he was afraid that he would one day be made to pay dearly for his excessive vitality and power of resistance. His foreboding was fully confirmed.

Gladstone had celebrated his eighty-eighth birthday at Cannes on 29 December, 1897 ; and in his worst moments he was occasionally heard to exclaim, "I cumber the ground !" He went to Bournemouth on 22 February, 1898, and there, on 18 March, the doctors abandoned hope. A new swelling had appeared on Gladstone's palate, and he was told that he could not recover. He returned to Hawarden on 22 March, and his son, the Rev. Stephen Gladstone, wrote (28 March) to Lady Aberdeen in Canada :

'It was a great relief to Father to be told he could not recover. He has long, though with entire submission, desired the end. For him I only fear that the (probable) months of waiting will seem terribly long. But now the doctors can feel it right to do all they can to relieve the pain . . . My Mother does not fully know yet. We dread the shock for her, and want her to understand gradually . . . It was most touching when we left Bournemouth. When we passed through the crowd . . . he turned and spoke his farewell : " God bless you all, and this place, and the land you love " . . .'

Morphia and music provided partial relief for body and mind during the final two months' agony, and Gladstone often asked wistfully when the hour of his release would come. His daughter, Mrs. Drew, had written (4 March) : 'no-one can say he is not an angel in the way he accepts the suffering, but I never saw anybody mind it as he does . . . he has the sort of organization that is knocked to pieces by it. I remember 20 years ago, when I had the nettlerash and he came up to see me, the sort of agonized expression of sympathy on his face : " My dear Maisie, I had the nettlerash once for 24 hours, and if I had had it another hour I should have been in Bedlam ! "'

Gladstone longed to die, and he sometimes complained that he was given over, like Job, for torment to Satan. More often, however, he broke into words of praise and love, and in his worst bouts he could often be heard repeating in a voice of extraordinary fervour, the first verse of Cardinal Newman's hymn : 'Praise to the Holiest in the height'. His faith remained undimmed, and there were times when he was almost his former self. On 18 April, for example, nine days after he had been out in the garden for the last time, Gladstone came down to dinner and talked about the history of the Oxford and Cambridge boat race. He described how he had witnessed the first race rowed in 1829, at Henley.

Messages of sympathy and affection poured into Hawarden ; one, which may have moved Gladstone most, came from the Hebdomadal Council at Oxford :

'. . . while we join in the universal regret with which the nation watches the dark cloud which has fallen upon the evening of a great and impressive life, we believe that Oxford may lay claim to a deeper and more intimate share in this sorrow. Your brilliant career in our university, your long political connexion with it, and your fine scholarship, have linked you to Oxford by no ordinary bond, and we cannot but hope that you will receive with satisfaction this expression of deep-seated kindliness and sympathy from us.

' We pray that the Almighty may support you and those near and dear to you in this trial, and may lighten the load of suffering which you bear with such heroic resignation.'

Rallying his failing powers, Gladstone dictated this reply to his daughter, Helen :

' There is no expression of Christian sympathy that I value more than that of the ancient university of Oxford—the God-fearing and God-sustaining university of Oxford. I served her, perhaps mistakenly, but to the best of my ability. My most earnest prayers are hers to the uttermost and to the last.'

Gladstone, at the end, became as quiet and gentle as a tired child. On Sunday, 15 May, Mrs. Drew told him that she was going to church :

' To Church ! How nice ! How charming ! Pray for me, Mary dear, and for all my fellow-Christians, and all the unhappy and miserable people.'

Thereafter there were only intermittent signs of consciousness, and at 4.00 a.m. on Thursday, 19 May—Ascension Day—Gladstone died without a struggle, in the presence of Mrs. Gladstone and all their surviving children, while his son Stephen read the last prayers.

The House of Commons adjourned immediately, and on the following day (20 May) Lord Salisbury in the Lords and Arthur Balfour in the Commons proposed that Gladstone should be buried at the State's expense in Westminster Abbey. Unanimous approval was accorded in both Houses, and tributes were paid to Gladstone by Lord Salisbury and Lord Rosebery, and by Arthur Balfour and Sir William Harcourt.

While telegrams poured into Hawarden from princes, potentates, parliaments, public bodies, and private persons, Mrs. Gladstone drove, on 24 May, to call on the widow of a young miner who had been killed in a pit accident on the previous day. They knelt side by side, and prayed together. The Gladstone family had been asked, in the meantime, to choose between a pompous funeral a month later, with a procession through the streets of London and stands for spectators, or a simpler and immediate ceremony. It chose the latter, and accordingly, on 25 May, Gladstone's body was taken to London by special train and laid in state in Westminster Hall. Before the coffin was sealed a jewelled Armenian gold cross was placed inside it—the gift of the Church of that persecuted and afflicted nation which Gladstone had tried to succour in his extreme old age.

Vast crowds filed through Westminster Hall, by day and by night, to pay their last tribute to Gladstone ; and soon after 11 o'clock on the morning of Saturday, 28 May, 1898, the body was committed to earth in the North transept of the Abbey, close to the statues of Sir Robert Peel, and Disraeli. A statue of Gladstone was erected later, almost touching that of Sir Robert Peel. The members of both Houses of Parliament marched in procession into the Abbey —the Commons first, behind the Speaker with his Mace, and the Lords afterwards, in rather better order, behind the Lord Chancellor with the Great Seal. The pall-bearers were Lord Rendel and George Armitstead ; the Earl of Rosebery and the Earl of Kimberley ; the Marquess of Salisbury and the Duke of Rutland (who as Lord John Manners had been Gladstone's fellow-member for Newark from 1841–1845) ; and the Prince of Wales (Edward VII) and the Duke of York (George V).

The Queen was displeased that her son and grandson should have acted as pall-bearers, and she could not be persuaded to announce, in the *Court Circular*, her regret at Gladstone's death. Her respect for the truth was too strong. She said that she had never liked Gladstone, but that she was sorry for Mrs. Gladstone, about whom she made frequent inquiries. On the day of the funeral the Queen sent Mrs. Gladstone a long and charming telegram : ' I shall ever ', it concluded, ' gratefully remember his devotion and zeal in all that concerned my personal welfare, and that of my family.' The Queen telegraphed at the same time to the Prince of Wales, to ask what advice he had taken and what precedent he had followed when he engaged himself to act as pall-bearer. The Prince, who was then aged fifty-seven, replied simply that he had sought no advice and that he knew of no precedent.

After the committal, while Handel's Dead March in *Saul* was being played on the organ, Mrs. Gladstone remained for some time kneeling in prayer by the grave which was to be opened two years later to receive (19 June, 1900) her own remains. Her sons gently raised her, and when she was seated on a chair which had been placed for her at the head of the grave, the Prince of Wales followed by the other

MAY 19, 1898

PUNCH, *May 28, 1898*

pall-bearers walked over to where she sat and stooped to kiss her hand. She spoke a few words to each, and she remembered that Lord Salisbury had been too deeply moved to say anything.

*   *   *

As the great congregation filed out of Westminster Abbey to the organ notes of Schubert's *Marche Solennelle* in E flat, many of its members must have asked themselves upon what foundation Gladstone's title to enduring fame would ultimately be found to rest. He had dominated the political world for as long as most of them could remember, and had rendered splendid service to his country and to the world. Yet the office of Prime Minister, which he held, in all, for twelve years, was not one for which he was temperamentally well fitted.

Gladstone's heart was not in politics, which he had chosen early as his field of action from motives with which he was never wholly satisfied. He had resolved, as far as possible, to make politics conform with the highest Christian ethic. He was conscious of the possession of great gifts, and he loved power for the opportunities which it gives ; but all his affections were centred upon the universal Christian society, and not upon any local temporal kingdom. After he had abandoned his exalted theory of a union between Church and State, he was content to see the Church become a voluntary body. But the problem of the right relationship between two societies—the one, eternal and divine ; the other, mortal and mundane—which has troubled the conscience of Europe for two thousand years, continued to torment Gladstone and to plunge his mind into a seething ferment of restlessness. Throughout the ages, the parties to that ancient dispute have constantly shifted their positions, and Gladstone also shifted his own position. The increasing secularization of nineteenth-century thought made him desist from the intellectual search for a unifying principle. He continued, however, to thirst for it emotionally, pending the full conversion of the leading nations of mankind to the Christian way of life.

Many, perhaps at first a majority, of Gladstone's contemporaries saw as clearly as he did the hand of God at work, behind all the transient phenomena of history, to propel mankind towards some transcendent and, as yet, imperfectly apprehended goal. No statesman in modern times, however, has made so little concession to human weakness ; and none has been in a position to dedicate such an extraordinary combination of qualities so unreservedly and effectively, on so grand a scale and for so long a period, to the task of giving effect in politics to the Christian religion. In that respect Gladstone's record is unique, and his approach to politics was as different from that of his colleagues as it was from that of his opponents.

Gladstone regarded Party as an alliance of enlightened individuals formed to serve a series of high moral causes, such as his mission to pacify Ireland. He conceived that it was his duty, as leader, to devise such missions, and he was convinced that the electors could be taught to respond to the voice of God appealing directly to their consciences. When his own class rejected him as a prophet he called the masses to his aid by extending the franchise. The study of Homer had helped him to persuade himself that the spirit of justice in its purest form had its habitation in the hearts and minds of the untutored masses ; and he argued with simple faith that the masses were less exposed than the classes to motives of self-interest.

Gladstone understood from the outset that Party ties—despite the practice of Lord Chatham, the theory of Edmund Burke, and the inchoate aspirations of many warm-hearted and self-respecting individuals—had seldom represented more than a tangle of alliances between groups of politicians competing for material satisfactions. Nevertheless, Gladstone indulged the noble hope that the evangelical spirit would prove as potent in purifying the nation's political life as it did in fact prove in restoring the religious life of the Church of England.

Gladstone was not interested in bread-and-butter problems, except when, as in the early part of his career, they were related directly to his transcendental purpose of setting individuals free. He left the details of Party organization and election programmes as far as possible in the hands of others, while he concerned himself with the task of creating, rather than merely inspiring, the unity and enthusiasm which held the Liberal Party together. The campaigns against Turkish misrule in the Balkans and English misrule in Ireland were products of the irrestrainable energy of a single dæmonic individual.

Gladstone would not have been able to remain in politics if he had not been successful in finding a series of high moral causes to serve. He was always intensely in earnest, and he discovered them usually after prolonged periods of self-absorbed concentration, and of partly sub-conscious brooding. He considered that his instinct for ' right-timing ' was his most striking political gift, and his high-mindedness

led him to suppose that others would attach as great a weight to
ethical considerations and as small a weight to considerations of
expediency as he normally did himself. He was, however, constantly
liable to overlook the need for nursing and preparing public opinion ;
he was capable of self-deception ; he did, quite unconsciously, persuade himself occasionally that an expedient course had become a
moral duty. Once he had found a compelling cause he was willing,
if necessary, to incur martyrdom on its behalf for himself and his
Party. In that way he eventually wrecked the Liberal Party which
was his instrument. He tore and wrenched its roots so violently
that at the end of his life they were left exposed and dry, and no
longer sunk securely in the life-giving soil of public opinion.

The seismic quality of Gladstone's mind bewildered his contemporaries, and caused a majority of them to believe that his methods
concealed a greed for power and office. He seemed to be bent upon
playing an heroic rôle against an Olympian background, and upon
plunging the country into an enervating ferment of excitement.
Many statesmen throughout the ages have drawn expertly upon the
reserves of elemental passion which drive men and nations on their
courses ; few, if any, during an epoch of comparative tranquillity,
have generated so much heat themselves. In periods of danger, a
Chatham, a Pitt, a Lloyd George, or a Churchill has hitherto always
been at hand to summon the spirit of the nation from its depths.
That spirit is, however, apt to sulk when it is summoned in counterfeit
emergencies.

Many of Gladstone's colleagues and most of his principal opponents
thought that his approach to politics was liable to make the best
cause become the enemy of the good. It seemed to them that the
nation was being made bilious on a diet of caviare and champagne,
when cheese and beer would have suited it better. Lord Beaconsfield
and Lord Salisbury, Lord Hartington and Lord Rosebery, did not
share Gladstone's belief that the masses would prove more politically
disinterested than the classes. They regarded the advent of democracy
as inevitable, and they considered that it had become necessary, in
consequence, to conciliate and serve a vast new range of varied and
interlocking group-interests. In such conditions, as Disraeli was
the first to discern, the possession of an efficient Party machine was
of more practical importance than a transcendental purpose ; furthermore, an ability to compromise, and to act as the chairman of a board,
was more valuable in a Prime Minister than a mission. It would

often have been possible to apply to Gladstone words which Oliver Goldsmith had once used about Edmund Burke—'too fond of the right to pursue the expedient'. If others were of the earth, commonplace and practical, Gladstone seemed to be of the heavens, nebulous and incalculable ; and sometimes of the underworld, sulphurous, in league with the devil to disrupt the empire and the social order.

At the apex of Great Britain's moral and material ascendancy during the nineteenth century, liberalism was the operative political creed of most Englishmen. Gladstone was gradually converted to it as a result of his experiences at the Board of Trade and at the Exchequer. Throughout his life those were the only great departments of State in which he took a deep and constant interest. He was excited sometimes by foreign affairs, when great moral issues were involved ; he disliked the Army and Navy ; he was bored by education ; and he seldom thought about India.

Liberalism, in Gladstone's hands, became a fiery sword which was used, at first with superlative success, to set the individual free. It was used later, with considerable success, to extend the ideal of chartered liberty throughout the world. That ideal was concerned with means ; the ends were never clearly formulated ; and the sword itself became rusted when, towards the end of the century, the economic and intellectual climates changed.

The means which liberalism had used were freedom of worship and expression, and freedom of enterprise and trade. Those means were found, in the end, to be inadequate, after the decline of religious faith had removed powerful restraints which had once seemed almost strong enough to hold aggressive nationalism in check, and to set a limit to the cultivation of material standards. In the absence of those restraints, human society was menaced by anarchy. It became increasingly apparent that welfare had been recklessly sacrificed to wealth ; and wealth itself began to appear increasingly insecure as other nations challenged Great Britain's commercial and industrial lead, and adopted protective practices in defiance of free trade doctrines.

It had become evident, before Gladstone died, that a new set of moral values was needed ; and Gladstone's appeal to the consciences of individuals led to results utterly at variance with anything that he had intended. He had told the masses to forget their fears and to curb their wants ; and the first incoherent attempts to formulate the modern ideals of freedom from fear and freedom from want released two new currents of opinion from both of which he averted his head in disgust.

The first of those currents was imperialism, which sprang, in England, from the uneasiness caused by foreign economic competition, and by the growth of militarism among the great European powers, after the adoption of popular nationalist policies had blasted the hopes of the organizers of the Great Exhibition of 1851. Confronted by swollen conscript continental armies it was natural that Great Britain should seek to redress the changing balance of power in the old world by extending and consolidating her ties with the new.

The second of those currents was social reform, which sprang, in England, from evangelical philanthropy. Prince Bismarck's example in Germany helped to convince some thoughtful sections of British opinion that there might be a case for embarking upon constructive action to remove the causes of distress, instead of concentrating, as heretofore, upon individual action to relieve its symptoms. During the late 1870s, and the 1880s, slumps, unemployment, riots, and strikes stirred the conscience of the classes and aroused the anger of the masses.

Gladstone coupled imperialism with militarism and called the compound 'jingoism'. He argued that jingoism would enslave the masses to mean passions, and that it would disqualify them from fulfilling the rôle for which he had cast them, of acting as a supreme tribunal on earth to which men and nations could appeal. He coupled social reform with socialism and called the compound 'construction'. He argued that construction would ruin the national character, sap individual initiative, and overturn the strict principles of economy on which British prosperity had been founded.

Gladstone had seen the power and wealth of the State expand during his lifetime beyond all precedent, and he was more afraid of misusing both than he was of neglecting problems. He considered that politics would be debauched, and divorced from the service of God, if policy were to be auctioned by Party leaders ambitious to buy votes from selfish and, possibly, unscrupulous pressure-groups. Behind the luxury and pride which capitalist industry had generated, behind Bismarck's ruthless concentration and use of force, behind the growing and almost universal demand for increased material satisfactions, Gladstone glimpsed monstrous shadow-shapes which danced convulsively in the fiery furnace of his imagination. The full measure of the twentieth century's shame was concealed from him. He did not foresee extermination camps; he did not foresee the enslavement of a vast portion of the human race to a non-Christian creed which denies integrity to the individual conscience and personality ; but he fought to the last against the tendency to replace the worship of God by that of Cæsar or any species of idolatry.

Gladstone was no mystic who lived withdrawn from the world. His genius ripened slowly in the mart and exchange of everyday human affairs, but he lived his life deliberately and consistently upon a higher plane than that of others who were similarly, if less conspicuously, employed. He was often compelled as a statesman to use a politician's arts, but he did so with visible reluctance, as when, in 1891, he propounded the ' Newcastle programme ' of social reform. Gladstone was a man of peace who loathed war as the greatest of human calamities ; but his boyish glee at the victory of Tel-el-Kebir in 1882 and the stand which he took against Russia during the Penjdeh crisis of 1885, showed that he could be as fierce and uncompromising as anyone when confronted by a challenge to his conscience.

In the last analysis what Gladstone was is of vastly greater significance than what he did. Mortal men are condemned to see mortal events ' through a glass darkly ' and the echo of dead political controversy sounds ever more faintly down the ages until it is barely distinguishable from that of the mythical war between the kites and the crows. Gladstone may be judged as a statesman ; few would venture to judge him as a man. He dedicated his life to the task of teaching men and nations to govern themselves by schooling their passions, and thereby to realize on earth the spirit of the Christian ethic.

By his radiant example, Gladstone did more than any statesman since the Reformation to give effect in politics to that ideal. In its service he started as the foe, became the agent, and ended as the prophet of the Liberal experiment.

APPENDIX

A SPEECH IN GLYNNESE

As an example of the correct use of the Glynnese language, Lord Lyttelton, in 1851, composed the following speech for delivery by Gladstone in the House of Commons :

' Sir, the Noble Lord opposite is such a phantod,[1] and the Honourable Gentleman next to him such a daundering [2] and wizzy [3] old totterton [4] that my take [5] must be to make an idiotic [6] speech [a faint ironical cheer from a young Gladstone, or Lyttelton, in the gallery]. What's that unearthly [7] little sound ? I shoot [8] the buckish [9] young mawkin [10] who fired away [11] that cheer ! I could throw my shoe [12] at him. Up and dressed [13] indeed ! Who's who and what's what ? [14] What sort of a result [15] is he ? . . . Here have I been sitting tight [16] all day, pompéissimus,[17] for the chance of showing my ring [18] on a subject I understand, and am I to be sat upon [19] by a dandy-major [20] like him who cuddles [21] with all the twopenny [22] people in town, and can do nothing but sit in the gallery like a grasshopper's uncle ? [23]

' Sir, I am sorry to see you looking so grubous [24] and taken out of [25] by the moral sag [26] of this long debate. I fear that is one of ours.[27] This House is in the chair [28] for rotgut [29] and offal [30] and false flash ; [31] and some of the debates are beyond.[32] Look at the hydra [33] on the table ! Than which,[34] Sir, I fear that while sitting there like a hen [35] you must have the Housums [36] terribly, and that no speech can be any break [37] to you . . . [Interruption] . . .

' Sir, I am addled [38] with these interruptions, and shall tangle my tongue [39] . . . I hold in my hand quite a circumstance [40]—a voucher [41] of grub [42] from an Honourable Member who is absent on account of bowdler.[43] Mr. Speaker, do you die ? [44] . . . The Honourable Member near me, with the little antic [45] on his nose, need not sit battening [46] with his eyes as if he were going to be niobe ! [47] [A voice : " He is gone to sleep ! "]. What a blow ! [48] But . . . though I am not human [49] from the manners of Honourable Gentlemen around me who are bursting [50] every moment, I will not let down my leg,[51] but will try to read, sanguine,[52] the cocked-hat [53] letter which I have mentioned.

' The Honourable Member was great audience [54] to an old Dolly [55] with whom he was an old shoe,[56] who was frantic [57] at having lost her shawl making her rather a witch ; [58] and she kept telling it to every passing pig-man [59] . . . He . . . took great rank [60] on his wisdom in telling the old lady to sit crosslegged [61] in a corner, while he went and curtseyed [62] with a policeman which of them should trapes [63] about and find it. And though at first she thought it gaunt,[64] . . . yet that went off in ginger-beer.[65] Viewing [66] that the old lady had been washing her hands, he ran off like a

447

lamplighter,[67] and found it squashed among the towels. What an ebb ![68] . . . But the Dolly [55] . . . was over the moon [69] with a magpie [70] sandwich . . . which she took like pork [71] . . . " Catch me again," he said, " doing such a blowing [72] thing for you ! A commander [73] like me having the kindness to do chars [74] for an old moth ! [75] . . ." '

[1] imbecile. [2] sloppy. [3] sallow. [4] prematurely aged. [5] best course. [6] in terms suited to a person of inferior intelligence. [7] nasty. [8] spy. [9] too familiar. [10] stranger. [11] uttered. [12] indicates irritation. [13] presumptuous. [14] indicates bewilderment. [15] indifferent person. [16] attitude of eager expectation. [17] jaded. [18] showing off. [19] brow-beaten. [20] little fellow. [21] associates with. [22] worthless. [23] worthless fellow. [24] dirty. [25] sickened. [26] strain. [27] characteristic. [28] pre-eminent. [29] badness. [30] rubbish. [31] sham. [32] indescribable. [33] disorder. [34] an elliptical method of expressing the superlative. [35] immobile. [36] political worries. [37] relief. [38] on edge. [39] make a [pre-Spooner] spoonerism—e.g. ' spit in that face ' for ' fit in that space '—an alleged Gladstonian one. [40] something worth while. [41] a letter just opened. [42] gossip. [43] stomach-ache. [44] are you amused ? [45] pimple or wart. [46] blinking. [47] to cry. [48] bore. [49] absent-minded. [50] laughing. [51] indulge in self-pity. [52] recklessly. [53] pompous. [54] involved with. [55] a dowager. [56] a friend. [57] anxious. [58] half-dressed person. [59] moaning about it. [60] plumed himself. [61] be patient. [62] talk politely. [63] bestir oneself. [64] tiresome. [65] was soon over. [66] taking into account. [67] as fast as possible. [68] miserable occupation. [69] in high spirits. [70] underdone. [71] without any feeling of gratitude. [72] conspicuous. [73] great man. [74] domestic chore. [75] an old lady.

SELECT BIBLIOGRAPHY

A. British Museum Additional Manuscripts 44086–44835.

It is difficult to list selected material of the most general interest. A start might be made with the autobiographical memoranda (Add. MSS. 44790–44791) and with another series of political and autobiographical memoranda (Add. MSS. 44777–44778).

Of great interest are the correspondence with the second Earl Granville (Add. MSS. 44165–44180), the eighth Duke of Argyll (Add. MSS. 44098–44106), the eighth Duke of Devonshire (Add. MSS. 44143–44148), the first Lord Herbert of Lea (Add. MSS. 44210–44211), James Hope-Scott (Add. MSS. 44214), the fourth Lord Lyttelton (Add. MSS. 44238–44240), Cardinal Manning[1] (Add. MSS. 44247–44250), the fifth Duke of Newcastle (Add. MSS. 44262–44263), the third Viscount Palmerston (Add. MSS. 44271–44273), Sir Robert Phillimore (Add. MSS. 44306–44314), the fifth Earl Spencer (Add. MSS. 44306–44314), Harriet, wife of the second Duke of Sutherland (Add. MSS. 44324–44329), and Gerald Wellesley, Dean of Windsor (44339–44340).

Of great interest, too, are Gladstone's account of his first interview with Queen Victoria after the death of the Prince Consort (included with Add. MSS. 44752), his memoranda about the Prince of Wales and the question of a royal residence in Ireland (included with Add. MSS. 44760), Gladstone's journals of continental travels, 1832–1850 (Add. MSS. 44818), a diary of secret political memoranda, 1832–1848 (Add. MSS. 44819), and Gladstone's notes of Cabinet meetings which he attended between 1835 and 1894 (Add. MSS. 44636–44648). Permission to examine Cabinet papers must be obtained from the Cabinet Office.

B. Gladstone's correspondence with Queen Victoria and the members of her family. Those papers form no part of the British Museum's Additional Manuscripts : they have been deposited in the Museum by the Gladstone Trustees on permanent loan, and permission to examine them must be obtained from the Gladstone Trustees.

C. The Diary (1880–1906) of Sir Edward Hamilton. Until 1956, permission to examine it must be obtained from the Trustees of the British Museum.

D. The Gladstone Papers in the octagon room and library at Hawarden Castle, Chester, in the possession of Mr. Charles Andrew Gladstone. Those

---

[1] Almost all Manning's letters are absent, as they were returned by Gladstone in 1862 to Manning who destroyed them.

papers include all Gladstone's correspondence with his wife and with the members of his family, besides much other personal and intimate material.

E.   Published works,[1] chronologically arranged :

W. Bagehot : *Mr. Gladstone* ; 1860 (reprinted in *Biographical Studies* ; 1881).

W. E. Gladstone : *Gleanings of Past Years* (7 vols.) ; 1879.

W. E. Gladstone : *Later Gleanings* ; 1898.

Sir Edward Hamilton : *Mr. Gladstone* ; 1898.

Sir Algernon West : *Recollections (1832–86)* ; 1899.

H. W. Paul : *Life of W. E. Gladstone* ; 1901.

John (Viscount) Morley : *Life of Gladstone* (3 vols.) ; 1903.

Lord E. Fitzmaurice : *Life of Lord Granville* (2 vols.) ; 1905.

(Sir) W. S. Churchill : *Life of Lord Randolph Churchill* (2 vols.) ; 1906.

A. C. Benson and Lord Esher (editors) : *Letters of Queen Victoria (1837–61)*. First Series (3 vols.) ; 1907.

C. R. L. F(letcher) : *Mr. Gladstone at Oxford, 1890* ; 1908.

D. C. Lathbury (editor) : *Correspondence on Church and Religion of W. E. Gladstone* (2 vols.) ; 1910.

W. F. Monypenny and G. E. Buckle : *Life of Benjamin Disraeli, Earl of Beaconsfield* (6 vols.) ; 1910–20.

Bernard Holland : *The Eighth Duke of Devonshire* (2 vols.) ; 1911.

A. Tilney Bassett (editor) : *Gladstone's Speeches* ; 1916.

Mrs. Drew : *Catherine Gladstone* ; 1919.

H. G. Hutchinson (editor) : *Private Diaries of Sir Algernon West (1887–98)* ; 1922.

G. E. Buckle (editor) : *Letters of Queen Victoria (1861–1901)* Second and Third Series (6 vols.) ; 1926–32.

J. Bailey (editor) : *Diary of Lady Frederick Cavendish* (2 vols.) ; 1927.

Viscount Gladstone : *After Thirty Years* ; 1928.

Philip Guedalla (editor) : *Gladstone and Palmerston ; Correspondence (1851–65)* ; 1928.

A. Tilney Bassett : *The Gladstone Papers* ; 1930.

Lucy Masterman (editor) : *Mary Gladstone—Diaries and Letters* ; 1930.

Lord Rendel : *Personal Papers* ; 1931.

F. W. Hirst : *Gladstone as Financier and Economist* ; 1931.

Marquess of Crewe : *Lord Rosebery* (2 vols.) ; 1931.

Lord Kilbracken : *Reminiscences* ; 1931.

J. L. Garvin : *Life of Joseph Chamberlain* (3 vols.) ; 1932–4 : and fourth volume by Julian Amery ; 1951.

Philip Guedalla (editor) : *The Queen and Mr. Gladstone* (2 vols.) ; 1933.

Francis Birrell : *Gladstone* ; 1933.

---

[1] All published in London, except where otherwise stated.

F. E. Hyde : *Gladstone at the Board of Trade* ; 1934.

W. E. Williams : *The Rise of Mr. Gladstone (1859–68)* ; Cambridge, 1934.

R. W. Seton-Watson : *Disraeli, Gladstone, and the Eastern Question* ; 1935.

A. Tilney Bassett (editor) : *Gladstone to his Wife* ; 1936.

G. M. Young : *Portrait of an Age* ; 1936.

R. C. K. Ensor : *England 1870–1914* ; Oxford, 1936.

J. L. Hammond : *Gladstone and the Irish Nation* ; 1938.

E. L. Woodward : *The Age of Reform (1815–1870)* ; Oxford, 1938.

Arthur (Lord) Ponsonby : *Henry Ponsonby—his Life and Letters* ; 1942.

Agatha Ramm : *The Political Correspondence of Mr. Gladstone and Lord Granville 1868–1876* (2 vols.) ; 1952.

J. L. Hammond and M. R. D. Foot : *Gladstone and Liberalism* ; 1952.

C. H. D. Howard (editor) : *A Political Memoir (1880–1892) by Joseph Chamberlain* ; 1953.

Catalogue of *Additions to the Manuscripts in the British Museum*—(Add. MSS. 44086–44835) : 1953.

INDEX

INDEX

Aberdeen, 4th Earl of, and Neapolitan tyranny, 99–100 ; leader of Peelites, 101 ; 'Government of All the Talents' of, 110–11 ; and Crimean War, 114 ; resignation (1855), 119 ; persuades Peelites to serve with Palmerston, 120 ; advises Gladstone against joining Derby, 133 ; and Gladstone's Ionian Islands' post, 137 ; death, 156 ; Gladstone's opinion of, 22, 120 ; Gladstone's letters to, 99, 122, 235. Mentioned, 69, 96, 129

Aberdeen, Marchioness of, 436

Aberdeen, Marquess of, 370, 379 ; Governor-General of Canada, 401–2

Acland, Sir Arthur Dyke, 402, 404

Acland, Sir Henry, 385

Acland, Sir Thomas, 92, 105, 402 ; tells Gladstone his faults, 176–7

Acton, Lady, 260, 365

Acton, Lord, on Gladstone and Disraeli, 244 ; his high opinion of Gladstone, 260–1 ; argues against Gladstone's retirement, 323 ; post for, 401. Mentioned, 365, 404, 418

Adams, Charles Francis, 206

Adullamites, the, 178

Affirmation Bills, 278–9

Afghan War, First, 53 ; Second, 262, 264, 285

Afghanistan, Penjdeh incident, 324–5

Alabama claims, 206–7

Albania, visit to, 136–7 ; naval demonstration off, 283

Albert, Prince Consort, influence of, on Queen, 96, 160, 426 ; congratulates Gladstone on Budget, 113 ; Gladstone's defence of (1853), 114 ; praises Gladstone, 146 ; death, 157–9 ; Irish demonstrations against, 209 *n*. Mentioned, 69

Albert Memorial, 183

Alexandra, Queen (Princess of Wales), 249, 285, 348

Alexandria, naval base at, 239 ; bombardment of, 287, 290, 294 ; Arabi's revolt in, 288

All Souls, Gladstone's visit to (1890), 383

Alsace-Lorraine, annexation of, 205

Althorp, 125

Althorp, Viscount, *see* Spencer, Earl

Alverstone, Lord, 373

American Civil War, 152–4 ; and *Alabama*, 206

Anglo-Turkish Convention, 252, 264, 430

Anstice, Joseph, 9, 11

Anti-Corn Law League, 53, 65–6, 80

Apprenticeship system in West Indies, 19, 32

Arabi, Colonel, 288, 290, 308–10

Arco, Baroness, 260

Argyll, 8th Duke of, Gladstone's friendship with, 143 ; Pope Pius IX on, 184 ; opposed to Irish land reform, 201 ; and memorial to John Stuart Mill, 226 ; Lord Privy Seal, 275 ; resigns on Irish Land Bill, 298, 319 ; refuses to serve under Gladstone, 343 ; story of guest of, 380. Mentioned, 122, 168, 234, 260, 270, 318

Armenian massacres, 430

Armitstead, George (subsequently Lord Armitstead), 378, 381, 396, 407, 418, 438

Austin, Alfred, 404

Army, conditions in, in Crimean War, 118 ; conditions in barracks, 167 ; abolition of purchase of commissions in, 221 ; pretensions of exclusive caste in, 380

Arnold, Dr. T., 52

Arnold, Matthew, 346

Ashanti War, 226

Ashley, Hon. Evelyn, 193

Ashley, Lord, *see* Shaftesbury, Earl of

Asia Minor, Gladstone reverses Beaconsfield's policy in, 285

Asquith, H. H., *see* Oxford and Asquith, Earl of

Athenæum Club, 176–7

Athens, 136

Audley End, 45, 118

Austen, Jane, 433–4

Australia, transport of convicts to, 78

Austria, ally of Prussia, 169 ; at war

5